RALPH ELLISON
Emergence of Genius

Lawrence Jackson

John Wiley & Sons, Inc.
New York • Chichester • Weinheim • Brisbane • Singapore • Toronto

Copyright © 2002 by Lawrence Jackson. All rights reserved.

Published by John Wiley & Sons, Inc., New York
Published simultaneously in Canada

Grateful acknowledgment is made to Fanny Ellison and Professor John Callahan for permission to quote from the Ralph Ellison Papers at the Library of Congress; to Random House and its subsidiary Modern Library for permission to reproduce from the following books by Ralph Ellison: *Going to the Territory,* copyright © Fanny Ellison 1986; *Shadow and Act,* © Fanny Ellison 1953 and 1964; *The Collected Essays of Ralph Ellison,* © Fanny Ellison 1995; *Flying Home and Other Stories,* © Fanny Ellison 1996; *Trading Twelves* by Ralph Ellison and Albert Murray, © Fanny Ellison and Albert Murray 2000; and to Duke University Press for permission to reprint portions of the essay "The Birth of a Critic" published in *American Literature,* © 2000.

This publication is designed to provide accurate and authoritative information in regard to the subject matter covered. It is sold with the understanding that the publisher is not engaged in rendering professional services. If professional advice or other expert assistance is required, the services of a competent professional person should be sought.

Wiley also publishes its books in a variety of electronic formats. Some content that appears in print may not be available in electronic books. For more information about Wiley products, visit our web site at www.Wiley.com

Library of Congress Cataloging-in-Publication Data:
Jackson, Lawrence Patrick.
    Ralph Ellison : emergence of genius / Lawrence Jackson.
        p. cm.
    Includes bibliographical references and index.
    ISBN 0-471-35414-7 (cloth : alk. paper)
    1. Ellison, Ralph. 2. Novelists, American—20th century—Biography. 3. African American novelists—Biography. I. Title.

PS3555.L625 Z74 2001
818'.5409—dc21
[B]

                                           2001022367

Printed in the United States of America

10 9 8 7 6 5 4 3 2 1

For
my mother,
Verna M. Jackson

and

in memory of
my father, Nathaniel Jackson, Jr. (1933–1990)

Contents

Illustrations follow page 236

Preface

And learn that streets loom larger in the mind than ever
Upon the arches of the hills:
That kisses linger in the memory as indelibly as pain
Or harsh words thrown through adolescent anger.
Fined too, the dream which went before the passion,
(That child father to the childish man) of him who dedicated me
And set me aside to puzzle always the past and wander blind within the present,
Groping where others glide, stumbling where others stroll in pleasure.
And now returning after all the years to crawl the paths most others
Had forgotten. My second coming into deep second, that frontier valley
Between two frontier hills, that world bounded by Walnut and Byers.

　　　　　—excerpt from the poem "Deep Second" in *Trading Twelves*

IN JULY 1953, Ralph Ellison returned to Oklahoma after an absence of nearly twenty years. He returned to Oklahoma a hero, nationally recognized by his literary peers and claimed by powerful and important people as a credit to the former Indian Territory. He was treated as the welcome child, the "red-cock crowing on a hill," as he described himself in a letter to Albert Murray. Ellison's stature grew at a time when racial segregation was beginning to crumble all over the United States, and quickly in Oklahoma, where it had been in place less than fifty years. The first Negro American awarded the National Book Award for fiction, he was an appropriate symbol for the intellectual promise of liberal democracy and peacetime American freedom. But after the dinners and festivities had quieted and Ellison was alone in his hotel room (his wife of eight years had not accompanied him), he had sober if not grave moments which he poured into a rare poem, an elegy to the main thoroughfare of the black community of his boyhood. The hub known as "Deep Second," or the "Deuce," was the emotionally charged landscape of the place that he had remembered and tried to forget. Oklahoma was the territory of his dreams.

The return to the ground of his birth was as poignant and nostalgic as any homecoming, but Ellison's concern with home would have enormous significance for American literature. Oklahoma would form the signal terrain of the novel Ralph Ellison could never bear to finish. For whatever past that lay buried there, for whatever monumental experiences that had formed him and were now behind, after the triumph of *Invisible Man* Ellison did not go on to publish subsequent novels. In his first book he had examined the geography of immediate significance to his own personal experience: a Negro college in the deep South, and New York City during the height of black "fellow traveling" with Communists. When he began the second piece of fiction, he intended to launch the novel from the base of his youthful experience in Oklahoma. However, despite notable exceptions, Ellison kept in his desk the voluminous work he drafted in the years immediately following the publication of *Invisible Man*. In a 1960 short story, "And Hickman Arrives," and again in a 1973 short story, "Cadillac Flambé," Ellison displayed his trademark razor-sharp irony and still considerable power as fiction writer. But whatever his need—either to perfectly craft the geography of his early years, or to escape it—he used the next symphony in prose mainly for his own enjoyment. He was satisfied to publish an occasional riff off the grand Ellisonian melody.

Ellison had accepted the Aristotelian view that, as a novelist who had produced a work of art, especially a tragedy, he had released "magic" capable of cleansing and purging dangerous and troubling emotions. His award-winning and comitragic book *Invisible Man* succeeded as a work of art, and brought with it a justification and a pattern for the decisions that Ralph Ellison had made in his own life. The novel in itself, and then all the machinery of its critical success, enabled him to confront and to triumph over the emotional wounds of his youth; that he emerged whole is due at least in part to a series of ritualistic recastings of himself in the guise of the narrator in *Invisible Man*. But something prevented Ellison from coming to the same closure about the story that included so much of his early life in the Southwest. While he was recognized as a novelist, for the remainder of his career, his reputation grew mainly through essays that stressed the rich racial ambiguity of the American legacy. At the age of thirty-nine, Ellison became the publisher of literary, artistic, and social criticism, and occasional short fiction.

Between 1954 and 1964, he wrote significant essays on American literature, life, and culture in general; and in particular, on the paradoxical freedom found in the discipline of Negro American life. Ellison's enduring genius shone in two essays in which he nimbly distinguished himself from among his critical peers: "Change the Joke and Slip the Yoke" (1957) and "The World and the Jug" (1963–1964). When well-meaning writers tried to substitute theories and statistics for the deep texture of black life, Ellison warned them to expect results outside of their narrow formulas. He carried that idea into the late 1970s with his last signature piece, "The Little Man at Chehaw Station."

Five years after his death in 1994, a segment of Ellison's unfinished novel was published by his estate. *Juneteenth,* the middle section of larger work, devotes much of its energy to the Oklahoma of Ellison's youth. He explores the past through two figures: Bliss, the orphaned boy of indeterminate race who spends his life playing ambiguously across the American color line; and Hickman, the grandfatherly black preacher who raises him. It is a novel rife with longing, and it remembers vividly the early part of the twentieth century, the time of Ellison's own boyhood. He seems to have written the core of *Juneteenth* in the 1950s, chiefly when Ellison was a fellow at the American Academy in Rome, and not too long after he had told his friend Richard Wright, "I am working on a novel that demands I go West." The time Ellison devoted to writing his post–*Invisible Man* fiction were years of steady transformation for him and American society. Ellison had moved from being an embattled social critic, a position he had occupied during most of the years he wrote *Invisible Man,* to being a symbol of America's willingness to accept talented blacks. He was a shining example of Negro American class and high artistry. The black boy who had grown up poor and fatherless had traveled far.

His career and his life hinged upon irony. Apparently untrained and untried, he had sent his first novel *Invisible Man* into the world and collected the National Book Award—the "bright hunk of gold," as he called it—all in his thirty-ninth year. His own father, Lewis Ellison, had died when he was thirty-nine. Ralph Ellison knew that his most intimate story lay in his earliest years, during the time he had turned himself into the writer of *Invisible Man.* Because, in spite of the lofty promise of the second half of his career, it was due to the achievement of *Invisible Man* that he entered the ranks of the great visionaries and writers of the American scene, which included Thomas Jefferson, Frederick Douglass, Herman Melville, Mark Twain, Jean Toomer, Ernest Hemingway, and William Faulkner.

That is the story that this book, the first biography of Ellison, has tried to tell. It is a narrative of Ellison's childhood, college education, and years as a writer in New York City until his acceptance of the National Book Award in 1953. The book, begun as a dissertation project at Stanford University, has taken six years to write; and while it is not an authorized biography, it was compiled with partial access to the closed archives of Ellison papers at the Library of Congress, portions of which have been available to researchers since 1998. This work draws heavily from both the restricted and unrestricted sources of that archive, supplemented primarily by Ellison's major literary correspondence with Richard Wright, Stanley Edgar Hyman, Langston Hughes, Kenneth Burke, and Albert Murray; and by interviews with his brother Herbert Ellison and with friends and associates.

When this work was begun, only rudimentary biographical data on Ellison's life existed, from a long 1976 interview by Jervis Anderson, and from the early scholarship of Robert O'Meally, who devoted both a dissertation and a scholarly monograph to Ellison's life and work. As the June 2000 publication of his correspondence with Albert Murray bears out, Ellison's life as a man of writing and of ideas is too important for such sparse treatment. Ellison is routinely ignored by biographers, literary historians, social critics, and social historians in studies of literary movements in New York City during the 1940s, even by biographers of Richard Wright. Ellison's active involvement in the socialist Left of the 1930s and 1940s, the black radical rights movement of the same period, and the literary circles around the League of American Writers, *New Masses,* and *Partisan Review* not only has never been documented before, but has rarely ever been a topic of public intellectual discussion. Daniel Bell declared Ellison a cousin of the family of "New York Intellectuals" in *The End of Ideology,* but he based that judgment exclusively upon Ellison's standing after 1953, when he could have been legitimately claimed by almost every major faction of American writers, from the New Critics to the Beats. Little has been done with the important friendships he shared with Richard Wright and Langston Hughes, or in fact, with the existence of an entire fraternal cadre of important leftist black writers and critics who lived in or frequented New York—William Attaway, Theodore Ward, Carlton Moss, Horace Cayton, C. L. R. James, and Lawrence Reddick. Ellison's life and work during the 1940s, his patient crafting of a novel that would bridge medieval belief and the atomic age, resonates as a singularly rich American struggle, perhaps *the* artistic struggle of our epoch.

Acknowledgments

I would like to thank first of all Horace Porter, my dissertation adviser, for believing that this work was important and could be completed. The project would never have been undertaken without his sage counsel and willingness to preserve the endeavor at its most vulnerable moments. I have never before received such unflagging support and friendship.

I owe my understanding of the writer's craft to the persistence and concern of Horace Porter, Sandra Drake, Richard Yarborough, Sandra Adell, George Dekker, Beverly Moss, Ike Newsum, and Roland Williams. As a black American, I am not sure that I can overstate, or properly acknowledge, the importance of their labors.

This work was made possible by several generous grants and fellowships: a Ford Foundation postdoctoral fellowship; a funded residential fellowship at the W. E. B. Du Bois Institute at Harvard University; three semesters' leave from Howard University; a Faculty Research Opportunity Grant from Howard University; a Walter and Theodora Daniel Fund Howard University School of Education grant; a dissertation fellowship and research grant from the University of Vermont; a graduate fellowship year at the Stanford Humanities Center; and the Graduate Research Opportunity Grant from Stanford University.

I presented portions of this work at Harvard University, Emory University, Boston University's Center for the Study of Race and Social Division, the University of Michigan, the University of Washington, and Stanford University. I wish to thank Rudolph Byrd, Mark Sanders, Glenn Loury, Eileen Kaizer, Alford Young, Shelly Eversley, and Geneva Lopez for giving me the opportunity to present and gain critical feedback on my scholarship.

Several libraries, librarians, community leaders, and local historians provided me with invaluable assistance during my research: James Johnson,

Charles "Ceedy" Morgan, and William "Tank" Jernigan of Oklahoma City; the Oklahoma State Historical Society and its staff; the family of Payton, Marjorie, and Julia Williams; Emogene Crittenden, registrar of Tuskegee University; Daniel Williams of the Tuskegee University Library; Rebecca Hankins of the Amistead Research Center; Rebecca Martin and Craig Chalone of the University of Vermont Libraries; Marva E. Belt of the Moorland Spingarn Library of Howard University; the Penn State University Archives and Manuscript Collection; Jason Purnell, my research assistant at the Du Bois Institute; Maureen Heaher of the Beinecke Library at Yale University; the Milton Eisenhower Library of Johns Hopkins University; the Schomburg Center for Research in Black Life and Culture; Ahmed Jones and the Library of Congress Manuscript and Archives; Roy Hurst of KPFK Los Angeles; and the Tamiment Library of New York University.

For permission to use portions of Ralph Ellison's writings, including materials from the Ralph Ellison Papers at the Library of Congress, I would like to thank Fanny Ellison and Professor John Callahan.

I owe a scholarly debt to several people who read sections of this manuscript in its early stages and provided useful criticisms: Michael Hill, Adam Bradley, and Biodun Jeyifo. I owe thanks to those who read the manuscript as it neared completion: John Reilly, Ross Posnock, Horace Porter, James A. Miller, Corey Olds, Jack Stallings, and Regine Ostine. For his wise criticism and consistent friendship, I thank W. S. Di Piero.

I would like to thank several individuals for their support and advice during the completion of this project: Jerry Watts, Barbara Griffin, Jon Woodson, Huck Guttman, Philip Baruth, Jim Miller, John Bracey, Akinyele Umoja, John Stewart, Kennel Jackson, Diane Middlebrook, Ramon Saldivar, Abdul Jan Mohammed, Sylvia Wynter, Avon Kirkland, Houston Baker, Henry Louis Gates Jr., Eleanor Traylor, Richard Newman, Alan Wald, Mark Lenzenweger, Edward P. Jones, and Charles Dugger.

As one of the first people to do sustained work on Ellison and as my undergraduate teacher, Robert O'Meally was generous and important in this project. Hazel Rowley, who has completed a biography of Richard Wright, generously shared her collected files and contacts and read my manuscript. Arnold Rampersad, who is writing a biography of Ralph Ellison, was charitable and kind and shared with me several facts about Mr. Ellison's life.

There are many people who agreed to be interviewed in conjunction with this project, usually at their homes or occasionally over the telephone, to whom I owe considerable thanks: Herbert Aptheker, Sanora Babb, Currie Ballard, Joe Frank, the late Dr. John Henrik Clarke, Marvel Cooke, Elnora Decker, the late Herbert Ellison, Saretta Finley, Carolyn Walcott Ford, Michael Harper, Juanita Vivette Harris, Ruth Jackson, Tracy McCleary, Darlene McLeod, Robert Meezy, Prentiss Nolan, Robert O'Meally, Nancy Packer,

Gordon Parks, Mike Rabb, Etheldra Robinson, Hollie West, Jimmie Stewart, Laly Washington, Freddie Williams, and Tommie Williams. For enduring repeated interviews, writing letters, and sharing original collections, I would like to single out for thanks Albert Murray, Ernest Kaiser, and Michel Fabre.

I apologize if I have omitted anyone deserving of thanks.

I have the pleasure of counting among my friends the brilliant and distinguished writer Ethelbert Miller of Howard University. He introduced me to my literary agent Jenny Bent, who found a publisher interested in the biography. This manuscript was completed under the clear direction of Hana Umlauf Lane, who was patient, judicious, and marvelously free from prejudice against a novice.

I would like to thank my mother Verna Mitchell Jackson, my sister Major Lynn S. Jackson, my stepdaughter Katani, and my wife Regine, for their unselfish love.

1

Geography Is Fate

1913–1916

OKLAHOMA CITY'S 407 East First Street buzzed with excitement as Ida Ellison, whom close friends called "Brownie," neared term in early 1913. She and her husband Lewis[1] lived in an apartment in a large rooming house owned by J. D. Randolph and his family. Because the Ellisons had already lost an infant son, Alfred, born shortly after their marriage,[2] the Randolph clan was paying extra-special attention to their "kissing cousin" from Georgia, assuring that Ida was well fed and comfortable, and had few chores to perform. On March 1, 1913,[3] matriarch Uretta Randolph and her mother Thomas Foster helped deliver the Ellisons' first healthy offspring into the world.

Lewis Ellison, then working as a driver, seems to have been principally responsible for his son's name. He named his second son Ralph Waldo after the famous American poet and philosopher Ralph Waldo Emerson. After the loss of his first child, Lewis Ellison had developed an acute interest in the correlation between name and destiny. He was determined to invest enormous potential in his infant son.

The choice of name showed no vague desire to link the boy's destiny with a famous American. Lewis wanted to think majestically about his son's future. He deliberately named his son after the founder of the American Renaissance in literature and philosophy, telling family and friends that he was "raising this boy up to be a poet."[4] Emerson was certainly one of the best-known writers and thinkers of turn-of-the-century America; he seems to have been Ellison's favorite writer. Ellison probably had read the easily available poetry

1

or essays of Emerson while stationed at a Southwestern military post. Certainly his landlord J. D. Randolph, the former principal of Oklahoma City's lone black school, had Emerson's significant works. And Emerson's famous poem "Threnody," addressing the death of a son, might have consoled Lewis and Ida after burying tiny Alfred. The name bestowed on the first boy had been a peace-making gesture toward "Big" Alfred, Lewis's father; this child would represent his own inclinations and dreams. Lewis named his son, hoping that the boy would not have to spend his life digging ditches or breaking stones. Besides reflecting Lewis's own literary interests, the name indicated enormous pride and a bit of pretension, if not outright showing off, about the potential of a black boy born outside of the South. Clearly, in passing over the name of the renowned black poet Paul Laurence Dunbar, for example, Lewis Ellison was expressing the wish that his son's life would not be as defined by race as was his own. Ellison felt strongly that black destiny in America was linked to literacy and social equality, even when it meant moving next door to whites and brushing aside the cherished customs of the South. Lewis Ellison would develop a close and affectionate bond with his son, who nearly shared the same birthday with him.

Born in the newly ratified state of Oklahoma, Ralph Waldo Ellison represented ambition to his parents. Like most black Oklahomans, Ellison's father Lewis was something of a pioneer, something of a refugee. Lewis Ellison—five feet eleven inches tall with light brown skin—had spent his youth as a soldier and as an entrepreneur. To Ralph, Lewis's travels would become legendary. Even after death, his father would remain the magnanimous and wise centurion, the sensitive but conquering hero.

Lewis Ellison, born on March 4, 1877,[5] grew to manhood in one of the most violent and racially contested regions in the post-Reconstruction era South, up-country South Carolina. The son of Alfred and Harriett Ellison, Lewis spent his childhood on a farm, not far from the town of Abbeville, the local county seat for Abbeville County, South Carolina. The county of his birth, just across the Savannah River from Georgia, where black citizens verged on outnumbering whites two to one, was marked by a high level of racial tension that periodically exploded.

Ralph's grandfather Alfred had been born a slave in Fairfield County, South Carolina, in August 1837. He and twenty-seven bondpeople were owned by widow Mary Ann Ellison.[6] Mrs. Ellison sold her plantation in 1855 to the ambitious entrepreneur of her generation, David Aiken. It is possible that ten-year-old Alfred moved with Mary Ellison into Abbeville; but if he was well-developed and strong, as his later name "Big" Alfred suggests, he probably headed into Aiken's cotton field. If he became Aiken's property, which is likely, then Alfred exchanged the temperate slavery of his youth for significantly harsher bondage as an adolescent and young adult.

The son of an Irish immigrant, Aiken owned several large plantations and "scientifically" farmed cotton. After serving the Confederacy as a colonel in the Civil War, he had become the most outspoken opponent of black enfranchisement in Abbeville County. An 1868 state investigating committee charged Aiken, a violent man, with administering scores of beatings, committing arson, and inciting whites to murder at least four blacks.[7] Whether Alfred Ellison served on Aiken's plantation or not, he could not have grown up without knowing of formidable opponents to black freedom. Alfred's inevitable experience with men like Aiken callused him and inspired his own self-determination. He became a member of the Union League, committing himself to protecting black elected officials such as Hutson Lomax, Abbeville's black commissioner of elections. Noting the severity of racial strife in his region following the Civil War, Lomax had proposed that a colored man should monitor each polling place in Abbeville to ensure polling booth equity.[8] During the era of the Reconstruction, when federal troops were garrisoned throughout the South, black people seemed poised to spring far away from their origins in servitude.

By 1870, the thirty-three-year-old Alfred, now a freeman of four years, was married to nineteen-year-old mulatto-looking Harriett Walker. The couple, along with Alfred's ten-year-old brother William, decided to make their home where they had gained freedom. Alfred and Harriett worked as domestics. Alfred Ellison could neither read nor write, but his wife Harriett could read. By the time Lewis was three, the Ellison family farmhouse on Magazine Hill, off Poplar Street, was filled with children: eight-year-old Janie, seven-year-old Creesy (Lucretia), five-year-old Sallie, and one-year-old James. William Ellison had become the local schoolteacher.[9]

While working as a domestic, Alfred grasped the reality of Southern racial politics and made the most of a tenuous situation. Relying on his common sense and robust physique, Alfred became town marshal of Abbeville in the early part of the decade.[10] His was a Faustian bargain. His youth as a slave in a cotton-heavy region had taught him to cultivate powerful white allies. He won the office with the influence of powerful whites like Aiken, who wished to abolish black rights. Part of the price of keeping his job was enforcing laws aimed at ending black enfranchisement.

After the pivotal election of 1876, known as "Big Tuesday," an event celebrated by local whites for the next seventy years, Republican rule—the party of Lincoln—ended, and with its ouster went the federal troops. Though black enfranchisement remained alive for some years under the benign white supremacy of Governor Wade Hampton (who had entitled his campaign pledge and booklet "Free Men! Free Ballots!! Free Schools!!!"), ultimately it, too, came to an end. Black men like Ellison, public figures, had little terrain upon which to maneuver. Factions of Democratic cavalry called Red Shirts and Ku Klux riders, sometimes numbering in the hundreds, routinely assaulted and shot up black Republicans—even U.S. marshals such as Louis Waller and A. M. Heard.[11] Four months before the election, white supremacists had helped guarantee its outcome by massacring the politically important black militia at nearby Homburg, South Carolina. Even though he ably performed his tasks and voted for the Democratic Party's candidate Hampton (a liberal on race issues), Alfred Ellison lost his job at the end of the Reconstruction period. While Ellison admitted voting for Hampton in 1876, he snorted to those who cared to listen, "I am not a democrat."[12] Neither his words nor his realpolitik could change the coming tide. In September of 1878, Abbevillians elected John Kirby as town marshal.

After the return of "Home Rule" to the South, the job of town marshal of Abbeville became nearly impossible for a black man to hold. The marshal's duties involved more than merely countenancing white supremacy. One of the most important functions was to enforce the rigid vagrancy laws of South Carolina, aimed at keeping available an abundant pool of cheap labor. If found on the street without the approval of a reputable white, black men were quickly imprisoned and then farmed out to various businesses under the brutal convict-lease system, which sometimes surpassed slavery in its harshness. Employers had little long-term interest in the convicts and worked them under inhuman conditions with minimal concern for their safety. Particularly notorious was the 1879 attrition rate of "Stockade No. 5" in Edgefield County, where 128 prisoners died, some of them not even fourteen years old.[13] The prisoners had been farmed out to the railroad, laying trestles in the swamp land between Greenwood, South Carolina, and Augusta, Georgia. Even though blacks constituted a majority of the population in Abbeville County, their political rights were in great jeopardy.

Throughout his youth, Lewis Ellison was a witness to racial brutality. When he was five, a black man, Dave Roberts, was taken from the town jail and lynched in the town square.[14] Alfred and Harriett Ellison sent their son to school in order to prepare him for a better life than their own. His uncle William apparently taught him to read and write; but Lewis, the first male child growing up on a labor-intensive farm, would have been extraordinarily lucky to have received schooling through the eighth grade. As Lewis reached the age of learning a trade in the early 1890s, the viciousness of racial prejudice set in. Some years earlier in 1885, shortly after the election of Grover Cleveland, the first Democratic president since the Civil War, the black Northern journalist T. McCants Stewart of the New York *Freeman* traveled to his native South Carolina to offer a candid assessment of Southern prejudice. He found almost nothing to complain about, and viewed the races operating in public places fraternally. "I feel about as safe here as in Providence,

R.I. I can ride in first-class cars on the railroads and in the streets."[15] But the ensuing decade had dashed any optimism about the Palmetto State. After the Supreme Court *Plessy v. Ferguson* decision of 1896, the triumph of negro-phobic politicians, and the erection of rigid barriers to prohibit interracial socialization, the economic exploitation of the Negro farmer and laborer would rival that of the former slave regime.

Lewis Ellison did not lack courage. In 1898 when he reached twenty-one, Lewis left Alfred and Harriett Ellison and the peace they had made with Abbeville. Obviously he wished neither to submit to the newly minted and insulting jim crow social customs nor to wind up in the county stockade. One of the few occupations open to him was laying trestles for the Southern Railroad. In 1900, his teenage brothers James and Robert were working as shop laborers for the Southern. Barely fifteen, Lewis's youngest brother, William, was an office boy at the local cotton mill. Lewis left—probably in May 1898. Before the year's end, another South Carolina racial massacre had taken place close to Abbeville in the village of Phoenix. Red Shirt cavalry mercilessly struck twelve blacks at random on November 9 and 10, following a botched attempt to organize black voters for the general election.[16] Instead of competing with the chain gang for unsavory jobs, or coming into open conflict with local whites or perhaps his own father over politics, Lewis moved, temporarily, to Atlanta.

In his heart he nurtured a dream of adventure and recognition, now tantalizingly possible. Congress had declared war on Spain in April, seven weeks after a deadly explosion aboard the USS *Maine,* anchored in the harbor of Havana, Cuba. With the ditty "Remember the Maine!/ To hell with Spain" in the air, and having heard glowing reports of Commodore Dewey's naval victory over the Spanish fleet in the Philippines, Lewis enlisted on May 31, 1898, in the Twenty-fifth U.S. Colored Infantry, under the supervision of Captain James Ord.[17] The Southwestern exploits of the Ninth and Tenth U.S. Cavalries—the fearless black Indian fighters called "Buffalo Soldiers"—were widely known, and not long after the commencement of hostilities, young Lewis Ellison had decided to join up. He entered the service to sustain his bid for independent adulthood. Lewis no doubt noticed the connection between being a soldier in uniform and his dad's old job as town marshal. He wanted to outmaneuver more than escape the older man.

Lewis joined the army in the era of American imperial expansion. Military service presented an opportunity for a black man to command the respect of the citizens he was sworn to protect or whose interests he would advance. There was no small amount of pride, too, in serving under the Ohioan and ex-Union soldier William McKinley and the Republicans, who had taken back the White House in 1896. In the uniform of Uncle Sam, whites might accord black men a degree of dignity and respect.

While the hostilities with Spain in Cuba caught all the newsprint, Lewis waited out the Spanish American War in boot camp at Chicamauga Park, Georgia, becoming accustomed to the rigor and discipline of life in the U.S. military. After he had mastered close order drill and platoon tactics, and learned to operate his Krag-Jorgenson bolt-action rifle, the raw recruit mustered into F Company of the Twenty-fifth Infantry on September 10, 1898, at Camp Wickoff in Montauk, Long Island.[18] Ellison joined a seasoned outfit. The unit had outfought Spanish Regulars in the war and had seen action at the battles of El Caney and Santiago in the first week of July 1898.[19] Ellison was among the new recruits bringing the regiment back up to full strength after the cessation of hostilities. Soon the War Department parceled out the all-black Twenty-fifth to the sparsely populated territories of the American West, where they caused little controversy and served outpost and garrison duties in New Mexico, Arizona, and Colorado.

Lewis Ellison went on a 2,600-mile train ride with F Company to Fort Bayard in what is now southwestern New Mexico. Established shortly after the Civil War, Fort Bayard guarded the Pinos Altos mining district and Silver City from Apache marauders. Not far from the Mimbres River, the fort sat at the base of the Santa Rita mountains. Ellison adjusted to the desert and then proved himself adept at several unsoldierly activities. One of them was gardening, the other was reading. After a few weeks on a post covered with cactus, the South Carolina native became the gardener of Fort Bayard. With nearly a half-dozen assistants, Ellison oversaw a huge agricultural project of perhaps fifteen acres, yielding many thousands of pounds in spinach, lettuce, cabbage, okra, celery, squash, tomatoes, and more. His fellow troopers appreciated the man who ably supplemented their meager rations. When not irrigating a field or answering a call for guard duty, Ellison made use of the fort's library, excellent by U.S. Army standards. His post carried fifteen subscriptions, including *Harper's Weekly, Puck,* the *New York Herald,* and *The Nation.* As a literate trooper, he also may have had the opportunity to teach or study in the extraordinary Chaplain Allen Allensworth's post school, specializing in elementary education for the black troops. Fort Bayard's Allensworth, one of the few black chaplains in the West, pioneered army educational services for enlisted men.[20]

Military service suited Ellison. He decided to reenlist after half a year in the dry desert heat. On March 2, 1899, Captain Ord judged him to possess a "very good" character—a superior evaluation—when he issued Ellison a recommendation for reenlistment.[21] Ellison was a man of quality, seemingly destined for a noncommissioned officer rank.

After six months on the Mexican border, F Company and the rest of the Twenty-fifth received orders to go to the Philippine Islands in the South Pacific to help quell the Filipino national independence movement led by the young general Emilio Aguinaldo. Since February, U.S. volunteer regiments had fought the superior forces of Filipino nationalists. The year before, Aguinaldo's rebel army had helped the American naval hero Commodore Dewey to take Manila, but Aguinaldo's plans for an independent state had run afoul of U.S. diplomatic aims. Whereas Congress had amended a clause to its declaration of military action preventing the annexation of Cuba, no such prohibition protected the territory of the Philippines, seen as a desirable ornament for the maintenance of global power. Ellison's regiment left for Manila from the U.S. Army's San Francisco military installation at the Presidio, close to the Golden Gate Bay. The unit arrived at the Philippine capital July 31.[22] When the black soldiers began to disembark onto the streets of Manila, white American bystanders spat out to them, "What are you coons doing here?" The proud black troops, vested in irony, and being scholars of the white American psyche, replied unflappably in the popular language of Kipling, "We've come to take up the white man's burden."[23]

More than sixty thousand American troops, or about three-quarters of the U.S. Army, were in the field by the summer of 1899. Lewis's company learned mainly about garrison duty and combat drilling following their arrival in the Philippines. The rainy tropical climate was bleak, and in characteristic fashion the black American soldiers were undersupplied. Many companies spent the war guarding telegraph lines. The Twenty-fifth regiment held a line between the towns of Caloocan and La Loma the first couple of months, until the troops engaged negroid-looking Philippine insurgents on October 9. During the ninety-minute defense of the lines, a musician from E Company was killed, but Lewis Ellison acquitted himself with particular valor and cool thinking, ably handling his Krag. The next day, Ellison had every reason to believe in the American dream of upward mobility. He received a field commission. Company commander First Lieutenant H. C. Clark appointed Ellison lance corporal, a promotion that brought increased pay and made him a noncommissioned officer.[24] Lewis may have set his sights on becoming a staff sergeant.

The company then moved to the mountainous Zambales province, the region where F Company spent most of the war. In December 1899, Missourian John Straat, a freshly appointed lieutenant, took over command of Ellison's unit. After a couple of weeks of rapid movement around the province, marching one hundred miles in four days and reconnoitering distant towns for enemy activity, Straat reduced Ellison back to his original rank of private. It is conceivable that there was an infraction of one of the many rules governing soldierly behavior in the field. The Missourian may have disliked the corporal, described in his military records with a scar over his eye, or thought him unremarkable and unnecessarily distinguished by two stripes. Despite a sterling reputation, Ellison rejoined the masses of black privates.

Meanwhile the damp war turned hot. An incredible boost to morale was the January 1–6 battle at Iba, Zambales, where one thousand of Aguinaldo's troops attacked F and I Companies and received over one hundred casualties from the by now well-acclimated black servicemen. The Twenty-fifth emerged unscathed. The open field combat of Iba would be one of the last traditional military battles of the war, as toward the end of 1899 Aguinaldo turned entirely to guerrilla warfare. During the same week as the success at Iba, other companies from the Twenty-fifth did not fare so well. The Filipinos captured three members of the regiment and tortured them to death, horribly mutilating the men. Many of the companies were in the field with young, untried superiors while their captains remained stateside or in major Philippine cities on detached service assignments. The guerrilla war made it difficult to tell the difference between civilians and enemy soldiers, and U.S. soldiers found themselves consistently retaking towns and territories where they had fought earlier battles. Malaria started to take its deadly toll on the black troops, who were imagined immune to tropical disease by higher-ups in the War Department. The winter and spring brought virtually no enemy activity, but on July 15, 1900, F Company sustained an attack that cost Corporal James Ward his life. The rest of the summer brought little action, and in early fall, F Company returned to garrison duty at Palauig.

Lewis Ellison slogged on through the tedious routines. On November 19, 1900, he participated in a raid alongside other specially selected soldiers.[25] He had nerve as a soldier, but the rigid structure of military life ultimately did not reward him. By December 30, after more than a year in the field, Lewis Ellison had contracted malarial fever and constipation severe enough that he had to be sent to the rear, probably to Manila. He returned to his unit in a weakened condition on January 22, 1901. His company was now stationed in the town of Botolan in the province of Zambales.

As a man into the third year of his enlistment, he earned more than many of the privates in his company and was generous, lending his pay to the men who indulged in cards. Lewis himself did not gamble. After taps on the evening of January 26, before evening gambling got into full swing, Ellison went into a small shanty off post to collect his money. Because gambling violated army regulations, to avoid reprimand, the men took their leisure off the base. While avoiding one military regulation, they were in violation of another, requiring them in the barracks after taps was blown. Mysteriously and without warning, Lieutenant Straat appeared in the off-post shanty that evening, accompanied by the first sergeant. Immediately, the lieutenant ordered every man present put on a list and punished. The soldiers were given two additional hours of drill in full packs per day, one session taking place from 2:30 to 3:30 P.M., the pinnacle of afternoon heat.

Two days later, Lewis Ellison requested that corporal Elijah Reynolds arrange an audience with Straat to explain his special circumstances: drill in full pack was impossible. Ellison still took medicine under a physician's orders to recover from malaria and constipation. Corporal Reynolds knew Ellison well and respected him as a soldier; he marched the private to their company commander. Reynolds briefly explained the situation to Straat, who quickly became enraged. Straat seems to have thought Ellison the ringleader of F Company's confidence men and shirkers. The lieutenant threatened to have Ellison hung by his thumbs if the trooper did not put on his pack and shoulder his rifle. Ellison sensed the situation getting out of hand and requested an audience higher up the chain of command with the regimental commander, Colonel Burt, a suggestion that further enraged the lieutenant. Straat again ordered Ellison to drill, and threatened him and the other men with death if they did not march the post. Led by Ellison, the men all refused and threw down their packs. They were arrested and taken to the stockade for confinement. Straat put in papers for Lewis Ellison's court-martial and dishonorable discharge, along with William Bell, William Bigby, Moses Fowler, Robert Jones, and Alexander Peyton. During the three months that Ellison was in the stockade awaiting trial, American commandos captured the Filipino general Aguinaldo, ending most of the organized resistance on the island.

On the morning of April 9, 1901, a military tribunal made up of the all-white officers from the Twenty-fifth tried Private Lewis Ellison with violating the Articles of War, numbers 20, 21, 31, and 62. Second Lieutenant George Deiss served as the judge advocate. The first two charges were most serious. Straat had accused Ellison of behaving with "gross disrespect, acting in an insolent, defiant and unsoldierly manner towards his Commanding Officer" and refusing to obey "a lawful command of his Commanding Officer 1st. Lieutenant John N. Straat."[26] Ellison pleaded "not guilty" to the charges and told a compelling story of personal illness as his reason for refusing the command of his superior. In the most formal and serious ceremony of his life, he told the tribunal:

> When the sergeant read the punishment to me I said "Sergeant I am just out of the hospital I'm not able to stand that punishment" and I said as this is my first offense in not discharging my duty properly and having been only 11 days out of the hospital I thought may be that if I could get to make an explanation to the Lieutenant that he might be more lenient and give me a court martial. But Doc Mauley told me before I left the hospital that to go to the hospital steward at Botolan every day and get medicine to work out of my system the malaria and cure my constipation. . . .
>
> Taking the lieutenant from the way he looked every day and the way he looked that day I thought him to be very very angry. Then he came down stairs he went outside and said "You men fall in here." I falls in he calls roll, after he called the roll being the first chance to see the lieutenant I said "Lieutenant, I like a chance to make an explanation regarding my case." After he would not give me a chance to make an explanation I said to him

"Lieutenant I don't think I'm being treated right." I said as this is my first offense "I'd like permission to make an explanation to the lieutenant if the lieutenant would give me a court martial instead of this punishment." As he would not let me speak to him and the lieutenant appeared to get more angry than at first, I said to him "Lieutenant I like to have permission to make an explanation." He ordered the First Sergeant [Haynes] out and hang me by my thumbs if I didn't serve the punishment. He said these men will serve the punishment or I will kill them.

The court briefly adjourned, and reconvened at 11 A.M. The only question the tribunal considered was whether Private Ellison had disobeyed a direct order from his commander. Despite accolades from noncommissioned officers Sergeant William Haynes and Corporal Reynolds, who determinedly made a point to mention Ellison's excellent service record during cross-examination, the court refused to excuse the facts. Repeatedly the judges fired the same question to each witness, culminating with Lewis Ellison's own damaging testimony.

RESPONDENT: Did the Lieutenant order you to drill?
ANSWER: Yes sir, after he came out.
RESPONDENT: Did you drill?
ANSWER: No sir.

After slight deliberation, the tribunal found Ellison guilty of each charge, with a few minor alterations. The court changed its charge of "lying out" of quarters after taps to "remain[ing]" and decided that though the private had not engaged in a game of cards, Ellison had still disobeyed the sixty-second article of war. The military judges remanded their prisoner to the stockades of the Presidio de Manila for two years at hard labor, followed by a dishonorable discharge. Ellison seems to have had his sentence reduced and to have left the service in July 1901, deprived of his pension and forfeiting all his pay and allowances. The only other dot on the historical record came in January 17, 1902, when Lewis, apparently stateside and free, requested a copy of the proceedings of his court-martial. After his muster out of the service, Lewis returned to his family in Abbeville, chastened and in less than vigorous health, stripped of the tangible benefits of three years of military service.

Civilian life at home offered little relief to the prematurely retired soldier. Abbeville had grown no kinder in its ritualized injustice toward black citizens. The U.S. Army under Republican administrations had been a logical place for a relatively ambitious but informally educated black man from the South just two years following the *Plessy* Supreme Court decision. Ellison's return to the South Carolina of racial demagogue "Pitchfork" Ben Tillman and the party of Jefferson Davis signaled personal defeat. He worked as a laborer for a few years, repairing his health and saving cash for another move. First Lewis, likely in partnership with his brother James, opened an ice cream parlor and confectionery for blacks in Abbeville,[27] who like other black Southerners routinely were forced to the rear steps and kitchens of every eating establishment in the South. This undertaking was short-lived, and may have foundered because of the intense determination of whites in all classes to eliminate black entrepreneurs. As late as 1916, Abbevillians would lynch Anthony Crawford after the well-off black farmer refused to have his cotton ginned at a store where he had been meanly insulted. An angry group of whites beat Crawford to death, raked his body with gunfire, then ceremoniously hung the corpse in the town square.[28] There would come a point during those days in October 1916 when even seventy-nine-year-old "Big" Alfred Ellison would have to make a rough but sincere plea before local whites to end the violence.[29]

Stunned at the tenacity of antiblack prejudice and the economic exploitation that fed it, Lewis had a decision to make regarding his future. Like thousands of his neighbors, who migrated en masse to faraway places like Philadelphia and Pittsburgh, he began to pick his way west.

Lewis Ellison seems to have had a connection with another disgraced black soldier and South Carolina native, Charles Whittaker. Whittaker would have talked excitedly about the new territories that Lewis had taken stock of on his way out to Fort Bayard in New Mexico. Whittaker had already determined to try them out on his own, and set out for the recently established state of Oklahoma in 1908. Ellison's service in New Mexico had given him a certain degree of confidence in his ability to survive on the frontier and a general familiarity with the Southwest. His years in the military also gave him status among other blacks and whites. Another advantage Ellison had was the family's work history on the railroads and in local construction projects. Most exceptionally, his tenure building railroad lines had included some experience with pouring concrete.

So Ellison moved west to Chattanooga, Tennessee, where he applied his skills in erecting concrete and steel buildings. The work was plentiful, but racial violence remained a constant threat. Many black Tennesseans sought escape by moving north, others west. Certainly a critical mass of black Tennesseans, particularly from the town of Gallatin, were making a concerted effort to get to Oklahoma. The promises of the Afro-American Colonization Company in Guthrie, Oklahoma, might have lured Lewis out to the new state, which had recently consolidated from portions of the former Indian Territory. Education was to have a new priority. The famous Oklahoman Edward P. McCabe, the former state auditor of Kansas and the highest black elected official outside the South, had already donated the land for Oklahoma's Colored Agricultural and Normal University at Langston.[30] And certainly Lewis recognized the names of some of the all-black towns—Boley, Langston, Taft, Vernon, and Lincoln City—where Negro self-determination was not a crime. Oklahoma loomed as a potential black Atlantis.

Though it seemed providential, Oklahoma City, a city founded by a land run and thus literally established overnight, promised to challenge even the most ardent settler. Oklahoma, whose name was a Choctaw neologism for "red people," differed remarkably from the old South. Blacks had obtained firm ground in Oklahoma City by the time Lewis Ellison pitched a tent on the banks of the Southwest city's largest estuary, the Canadian River. Negroes had been among the six thousand "Sooners" who settled Oklahoma City in the Run of April 1889, when the Southwestern metropolis consisted of empty prairie, tracks from the Santa Fe railroad, and a tree line by the fork of the North Canadian river.[31]

Prior to the Civil War, the entirety of the Territory had been the exclusive province of Native Americans. The Five Civilized Tribes, as the former East Coast Indian nations were collectively known—Choctaw, Creek, Cherokee, Chickasaw, and Seminole—had moved west for resettlement in the 1830s and brought slaves with them.[32] But the plantations of Cherokee and Choctaw had not been in the same league as those in the rebellious Southern states, and in 1860, Oklahoma contained fewer than eight thousand bond-people.[33] Still, during the Civil War, landholding Native Americans had aligned themselves with the Confederacy, and after the war had their lands reapportioned as a punishment for their secession. The federal reapportionment following the Civil War marked the end of Native American sovereignty in Oklahoma and began the process of carving up chunks of land for new settlers. Officially the 1889 Springer Amendment opened the remainder of the vast Oklahoma territory to non-Native American settlement. For the former bondpeople of the relocated Indian tribes, the Territory possessed a tradition of slavery, which the former slaves, known as "natives," were now conspicuously throwing off. In fact, some of the "natives" resisted the flood of Negro migrants to Oklahoma because they considered the Southern black newcomers timid and submissive to whites.[34] But around the time of the first land runs in the late 1880s, the tensions between whites and blacks were slight. Land was plentiful, and white settlers at the time worried more about their crops in the field than matters of politics and racial caste.

In Oklahoma City, black migrants initially clustered on a couple of acres in the southeastern portion of the city called "Southtown," an area bounded by old Washington Street and extending north to Choctaw Street.[35] Bracketed to the north and west by rail lines, and teeming with drifters and ne'er-do-wells, Southtown was the least-desirable quarter of the city. By the early twentieth century, black families had expanded well north, across the railroad tracks, south of Second Street and three blocks east of the city's main business center. Less well-off black settlers had taken to tent life along the sandy banks of the Canadian; one of their prominent communities became known as "Sandtown" because of the amount of sand brought into their homes after routine river flooding. Affluent and tenacious blacks arriving in Oklahoma City attempted to get north of the Rock Island railroad line to First Street, breaking the confines of the black ghetto. Ellison had no illusions about which side of the tracks he hoped to spend his life on.

Lewis Ellison was not quite a young man in the summer of 1909 when he made Ida Millsap his wife.[36] Born on December 19, 1884, Ida had left her own parents, Polk and Georgia Millsap, and her younger siblings still share-cropping on a farm in rural Walton County, Georgia.[37] She and Lewis had in common their refuge (though brief) in the city of Atlanta, where both had fled in their early twenties to escape rural life, and the couple apparently met in Tennessee.[38] An extremely attractive and shapely woman in her mid-twenties, Ida had seen quickly the advantages of a relationship with the former soldier in the open country. Good-looking and single, Ida attracted a great deal of attention. And Lewis was quite singular. Despite his tough exterior, he read poetry, introduced her to influential people in the city, and talked politics with her. The pioneering Ellisons certainly felt that Oklahoma had more to offer than Atlanta with its palpable race prejudice, that city's deadly riot of 1906 still being described in lurid detail as a catalyst for movement north or west.[39]

In the late teens and 1920s, the 300 block of Second Street became the black mecca for business and social life. Eventually it would be surpassed by Fourth Street, which would give way to Tenth Street, finally to be eclipsed by Twenty-third Street, in a steadily expanding northward stream of black Americans on the east side of Oklahoma City. But in 1910, when Lewis and Ida Ellison were first setting up household, Second Street was just a row of intermittent "ready cut" Sears and Roebuck frame bungalows, shotgun houses, wooden tenements, and false-front stores. While the generally temperate Oklahoma climate could shift swiftly to violence as gentle breezes spiraled into tornadoes, the area lacked the sticky heat that freedmen and their descendants had known along the Atlantic seaboard and the Mexican Gulf regions. Even to those living in sod dugouts, the new land seemed good, salubrious even. One of the new migrants to the area, Dr. W. L. Haywood, had come out to Oklahoma because the dry air was supposed to be good for his lungs. But most of the blacks pouring into the city on foot, by wagon, or by railcar came with the hope of encountering new freedom that the rude compromise of 1877 had ended in their native South.

By 1910, the Ellisons, married six months, were rooming with the three adult Randolphs and their five children in the large, two-story frame house at 407 East First Street, barely east of Stiles Avenue and next door to the Colored Methodist Episcopal Church. Ralph Ellison would later describe the man who became his adopted grandfather as tall, "brown as smoked leather," and Indian-looking in appearance; but mainly J. D. Randolph was a prosperous man, well-liked by all races in the new state.[40] Born on October 19, 1862, in Adarville, Kentucky, to a Cherokee father and black mother, Jefferson Davis Randolph was named after the president of the secessionists and later adopted the surname of Randolph from the plantation where his family worked. He grew up in Gallatin, Tennessee, receiving his education from a private German tutor named Zanderwich. Randolph lit out for Oklahoma freedom with the other Boomers in 1898; he served as first principal of the public Douglass School for colored, and published the Territory's first black newspaper, *The Occidental Lighthouse.*[41]

Meeting the Randolphs was an unusual stroke of good fortune for the Ellisons; and it is possible that South Carolinian Johnson Whittaker introduced the new couple to the pillar of Negro Oklahoma City. J. D. Randolph had made something of himself and wanted in on the establishment. A man capable of voting for the Democrats, Randolph put himself in the path of political plums. While he headed Douglass, he earned the same salary as any other white Oklahoma instructor, $60 per month, a feat impossible in the old South.[42] But Randolph suffered on account of his political ambition, which some thought unprincipled. He was forced out of education by black Republicans for making alliances with the Democrats. After leaving the education field, he opened a drugstore and real estate business in conjunction with his son-in-law, W. H. Slaughter, another aggressive entrepreneur.

The Ellisons lived with the Randolph family, probably in a separate or semiprivate apartment attached to the main house on First Street, until after 1914. On the 1910 census, thirty-three-year-old Lewis listed himself as a "streetworker," like many of the other men on his block, involved in the rapid expansion of Oklahoma City's paved roads. His twenty-six-year-old wife answered the query of occupation with "none."[43] Lewis Ellison apparently had invested all of his money with his brother in a Tennessee venture and was now starting from scratch in Oklahoma. But his travels abroad, his military discipline and organizational expertise, and familiarity with weapons were strong assets in the new state.

Another asset was his significant prior contact with powerful whites— military officers, judges, quartermasters, lawyers, and businessmen. Ellison wasn't easily intimidated by loud talk, big words, or white skin. His counsel was valuable during the tense moments of the spring 1911 streetcar strike when Oklahoma Governor Charles N. Haskell declared martial law and deputized four hundred men under the leadership of building magnate Charles Colcord.[44] Organizational talent and the ability to read well separated Lewis Ellison from most of the other black workers who streamed into the territory. Given his important contacts in the black community, his goal of home ownership and economic security seemed within reach. He struck up a relationship with J. D. Randolph, who had become one of the black community's most important men.

In addition to his tasks paving city roads, Lewis may have hired himself on to finish construction at the Colcord building, erected in 1910, one of the first steel and cement structures in the city. Colcord wanted his building to withstand such fires as the apocalyptic San Francisco fire that had melted steel frame structures; a worker with expertise in concrete and steel would have obtained immediate employ. Enormous packinghouses also went up in 1910 that required heavy labor; and the general boom of the period afforded work for anyone familiar with brick masonry.

On his job Lewis came in contact with other veterans who gathered and drank at the local Spanish American War club. Socialists and their theories of state-controlled utilities and well-stocked schools percolated on the political scene, attracting the constituency left from the Populist movement of the 1890s and the unfulfilled progressive promises of the Democrats. With growth lapping over its belt, Oklahoma offered the chance for even the black migrants to enjoy something new and precipitous.

But the tension over precisely how much blacks would be enabled to prosper and exercise freedom, precisely what form would their social and political acceptance take, never disappeared. Soon enough on East First Street, the question of black enfranchisement became cloudier. Segregation had arrived in Oklahoma when the Democrats took over the legislature during the constitutional convention of 1906–1907. Race prejudice began to thicken, with white Oklahomans segregating the new state, making it remarkably similar to Texas and Arkansas in custom and mores. William "Alfalfa Bill" Murray wrote into Oklahoma's state constitution her segregated schooling clauses, legalizing jim crow. In October 1910, the state legislature passed a notorious grandfather clause, automatically enfranchising those whose relatives had voted prior to 1866 and requiring everyone else to pass a rigorous literacy test. Only blacks who could read, write, and recite the state constitution would be allowed to vote, a test that could be passed or failed according to the mood of the interviewer. By the time Lewis and Ida moved to their rooms in the Randolph home on the hill overlooking the Rock Island and Pacific rail yards and switching station, "colored" and "white" were identities gaining more distinct and polarized significance. Black settlers responded to the change in racial attitude with their feet. More than a thousand migrated to the Canadian plains in Saskatchewan and Alberta between 1908 and 1911.[45] The continued race prejudice and swelling race pride affected a small minority quite profoundly. Organizing throughout the state's all-black towns, Chief Alfred C. Sam of the Akim Nation repatriated sixty Oklahoma Negroes to West Africa in 1914.[46]

About eighteen months following Ralph's birth, anxious for more space and privacy, and preparing themselves for more children, the Ellisons moved out of their rooms with the Randolphs and into a single-family house at 218 North Stiles Avenue. Though faced with the demands of a baby, Ida spent considerable time in political meetings and canvassed local neighborhoods for the socialist gubernatorial candidate, coal miner Fred Holt.[47] Under the socialist platform Ida espoused, state government would take over ownership of large-scale mining, oil, cotton, and telephone industries; provide free schoolbooks for students; dispose of poll taxes; admit women to suffrage on the same terms as men; and institute an eight-hour workday.[48] Wanting to invigorate local politics, Ida was drawn to the socialist agenda. The Republicans in Oklahoma had chosen to sacrifice their black constituency by selecting a lily white platform that appealed to white voters with traditional Southern prejudices. The Democratic Party, despite well-publicized exceptions and the occasional backroom deal, was anathema to black people, basing its platform on the racist principles of the Confederate South. In presidential election year 1914, Ida continued her pollstering, and supported Socialist candidate Eugene Debs for president.

Notwithstanding the hard conditions for blacks in Oklahoma, the dream of a better way of life did not fail Lewis and Ida. The house at 218 North Stiles was a recently built, narrow, single-story, wood-frame house, only two blocks around the corner from J. D. Randolph. Though a substantial number of blacks still lived in Southtown, Lewis and Ida were part of the black vanguard, pushing north and east in search of decent, affordable housing. Unhappy with the vice and the disease associated with the Black Bottom, they were resisting residential segregation. The Ellisons were part of a boom that saw a quickening black real estate explosion as their relatively new neighborhood, the Military Addition, filled up and gave way to the Phillips Addition, extending several blocks east. They had not moved to the remote American West to remain locked in patterns of residential jim crow.

Community stalwart J. D. Randolph probably rented the Stiles Avenue home to the young family. The Ellisons occupied the last house on the eastern side of the avenue, on a slight ridge overlooking the rear of Second Street. By 1914, Second Street was a promising black commercial hub of wood-frame businesses, including Andrew Rushing's cafe and Dr. Webster Slaughter's office on the floor above the Cove Pharmacy. Edna Randolph Slaughter served as proprietor of the pharmacy while her dentist husband T. J., Lewis's close friend, administered to patients upstairs. Lewis got to know the restaurateur Andrew Rushing's reliable teenage son Jimmy and made regular visits to his friend Slaughter. The era of the first large settlement in Oklahoma was auspicious for the ex-slaves and their descendants. Black men like Rushing and the successful S. D. Lyons, a hair cream salesman, were beginning to make names for themselves. Even small shop owners with little book learning could lay claim to the middle class and surge over the boundary of the railroad tracks. After saving his money from his jobs in construction, in street work, and as a teamster, Lewis went into business for himself, becoming an ice and coal dealer.

By 1916 the ice and coal business was prosperous enough for the Ellison family to move a block east of Stiles Avenue to 314 North Byers, a spacious home overlooking the Bryant School. Again, Lewis and his family were the ambassadors of the colored race, facing white families at the 400 block of Byers as well as on the entirety of Third Street. For the time being, relationships with whites were amicable. The move to North Byers took the Ellisons to the edge of Third Street, a quiet block whose only black resident was Abraham Baxter. Third Street heralded success, with its paved roads, well-groomed lawns, and backyards for playful children. Lewis was fulfilling the American dream, moving his family into a tree-lined residential neighborhood and putting a quarter-mile between them and the crowded rooming house where they had started. J. D. Randolph, too, had made a move, selling his home on First Street for a more serene dwelling, while an economic upswing jammed Second Street with doctors' offices, undertakers, and restaurants. The eateries and entertainment places catered to a younger, transient crowd, and Second and First Streets gained a reputation as being a little unruly. By the 1920s, when a scuffle or the report of a pistol was no longer unfamiliar, one name linked to the section was the "Bloody Bucket," though the business area never quite duplicated the squalor of East Main and East Grand Streets south of the railroad tracks. The different expectations of black and white pioneers in the new city continued on their separate courses. Oklahoma City was fast trying to lose her image as a Dodge City, with an urbanizing spirit that affected Lewis and Ida as they moved to gain more respectable neighbors. The city directory in 1916 announced that Oklahoma City was "splendidly governed and free from any 'Frontierism.' "[49]

The unruliness of parts of the new city grated less against the Ellisons than did their gradual but effective exclusion from city and state politics. They had anchored themselves to the Territory with Booker T. Washington's idea that political influence was based on economic leverage. Lewis and Ida aimed to provide a completely different life for their children, psychologically and materially. They spent evenings talking about the effects of environment on children. They hoped for stunning success for their young child, who was two generations removed from slavery and far from the plantations. This boy would have as many material advantages as they could afford, and they wouldn't fasten the chains of caste to his spirit. He was not to spend his life laying railroad trestles or facing down a judge advocate's decree. After their son's birth, they made a point of cerebrally engaging little Ralph, easing the boundaries between the world of the adult and the world of the child, expecting a focused attention span and a surefooted memory. The Ellisons' unusual program paid off, and little Ralph seems to have shown exceptional early mental development. The family legend held that he walked at six months and spoke sentences at the age of two.[50] He read just as easily and quickly, and enjoyed his family's attention.

As a toddler, Ralph was unaware of the unusual aspects of his relationship with his father. Lewis Ellison and his son Ralph were inseparable. As soon as the little boy could ride on top of the wagon, Lewis took Ralph with him when he made his coal and ice deliveries. Instead of inhabiting a world with a sharp boundary between feminine care and masculine discipline, Ralph went to work with his father and enjoyed the former soldier's nurturing. His relationship with other adults was unusual, too. The circle of adults frequenting the Ellison household included the Randolphs, the Slaughters, and the Rushings, among other literate blacks—and even whites, like Metropolitan Life insurance agent Mr. Lilly, who came over to break bread with the family. They all were intrigued by Ralph's curious middle name.[51] All seemed to take pride in revealing their knowledge of Emerson, America's premier philosopher, perhaps to one another as much as to the three-year-old child. Ralph felt the extra attention turn sour as the intense focus on the "Emerson" hiding behind his name obscured the existence of Ralph Waldo *Ellison*. He had no idea why the "Waldo" part of his name attracted such regard. Ralph battled to assert his own individual personality and character.

In the two-block radius bounded by Walnut, Stiles, First, and Second, the growing black community satisfied its social needs. The small family enjoyed evenings on Peach Avenue with Lewis's sister Lucretia Brown and her family. The Browns, who had migrated to Oklahoma around the same time as Lewis and Ida, lived in Westtown, one of the small black enclaves distant from the eastern part of Oklahoma City.[52] In the years before widespread radio and cinema, families entertained themselves, especially with music. Ellison told interviewers that his earliest memory was of learning the song "I'm Dark Brown, Chocolate to the Bone" from his father and being schooled in the proper way to perform the Eagle Rock, the popular blues dance step of the early 1910s.[53] While Ralph's Peach Avenue cousins played "Squeeze Me" on the piano, Lewis taught him how to cock his head and rock his hips to the music, likely meriting an eyebrow of caution from Ida.

Ralph's early years had an aura of gentle invincibility. In the backyard of the house on Bryant Avenue, he raced his tricycle and tried to make friends with the fighting cocks that roamed the alley.[54] Some days, when not imagining himself a fireman, he observed the transformation of the wooden Bryant elementary school into a modern brick structure. Ralph began to meet the children of the vibrant and influential preacher Ezelle W. Perry of Tabernacle

Baptist Church, including Darlene, who was his age. And Ida was pregnant again. Though life was hardly easy, the future looked bright for the Ellisons.

On June 19, 1916, Lewis was carrying Ralph with him as he made his way over to Stephens Ice and Ice Cream company, where he loaded up several blocks of ice, and then picked his way through the crowded streets to his customers. His custom was to sit his small son on the wagon, which was covered with sawdust and canvas to keep the ice from melting, and to drive his team around to local grocers and private homes, talking to the boy throughout the day. This was an act of affection for Ida as well as Ralph, since it eased her burden of caring for a rambunctious child while eight months' pregnant. Lewis loved being his own boss and conducting his own transactions, getting to know the city and making connections. Still, his work could be demanding, depending upon the weight of the blocks of ice he was trying to move. Off and on he employed Andrew Rushing's fourteen-year-old boy Jimmy, short but powerfully built, to help him with his deliveries. Of greater concern to him was the compounded medical condition he seemed to have developed during his years in the Army. His stomach pains had become less bearable, and he was frequently doubled over in pain. On that hot June day when grocers would buy all the ice that he could haul, Lewis and three-year-old Ralph brought a delivery to Salter's grocery store. Lewis propped open the large metal plates in the sidewalk, hoisted a block of ice onto his shoulders, and headed for the dirt cellar, his young son on the wagon. Ralph heard him slip halfway down, heard the thud of the ice. The block sliced into Lewis's side, puncturing the stomach wall inflamed by an ulcer and causing massive hemorrhaging.[55] Lewis was rushed to the University Hospital at the northeast corner of Second Street and Stiles, and someone took the shaken youngster home.

Doctors expressed little hope for Lewis's condition from the beginning. While they had stopped the bleeding, they'd been unable to close the wound because of excessive inflammation and infection. Ida herself was in little position to be of much help as she recovered from giving birth to another healthy son, Herbert, in June. While doctors debated the appropriate surgery to take, Lewis's infections spread. Around the middle of July, they determined to try an experimental surgery. Ida and Ralph went to the hospital on July 18 to see Lewis before the operation, which was dangerous and uncertain enough to warrant the admission of a small child into the hospital ward room. The family huddled together briefly, with Lewis concealing his pain from his son. It was a meeting that became a poignant memory for Ralph, and it was also the beginning of his loneliness. In 1956, Ellison rendered the final interaction with his father in vivid and understandably celebratory detail. While it doesn't necessarily provide the details of historically verifiable reality, this passage excerpted from "Tell It Like It Is Baby" suggests a great deal about how Ellison emotionally responded to his father's sickness and death.

We had said good-by and he had made me a present of the tiny pink and yellow wild flowers that had stood in the vase on the window sill, had put a blue cornflower in my lapel. Then a nurse and two attendants had wheeled in a table and put him on it. He was quite tall and I could see the pain in his face as they moved him. But when they got him covered his feet made little tents of the sheet and he made me a joke about it, just as he had many times before. He smiled then and said good-by once more, and I had watched, holding on to the cold white metal of the hospital bed as they wheeled him away. The white door closed quietly and I just stood there, looking at nothing at all. Nearby I could hear my mother talking quietly with the physician. He was explaining and she was asking questions. They didn't talk long, and when they finished we went out of the room for the last time. Holding on to my wrist as I clutched my flowers in my fist, my mother led me down the silent corridor heavy with the fumes of chloroform. She hurried me along. Ahead of us I saw a door swing ajar and watched it, but no one came out, then as we passed I looked inside to see him, lying in a great tub-like basin, waiting to be prepared for his last surgery. I could see his long legs, his knees propped up and his toes flexing as he rested there with his arms folded over his chest, looking at me quite calmly, like a kindly king in his bath. I had only a glimpse, then we were past. We had taken the elevator then and the nurse had allowed me to hold the control and she had laughed and talked with me as we went down to the street. Outside, as we moved along the winding drive into the blazing sun, I had told my mother but she wouldn't believe that I had seen him. I had though, and he had looked at me and smiled. It was the last time I saw my father alive.[56]

Ellison's memoir provides some clues to the gravity of the situation. Ida brought Ralph to the hospital on that day probably because she knew that the surgeon, Dr. L. E. Sauerport, was gambling with her husband's life on the operating table; she wanted to give the boy a final chance to see his father alive. Lewis was majestic for the occasion and bestowed gifts of beauty on his tiny son (who began to see himself as a prince or an heir), dressed up for the visit and somber. Ralph probably had been kept out of the hospital and was pleased to glimpse his father, whom he saw as a giant man of huge proportions, a figure whose immensity could only be taken in through snatches of vision. The elevator operator missed the gravity of the situation and joked with Ralph, letting him control the machine as they sped toward earth, leaving Lewis in the sky.

But most consequential to Ralph's development was Ida's refusal to believe her son's words, despite his attempts at explanation. Ida played the role of skeptic, refusing to believe that her son had seen his father in the operating room. Throughout Ellison's life, his mother would personify the forces of realism and materiality, pulling Ralph when he wanted to linger, and ignoring the precious gift from Lewis, yoking the little boy by the same arm that had held the precious flowers. Ida's challenge to the young boy's version of reality in an extremely powerful emotional experience, a reality perceived surreptitiously—a snatch of a glimpse around a corridor—appointed the imagination as a potential conduit to continue his paternal relationship. Ralph's inability to persuade his mother that the glimpse was real surfaces as an important moment in his incipient understanding of the limitations of his language; his sense of reality was shaken because he could not find words to convince his mother. In his tearful experience, this inadequacy of language fostered his creative imagination. His determination to find ways to prove his experience and substantiate himself combined with the perplexing and unique name he had been stuck with and was unable to figure out produced the "dreamy" quality attributed to the young boy by his peers. Confronted with a profound moment of youthful experience, he had been unable to find the words to make it real. Ralph became a little boy looking for something.

One day after the experimental surgery, on July 19, 1916, Lewis Ellison died.[57] The Ellison family patriarch was killed by an abscess, or pus-filled lesion, of the liver. Ida scraped together enough money to pay Tucker's funeral home and on July 23, 1916, four days after his death, had her thirty-nine-year-old husband buried at the integrated Fairlawn Cemetery on the west side of Oklahoma City.[58] Numb during the entire ceremony in Lewis's honor, Ralph felt, as he later wrote, "bewildered" and "horrified," his senses too overcome even to allow him to shed tears.[59] Of his visits to the cemetery, he always remembered the "raw red clay mounds, the crude granite stones, the wild countryside."[60] Undoubtedly the older men and women at the funeral implored the young boy to be courageous and repress his emotions. One thing that he carried away from the funeral was an intensifying sense of willpower that refused to let him forget the day or what Lewis looked like. For Ralph Ellison, apparitions of his father would remain with him through-out the rest of his life, as he hoped for a reunion with the loving father he had known only too briefly.[61] In Ralph's earliest years, his family had been only moderately prosperous, but upwardly mobile; and he strove throughout his life to uphold that vision, that special aura, of his family. Without much to keep alive his connection to Lewis, Ralph pressed his early years tightly to his heart and turned bitter times attractive. He generally described his childhood years of lack as though filled with charm.

The death of Lewis Ellison devastated the family emotionally and finan-cially. Lewis's death marked the beginning of years of no-frills living, when Ralph disciplined himself to obtain essentials and regularly went without. The little boy on Byers Street began to know the meaning of sacrifice. On Lewis's death certificate, Ida Ellison listed her young family's address not at 314 Byers but at 406 Byers, an address that did not exist, and in a block where no colored people lived. Lewis's stay in the hospital probably had wiped out whatever savings he may have squirreled away, and the address at

406 Byers may have been a ruse to defeat bill collectors. Or Ida may have already been asked to leave her new home for temporary lodging with a generous neighbor. When Lewis died, the Ellisons had been on the upswing; Ralph had a tricycle. Now he wouldn't ride a bike until he started working for Randolph's pharmacy as a teenage delivery boy. As the country eased out of its wartime boom economy, many of Ralph's classmates knew that in theory they were poor, particularly in comparison with whites. Yet few were as poor as the Ellisons.

In his grief over Lewis, Ralph was either glum and withdrawn or furious. It was probably around this time that he began stuttering, a condition that struck him especially during his wrathful moments. Ida, engrossed with the newborn infant she had decided to name Herbert Maurice, had less time for Ralph. Other adults were of little comfort. The "Emerson" queries and ribbings now turned gravely sour and made Ralph silent as he came to terms with the death of his father and the deep pain at permanently losing a guide, comforter, and friend. He had suffered the amputation of a considerable piece of himself; gone was the figure for him to emulate happily. Now Ralph indulged in revenge fantasies, cold with what he called "blue murder," to eradicate those who called him Emerson, partly, no doubt, because the neighbors and friends threatened to erase his surname and hence Lewis's presence.

In moments of solitude, Ralph comforted himself with a recurring fantasy in which he emerged from the cold of the street into the warmth of the sun to see Lewis "rushing toward me with a smile of recognition and outstretched arms." Until he was thirteen, Ralph felt that the grim "processes of time and the cold facts of death" were held in abeyance through the power of this dream.[62] The trauma also seems to have influenced Ralph's youthful approach to people; a welcome smile and surface grace would give way to a refusal to become deeply intimate or to make himself vulnerable. Ralph became affable, but always managed a considerable emotional reserve. He was thought both quiet and aloof. And then, to cauterize his grief and to begin finding his own sense of self, Ralph began to experience more complex feelings toward his father. Instead of solely blind adoration and loneliness, Ralph began to feel abandoned and misdirected, perhaps even angry. Lewis Ellison's absence, coupled with Ralph's peculiar name, caused the youngster to resent the older man. The young man put his conscious mind to the task of asserting a distinctive identity, unassociated with the painful episode. One of the earliest references to Lewis in his writing is characterized by a prickly, almost indifferent tone. Lewis had "named me after someone called Ralph Waldo Emerson, and then, when I was three, he died."[63] Lewis's ritualistic act of naming, in congruence with his sudden death, confounded the young boy, just as the puzzling last words of the grandfather in *Invisible Man* mystify his heirs. However unintentionally, Lewis had set Ralph a-running.

2

Renaissance Man

1916–1925

AFTER LEWIS ELLISON'S DEATH, Ralph's mother became the chief source of his guidance and development. She was a woman alone in the rugged land of Oklahoma, far from relatives and in need of friends. But Ida Millsap Ellison was an unusual woman for her era. She had been the first person in her immediate family to learn how to read and write, and she had attended formal school as a teenager—a rare opportunity for the daughter of sharecroppers. Ida was probably being groomed to be a teacher. Her decision to break with her past and move out to Oklahoma City suggests formidable self-confidence and willpower. Whereas Lewis's travels to Atlanta, Long Island, New Mexico, and the Philippines fit neatly into the mold of a young man chasing a dream of military valor, Ida's pilgrimage from Walton County, Georgia, to Atlanta, and finally to Oklahoma City, implies an uncommonly vigorous and independent mind, one confident in its ability to ignore or even defy convention. She also possessed two extraordinary assets. According to Ralph's brother Herbert and J. D. Randolph's second son Taylor, Ida was both "smart as hell" and "beautiful."[1]

Ida had moved to Atlanta, away from the rural Georgia plantation in Walton County where she was born, to escape the repressive social relations as much as the poverty. In Oklahoma City, she cultivated the refinement and taste of a woman beyond her actual economic standing. After Lewis's death and Ida Ellison's inevitable acceptance of work as a domestic, she continued to associate with Edna Slaughter, a physician's wife, with whom she sipped tea after work, and Uretta Randolph, who helped J. D. in all of his real estate deals.

23

On her days off, Ida and Edna gathered up their children and window-shopped on Broadway and Main Street, evaluating the finery and opulence and day-dreaming about a better world. She strove mightily to ensure that Ralph would never be shut off from the world beyond black Second Street. Ida made certain that Ralph grew up knowing his pediatrician Wyatt Slaughter in the informal context of his home, where Ralph heard the doctor utter his favorite aphorism, "Prudence is the better part of valor."[2] She was not of the same class as women like Edna Slaughter, but she encouraged both of her sons to feel comfortable in a wide range of social environments. Ralph not only accepted the Randolph-Slaughter clan but viewed them as the equivalent of blood relatives.[3] Ida considered the relationship a solid achievement. She began counseling Ralph not to limit himself just because they didn't have material things at home. Her practical counsel and straightforward manner shot her bright son up beyond his years, preparing him to accept responsibility early on. For young Ralph Waldo, however, there was a significant drawback—Ida did not cuddle.

Other than the occasional afternoon visit with Edna, during which Ralph and Saretta Slaughter would leap onto her mother's ample featherbed, Ida had two constants: work and church. Looking for a job with consistent hours and regular pay, she worked as a chambermaid at the Hadden Hall Family Hotel on 215 West Tenth Street. Daily domestic work did not pay well enough to keep a family afloat. Many women took in laundry, cooked lunch and dinner, and cleaned for white families, but these demanding occupations were not quite full-time employment. And Oklahoma City had no ensconced gentry with deeply established ties to black families, a personal connection that might have compensated for the widow Ida's poor leverage in the marketplace.

By nursery school, Ralph was struggling with the demands placed on his mother who used to have time to play and respond to his dizzying array of questions; now she came home from work fatigued and with her mind heavily weighed down with worries about her family's survival. The change in family fortunes, however, would have its greatest effect on Herbert Ellison, who clung to his mother, brother, and adopted family. He would remain the baby and ward of the family until Ralph came to resent caring for him.

As the specter of race continued to hover over their lives, Lewis's absence made them vulnerable. The Armistice in France brought increased racial tensions back home. Planes routinely blanketed the Deuce with cards and brochures warning blacks to stay away from the polls. From his front porch on Byers Avenue, Ralph watched workmen with bricks and mortar transforming the wooden structure that had been Bryant Elementary school into one of the most modern schools in Oklahoma City, complete with playground swings. The four-year-old boy excitedly imagined that some day he would go to Bryant. Ida began his education in jim crow custom and plainly told him that the school was for whites.[4]

Oklahoma blacks faced more than white brutality in their "promised land." Frontier conditions were difficult, and few people could rely upon the kinds of elaborate kin networks that had developed in the South over decades that were so essential for survival. In 1918, the Ellison family shuttled from Byers back to their former rental home on 218 North Stiles, the Randolph-owned property that had previously signaled their climb toward middle-class success. On their way down the economic ladder, the Ellisons now had to rely on others for help. A stirring example of black communal support for the Ellison household seems to have occurred after Ida moved the small family into that house. She had gone off to work in downtown Oklahoma City on an early morning during the winter of 1918–1919 when a blizzard ravaged the town. Ida Ellison was an unskilled worker in a harsh economic environment. Rain or shine, blizzard or not, if her family was going to eat, she had to go to work.

She told Ralph to keep the fire going in the woodstove, the only heat available in the house. This was not a simple task for her oldest son, who was now attending kindergarten at Avery Chapel A.M.E. under the guidance of Corrine Eagleton, Camille Boyer, and Sallie Floyd.[5] The fire went out, but like a maternal saint, Uretta Randolph came to the children's rescue.[6] The adopted grandmother found Ralph and Herbert huddled together, the embers cold in the fireplace. She removed them to a warm house, probably her son T. J.'s on Second Street, until Ida got home from work.

Ralph had failed to accomplish a grown-up task at a child's age, an experience that emphasized his city upbringing in comparison with the rural experiences of some of his classmates and parents. As a mature adult, he would remind people of his childhood in the city. "I had none of the agricultural experiences of my mother, who had grown up on a farm in Georgia. . . . I shared none of the agricultural experiences of many of my classmates. I was of the city."[7] In the struggle with the stove, he was face-to-face with the sort of survival skill that might have come readily to a rural child. The fire needed fuel and steady attention. But the requirements were beyond the youngster, nearly six years old. Without a father on the urban frontier, Ralph learned that he would have to look out for himself and his family. And through this kind of experience, he was confronted with the necessity of being his own father. At that young age, Ralph realized that he would face the challenge of manhood soon, and despite the paramount influence of his mother, he would face it alone.

Ida clearly relied upon her young son for labor in the family unit. Ralph was given more than light chores from an early age, and he substantially assisted in raising Herbert. His mother expected him to learn fundamental tasks quickly, without the extensive benefit of trial and error. She needed him to move beyond his years. Ralph would not have the luxury of achieving adult discipline as incrementally as would his peers. As he grew older, Ida told her young and quietly articulate son that his generation would have to be responsible for improving the racial situation: she never counseled him to expect pioneering leadership from his elders, but infused him with the very Emersonian creed of self-reliance. Ida told Ralph when he tirelessly questioned the intractability of black oppression that "the hope of our group depended not upon older Negroes but upon the young, upon me."[8] Over time, as he met Ida's steadily mounting expectations, the maturation of the self and the race meshed.

That Christmas was the little boy's best, a feat that his mother would be unable to duplicate in the future. His Christmas gifts gave Ralph an inkling of his mother's ambition for her precocious five-year-old reader. Probably with the help of her more affluent friends, she gave him a roll-top desk, a straight-back chair, and a toy typewriter.[9] Ida wanted to groom her oldest boy in the image of her brilliant friend Roscoe Dunjee, insurgent editor-in-chief of the Oklahoma City *Black Dispatch.* Dunjee had founded the newspaper in 1915 to fight the political schemers who had toppled Langston University's popular black president Inman Page.[10] The editor and his equally eloquent sister Drusilla decried racism not merely in the words of moral indignation. They exposed the unconstitutionality and blatant inequity of economic preferences and social privileges for whites. Roscoe Dunjee was a gadfly who attacked the state's "separate but equal" segregation policy by drawing attention to the unassailable reality of the dismal facilities available to blacks. The editor had impeccable integrity; he refused to accept advertising from anyone attempting to manipulate the Negro vote.

Ida infused her young boy with pride and challenged him to build a better world. During energetic moments, she filled her house with words, talking to Ralph as if he were her peer, weaving elaborate stories about his father: Lewis had fought the Spanish Army in Cuba, journeyed to the Philippines, and even put down a rebellion in far-off China. She told him that his father had opened businesses in Abbeville and in Chattanooga, and had risen to the position of construction foreman in Tennessee and Oklahoma.[11] The little man's deeds, she told Ralph, were to be as mythic as his daddy's. She knew that Lewis, like the men of the Twenty-fifth Infantry dishonorably discharged after Brownsville, had suffered deeply and silently in the military; but that story was unsuitable for a boy alone in the world. Ida managed to promote in her son an optimism that was rapidly disappearing from her own life.

The passion of Ida's life was the African Methodist Episcopal Church. Avery Chapel A.M.E., built at 201 North Geary in 1903, became the focal point for the Ellisons' family activity. The A.M.E. tradition included fire-and-brimstone rhetoric from the pulpit, but featured a core of intellectual sophistication and political radicalism, evidenced in the works of the founding bishop Richard Allen or the back-to-Africa proselytizing wizard Bishop Henry McNeal Turner. The A.M.E. churches had accomplished a remarkable conversion feat in the postbellum South by transforming the belief of a small, urban, Northern congregation into an overwhelmingly popular faith among Southern rural freedmen by the turn of the century.[12] The generally progressive, nonaccommodationist politics of the A.M.E. appealed to Ida. Immediately after the Civil War, radical Bishop Turner, the most famous A.M.E. minister, had preached a sermon titled "God Is Not White" and banned his district from singing the hymn "Lord Wash Me and I Shall Be Whiter Than Snow."[13] In Abbeville, for example, the young A.M.E. missionaries with their college training and formal approach not only had been successful in recruiting members for the church but were also political radicals. At Avery, the undercurrents of politics in Reverend Turner H. Wiseman's sermons on Negro "sobriety and industry" escaped little Ralph, but certainly another aspect of the church service was more readily accessible: the music.

Ida had probably never shared her husband's fondness for earthy, down-home musical entertainment. In her own experience, colored women had to struggle furiously to maintain a virtuous reputation in a society that was speedy to condemn their slightest flaw. The popular blues and rags of her era had succeeded in ruining many a good woman either by luring her to the wrong place at the wrong time or merely by association. The widow Ida turned away from entertainment in the secular world and became more passionate about her duties at Avery Chapel. While the church did not offer popular entertainment, it did emphasize music. Dentist William Haywood led Avery's prominent church choir. A graduate of Tennessee's Fisk College and Meharry Medical School, Haywood was not a musician, but he had a flair for conducting and an enthusiastic passion for Handel. The strict conductor, known to expend as much energy on choir rehearsals and performance as he did on dentistry, shaped the choir to present the most traditional sound possible.[14] Haywood exemplified the school of black refinement and probity, filling the religious service with anthems; and joined by organist Ruth Lewis, converting the psalms into lyrics for song. Embracing the most formal classical music traditions proclaimed for many African Americans their attaining high civilization—though this tendency had the nasty side-effect of blotting out their own rich vernacular musical heritage. Haywood completely rejected even slightly less formal religious music, like the Negro spirituals. As for the popular music of black musicians, Avery's leadership was intolerant. Ellison would write that if Haywood had so much as found such music or notated scores, he would have "destroyed them and scattered the pieces."[15]

On Sunday, wearing a starched white nurse's dress, cap, and shoes, Ida served the church as a steward and nursed her own spirit and mind. There she could receive emotional consolation after her week of toil. During the thundering sermons of Reverend Wiseman, Ida took a post in the Amen corner. And the metaphorical scheme of Wiseman's stentorian sermons appealed as deeply to Ida and the other desperate parishioners as it had to their slave-born parents: the Israelites knew it was their duty to turn Oklahoma into Canaan, despite the work of pharaoh. Avery members from the 1920s, like Mrs. Tommie Williams, a younger contemporary of Ralph's, remembered the sweet-faced Ida's words of joy and ebullience. She told them after the service, "My soul is happy."[16]

Avery also attracted the black middle and upper classes, cementing the ideologies of black nationalism and religious activism with the American middle-class doctrines of thrift, sobriety, industry, and conservation. Doctors, entrepreneurs, and teachers attended Avery. The church hosted such secular activities as musicals, vocal recitals, educational talks, and political speeches. With its conspicuous message of upward mobility and political independence, Avery became Ida's social bedrock, the source of the faith that she and her boys would survive. And everyone recognized Ida's God-fearing devotion. Her publicly recognized piety was a good thing, since after the brutal winter of 1918, Ida's indigent financial circumstances forced her on the mercy of her church to give her a place to live.

At some point in 1919, the Ellison family moved into the Avery Chapel parsonage at 207 North Geary, twenty-five feet north of the A.M.E. Church. Reverend Wiseman had moved on to greener pastures, and the new minister, Reverend J. E. Toombs, had secured his own home and had no need for the church-owned property. Dissatisfied with hotel work and the sleazy assumptions of the guests, Ida accepted a position from Avery's vestry as sexton of the church.[17] Now that his mother wore keys and brandished a mop while the Randolphs, Slaughters, Vivettes, and Pages dressed for church, Ralph was considerably more distant from the elaborate religious ceremonies than his classmates. He lived in the parsonage with a mother who worked on Sundays and discussed the practical matters of creating the pious atmosphere and ritual in the church instead of venerating it.

The parsonage itself was another country. The church-owned home was the largest and most elaborate house Ralph lived in while a resident of Oklahoma City, far superior to the series of narrow, "ready-cut," shotgun houses the family ordinarily inhabited.[18] But there was something else at Avery far more important than the physical space. The ample library gave him many joyful hours of amusement. Built up over the years by Reverends Wiseman, C. R. Tucker, and John N. Abby, and local parishioners, its holdings included adventure novels by Rex Beach and other material accessible to the six-year-old.[19] Ralph began a lifelong passion for reading in the quiet library, a place of mystery and unusual wealth for a black Oklahoman. Many children went home to loving parents, but Ralph may have been the only Negro child going home to an extensive library, with the curiosity and resolve to engage himself with books. Ida encouraged reading not only because of the value that she placed upon education but because it had the practical result of keeping her little son inside the house instead of visiting the busy commercial intersection at Second Street or running pell-mell over to Byers Avenue to the playground and his former playmates. When not reading, however, Ralph roamed the other side of the alley, where he found a couple of playmates, including six-year-old Arzelia Wells and seven-year-old Raymond Dawson. Ralph had immediately gravitated to the alley, a place of "superiority over playgrounds,"[20] because he could indulge in creation, rifling for poor man's treasure in the neighborhood garbage cans. The family's stay in the parsonage through 1920 cemented their connection to Avery Chapel, though Ralph, less awed by church ceremonies due to his daily familiarity with Avery personnel, and not wanting to be mistakenly identified as the pastor's son because he lived in the parsonage, looked elsewhere for magic and reverence.

In the fall of 1919, Ralph Ellison began the first grade. His mother had already bluntly informed the boy that he'd be attending Douglass, an institution distant from home, and now her words took on concrete meaning.[21] Save for one brief period, Ralph would attend the segregated Frederick Douglass School throughout his entire academic career in Oklahoma City. Spirited black Oklahomans had named the school after Frederick Douglass as opposed to the popular public figure Booker T. Washington, the "Wizard of Tuskegee." But Ralph's first view of the school was disappointing. The newly named Douglass School for blacks was actually the old Webster school for whites, and couldn't compare with the new Bryant building on Byers. He felt let down that he wouldn't be attending the school close to home with its vast ball fields.

Black education in Oklahoma City was the center of many of the debates over the legality of "separate but equal" segregation laws. One of the first laws approved by the Oklahoma state government had been to institute segregation in the schools.[22] Negroes were happy merely to have education for their youngsters, and were gleeful at the prospects of a high school. When J. D. Randolph had opened the first colored school in Oklahoma City in 1891, he had started with a two-room shack located next to an aromatic livery stable at Reno and Harvey Streets. After a 1903 fire burned down somewhat better accommodations on 400 East California Street, black parents began pushing to see that their children got a brick school building, just like white kids. By 1904, black students had moved into the old Webster School at 200 East California, formerly for exclusive white use. Riverside Park across the street provided a place for young people's diversions, and the fire escape chutes on the front of the building offered the thrill of a roller coaster for those bold enough to risk a spanking from the teachers.

Ralph's long walk to Douglass, probably begun with his other Geary Street friends Arzelia and Raymond, was an adventure. The children went through the alley to the booming businesses and adult world of East First Street, then headed west, up the hill. At Walnut Avenue they went up a couple of flights of stairs to reach the wooden plank floor of the steel viaduct, which gave the children safe passage over the switch engines and trains from the Chicago, Rock Island, and Pacific lines. Once down the other side of the viaduct, which was scary and slightly dangerous to the youngsters, they marched straight down Walnut Avenue, under strict orders from their parents never to talk to strangers on Main or Grand Street. Parents who lived north of the railroad tracks feared the underworld corridor south of the Rock Island line and west of the Canadian River, which was basically Douglass's neighborhood. Ellison later described the experience of walking past the whores and their johns as if it were a smorgasbord of culture: "And that once the tracks were safely negotiated you continued past warehouses, factories, and loading docks, and then through a notorious red light district where black prostitutes in brightly colored housecoats and Mary Jane shoes supplied the fantasies and needs of a white clientele."[23]

Though the youngster may have noticed the racial dynamics of the sexual exchange, Ralph's time spent in the parsonage and the influence of his pious mother would have made the scene look shocking, if he even understood what took place there. Besides, as an elementary school child, he really did not receive the education of the ruinous streets, since his path on Walnut Avenue did not take him along the corridor of vice. He would soon come to realize, if he did not know it the first day, that there was a far more expeditious route straight down Geary to California that would cut several blocks off his journey, but ambitious and respectable black parents devised elaborate routes to keep their children from spending any time on Main, California, or Grand Street. The lures of prostitution, gambling, narcotics, and saloons threatened the schoolchildren as much as the lynch mob's noose or the chain gang.

At 200 California Street, at the corner of Central, stood the Frederick Douglass School—a "people's college," the rock of higher education for blacks in Oklahoma City. Though the city had imported many traditions of the old South, the presence of a public school that catered to the upper grades without a unique emphasis on manual trades was an indication of the freedom that blacks found in Oklahoma. To begin with, a public high school education of any kind for a black Southerner was a rarity. In 1916, of the slightly more than twenty thousand African Americans enrolled in high school, only a quarter were in public high schools.[24] The Bourbon aristocracy that controlled the South bitterly opposed black education beyond the elementary grades. High schools sprouted up in the former Confederacy only as a result of large migrations of black youth to Southern cities, glutting a soft job market. Public schools were designed to occupy black youth during the day and socialize them to pursue the "Negro job" field of the coarsest unskilled labor.[25]

In contrast, black Oklahomans themselves determined the curriculums within their separate schools; what they lacked were facilities. The network of separate schools and supporting churches (the huge Calvary Baptist Church on East First Street ordinarily held the high school graduations) promoted athletics, plays, oratorical contests and the like for the youngsters, and angrily opposed the appropriation of virtually every black tax dollar for white schools. Black Oklahoma City folks waged war on the school board for fifteen years to get them to erect a new building in a more savory part of town, and Dunjee's crusading *Black Dispatch* ran articles describing the dangers of the East California Street area, especially to the young women forced to endure its gauntlet. According to Dunjee's spring 1918 editorials, Douglass's principal Stafford Youngblood had "worn himself out" keeping "rounders" from spinning lies and corrupting female pupils.[26] Parents feared also that their kids would take a shortcut across the rail yard tracks and be injured by the trains. One boy had his toes cut off by a fast-moving switch engine.

When Ralph crossed the school's threshold in the fall of 1919, Stafford Youngblood was still principal of Douglass. Youngblood had been a chairman of the history department at Claflin University in South Carolina as well as a teacher at the Colored Normal and Agricultural School at Langston. A stern, religious man, Youngblood brought a rare intellectual and organizational expertise to the school. Even though the building was not new, and had never been designed as a high school, Douglass managed to thrive in the face of segregation. Inside the school, which handled youngsters from the first through the twelfth grades, black Oklahomans had created a mighty fortress for the ideals that they held sacred. The stately-looking main structure teemed with so many students that four barnlike compartments dotted the school grounds to deal with the surplus of young African Americans attempting to educate themselves and their families out of the cotton patch. Jim crow politics made it impossible to get new equipment or repairs for the school. Douglass used castoffs from Classen and Central and the other large white schools. Nevertheless, even without electric lights or adequate supplies, and though surrounded by a slum, Douglass made an indelible impact upon its students with an incredible coterie of black educators. The virtual exclusion of blacks from fields like law or business made teaching, medicine, and the ministry the only viable professions through which to display talent and achieve status. Teaching was perhaps the only profession open to exceptional women. During his elementary years, Ralph took his classes in English grammar, reading, arithmetic, orthography, penmanship, U.S. history and civics, health, geography, and agriculture from a staff of competent and deeply concerned educators.

But Douglass's impressive schoolteachers couldn't occupy all of their students' time. After 4 P.M. and on weekends, the young people demanded amusements suitable to their age. Near the time that Ralph began to attend Douglass, he hit another boundary of segregation. At the city zoo in Wheeler Park, his family met with the white community's stiffening resolve to institute jim crow. Oklahoma City had segregated her parks along with the schools, but for many years had not strictly enforced the laws. Black Baptists holding their Sunday school picnic in Wheeler Park in September of 1907 had made the front page of the *Daily Oklahoman,* but the confrontation had not turned into an ugly incident.[27] A Republican member of the city park commission had encouraged the Baptists to leave, telling them their presence might cause white "attendance to fall off," which in turn might discourage the extension of a streetcar line to the park. The streetcar line went through, but black usage of Wheeler Park did not. From then on, the racial attitudes of white Americans in Oklahoma and beyond became increasingly negrophobic; devastating riots swept East St. Louis in 1917 and again two years later when black soldiers returned home from World War I. The nasty racial climate had turned public places into battlegrounds; in Oklahoma City, the zoo was one of the frontlines.

Around 1918, Ida Ellison had begun to meet resistance when she attempted to enter the public zoo at Wheeler Park. The gate attendants told her to use the park set aside for colored, Riverside Park. She could remember a different time in Oklahoma City history. She had had privileges—rights. Now they had been roughly removed, and as a taxpayer, she resented it.

At five or six, Ralph had been sheltered from the more punishing realities of his race. He couldn't understand why his mother had become reluctant to return to the zoo. The episode was uncomfortable, and it resurfaced throughout his life in memory. In the years before his death, Ellison reconstructed portions of the dialogue he had had with his mother on the day she began balking at his requests to go to the zoo. At first, Ralph asked her questions about the animals' health, as if he were designing a hypothesis.

> Had someone done something bad to the animals? No. Had someone tried to steal them or feed them poison? No.[28]

And then he recognized the new element that had begun to weigh upon his consciousness. "Could white kids still go?" he asked his mother. When she told him that white children were still going to the park and he asked why he was yet prohibited, Ida revealed her bitterness to her smart young son. "Quit asking questions; it's the law, and only because some white folks are out to turn this state into a part of the South."

Ida had a choice to make. She could give up the dream that she and Lewis had carried and slowly watch the spark of intelligence and imagination in her son's eyes fade, or gird herself for confrontation. She made her decision, and loaded the boys onto the streetcar for another trip to the zoo. At the end of the visit, which had passed without incident, a plainclothes guard demanded, "Where are the white folks you come out here with?" Ida's flavorful response showed courage and honesty. She was a believer in Frederick Douglass before she was anything else, and she spoke white-hot truth to power. Teeth clenched, she barked to the guard, "I'm here . . . because I'm a *tax-payer,* and I thought it was about time that my boys have a look at those animals. And for that I don't *need* any *white* folks to show me the way." The guard, determined not to lose face to the ornery black woman, told her to see that she got herself on the streetcar—"You and your chillun too!" On the ride home, Ida broke into laughter—though it would be their last trip to the zoo. Ralph hesitantly joined in her mirth, deeply impressed with his mother's stand against injustice, with her mettle under fire from authority. The guard's rebuttal gave Ralph and Ida the basis for their own private joke, a comic loop, a refrain they used to close tales of day-to-day tragedies and racial imponderables, an affectionate way of putting a smile on a sour-tinged situation. As he grew older, Ralph looked back on the incident, which he always thought of as his introduction to real race prejudice, with a cultivated wryness. He realized that though broad claims were proffered by legislative bodies, newspapers, and the police, the truth was more subtle, and more ironic. Ida, if sitting at the front of a streetcar or entering the zoo with little white children, was invisible. Only after acknowledging her own children and denying the presence of any employers—her white folks—did her presence become offensive to the guard. Whites did not always object to the presence of blacks; in fact, under certain circumstances, they did not see them at all.

The loss of an accustomed privilege for such an abstract reason as race confused the young child. Ralph had already found disconcerting the incongruity of being able to see Bryant Elementary a block from his house on Geary and then having to walk eight blocks to Douglass. His welcome to Southern customs bred a cynicism in the young boy that he may have carried over to the classroom in Douglass, and toward authority figures in general. The manner by which jim crow made vulnerable the powerful figures in his life—such as his mother and J. D. Randolph—had a similar effect to the painful abandonment he suffered from Lewis's early death. Ralph was looking for someone capable of taking on Lewis's role. Through his powerful imagination, he inflated the prowess of his temporary heroes for the task; but when his surrogates were defeated or were inadequate, as a precaution against reliving his early trauma of abandonment, he became capable of striking them down.

Even though Ralph's initiation into jim crow had been more embarrassing than painful, life in Oklahoma could reveal the more barbaric aspects of racial relations between blacks and whites. The entire lower half of the state had earned the nickname "Little Dixie" on account of its thoroughgoing institution of jim crow practices. The black migrants to Oklahoma did not succumb quietly to brutality. When Claude Chandler was lynched in Oklahoma City in 1920, the black newspaper in Tulsa, the *Star,* roundly criticized the *Black Dispatch* for failing to issue editorials sounding the call for black self-defense. The Tulsans feared that black passivity had allowed for an environment conducive to lynching.[29] But during the early 1920s, even confirmed radical black politicians and newspapers such as the *Dispatch* had to contend with a well-organized and deeply influential Ku Klux Klan, or "Knights of the Invisible Empire." The modern Klan organization did not restrict itself to murder, night riding, and random acts of brutality and lawlessness, but was a consequential political third party actively promoting its regime of white supremacy and Christian values through a coherent political and moral agenda. At the time, half of the police department in Oklahoma City had pledged allegiance to the Invisible Empire.[30] A 1920s chronicler described the deeply Klan-influenced attitude of Oklahoma as a combination of "the Old South, the pioneer West and hustling modern Rotary Club Babbitism."[31] Another nuisance for blacks were the white Texans transplanted to Oklahoma because of the oil boom, who demanded that Negroes cow in the Longhorns' wake. In this mix, black acts of racial solidarity were not only common but de rigueur. Despite the escalating tensions over racial attitudes, black settlers continued to pour into the territory to escape even worse violence and subjugation in the old Confederacy.

At school, Ralph's racial education expanded beyond the classroom. During recess, he listened to, then recited on his own, the children's versions of the folk wisdom regarding race relations. This was his youthful education for survival. On the playground, when teacher H. V. Gear had his back turned, the younger children would ritually chant the words:

> My name is Ran,
> I work in the sand, but
> I'd rather be a *nigger*
> Than a poor white man. . . .

and

> These white folks think they so fine
> But their raggedy drawers
> Stink just like mine.[32]

The chants and boasts made him feel mannish and a bit more courageous. Ralph well understood that he and his mother and baby brother lived alone; he knew that Lewis could not come charging with a rifle to his rescue.

Such boasts counteracted a steadily mounting psychological pressure that resulted from the segregation of public facilities and the perpetuation of mythic black inferiority, inevitably encountered whenever the kids ventured away from home or school. The vulgar ditties were infectious to the children, though their parents would have switched them thoroughly had they heard them uttering profanity or talking "underneath of people's clothes." They helped to toughen the Douglass students mentally and prepare them for what grown-ups talked of in whispers. By school age, when a young person would begin to interact with the white world without the protection of home and family, it was necessary to have a built-in sense of pride to offset the oppressive antiblack climate. As a black boy fending for himself, Ralph could not afford "the luxury of being snobbish or provincial" in dealing with whites.[33]

Despite racial prejudice, or perhaps because of it, music—all kinds of music—permeated Ralph's childhood. Blues shouters on Second Street, Holiness churches screeching what some thought of as "rock" and "roll" music, and especially the brass section in the Elks military and concert band punctured the serene demeanor that young Ralph tried to present to the world. The dignified Avery Chapel music filled the heart by way of the mind, never descending below the sash or belt buckle. At regular intervals the church held vocal recitals and performances by out-of-town guests, as well as special appearances by the choir. Ralph listened attentively, and enjoyed the beauty of the traditional musical fare.

Music became a part of the educational program at Douglass because it was such an excellent means of demonstrating black capability to a hostile white world. Members of the Oklahoma black elite thought that inherently enlightening classical music should serve as a ramrod, straightening the school curriculum. In 1918, Zelia Breaux took over the music curriculum in black Oklahoma City schools, and became in the process Ralph's most significant teacher until college, one "who for years guided me [Ellison] in the path of art."[34] Zelia Page Breaux came from perhaps the best-educated black family in Oklahoma. Her father Inman Page had graduated from Brown University. Born in 1880, she had earned her undergraduate degree from Lincoln University in Jefferson City, Missouri, and directed the band at Langston University, where her father served as president. Breaux noticed Ralph in her music appreciation class as early as 1920. Sitting at the piano, the music teacher played for her students the standards of the classical tradition, quizzing the second graders until they could distinguish Handel from Haydn, Beethoven from Brahms. Promoting black Victorianism as well as turn-of-the-century black nationalism, Breaux designed the course to familiarize the black youngsters with Western classical music. It was thought that mastery of classical music—difficult to gain access to unless one was a member of Avery or Redeemer Episcopal—would not so much make blacks white as speed the collective destiny of the race toward higher culture.

Something about the youngster caused Breaux to begin what would be Ralph's most significant mentoring relationship, and it may not have been effervescence.[35] A photograph of Ralph with his first-grade class is remarkable for capturing a kind of tight-lipped sadness in the little boy's face.[36] Whatever his temperament at the outset of the relationship, the little boy opened up to the music teacher. Soon enough Breaux involved Ralph in all aspects of music in the school, and by age eight, Ralph was probably attending band concerts and marching band events, though he did not join the band until he was thirteen.[37]

Within a short time, Ralph learned the price of musical discipline and the tension between thinking and feeling. Breaux was soft-spoken, a gentle woman, but she also commanded the respect of the class, and like other Douglass teachers, permitted little in the way of disobedience. During a second grade rendition of Saint-Saëns's *Carnival,* in which students were instructed to play the roles of animals, one of Ralph's more rambunctious classmates dramatically acted out the mannerisms of a vivid green snake instead of the snowy white bird suggested by Breaux. Despite a remonstrance or two from Breaux, as Ralph later recalled, his "stalwart classmate held firm" to the form of the green snake, while Ralph and the rest of the class "lied like little black, brown and yellow Trojans about the swan." For his disobedience, Breaux spanked Ralph's young friend, a punishment that moved her to tears. The cost of holding true to one's principles could be a humiliating spanking, "but truth, reality and our environment were redeemed" through the young boy's virtuous expression.[38] The boy had behaved heroically in the face of the odds, and without any help from his peers. While Ralph learned discipline and high standards from Breaux, he also learned the discomfort of squelching his own inclinations. But the relationship with his teacher and the vitality of the music were sufficient for him to willingly sacrifice his own impressions. Ralph threw in his hat with the strivers in the status game that was classical music.

While music class began to sustain him in school, Ralph's home life did not seem nearly as secure. The family left the Avery parsonage around 1920, and Ida Ellison did not feel comfortable accepting charity from the Randolphs. The impoverished family moved in and out of rooming houses and rental properties all over the east side of Oklahoma City, loading into a wagon their trademark piece of furniture, a table that opened up into a bed.[39] But even after finding a temporary home for her two boys, their prospects in Oklahoma City seemed dim. Around 1921, Ida took to the open road to find a decent home for herself and the children. In late 1920 or early 1921, Ida decided to move in with her brother, an employee at the huge U.S. Steel manufacturing plant in Gary, Indiana. On their way north, the family passed through the famous black Greenwood business district in Tulsa, about one hundred miles northeast of Oklahoma City, and stayed with another one of

Ida's relatives. Before the end of summer, the family was making their way back to Oklahoma, after her brother's good fortune had sunk due to a dip in the U.S. steel market. The Ellisons again passed through Tulsa, and found the once-prosperous black neighborhoods and businesses obliterated after the systematic bombing, looting, and burning by Tulsa whites during the race war of June 1, 1921, commonly called the "Tulsa Race Riot."[40]

To call what happened in Tulsa that spring a "riot" is a misnomer. It was a distinctive white American racial pogrom, designed to diminish black political and economic leadership. And contradicting the logic of Tulsa's rugged black paper, the *Star,* black Tulsans' self-defense tactics fueled white wrath. The conflict began on May 31 in a violent clash outside the jailhouse where police held a black teen, Dick Rowland, on charges of assaulting a white elevator operator named Sarah Page.[41] A large group of armed blacks, inspired by Hubert Harrison's nationalistic editorials in Marcus Garvey's *Black World* and heavily made up of veterans, vowed to protect the boy until the trial. Thousands of armed whites showed up to lynch Rowland, initiating an armed conflict. After airplanes dropped turpentine balls and dynamite over the black community, whites burned down Tulsa's entire proud black business community and shot scores of black men, women, and children.

Similar tensions were inescapable in Oklahoma City. As an eight-year-old, Ralph began to realize the danger of having brown skin, and as an adult he would never underestimate the potential scope of white violence. But more painful for him than the apocalyptic scene in Tulsa was the continuous jerking and shuffling of his family. The Ellisons' frequent travels and apparent rejection by relatives and friends left deep psychological scars.[42] Back in the city of her children's birth, Ida probably settled her family briefly with Lewis's sister Lucretia Brown on Peach Avenue until she could set their rudder for the rest of the year. The reason for the return to Oklahoma City is uncertain, for Ida had a sister in Cincinnati, Ohio, and of course, she had family in Georgia. When she had left for Gary, Indiana, a city with boundaries nearly contiguous to Chicago, clearly she had imagined that she would find a better financial and racial climate. Ida may have received a friendly word from the Browns about a job or a place to live in Oklahoma, but it is quite likely that she never considered returning to Georgia because she simply refused to raise her sons in the South.

According to Ralph's recollection, his family moved when he was eight to a new neighborhood, "one of the white sections" he had passed through on the way to visit Lewis at the integrated Fairlawn Cemetery. His mother worked as "custodian of several apartments" and the family lived in comfortable "servant's quarters . . . of four small rooms, a bath, and a kitchen."[43] Having lived in a white middle-class neighborhood would be of paramount importance to the mature man. It was the anchoring point for his effort to sidestep the pit of race prejudice; Ralph Ellison neither idolized nor vilified whites, because in his youth he had been fortunate enough to live near them, becoming friends with a white family at what arguably was the height of American racial antipathy toward blacks.

In neither the 1921 nor the 1922 Oklahoma City directory was his family listed as living in what Ralph later called, in the consequential 1961 interview with Richard Stern, a "white middle class neighborhood."[44] During some period in 1921, Ida had the family at 428 North Phillips Street, where the next block was indeed white; but the outskirts of the black east side community was not the neighborhood of Ralph's near legendary contact with the white world that he would later write about. Ida probably moved the family into this tiny rental home on Phillips for only a few months in the early part of the year; it was one house over from the Randolphs, who now lived on Third Street. J. D. and Uretta probably owned the house at 428 Phillips. By 1922, when Ralph was nine, the family had moved a block down Phillips to 827 East Second Street, one house from the corner, and solidly in the heart of the black east side.[45] If Ellison's memory served him right and the servants' quarters in the apartment building did consist of six rooms in total, then the experience was particularly memorable for another reason as well: he had the rare luxury of his own room.

It is quite possible that Ida briefly took her family into a white neighborhood, long enough for her older boy to get a clear sense of his surroundings and for him to find a white playmate, but too brief to be picked up by the Oklahoma City directory. It makes sense that her demanding job as maid for several apartments allowed her a rather large apartment; this was a substantial job, an unusual enough opportunity to prompt her to move from Gary. The job also provided Ida with enough spare income to buy Ralph a cornet, a luxury item, within the next year or so. Ralph described the apartment building as housing on its street floor a U.S. Post Office and a Piggly Wiggly, a forerunner to the modern-day emporium-style supermarket. The only place in the city where two such businesses would have been in any sort of proximity was on West Main Street, the direction the family would have traveled to reach Lewis's plot at the Fairlawn Cemetery at Western Avenue and Twenty-seventh Street. In this busy downtown area, Ralph might have had a decent amount of time for unsupervised exploration before Ida came home from working in the apartments and when he wasn't responsible for Herbert.

While servicing apartments on Main Street, Ida Ellison began bringing home articles of interest for her eldest son, whose precocious curiosity and remarkable memory had marked him already as singular. Ralph's mother sought for him the same kind of leap in learning that she had shown her own parents thirty years earlier. In an effort to stimulate her son's intellect, and to keep him indoors in the busy downtown neighborhood, Ida brought home discarded copies of *Vanity Fair, Literary Digest,* and occasional opera recordings. These unexpected gems thrown away from the white apartments would not have been the sort of thing a Negro child, or a Negro adult for that matter, would readily have had access to in Oklahoma City. None of the children that Ralph knew, and only a handful of the adults, would have heard of the writers T. S. Eliot, Marcel Proust, Edmund Wilson, or Kenneth Burke, found in *Vanity Fair.* Ralph had the luxury of becoming familiar with famous names and the high culture associated with them. Though not as materially privileged as other kids, he was learning that class and taste were largely mental, not material, attributes. The magazine included the artwork of Picasso, reviews of the music of Stravinsky, and poems by Edna St. Vincent Millay. The columns "In and About Theater," "The World of Art," "The World of Ideas," "Literary Hors d'Oeuvres," and "Satirical Sketches" presented a world of refinement and taste formerly unavailable to Ralph, and he didn't even need to pay the exorbitant 35-cent newsstand fee.

Near the time that Ida was bringing home these artistic and literary magazines, Ralph had taken to reading the newspaper touting white supremacy, the *Daily Oklahoman,* mainly for Oliver Odd McIntyre's syndicated column, "New York, Day by Day." McIntyre's jaunts through New York's Bowery, Tenderloin, and Upper West Side, written from the viewpoint of a small-town Midwesterner, greatly appealed to the young man and initiated his fascination with the East. Columns like "Be Yourself!" and "Just a Country Boy in the Big, Wicked City" used irony and mild sarcasm to defend the importance of regional identity.[46] McIntyre insinuated that big cities like New York had no exclusive right to sophistication or vice. His folksy but simple language and sly humor developed Ralph's own sense of comedy. In his own tales to Ida and Herbert, he refined a talent for turning teary incidents into droll stories. Ellison later described his feeling that *Vanity Fair* and McIntyre, "accidents" of literacy and exposure to something new, had painted for him a world "broader and more interesting," "not really a part of my own life."[47]

Even as her family changed addresses, Ida kept up with Edna Slaughter. The two women continued to take their family walks together on Sunday. Ida marched her young sons through wealthy white neighborhoods in Oklahoma City to present them with a more elaborate and diverse concept of the world. The two families would trek up Robinson and Broadway on Sundays, admiring the fine homes and indulging in wishing games and fantasy. Looking through the windows of the wealthy oil barons and real estate tycoons of Oklahoma City was a blissful experience for Ralph:

> [T]here was a world in which you wore your everyday clothes on Sunday, and there was a world in which you wore your Sunday clothes every day—*I* wanted the world in which you wore your Sunday clothes every day. I wanted it because it represented something better, a more exciting and civilized and human

way of living; a world which came to me through certain scenes of felicity which I encountered in fiction, in the movies, and which I glimpsed sometimes through the windows of the great houses. . . .[48]

New clothes and cars had an immediate appeal to a poor child accustomed to birthdays and Christmases without gifts. But Oklahoma City's elite class whose homes Ralph admired was chock full of robber barons, land grant schemers, and esquired swindlers. According to historian John Thompson, the southern half of the early state was "an isolated premarket society," where prices were determined not "by economic laws but by coercion."[49] Ida Ellison, who had been a Socialist ticket supporter and forceful civil rights proponent, definitely wanted her sons' dreams unhampered, but would have discouraged any romanticism about the accumulation of wealth. Most likely, on the Sunday walks alongside what Ralph described as "shop-window displays of elegant clothing, furniture, [and] automobiles," she imparted pointed lessons on the peculiar sources of that wealth, the banefulness of avarice, and the reality of American slavery. Eight-year-old Ralph may have found confusing Ida's warnings, but as a sensitive boy he probably took his mother's words to heart. Ida also reinforced class realism at home every chance she got, being more explicit than was fashionable regarding the family's economic condition.[50] She told her sons how much she earned, the cost of rent and food, schoolbooks and clothes, and persuaded the young men to gauge their expectations accordingly.

Herbert had a more difficult time than Ralph, less with his family's economic situation than with their isolation. Herbert understood very little about his father and always wished for a larger family, one that celebrated holidays and held family outings and reunions. Apparently not even Ida's pan-toting relieved the sparseness of their dining room table. The Ellisons did not customarily celebrate Thanksgiving or Christmas at their own home, but went to the Slaughters and Randolphs for a more bountiful meal.[51] Besides, hotels did a thriving business during the festive season, and Ida had to work. Ralph did not complain at the noontime meal of beans and a biscuit at the canteen on Douglass's yard.

In the early 1920s, Ralph, Ida, and Herbert saw another black family strolling through the same white neighborhoods where they walked. Future jazz guitarist Charlie Christian, his older brothers Eddie and Clarence Jr., nicknamed "It," and their blind father Clarence Sr. traveled in Oklahoma City's well-to-do neighborhoods on Sundays as well. For the Christians, as Ralph learned later, wealthy whites were not merely an outlet for the imagination but a very real component of day-to-day survival. The men were entertainers, serenading white passersby with renditions of folk-band classics and the blues. Ralph admired the musical skill of the family and the relaxed atmosphere at Eddie's home on South Geary Street, a slum near the Douglass

School where "all the forms of disintegration attending the urbanization of rural Negroes ran riot." The Christians took on the common roles of black mendicants, though the troubadours did so with a great deal of dignity. Even though the Christian family were using their musical ability to stave off starvation, Ida might have encouraged her musically inclined eldest son to look beyond simple entertainment as a vocation. Ralph viewed the skillful street-corner panhandling as a standard by which to evaluate his own success and mold his own goals. Ralph saw the excellent musicians humbled before uninterested whites, and he well knew the reservations of his teacher Zelia Breaux and other members of the black elite who found vernacular music a "backward, low-class form of expression."[52] He wanted his own dream to be impressive, inspiring Edna Slaughter's praise instead of her frown or quickened pace past the blues players.

Encountering the dirt-poor Christian family on their jaunts window-shopping and admiring fine homes brought out the ambiguities of Ida's strategy for cultivating her son. She had acculturated Ralph to white Oklahoma City; her boy now stuck his nose into the neighbors' trash looking for ice cream cartons and other odds and ends. Encouraged to emulate the heroic manners and deeds of his father, Ralph sought adventure. Refuse was richer in the white neighborhoods, and he would roam farther to seek better treasures. At some point in 1921 or 1922, when the Ellison family lived in the white neighborhood on West Main, Ralph became friends with a young white boy named Henry "Hoolie" Davis. For Ralph to have stumbled upon the young Davis boy, who was kept near to his home because of a physical ailment, he would have had to venture some twenty blocks to Davis's house at 1823 West Sixteenth Street. The formidable distance was longer than the trek back to Geary or Phillips, where Ralph longed for his friends from Douglass.[53] The resourcefulness and temerity required for adventures so far from home is uncommon for a youth known for his patient interest in literature. Ralph did not traipse back over to the neighborhood of his church or school but in the opposite direction, toward the manicured lawns and brushed sidewalks of white Oklahoma.

Henry Davis, whom Ralph knew as Hoolie, was the son of Reverend Franklin Davis, the prestigious pastor of St. John's Episcopal Church on Classen Boulevard. Henry's mother Maude was a Northerner, born in Pennsylvania,[54] which perhaps explains why she didn't take automatic offense to her son playing with a young Negro boy. It seems that the boys played together during the school year, apparently when Henry's older brother Franklin Jr. was away and during a period without school responsibilities, when Ralph had enough idle time to explore the streets.

Ralph's forays into the city's western "whites-only" neighborhoods helped him envision a world of grandeur, but they were dangerous. Despite his youthful innocence and superior manners, many whites did not take kindly to the appearance of Negroes at all. Oklahoma City Judge Joel Estes, who lived close to the Davises, told litigants to his bench that sighting blacks in a Ford Model T surpassed the misfortune of crossing thirteen howling jet-black tomcats.[55] Negroes weren't just unsightly, they were bad luck.

Ralph first met Hoolie one afternoon, probably around the spring of 1922, when he stumbled into Davis in an alley, searching for equipment to build crystal sets, the small, one-tubed radios of the era. When the two boys realized that they were both looking for ice cream cylinders to wind their tuning coils, they quickly collaborated and began a joint project that continued inside Hoolie's home. To Maude Davis, Ralph probably seemed innocuous rummaging through the alley garbage cans. Clean, respectful to elders, and articulate, the caramel-complexioned boy impressed her as a suitable playmate for her son. The refined Davis home, quite different from the tiny bungalows Ralph had lived in, would have been impressive and added to the prestige of the event. Ralph would later remember that in this relationship he was treated as a guest in the Davis household. And as the wife of a pastor, Maude enjoyed a little more flexibility in matters of caste than did her neighbors. Ralph later recalled thinking that Hoolie's mother was "glad to have someone around" to keep her son company; though he only claimed to have been "helping" in the white youth's radio experiments. Hoolie was a year older than Ralph, part of the reason for the deference that Ralph seems to have accorded the other boy. Ralph rejoiced that Davis accepted him as a playmate on somewhat equal footing. Taught at home by a tutor because of a rheumatic heart, young Henry Davis challenged Ralph mentally, and simultaneously helped to eradicate notions of the white mystique. Ralph admired Hoolie's intellectual aggressiveness and daring: "Knowing him [Hoolie] led me to expect much more of myself and of the world."[56] Now he didn't have to imagine what whites were like to make a comparison to himself and his black friends.

Ralph cherished the rewarding experience with the white Davis family because it offset the poverty of his own life, which had begun to shame him. He later revealed that "the idea of [his] mother living in service" caused him a great deal of distress.[57] Ida did not stay long on the taxing job in the apartment on West Main Street. By the middle of 1922, she had taken up residence at 827 East Second Street. Once the Ellisons moved back to Deep Second, Ralph never saw Hoolie Davis again.

Becoming more internally focused, by the end of 1921 Ralph gained access to a corner of the world that women like his mother and Edna Slaughter did approve of, the public library. After the Carnegie Library in downtown Oklahoma City refused to open its stacks to black Episcopalian Father Kilpatrick, the city council, to avoid a Dunjee-inspired lawsuit or publicity fusillade, hastily set up the Dunbar Branch Library for colored. A committee turned a former pool hall in the 300 block of Stiles Avenue into a Negro library and reading room, under the direction of Miss Alphenia Young and Lillian E. Youngblood. Ida and her young son were ecstatic. Ida beamed at the demise of the pool hall, an institution she "fervently opposed," as well as the hustling sweet men associated with it.[58] Ralph and his Douglass playmates Tracy and Willard McCleary and Hilliard Bowen made a pact to read every single book in the library, whose holdings were scant enough that the youngsters included reference material and other nonnarrative matter in their contest. Having gained confidence by his Avery parsonage experience, he scoffed at his playmates' fear of the large volumes and unpronounceable words. The boys raced through the secondhand materials, castoffs from Carnegie and private collections that included the Haldeman-Julius Blue Books (a set of helpful plot summaries), long before the librarians had had time to categorize the books by age group. Excited to have access to adult books on the sly, the boys tried to crack the meaning of the challenging words and mature themes. Instead of limiting themselves to materials designed to protect their innocence, they nibbled at sexually mature themes in Shakespeare and the stark social realism of Theodore Dreiser and Sinclair Lewis. And the young readers devoured the popular cowboy stories and typical boys' books. But try as the boys might to outdo them, the girls, Vickinia Norman, Elvira Fleming, and Elmira Richardson, read more. With the new library, Ralph held on to his early exposure to books and reading. Literature became a sanctuary where he could access his fullest emotional range. Though the outside world forced him to exhibit a demeanor of unassailability or, when he felt most devastated, numbness, with his books Ralph could cry. He reread fairy tales until junior high because of the enchantment and possibility in them; their magic supported far-flung hopes of a returning father.

Ralph associated reading far more with the building on Stiles Avenue than he ever would with his school, where students had to bring their own textbooks, where apparently there was no library. In place of books, the school relied upon people. Ralph came to know and admire the school principal, Johnson Chestnut Whittaker, who doubled as physical science teacher during the 1922–1923 school year. A South Carolina native and an 1876 appointee to the United States Military Academy at West Point, Whittaker was an extremely important figure to Ralph. By nine years of age, Ralph had grown used to the absence of his father, and to keep him alive had begun to memorialize his deeds. What would have been especially attractive to the young boy in the period immediately following the First World War were his father's military exploits. For this reason, Whittaker served as an excellent surrogate male figure.

A former soldier and lawyer, Whittaker had light skin, blue eyes, and a goatee, and he maintained "erect military bearing." Ellison fondly recalled that the old principal introduced "elements of West Point style and military discipline to young Oklahoma Negroes."[59] Whittaker's strategy for instilling orderly conduct into the young children included training students to form crisp lines in front of the school building in the morning to the sound of a triangle. He commanded good behavior, tolerated no back talk, and carried a quirt with which to punish malingerers. Despite his fair complexion, Whittaker was an early example for the boy of what was possible for him. Whittaker had attended West Point during the Reconstruction, but had suffered disgrace and expulsion after his classmates and officers learned of his black ancestry. To force the ex-slave's dismissal, his fellow cadets tied him to a cot and mangled his ear with razors to make him physically unfit for the academy's standards of cadet appearance. He was court-martialed by West Point officials, who claimed his wounds were self-inflicted; but he had the court-martial overturned by President Chester Arthur. West Point professors then expelled him for failing an unscheduled, closed-door, oral philosophy examination shortly before graduation. Undaunted, Whittaker went on to become a lawyer in his native South Carolina.[60] Whittaker symbolized not only perseverance and survival, but resilience and personal dignity.

Ralph became more comfortable at school, but his home life churned with upheaval. Later in life, Ellison revealed little of his impoverished childhood, beyond an occasional gruff simile to an interviewer: "We were poor as hell."[61] However, even casual observers on the east side saw the devastating impact of poverty on Ralph's fatherless family. The ragtag pilgrimage of the Ellison family from house to house across Oklahoma City became the nine-year-old boy's unspoken shame. The constant relocation could not be helped, though—the result of a combination of miserable wages, unbearable conditions, and terminated contracts, probably more often by Ida's employers than with her landlords. Ida earned roughly six dollars per week, and faced a rent close to $10 per month, roughly a third of her take-home pay.[62] The working woman's one means of protesting an unfair arrangement was to quit the job or move, and spunky Ida did both. After her struggles at the Hadden and being "in service" at the Main Street apartments, Ida had a job washing test tubes at University Emergency, where Lewis had died. She also seems to have stuck exclusively to the larger hotels for work. One method that she used to reinforce her conception of herself, despite what any employer thought of her, deeply influenced Ralph. With a rural education that perhaps went beyond the eighth grade, she gave herself creative titles to dignify her labor to Ralph and to anyone else who asked about the work she did. Ida titled herself "janitress" when working at Avery and "custodian" while living in service at the apartment complex.[63] She aimed to deeply instill a sense of pride in her son about himself and his parents. Some of their neighbors interpreted the strategy as "putting on airs."[64]

In 1923, Ida defied probability and moved a peg up the ladder, to 822 East Fourth Street, a home with as much significance to Ralph as the cottage apartment on Main Street. Fourth Street, alongside the streetcar line, was an avenue signifying success for black Americans. Not long after he had had his demystifying racial experience with Hoolie, Ralph's imaginative landscape expanded. Next door to him lived eleven-year-old Frank Meade, who sparked Ralph's interest in drawing and painting. A little more than a year his senior, Frank was simply the "hero of my [Ellison's] childhood."[65] The older boy filled notebooks with expertly drawn cartoons whose subject matter was mostly the east side of Oklahoma City. The characters in his early fictive landscapes were black cowboys and bulldoggers, local gangsters and badmen, Bill Picket, Second Street detectives like Baker and Earnest Jones, and of course, Jack Johnson. After the boys had been friends for about a year, Frank's father Joseph Meade, the local barber, took them both out into the backyard, and in an act of fatherly charity, taught his son how to play the trumpet and taught Ralph the E flat, or "peck" horn. The boys' days of cartoons were over; the serious work of music had begun.

Following what seems to have been an uninterrupted year at 822 East Fourth Street—sometime between 1923 and 1924—is another gap in Ralph's life in east Oklahoma City. At some point in early 1924, Ida seems to have moved the family in with Lewis's sister Lucretia Brown in a house on Peach Avenue. Possibly Ida moved out of the east side neighborhood because her political opposition to jim crow left her vulnerable to attack. In 1923, Dunjee had encouraged black city resident William Floyd to test the housing legislation by moving into a building on Second and Walnut. The next year, blacks began pushing segregation boundaries farther by moving north and east, beyond East Fourth and Byers. White vigilance committees responded with bombing attacks.[66]

This sentiment of white enmity encumbered all of Oklahoma City at that time. It could not be avoided. On Peach Avenue, Ralph saw the white children of their local corner grocer decked out in white sheets and hoods, waving rebel flags and holding a mock parade as the adults looked on in approval. Ellison's aunt quit trading with the grocer in response.[67]

Another possible reason for the move to Peach Avenue may have been that Ida was out of work, or was close to losing a job. Whatever her motive, sometime during the early 1920s Ida lived on Peach Avenue long enough to enroll the boys at the Orchard Park Elementary School, a block up the street at 3 North Peach. The Orchard Park school consisted of two rooms in an old frame house, which housed a family in its upstairs compartments. At Orchard Park, Ralph met Jimmie Stewart, who became a sparring partner and a friend to help raid local peach trees.[68]

The two Ellison boys by this time had developed in two distinctly different modes. Ralph gravitated toward reading and talking, could be quiet and musing, and played with other kids. Desperately attached to his older brother, Herbert shunned other children and didn't read well. Largely silent, Herbert was afflicted with a stutter that slurred his speech severely enough that Ralph often had to serve as translator for his younger brother. In the words of Saretta Finley, longtime friend of the family, "Ralph was Herbert's protector. Herbert idolized him."[69] Local children brutally ridiculed Herbert's academic performance, which made him further introverted. Ralph easily mastered the King's English spoken by schoolteachers and the well-educated Randolphs, Slaughters, Haywoods, Pages, and Breauxs, as well as the Southern black vernacular spoken at home. His little brother always remained a speaker of the home language and a stutterer, never attaining the polish of his older sibling. Herbert bewildered his relatives by being naturally left-handed, and his Aunt Lucretia rarely spared the rod in order to turn him toward "proper" dexterity. When Ralph got out of school, he customarily played with neighborhood boys as long as he thought it prudent, considering his mother's dictum that he must watch his baby brother and finish his household chores. In contrast, Herbert went straight home. When the family lived on the east side, he generally found sanctuary in Randolph's drugstore or under the table of his adopted "aunts," Edna Slaughter and Uretta Randolph, fetching a fallen needle or spool of thread while the women quilted.[70]

Ralph felt burdened by a brother whom the other kids ridiculed and who seemed incapable of maturing into a fitting comrade. He also retreated emotionally from Herbert because the boys shared so much physical space, and because Ralph had almost a father's responsibility for protecting him. Herbert's emotional response to his brother's caretaking duty—adoration, blind trust, and irritability when not receiving frequent attention—endeared him little to Ralph, whose sentiment at this stage had begun to flow in the opposite direction. The older brother increasingly valued silence, contemplation, and serenity. Adding to the distance between the two, Herbert had no recollection of his father Lewis. He was unable to take part in his older brother's imaginative connections with a fallen hero. Ralph found relief when the family stayed at Peach Avenue and one of his older cousins helped care for his brother.

Ellison offered sparse comment on his relationship with Herbert. His 1943 short story "That I Had Wings," based upon an afternoon in the backyard with his brother, explores the different voices of the slightly daring, slightly mischievous Riley and his friend Buster.[71] The Ellisons, like most families, had a chicken coop in the backyard for eggs and meat. The setting of the story seems to reproduce the home on Peach Avenue. Ida had a favorite rooster, trained like a dutiful and mildly vicious watchdog, who would come up to the porch when called. After experimenting with pieces of iron, Ralph and Herbert dropped baby chickens from the top of the henhouse down to the ground. Their next-door neighbor told Ida, and the children were punished. In the story, Ellison elaborates his interest in birds and flight, but offers an analogy comparable to his relationship with Herbert: "First the mama bird would fly a piece and chirp to the young bird to follow her. But the little bird didn't move. Then the mama bird would fly back and peck the young one and circle around and try to push it off the branch and the little one held on, afraid."[72] The story ends with a failed attempt to make parachutes for the birds. Flying, Ellison's favorite metaphor for growth and freedom, ends in death for the chicks and punishment for Riley. Faithful as he was, Herbert, like Buster's brother Bubber who constantly cries, would never build wings strong enough to fly alongside Ralph.

Soon the living quarters on Peach Avenue became cramped and unsatisfactory and, perhaps near the spring of 1924, Ida proposed a new scheme for solvency. She landed another job "in service" in McAlester, Oklahoma, a day's train ride away.[73] The family's passage to the small town left an unusually profound imprint upon Ralph. More than twelve years later, he would use the trip as the source of one of his earliest known short stories, a work constructed heavily from autobiographical material. Ellison wrote "Boy on a Train" in Dayton, Ohio, between 1937 and 1938.[74] James, the eleven-year-old protagonist, rides the train with his mother and his brother Lewis, described repeatedly as a "baby," to McAlester from Oklahoma City in 1924. The details in the short story mirror the Ellison family structure at the time. Ralph, like the character James, was eleven, and his father had passed away after coming West from the old South for freedom. Like the pretty widow in the story, Ida was uncertain about the future for herself and her young sons, one of whom, though eight years old, still acted like a baby.

In the story, the reader learns of the inconvenience of the jim crow car, stiflingly hot behind the engine and outfitted with inoperable windows to keep out cinders and ashes. The specter of white violence looms in the enigmatic ritual of beefy, red-faced whites retrieving a casket from the train at a small depot. The story contrasts James's desire for the world of childhood, candy, bicycles, and trips to the zoo with his growing understanding that he must become the defender of his family in a racially hostile world. His mother, who has already faced sexual assault on the train from a candy vendor, recounts her and her husband's dreams on their way out to Oklahoma. With her husband dead, she implores her son to remember the family's dogged pursuit of freedom. James's mother, Mrs. Weaver, tells her son the reason they move for a better life. The impassioned speech, followed by a prayer, was common for Ida Ellison.

> You must remember this, James. We traveled far, looking for a better world, where things wouldn't be so hard like they were down South. That was fourteen years ago, James. Now your father's gone from us, and you're the man. Things are hard for us colored folks, son, and it's just us three alone

and we have to stick together. Things is hard and we have to fight . . .
O Lord, we have to fight![75]

Ralph viewed his youthful journey to McAlester as a turning point on the road to adulthood. Not long after, the family returned to Oklahoma City. Despite the assurances of her employers, Ida's job in McAlester had fallen through. When the world pressed Ida, she cried aloud to the Lord.[76] Ralph's mother quietly ushered the boys back to the house on 822 East Fourth Street. Ralph had toughened enough to take the move from one place to another in stride, and perhaps was even pleased, since he had greater access to books in Oklahoma City than in McAlester.

At the home of Dr. Haywood, Ralph and a young friend pulled down a copy of Sigmund Freud's *Interpretation of Dreams*. A streetwise Ralph avidly deciphered some of the pages until he realized that the Viennese psychiatrist's text was not a guide to exposing winning numbers for lottery tickets.[77] These unsupervised, heavyweight intellectual exercises, along with Ida's growing reliance upon her eldest boy, who now pursued his first consistent part-time job with a paper delivery business at 4 A.M., began to produce a vigorous and fierce independence in young Ralph. In his own words, he also became "quick-tempered and impatient."[78]

Not long after they returned to Oklahoma City, Ida opted for a new course for her family, a direction that perhaps initially appeared to Ralph more as betrayal. On July 8, 1924, Ida Ellison wed a Texan named James Ammons, a literate common laborer, at Avery Chapel Church in Oklahoma City, with the Reverend J. E. Toombs presiding.[79] Still an extremely attractive woman in a frontier land where women were few, she generally had had to keep suitors at arm's length. Ida walked down the aisle again, almost exactly eight years after her first marriage had ended with the death of her husband. Ammons may have provided some of the backing that enabled the Ellisons to return to Fourth Street. Succumbing to mild vanity, Ida seems to have led the twenty-nine-year-old laborer to believe that she was thirty-five, still in her child-bearing prime. However, in the 1920 census she had listed her age as thirty-five; and on her death certificate, Ralph indicated that his mother had been born in 1884. Thirty-nine-year-old Ida had chosen a man who, while literate, was ten years her junior. Following the ceremony, Ammons gave up his home at 308½ East First Street and moved in with his new bride and her two rapidly growing sons on Fourth Street. Ammons was probably as undaunted by the circumstances of the ready-made family as he was ignorant of his wife's true age; Oklahoma still had many aspects of the frontier, and all but the elite blacks generally lived in close quarters. From a woman purportedly in her thirties, Ammons probably expected children. Ida would have warned Ammons (probably an avid attendee of Avery Chapel) about her precocious son Ralph, who had walked at six months and read at two. In fact, Ammons's presence in the household had a stunning affect on Ralph; he ceased to fantasize about Lewis's inevitable return.[80] Seeing another man receive intimate affection from Ida no doubt played a major role in cementing the immutability of Lewis's death.

Despite his touchiness, and his eight years of immortalizing his father, Ralph got along well with Ammons, who taught him how to hunt. His stepfather would take him out a mile beyond the city limits with a well-oiled Winchester automatic shotgun and .22 rifle to look for pheasants, rabbits, and squirrels. This was manly activity that enabled him to escape the confines of his mother's oversolicitousness. Ellison remembered the winter of 1926 in his first lengthy fictional effort, the abandoned manuscript of 1939 called *Slick*. In his unpublished novel, a young black Marxist named Booker Smalls from Oklahoma fondly recalls tales of hunting in the cotton fields and game preserves of Oklahoma with his out-of-work stepfather in the winter of 1926.[81] Apparently Ammons taught Ralph how to catch rabbits in the snow beneath cotton stalks by their legs and then to shoot them in the back of their heads. Although the family had little money, Ellison cherished the memory of the suppers of rabbit during that winter. The scene that Ellison rendered in fiction was touching, and suggested a deep connection between stepfather and stepson. Ellison's reverent retelling of the interaction between a character much like himself and his stepfather in his early fiction suggests that he accepted his new caretaker.

Ralph made the adjustment to the new presence in his house and overcame his eleven-year-old's jealousy or resentment toward the man taking over his own father's place, which might have been considerable. But his renewed affections did not—indeed, could not—last long. It seems that within a year of moving into the Ellison household, Ammons died. By 1926, a year after the East Fourth Street home was listed in the directory as that of "John [sic] and Ida Amons," the Ellison's family economic worth plunged to a new nadir. The three survivors now moved into a small room at 415 North Stiles, a home owned by Cyril House, a porter for the National Cash Register Corporation, and his wife Edna.[82] Ralph responded to the tragedy by plunging more deeply into the imaginative realm of fiction. He read *The Last of the Mohicans* ten times.[83] Ida referred to herself, for her boys' sake, as "Mrs. Ida Ellison."

Now in his preteen years, Ralph had cultivated a group of friends with whom he explored the urban landscape of Oklahoma City, among them the leaders from school, Albert Alexander, Tracy and Willard McCleary, and Hilliard Bowen. He'd already had adventures on his own: wandering the west side of Sixteenth Street to see Hoolie, and living near the busy main thoroughfare of West Main. Now he had new experiences as a delivery boy on a

bicycle (and later a motorcycle) for Randolph's Drugs. Part of his adventurousness had to do with the impossibility of his hardworking single mother to
supervise his after-school hours. As a testament to the hours logged in the
library, Ralph and the boys in his group took the fifteenth-century Renaissance man as their ideal. Ralph later would write that he had thought that the
Italian-flavored concept, filtered to them from a Northern-influenced black
educator a "dreamer, seeking to function responsibly in an environment which
at its most normal took on some of the mixed character of nightmare and of
dream." The Renaissance men of Deep Second were young barnstormers,
infused by the dream, and unintimidated by Oklahoma's frequently nightmarish conditions. They took to heart their birthright as "natives" to the state
and went to lengths never to appear passive or diffident. His afternoons
devoted to what he dubbed "emphatic adventuring" and self-development
enabled him to lay claim to what he saw as "Negro American style." Typically
consisting of speech styles and walking rhythms, ways of self-defense and self-
promotion, black style seemed to combine perfectly the familiar and the foreign, the welcome and the prohibited, a blend carried off not only by formal
competence, but also by "reckless verve."[84] With a crew of roughnecks, readers, and athletes as his companions, Ralph began to feel confident that he
might make something of himself.

Ralph was not always easily accepted by the group. Nor was he the most
popular boy among his comrades. Some of his friends felt that Ida was acting
above her circumstances in the years following Ammons's death, and thought
her snooty. She aimed to cultivate Ralph and infuse in him the idea that he
was better than the common lot. His classmates called him prissy and hazed
him about his pretentious-sounding middle name. The Baptist-bred east
siders thought the A.M.E.s and their sanctimonious music were stuck-up,
anyway. Ralph tried to prove himself by running with the gang over to the
fairgrounds, or collecting whiskey bottles in back alleys for the bootleggers.

For the most part, junior high school did not promise an educational
adventure comparable to the lures of the east side, with the notable exception
of social studies and the lessons in race pride. Since he distributed the *Black
Dispatch*, it was impossible for him to miss the dire crisis of blacks in America. Roscoe and Drusilla Dunjee, Oklahoma City's crusading writers, strove
tirelessly to inform and agitate black Americans regarding the quagmire of
American racial relations. And in his junior high classroom at Douglass, Ralph
received a complementary analysis of an unusually sophisticated caliber. Mrs.
Lamonia McFarland, a regular subscriber to black journals such as the *Crisis*,
taught the youngsters at Douglass about the New Negro Movement and, as
her former students recall, militant race pride. McFarland hailed from Mississippi, where both of her grandfathers had been Europeans, one Dutch, the
other Irish. The brown-skinned woman had known both of them, and out of

this complex experience determined that "I am not an African since I am many generations removed from my African-born ancestry, born in America of a mixed blood parentage. . . . I am an American."[85] McFarland imbued the youngsters with a complex understanding of their racial identity that included solid pride regarding the "Americanness" of their experience. She taught that they were to inherit the fruits of their forefathers' labor, and that their progenitors had been both black and white. She promoted black intellectuals such as Phillis Wheatley and W. E. B. Du Bois. In McFarland's vanguard social studies classes of the mid-1920s, black Oklahoma City children read Langston Hughes (whom she quoted from memory), Countee Cullen, Claude McKay, and James Weldon Johnson, among others.[86] Ralph, who at the time cared little for poetry, listened to the lyricism and music in the words, waiting patiently for music class.

His mother could not guarantee that the refinements of *Vanity Fair* would win out over the lures of the back alley. The same fury that ignited her battle for social justice also stewed inside the boy, whose achievement of manhood was by no means guaranteed. Though Ida prided herself on Ralph's intelligence, around the time he entered junior high school, he began to use his fists as regularly as his words. The warfare may have stemmed from the noble impulse to defend his younger brother from bullies and insults, or it may have had less sentimental origins. Ellison casually recalled of the period that he "was constantly fighting."[87] His maturation process was rough-and-tumble, like the homes he'd lived in. One incident occurred sometime around 1926 or 1927, an altercation with his pal from Peach Avenue. Jimmie Stewart was a fast talker, and at about five-feet-six, was out to prove that even though he was from Westtown, he could hold his own with the boys from the Deuce. It may be that Stewart challenged one of Ralph's ready statements about his father's unusual talents and qualities. Ralph readily told young and old alike that Lewis had led crews erecting the towering Colcord building, soldiered in Cuba, the Philippines, and China, and read literature. One way or another, Stewart provoked Ralph, and the two boys carried out their battle underneath the Walnut Avenue viaduct, to avoid the watchful eyes of school authorities.[88]

Ralph's pugilistic contests spilled over into school, one of them culminating in a confrontation of epic proportion with Inman Page. The "Grand Old Man" was the premier black educator in Oklahoma. Born a slave in Warrenton, Virginia, Page had gone on to become the first black to graduate from Brown University, and had been chosen the class orator. He came to Douglass in 1921 after a successful thirty-year career as president of the Colored Normal and Agricultural School at Langston and then as the chief of Lincoln University in Jefferson City, Missouri. Then he returned in the fall of 1923 to head Douglass following the brief tenure of Johnson Whittaker.

One of Page's favorite tasks, which added to his mystique among the students, was expounding upon Saint Paul's Letters to the Corinthians during the school's morning religious services, at which all grades were present. Page had a distinctive command of language and intoned the biblical passages with enough timbre and vitality to evoke a later description by Ellison that included the words "magic" and "joy." Even as late as the seventh grade, Ralph was still heavily intimidated by the imposing figure of Page. He was a man to be listened to in silence, not an educator to engage in dialogue. To Ralph's youthful sensibility, the former bondman Page was persuasive because he "expressed authority in every gesture."[89] Slavery-born black folks had an aura of power and confidence for Ellison's generation.

Despite the educator's severity, mild pandemonium frequently broke out during the lectures in the chapel, largely because the auditorium was never designed to hold anything close to the two thousand students who packed into the school every day. Students jammed aisles and even windows, creating a gross fire hazard.[90] Boys at the junior and senior high school level were seated on the auditorium stage, an effort to encourage their good behavior and self-discipline, since the eyes of the entire school were upon them. But notwithstanding the seriousness of the chapel-like environment and their prominent seats upon the stage, the young Douglass men found the two stairways leading up to the main floor of the stage to be "favorite sites for horseplay."

Ralph had begun to receive singular treatment from the other boys. His independence of character won as little prestige from them as his appetite for reading. In his own words, he was "somewhat out of sorts" with his peers. But the Douglass boys weren't just anti-intellectual. They probably picked on Ralph because they thought he was a mama's boy. One day, Ralph had been pushed to his limit, and told himself that "if some guy pushes me, I'm going to swing on him and start punching." When the inevitable shove occurred, the twelve-year-old went berserk. In his fury and blind rage, he managed to swirl from the curtain area on the wing over to the center of the stage and accidentally strike Dr. Page. Incredulous, Page grabbed the offensive youngster, who added to the pandemonium by flailing into the stage pulleys that lowered the massive curtain, toppling the dignified principal off the platform and onto the ground. The principal immediately became enraged—"What do you think you're doing, boy. . . . What do you think you're doing!" Ralph's shocked and fear-filled reply came forth shrilly, "We fell, Mister Page! Mister Page, we *fell!*"[91] Page pushed the offending youth off and subjected him to a teeth-chattering shaking. Then, wonderfully, Page initiated Ralph into one of the mysteries of adulthood, collapsing the distance between child and man. The older man chuckled. Page laughed loud enough for Ralph to hear the merriment in his voice, then, still shouting, chased the boy out of the auditorium, threatening him with expulsion. The other students were delighted, the morning chapel service turned into a circus, and Ralph felt disgraced enough to question whether he had heard the principal laugh. The next day, he was readmitted to Douglass, and from then on he studiously avoided Dr. Page until he received his diploma some years later.

Ralph's shift from disciplined bibliophile to pugilist boded disaster for his mother's careful plans. For a boy of much promise to have such a melee as his prominent memory with the premier educator of his generation suggests that Ralph did hit a crossroads in junior high. In part due to the almost itinerant lifestyle of his family, Ralph never settled into a scholastic routine at Douglass, except for his music classes, and sometimes not even those. Schoolbooks, which students were expected to buy before the beginning of the term, were a luxury sometimes beyond his family's means. His pride would only let him ask other students and friends for so much. He was a loner, separate from the crowd and quick-tempered with people. Certainly his obvious poverty fit unsnugly with how Ida had groomed him. He referred to his father as a foreman and his mother as a custodian, while other kids' parents were hod-carriers and maids. His literary explorations were a more pleasant world, entirely distinct from the stuffy rooms and stiff wooden desks of 200 East California Street. But if his adolescence tripped over everybody's expectations, perhaps a single unadulterated note stands out: Ralph loved distinction.

3

The Horn of Plenty

1925–1932

A YOUNG OKLAHOMA CITY Negro seeking acclaim in the 1920s really only had one option: membership in the Frederick Douglass Junior and Senior High School Band. Formed by Zelia N. Breaux in 1923, the band was modeled after Major N. Clark Smith's memorable boy bands in Kansas City, and membership in it established the reputations of twenty-five lucky young men. The players were minor celebrities, participating in the April 89er Day Parade and the May Day gala festival, in addition to all of the national and religious holidays. They opened baseball season at the Oklahoma City Western League Park and solemnly rendered classics and spirituals in the multitude of east side black churches. The Douglass band's music broached the racial divide. In a world fouled by race prejudice, black marching bands were simply the best, most elegantly symbolized by James Reese Europe's extraordinary marching band from the U.S. 369th Colored Infantry, which had strutted down Fifth Avenue in New York City to celebrate the Armistice.

Ralph's neighborhood, the "Deep Deuce," was the musical focal point for Oklahoma City and boasted about its superior adult marching bands from early in the century, such as one led by confectionery shop owner Andrew Rushing.[1] The racially mixed crowd's enthusiastic applause promised to knock jim crow hokum off its feet. Though Douglass's students had to dodge manure during the parades (inevitably they followed the horses), and were refused competition with white groups, when they rounded the corner from Broadway to Main Street during the parades celebrating Oklahoma's birth, the salt and pepper crowd roared with hearty approval. Blowing his horn in a crisp uniform that erased his poverty, sometimes before the city's white elites, Ralph could distinguish himself.

Ellison came of age during a musical shift whose effects would linger for the rest of the century. Around the time that Ralph had left kindergarten, New Orleans funeral bands were perfecting the crisp tones and beats of European military and classical music, inflecting them tonally with a Negro wail, and ragging their timing, transforming the music into something electric, something very hot to the ear and infectious to the feet. Although the music was known in Oklahoma City as "stomp," Easterners felt more comfortable with a tamer version and called it "swing."[2] Jazz was born. The adolescent Ralph immediately understood that musicians and the new music were the determining ingredient in social affairs, the means through which he might be accepted by his peers. Learning to play the trumpet, and later aiming to become a professional musician, offered him a Frederick Douglass–like moment of self-creation. Music was simply the best route for self-definition, given his background, he later acknowledged. Although he had other claims to distinction, such as his knowledge of books, Ralph understood that, starting with Oklahoma City's east side, recognition from blacks and whites began with music. "On the level of *conscious* culture," black Oklahoma City was "biased in the direction of music" and, important for the boy who loved reading, "starkly lacking in writers."[3] Though Ralph continued to read ravenously, he saw no one around him who felt a profound joy in the written word. To most, what the written word imparted was pain and frustration, as with Dunjee's impassioned *Black Dispatch* editorials about racial injustice.

By the mid-1920s, all the boys looking for a popular and competitive extracurricular event wanted to join the Douglass band; the football team, by contrast, was dismal.[4] At age thirteen, when he was finally old enough, Ralph joined Breaux's group in the fall term of 1926, a year or so after his friend's father Joe Meade had taught him to play the brass alto horn underneath the Meades' apricot tree on Fourth Street.[5] And after a summer trailing Frank Meade down to Ed Christian's house on South Geary to jam with that incredibly talented musical family, Ralph had become carried away with the peck horn. So with his mother's hearty approval, he began to take lessons in the trumpet under Breaux three times a week in the Douglass Chapel, until after six o'clock in the evening.[6] Ida Ellison saw her son's membership in the dignified band under the direction of the tasteful Breaux as a harbinger of his future achievements. She welcomed the enthusiasm that Ralph had for the instrument, and she managed to scrape together enough money to get him a secondhand cornet, happy that her boy was showing interest in something that would keep him out of the alleys and away from the bullies' fists. Financially pressed after her second husband's death, she nevertheless supported activities that would provide structure and cultivation. Though the band played popular classics like the "William Tell" and the "Light Cavalry" overtures, the marchers also had to be fluent in popular tunes of the day, which included some rags. But as befit an ensemble that practiced in the chapel, they did not play jazz.

His teacher Lamonia McFarland's comments in social studies about New Negroes, and the passages from Countee Cullen and Langston Hughes that she recited by heart, bounced off ears buzzing with John Philip Sousa, Igor Stravinsky, and Louis Armstrong. Ralph cultivated a love for music and the trumpet not only because he enjoyed it but because he began to see music as a profession. He devoted himself to a craft that would call him out from his family's single rented room, exposing him to a vision of a life beyond the cramped quarters at 415 Stiles. The boy took to his horn as to a life buoy. When adults asked the no-longer-little adolescent, "What do you want to be when you grow up?" he was comfortable proposing a future as a musician.

When he joined the band, Ralph's relationship with Zelia Breaux blossomed.[7] As a band member, he fulfilled the music teacher's personal crusade. Breaux vigorously advocated instrumental music teaching because she thought it capable of having a near transcendental effect upon the children. In her master's degree thesis for Northwestern University, Breaux said that when young people were introduced to the classical tradition, "feeling finds a vent, is ennobled and purified."[8] She deeply believed in elevating the creative impulses of her students to the highest levels of conventionally accepted musical art. By teaching the boys and girls to crook their little fingers and pronounce the composers' names correctly, she believed that she was helping them shake lives of degradation.

Ralph now began "one of the most important relationships" in his life; he would later refer to Zelia Breaux as his "second mother."[9] Breaux was a fortunate choice for Ralph, personally and professionally. She was a well-established woman who split her time between Oklahoma City and Langston, where her husband lived. She owned rental properties and half of the Aldridge Theater on Second Street, and had her meals prepared for her by a live-in cook at a large two-story house at 901 East Third Street. Whereas many had education with no property, and others possessed riches without any cultivation or elegance, Zelia Breaux united these qualities as did no other black in Oklahoma City. Ralph later would see Breaux, and her lessons in the value of elite culture, as one of his chief sources for adequate "equipment for living." The matronly teacher introduced artistic discipline through the dogged pursuit of the unfamiliar, but always gave the youngsters the idea that they were capable of mastering complex forms. Ralph pointed to Breaux as his earliest source for artistic discipline. Good music simply wasn't created without practice. As a conductor who demanded a working relationship with Ralph, Breaux became an early adult friend.

"Mother" Breaux encouraged Ralph to channel and direct his energy, and never allow the explosiveness that sometimes lurked behind his anguished countenance to get the best of him, even when it was the result of his most forthright impulses. She told him after he made a sarcastic remark back to her in class one day, "Ralph, with you the first thing comes up is the first thing out. You've got to watch that or it'll land you in trouble."[10] Breaux had her sights set on institutionalizing music in black Oklahoma City's school curriculum, and she wanted to keep as many of her disciples on the straight and narrow as possible. She implemented the Public School Music Program, which produced orchestras, operettas, choral groups, and famous marching bands. Breaux advocated instrumental instruction at a time when anything more than vocal instruction was unusual at black schools. Though she was confident that "the Negro can sing as perhaps no other race can," Breaux recognized the handicap blacks might suffer without access to the ensemble, the band, and the orchestra.[11] She also felt strongly that music classes in the public school should be offered for credit toward the diploma. Because of her influence in Oklahoma City, where she directed musical education for the entire black public school system, black students began musical instruction in elementary school and received academic credit for their work.

Breaux was not a snob. She realized the lure and purpose of vernacular culture, but chose to aim her students' expectations beyond the ordinary. Any student could hear barrel-house music on the 300 block of Second Street, coming from Honey Murphy's, Hallie Richardson's, or Ruby Lyon's. However, her desire to teach the classics in the schools did not cause her to condemn folk art. In the interest of providing the black public with first-rank popular entertainment, she had opened the city-famous Aldridge Theater in the heart of the Second Street commercial district in 1919. The theater, named after the nineteenth-century black British Shakespearean actor Ira Aldridge, gave everyone from millionaire S. D. Lyons to the lowliest hod carrier a forum to hear King Oliver, Ma Rainey, Ida Cox, Blind Boone, Pigmeat Markham, Dusty Fletcher, Butterbeans and Susie, and Bessie Smith.

Ralph learned sight-reading as a part of the school curriculum, and gained appreciation for varieties of musical styles through another novel approach for an early 1920s public school, the use of phonograph recordings. Breaux, moving from school to school throughout the week, instructed her young pupils in theory, elementary harmony, and music appreciation. On the lookout for aspiring musicians, she had developed a program that made music a core course in black grade schools throughout the city. Music became an elective in the ninth grade. Breaux realized that training in the elementary school would help to prepare players for larger high school groups, and she also believed that with sufficient guidance during the early years, the youngster would choose to take musical classes in high school. Ralph was one of her early successes, a boy who made the transition from mandatory classes in elementary school to musical electives in high school. Another reason for Breaux's success in implementing music into the curriculum was her family connections. The Oklahoma City school board had hired her father, Inman Page, as principal for the princely sum of $3,300 in the 1923 school year. The same year, Douglass purchased two Kimball pianos, several Victrolas, and $974 worth of band instruments.[12] Youngsters flocked not only to the remarkable teacher but to the newest equipment in their undersupplied school.

Though Ralph followed Breaux's well-planned script for enlightened black youngsters, he made one choice independent of his teacher's influence, a choice indicative of his personality. Beyond the fact that it was Frank Meade's instrument, the trumpet was the obvious instrument for a youngster with a purpose. The 1920s was the decade of impressive horn soloists. Ralph's musical exploration by way of the trumpet owed a significant debt to King Oliver, who frequented Oklahoma City, and the national ascendancy of Louis Armstrong, the genre's first great soloist to reach superstar status. Though he'd started in New Orleans, Armstrong spent a good portion of time in St. Louis; Ralph was perhaps encouraged to see him as a regional comrade and forebear.

In the early 1920s, the Southwest touted an abundance of jazz bands. Around 1924, Joe Meade may have let Ralph and Frank stay up and listen to the highly successful Alphonse Trent Band, based in Dallas and broadcasting nightly from the Adolphus Hotel on radio station WFA.[13] Trent's was the best-known black band in the Southwest, superseded only by Coon-Sanders's Nighthawks from Kansas City. All three would have listened attentively to the superb style of trumpeter Terence "T" Holder, who went on to manage the band. Not known as a swinging band, the Trent group even managed to do justice to classical numbers, featuring their superb violinist Claude Williams. But Holder, two hundred miles south, didn't hold Ralph's attention too long. By the time Ellison was a bona fide member of the Douglass band, with his white shirt, white pants, black tie, and black cap, another idol named Walter Page had captured his musical imagination. Page's Original Blue Devils, featuring the fiery Oran "Hot Lips" Page on trumpet, initiated a spectacularly fecund era of music for the city.

Ralph probably practiced his horn more during the school year than during the summer. The months of school recess were devoted to whatever jobs the youngster could manage. But before going down to Second Street to sell the *Dispatch*, Ralph started his day by blowing sustained tones out of the window. Papers sold, he checked in with dentist T. J. Randolph at Randolph's Drugstore to see if there were any deliveries to make. Randolph had taken on Ralph as an errand boy and general shop clerk at the drugstore and dentist's office. He once let Ralph prepare the molds for a set of false teeth.[14] The errands and deliveries for medical supplies took Ralph several times a week to the Hettinger Brothers company for supplies, located on a floor inaccessible without walking past the offices of the Grand Dragon of the local Ku Klux Klan. Surmounting his "revulsion" and "hate," Ralph turned out to be fascinated by the blue and red lights that glowed behind the Klan's window emblem. On his trips, he always stopped to stare for a few seconds.[15] Between these errands on foot or on bicycle, he sandwiched in M. Arban's venerable double- and triple-tonguing horn exercises. He enjoyed his afternoon rambles through the east side, and by the late 1920s had use of the Randolphs' motorcycle to make his runs. Ralph jerked sodas in the drugstore of his adopted family during the summer and after school, amiably chatting with Roscoe Dunjee, when the *Black Dispatch* editor stole away from his office around the corner at 225 Stiles. At home in the late afternoon, he devoted himself to imitating the rowdy solos of Hot Lips Page, pianist Earl "Fatha" Hines, and Louis Armstrong. When he tried to make the trumpet sing, he was met with the mixed approval and consternation of his neighbors, like W. G. Sneed across the alley and Mrs. L. J. Tye on the other side of the street.

As a mature writer, Ellison would playfully recall the support he received in his early trials.

> "Let that boy blow," they'd say to the protesting ones. "He's got to talk baby talk on that thing before he can preach on it. Next thing you know he's liable to be up there with Duke Ellington. Sure, plenty Oklahoma boys are up there with the big bands. Son, let's hear you try 'Trouble in Mind Blues.' Now try and make it sound like old Ida Cox sings it."[16]

As he grew more assertive about his passion, he encountered more obstacles. Dentist T. J. Randolph's concern for Ralph prompted the suspicion and ire of his wife Hattie. Jealousy cropped up in the relationship of the childless couple as Hattie Randolph, known in the community for being pretentious and liable to publicly project her own insecurities onto friends and family members, began to circulate rumors that T. J.'s kindness to Ralph stemmed from her husband's guilty conscience. She told people that Ralph was T. J.'s bastard son, and that Ida was his mistress. Hattie's scandalmongering gossip deeply wounded Ralph's pride, all the more because the rumor circulated among people he had loved and trusted as kin. Infuriated, he brashly talked of revenge to his mother on the porch of 419 Stiles, but she refused to allow the young teen to take the incident further. The entire community recognized Hattie as unbalanced, and that was all there was to it. Ida told him, "She's crazy. So use your head. She doesn't have to be put in an institution, but you have to understand and accept the fact that she isn't responsible."[17] Ralph bottled his rage, but the relationship with the Randolph family was damaged and never regained deep intimacy.[18]

The incident with Hattie Randolph demonstrates Ida's own precarious class situation. A bright and articulate woman, the widow posed a threat with her good looks and her forthright manner. Her conversation, filled with references to gender and racial equality and public affairs, seemed too radical and outspoken to genteel women. Ida could not attend the meetings of the Phillis Wheatley Club, the Stepping-High Whist Club, the Social Uplift Club, the Laff-A-Lot Club, the Progressive Outlook Club, or the Royal Garden Syndicate, the stomping grounds of Oklahoma City's black petite bourgeoisie. While women like Mrs. L. P. Brockaway, one of the east side's busiest socialite, talked about books in their reading clubs, planned card and garden parties, and prepared elaborate luncheons, Ida rested her feet after a taxing day's work or prepared supper for her boys. Only women who didn't have to labor could partake in club life and its trappings. Ralph recognized that his mother "didn't strive to be a part of the social leadership of the black community; that was left to the wives of the professional men, to teachers and to preachers."[19] For her part, Ida found the club women's catty behavior and the preoccupation with paper-thin social credentials boring and childish. The hardworking domestic appreciated the finery of the black upper class, but she refused to feel ashamed of her down-home origins or to be embarrassed by her current situation. As a result, other women resented her. Because she was of light complexion, her remarks on Ralph's future, and the unworthiness of some of his associates, made some think her vain. In the words of one of Ralph's playmates, "I don't remember his mother as a nice person."[20]

Ida's ambition for her son to have all of the refinement and erudition available from Breaux and the successful Randolphs caused Ralph some anguish. Along with his peers, he gravitated to blues and jazz, the music of the lower class which in Ralph's youth was discredited as evidence of African barbarism. But despite his cultured role models, Ralph saw tantalizing examples of native black style all over the Deuce, and not exclusively in music. On sultry summer evenings, Ralph got to indulge the marching and strutting aspect of his new vocation. Veterans from the Spanish American War and World War I delighted in training the young east Oklahoma City boys in complicated military drill patterns on the whites-only Bryant School grounds at Byers and Second Streets. The men had been in the Tenth Cavalry Band, and some had seen service with Lewis Ellison's famous regiment, the Twenty-fifth Infantry. Also prepared to offer their instructions were various lodge members: the Elks, the Knights of Pythias, the Odd Fellows, and the Shriners. The old soldiers and lodgemen, embittered and despairing after the court-martial of scores of black soldiers following the Brownsville Affair of 1906 and the lynchings and race riots of 1919, took distinct pleasure in taking over the Bryant School and expertly drilling in front of whites. They taught the tennis shoe–wearing boys complex formations and drill patterns by moonlight, if need be. Meanwhile they passed on information to the young boys that Ralph found invaluable. He had the opportunity to hear the details of a black soldier's life during the turn of the century, and he proudly told the veterans the dates of his father's service. Under the "hep, hep" of strict military cadences, the boys displayed intense effort for their teachers, who were always encouraging if gruff. For Ralph the summertime drilling offered an enjoyable cultural lesson. Despite the strict, standard form employed by the drillmasters, sooner or later, he recalled with pride, "as we mastered the patterns, the jazz feeling would come into it, and nobody was satisfied until we were swinging."[21]

Ralph felt the sonorously rich connections all around him. He had taken to music at the height of the Jazz Age, but at a time when the rural blues origins of the jazz form existed comfortably in the same bawdy houses and juke joints as the finished urban product. He linked his awakening to the joyous powers of music with the earthy and pleasurable call of the watermelon hucksters in east Oklahoma City. Keeping their calls in time with the horses' hooves, these shouters, whose voices were like "mellow bugles," advertised their business by consistently hitting a throaty, high-pitched cry that carried for blocks. Jazz was less a specific form of music than an essential element of black style, obvious in football and boxing, bootlegging and preaching. Horns, jazz, and swing were ubiquitous.

When it came to pursing his lips and pushing air through the trumpet's mouthpiece, however, Ralph discovered his limitations. "I was no embryo Joe Smith or Tricky Sam Nanton." He was not born gifted enough to play in Duke Ellington's band. For Ralph the path to a life's work required the combination of raw enthusiasm and dutiful practice. Before school, he would enthusiastically blow an "exhibitionist" morning reveille, inspired by the military tradition of father and principal, announcing himself to the Houses, who rented his family their room. Evening taps, played long and slow, carried in it a color guard's ode to Lewis Ellison, and also invoked the tragedy of a young James Ammons, the stepfather who had taught him how to hunt. After school, Ralph shuttled back and forth from the street-level drugstore at 331 East Second Street to Room 206 of the Slaughter Building at 331½ to serve as T. J. Randolph's office boy. Offering encouragement in the direction of a proper musical tradition, Randolph had Ralph blow Schubert's "Serenade" to muffle the cries of yelping patients in the dentist's chair. At the time, Ralph admittedly felt confused, pulled in two directions—one that demanded strict adherence to codified standards and hierarchy; and the other, more prone to allow the expression of his individuality. In later years, he would characterize the confusion: "Caught mid-range between my two traditions, where one attitude often clashed with the other and one technique of playing was by the other opposed, I caused whole blocks of people to suffer."[22]

He found the varying notes and tones of blues and jazz enticing, in no small measure because they afforded the chance to mend some bridges with the guys at school. It was a choice. Ralph knew that his teachers and church elders tended to view jazz as the last vestige of primitivism. For his prudish elders, the music was simply lewd. Their opprobrium stemmed less from aversion to black vernacular culture than from the nobler urge to defy the popular caricatures of the vaudeville tradition and the current revue shows. Despite the convincing work of an entire generation of black scholars, militants, ministers, and teachers, the new media of radio and film enforced the image of barbarous and lusty blacks (Africans or Americans), pulsing to the beat of jazz music—generally advertised as the genuine sound of the African jungle. So powerful was the connection between jazz and African nativity that New York's Cotton Club ran a revue featuring scantily clad black flappers and Ellington's hot urban music as an "authentic" representation of the African jungle.[23]

Ralph managed to incorporate the two genres of music, but musical expertise demanded patience from a boy well on his way to becoming impetuous. One way to learn the art of waiting was from the old men who gathered at Randolph's drugstore or in front of Edward's funeral parlor down at the corner of Second and Central. At these classic preserves of idle talk, Ralph came in contact with older Negroes under less rigid and formal circumstances than at school. These were men who had seen slavery and knew a great deal about black folk culture. As the older men lit their pipes on rainy afternoons, they recited hometown versions of classic tales of buried treasures and headless horsemen. Ralph heard the popular folk verse "The Shooting of Dan McGrew" along with tales of Jesse James, John Henry, and the legendary black cowboy Bill Pickett; and the exploits of black U.S. Marshal Bass Reeves, and of blacks who had become chiefs of Indian tribes.[24] The older men revealed that an itching palm rubbed over a pocket brought fortune, and that brooms swept over feet were bad luck for marriage.[25] Best of all, the august crowd helped to keep his father's memory alive. The men remembered Lewis as an extremely gifted raconteur.

Through the Second Street scuttlebutt, he also heard views rivaling the white supremacy–toned Oklahoma City *Daily* or the black nationalist *Black Dispatch*. One of the older men still around in the 1920s who had a claim to legendary status in Oklahoma politics was Jim Noble. Noble was a lackey, a black yes-man in social circles that treated blacks pitifully, but one who cannily understood his position in the scheme of things, and took proper reward. Under the order of William Anthony, secretary to then Oklahoma Governor Haskell, Noble had been responsible for physically carrying the state seal from Guthrie to Oklahoma City during the tumultuous battle of 1910, when the two cities had slugged it out to determine which would become the state capital.[26] Oklahoma City courted Haskell and the rest of his Democratic constituents by promoting the disenfranchisement of blacks and the subsequent absence of black elected officials, unlike the Republican stronghold of Guthrie. Noble took the seal to Oklahoma City's Huckins Hotel, where the government remained until the state capitol was completed on Lincoln Boulevard. Regardless of the irony of the affair, Noble's duty became a source of pride for Oklahoma Negroes. Noble, who called himself William Murray's "messenger boy" and a "darky," also bragged that he had made barrelfuls of money, a hundred dollars per week, sometimes in gold.[27]

Another bridge to the antebellum era was Emmitt Carruthers, owner of the Baltimore Barber Shop, a Negro thought very well of by the white community. In the 1920s, most of Oklahoma's powerful men—Anton Classen, Colcord, Stafford, and J. H. Wheeler—patronized the black man born into bondage in Tennessee, sometimes asking the stooped barber's advice on business deals. Carruthers silently lathered faces and stropped his razor, holding true to Southern decorum, and "never offered his advice unless it was sought."[28] Both Carruthers and Noble had been traditional members of the black middle class. Now they were being replaced by Meharry Medical School's legions and other professionally educated blacks. The college elite replaced the informally educated but powerfully connected black ward bosses and petty politicians. The new breed—the so-called New Negroes, in black philosopher Alain Locke's sense of the word—had plenty of intellect and cultural refinement; but unlike those involved in the messier political logrolling and wildcatting of an earlier era, they had virtually no influence with the downtown white politicos.

Ralph's surrogate "grandpa" J. D. Randolph was a Democratic crony as well, though with his thorough education on a Tennessee plantation from a German tutor and his business acumen, he commanded more respect than other slave-born men. J. D. rarely spent an entire afternoon on his duff with the idlers. Thousands of burnt matchsticks littered the ground in front of Randolph's porch on Third Street, testament to the conversations that J. D. had over pipe or cigar with lawmakers and influential men, white and black, who came to his house seeking the old pioneer's counsel.[29] In 1927, Randolph maneuvered his influence into a job in the capitol building, where he was janitor of the law library until 1934.[30] Though his title was unimpressive, like Noble, he had access to important documents and powerful people, which the discerning real estate owner used to his advantage in his own business deals. Randolph took Ralph, now a high school freshman, with him to the capitol during slow days at the drugstore, at nights, and on the weekends, to begin showing the young man potential careers. Often while Randolph wrung out a mop or emptied a wastebasket, white legislators asked "Uncle Jeff" questions regarding technical aspects of the law. The former school principal fired back articulate, well-conceived responses, generally without having to consult the law books at hand. Ralph knew too well why his grandpa wasn't a lawyer. The atmosphere in Oklahoma bred condescension to all Negroes. In Ralph's words, it was impossible for him "to ignore that race was the source of this rot . . . the law was colored and rigged against my people."[31]

Ralph grasped the rough irony behind the facade of racial segregation. White lawmakers around the capitol building—the very same legislators who daily upheld laws and customs based upon the assumption of black mental inability—highly valued Randolph's opinions. Ralph grew fond of the encounters, glowing at the subtle deference paid to his grandpa. He learned to look past the appearance of a situation and see more deeply into issues of power and control. While J. D. Randolph's title was incommensurate with his ability, and it was generally the lawyers who set the conditions for the edifying conversations, Ralph learned that his grandpa's own estimate of himself was closer to the truth, and ultimately was what mattered most. Understanding that there was strength as well as dignity in humble competence helped ease his insecurity about his clothes and shoes at school. But despite Ralph's great affection for the man, as he neared his own maturity, he bristled more and more at Randolph's counsel of endurance. Randolph touted the common sense of an unsentimental pragmatist: "I never tackle anything unless I have measured the distance and know that I can jump that far."[32]

Randolph's caution was well-founded. Oklahoma brimmed with foul characters in high places. Oklahoma Circuit Court Judge Joel Estes and the citywide imposition of "Texas Law" (a salty euphemism for racial segregation) made the young man cynical regarding the potential for black social equality and unbiased legal justice. Articles invariably appeared in Dunjee's weekly paper covering the last moments of a condemned Southern black who had tired of racial prohibitions, killed the insufferable white man, and suffered the ghastly consequences. (In one earlier incident, in 1919 at Fourth and Philips, a Negro had shot and killed a white streetcar conductor over a racial slight.[33]) As Ralph grew painfully conscious of the racial climate, he ventured youthful skepticism. When he looked back on the period of his early teen years, he recalled finding "no hope in the law . . . [and] in instances of extreme pressure, it was to be defied, even at the cost of one's life."[34]

Ralph took this skeptical armor with him to the classroom, along with a few schoolbooks. His dubious perspective was unwelcome, as it exposed the flimsy bunting used to make the black American dream attractive. Teachers like the sedate Breaux and her incomparably dignified father Inman Page warned Ralph to hold his tongue and curb his defiant opinions. One of the opinions he would have been discouraged from holding was any favoritism toward contemporary jazz music. He wanted acceptance from the important members of the Oklahoma City community and to play jazz, but a career as a popular musician seemed nearly a repudiation of the lives of the dignified educators who taught him at Douglass.

By ninth grade, Ralph had decided to think of himself as a musician. He needed something to feel proud about. By now, his brother Herbert's academic irregularities were legendary, and his family fortunes were bleak. It had taken a year of stiff economizing after Ammons's death for the three of them to get their own address at 419 Stiles, in a building or group of rooms probably connected to Willis Taylor's larger home at 417 Stiles. As a signal of the way Ralph thought that he might reconcile the dilemma of choosing between classical or vernacular music, as well as increase his own stock with Zelia Breaux, he joined the school orchestra, doubling the time that he spent on his instrument.

Nineteen twenty-seven marked the arrival of Douglass as a music powerhouse. That September the Douglass band opened the Oklahoma State Fair.[35] Excited by the exposure and fanfare, Ralph focused his attention on music and relied on his extracurricular reading and verbal ability to keep him afloat in the classroom. His purpose was to pass his classes and bring home a high school degree, an achievement that had eluded even the most astute members of his family. At the time, Ralph had little reason to put academic excellence on par with his determined pursuit of musical distinction. Douglass faculty certainly hoped for academic brilliance from their students, but tended rather to emphasize the discipline of the body and moral uplift of the mind. Independent thought was not encouraged. Brown University salutatorian Inman Page's main duties consisted of patrolling the building's halls, enlisting a truant officer to collect errant pupils, and conferring with a matron to keep the girls away from the rounders and fancy women of East Main Street. The same sort of conformity was true with the musical instruction. Had something like Ralph's budding orientation toward swing music gained attention, teachers would have tried to help the poor boy by stamping it out of him. The gifted Charlie Christian, three years behind Ralph and by then a superlative string musician, never once played in any of Breaux's esteemed orchestras or ensembles. Christian refused to completely disavow the music favored in the South Geary Street slum where he lived, and therefore was unacceptable.

To complicate Ralph's struggle, the cosmos seemed aligned so that he couldn't miss out on any music, especially stomp. Ralph had already picked a fortuitous year to learn the horn. Near the time that he lived on Fourth Street and pushed down the first and last valve to blow a D, tuba and bass player Walter Page reached a crossroads about six blocks away. In 1925, Billy King's Road Show had disbanded after reaching Oklahoma City. They had been a vaudeville outfit featuring the then relatively unknown Page. A Kansas City protégé of Major N. Clark Smith, the tuba player considered continuing his music education at the University of Kansas, but instead rounded up the other musicians from the troupe and rechristened them Walter Page's Original Blue Devils. With original members Oran "Hot Lips" Page and Jimmy LuGrand (trumpets), Dan Minor and Eddie Durham (trombones), Reuben Ruddy and Ted Manning (reeds), Thomas Turk (piano), Reuben Lynch (banjo), Alvin Burroughs (drums), and Page (string bass, tuba, and baritone saxophone), the Blue Devils eventually became one of the best-known jazz bands of the Southwest. The musicians played out of Oklahoma City until about 1932, when many of the men joined forces with their regional rival from Kansas City, Bennie Moten. By that time, their numbers would have expanded to include a piano player named William "Count" Basie and a saxophonist named Lester Young. The combination of Moten's reputation and Kansas City boss Tom Pendergast's fortunes pulled away all the star players—the two Pages, Young, and Basie. But in 1925, they had just begun. One of the first local musicians hired was trumpeter Harry Youngblood. When Ralph was in high school, the band's popularity soared when it employed another local boy who had grown up next door to Second Street's Aldridge Theater with all of its wonderful blues entertainment, the powerfully lunged Jimmy Rushing.[36]

The Blue Devils were either classically trained, sophisticated musicians, like pianist Willie Lewis, a great "sight" reader and "very smart," or exceptionally gifted soloists like Buster Smith. The 250-pound Walter "Big-un" Page, a jazz innovator who substituted the string bass for the tuba in the rhythm section of the band, was easily in a class by himself. The group frequently won magnificent musical contests, known as "battles of the bands," held at Forest Park, the Ritz Ballroom, and the third floor of Second Street's Slaughter Hall. Though other bands played in Oklahoma City, the Blue Devils competed with the very best from the Southwest: "T" Holder's Twelve Clouds of Joy from Dallas (renamed after Andy Kirk in 1929), which used arrangements rivaling Fletcher Henderson's and Duke Ellington's in complexity; George E. Lee's Kansas City Band; Jessie Stone's Blues Serenaders; and Moten's nearby Kansas City outfit. The bandsmen prized versatility and strove to combine multiple playing styles. Audiences in Saginaw, Michigan, wanted waltzes and "sweet" music, just like Guy Lombardo played. Bottles at the ready, blacks in the frontier lands of Oklahoma and Arkansas demanded Texas swing music, in the style of Bob Wills and the Texas Playboys. But the Blue Devils' strong suit was the freewheeling, caterwauling, gutbucket stomp music, redolent in Hot Lips Page's rowdy solos on their only known recordings, "Squabblin'" and "Blue Devils" (1929). Territory bands started out playing for dances; staying true to their roots meant satisfying audiences that wanted "hot" music—rhythmic, hard driving, and sometimes "progressive" or freely innovative. Comparing the Devils to Moten's better-known group, saxophone player Buster Smith said, "We tried to be a band that could just get off instead of just read the music."[37]

Though "reading," or formal training, was a necessity for a musician, it was not the end-all or be-all. As Smith (himself not a great reader) suggested, the Blue Devils saw their distinction as being able to do more than read. For Ralph and other local band members, Walter Page and Icky Lawrence were especially heroic and admirable. The men frequently impressed Second Street and silenced the objections of black critics like Breaux and Avery choir director Haywood by playing the raunchiest blues-driven stomp music, then with only the slightest preparation, tackling the music scores in any theater pit in town. An impresario like Page was a model for mastery of form and truth to the idiom. Ralph observed little difference between the aspirations of a musician who desired the jazz bandstand or the classical orchestra: "There wasn't always this division between the ambitions of jazz musicians and the standards of classical music."[38]

Jazzmen exhibited an even more important quality for Ralph than merely discipline and excellence. They were clear examples of virtue during a time when adolescent Ralph was experimenting with different styles of behavior to see which one fit him best. He found a purity in musicians who mastered their craft, and most that he knew and respected were black and played jazz. For Ralph, musicians were nearly religious martyrs: "Their driving motivation was neither money nor fame, but the will to achieve the most eloquent expression of idea-emotions through the technical mastery of their instruments (which incidentally some of them wore as a priest wears the cross)."[39]

For the church-raised teenager, jazz musicians had followed a higher calling, and they elevated music to a sacred ritual performance of life. There was virtue even in the players' Dionysian Sunday night excesses, since they were not hypocrites like some of Avery's Amen corner, who every young person knew had been carousing at full throttle Saturday night. Jazz music afforded, even demanded, being true to self-inclination, while the classical tradition that was enforced at the black public school represented a denial of black vernacular music. Ralph sensed that Breaux and her supporters were doing the right thing for the wrong reason. Classical music had a constructive role to play in the schools, but not because it had an abstract "civilizing" quality. For Ralph, working to learn and understand how one produced the range of sounds of the contemporary orchestra, the techniques of harmony, melody, and counterpoint, creating an emotional mood through instruments, afforded him an inchoate perspective on the historical progression of classical music through its various eras—from roots with Greek lyres and Spanish troubadours through the more complex articulation of the baroque, romantic, and modern periods. His education removed much of the veil over the European cultural mystique. To Breaux's young musicians who had acquired the power of critical insight, classical music could be understood as one form among many.

Not a spectacular soloist, Ralph flirted with the idea of emulating a composing group leader like Walter Page or Bennie Moten. Page and Young were the suitable role models for black youth growing up under successive waves of devastating race oppression and economic insecurity. Negro ancestry might still be an ignoble stain in the eyes of the world, and the rewards of the American Dream might have failed to materialize, but there was still the higher calling to the jazz priesthood, capable of transcending the dissatisfaction with American law and custom.

If he wanted to live the music as seriously as those he admired, Ralph realized he would have to obtain private lessons. His fellow bandmates looked down on people who played only one instrument, and Ralph wanted to continue, in his own way, to feel superior. Likely toward the end of freshman year, Ralph connected himself with a leading Oklahoma City musician who gave him elegant bragging rights. He rode a streetcar over to 2120 North McKinley Avenue, on the west side of the city, and mowed Ludwig Hebestreit's lawn in exchange for advanced trumpet lessons.[40] Hebestreit was the music instructor at Classen Senior High School and had also formed the nucleus of the Oklahoma Symphony Orchestra. It's quite possible that Breaux, concentrating on Malcolm Whitby and Lawrence Davis, her star pupils, did not have time to give Ralph more complicated lessons, though undoubtedly she was capable of pushing the ninth grader. He had been in her band for only a year and showed promise, but not exceptional ability. Or it may have been that Ralph took the lessons from Hebestreit instead of Breaux in 1930 or even as late as 1931, when meeting the requirements for her Northwestern B.A. in educational music consumed Breaux's time. Her degree was awarded in the spring of 1931.[41]

The tutorials with Ludwig Hebestreit represented one of the continuing anomalies of black life under segregation, similar to J. D. Randolph's incongruous role at the state law library. Ralph could not attend the prestigious Classen Senior High School, where the conductor taught, nor could his family afford costly music lessons from the area's best music teacher, not to mention that it may well have been socially inadvisable for the white conductor to teach a Negro boy out of his home. However, pushing a mower on Hebestreit's front lawn fit in well with the white community's assumptions about a black young person, so much so that they may have ignored the fact that Ralph emerged from the streetcar with his trumpet case.

Inside the McKinley Street house, Hebestreit's demeanor reversed the assumptions of an unkind world. He offered the Douglass High kid an insight not only into the intricacies of his instrument but also into those of conducting. The German immigrant provided lessons in structure, chord patterns, modulations, and other composition and conducting techniques. For Ralph, the lessons in composing and the complexity of orchestral arrangements were challenging. He would play a score, and then the older man would show him his strong points and errors. Despite the difficulty of the material, Hebestreit brimmed with enthusiasm about Ralph. He helped the youngster to understand the way the symphonic effect was produced in his favorite compositions. Hebestreit was indulgent whereas some of the black jazz musicians Ralph knew, like the piano-playing custodian of the Slaughter Building, were not.[42] "You like such and such a composition, don't you?" Hebestreit asked. "The strings are doing this . . . and the trumpets are playing this figure against the woodwinds." Hebestreit helped Ralph understand the logic that lay behind the music scores and offered strategies to help him, as he recalled, "attack those things I desired" and "pierce the mystery and possess them."[43] Ralph may have thought of himself as a young swinging soldier in the advance guard of Walter Page or Benny Moten when he started going over to McKinley Avenue; but by the time he finished his chores at Hebestreit's, the idea of more traditional conducting had settled in his mind. The experience also fed into the intelligent teenager's sense of his own uniqueness, his peculiar ability, like J. D. Randolph's, to hurdle certain racially imposed obstacles. Douglass stars like Whitby and Davis may have been the favorites, but Ellison had found the musician's catbird seat.

Ralph had other kinds of experiences that emboldened his resolve for unique exploration. During the late 1920s, the Ellisons were privileged to host an unusual houseguest. A black woman from England named Clark would come and stay at the Ellison household during the theater runs of Emma Bunting's company. For Ida, the visits, and the performances, which she enjoyed, elevated her sense of herself. Perhaps she had been bringing home *Vanity Fair* as much for herself as for Ralph. As Bunting's personal maid, Miss Clark had access to the exciting world of professional theater. She appears to have stayed with the Ellisons at least three seasons, perhaps during the late 1920s, when the family had stopped moving so frequently and had room to put up another adult somewhat comfortably. The good-looking Miss Clark intrigued Ralph, who was beginning to have crushes on his teachers at Douglass, including the uncommonly attractive, fair-skinned instructor Odessa Eudailey. Clark introduced an unfamiliar accent and speech pattern into the house and delighted Ralph with her own renditions of high society theatrics. She not only revealed to him the wonder of English society, but also served as another example of social and cultural mobility. She showed him how blacks might fit into the world of Shakespeare and Big Ben, places that Ralph might have been inclined to imagine himself excluded from. Emma Bunting herself, the star of the company, brought Miss Clark over to the Ellisons to stay—an interaction with a celebrity that delighted the family. Ida proudly carried a lace bag that was a gift from Bunting. Encouraged by his unique visitor, by sophomore year Ralph had joined the school drama team and played a role in Breaux's spring operetta "Gypsy Rover."[44]

Around 1928, the Dunbar Branch Library moved to a new building with the Colored Women's Federated Club on 615 East Fourth Street, a block that had come to represent the height of black middle-class prosperity. Between Byers and Durland Avenues lived the dentists S. R. Youngblood and A. B. Whitby, and further down the block, Reverend Toombs, formerly of Avery Chapel. Oklahoma City now boasted a proud and secure black middle class. At the library as a high school student, Ralph determinedly handled heavier literary material, propelled by, if not in private contest with, a brilliant and overachieving young man named Hilliard Bowen, who was also growing up without a father.

Dunbar's used books and eclectic hand-me-downs did not satisfy Ralph's growing appetite for reading material. The glossy *Vanity Fair* magazines that he kept carefully stacked at home, Dunjee's rapid-fire *Black Dispatch* editorials, and O. O. McIntyre's posh journalistic understatement in the *Daily Oklahoman,* had prepared him for engaging adult material. With the library's resources consumed by the new building, librarian Young was hard-pressed to secure new books, and Ralph found intellectual sanctuaries elsewhere, as in the home of Mr. and Mrs. Harlish Gear, teachers at Douglass. Harlish Gear, like Douglass English teacher Harriet D. Christburg, had been educated at Knoxville College in Galesburg, Illinois.[45] "I read my first Shaw and Maupassant, my first Harvard Classics in the home of a friend whose parents were products of that stream of New England education," recalled Ellison in an early 1960s conversation.[46] This confluence of Northeastern influences and the development of intellectual abilities is not surprising, and reflects the typical source of intellectual light in Southern-reared, post-Emancipation black communities. The Gears, or perhaps the A. B. Whitbys, whose children were educated at private schools but knew Ralph, had a complete set of George Bernard Shaw, and also a smattering of Nietzsche's writing on folklore.

Shaw's references to Wagner probably helped create a bridge to Nietzsche, whose work he found on the teacher's shelves. Ralph seems to have explored the philosopher's recently translated material and uncovered a connection between the use of folklore in Nietzsche and his newfound playwright. The trumpeter understood the layers of mythology invested in folklore, and he discerned the same mythic strands woven through black spirituals and the lyrics of the blues.[47] His literary wanderings were picking up speed, and he found himself enjoying the digging necessary to gain understanding.

At Douglass, Ralph kept an eye on his course work, and at the same time developed a certain reserve. He contented himself with Cs, an occasional B, or an occasional D in T. R. Debnam's math class.[48] Earl Byrd, Ralph's physics teacher, rode herd if he even suspected that a student was uninterested, and he told his class at the beginning of the year that he didn't give As. Juanita Vivette Harris, who had been a year behind Ralph at Douglass, recalled Byrd offering to all who squeaked by in their measurements of velocity and height the adage that "the mills of the gods grind slowly."[49] Teacher Ida Wright gave Ralph's class their composition and literature lessons as he approached junior year in high school. Henry Berry, who also read Hebrew and Greek, taught him four years of Latin. The Latin classes were a significant indicator of the liberal arts bent of the school, offset only by Professor Youngblood's yearlong course in agriculture, which mildly infuriated the young people, who disdained any connection with manual education. In Breaux's harmony classes, Ralph made his most consistent effort, earning three Bs and three Cs. Although he was physically in school, his mind was elsewhere, probably combining the themes and rhythms of Second Street with the techniques of Hebestreit. Ralph's attitude was also quite strategic. He knew that the black colleges to which he would be limited didn't require full transcripts, only the students' own record of the classes they had taken. The significant questions were whether one had earned the high school diploma and if one could get a glowing recommendation.

Despite the intensity of his focus on music, Ralph paid attention to literature and also to writing. His first genuine writing experience took place in his junior year under English instructor W. A. Jackson in 1930, when the school nurse Mrs. Waller ordered Ralph to University Hospital to have his lungs checked. Having heard his hacking cough for several weeks and knowing the circumstances of the family, she feared tuberculosis. The nurse's insinuation slightly humiliated Ralph, who was accustomed to struggling through the winters. His resentment changed dramatically, however, when he reached the waiting room at the hospital where he had last seen his father alive. Ralph experienced mild horror sitting next to the other more seriously ill people in the hospital common room. The two emotions, indignation and repulsion, prompted him to pick up pen and paper. He wrote a journalistic piece, detailing the scene and the symptoms of the ill from the vantage of a healthy outsider, in the vein of O. O. McIntyre and with what he hoped was Shavian perspicuity. He showed his essays to Douglass's Professor Jackson, who was astonished that Ralph had extended himself beyond the required course work. Ralph also experimented with poetry, moved to verse by a serialized novel from the abolitionist-minded late-nineteenth-century fiction writer Albion Tourgeé.[50] Ralph likely read a copy of the then forty-year-old *Our Continent* magazine, edited by Tourgeé in the early 1880s. In 1882, the Yankee and former Union soldier Tourgeé published his serial novel *Hot Plowshares* in the magazine. The August edition featured the chapter "Hargrove's Quarter," impugning slavery and detailing the demise of a plantation in the swamp country of the mid-Atlantic region. The rich images of the story and the heavy myths of the cavalier planting class impressed Ralph. Up to then, he had shown only the most cursory interest in class—a slick boy doing just enough to pass. His unprecedented effort with the additional essays and a poem or two are probably what netted him his single B grade in English.[51]

Practicing his horn and working after school left Ralph with less and less time for homework. He learned the majority of his lessons in the hep new music when as a sixteen-year-old he wandered into Hallie Richardson's new shoe-shine parlor at 308 East Second Street, bastion of the red-light district on Second Street. The Deuce had long been the hotbed of black entertainment, and it quickly had become the center of the latest craze in music. Richardson's place, along with Ruby Lyon's Cafe and Lyons Den, the billiards place at 321 East Second Street, were the reputable places of ill repute. Hallie Richardson, known as "Fat Hallie," ran an open-air bootlegging establishment. According to musician Count Basie, Richardson was "fat" because he always had an enormous paunch, carefully concealed in a huge raincoat. On evenings at the public dances at Slaughter's Hall, Richardson went in and distributed the inebriating contents of his paunch, for a small fee. Ralph got into Hallie's by sweeping floors and shining shoes, and soon yearned to go to the popular breakfast dances and to Honey Murphy's after-hours jam spot off Second Street, where Basie, an unknown piano player from New Jersey, cooled his heels.[52] Ida was unimpressed with Ralph's workplace; she didn't want him running off with a band.

But vital to the budding musician's development were the sorts of people attracted to the free-floating environment, where the rules of middle-class society were suspended. During Ralph's junior year, saxophonist Lester Young, a future great with Count Basie, came down to Oklahoma City and turned the Deuce out with the layered complexity and unassuming style of his play. Young immediately set himself apart from the other men, well known for their Apple caps and natty suits, with his white sweater and blue stocking cap, and his trademark outthrust style of playing a silver saxophone. He introduced a melodic vein into the cutting contests and the bandstand solos, making an immediate impact on music in the city, influencing what instrument people chose and how they played it. Not many years older than Ralph, "Prez" challenged the members of the Blue Devils—Page, Lem Johnson, and Ben Webster—whereas Ralph had been struggling to get into one of Hallie's shine chairs to go against them.[53] He began to understand what real dedication to an instrument looked like. Through exposure to musical virtuosos like Young, Ralph began to make concrete-solid the new dream in his heart, one that might make use of all of his faculties, particularly his increasing analytical skills. He would study to become a conductor, though not necessarily of the new music. He began to see classical music as the means to continue to separate and elevate himself in the face of stiff competition.

As a high school junior under Ida's hawk eyes, Ralph didn't stay long in Hallie's without his shine rag. But occupying a space with the Blue Devils was the pinnacle of a young man's social achievement and reputation, one that would put him on a par with fellow Douglass band member Frank Meade. Ralph bartered his way onto the bandstand during practice sessions. Occasionally he went in and let Oran Page borrow his mellophone (a brass instrument similar in tone to the French horn). In exchange, Ralph politely suggested that he be allowed to sit in with the men, and when music sheets were passed around, Ralph jumped on the opportunity to prove his sight-reading skills. On occasion, he read better than a Blue Devil, and due to his impartiality, was sometimes asked to arbitrate disagreements on interpretation when the patrician Walter Page missed the informal rehearsals.

Playing inside the cramped shoe parlor had all of the ritual and ceremonial import of a debutante ball to the young Oklahoman, who was now concerned about the cut of his hair, the proper portion of pomade, and the ridges produced by a hot wet rag applied to the scalp. After formidable and intricate warm-ups involving tones and scales, but designed to carve out space to play, the trumpeter would blow the collected spittle from his horn and announce himself ready. In the crowded and stuffy parlor, one man would begin to blow and play until challenged by another, who now had to incorporate and improve upon the theme laid out by the initial musician. This was "cutting." Earning his chops at Hallie's enabled Ralph to join Edward Christian's band, the Jolly Jugglers, sometime after tenth grade. But Ida still held his reins and forbade participation in the evening jazz events with the older men, especially the nefarious public dance.

Ralph learned that the dignified, quirky, and irrepressible musicians were absolutely serious about their art and the ritual of creation. The Devils and their competitors practiced a discipline and self-sacrifice unsurpassed by anyone Ralph knew. And some musicians were capable of exceeding the barriers of the world as he knew it, with a talent and dedication that proved capable of trouncing even the most cherished of society's sacred cows. In 1929, Louis Armstrong came to town, generating so much excitement that white women crashed Slaughter's Hall and the races mingled freely and illegally on Second Street.[54] For a night, segregation's greatest taboo lay dead on the dance hall floor.

However, the jazz musicians' divine powers inevitably led to a less than sacrosanct view of the Sabbath. The Blue Devils normally practiced on Sunday mornings, somewhere in the 300 block of Second Street,[55] where Ralph walked on his way to church on Geary Avenue. He felt seduced by the hot music pouring out of the Second Street clubs on a Sunday morning as he made his way to Avery Chapel to hear choirmaster Haywood's renditions of European baroque. Then later in the day, the Devils, a blue imp emblazoned upon their bass drum, played gigs, indulging in a revelry wholly at odds with the fire and brimstone seething out from most of the black pulpits. Ida made sure that her son was in church, where Avery's Reverend Jordan filled his house with such sermons as "The Dying Request" and "The Nearness of Jesus."[56] When not endorsing Reverend J. T. Jordan's powerful sermons, Ida entrusted her son to Mrs. Breaux, who had him playing excerpts of her latest operetta, the "Bells of Cornville," at Calvary Baptist Church that May.[57] After his row with Inman Page in junior high, Ida tried to keep her teenager on the path to success.

Other factors influenced Ralph's adolescent shifts—his pull away from Avery's junior fellowship and Zelia Breaux toward the world of the Deuce. In the middle of his high school education, the Ellisons moved to 710 East Second Street, Ralph's final home in Oklahoma City. More than likely, the added income of Ida's latest suitor made the move to a larger home possible. Now the twice-widowed mother of two was being courted by John E. Bell, a former servant, originally from Tulsa.[58] The year before, Bell had either just divorced or buried his wife Nurleen, with whom he had shared a home in 1928 at 116 North Geary, a block down the street from Avery. Brown-skinned and small, Bell accompanied Ida to the main church services while the boys took part in Avery's junior fellowship.

Herbert Ellison claimed that neither he nor his brother thought well of Bell.[59] Ralph ignored the courtship by going off further into music. He decided that he would enjoy the noise of his new neighborhood, tougher than middle-class Fourth Street. At least the chaos drowned out the sounds of his mother's latest suitor. The Ellison family now lived next door to Ralph Canty's auto repair shop, adding the roar of the combustion engine to the already powerful noise of the Rock Island Round House, the railroad switching station about three blocks away. Even from that distance, Ralph recalled hearing "a steady clanging of bells and a great groaning of wheels along the rails, switch engines made up trains of freight unceasingly." A variety of sounds wafted through his house, from guitar players in the alley to Victrolas blaring records bought from the East Side Record Shop. Just across the other side of Ralph's alley, in the rear of 707 First Street, was a series of apartments full of more revelry than he knew at home. In the springtime during quiet evenings, he could hear Jimmy Rushing piping for the Blue Devils at Slaughter's Hall on Second Street. As a teenager, when he wasn't old enough to attend the evening dances but was "old enough to gather beneath the corner street lamps," Ralph and his young buddies joked about the Blue Deviled folk heroes "raising hell down at Slaughter's Hall," as the music drifted eastward toward them, four blocks away:

"Now, that's the Right Reverend Jimmy Rushing preaching now man," someone would say. And rising to the cue another would answer, "Yeah and that's old Elder 'Hot Lips' signifying along with him; urging him on, man." And keeping it building, "Huh, but though you can't hear him out this far, Ole Deacon Big-un [the late Walter Page] is up there patting his foot and slapping on his big belly [the bass viol] to keep those fools in line."[60]

Dreaming of the Blue Devils and the dance hall did not prevent him from coming to know a great deal about his mother's suitor. Within weeks of the stock market crash, Ida Ellison took another name. Oklahoma City district judge Wyley Jones married thirty-three-year-old John Bell to Lucy Ida Ammons on December 9, 1929.[61] Ida told Bell her real age, not hiding the significant disparity between her forty-five years and her husband's thirty-three. Despite her honesty to her betrothed, Ida seems to have recoiled from the process of making legal records. When she married, she used her middle name Lucy and James Ammons's surname. She also declined to marry in her church. One of Ralph Ellison's rare public statements regarding the men his mother would marry hints at the thorny relationship between the adolescent and the new husband. "I was quite touchy about those who'd inherited my father's position as head of my family."[62]

Music and dancing kept him upbeat. Probably around the time of her wedding to Bell, Ralph asked permission to attend a morning breakfast dance following Avery's Christmas service, a reverent occasion never sullied with frivolity. But this time, though disinclined toward social events that took place following church, Ida, "quite pious," allowed her boy to go.[63] As her son stretched toward manhood, Ida Ellison Bell attempted to give him room to grow.

Despite his dedication and know-how, Ralph understood that he didn't have the superlative gifts of musical genius that Eddie Christian's little brother Charlie, the local wunderkind, did. Nor did he possess the no-holds-barred adventurousness of fellow trumpeter Tracy McCleary, who, seized by Lester Young's influence, moved to Baltimore, where his abilities were proclaimed to all the musical depth of the Southwest.[64] Even with the dedication and expertise Ralph showed in his new vocation, he still faced the issue of remaining true to the desires of his inner self and his love for the Deuce, in contrast to the mandates of authority figures. Toward the end of high school, he developed his own perspective on the tension between jazz and the classics. As a partial resolution, he evolved toward writing symphonies with melodic themes borrowed from the Negro vernacular. Beyond its cachet in elite circles, Ralph liked the symphony because of the depth of mood that it was capable of invoking and the diverse body of listeners attracted to it. Ralph never doubted that there were bigger audiences beyond Second Street. The intelligent appeal of the symphony could shape the tastes of the educated elite of both races, as much as it could compensate for his inability to become a pioneering soloist. Partly by listening to the music of Duke Ellington, Ralph began to realize that, as he said later, "jazz possessed possibilities of a range of expressiveness comparable to that of classical European music."[65] He counted on his fluency with black vernacular forms to provide him with symphonic originality. Instead of imitating the flash of the soloist or the flamboyance of the band leader, Ralph borrowed their tonal and stylistic originality and modeled himself in the statelier image of Breaux and Hebestreit, perhaps with a distant vision of Robert (Nathaniel) Dett or Jim Europe as the apotheosis of his image. As a conductor, one needed to be in vogue and well aware of avant garde techniques and innovations, but one didn't have to invent them. The challenge of the career was to muster dedication enough to master the array of instruments necessary for the orchestra's instrumentation and to develop an aesthetic sense capable of pushing others to higher degrees of achievement.

Roscoe Dunjee may have helped Ralph shape his elite musical goals. The editor rocked the newsboy's cynicism about white justice and supposedly white traditions by ridiculing teachers who encouraged students to embrace racial myopia. On one occasion he condemned the "rut of narrow subjective thinking" that led black contestants at a state oratorical contest to dwell exclusively on the Thirteenth, Fourteenth, and Fifteenth Amendments to the Constitution, as if those passages represented all that was useful to black Americans. Ralph must not content himself with thinking "black on every subject,"[66] the editor warned. Dunjee encouraged him to desire a career loaded with potential, in which he could be unique. And of course, there were but a few select men with the training of William Marion Cook, Duke Ellington's formally schooled aide in composition. Ralph wanted to follow in the footsteps of such composers.

He at least wanted the appearance of classy success. A boy whose only claim to pedigree was through a tenuous link to the Randolphs and Slaughters, Ralph grew less comfortable with being thought some sort of ward of well-known black Oklahoma families. More to the point, he had not recovered from the insult of being thought Randolph's illegitimate son. And he still had rows with his peers. He tried gamely not to let his self-esteem dip when he couldn't attend a party or a jazz show because of his mother's strict rules or his after-school jobs. As he grew up, he became capable of striking a balance—living up to requirements of the black classicists, who were impressed by his manners, without being ostracized by his peers. Even though determined to have a polished and refined career, and cultivating a sophisticated manner, Ralph resisted the tightest strictures of the bourgeois path of success. For him, the boys like Hilliard Bowen, whom his mother hoped he would befriend, were too much like the adults at Douglass. Ralph would be more of a maverick, refusing to reject out of hand the back-alley sharpies like Hallie Richardson and Bill Creekmore or vagabond jazzmen. From what he could determine, the playwright Shaw supported the folk passions of hips swinging to jazz and the catcalls of a grinding blues. Ralph began to think that he could complement his ambition to achieve status with never losing sight of who he had been, or the deepest blues of his experience.

Ellison's own regard for his earthier and less directed experiences grew over time. Even after he had attained the success of his adult life, Ellison was still in contact with two men from Oklahoma City who helped him reconstruct his experiences: Virgil Branam, a classmate, and singer Jimmy Rushing, who had been more than a couple of years ahead of Ralph at Douglass. Though both could well remember Breaux, neither man was interested in or capable of affirming the years of striving for straitlaced success that had characterized much of Ralph's adolescence. Ellison decided to remember the place as the Mississippi River, and himself as Huck Finn. (Ironically, when he had lived there, it was his brother Herbert whom he had called "Huck.")

At school, the classy trumpeter went as far as he could to appease some of the other boys. Douglass included among its students some band members who didn't listen to adults at all, whom Ida deliberately kept her son away from. Ralph was growing in size and felt the need, and had the capacity, to assert himself. He had anguished throughout high school, wanting, he later said, "to be out on the front lawn throwing and kicking a football, showing off in front of the girls."[67] Athleticism and toughness could be displayed on the football field. Increasing his campus popularity, Ralph joined the Douglass Red Machine in the fall of 1929.[68] In a poignant moment, classmate Lance West recalled, he went out for the football team in an effort to prove himself.[69] Years of reading and playing the horn had not exactly prepared Ralph for a consequential position on the Machine, which still enlisted graduates from bygone years and any good-sized locals to help beat rival Booker T. from Tulsa. Ida's motherly advice for him to finish his studies, if he was "going to get anywhere with a woman," fell on leather-helmeted ears.[70] It was a trade-off. Ralph lost points with Breaux over his extracurricular football, which would have excluded him from any number of band activities by the beginning of senior year in the fall of 1930. In a contested battle, he lost out as band conductor to cornetist Lawrence Davis.

He approached the end of his high school years by broadening his interests and exploring new talents. In early March 1931, the impressive Wiley College debate team, headed by poet and English professor William Tolson, debated Oklahoma City University at Avery Chapel. Ralph watched the match with a great deal of pride and interest as the small but intense brown poet led his Texans to victory.[71] Soon after the debate, Douglass started practicing for the annual spring operetta. Breaux produced her spring musical in May, "Sonia: The Girl From Russia," deciding to use Ralph's talents on the stage instead of in the orchestra pit. He played the role of the villain Boris, acquitting himself well and engaging in an intricate dance with the attractive Dorothy Cox. In the operetta, he played second fiddle to Alonzo Williams, who the *Black Dispatch* thought "represents the best in high school artists." Williams was a popular youth known throughout Douglass as a look-alike for moving picture actor Lon Chaney. Nor did Ralph gain anywhere near the celebrity of Red Machine quarterback McHenry Norman, who was cheered by the audience every time he walked on the stage.[72] The operetta ran on the evenings of May 11 and 12 at the Aldridge. Ralph played his role well, but perhaps had expended too much energy on it. By June he had run into serious academic difficulty in Latin and math. He was stunned when told that he would not be able to graduate with his class. Ralph would finish Douglass in 1932, a year after his classmates.[73]

The crowning achievement of the popular Douglass High School Band during Ralph's years would be its July 1931 appearance in the parade in Denver, Colorado, at the Elks' Middle Western Association meeting. They had traveled to Tulsa, Topeka, Muskogee, and even to Wichita, Kansas, but the Colorado trip would introduce them to the America beyond the middle Southwest.[74] None of the boys had ever been that far from home. To pay for the trip, they conducted a three-month-long fund-raising drive, which dominated Ralph's activities, either taking his mind off finals or consuming energy that should have been devoted to them.

To help the boys raise money, the *Black Dispatch* sponsored a parade and used the event to galvanize black community support, rallying Oklahoma City's fifteen thousand Negroes to think of themselves as a unit instead of as individuals, a consistent *Black Dispatch* theme. Dunjee's newspaper insisted that the trip would have immeasurable value not only as a teaching tool to demonstrate the power of that many economically unified black Oklahomans, but also as an important experience for the twenty-five young men: "Giving the boys of Douglass high school band an annual trip is a fine constructive program for the citizenship. It will make their imagination more practical and elastic, add to their fund of knowledge, and spur them on towards a more definite program in life."[75]

The "Denver or Bust" parade was a black gala. Swinging in lockstep down Fourth Street in a rich Douglass band uniform with a plume on his cap, Ralph alternately cradled and blew his horn. He was a proud eighteen-year-old, in a position of great responsibility and respect. The band had earned a platinum reputation with their concert in the Topeka, Kansas, rotunda, and were now allowed to march in front of the horses. Alongside the band were the James Europe Post of the American Legion, the Ladies Drill Team of Victoria Temple, the Boy Scouts, and a decorated car filled with Douglass's prettiest young women, who stopped in front of the crowds to sell subscriptions. The parade netted $87, leaving the band $100 shy of their goal.

While the community as a whole supported the band, the Business League placed unusual store in one Douglass youth, a boy who carried no instrument. Hilliard Bowen attended the conference as the Oklahoma entrant in the Elks' oratory contest. The brilliant young Douglass high school orator would get his travel funds from the collections of the band members.[76] On Thursday, June 25, the band and Hilliard Bowen made off for Denver, due to arrive by June 28 in time for the Monday festivities. In Denver, Ellison watched the adult Elks match their marches step for step. He could still see them vividly almost thirty years later: "[T]hose tall, Watusi-looking moses, wearing capes and fezzes and leaning on a pivot like a stage coach taking a sharp curve, their shoulders touching, their faces skimming across a cymbal lightly."[77] On Tuesday evening, the biggest event took place. Bowen won the oratorical contest and clinched a $1,000 scholarship with his talk, "The Constitution and Slavery."[78] Bowen was a favorite of Dunjee, who influenced his choice of subject matter, and later personally drove him to Philadelphia, where the boy competed in another national oratorical contest. Somehow Bowen always managed to steal Ralph's thunder.

On the two-day trip up to and back from Denver, the boys on the bus stuffed paper in their sleeping classmates' mouths and roamed into farmhouses whenever the bus stopped. A cheering event took place at the Denver YMCA, where the boys were given their first opportunity to use an indoor swimming pool.[79] In Oklahoma City the only swimming hole was a ditch near the railroad tracks. The bus passed through Kansas and Colorado, and while the boys strained to see the snow on top of Pike's Peak, Ralph pondered his future. He had taken graduation pictures with his class but he had not received a degree. Ralph nursed a dream but had little to go on in the way of obtaining it, particularly regarding college prospects. Oberlin was the most renowned school for training musicians that admitted blacks, but Ralph had no grades or scholarship. Admission to Hampton or Fisk was impossible for the same reason. Taking some counsel from Breaux, a consoling woman even to football-playing trumpeters, he set his sights fifty miles away, on the Colored Normal and Agricultural Institute at Langston. But first Ralph had another semester at Douglass to consider.

He hoped to enjoy the rest of the summer, but he needed work, like most of the other young men in the city. His days at Randolph's, where his pay was on an uncomfortable sliding scale—sometimes something, sometimes nothing at all—left him with little choice but to try to get another job. Near the beginning of the summer, he ran into a classmate who told him about a job on Broadway, if he could hustle over there. By the time Ralph made it up to Greenlease-Moore Used Cars on 1016 Broadway, between Ninth and Tenth, he was sweating freely. The white lot manager invited him to sit down on a crate and rest, while the sun hovered overhead, pushing the mercury past

100 degrees. Thankful for the rest, Ralph responded freely to questions about his family. The friendly interview continued until he felt sure that the salesman was about to make a job offer. Seconds later, he felt a strong surge of electricity in his tail. He shot upward, electric current spurring him off the crate, and landed in the dust, the laughter of the salesman ringing in his ears.[80] Holding himself as he walked away, Ralph realized that the entire interview had been a set-up. He knew of other cruel games. In Kansas, whites would hide an occasional gold piece and multiple brass coins in a barrel of flour, then force colored boys, arms tied behind their backs, to fish through the barrels with their open mouths to secure the booty.[81] Ralph was developing an almost palpable rancor toward his hometown and region.

There was plenty of anguish to go around in Oklahoma City. Ralph and his peers were devastated by the early June death of nineteen-year-old John Walton. Walton had lived with T. J. and Hattie Randolph as an adopted boy until leaving for Wichita in 1928. A self-taught mechanical genius, in a fit of bravado and pride, Walton had cut away several of his own fingers, which had been severely burned while he was working on the electrical system of a Model-T. The boy died of peritonitis.[82]

Band activities provided some respite, though little material reward. On July 24 at 8 P.M., the band gave an appreciation concert at Slaughter's Hall. Ralph probably enjoyed reaching the bandstand in the new brick Slaughter building more than the neo-Victorian social life of the black middle class. His girlfriend Vivian Stevenson had helped found the Novem Amicus club, a group dedicated to improving social etiquette. Spearheaded by Clytia McMurray, the club regularly honored Maxine Randolph, T. J.'s daughter, who attended prestigious Fisk University.[83] On Thursday, July 16, the girls invited their beaux over to the Randolphs' home on Twenty-third Street for "Guest Day." Affluent blacks had steadily pulled away from the confines of Second Street, as neighborhood disputes there more frequently ended in cuttings and shootings. Included at the formal party were the most popular young men on their way to college: Hilliard Bowen, Floyd Alexander, and Virgil Chandler.[84] Ralph was included in the elite group, but he did not share their sunny prospects.

Almost graduating from high school brought Ralph new independence, which he found quite timely. That year, Ralph saw Duke Ellington splash into town over at Slaughter's Hall. The Ellington orchestra was a grand and complex affair. Circulars and billboards up and down Second Street had announced the New Yorkers' arrival for weeks. The appearance of the sophisticated band members in elegant uniforms with "golden horns" and "flights of controlled and disciplined fantasy" impressed and enraptured concertgoers. Ralph copied the style of Ellington, America's most popular and accessible black entertainer. Ralph had tuned his crystal set to CBS to hear the Duke and his orchestra broadcasting live from the Cotton Club beginning in 1927, listening to such important works as "East St. Louis Toodle-oo" and "Black and Tan Fantasy." The Duke's "East St. Louis Toodle-oo" was the veritable black anthem of optimism during the Depression, while deeper, more probing pieces like "Black and Tan Fantasy" plumbed the somber side of life, reminding everyone of the necessity of humor. Ellington and his orchestra had been featured in the 1930 Amos and Andy movie *Check and Double Check,* which was run at the Aldridge. The Duke had enviable style and elegance and a budding international reputation. In Ellington, Ralph found a formidable example of flair and mastery in the not always encouraging world of black Americans. The worldliness, elegance, and sardonic imagination expertly used to outmaneuver racial limitations became a defining attribute of Ralph's personality. The Ellingtonian presence wasn't entirely about music; it also offered a means to navigate social class and Negro racial space. Duke the "culture hero" influenced "even those who had no immediate concern with the art of jazz."[85] By this time, Ida had begun to allow her eighteen-year-old son more freedom. She even confided to him that she hoped that someday after the completion of his musical studies, he, too, would have a band like Ellington's.

During the fall cotton picking season, a veritable wing of the Douglass Junior and Senior High School would depart for Beckham County, Oklahoma, in search of jobs to earn money for the winter. But that year, Ralph didn't have to worry about rushing off to pick cotton, an experience that many poor black parents like Ida specifically wanted their children to have no contact with. He was working full-time at Lewinsohn's Clothing Store on Main Street. Ralph was excited that now he'd be able to have a bit of a wardrobe, and he liked the store owner, Milt Lewinsohn, to the point of imitation. Recovering from a hip injury on the gridiron, Ralph modeled his walk after Milt's. But he hadn't been on the job long before the manager sent him home one day near tears. One of the store's managers demanded that he call a white female elevator operator "miss" and he complied.[86] She was Ralph's age, a peer whom he'd become friends with. Now he knew how little such things mattered. Returning home, he told Saretta Slaughter as much as he could without breaking down and telling her he had felt crushed. Not only did he feel like a peon, but he couldn't even valiantly quit the job. All the pleasantries at work, the genial environment, had hid the existence of underlying prejudice.

In May 1932, Ralph received his Douglass diploma in all of his glory at Tabernacle Baptist Church, the forum of Reverend P. P. Barbee. After gaining the coveted sheepskin, he groomed himself for membership in the music band at Langston, Oklahoma's state school for Negroes. Ralph took as much work as he could to earn the money that he knew he'd need to finance his education. He got a job waiting tables at a country club in Nichols Hill, where the boys had to travel in groups to fend off the dogs set upon them by whites when they walked from the streetcar line.[87]

Ralph had learned about Langston when it was headed by Zachary T. Hubert, a former president of the Oklahoma Association of Negro Teachers. Under Hubert's administration, students gained new rights and privileges, changes that earned the disapproval of the state board of regents.[88] Ralph had even gotten to know Zack Jr. and Wilson, President Hubert's sons, probably when Breaux visited the school with her Douglass choir and musical groups in 1929, during President Hubert's years.[89] But by 1932, Democrat I. W. Young had regained control of the school. He'd been appointed by Jack Walton from 1923 to 1927, and after "Alfalfa" Bill Murray took the Oklahoma governorship in 1931, Young resumed leadership of the school. At some point before the fall of 1932, Ralph took a bus out to Langston University to have a talk with Pope Benjamin, the director of the school's forty-four-member band. He traveled for an hour and lost a day's worth of work, but band director Benjamin postponed the appointment indefinitely, then feigned ignorance of the meeting entirely. Ralph had followed an errant lead. He then learned that Breaux had been wrong about his scholarship. He had no position in the Langston band.[90]

4

Down South

1932–1933

OKLAHOMA WINTERS are not generally harsh in terms of quantities of ice and snow. But for a family like the Ellisons, without adequate stove wood or shoe leather, every winter's chill brought with it the necessity of renewed struggle for survival. With the onset of foul weather, Ralph worked hard at being amicable to customers while operating the elevator at Lewinsohn's. He beamed at the white patrons in accord with the demands of jim crow courtesy, but became further determined to make it out of Oklahoma City after the lost opportunity at the Colored Agricultural and Normal School at Langston. But he had little time for brooding, at least not if he wanted to blossom into a better musician. He devoted his free hours to the "cutting" contests with the jazz immortals of Second Street.

But at the end of 1932, Ralph's college prospects brightened considerably. A new possibility entered the field: Tuskegee Normal School and Industrial Institute. Two days after Christmas, while listening to the radio, Ralph heard the Tuskegee Institute choir open Radio City Music Hall in New York.[1] Duke Ellington's Cotton Club show wasn't the only program featuring black artists coming over the airwaves and into the Ellison-Bell house at 710 East Second Street. Ralph was delighted by the powerful range and brilliant execution of the choir. He admired, if he did not slightly envy, the black college students who were making their debut in America's only megalopolis on such a prestigious occasion. New York's might had intrigued Ralph since his preteen years, when he read O. O. McIntyre's syndicated columns in the *Daily*

Oklahoman. Now he became aware of students just like him who had made it to the big time, in spite of the obstacles.

Beyond the success of the students, the vision and accomplishment of the young black conductor who had brought off the entire affair appealed directly to Ralph. In spectacular fashion, William Levi Dawson, Tuskegee's virtuoso conductor, had woven American Negroes into the gala national affair. Within the next few weeks, the Tuskegee One Hundred went on to play sold-out shows at Radio City, Carnegie Hall, and Philadelphia's Symphony Hall.

Ralph knew how to measure competition, and he saw that Tuskegee had something to offer. He had dreamed wistfully of applying to Juilliard to continue his studies in music composition and the trumpet, but he knew that the school was beyond his reach.[2] Instead of honing finishing-school manners, Ralph had spent several years woodshedding in Oklahoma City's Deep Deuce; he hoped that fate would not select him to spend a lifetime picking splinters out of his hair. After hearing Tuskegee's standout performance at Radio City, Ralph could imagine himself as an undergraduate at the brand new and nationally recognized music school in Alabama. Zelia Breaux and Ralph plotted a strategy to get him to Tuskegee, where she had contacts with the music school.[3] Following a few wintertime conferences with his former music instructor, Ralph wrote to Tuskegee requesting a catalog.

Tuskegee was a bright jewel in the red clay hills of Macon County, Alabama. By the 1930s, it was rapidly expanding beyond its foundation as a secondary school and vocational and technical institute. Founded in 1881 under the leadership of a young Booker Taliaferro Washington, the Normal School and Industrial Institute had blossomed from a one-room schoolhouse for local freedmen into a world-renowned black magnet school of a thousand and a half students. Tuskegee of the 1930s boasted a physical plant of multistoried, redbrick, white-columned academic buildings and dormitories nestled together on a 2,500-acre campus. The school flourished because of Washington's superb tact when dealing with wealthy white industrialists and conservative Southern politicians. During the repressive 1890s, Tuskegee had grown with the help of the Alabama state legislature. Of course, Washington's success came with a considerable caveat. The famous black leader had endeared himself to America by his 1895 speech at the Cotton States' Exposition in Atlanta, where he had countenanced the separation of the races and scoffed at black Americans' pursuit of social equality.

Robert Russa Moton took over the school in 1915 after the death of Washington, affectionately called "the Founder" in Macon County. Moton ably steered the school into the modern age, though he lacked the unique charisma and determination of his predecessor. The Great War, increasing mechanization, and shifts in the Southern economy demanded immediate alterations to the school's curriculum, which previously had been geared toward providing a secondary education. In Moton's era, enough black students had benefited from public schools and laws restricting child labor to produce a tier of students capable of handling college material. In 1925, the trustees added a College Department to the normal (secondary) school, and created a school of agriculture, a school of education, and a school of home economics. By 1929, Tuskegee was graduating students with bachelor's degrees and within ten years, most of Tuskegee's pupils had gravitated toward these newly constructed divisions.

Despite the changes of the late 1920s and early 1930s, Tuskegee still carried the scar of intellectual backwardness, a souvenir of Washington's mocking public tone toward the liberal arts. The school never adequately bridged the traditional fissure between its departments of industry and trade and the academic department, even though the publicly conservative Washington had advanced the inevitable shifts toward scholastic rigor in Tuskegee's classrooms. After a 1905 curriculum revision, he abandoned courses in the Bible and music to allow instructors more time to train the students properly. Washington's strategy had been "correlating," meshing proficiency in academic subjects with the practical demands of modern industry. The internationally known president had encouraged his teachers to ignore abstract applications of mathematics and English and instead to "practice mathematics in the carpentry shop and write essays on plowing a field in English."[4] Still, the tension remained. Would Tuskegee remain an industrial school or become a first-class academic institution?

Washington's tactic of publicly ignoring white brutality did not enhance the rigor of the classroom but rather symbolized the school's priorities: appearance over substance. During the years of Tuskegee's propitious growth, the political quietude that blanketed the campus could be deafening. Langston Hughes visited Moton's Tuskegee in 1932 and was warmly received, but the poet was appalled to find few conversations, let alone activism, on behalf of the Scottsboro Boys, charged with raping two white women and on trial for their lives so near to the campus. In the magnificent halls built by the students' own hands, Hughes heard "no discussion whatsoever" regarding the fate of the nine black youths whose chief accuser had recanted her own testimony.[5] Tuskegee's intellectuals and politically inclined students suffered from the reluctance to debate race and politics in the United States. This was the crippling ambiguity of jim crow colleges. On the one hand, the school offered unparalleled resources and outlets that made the college a completely unique experience relative to the meager educational opportunities available elsewhere to America's blacks through the middle of the twentieth century. On the other hand, in terms of it being an intellectual haven for the promotion and protection of black rights, the school had barely crept into the modern era.

Even the training promoted by the institution was not without its blemishes. By the mid-1930s, the full-fledged impact of the Depression called the entire vocational focus of the school into question, exposing the fragile

nineteenth-century logic upon which the argument for vocational and agricultural education was based.[6] Tuskegee's narrow vision of black advancement
relied upon the tactic of public acquiescence to the agendas of Northern industrialists and Southern politicians. The strategy had left the school unequipped
to deal with the lightning-fast changes of the modern academic world.

However, the school's limited academic curriculum did not result entirely
from wrong-headed black administrators; the climate in the South was hostile
toward black culture in general and black education in particular. In 1930,
there was no public senior high school in Montgomery, Alabama, for blacks.
The economic disaster of the 1930s only made wider the already significant
disparities between black and white educational opportunities. Tuskegee's
manual training programs and academic departments, which concentrated on
secondary school preparation, at least helped to fill an educational void.

Ralph had heard of Tuskegee and its world-famous founder when he was
still in short pants (the Oklahoma City *Black Dispatch* regularly reported the
activities of the famous school). Now that the school's curriculum was becoming more academic, it devoted specialized treatment to music. Including music
in the curriculum at black schools was customary, as it had been at Douglass
in Oklahoma City, and at its founding Tuskegee had required vocal instruction for its students.[7] Washington recognized the importance of music in his
program of acculturating poor rural students to middle-class habits and mores,
and after the stunning financial success of the Fisk Jubilee Singers, who
toured internationally, he was well aware of the potential profit to be made
from black students singing Negro spirituals to white audiences.[8] Moton had
revived and enhanced the Founder's vision and increased the school's visibility to philanthropic contributors in the 1920s by funding a full-blown school
of music.

Ralph was interested in Tuskegee primarily because of Breaux, who had
sent several star pupils down to William Dawson, a Tuskegee alumnus and
former trombonist for the Chicago Symphony Orchestra. Dawson had come
on board in 1932 after Tuskegee President Moton granted him carte blanche.
As evidence of the sweep of his power, Dawson had what no other Tuskegee
department head could have dreamed of—the power to hire faculty and build
his school from scratch. His Music School boasted three departments and
about twenty faculty. Dawson's entry description in the school catalog stressed
the Music School's ambitious new program offering "the theory of music and
correct discipline in the technique of vocal and instrumental music."[9] Another
important area of the chairman's power was the treasury. He could offer students scholarships and sometimes post their fees, a feature without which
Ralph would have been unable to attend school.[10] Booker T. Washington
had loved the spirituals; after sixteen years of leadership and well on his way
toward retirement, Moton had carried the Founder's legacy to the next level,

introducing a professional, first-rate music school, the likes of which the deep South had never seen.

At last something looked promising. Ralph leafed excitedly through the catalog, dreaming of a career for himself as a symphonic composer. He aimed for that profession, confident that he could at least obtain a career as a public school music teacher. By setting his ambition high, he made the practical destination of high school music teacher an easily realizable secondary goal. Though his mother had encouraged his pursuit of distinction and elegance, Ida Ellison-Bell had also instilled in her son a bedrock layer of practicality. And Ralph dearly wanted to leave Oklahoma City. He felt keenly his own limitations as the store managers at Lewinsohn's rudely reminded him to remember his "place." For his sense of himself to grow, he had to escape the stunting prejudice and parochialism of Oklahoma City. He was restless, too. He had graduated school at nineteen, then spent a year working while the Hilliard Bowens, Malcolm Whitbys, and Robert Alexanders vigorously pursued their distinguished undergraduate careers. Instead of studying with impressive musicians and thinkers, Ralph earned side money by playing background music at black Oklahoma's upper-class social parties and teas. Though Ralph knew well and admired the people who paid him to quietly play the classics on their patios, the situation did not elate him. He wanted to be at least their social equal, not the hired help.

Ralph realized that if he could graduate from the Tuskegee conservatory, he would have both a prestigious bachelor of science degree in music and exposure to Dawson, who knew firsthand the international world of conducting and composing. Also, Tuskegee's black music faculty were simply some of the best trained anywhere; many had studied in Europe with renowned classical musicians. He was aiming not only to gain sophisticated training, but to earn his college degree from a school that far outshone Langston. Ralph wanted to erase his humbling experiences in Oklahoma by flourishing at Tuskegee.

Even though he knew about the program, by the spring of 1933 Ralph still hadn't made the decision to matriculate, likely because of financial complications as the full impact of the Depression choked the country. But the ambition to attend the prestigious college won out over indigence, and on June 15, he mailed in the application, completed in his own handwriting. The most important admission criterion on the application was "CHARACTER— Good habits, strength of character, trustworthiness, and earnestness of purpose," which was "required of all students."[11] For black education in the South in the 1930s, an era of uneven primary and secondary school preparation, an estimate of the student's inner fiber played the pivotal role in admission. Moton's Tuskegee was still about the business of molding black gentlemen and gentlewomen, confident in the black race's future in the agrarian

South. Ralph's inconsistent performance in the Douglass classrooms would not stand in his way.

Zelia Breaux wrote his lone recommendation. She vouchsafed his "fine" character, noting that Ralph was "industrious" and a "very splendid scholar."[12] Though a brief two sentences, Breaux's estimation counted a great deal. She had a formidable reputation in the Southwest and had known the Tuskegee conductor Dawson from his days as a young music teacher in nearby Kansas City. Breaux guided her star music pupils to Alabama; the year before she had sent two of her best musicians to study at Tuskegee.

Ralph received the pleasing news of his acceptance within a short time after submitting the application. His grades and the brief recommendation from Breaux had been promising enough to win him a Tuskegee Music School scholarship. The scholarship was indispensable; the Music School charged one hundred dollars more in tuition and fees per year than the rest of the college.[13] And Ralph wanted to go to Tuskegee wearing the latest collegiate fashions. A sleek-looking wardrobe would mildly compensate for his delayed matriculation to college. At the end of April, he had paid $5 cash money for a May Brothers felt hat.[14] The emphasis on sartorial chic also stemmed from his childhood desire to live in a world of Sunday dress-up clothes. He had created his own unique self-image through the clothes that he wore, an image distinct from the unimpressive rented rooms and hard-scrabble shotgun houses he had grown up in.

But Ralph had more pressing concerns than his attire. After twelve years as a musician, it had long been time for a new horn; his pawnshop cornet from the early 1920s was inadequate for his burgeoning musical career. Any reputable music school expected its students to bring their own instruments, and certainly Ralph knew that a serious commitment to his craft demanded the investment in a professional horn. On April 22, 1932, he settled upon a sparkling Conn Cornet from the Jenkins Music Company at 225 West Main Street. He agreed to pay $157.50 for the horn, in installments of about $2 per week. In the spring of 1933, he calculated that with the help of Tuskegee's scholarship and a few more months of work, by fall he could scrape together enough money to get down to school and finish paying for his cornet.[15]

Near late June, a bombshell burst. The terms of his scholarship required an early summer matriculation, well before fall instruction began. The Music School faculty demanded an audition from the pupil admitted scant weeks before the beginning of the fall term. Led by Dawson, band director Frank Drye, and orchestra conductor Andrew Rosemond, the Music School ordered Ralph to appear in early July at Tuskegee.[16] The hastily made request indicated the youth of the program. In 1933, Tuskegee had not yet graduated a student with a music degree. They needed to admit and to cultivate talented musicians, but they also needed an idea of how well the students could perform in the program. Though the classroom atmosphere was formal and exacting, the Music School operated as something of a family, with almost a one-to-one ratio between majors and faculty. Classes were small and the environment was intimate; generally there were nine or ten music majors.

Ralph had thought that he would have the entire summer to stock up resources for a mid-September trip, and he still owed about $12 on his instrument and the beginnings of his collegiate wardrobe. He had only $32 for train fare and for his most considerable expense, room and board, once he got to Tuskegee.[17] Though conceivably he would have earned only another $16 or so during a summer of delivering passengers in Lewinsohn's elevator, the unforeseen Tuskegee command created a hardship.

It may have been Zelia Breaux who motored over to the Ellison-Bell house (they didn't have a telephone) on Second Street with the news of the early summer audition at Tuskegee. Ralph walked to T. J. Randolph's spacious home and asked for help from the man who had been a surrogate father. Wasn't someone whom the dentist knew on his way to Alabama from Oklahoma City? The Randolphs thought that Ralph might be able to ride down to Tuskegee with another man. But within a day or two, the opportunity fell through; the traveler expected his passenger to handle the wheel part of the time and take care of minor repairs. Ralph had not learned to drive.[18] The fabulous opportunity for a college degree seemed in jeopardy.

He considered his options: delay school another year, with his prospects for a college degree slipping further and further away; sell back the nearly paid-for horn in order to book a passage in a jim crow railroad car; or hobo his way down to Tuskegee as best he could. The desire to attend school in the fall and finger the horn won out. Of the books Ralph had disciplined himself to read while out of school, he had recently reread Twain's *Adventures of Huckleberry Finn* with interest, but from a certain distance. Now he found himself preparing to take a ride on a mechanical raft down his own Mississippi, the Louisville and Nashville railroad line. Something other than peril hung in the air about the trip. Ralph was staking out his own freedom, moving outside his mother's authority and that of the man she had married. There was even a certain dignity to hoboing; the ravages of the Depression had reduced many Americans to the risky and illegal form of free travel. After consulting with the Randolphs, Ralph determined to hop aboard freight trains, and hobo in the grand tradition of Jack London and Carl Sandburg.

While the Randolphs couldn't help him get to college, J. D. Randolph had a scrappy in-law named Charlie, a black man light enough to pass for white, who promised to teach Ralph the hobo's craft and to get him to Alabama in one piece. Charlie mesmerized the Randolph and Slaughter children with his stories of riding trains all over the country. Justifiably fearing the hazardous journey, mother Ida initially rejected the idea. As the somber reports of the Scottsboro Boys indicated, hoboing through Alabama had proven a dangerously wrongheaded decision for black men. Ida Bell preferred a living, breathing, frustrated son, over an ambitious and courageous dead one. At twenty, Ralph faced one of his first major tests of adulthood: pursuing a well-reasoned goal in the face of opposition. Actually, he was in the same position that Ida had been in when she had blazed out to the uncharted Oklahoma Territory a quarter of a century prior. Once the idea had taken root, Ralph never let up, and he badgered his mother for a few days. It required a "great deal of pressure," he recalled, to move the religious woman, who only very reluctantly gave in as she realized that her boy, Lewis's son, would obtain manhood on his own terms.[19] Eventually she threw up her hands in her characteristic gesture of letting go, and entrusted her son to the Lord. She would pray for his deliverance. Ida told Ralph to write her when he arrived and that she would finish the payments he owed, then send his instrument and clothes.

Charlie didn't know if Ralph was up to the task, so he staged a small trial to test the youth's dedication. He told Ralph to wait for him at the water tower on the train tracks, then promptly ignored the rendezvous. Determined to go to college, the anxious trumpeter found Charlie in a house serving home brew off Second Street and angrily reproached the older man. A day later, the two met and took off. To pronounce his new identity as a college-bound scholarship student, Ralph wore a beret—but he protected his frontier-bred independence (and his life) with a switchblade in his pocket.

Despite his years spent living within sight of the Rock Island roundhouse and crossing the numerous rail tracks to get to Douglass High, jumping trains was foreign to him. The tandem squirreled their way onto a northbound Rock Island train and pushed on to Wichita, the first large stop before coming to East St. Louis, where they would switch lines.[20] Cursing freely, Charlie told Ralph how to clamber on board a swiftly moving freight train, a technique called "flipping." Even more important, he taught him how to read the manifest nailed to the side of the train to determine its destination. Charlie also taught Ralph what to be afraid of and how to defend himself. Mainly they had to stay alert for "bulls," or railroad detectives, prowling on the trains and lurking about the yards. Some of these men were keen to kill and maim hoboes, a term that, considering their low status, ironically seems to have derived from the Latin *homo bonum,* or "good man."[21] Charlie gave him an invaluable lesson in self-defense—how to ward off thieves, sexual predators, and other bums wanting to make an example of a lone black boy. Race prejudice could be thick and violent, even among the down-and-out. The two men spent a good portion of time clinging to boards between and underneath swift-moving freight cars to avoid the detection of vigilant bulls. When they traveled on top of the freights, the men endured engine sparks, cinders, and thick smoke—the ambrosia of the huge four-eight-four steam locomotive. Inside the rough-hewn boxcars, Ralph learned to squat flat-footed and rest on his palms, his rear end off the car's floor, to absorb sudden shocks. He was counseled never to sit with his legs dangling off the side of a boxcar, whose door might come loose and lop off a leg. When the highballing trains jumped and jerked on the track like a roller-coaster ride, Charlie consoled Ralph in the rough words of the frontier: "She's running like a bitch with the itch." The two developed the familiarity of comrades, and in the flush of excitement, Ralph learned to laugh off the trip's hardships.

The most important piece of advice and experience that Charlie brought to the table was the route. The men would travel north to St. Louis, then east over to Evansville, Illinois, to pick up the L&N line through Kentucky, and finally make their way south, through Tennessee, down to Alabama.[22] Arkansas, immediately east and the speediest path, was to be avoided at all costs. Charlie candidly told Ralph that if he got caught in Arkansas hopping a freight, "they're liable to shoot you or throw you on the chain-gang."[23] Ralph swallowed another lesson in Southern realism.

Black skin meant other restrictions. Besides the obvious difficulties associated with flipping trains—hours on end in cramped quarters with no possibility for food, fresh water, or sanitation—Charlie could pass for white and avail himself at least of some public amenities entirely unavailable to Ralph. Part of Ralph's education included a straightforward lesson in transacting business for his necessities through the informal networks that existed in poor black communities throughout the country and in the "jungles," hobo camps located on the railroad line on the outskirts of larger towns. They met another obstacle in East St. Louis, where Ralph had to walk past a bridge guard in order to make a connection.[24] Railroad detectives and armed guards patrolled the tracks to turn away blacks on their way to the World's Fair in Chicago. For Charlie, crossing the bridge was no problem, but the officer challenged Ralph. Where did he think he was going? Ralph sidestepped the officer with the truth—he was a college student on his way to Alabama to take up his scholarship. He invited the guard to share in his success and was allowed to reach the other side of the bridge.

The train ride in the summer of 1933, a peak Depression year, was an education in itself. Ralph saw people of position and stature using the rough form of illegal travel. He seems to have had at least one pleasant experience with an older white couple who shared food with him, a welcome improvement over the mulligan stew of bologna and cornmeal served in the hobo jungles. But even this contact emphasized the tightrope Ralph walked. Raised to respect authority and his elders, he also felt compelled to stand tall for his personal dignity and his race, wherever the two were not indistinguishable. Four brief years after his train ride to school, Ralph composed a fictional account of the experience, peeling free the layers of tension felt by an articulate black hobo who wants friendship, but wants more dearly to preserve his own integrity. Even in a conversation with an elder, the male protagonist, who is Ralph's age and has the same education, refused to call the white man "sir": "I was having a hard time trying not to hate. . . . Saying 'sir' was too much a part of knowing your place."[25] Ralph didn't want to believe that all whites were contemptuous and scornful of him, but he refused to even hint at the fawning, timid behavior attributed to blacks and popularized in the American cinema of the 1930s by Stepin Fetchit.

Ralph's encounters on the trains also helped to make tangible his own inchoate ideas about human brotherhood and the socialist politics that had been a part of his earliest upbringing. The lines of racial caste were not sacrosanct and inviolable in the open community of the poor and déclassé who rode the rails. The humble freight cars introduced Ralph to a more egalitarian world which, although dangerous, offered personal relationships based upon sincerity and genuineness of character. Not only had he left his mother's home for full independence, but his first solo encounter with the adult world was one of little pretension and illusion. The same qualities of spontaneity, equality, and struggle that made hoboing attractive would become essential components of his personality.

After the two men reached St. Louis, Ralph quickly learned that Charlie drank to excess. Though not physically intimidating (Charlie was the size of a jockey), the hobo-teacher hit up the five-foot-ten, 153-pound twenty-year-old for some of his limited funds to buy liquor. Once they arrived in East St. Louis, Charlie somehow managed to find a bootlegger who sold him two quarts of home-distilled alcohol. He drank the concoction throughout the sweltering July day until he fell off their southbound train somewhere in Missouri or Illinois, afflicted by sunstroke. Ralph entered a white-only store, requested water for the prone "white" man in the gutter, revived Charlie, and then gave him $2.50 to go see a doctor. After getting a few somber words of encouragement and advice from the professional tramp, the young man continued his journey alone.

While Ralph was speeding down the rails into Alabama, smelling the pine trees and hearing the mockingbirds, nine black youths were feeling the fist of Southern malice. For over two years, Ralph had been reading newspaper articles about the trial and retrial of the black hoboes accused of raping two white women on an Alabama train, not far from the town of Scottsboro. In November 1932, citing a violation of the Fourteenth Amendment, the U.S. Supreme Court had overthrown their convictions, ruling that the state's all-white juries indicated evidence of bias.[26] Alabama first retried Haywood Patterson in the spring of 1933, a young man so numbed by the process that he sat listlessly while hearing his second guilty verdict and sentence to the electric chair being pronounced. Ralph, with his intelligence and well-formed skepticism of white America's justice, realized the impossibility of any of the boys receiving a fair trial in the South. In the Alabama kangaroo court, the guilty verdict and the death penalty were a mere formality. Even the NAACP dragged their feet before getting involved in the boys' defense. After a prosecuting attorney's mention of the black boys receiving support from "Jew money from New York," Decatur jurors had found Patterson guilty on scant evidence in the obscenely short period of five minutes.[27] Xenophobic prejudice and an almost comic attitude toward Negro mortality characterized the region. (In Tuscaloosa in June, local authorities preferred to send three blacks accused of rape and murder to an impromptu firing squad than to risk the publicity of trials.) While his pending music examination should have consumed his attention, Ralph could not escape a sense of apprehension fueled by the "macabre circus" in Decatur that took the place of an impartial trial.[28]

And even if he could mentally ignore the infamous Alabama case, he had the memory of the chilling and brutal murder of Henry Argo in 1930 by a white mob in Chicasha, Oklahoma,[29] to needle him with anxiety as he jumped onto boxcars. Though the *Black Dispatch* had valiantly crusaded against white barbarism, and had secured at least an indictment of several of Argo's murderers, subpoenas and printed words were of little comfort in the face of a pistol and a mob. Perhaps one distinction comforted him. While Ralph despaired for the Scottsboro Boys, he also likely considered the difference between himself, a successful scholarship student, and the country-tough, poor, uneducated black youths pulled off the train. Ralph was taking the freight ride because after two restless years at home following high school, he had a once-in-a-lifetime opportunity to become a musician. Though he didn't quite have the luxury of blissful ignorance, Ralph understood himself as special, and trusted that his exceptionalism would differentiate him from the pack.

As the L&N tucked into Decatur, Alabama, more than two hundred miles north of Tuskegee, two detectives brandishing nickel-plated .45s rousted all illegal passengers from the trains. Milling in a large gang, Ralph was flooded by straight-out fear. Indiscriminate white fury might this time select him as its black scapegoat. Though he never completely revealed the episode in any of his writings, from the scant historical facts available, it seems that Ralph became that scapegoat, the black victim treated with cruelty. When he wrote his first short story in 1937, he pointedly explored the brutality of the railroad detectives, who used blackjacks and gun butts on Negro hoboes like they were "cracking black walnuts with a hammer."[30] In an essay published in 1976, he claimed only that when a group of whites made a run for it, he took advantage of the confusion and joined the stampede. He ran across the terrain broken-field style, "closer to the ground than I had ever managed to do as a high school football running back." He tuned his ears for explosions, tensing his skin for the burning sledgehammer blow of a bullet. Escaping the detectives, who did not discharge their pistols, he hid underneath a shed near the railroad loading dock and remained in hiding until dawn. After a harrowing night of vigilance in the hole, Ralph caught, he admitted later in an interview, "the first thing that was smoking and headed south."[31] He would reexperience the train-yard nightmare in his dreams over and over for the next ten years.[32]

However, a great deal more had happened to him than a dash away from railroad detectives. When Ellison arrived at Commandant Colonel B. O. Davis's office in the Tuskegee Institute Administration Building to have his entrance photograph taken, he was promptly sent to the school physician. Tuskegee officials were surprised he could walk. Ellison had arrived at the campus with two head wounds, as fresh as they were severe. The Institute entrance picture shows him with the left side of his forehead heavily bandaged, and an open gash alongside his right eye, just below the temple.[33] He was weary, but in spite of his condition, he had survived, and endured his first test of independent adulthood. Now he occupied the newly won psychological terrain of self-determination. Ellison classed his run-in with railroad authorities as unremarkable, indicating not only the sharpness of his experience in Oklahoma City but also his refusal to let anything stand in the way of his education at Tuskegee. It seems likely, for example, that he never wanted his mother, or Breaux for that matter, to know of his encounter with the railroad detectives. He recognized that admitting to the chaos of the world might frighten her and stimulate her overprotection. He didn't want the freedoms and privileges that he needed to thrive to be limited. Instead, Ellison would go on to deny the personal impact of chaos, brutality, and hardship. He repressed the incredibly violent train-yard episode, refusing to attribute value to accidents of fate.

The wounds that he gained on his journey to Tuskegee, and his repression of its violent memory, signaled a growing separation between Ellison's public and private personalities. He nurtured a tough, gnarled side of himself for survival, but kept the conditions and purposes of this private self under the surface in public. Ellison never wanted to appear a thug, though the aggression and selfishness of the bully were the underside that enabled him to ignore pain and make inconsequential adversaries and adversarial situations. The balancing act did not fool everybody. William Dawson viewed the bandaged trumpeter with suspicion. The Music School chief had made his peace with the South, voluntarily moving back to Alabama at the height of a stellar professional career in Chicago; Ellison's scars may have seemed evidence of an unhealthy amount of pluck. When his new campus friends pushed too far into Ellison's inner world, asking questions about his fresh scar, he closed up and looked past them. In the words of classmate Mike Rabb, Ellison was moody.[34]

The commandant assigned Ellison a room in Thrasher Hall, the "little boys room," the domain of dormitory monitor Captain Walter J. Love. After finding his room, Ralph learned the house regulations: no fighting in the dining hall; and to prevent fire, ironing clothes was prohibited. Tuskegee men were expelled for infractions of the rules, though he quickly learned that instead of trotting outside to the bathhouse, most of Thrasher's boys used the third-floor window as an open-air urinal.[35] Love told his new charge where to purchase his school uniform, the blue serge regulation suit, cap, and belt, white duck trousers, black four-in-hand tie, and black shoes. The well-kept campus, with its rolling, manicured lawns, shrubs, and paved roads impressed Ellison. A spirit of improvement and hard work kept the campus looking good.

Tuition at Tuskegee could be had for a song. Between 1933 and 1936, it stayed at $51 per year.[36] An additional $9 went for students' athletic and "Lyceum" fees. The other cost for the Tuskegee education for nine months was a significant $20 per month for room and board, $180 per academic year. The total went well beyond the range of a poor boy like Ellison, living off $100 a year. On his application, Ellison had asked to be classified not as a "day," "night," or "special" student, but his own concoction, a "work" student.[37] Without a campus job, he had no prospects for making ends meet; and as a night student, he'd have no way to attend the music classes. But as a Music School scholarship student and a member of the elite Conservatory Division, Ellison could find a way where there had been no way.

Despite his cuts and bruises, his first moments of arrival had been exultant. The young bibliophile was undoubtedly struck by the latest addition to the campus, just north of the train depot, the Hollis Burke Frissell Library. Completed in 1932, the three-story library evoked the Renaissance style and housed more volumes in one place than anywhere Ellison had previously had unlimited access to. Frissell's magnitude dwarfed the Slaughter Building and Oklahoma City's new Dunbar Library on Fourth Street. Slightly behind the library lay another new building of significance for the young musician, Logan Hall, the modern facility used to accommodate the huge crowds that came to Tuskegee on Founder's Day and at Commencement.

After the intimidating audition before a committee of Music School faculty, the summer months of July and August were relaxing and event-filled. Ellison immediately became acquainted with the musicians on campus, and gravitated toward those who were comfortable with jazz. He started playing trumpet in a band under Philmore "Shorty" Hall. At four feet tall, Shorty, in Ellison's words, blew "the hell off of a big-bore symphonic trumpet." Hall had studied under the irrepressible Captain Drye at Tuskegee, and he would have appealed especially to an ambitious youngster like Ellison. Shorty graduated Tuskegee in 1929 and had been a campus phenomenon: ROTC captain, student band conductor, president of the Triple Octans Glee Club, and conductor of his own band, Hall's Orchestra. After finishing at Tuskegee,

Hall went on to make his mark on the music world outside Alabama, giving lessons to a young trumpeter from North Carolina, named John "Dizzy" Gillespie. Ellison compared Shorty's musical facility to that of the New Orleans trumpeter Al Hirt, because Hall had mastered all of the complex variations and difficult triple-tonguing techniques, and he specialized in the traditional Dixieland style. As a member of Hall's Orchestra, Ellison traveled to regional hot spots Columbus, Georgia, and Montgomery, Alabama, where he got to see Erskine Hawkins's Alabama State Collegians, the region's best dance band, perform their soulful hit "Tuxedo Junction."[38] Hall's group played at local dances for teachers as well as for the physicians who staffed the Veterans Administration Hospital on Tuskegee's campus. In Hall's Orchestra, the twenty-year-old Ellison, who had been restrained from fraternizing with jazzmen most of his adolescence, was finally free of his mother's watchful eye.

During the weeks before school opened, as Ellison bustled back and forth from the post office to collect his clothes, he had the opportunity to take stock of his new environment. Tuskegee students were overwhelmingly from the rural deep South. Alabama contributed the bulk of the Tuskegee student population, 745 out of 1,578 in Ralph's first year. Texas was a distant second, sending 133, followed by Georgia's 116. The North sent a handful, mainly Midwesterners from Chicago and Detroit. Rarely did a student travel from New York City or Philadelphia to the jim crow South of Tuskegee, Alabama.[39] On a campus where class levels began with "c-prep special," about the equivalent of the fourth grade, Ellison's well-developed taste in literature and passion for music distinguished him among his peers.[40] He was not entirely singular, as there was a cadre of bright, provocative, and energetic students in every class who excelled and whose activities were splashed across all of Tuskegee's publications. They were walking, breathing advertisements for the overall advancement of the race. Ellison met many black students inclined toward the same sort of achievement he was familiar with, and some who were more inclined. But even the most refined students from the deep South tended to view themselves as members of a large group, bound to the past and with a predetermined future. They exchanged ambition for gentility, contenting themselves with their status as the elite among blacks.

Ellison cultivated his legacy from the Southwestern frontier. Taking advantage of the vital example of Oklahoma City and Kansas City jazz music, he maintained a posture of rugged individuality and meritocracy. He was something of a loner, and he resisted efforts to control him—both hallmarks of the West.[41] Southern lore and mores would shape his identity as well, however, particularly the so-called Cavalier Myth, still flourishing in the South during the early 1930s. The myth of the noble aristocrat of the plantation, who in the words of scholar Daniel Singal "could use his great stature and remarkable personality to stop the drift towards chaos," explained the differences between Southern and Northern economies and promoted the viewpoint that slavery was a system that had been devised to civilize the African.[42] Members of the black elite helped to enforce the myth of the dichotomy of civilization and savagery by their overwhelming preference for the classics over jazz. The plantation brought Negroes in contact with "Culture," went the familiar argument, which was, if not quite an endorsement of Southern slavery, then an apology for the regime. While Ralph had encountered and, to some extent, assimilated the myth, he had his experiences with music on Second Street in particular and the Southwest in general as a buffer. He didn't deny or apologize for the difference between his sense of fluid Southwestern traditions of social status and the rigid social hierarchies of students fresh from rural farms and plantations. In Alabama, Ralph came face-to-face with what would become a lifelong intellectual grapple between the genius of authentic American black folk culture and the complex of American social institutions that drew on the same folk materials to enforce the myth of black inferiority.

5

The Trumpet and
a Barrel of Crabs

1933–1935

COLLEGE DID NOT BEGIN as much of a scholastic wrestling match. In the
fall of 1933, Tuskegee officials attempted to keep student life almost as orthodox and regular as the military. For the young men, required to drill in uniform three days per week, it nearly *was* the military. Most tightly monitored
were freshmen, who were required to study in the library three hours per
night and had to get pink permission slips from dormitory monitors to go
across the street to the "Block," a series of small shops and cafes. Only upperclassmen could venture to downtown Tuskegee, and no one went alone. After
five days of registration, with immense lines originating from all sides of the
administration building and swelling the campus, life settled down. Ellison
completed orientation after a mandatory reading of Washington's *Up from
Slavery,* which he found unremarkable, then the official quarter began on
Thursday, September 13.[1] Students rose to the 5 A.M. gong of the bell in
Thrasher Hall, put on their uniforms, and hustled down the hill to Tompkins
Dining Hall. After bolting corn bread and molasses, if it was a drill day, they
stood in formation at the parade ground while their rooms were inspected.
Classes began promptly at 8 A.M.

Ellison would spend the lion's share of his academic career in the music
studios in Huntington Hall, Rockefeller Hall, and the Chapel, where much
of his Oklahoma pride was clipped. The culprit who trimmed Ellison's musical ambition was William Dawson. Dapper, good-looking, and with a broad

reputation, Dawson had more ambition than any man on the Tuskegee campus. Aside from the widely hailed philosophy of Booker T. Washington, it was the music department chairman and his choir that put Tuskegee on the national map in the 1930s, making him a cardinal member of the Tuskegee team. Though Dawson personally had approved Ellison's scholarship, he dealt little with musicians, focusing nearly all of his attention on his marquee choir. Dawson, well-known for his exacting standards of excellence and the rigidity of his discipline, taught harmony and solfeggio, both required classes in the music major. Though admired for his accomplishments and respected for the caliber of achievement he pulled from all of the students who worked with him, Dawson appeared pushy to most. The conductor had a knack for embarrassing and humiliating students, whether for missing notes or coming in late to the Chapel for rehearsal. He expected choir to be the students' number one priority, at the expense of other academic disciplines. According to contemporaries, Dawson had the tendency to be "self-centered," and more extremely, "inclined to polish the halo he wore."[2] The nattily dressed conductor, whose salary was second only to President Moton's, considered himself an elite, professional musician. He demanded businesslike perfection and commitment from his students, as if they, too, were handsomely paid professionals.[3]

The other music faculty included Abbie Mitchell, head of voice culture and repertoire; violinist Andrew Rosemond, head of the concert orchestra; Frank Drye, who retaught Ellison how to play trumpet; and organist and orchestra conductor Orrin Clayton Suthern. Also in the department was Booker T.'s own daughter, Portia Pittman, who taught piano and choir, and serenaded students Sunday evenings with recitals from Franz Liszt.[4] Most influential in Ellison's college instruction were piano teacher Hazel Harrison and band director Drye.

The Collis B. Huntington Memorial Building housed the music studios, where Professor Hazel Harrison had an office for her Steinway and several cherished original Sergey Prokofiev scores. A social recluse on campus and an insatiable practitioner of her craft (she wore down to the wood the keys of a brand new Steinway in four years), Harrison was a large, matronly woman, single and in her early fifties. The incredible black pianiste of her generation, at one time a student of Ferruccio Busoni in Berlin and an intimate of the composer Sergey Prokofiev, she tempered the provinciality of campus life with her international flair. Ellison introduced himself to Harrison, whom he took piano from that fall. He entertained her with stories of George Washington Carver chasing him out of Rockefeller Hall where Ellison went to practice his harmonic exercises, and impressed the broadthinking teacher with his serious literary interests.[5] Harrison became Ellison's confidant and wise matron in place of Breaux, offering the talented youngster advice and instilling in him the importance of practice and discipline.

All of Ellison's summertime jazz swinging and stomping ended with the beginning of fall semester. He joined the mass of other freshmen—heckled on the campus as "crabs"—particularly in the Chapel and Huntington Hall. The Music School's policy was that the performance of spirited jazz pieces was degrading to classical technique. In an eye-blink, Ellison faced the same snide middle-class prohibitions toward black vernacular culture that he had known in Oklahoma City; only now he had no nearby Blue Devils or Second Street for relief from the elites. Music students were bade to shun jazz, which dealt a blow to Ellison's social life. The popular campus jazz musicians—the Melody Barons, the Rhythm Boys, and the Harlem Revelers—performed at student functions and built the local reputations of their members. Tuskegee music teachers discouraged their students, to the point of penalty, from affiliating with music groups that obviously brought pleasure and employment.

Ellison quickly learned that the Music School's sovereignty extended even further. On September 11, the freshman went out for varsity football. The Golden Tigers were scheduled to play Wilberforce on October 21 at Soldier Field in Chicago.[6] The team would travel in their own Pullman car and would also get to see the World's Fair exhibit. Ellison had never visited Chicago; but he had no idea that all of his time belonged to the Music School. Rough-talking Captain Drye, the ex-bandmaster from the Tenth U.S. Cavalry, freed him of his illusions in no uncertain terms: "Here I'm teaching you to use your lips and fingers and you want to go out there and get the shit kicked out of you."[7] If the music department was awarding him a scholarship and putting time and effort into his embouchure (the lip-pursing techniques required to produce a tune) and his fingering exercises, there would be no jeopardizing of their investment on the gridiron. Ellison would have to find another way to shuck the inevitable accusations from the campus jocks and the hardy agricultural students that he was an effete musician.

Despite his harsh demeanor, Captain Drye had faith in Ellison. One of the nicknames that Ellison earned freshman year was "Sousa," after the renowned American marching-band leader. When occasionally called away for an engagement, Drye left the direction of the band in the hands of the Sousa from Oklahoma City.[8] Soon after the quarter began, Ellison came to realize on his own that he had little time for as demanding an extracurricular as football. He regularly got out of bed at 5 A.M., to the pain of his hallmates, to blow an hour's worth of sustained tones and scales for Drye's class.[9]

Drye commanded his students unequivocally to abandon the smears and mutes of popular jazz techniques for the great "dignity" of the trumpet. Basing his lectures on the historical evolution of the instrument from the horn of the ram to the valves and slides of the modern trumpet, Drye refused to dignify the infectious popular sounds of jazz with the title "music." In Ellison's earliest drafts of *Invisible Man* describing the college, he included a music instructor who mouthed Drye's patented estimate of jazz: "Why it is a disgrace to the whole of human history! A disgrace and our people are the greatest offenders, and some of you are even proud of this assault upon the human ear." Ellison's character claimed that the sounds of the Tenth Cavalry mules had been more pleasant than the "razor toting so-called music that belongs in back alleys and on the levees." After impressing the young musicians with the low registers of the horn, evoking vast landscapes and tearful emotions, the fictional bandmaster bade his trumpeters to "play this goddamn music as it's written."[10]

The registration week concluded with one of the more important aspects of a music student's life: Chapel. Tuskegee required attendance for students and resident faculty, and used its Music School to enhance the program. Students soberly marched to the Chapel for religious services in the morning, their steps accompanied by symphonic notes from the band. In the early evening, the campus returned again for vespers and an address. The orchestra sat in the front during the Sunday evening service, but the main attraction was the inspirational address delivered by the school's president. Tuskegee chief Robert Russa Moton used the Sunday service as a pedagogical forum and preached in conservative Macon County tones.

By 1933, President Moton represented fully the principles of Tuskegee. A tall, broad-shouldered, brown-skinned man in his late sixties, Moton traced his ancestry to West African, probably Mandingo, royalty.[11] His genealogical précis in the introduction to his autobiography, *Finding a Way Out* (1921), assured white readers of the potential for cultivation of the unadulterated African. Tuskegee students revered their president, with his affable and easygoing manner.[12] He stood as a direct link to the Institute's illustrious founder and as a monument to the strategies of gradualism and accommodation. Moton didn't have Washington's drive or his unique vision for constructing an institution, but what he lacked in originality he compensated for by an unswerving faith in the path laid down by the Founder. Moton had had some difficulty in the post–World War I age of black radicalism in maintaining Washington's role as the principal spokesman for black Americans. Washington had never had to contend with Marcus Garvey, the apocalyptic race riots of 1919, or increasing black interest in socialism. Still, Moton easily ranked among the most influential blacks in the country. Under him, the Institute thrived, expanding the size of its physical plant and extracting support from white philanthropists.

Moton's views of black ability and character were mildly progressive, but he was prone to make concessions despite his better intentions. For example, though he personally suspected that whites derived only cheap amusement from black spirituals, he complied with Washington's inclusion of the soulful melodies in public ceremonies and speaking engagements. Born in Virginia two years following Emancipation, Moton mouthed the doctrines of racial essentialism, writing that the "Negro, as we have long known, is cheerful and buoyant, emotional and demonstrative, keen of apprehension, ambitious, persistent, responsive to authority, and deeply religious." The insertion of ambition and persistence into the well-recognized pantheon of black comic and pathetic characteristics represented Moton's progressivism, his attempt to destabilize the long-accepted assumptions about black passivity. He realized early that blacks had the same drive as whites—sometimes more—but rarely the same preparation. As an adolescent in Virginia during the Reconstruction period, Moton had been encouraged to run for state legislature, as one of a handful of Negroes in his district who could read. His lesson from the incident, beyond confirming Southern suspicion of Reconstruction era excesses, was to see himself and other blacks as possessing an "earnestness that often outstrips [his] development."[13] In the national role of race leader—whether in France in 1918 quieting rumors about black soldiers ravishing white women, or participating on the South's General Education Board—Moton counseled preparation, patience, and cooperation.

On Sunday, September 10, at 6:30 P.M., Ellison attended his first Chapel address. Moton called his fireside chat "Believing in Yourself." In his deep baritone, he compared blacks to South Asian "Untouchables" and tackled the "subconscious inferiority complex" that he believed stood in the way of group solidarity and individual self-respect. Moton even referred to chatteldom to bring his point to its roaring crescendo—bondage was a taboo subject among blacks. Despite trials and handicaps, and even the ignoble stain, "yes, and slavery if you please," Moton told Tuskegee students to have pride in their race, because it evolved into pride in themselves. As a speaker and writer, Moton mixed an educator's message with a preacher's bombast. Though his speeches were pleasant-sounding to the ear, their themes could be hard to follow. His sentences, liberally punctuated with "so far as," sometimes included as many as ninety words. Moton's style was to stray from his main point to deliver a folksy analogy or homily. But the analogies were difficult to make sense of, not because they were particularly complex but often because the straightforward axioms failed to expand or coherently relate to the arguments that had preceded them. And, as in most of the official rhetoric aimed at blacks in the South during the era of segregation, there was always an underlying hint of condescending patronage. In this first address for the term, Moton followed his technical opening about the "inferiority psychosis or complex" by encouraging his students to "see that you are clean and dressed neatly and that you look as well as you can look."[14] Ellison, as a member of the band, always had a behind-the-scenes vantage point from which to view the Tuskegee president's wizardry; he helped to create it. Sitting patiently in the orchestra pit during the evening address, he got to see a great deal of the fallible flesh behind Moton's public mask. After a while, the ritual pomp would become familiar, then tedious.

Another senior member of the Tuskegee staff made himself known to all the first-year students, particularly the men. Captain Alvin J. Neely, dean of men of Tuskegee, had a reputation as a no-nonsense administrator with the personal courtesy of a military drill instructor. Of medium height, dark-skinned, and heavyset, the voluble dean led Wednesday evening vespers underneath the dining hall, where he instructed his brood in the age-old teachings of Booker Washington, the "gospel of the toothbrush"—a famous Washingtonism about hygiene. He soon singled out Ellison as a problem, a potential bohemian on the campus, which was evident to him from Ellison's heavy reading and slick city clothes. A sneaky man, Neely would offer students a patently false smile as he sized them up, then discharge his favorite salvo: "Boy! Why don't you behave yourself?"[15]

First-year students worried about no tricky series of course selections: students accepted a well-regimented program from their major departments. Ellison signed up for the conservatory's Instrumental Supervisors Course for Band and Orchestra Supervisors and Teachers. As a trumpeter, Ellison listened to Captain Drye in the classroom three hours a week and had three hours of daily practice on his horn. Harmony—which included scales, intervals, triads, chords, coordinating bass and soprano melodies and original composition, as well as solfeggio (ear and sight training)—was taught by William Dawson. Ellison took Hazel Harrison for piano; and he finished out his schedule with English composition—Ellison's least important class—from the chair of the English department, Morteza Sprague.[16]

Besides mandatory playing at the Chapel, football games, and special events, music students had another required performance that was a more official part of their curriculum. On October 28, Ellison underwent the first of the Music School's ritualistic trials, the student recital. In an atmosphere ceremonious enough to be gaudy, the recital was held in the Chapel. Attired in a rented tuxedo, which Tuskegee men wore at all formal student events, Ellison played J. R. Thomas's "Must We Then Meet as Strangers" on cornet.[17] Though he was not the only performer, he was the only cornet soloist. Mabel Hayes played Haydn, James Barr played Dolmetsch, and Victoria Howard offered Mendelssohn and Bach. The audience could see Dawson hanging fire until the conclusion. When the last student had finished, he analyzed what he had heard with pointed barbs, wasting little breath on anything that fell below his demanding standards of performance. These recitations constituted perhaps the most intimidating aspect of the Music School, and they were appropriately dreaded by the students. To begin with, the higher Music School tuition and fees fostered a sense of elitism. The demanding classical repertoires that the students had to master stood in open contrast to the agrarian peonage of the larger community of black Alabama and the sometimes remedial aspect of education at Tuskegee. Music students had reached the next level of culture and decorum, and lived, at least partly, in another world. But membership in the elite strata was conditional, if Dawson had anything to say about it. He generally used the recitals to thunder out criticism. The other teachers backed him up.

A couple of days later, as Ellison continued to ponder the critique from the music department, the campus film committee showed the movie *Emperor Jones,* featuring Paul Robeson. Tuskegee's Lyceum Committee provided first-run motion pictures in Logan Hall, relieving the isolation and boredom of the college students in that sleepy Southern cotton town. Meanwhile, the testy Dawson still ruled harmony, solfeggio, and special events with an indomitable and brutal will, throwing chalk and hymnals until students played to his satisfaction.[18] Ellison was learning the high price of brilliance.

One faculty member who did inspire Ellison to push the limits and boundaries in a more congenial manner was the startlingly young head of the English department, Morteza Drexel Sprague. At twenty-four, Sprague had been the chairman of English at Tuskegee for three years. Sprague thought well of the trumpeter from Oklahoma in the freshman composition class, who performed ably on his feet but seemed less than fully devoted to his English lessons, particularly spelling. Outside of class, Sprague talked informally with Ellison, in the same low tones of confidence that he used while lecturing.[19] Ellison, with a shy smile that disarmed everyone except William Dawson, brought to the class unusually well-honed taste and a facility for analysis. Only four years his senior, Sprague took a liking to Thrasher Hall's freshman reading phenomenon; their friendship was the most significant intellectual bond Ellison would form at Tuskegee. Ellison ultimately recognized the important influence the relationship had on his ability to write cogently and to think critically by dedicating his 1964 collection of essays, *Shadow and Act,* to his Tuskegee professor.

Morteza Sprague had earned a bachelor's degree in 1929 from Hamilton College and in 1930 a master's from Howard, the academic stronghold of black criticism at the time.[20] At Howard, Sprague came under the influence of two renowned black thinkers, Alain Locke, the foremost black humanist of his generation, and Sterling Brown, a well-known poet and critic. Rhodes scholar and Harvard Ph.D., the philosopher Locke had collected the essays for *The New Negro* (1925) anthology, and had provided organizational and intellectual leadership to the Harlem Renaissance arts movement. Brown's collection of poetry, *Southern Road* (1932), brought out an entirely original and authentic vernacular black voice, leaping the pitfalls of dialect poetry and tackling modernism through the form of the blues stanza. A Williams College graduate with a Harvard M.A., Brown had authored the highly original *The Negro in American Fiction* (1928). His most enduring contribution was the influential essay "Negro Character as Seen by White Authors" (1933), in which he exposed the most common stereotypes used by popular writers, stereotypes that effectively distorted black American life. The two theoretically minded black teachers created an environment at Howard that stressed the simple superiority of the black folk tradition, in spite of both men's unambiguous membership in the black middle class. With a firm belief in the primacy of vernacular folk products as the foundation for high art, Howard graduates challenged the plethora of black stereotypes masquerading as the real thing in American popular culture. Brown and his acolytes instead promoted Negro authors as "the ultimate portrayers of their own."[21] Sprague's Howard training also rejected the feasibility of racial distinctions. Brown, who taught Sprague in the English course "The American Drama," wrote in the introduction to *Negro Caravan:*

> "Negro literature" has no application if it means structural peculiarity, or a Negro school of writing. The Negro writes in the forms evolved in English and American literature. . . .
>
> The chief cause for objection to the term is that Negro literature is too easily placed by certain critics, white and Negro, in an alcove apart. The next step is a double standard of judgment, which is dangerous for the future of Negro writers. "A Negro novel," thought of as a separate form, is too often condoned as "good enough for a Negro." That Negroes in America have had a hard time, and that inside stories of Negro life often present unusual and attractive reading matter are incontrovertible facts; but when they enter literary criticism these facts do damage to both the critics and the artists.[22]

In their private tête-à-têtes, Sprague impressed upon Ellison the dangers of double standards and the importance of an authentic black voice, influenced by the latest innovations in literature. Dressed in Ivy League–cut suits and wing tips, and delicately chain-smoking, the young professor brought the aura of intellectual brilliance and independent thought to the campus. Extraordinarily popular among students, Sprague served as the mentor of the debate society, frequently lecturing on literature and drama at the Ki Yi Club, the YMCA, and the Dawson Society for Music.

During the fall of 1933, Ellison took advantage of another haven for intellectual development on the campus, the home of an Oberlin College–educated teacher, Bess Bolden Walcott. In a cottage between Sage Hall and Tompkins Dining Hall, the retired English teacher had an open-house policy and welcomed young Tuskegee men and women to her capacious library and parlor for discussions. Mrs. Walcott's pretty daughter Carolyn, a student in the class of '35, participated in the talks. Carolyn Walcott later would remember Ellison as shy and soft-spoken in demeanor and intellectually curious, and as an insatiable consumer of books, despite his demanding music schedule. Ellison encountered a clique of well-read, studious, and energetic students at the Walcott cottage, like suave Minnesotan Leroy Lazenberry, William Pipes, Laly Washington, and Letitia Woods. Many were members of the intellectually inclined Ki Yi Club. The cerebral types frequented the Walcott home, gathering around their enormous oak dining room table for vigorous and engaging discussions about art, music, and literature, as well as a sandwich or some fudge. These sorts of discussions were a rarity at the Institute.[23] The Walcotts provided Ralph with a place to indulge his passion for reading and simultaneously to gain acceptance from his peers. Despite the popularity and intellect of most who came to the house, there was little competition and pretension. Mrs. Walcott, who referred to race prejudice as an "infectious national eczema" (in need of "panacea"), talked to Ellison about the latest new books, such as James Weldon Johnson's autobiography *Along This Way,* published in late summer. Ellison enjoyed the discussions of Johnson's life of distinctive and sometimes spectacular achievement.[24] Soon after, he picked up Johnson's *Black Manhattan,* which fed his interest in New York City that had been inspired by O. O. McIntyre's syndicated column in the *Daily Oklahoman.* For reasons of especial interest to Ellison, who had already experienced Southern violence, New York appeared especially attractive. According to Johnson's *Black Manhattan,* "New York, more than any other American city, maintains a matter-of-fact, a taken-for-granted attitude towards her Negro citizens. Less there than anywhere else in the country are Negroes regarded as occupying a position of wardship; more nearly do they stand upon the footing of common citizenship."

Manhattan held unique promise for blacks; it was a world beyond the separatist rancor of Alabama. Johnson's rigorous scholarship excited Ellison, emphasizing black tenacity and informing him of the role of blacks in the development of Broadway theater and music. Ellison learned proudly that Tuskegee music teacher Abbie Mitchell stood among the "great Harlem favourites," and had the distinction of being thought "important in Negro musical comedy and dramatics."[25] Walcott's home library helped to fill in gaps from the Institute's library. The former professor had mildly controversial new materials, like *The Sun Also Rises* and *Remembrance of Things Past,* along with traditional pedagogical materials such as *The History of English Literature* and *The Introduction to American Literature,* as well as classic fare like *Moll Flanders,* Boswell's *Life of Johnson,* and *El Cid.*[26] The Walcott house emerged as a little oasis amid the drudgery and tomfoolery of dorm life and the regimentation of the music department.

Even more intriguing than an evening at the Walcotts was the October 11 meeting of the Ki Yi Club at the Oaks, President Moton's home. Presided over by Thomas Campbell, Tuskegee's premier club heard an address by Mort Sprague and greetings from other faculty members such as William Campfield, who taught business, and Theodore Stafford of the hospital staff. Ellison undoubtedly struck up a conversation with Sprague, and may have known Stafford from his summer performances with Hall's orchestra at the VA Hospital. The elite club merited regular notice in the student paper, unsurprising since Ki Yi's generally staffed the *Campus Digest.* Even before mid-October, freshmen interested in the club had earned identifying appellations: John Batcher, "president of the class"; Robert Murdock, "the fiery orator"; and Alton Davenport, "the crooner."[27] It was club member Mike Rabb who had named Ellison "Sousa" after the famous conductor. At the meeting's conclusion, refreshments were served—a definite plus to supplement the miserable food service on the campus—accompanied by the soulful music of Cab Calloway over the radio.

Toward the end of his first quarter, Ellison was finding the most intellectual stimulation in literature-related fields and activities. Besides its musical and agricultural divisions, Tuskegee devoted a great deal of attention to its English department. Including those who taught in the high school, the large English department boasted a well-trained faculty. During Ellison's tenure in Alabama, the English department included Sprague; Neal F. Herriford, with an M.A. from Harvard; Fred B. Syphax, a Yale man; Grace Walker, trained at Emerson College in London; Martin Bethel, who had an M.A. from Lincoln and a Princeton theological degree; and Henry Jerkins, a University of Wisconsin M.A. The high school teachers of the Academic Department had degrees from Fisk, Talladega, the University of Maine, and the University of Michigan.

A week after an early November home football game against Morehouse, Moton addressed the student body on the anniversary of Washington's death. Ellison and his schoolmates were offered Tuskegee's unique spiritual food. Moton's talk, "The Force That Wins," did not eulogize the Founder, whose heroic bronze statue lay a footpath away from the Chapel, because "these grounds make quite a sufficient monument and quite an adequate eulogy." Moton played upon familiar themes, recounting Washington's great victories and touting the clearheadedness of political and social gradualism—"the sane path, the right path." The president emphatically told the students that Washington "caused the world to think of the Negro in terms of manhood," a condition that would engender "humanity . . . justice and equality."[28] But at the conclusion of the talk, he addressed his audience more familiarly, and in far less empowering terms: "Can you do the same thing boys and girls?" Moton championed forthright behavior and action in his students, but he also limited the scope of their ambition—the paradox of Tuskegee.

The same month, Tuskegee released the reports of an analytical survey that the school had commissioned by Dr. E. George Payne of New York. The survey was to show "how closely Tuskegee has hewed to the line of the original purpose of the school while making the adjustment necessary to meet the needs of present day conditions." Resembling a pep rally more than a report card, Payne's findings were at least mildly disingenuous. Predictably, the researcher found Washington prophetic in the same vein as America's philosophers and pioneers in educational theory, William James and Thomas Dewey:

> William James . . . announced a new conception of knowledge and defined education in terms of behavior and thus, along with others, like Dewey, contributing to this movement, laid the basis for a new educational conception which may be stated that education consists in learning to do better than we have done, those things which we are going to do later in our lives. This theory then was exactly the one underlying the practice of Booker T. Washington. . . . Therefore, Tuskegee has a long and honorable record in practice in modern education and in the midst of educational reconstruction it finds itself ready to go forward along the lines of its historical foundation without radical reconstruction because the institution has set the pace for public and private education through the wisdom of its Founder and successor.[29]

Effective as a public relations tool, Payne's study took a close look at the glass half full. The everyday experiences of educators and students in the Tuskegee classroom were perhaps less satisfying. Payne's analysis seemed almost satirical, suggesting that due to its emphasis on trades and industrial arts, Tuskegee had maintained a "long and honorable record in practice in modern education." Another clue to an overall tone less than academically serious was the pro-Confederate pun that the school had shone "without radical reconstruction." Booker T.'s sagacity would remain inviolable. The investigation of Tuskegee did not present a quantitative accumulation of data, but instead relied for evidence on the researcher's experience as an educator. Curiously, Payne ignored the radical shifts the Institute had made after Washington's death, especially since 1925, when it began granting bachelor's degrees. In Payne's praise-song, Tuskegee had rapidly advanced from her core curriculum of "c-prep special" to the ranks of Ph.D.-granting institutions.

While Tuskegee congratulated itself, Ellison's uneven high school preparation caught up with him. The fall composition class under Sprague was hard but fair. It initiated Ellison into the nuances of thematic organization, documenting sources, sentence and paragraph structure, vocabulary, and punctuation. He was returning to English after a two-year hiatus, and his classroom approach bore a little rust. The class work for the term involved mostly blue-book examinations, allowing Ellison little chance to discuss his own reading. But of significant importance, the teacher and student had a uniquely honest relationship. Ellison gave priority to his music classes beyond everything else and was a little divorced from English composition, a remnant of his high school attitude. Sprague, on the other hand, played no favorites with the student he openly had taken under his wing. To stay afloat fall quarter, Ellison had to withdraw from physical education, but still earned only average marks under Sprague.[30]

Ellison initially approached his college responsibilities and commitments with the same juggling techniques he had used in Oklahoma City. Due to his limited finances for the year 1933–1934, the registrar enrolled him for only part of the term,[31] surely an unsettling situation that caused Ellison to focus on the Music School curriculum, the source of his scholarship, to the exclusion of other subjects. His campus job could do little to ease his financial burdens; it paid only fifteen cents an hour.[32] And, though the requirement was self-imposed, twenty-year-old Ellison had the additional pressure of looking sharp and representing his hometown flavor. He wouldn't want to wander around campus looking unkempt, without his trademark tapered haircut, or minus creases in his pants. Whatever the case, the hard work in music courses paid off. His classes under Drye, Dawson, and Harrison went well, and he earned above average grades overall for the fall term—something he hadn't done at Douglass.[33]

Probably the end of the exam week culminated with Ellison's Ki Yi Club initiation, a mildly harrowing evening out in the woods with paddles, blindfolds, and sacred lore, concluding with instruction in the secret handshake from the club president. Though his name did not appear with the other fall inductees in the *Campus Digest,* Ellison joined the club before the end of the year. The organization included many dynamic Tuskegeeans like Bobbie McClaskey, and fellow frosh Alton Davenport, both of whom would participate alongside Ellison in the Negro History Week production "Drum Beats." Ki Yi's mission of "social and cultural improvement and unexcelled scholarship"[34] was unequivocally Ellison's own mantra.

The winter quarter began on December 14, 1933, and included a surprisingly full Christmas break from December 23 through January 2. Ralph corresponded with Ida and Herbert, wishing them well for the holiday season, but like many of Tuskegee's students, remained on the campus for the break, too poor to travel home. Besides, it was customary for the Christmas holiday to consist of a half-day on December 24 and a full day on December 25. For an Oklahoman, holidays with the family were an impossibility. And for any member of Dawson's Music School, the Christmas season bubbled with activity. The year before, the choir had gained international recognition at Radio City Music Hall. This December 24, Dawson presented excerpts from Handel's "Messiah" in the Chapel, the choir fully accompanied by the orchestra.

For the winter quarter, Sprague's class covered letter writing, oral composition, and expository writing.[35] Ellison had earned kudos in the music department, but still hadn't impressed his friend in English, at least not in the classroom. Sprague typically assigned a six- or seven-hundred-word assignment due the following day, which would have required an unusually large expenditure of time for a student with basic competence in a subject that still required meticulous effort. Since English remained a low priority, Ellison dashed off his assignments.

Ellison was perhaps not alone in his negligence. During the mid-1930s, the cultivation of accurate grammar and precise vocabulary became an increasingly public priority at Tuskegee. In December 1933, Neal Herriford, a teacher in the high school department, challenged Tuskegee students on a perennial theme: proper diction and grammar. Tuskegee grammarians encouraged students to put their best "tongues" before the world: "Errors in English, spoken or written, stamp a man at once as being uncultured. They indicate a mental shoddiness that is far from respectable." Herriford's essay, "Transforming Calibans into Ciceros," revealed one of the major goals of the school, respectability. Herriford counseled student "Calibans" to move beyond *True Detective* and *True Confessions* and become "Ciceros," digesting the British and American classics and "some of the moderns." The English department teachers tried to reverse the traditional bias against a liberal arts education. Impeccable language skills improved social acceptance, teachers told Ellison and his classmates. According to the faculty, students' ability to transcend jim crow would operate in proportion to their use of "Good English."[36] If anything, Herriford probably influenced Ellison, growing comfortable in his identity as a campus Renaissance man, to read more challenging works.

Holding steady in his other classes and perhaps slightly more conscious of English, Ellison pursued extracurricular activities in the winter quarter. As a new Ki Yi, part of his efforts included developing greater breadth. He played a central role in the February production of "Drum Beats," a broad-based dramatic program organized to celebrate black history. For the eighth time, the Tuskegee campus celebrated Carter G. Woodson's "Negro History Week." The events began with a rousing speech by Rayford Logan, professor at Atlanta University. Logan's black history talk was of the vindicationist sort. Aiming to expose African contributions to world history, the lecture coursed through the contemporary debates of anthropology and ancient history, exposing tendentious erasures of the African presence. Not long before, writers from *National Geographic* had rejected the standard opinion that Abyssinians were Negroes, suggesting that the medieval-looking ruins in Zimbabwe were not from 1500 C.E., but actually had Semitic origins dating to 1000 B.C.E. Logan presented the harsh facts of the ongoing whitewash of black achievement in history: "In brief, an effort is being made to show that any Negroes who have done anything worthwhile have done so in spite of the fact that there was Negro blood in their veins; that in each case you would find some strain of foreign blood in them."

After describing the scope of the problem, Logan proposed a series of historical correctives. Using easily available sources, from Minoan frescoes and descriptive passages from the *Iliad* to Logan's personal relationship with West Indian Commandant Mortenol, who had defended Paris from German aerial bombardment during the war, the professor verified the black African presence during pivotal moments of Western development. The stimulating lecture was a rare occasion to hear someone knowledgeable about African contributions to world civilization and independent government. Logan intended his even-handed, dispassionate paper to be a rectification of current publications like Gerald W. Johnson's *Secession of the Southern States* (1934), which had gone to great lengths to suggest that blacks had foundered since Emancipation, and that the only accomplishments they had made were owing to "white men with a touch of the tar brush." Tuskegeeans, Logan argued, needed to be "up and stirring in order to preserve those records that are still available" in the face of the "conspiracy to make the worthwhile Negro vanish."[37] Ellison had gone to school to concentrate on music, but soon enough he was feeling the thrust of historical responsibility.

The student portion of the black history program took place during the weekend. The Chambliss Children's House hosted the first half of the performance, starring Leroy Lazenberry, who was Carolyn Walcott's boyfriend and center of the debate team. Lazenberry's program spoofed Hollywood, featuring him as a director putting together a film on black life. The different skits that made up the "movie" included West African drumming and a blues number, followed by jazz selections highlighting the connections between West African drum rhythms and contemporary black music. The musical production culminated with the performance of an African folk dance. Lazenberry's movie concluded with poetry: Langston Hughes's "The Negro Speaks of Rivers" and selections from Sterling Brown's recently published *Southern Road*.

Moving the audience down to the Little Theater for the second half of the program, director Grace Walker presented Willis Richardson's folk play *Compromise*. The father of modern black playwrights and the first black to have a serious drama performed on Broadway, Richardson had written a stark play about agrarian peonage and the destruction of black family life.[38] Ellison had turned his years in Douglass's operettas to his advantage and taken the central male role of Alec Lee, a hotheaded young man determined to avenge the "compermises" of his mother and sister. He played opposite the popular Tuskegee dormitory matron, Queen Shootes, who headlined the play as Alec's mother, Janie Lee.[39] The drama involved working-class themes and race in a way that resonated for Ellison, accustomed to his mother's critique of capitalist exploitation and her refusal to bargain with vicious employers or landlords. Reviewer Zora Lee Barnes found it "representative of the best in amateur dramatics" and reserved highest praise for Queen Shootes, whose acting was "superb."[40] The play's denouement comes after a long exchange between Janie and landowner Ben Carter, the white man responsible for the death of Janie's husband and oldest son. Alec learns that his younger sister Annie has been "got into trouble" by Carter's son Jack. Knowing that the hotheaded Alec will kill Carter, Janie removes the rounds from a family shotgun; but Alec delivers "one lick" to Jack Carter, breaking the white boy's arm and ending the possibility of further "compermise" with the well-to-do white family. Ellison, having faced the horror of violent race prejudice in the Decatur freight yard, gravitated toward the character, determined to impart realism and meaning to the role. Though the other actors knew segregation firsthand, most had never ventured beyond the protection of home. Ellison felt that he had singular access to the justifiable black rage of Alec Lee. For the politically and socially conservative campus, the play was avant garde, particularly since it rejected the potential value of education because of the contemptible terms of the bargain, or "compermise," that was necessary to obtain it. Alec chooses retributive violence over further conciliation that clearly promises upward mobility. The play and the role were a harbinger of sorts for the attitude Ellison would develop toward his Tuskegee education. *Compromise* did not offer too much, however, in the way of release from the Music School faculty. The play was staged and conducted with the assistance of Drye and Dawson.

On March 3, 1934, an especially attractive event took place for the young trumpeter. At 7:30 P.M., after their audience of some two thousand had weathered the rain in formal attire, jazz great Noble Sissle and his orchestra took the stage at Logan Hall before the large crowd. In accordance with the South's traditions of racial separation, whites sat in the balcony overhead to hear the world-renowned band. Famous for his signature song "Hello Sweetheart, Hello!" Sissle's group featured singers Billy Banks and Lavada Carter. After the vocal portion of the performance, the band broke into dance numbers and played late into the night.[41] The premium concert was an excellent means for Ellison to let off steam after finals. He had proved himself in the music department, earning decent marks under Drye, Harrison, and the sometimes insufferable Dawson. Two days later, the spring quarter was under way. The chairman's spring solfeggio course promised "part singing" in folk melodies, an obstacle for the trumpeter with a slight lisp.

Founder's Day, a ceremony commemorating the school's origin, took place on Saturday, April 7, introducing Ellison to another venerable Tuskegee tradition. The educational director of the Phelps-Stokes Fund, Dr. Thomas Jesse Jones, along with the full complement from the board of trustees, chaired by Dr. Thomas Schiefflin, swept down upon the campus. The *Messenger* reported that the Founder's Day visit was unparalleled in the anticipation it caused, particularly in "these days of financial uncertainty."[42] Ever since the imposition of the income tax law in 1913, philanthropic grants had not come as easily as in the era of Washington.[43] Consequently, visits from the trustees and other well-to-do donors were vital to the livelihood of the school; they were accorded much pomp and reverence. As soon as the trustees reached campus on Saturday afternoon, they toured the student halls and agricultural buildings, then formed a line and reviewed students as the cadets marched four abreast to dinner at Tompkins Dining Hall. Depending upon the regional composition of the visiting groups, Moton would stand in a receiving line with his hands behind his back so that Southern whites would not have to shake hands with him.[44] The trustees received distinguished treatment; after lunch they attended student programs and exhibitions, ranging from dance numbers to dumbbell exercises. In the evening, the trustees' eyes focused on Tuskegee's centerpiece attraction, Dawson and his choir. In a concert that went late into the night, Tuskegee officials entertained, fully exploiting the potential of black spirituals. After Dawson's first-rank choir, two children's choirs sang for the celebrities, the bill finally completed by the efforts of a second college choir. Rufus Sampson of the class of 1914 paid homage to Washington, as well as to various philanthropists influential in the development of the Tuskegee idea: Seth Low, Julius Rosenwald, Mr. and Mrs. William G. Wilcox, Victor Tulane, and Andrew J. Wilbourn. Ceremonies concluded with a parade for the trustees on Sunday morning, led by the marching band.

Band members endured the light spring rain as they played to the trustees, but more interesting than their melodies were the upcoming debate team competitions. A tribe of enormously popular students spearheaded the team: captain Leroy Lazenberry; William Pipes, conductor of the campus band The Melody Barons; Alfred Taylor; and Major Lightfoote, the editor of the *Campus Digest*. On April 9, Florida Agricultural and Mechanical visited Tuskegee's Golden Tigers; the home team was represented by Ellison's classmate of similar name: Ralph Waldo Emerson Powe. Eleven days later, Pipes and Lazenberry attacked Alabama State Teachers College; and on April 29, the final home meet of the year took place in Logan Hall against the powerful Morehouse team. The wordsmiths faced Depression-era topics, such as whether the federal government should operate and control heavy industry for four years, or if states needed to implement unemployment compensation laws. Piquing the Oklahoman's interest was talk of scheduling a debate between Tuskegee and England's Oxford University, reminiscent of skilled Wiley College's powerhouse battles of years before.

Final examinations for the year began on May 14, but Ellison channeled his energies into his trumpet recitation scheduled for May 18. Choosing among pieces from Coleridge-Taylor, Chaminade, Tchaikovsky, Mendelssohn, Schumann, Bach, and Debussy, he still looked for acceptance in Dawson's Music School.[45] Ellison skirmished with familiar musical proscriptions, the boundary between classical music and vernacular music, and the difference between rigid adherence to the written notes and the freedom of personal interpretation. After one such recital, his teachers criticized him for employing musical showmanship in the place of diligent execution of the music as it was written. In later years, he recalled that during the recital he had "attempted to slide by on mere technique," whereas to fully convey the theme of the music a "passionate involvement of the heart and intellect" was necessary.[46] Though aptly skilled, Ellison had not delivered inspiration. Tuskegee faculty responded unfavorably, put off by the freshman's emotional distance. The teachers stung Ellison's ears with their rebuke.

Ellison's poorly received performance in the Chapel was the result of a broader cultural dynamic, however. Tuskegee was not the place to waffle over one's emotional commitment to formal music. The Harlem Renaissance of black culture had not yet performed its task of solidifying the black elite and the black masses when Ellison entered Tuskegee in 1933. Educators like Breaux and Page, and Dawson and Drye inculcated talented black youngsters with white elite cultural forms in an attempt to preserve connections with the white industrial world, a world that had been forcefully severing its ties with black masses as well as black elites since the collapse of the Reconstruction. At the same time, white academics and critics acted to purify and homogenize American culture, and to completely detach themselves from any vestige of commonly shared cultural ground with blacks.[47] In Nashville the year before Ellison matriculated, the city's leading white scholars and critics refused to attend a social gathering with Langston Hughes and James Weldon Johnson because of the maneuvering of Vanderbilt's famous critic Allen Tate. Tate had scuttled the engagement by circulating a letter which suggested that socializing with Johnson and Hughes was comparable to entertaining one's hired Negro servants.[48] Tuskegee offered a conservative approach to the problem of social inequality. Dawson had designed the Music School curriculum to ensure his students' technical competence and usefulness to elite social networks; and to that effect, his structure encouraged order, obeisance to decorum and, principally, unambiguous European musical standards. And of course, the conductor wanted something more from Ellison—an obedient spirit that announced to the world, but especially during recital, his pride in and enthusiasm for playing a part in Tuskegee's grand aims. With a keloid scar beside his right eye, Ellison may have thought that emotional closeness was unreasonable. Part of him began to chafe against the imposition of austere Dawsonian authority.

Yet Ellison sought approval, and he deeply respected his teachers. Fulfilling the highest dreams of his family, he could do no less. Following the recital, he did not have a unique artistic sensibility in place that would sustain him after the faculty's criticism; he was devastated by the articulate critique. He went to Hazel Harrison immediately following his humiliating dressing-down. Ellison and his well-traveled piano teacher had become close precisely because of her broad understanding and flexibility. However, despite her opinion of the stiff climate of the Chapel, rigid in its interpretation of European form, and Dawson's pretentiousness which the two made light of, Harrison lost her patience with Ellison. He had shown moments of fortitude, but in this situation he had behaved immaturely, unlike a professional musician. Harrison demanded renewed vigor in practice. Away from family and friends for the first time, Ellison had sought extended solace from the virtuoso pianist too frequently. His sour attitudes and need to be reassured, she told him, were "adolescent." He had been unprepared for the endeavor and had been upbraided for his lack of preparation, no more, no less. Still, Harrison's manner soothed her "baby," a term she used for students, maintaining their easy familiarity. Introducing a famous analogy, she told Ellison to "*always*" play his best, even if he was just biding time at the ramshackle Tuskegee train station at Chehaw, because "when it comes to performing the classics in this country, there's something more involved."[49] Ellison needed to play expertly and passionately, because he would find connoisseurs, teeny critics listening to him from behind even the dingy station-house stove, holding him to the highest musical standards. Harrison suggested that as an artist, Ellison should prepare himself for criticism from all corners, especially at a school like Tuskegee. If white Americans were not to think that at a black school, stringent classical standards were lowered, then as a black American he needed to prepare for the most rigorous evaluative criteria. Ellison had to have the capacity to surpass "something more" than what he might logically expect. To Ellison, it was confusing advice at the time. In those minutes in her basement office, Ellison thought Harrison unmercifully cryptic in his time of need. Harrison began practicing Liszt to signal the end of their conference, while the young trumpeter leaned into the curve of her piano, hoping for more advice. Though Ellison deeply respected her accomplishments and tried to figure out meaning from her explanation, the twenty-one-year-old left her office with only a riddle.

At the semester's conclusion, Ellison settled into the routine of college and held his own, earning above-average marks in his major.[50] He had arrived as a scholar, and he maintained his scholarship with his first distinctive academic performance. Commencement exercises began on Sunday, May 27, lasting until graduation day on May 31. Members of the band played integral roles in all of the exercises. For the first time in school history, a black woman gave the commencement speech. Nannie Burroughs, president of the National Training School for Women and Girls, talked to the students regarding the "Challenge of the New Day." Despite a deplorable job market and a mean racial climate, Burroughs bade the students to take advantage of the rough side of life because it would transform them into "a new group of men and women, strong and with powerful characters and lasting influence."[51]

More revealing about the actual nature of the hardships and difficulties that students faced during the spring of 1934 at Tuskegee was Moton's gloomy Sunday evening finale for the term. He indicated that during the year, "we have had some very, very disagreeable things happen" including "defeats" and "many sorrows." Moton blamed these unfortunate occurrences on the fact that "the people who caused them were deficient mentally no doubt." But he refused to elaborate on specifics, so well understood and inflammatory, if not dangerous to mention, were his points of reference. The unnamed defeats were racial in context, and reflected the peculiar penalties facing down American blacks—specifically, the penalties administered for operating an educational institution in the deep South. Needless to say, Moton did not explore the negative. Despite the misery of white racial hatred and abuse, the president angled his talk away from fomenting an us-versus-them mentality, a danger at Tuskegee since hundreds of Ku Klux Klansmen had staged a midnight march onto the campus in 1923. Moton did use the occasion to point out that recently an injured colored woman had died because a black undertaker, at the request of whites, had refused to use his vehicle to take the woman to the closest hospital unless the barely conscious woman "put the money down."[52] Evil and selfishness were perpetrated by those of deficient moral character, and no race of people had a monopoly.

Ellison spent the summer of 1934 working as an assistant to Walter Williams at the Frissell Library. A staunch public advocate of Tuskegee's practical education, the library head had been educated at Williams College in Massachusetts, and he soon familiarized Ellison with the library system.[53] For a diligent reader, getting the summerlong library job was a coup. Ellison enjoyed the more serious company of the older debaters who worked at the library during the summer, like Thelma Bradley and William Pipes. They organized an informal society of critics, such as they imagined were being formed at a rival school like Harvard, and read their poems and essays to each other in William's rooms. Out of these collaborations in creative writing and criticism came Ellison's lone published poem, but to him the camaraderie meant much more. "[I]n a school where only the manual and agricultural arts were respectable, this group was important in keeping my interest in writing alive."[54] When Ellison worked on his essays, he returned to the prefaces of George Bernard Shaw for pointers, which he remembered from the plays he had read at home. Exposure to Shaw's sophisticated, self-conscious record of the act of writing plays stimulated Ellison's own interest in writing his English compositions. "I tried to get some of the Shavian quality in my writing, but there again no one paid any attention to it and I didn't take it quite seriously."[55] Shaw's wit, irreverence, self-deprecating talent, and cold asperity toward the literary establishment appealed to Ellison's mental impatience, which he nearly always masked to friends, helping to produce the abstracted quality that they thought of as "dreamy." The self-conscious intellectual banter of Shaw's prefaces impressed Ellison as much as the words he looked up that the playwright used to pinpoint a character's physical movement and swift-changing facial gesture. Shaw rendered dialect impeccably, adding credence to Ellison's own intuition about the uncanny distinctiveness of the variety of black dialects he had heard in Oklahoma City and now in Alabama. He had found a bit more to life than playing and composing.

During the summer, he could also devote more time to jazz, or just take in a movie with some of his spare funds. The Institute had provided silent movie entertainment at the Chapel before the construction of Logan Hall. With the new facility in place, students could see movies and glorious shows, like the Radio City Rockettes or *Green Pastures,* in the comfort and psychological safety of their own campus. During the summer months, however, the Lyceum Committee offered fewer diversions, prompting students to venture to Tuskegee proper for entertainment. Since there were not as many students on the campus to look after, the rules requiring pink slips and safety in numbers were relaxed as well.

Enjoying his first spare time in months and having advanced beyond freshman year prohibitions, Ellison made his way down Old Montgomery Road to Main Street, took a right, and headed south to the city square, with its imposing statue of a Confederate soldier. Ellison watched the latest Hollywood films in the brand-spanking-new Macon Theater, a swank model of Alabama's commitment to jim crow. The movie theater offered its colored patrons ironic dignity. Instead of denying them access to the movies, or reserving the theater for them for an occasional day of the week, the Macon built a ticket window exclusively for blacks and a black entrance to the movie theater, which led into a divided screening room. Still, the rank aroma of racial bitterness clung to Ellison's nostrils. Despite the fact that the theater's double entrances for white and colored were a reasonable example of "separate but equal," Ellison found them "a product of social absurdity" and resented "the restriction of our freedom." He managed to enjoy the latest films in the new theater, nevertheless, aspiring less to win racial equality than to have a place to relish an afternoon. And he admired silent dignity in the face of racist treatment; it was low-class to always make a row. He told himself that he went "to the movies to see pictures, not to be with whites."[56] Certainly he did not go to the motion pictures to be in the company of whites from Macon County, few of whom were as well educated and polished as the students from Ki Yi, the debate team, or the Music School. However, Ellison did not go to the movies to be with uneducated black farmhands, either. A social climber, he sought out exclusive black circles.

Though the physical segregation of the town could be nearly tasteful, the white residents of the surrounding counties, particularly on Saturdays and during large public gatherings, were inclined to remind the black students of the rigidity of caste. Because of his greater goal of a music degree, Ellison publicly conformed with mechanical obedience, while revolting internally against the restrictive racial mores and patterns of conduct. Ellison had to repress his sense of himself as a Westerner and a pioneer when he ran up against ordinary instances of Southern racial hierarchy in the Reese Apparel Shop, McDonald's Shoes, or Rice's Clothing Store. He erected elaborate psychological buffers to protect himself from white condescension and to withhold any potentially explosive reaction. He felt "crowded . . . continuously" by the demeaning, if not homicidal, attitudes of back-road whites who demanded his supplication. On occasion, in response, he was tempted to believe them inhuman.[57]

During these times of severe distress and frustration, Ellison wanted to take the next step and assign this class of whites to another category, what he later wrote of as "a limbo beneath the threshold of basic humanity." Instead, as a coping mechanism, he adopted the strategy of "cool" to resist racial provocation by way of insulting epithets or taunts. But the "plaster cast—or [a] bullet proof vest" of "cool" had its own blemishes. Toward the end of his Tuskegee career, the tactic of "cool" provided only a passive Band-aid instead of a forceful riposte—what he called a "psychologically inadequate" prophylactic.[58] Ellison also tried the most direct method; entirely avoiding the Depression-ravaged white farmers and mill workers. But neither policy solved the real problem of acute powerlessness, which had begun to sap precious mental vitality. The experience with stark segregation helped redirect his efforts toward the imaginative playground of literature. When he ran out of cool, he found another procedure to succor himself against psychic assault and slip his head out from the mental beehive of the South. In another thirty years in his most important essay on black identity in America, "The World and the Jug," he would say of his experiences off campus: "I learned to outmaneuver those who interpreted my silence as submission, my efforts at self-control as fear, my contempt as awe before superior-status, my dreams of faraway places and room at the top of the heap as defeat before the barriers of their stifling, provincial world."[59]

Imaginative displacement and knowledge of the metropolitan world beyond Macon County enabled him to endure. Literature became a hiding place where Ellison gathered himself and braced his identity, as he had done when emotionally wounded by the loss of his father. Despite the intellectual fruit and stoic maturity produced by this manner of dealing with racial oppression, Ellison well knew that there was no adequate balm for racism's psychic ravages. Ellison's rugged frontier mentality, which advocated direct confrontation, took a thrashing. Tuskegee added a damper to Ellison's youthful tendency. With an arm tied behind his back, he esteemed less the knock-down, drag-out, no-holds-barred fisticuffs.

The threat of Southern violence did not curb entirely his activity. In an automobile driven by Booker T. Washington III and with older students like Mike Rabb, he traveled with his friends to Columbus, Georgia, through a gauntlet of tough police patrols. Columbus offered outlets for jazz music and for dancing, mainly in the red-light district on Eighth Street, with a beer garden run by a Mrs. Outlaw.[60] The visits to Columbus offered some respite from the Puritan mores of the campus, dictated by the philanthropist, where students were routinely suspended when suspected of sexual activity.[61] At the Columbus getaway, Tuskegee men indulged in weekend picnics and parties with local girls who were as impressed by collegiate status as they were without prudish attitudes toward sex. After a visit to the local bootlegger, Ellison and his homeboys indulged in more intimate relationships with the local girls, though Ellison probably shied away from a conjugal tie. Decidedly, the young men's sexual promiscuity took place well away from the campus where many of them expected to find wives. The Columbus escapades, though important in building youthful friendships, levied an unwelcome toll. The forty-mile route between Georgia and Alabama took the students through the infamous Phoenix City, Alabama, where law enforcement officers took especial delight in brutally harassing young college-going blacks. Ellison tried to adopt the "ancestral wisdom" when no answers were good enough for the white police, and shrug off these terrifying confrontations with white law enforcement through dismissive laughter. While it was perhaps similar to the strategy he used to control the painful memory of the Decatur freight yard, it was not completely effective. At times, he found himself brooding and melancholy, facing "whiteness" as a "form of manifest destiny which designated Negroes as its territory and challenge."[62]

The summer concluded with campus activities, which lacked the stressful relationships with whites. In early August, the student entertainment committee presented "The Forgotten Student," with prologue and epilogue sung by fellow librarian Thelma Bradley. The main section of the pageant was a monologue, done well by Ralph Powe, which, unsurprisingly, explored the life of Booker T. Washington in majestic terms.[63]

The joy and sorrow of sophomore year began on Tuesday, September 12, 1934. Ellison took a permanent room assignment in the upperclassmen dorm, Sage Hall. When he trod the campus footpaths and streets, he stumbled over the multitudes of new frosh, many of them from Texas. Ellison accepted his new status as a full member of the college community, one without a freshman's cap. Now Ellison took his meals in Tompkins Hall at the Ki Yi Club table in the company of attractive and popular coeds like Laly Charleton and cellist Lennie Whitfield, known to everybody in her circle as "Sue."[64]

Departmental instruction began the day after registration. As a sophomore, Ellison knew the terrain, and he took a heavier load. He carried his normal Music School core of trumpet, piano, harmony, and solfeggio, now at the more advanced levels, as well as the introduction to music history. When a freshman, Ellison perhaps had felt that English department chairman Morteza Sprague's composition class imposed unnecessarily upon his limited hours. But in sophomore year, he was expected to earn his marks in other fields. Dawson's curriculum proposed English courses in public speaking, but Ellison was not interested. The speech class emphasized a typical Tuskegee goal—academic instruction with thoroughly practical applications. Designed to "meet in a more practical way the speech demands of today," the course drilled intensively the "special forms of speech address."[65] Though the class undoubtedly benefited many Tuskegee students from isolated Southern rural society, who had had little exposure to urbane speech communities, the emphasis on thinking on one's feet and talking with poise before groups was superfluous for Ellison. He chose instead to take Education 101A, "Introduction to Psychology," a course scheduled for junior music majors. The psychology course reintroduced him to Freud, whose *Interpretation of Dreams* he had already encountered in W. L. Haywood's library in Oklahoma City. Taught by University of Chicago Ph.D. Alva Hudson, the class stressed the "application" of psychology to solve problems, and probably made Ellison and his classmates familiar with the terms of Freudian psychoanalysis.

Trumpet that year, again under Frank Drye, focused on embellishments, diatonic and chromatic intervals, velocity in keys and rhythms, St. Jacome's duos, practical transpositions, classical and standard solos for piano and ensemble accompaniment, style and interpretation, cadenzas, and recitatives. For Hazel Harrison's piano class, Ellison performed scales and arpeggios at different rates of speed, and studied such composers as Czerny, Hanon, Bach, and Haydn, but with particular emphasis on the modern black composers Samuel Coleridge-Taylor and Robert Dett.[66] In harmony, Ellison faced Dawson and the dominant seventh, ninth, and altered chords. After analyzing passages and drills, students would be responsible for short vocal and piano compositions. Solfeggio, also with the Music School head, drilled students in scale and interval singing of the seventh chord and the altered chord, as well as singing in the melody C clef. Ellison's difficulty with choral singing had a significant impact on his performance in solfeggio class. An unsympathetic and fervid pedagogue, Dawson would have made solfeggio extraordinarily difficult for a nonsinger. Ellison recalled that "giving me hell" constituted the singular component of the conductor's strategy to improve his performance.[67]

His relationship with Dawson began to sour officially around this time. Ellison never formed a close friendship with the Music School chairman, a deficiency that contributed to Ellison's ultimate separation from Tuskegee. Though Dawson may have seen something of himself in Ellison—ambition, courage, independence from family, even Ellison's poverty with style—the mature twenty-one-year-old student desired a mentor and not a demagogue.

And Dawson could only regard the trumpeter's considerable interest in reading as a distraction, a sign that the young man had not fully committed himself to music. To complicate matters, Ellison, already thought to be a tad independent by school administrators, was deeply invested in verbally engaging his professors. Ellison respected Dawson, but the relationship never advanced beyond that of teacher to student, and a student with much to learn. Despite Ellison's nostalgia when referring to Dawson and Tuskegee's "rather thriving music school," the only specific memory he publicly recorded elaborating his years with Dawson was an incident in solfeggio class where the hotheaded music conductor boiled over and threw a piece of crayon at Ellison.[68]

Dawson was not lenient with students; the previous year he had sent home Ellison's classmate James Barr, a musician from Tulsa. Between 1932 and 1934, Dawson's own career reached dizzying heights. In addition to his choir's stunning success at Radio City Music Hall in 1932—the event that had lured Ellison to Tuskegee—Dawson continued to refine and polish his path-breaking composition, *Negro Symphony No. 1*. The eminent Philadelphia conductor Leopold Stokowski performed the Music School director's symphony in November 1934 at Carnegie Hall. So impressed were they with the power of Dawson's composition, the audience broke the house rule of no applause during movements. At the symphony's conclusion, the white crowd summoned Tuskegee's composer to the stage with a deafening ovation. A week prior to the Carnegie Hall performance, Stokowski's orchestra had performed the symphony's world premiere in Philadelphia, transmitted over the Columbia Broadcasting System radio network to an estimated 25 million Americans. Dawson and his music were the rage of the campus and, arguably, the South.[69]

White adulation of the black classical composer went further. The printed reviews were kind, and this only two years after a journalist had covered Tuskegee's Radio City debut with the headline "Singing Darkies." Reviewer Leonard Liebling found in the symphony precisely what Dawson and others, convinced of the uniquely "American" and artistically rich nature of black folk materials, had argued all along: "The whole production impresses me as the most distinctive and promising American symphonic proclamation which has so far been achieved."[70]

By combining talent and hard work, blacks not only could acquit themselves as equals to whites, but might achieve new vistas untouched by any American, regardless of race. Dawson's purpose was straightforward, one that he undoubtedly conveyed to his students: "I have never doubted the possibilities of our music, for I feel that buried in the South is music that somebody, some day, will discover. They will make another great music out of the folk songs of the South. I feel from the bottom of my heart that it will rank one day with the music of Brahms and the Russian composers."[71]

The directive to black artisans was unequivocal: produce masterpieces to rank with the Western best. Though modest in his printed comments, undoubtedly in the small music classrooms and Chapel exercises, Dawson used his prestige to push students like Ellison to the limit of their potential. He loudly repeated the irrefutable fact that *he* had made great music from the black Southern folk songs. If a poor boy who had run away from home at thirteen could do it, what excuse did his group of coddled musicians have to offer? Dawson made Tuskegee's Music School into a hotbed of nationwide notoriety, aesthetic universalism, and most important, black exceptionalism. Ellison had come to school with the ambitious dream of emulating Wagner and writing a symphony by the age of twenty-six, combining his Oklahoma heritage of jazz and the classics.[72] At thirty-three, Dawson had accomplished many of Ellison's dreams: he had already been a premier musician, he conducted a renowned choir, and now he was a revered symphonic writer. Dawson stood as a near Oedipal father in Ellison's path, but perhaps a patrician too mighty to slay on his familiar ground.

The *Negro Symphony* and Dawson's unyielding personality represented the mark and the exacting price of excellence. Ellison, too, wanted to achieve brilliance and fame; but unlike Dawson, raised in Tuskegee, Alabama, Ellison resented a punitive authority that dismissed innovation out-of-hand. And if Dawson was the guiding light of black achievement, he was also the lion in the path of the future generation. Dawson's national popularity and excellence created a formidable challenge to faculty and students. Though only thirteen years Ellison's senior, Dawson loomed larger than a big brother because of his stature as director of the Music School. But perhaps this role of overarching leadership was not entirely of his own choosing. Dawson had under his direction many accomplished adults old enough to have raised him; he lived under a microscope of his black peers and the broader white music world. And unlike some blacks who were crushed by the probing public glare and double standard of excellence, Dawson found ways to thrive. He had won his job as the only African American member of the Chicago symphony in the late 1920s through an outstanding audition where he played the trombone in the alto clef.

As Ellison continued his education, his repugnance grew for his most consequential professor at Tuskegee, a man he could not afford to alienate. To begin with, Dawson's pedagogical style emphasized training over thinking. Ellison would remember that Dawson and others in the music faculty took students "away from the uses of the imagination."[73] The Oklahoma sophomore's desire for creativity, repartee, and intellectual engagement with his professors went unfulfilled. Dawson's and Drye's disregard for jazz music, the idiom of complex modernity, and the blues, the music of the modern vernacular, was a rejection of a good deal of what Ellison had personally cultivated. In the informality of Oklahoma City, he had known Walter Page, the redoubtable innovator who replaced the tuba with the string bass, ushering in the modern jazz swing sound sweeping the country. And Ellison had not come to Tuskegee fresh from high school. For eighteen months following his high school graduation he had set his own musical, intellectual, and social boundaries; now he had to conform to an environment more rigid in many ways than Douglass's.

Ellison was familiar with the contours of a complex problem. He could recall his having to accept Hattie Randolph's vicious rumor about him as a teenager. He realized that his teachers demanded compliance not just because they enjoyed obedience from their students. It was evident that blacks counseled their young and fellows to follow the path of accommodation and traditionalism to protect them from destruction and frustration. Their priority was the noble goal of longevity. But he also came to recognize this group homogenization as an almost atavistic yearning for simpler times, which the Depression era was not. For an energetic, intelligent student, bent on taking advantage of all that the campus had to offer, artificial distances and ornate protocols were incredibly obstructive. Other Tuskegeeans also acknowledged the lack of dialogue between students and faculty. Without even a student government for representation, many classmates, like Cleveland Eneas, felt that "the space between us, the faculty and the Administration, was too wide for comfort."[74]

Ellison disliked those professors who refused to speak to students outside of class, a prevalent custom: "I could never take them seriously as teachers. Something was in the way. Some fatal noise had been introduced in the communication."[75] Unfortunately for Ellison, the "fatal noise" was loud between him and William Dawson.

Tuskegee's faculty of the mid-1930s represented a broad body of contrasts. Many of the teachers were recent black graduates from elite white universities. Their teaching opportunities, irrespective of their intelligence or the excellence of their training, began and ended with all-black educational institutions, geared toward providing fundamental education to the descendants of slaves. These young academics were not in a position to challenge school administrations that mandated industrial education and its liberal arts counterpart; everyone knew Ph.D.s who were toting luggage in train stations and sorting mail all over the country. With horizons dimmed, the teachers accepted their position with cynicism, which could turn to conceit in the classroom.

As the only black institution of higher education that was taught and administered exclusively by blacks, Tuskegee presented an irreproachably conservative aura to the world, always on guard against traditional criticisms of black inefficiency. School officials used the black composition of the faculty as a talisman to ward off critics who desired more progressive or radical thought in the classroom. Tuskegee also carried an old guard of black education, teachers who firmly believed that just as important as their college lectures were their bridled demeanor and aloofness from the provincial student body. Students might not automatically assimilate bourgeois deportment, but surely they could observe it. Status was one of the few perks of a Tuskegee professorship. In an educational setting with the onus of high school teaching connected with it, the lines blurred between the expertise of college students who had firm high school training and the credentials of the faculty of Moton's era. The faculty arrogated their authority, in a sense, and sometimes conspicuously wielded it over their students.

The boundaries were harsh, if artificially drawn. Professors took to the stage as walking examples of black propriety and decorum in a Southern world that validated segregation on account of the Negro's supposed immutability to cultivation. Black educators in turn strove to appear refined and highbrow, an effort that truncated intellectual pursuits to the extent that it demanded imitation of attitudes and not the exploration of ideas. In an early 1930s conversation with the sociologist and writer Horace Cayton, Tuskegee sociologist Ralph Davis bluntly explained the conservative character of the school that gave rise to the distant attitudes of the faculty. "We lean over backwards trying to show the white folks that Negroes are as good and moral as white people. . . . [W]e have to get the money to run the school, and white philanthropists want to think of the Negro as being pure as angels."[76] "Purity" for teachers implied greatly exaggerated bearing and proper demeanor. Many teachers—like George Washington Carver, for example—were as interested in establishing cozy relationships with Southern whites as they were devoted to educating rural blacks.

Tuskegee instructors were supposed to look and talk like *professors,* which meant not like students. The *Messenger* proudly "quoted" a speck of casual conversation lamenting student deficiencies in speech, barely "overheard" at the conclusion of a faculty meeting: "Why grow emotional over modern youth trailing its clouds of glory through the mud and mire of slang and verbal inaccuracies? Many of us who are not students are none too careful about trampling the flowers of rhetoric and taking short cuts across the lawns of correct usage. The law of imitation still holds."[77]

The self-criticism in the guise of ornate Edenic metaphor—"clouds of glory," "trampling the flowers of rhetoric," "short cuts across the lawns of correct usage"—revealed the tension felt by the faculty. The philanthropists, local whites, and school administrators expected not only confidently spoken English from the teachers, but poetry in their casual diction, on a par with Harvard's Shakespearean scholar George Kittredge, at least in print. In reality, black faculty members' lives differed materially very little from those of the black townsfolk and city workers.[78] Some rejected a totally absorbing life of intellectual discourse not only because so many of the substructures necessary to support any scholastic exchange did not exist in Macon County, but also because of the absence of an essential practical motivating factor, prestige. Regardless of the immensity of their acumen, socially marginal black intellectuals gleaned few rewards for undertaking daring academic endeavors. Tuskegee teachers maintained their status as members of the black elite, the high-water mark of development dangled before the students, by means largely superficial. To entrench their position, professors remained aloof and condescending.

Teachers were not entirely to blame for the narrow mental compass of Tuskegee. Before long, Ellison was freely criticizing his fellow students, too, most of whom were not up to his demanding intellectual standards. Some of the more provocative students cultivated an ethnic chauvinism, an exaggerated response to white theories of black deficiency. Ellison undoubtedly enjoyed the humor of their cynical rhetoric and perhaps availed himself of the opportunity to socialize with them. But at bottom, he ranked such Garveyite tendencies of these privileged college students as the outward manifestation of an internal fear of competition with whites; an isolationism that ran counter to his purpose for attending college.[79]

Tired of the redundant genuflection to Tuskegee's tome, *Up from Slavery,* Ellison forged ahead with a ravenous reading appetite, traveling the campus with an armful of books. His undisturbed hermitage at the Hollis Frissell, with its forty thousand volumes, bespoke the library's chronic underuse, another unconscionable defect of the favored black student. Tuskegee students remained too hamstrung by proscriptions and prohibitions, in Ellison's view unable to "extend themselves," particularly in the realms of the imagination.[80] Ellison connected this conceptual sterility in many of the students to the dustiness of the books on Frissell's shelves. He saw black American life as something of a challenge, a discipline requiring mastery. His classmates' reluctant literacy, he felt, contributed to their exclusion from broader American society.

Around that time, while Ellison thought that the black chauvinist suffered from the mentality of the cloister, he also created psychological distance from foreign-born blacks. Tuskegee's student body included Dabiete Ayisi from Sierra Leone, and the outstanding Cleveland Eneas from the Bahamas; in total there were more than twenty students from Africa, the Caribbean, and South America. Revealing a jingoistic xenophobia that would have puzzled local whites, Ellison thought the international students "quite British," and tended to "link them all together." Eneas was popularly known as a "cocoa-nut head." It is possible that Ellison, conditioned to accept the complex skin-color and class hierarchy of Negro Americans, had little space in his world to add additional players, especially ones who already saw themselves as elites. Ignoring the international students also reinforced Ellison's own ego; it was unnecessary to compete with this formidable group of students. Capitulating to popular national prejudices, he rejected "cultural identification" with foreign blacks because the "sense of the alien was strong."[81]

Chapel remained the great equalizer and melting pot for the broad student body and staff. Despite rank, faculty and students alike were expected to promptly attend Sunday evening lectures. President Robert Russa Moton gave his 1934 inaugural talk on the second Sunday evening of the quarter. Moton's speech stressed the familiar trio of "usefulness, service and happiness," but he grounded his talk in Saint Paul's letters to the Romans. Moton used Saint Paul's rejection of heavenly or earthly impediment (by way of the strength of the "love of God which is in Christ Jesus") to encourage the new and returning students to embrace a particular spirit in Tuskegee; "I don't call it charity but love." Ellison would have been reminded of his high school principal Inman Page; but different from his Oklahoma mentor's exhortational style was Moton's crescendo, a Booker Washington tale. The Tuskegee president first invoked Christian charity and love to set up a straightforward parable of accommodation. Even the impeccable Washington had sold his own property at a disadvantageous price in order to allay white benefactors' suspicion of even the remotest hint of financial impropriety. The gospel according to Booker T. was dogged perseverance. "Nothing . . . shall interfere with my work at Tuskegee."[82] Moton was signifying that the school yet suffered under a microscope and that the best way of enduring the sometimes mean-spirited observation from whites was with unflappable faith.

The president's well-understood message of accommodation began to seem archaic to many within the next couple of weeks. In October, a group of citizens in Marianna, Florida, tortured, mutilated, then lynched a black man named Claude Neal in an incredible public spectacle that became nationwide news. Particularly upsetting to Tuskegeeans, the murderers had abducted Neal from his jail cell in Alabama, where he had been taken for safekeeping, and literally dragged him over the border to Marianna. Alabama's Governor Bibb Graves, a frequent Tuskegee visitor, had not so much as lifted a finger against this violation of the law. To express its outrage and to help revive support for the federal anti-lynching bill languishing in Congress, the NAACP flooded black communities with an unusually descriptive pamphlet about Neal's castration and murder, "The Lynching of Claude Neal." The graphic pamphlet stirred so much unrest that even editorials in the Birmingham newspaper assailed the brutality.[83]

Piano teacher Hazel Harrison remained unique amid the uninspiring administrators and distinct from the shadow of Dawson's celebrity. Ellison's pressurized contacts with Dawson made the young man's intimacy with Hazel Harrison even more important than her guidance had been the first year. With her sophisticated airs and Old World refinement, Harrison could scale down Dawson's Tuskegee-bred arrogance when she talked intimately with Ellison, particularly since Dawson's unending scrutiny made uncomfortable her friends in the department Abbie Mitchell and Portia Pittman. Ellison ingratiated himself to Harrison because, with a reputation beyond Tuskegee, she could protect him from Dawson. The internationally known pianist was frequently trotted out before white American audiences as a formidable example of black higher learning and cultivation.

In November of the fall quarter, Tuskegee sponsored a Negro Achievement Week, in which Harrison headed the bill. On Sunday afternoon, November 11, Harrison, perhaps with one or two of her exceptional pupils in tow, broadcast a concert performance over radio station WSFA in Montgomery, Alabama.

During this November celebration of black achievement, interested Tuskegee collegians had the chance to hear articulated again and again the important contributions of Negroes to American society. Though Ellison was well aware of the importance of black contributions to America, his ideas about the nature of black and white in American society began to crystallize in new and important ways. He didn't have to invent new concepts, but culled some of his more profound insights from the black staff physicians at the Veterans Administration Hospital on the Tuskegee campus.

Built in 1923, the VA Hospital was an anomaly in rural Alabama. Staffed and administered by blacks, the hospital had brought some of the most impressive medical talent in the country down to the pine woods of Macon County. When it opened, local whites had angrily resisted the idea of black professionals monopolizing a federal facility, but a resolved Moton weathered a midnight march from the Ku Klux Klan. After the demonstration, Moton demanded that at least black doctors be allowed to serve at the hospital. Federal officials responded by placing a white director in charge of a partly black staff for the time being, until local dissent died down.[84] Soon the hospital shifted entirely into black hands. The doctors, educated in the North and at Howard or Meharry, and the World War I veterans they served, cultivated attitudes of aggression and indignation. With their privileged educations and global experiences, they refused to accept second-class citizenship.

Hazel Harrison's concert was followed by a lecture from VA Hospital physician Prince Barker. Dr. Barker offered a concise elaboration of the idea of a miscegenated national American identity, which remained an essential theme for Ellison throughout his life:

> The Negro, successfully hurdling geographical, ethnic and economic barries [sic], has obviously cast in his lot with his Anglo-Saxon neighbor. He has not built a modified African culture. Unlike immigrant groups, he has modified the American order of things in the same proportion as he has been modified and of all the so-called amalgamated groups he has become the

most thoroughly Americanized. His absorption has been national and along all fronts of our complex national life. This assimilation has not been marked by revolution or radicalism. The Negro has subscribed fully to the principles of democratic government. The economic system cannot be healthy if a significant segment is diseased.[85]

Barker's creed rejected radicalism out of hand, but put well the unfolding dynamic of black and American cultural identity: "[H]e has modified the American order of things in the same proportion as he has been modified." In an elevated scholarly tone, the talk confirmed a kernel of Ellison's sense of identity—a rebuttal to the back-to-Africanists and the negrophobes alike. Whites had no claim to the entirety of the American experience; rather, whatever they labeled as "American" was unequivocally mulatto. In Barker's speech, Ellison heard his junior high school instructor Lamonia McFarland echoed, and perhaps for the first time he understood what his social studies teacher had been getting at.

Furthering campus critical thinking was a lecture on November 24 by the Negro poet William Stanley Braithwaite. Born in 1878, the eminently respectable critic and poet compiled a yearly *Anthology of Magazine Verse,* which appealed to Tuskegeans because the poetry collection emphasized craft and not race. In his Wednesday afternoon talk at the Institute Chapel, he urged students to disregard the stigma attached to slavery, since all racial groups "that have achieved" had endured bondage.[86] Ellison probably attended the midweek lecture of the gray-haired Boston poet. Braithwaite would have been remembered more for his literary and cultural criticism than for his poetic compilations. He had the distinction of being one of the original black writers to tackle the predicament of black representation in American literature. Alain Locke had published Braithwaite's seminal essay, "The Negro in American Literature," in the vanguard *New Negro* of 1925. Braithwaite carefully surveyed American literature, particularly the explosion of interest in black characters in the twentieth century, to insist on historically accurate, three-dimensional representations. The aesthetic principles upon which Braithwaite based his essay were widespread, but in particular his authoritative descriptions of the agenda and patterns of American fiction surely had had a strong impact upon Sprague, who had entered college as a literature major in 1925, then studied with Locke's colleague Sterling Brown (who went on to expand Braithwaite's aesthetic criteria) in 1929 and 1930.[87]

Braithwaite viewed literature as the culmination of ages. Black literature as a body had moved, thankfully, from the "dull purgatory of the Age of Discussion" into the more profound and deep "Age of Expression." Instead of discussing at length the Harlem black writers whose work had appeared within the previous fifteen years or so, Braithwaite anchored his discussion of black letters to the Civil War, an orientation point that resonated for Ellison.

The middle of the nineteenth century is where Braithwaite found the source of the enduring literary images of American Negroes. Black characters in American literature were flawed, he said, and black writers had erred in the antebellum era by embracing "the distortions of moralistic controversy." In the postbellum world, writers had offered only "condescending reactions of sentiment and caricature." Ellison, formerly unconcerned with black literature per se, now saw in bold script the pitfalls that hindered the efforts of black writers: moralism and stereotype.

Braithwaite's essay, "The Negro in American Literature," also helped Ellison to understand the conundrum of the actual value of folk culture. Braithwaite gave the poet Paul Laurence Dunbar, whose work was well-liked on campus, both kudos and criticism. Dunbar's achievement was "the first authentic lyric utterance" supported by his "faithful rendition of Negro life and character." But the great poet, who had written Tuskegee's school song in stiff, British-style verse, lacked "any rare or subtle artistry of expression"; he had excelled at content but failed in formal innovation. After Dunbar, black poets foundered until the work of James Weldon Johnson, whose *Fiftieth Anniversary Ode* (1917) rescued the ebony bards from the "mediocrity into which the imitation of Dunbar snared Negro poetry." Braithwaite clearly demanded that authentic folk materials be combined with artistic subtlety and innovation. In an inspirational tone, Braithwaite's essay reinforced the primacy of Negro slave culture, calling it "the finest expression of emotion and imagination and the most precious mass of raw material for literature" produced in America. Braithwaite's version of literary history challenged black college students to engage themselves artistically. His essay dramatically asserted that "the Negro novel is one of the greatest potentialities of American literature."[88] Black Southern life not only was culturally rich, but was the originating point of the great American epic, yet unwritten. Students would have left the lecture infused with the mission of advancing the program of the New Negroes.

After a surprise visit from Chicago Congressman Arthur Mitchell, a Tuskegee alum, the winter quarter began on Monday, December 17, with the holiday between December 24 and the New Year. As a Christmas gift to students and faculty that year, Moton arranged for the Logan Hall screening of the film *Imitation of Life*, based upon Fannie Hurst's novel, popular among students and faculty at Tuskegee. Louise Beavers's performance as the "mammy" Delilah appealed to the black theatergoers, who found convincing her blend of pathos and drama, which formerly had been absent from the screen.[89] More astute Tuskegeeans may have agreed with Sterling Brown's assessment of the novel and the movie: "It requires no searching analysis to see in *Imitation of Life* the old stereotype of the contented Mammy, and the tragic mulatto. . . . Once a pancake, always a pancake."[90] Nationally, black educators voiced greater discomfort with black representations in popular culture.

Christmas was a glorious time around the campus, when the restrictive puritanical decorum gave way to a more relaxed environment, and students from other black colleges and universities trekked to Tuskegee to visit friends and relatives. Ellison spent his holiday at parties in the Greenwood section of Tuskegee, at the fairly luxurious homes of the black doctors who staffed the VA Hospital, and with the Tuskegee clubs. Most of the clubs hosted breakfast dances and afternoon tea dances, vestiges of an era where adult supervision of young people was the rule and best enforced at early, multigenerational affairs. The dances took place at the homes of affable faculty members like Bess Walcott, host of the Pre-Frat Club's activities.[91] The Diaz Cafe, located in the Chambliss Building and featuring Cuban and French foods, also held several celebratory gatherings of students.

When he received his fall term grades, Ellison knew that the fall of 1934 had been his best quarter and his worst quarter, in the same breath. He earned his first distinguished grades at Tuskegee, the most impressive achievement coming under Captain Drye's tutelage in trumpet, an excellent accomplishment and one that consolidated Ellison's role as a student leader in the Music School. He had understood well the teachings of Hudson in psychology, and performed with excellent grades there and in music history. In harmony and piano he gave a solid performance, but a poor singing voice and simmering resentment caused him to nearly fail Dawson's course, solfeggio, though it was important to his degree and affected his average for his scholarship.[92]

Determined to make the dean's list in the winter term, Ellison avoided extracurricular activities and electives in order to buckle down for Dawson's class, in which he had to sing musical scales. As the cold weather settled on Alabama, the winter quarter continued with exactly the same courses as the fall, minus gym. For Ellison, it was time to hibernate. Throughout February, his favorite teacher Hazel Harrison attended recitals in far-off Pittsburgh and Washington, D.C. On the campus, the proper use and flagrant abuse of the King's English again assumed prominence in the school papers. The January meeting of the faculty featured English professor Sprague reporting on the results of the "Cross Comprehensive Examination in English," a broad test that had been administered to the freshmen in September.[93] The results suggested that Tuskegee students needed more concentrated efforts in pronunciation and in differentiating between idiomatic expressions and proper speech. After proposing a number of solutions, from reading clubs and public speaking exercises to more mandatory English classes, the faculty determined that it would be helpful if they led students "not merely by precept but by example." The desire to have faculty lead by example ironically exposed the underbelly of the Tuskegee education. At its best, with select students spending Sunday evening in Moton's drawing room reading poetry and drinking tea, the education could be sterling.[94] However, en masse, professors generally snubbed their students outside of class, refusing to acknowledge them, let alone engage them in conversation. Faculty could not set an example for student diction as long as most of the teachers embraced the rules of a rigid social hierarchy.

With some faculty prompting, Tuskegee students undertook to improve the perceived deficits in English grammar. Ellison's sophomore class took the leadership role in alerting students to the importance of diction and usage. The January 12 edition of the *Campus Digest* carried the headline "Sophomore Class Sponsors Campaign for Better English," and devoted the entire front page to anecdotes and spoofs designed to bolster respect for the King's English. Tuskegee still held its post as flagship black institution during the era; scolding its students for inferior pronunciation (the newspaper contrasted "Where'd yuh git" with "Where did you get that") reflected the school's desire to stamp out their rural Southern pronunciation habits and infuse them with Tuskegee starch. Other common problems in language, particularly usage, indicated the meager scholastic preparation that all but the elite of the student body had had. Many of the *Messenger*'s short pieces invoked a creed of social uplift and encouraged student patriotism to combat poor grammar, punctuation, and usage:

Stop using slang.
Look out for mistakes.
Listen for good English.
Let there be no traitor to the English language.
Are you a glutton who swallows the last syllable of every word?
Are you afflicted with the "this here" and "that there" disease?[95]

Ellison championed formal standards and technique, emulating the virtues of the black middle class, drilled into students at Tuskegee.

Ellison exerted himself mightily during the winter quarter examinations but succeeded only in duplicating his fall results. To his dismay, the March 4 examination period included another scotched solfeggio final. The Ki Yi's scheduled their anniversary dance an inconvenient two days before the beginning of finals, which may have moderately affected Ellison's exam performance. It was a dance he had to attend. His friend, senior Mike Rabb, earned his certificate from the Ki Yi's, and club co-sponsor Morteza Sprague (the other sponsor was Bess Walcott) gave the formal speech.[96] Ellison crept closer and closer to academic distinction but solfeggio, the bane of his existence, kept him off the dean's list.[97]

6

The Wasteland

1935–1936

Ellison stood at the crossroads on Monday, March 11, the first day of spring quarter classes. He had his destiny as a music major at Tuskegee in plain view. He'd either improve his ability to sing chords and recognize notes or he'd be forced into a ticklish position concerning the terms of his support from the Music School. He might have made strategic visits to the new voice teacher Florence Cole-Talbert, who had replaced Abbie Mitchell, to enhance his abilities in solfeggio. But he refused to let Dawson's Music School dominate his intellectual and creative life, as it had during the winter quarter when he had shut himself off from the world to master his departmental load. He decided to explore new aspects of his personality and talents. Perhaps because of the Aaron Douglas portrait of Dawson hanging in Hollis Frissell Library, Ellison flavored his stew of music department classes with Eva Hamlin's watercolor drawing course in advanced art.[1]

By late in the second year, the huge Founder's Day and Commencement exercises at Logan Hall had lost their solemnity and power for Ellison. The combination of an untoward local population of whites, a politically diffused black mass, and an aloof black professoriate made life at Tuskegee more and more disagreeable to him. Ellison felt insulted when a group he called the "high-powered word artists" swooped down upon Tuskegee at Commencement to tell the graduates and other students how they should feel about a broad spectrum of social and political issues. He also could have done without their patronizing thoughts on the merits of social equality.[2] Ellison was in

132

the process of internalizing the cultural nationalist rhetoric of Rayford Logan, the compelling black history speaker of his freshman year; Dr. Barker's thesis on cultural admixture; and William Braithwaite's analysis of black American literature. And Ellison had encountered Karl Marx during his nomadic rambles through Hollis Frissell, and had become slightly more familiar with the global debates over imperialism and socialism.[3] Though he did not see how they complemented each other, the psychological studies of Freud and the labor theories of Marx had given Ellison new conceptual language to articulate more precisely the reality behind the pomp and decorum of certain campus ceremonies. He became less and less amenable to the message of gradualism that was both Tuskegee's legacy and lifeblood. In particular, the campus practice of segregation shamed him. The Moton administration lavishly entertained dignitaries and still reserved Dorothy Hall exclusively for whites; in the meantime, students ate hastily prepared meals in the dining hall. In rebellion, Ellison began to steal away from the orchestra pit during the hollow ceremonies. Instead of upholding the ritual, he wandered over to the old football field where Tuskegee's rural black cotton farmers held their yearly picnics and athletic contests. Though he only casually observed, feeling cut off from agrarian blacks because of his city roots and college status, he found the "unrhetorical" joy and style of the farmers more significant than whatever the Northern and Southern "big shots" had to say. Though not all-out like his mother Ida, Ellison became increasingly critical of class and power relationships. No longer reacting to the dilemmas of racism, but now consciously alienating himself from black middle-class upward mobility, he began a delicate soul-searching.

Ellison probably had cause to first abandon his orchestra post at the April 7, 1935, Founder's Day address by Dean Kelly Miller of Howard University. Miller, the black sage of social science, had been a well-established academic during the turn-of-the-century imbroglios between Washington and Du Bois. While never a true adherent of either the industrial or liberal arts side of the debate, by the time he arrived to give the memorial address in Logan Hall, Miller had become an elderly conservative. At his lecture, he carried race thinking back from its recently established nonbiological precepts and revived the turn-of-the-century logic of racial essences: "The Negro, in his unsophisticated state, represents the Christian virtues and graces to a degree unequaled by any other variety of the human family. Meekness, humility, long-suffering, loving-kindness, unresentfulness, and forgiveness of spirit are inalienable coefficients of his blood. He is incapable of deep seated hatred and revenge."[4]

Miller's subject at Founder's Day was, of course, the great man, and naturally he strove to recount Washington's salient characteristics. What perhaps occurred to careful listeners was the ambiguity of Washington's own complex biracial ancestry, which derailed Miller's arguments of essences. In Miller's melodramatic elegy, he invoked Washington's innate and unerring "inner light"; the Founder "knew without learning; he understood without being taught; he was born with a caul over his face."[5] Ellison, frustrated with Dawson's tirades in class coupled with what began to seem a repetitive and uncritical fawning over the achievement of a man only twenty years dead, sought relief by watching the country people play on the ball fields.

After a jovial Spring Carnival weekend came the highlight of the year, the performance of Duke Ellington and his orchestra on Tuesday, April 16. They were billed to begin playing at 2 P.M., but for some reason Ellington thought the engagement at Tuskegee had been canceled, and then he ran into difficulty making his way to Montgomery. A Washingtonian who had spent much of his life in New York, Ellington had only recently begun to tour the deep South. He and his stellar orchestra, fresh from Europe, resented the provincial traditions of segregation, though displeasure rarely showed itself on the Duke's composed exterior.[6] Only because of the persistence of Tuskegee's secretary to the president, Dr. G. Lake Imes, who tracked down the orchestra by wireless, then motored to Montgomery to personally allay Ellington's suspicion and bad humor, did the celebrities make it to the campus, where a crowd of four thousand awaited them. When Ellington took the piano seat at 4:30 P.M., Ellison was among the crowd, probably close to the stage if not in the wings, as Dawson's musical elite would have received special privileges in Logan Hall. Ellington and the orchestra played fifteen numbers, including all the popular jazz staples such as "Creole Love Call," "Sophisticated Lady," and "Rocking in Rhythm." The orchestra featured Ivy Anderson singing the smash hits "In My Solitude" and "Stormy Weather." Ellington allowed enchanted students like Ellison and a few others from the Music School a brief audience at the conclusion of the concert. Gracious and warm, the Duke listened as an eager Ellison told him how long he had followed Ellington's orchestra. The glowing sophomore also revealed his dream of composing; and perhaps to Ellington, offered a vision of symphony different from Dawson's *Negro Symphony*.[7]

As if to underscore the arc and reach of Dawson's accomplishment and the distance of Ellison's dream, a few weeks later Birmingham's Civic Symphony Orchestra came to campus and performed Dawson's symphony. It was a crowning irony of Ellison's education that the disagreeable music conductor had the power to overcome segregation. As parochial as race relationships were at Tuskegee and in the South in general, Dawson's achievements continued to establish the Institute as a special and distinct beacon of artistic advancement and relative social freedom.

Sometime after the commencement on May 23, Ellison learned the results of the spring quarter. He'd admirably raised solfeggio to a satisfactory level but only by sacrificing his excellence on the trumpet. But Ellison had surprised himself in an entirely unfamiliar field—at least, strange at the beginning of the 1934–1935 school year. He earned an excellent grade in his advanced art class. His relationship with Hamlin had bloomed. A Pratt Institute graduate, the fine arts professor told Ellison all of the latest news about the black art movement taking place in New York City, especially the energetic artist Augusta Savage and her 125th Street studio. Ellison delighted in discovering a new artistic talent, but at the cost of established prowess. Art was the only superior achievement in the classroom that spring of 1935, and the quarter was a letdown. For perhaps the first time, he felt doubtful about his career; and to make matters worse, his favorite teacher, Morteza Sprague, would be spending the summer at Columbia University as a graduate student in the English department.[8] Hazel Harrison also would be gone, leaving Dawson in total command.

Ellison had other difficult, if not traumatic, social experiences at Tuskegee. The traditional rift between the rough-and-tumble agricultural and mechanical students and the jays drawn to the liberal arts curriculum led to personal disagreements. Vulnerable as one of the few males pursuing a degree in music, Ellison knew the same razzing he had encountered in seventh grade. Other male students, especially the older ones in Tuskegee's high school, were liable to equate "aesthete" with "effete." He suffered ridicule for his cultivated sensibility. Strong-backed farmworkers derided his attempts at eloquence when he read poetry to Sue Whitfield or played classics for Laly Charleton on the grounds. There was an incident with Pittsburgh athlete Jody Harris, who drew his cadet saber on Ellison for socializing with Sue Whitfield, who was Harris's girlfriend.[9] Ellison did nothing, but carried his switchblade for the dark nights across the campus. His high visibility also caught the attention of another group, a powerful clique of male professors and department heads, well-known for their predatory interest in attractive and muscular male students. Ellison frequently had run-ins with Dean Neely, whose sidelong looks and joking had moved beyond innuendo. Ellison now avoided Neely and gym teacher William O'Shields, whose awkward excuses never quite explained why male students were not allowed to wear trunks during swim classes.[10]

Ellison may have decided early in 1935 to spend the summer with his family. He hadn't seen them in almost two years, but long absences while completing an education were not unusual. Although he may have missed the love and affection of his mother, it's unlikely that Ellison would have missed much of Oklahoma City poverty, or his stepfather John Bell. Certainly he did not miss sharing a room with Herbert, the younger brother whom he had had to care for and protect. Contributing to the animosity that flared between the brothers, both of whom had now grown to manhood, Ellison craved distance. Herbert obviously reminded him of his humble origins and his uncertain future. Where Ralph Ellison was engaging and polished, Herbert was reticent and humble; where Ralph was learned, Herbert was casually literate, and he stuttered. That Herbert could not add one iota to the memory of their father Lewis Ellison certainly did not help matters. But Herbert and John Bell probably figured little in Ellison's mind. He went back to Oklahoma to see his mother Ida, the strong-willed head of the family, to whom he wrote frequently. Indeed, he may have been commanded home to help in its defense. In 1935, the Ellison-Bells left their house at 710 East Second Street in the Oklahoma City black belt, moving well into white territory to a home at 812 Stonewall Avenue. Far to the north of Seventh Avenue, Governor William "Alfalfa Bill" Murray's martially enforced racial dividing line for the city, the Stonewall address represented a front line in a shooting war over racial segregation.[11]

Undoubtedly, Ellison's decision to leave Alabama for the minimally structured learning environment of Oklahoma City did not sit well with Dawson, who had run away from home penniless to study at Tuskegee. Dawson likely suggested that Ellison perform more work in solfeggio during the summer and reduce his extracurriculars, a choice that may have been unpalatable to Ellison for any number of reasons. By spending the summer of 1935 in Oklahoma City, Ellison broke with the Music School, and in symbolic terms, rejected its patronage.

It may have been that Ellison was lucky, and Milt Lewinsohn took him back in his store for a few weeks over the summer, though returning to labor-intensive work at eight dollars per month would have been frustrating. But the Depression raged, and the economy offered few opportunities for a college student trained as a composer, symphonic conductor, and classical trumpeter. The summer break did allow mother and son to rekindle their intimacy in the new home on Stonewall Avenue, and the sparky racial attitudes of his mother Ida and newspaper editor Roscoe Dunjee invigorated Ellison after his return from the torpid deep South. More than his political senses were enlivened that summer. Even though the Blue Devils had disbanded, jazz still thrived, and Ellison collected praise as a local boy and musician who had gone to famous Tuskegee for his education. On the occasions when he ran into Zelia Breaux, J. D. and T. J. Randolph, and Roscoe Dunjee and told them about Tuskegee and his travels, he probably did not realize that he would never see them again.

Summer brought with it a delightful literary harvest. Lounging in a chair at the barbershop, Ellison read his first Ernest Hemingway while waiting to get his hair cut.[12] As he waited for an open chair, Ellison thumbed through old copies of *Esquire,* the mildly ribald men's fashion magazine that had begun as a quarterly in the fall of 1933 but was popular enough to turn monthly by early 1934. Taking in advice on bat-ties and dinner jackets, Ellison also noticed that the editors constructed the masculine sensibility of the magazine around the personality of a single writer. Nearly every *Esquire* for the magazine's first several years prominently featured a travelogue or American sportsman piece by the writer Ernest Hemingway. Ellison happily consumed such Hemingway essays as "Marlin off the Morro," "The Friend of Spain," "a.d. in Africa," "Shootism versus Sport," "Sailfish of Mombassa," and the influential "Remembering Shooting-Flying." Ellison's Oklahoma senses were attracted to this man, a writer whose every utterance, down to his style of description, exuded masculinity.

Ellison was impressed by the combined laconic style and braggadocio of the writer everyone seemed to love to hate. Hemingway caught the 458-pound marlin, wrote knowingly of Paris, talked about writing technique and safari in Africa in the same passage, and most important to an Oklahoman who had been hunting since he was twelve, described the intricacies of wing-shooting. In "Remembering Shooting-Flying," Hemingway sent Ellison back to pleasurable autumns in his childhood with James Ammons, tramping across the open prairie south of town for excellent-tasting birds and rabbits. Even more important than the memories ("How the jacksnipe rose with a jump and you hit him on the second swerve"), Hemingway's sports essays also provided a booklist:

> (and I would rather read again *Anna Karenina, Far Away and Long Ago, Buddenbrooks, Wuthering Heights, Madame Bovary, War and Peace, A Sportsman's Sketches, The Brothers Karamazov, Hail and Farewell, Huckleberry Finn, Winesburg, Ohio, La Reine Margot, La Maison Tellier, Le Rouge et le Noire, La Chartreuse de Parme, Dubliners,* Yeats's *Autobiographies* and a few other than have an insured income of a million dollars a year).[13]

And though *Esquire* indulged in the popular comic cartoons of blacks as indolent, playful, and irresponsible, it also allowed black writers like Langston Hughes and Chester Himes to publish. Hughes's short story "The Folks at Home" hit a familiar chord for Ellison, and showed the magazine's modernist racial consciousness. In the piece, protagonist Roy Williams, a European-trained concert violinist, returns to his native Missouri, slightly breaches local racial etiquette (he embraces a former teacher, a white female), and ends up the victim of the howling white mob.[14] In its editorial breadth, *Esquire* saw itself as sophisticated enough to simultaneously joke at common Negro stereotypes and publish protests against the national problem of lynching. More daring, the magazine's February 1934 issue carried a piece of prison fiction by the young black convict Chester Himes, "To What Red Hell." Hughes and Himes were in good company. The editors pitched the literary tastes of the magazine high, featuring writers like Erskine Caldwell, Ezra Pound, and Thomas Mann.

Summer break also involved more significant decisions for the Bell family, in which Ellison may have taken part. Ida's staunch resistance to the jim crow law began to jeopardize her and Herbert's safety and cause friction with her husband. Almost an original pioneer, Ida refused to accept the imposition of legally sanctioned racial segregation and the increasing dominance of Texas attitudes in Oklahoma City. Ida still maintained vivid memories of an earlier age when race relations had been less backward and when blacks had moved to Oklahoma as a promised land. Recent housing legislation in support of segregation threatened to erase that past completely. At the same time, fifty-year-old Ida was slowing down a little bit. The cream of her youth had gone to providing for the boys, and mainly for Ralph. She realized that her ambitious son might never return to the Southwest of his youth. With his considerable intelligence and collegiate refinement, he had outgrown the frontier city. He had the gleam of Chicago, Washington, D.C., or maybe even New York City in his eye. Ida began to consider moving with her family to Ohio, where she had more relatives, and where the racial climate was less ugly.

Ellison returned to the Tuskegee campus the first week in September, perhaps by motoring with other students from Oklahoma City like sophomore Mabel Evans or senior Zelma Robinson. In the fall of 1935, Ellison reached a milestone that was in many ways more significant than his original trek to Tuskegee. He broke with the music department. Though Ellison was still receiving a Music School scholarship, either he was refused registration in his classes because of his own rejection of summer work in solfeggio with Dawson, or he refused the music department curriculum out of hand, including his course work in the trumpet. Dawson may have been unsure about allowing Ellison to continue to the next level of theoretical course work, counterpoint, considering his tenuous solfeggio performances in sophomore year. Dawson, referred to by Booker T. Washington's daughter and music faculty member Portia Pittman as a "degree fiend," demanded immaculate records from the faculty and students in his fledgling program.[15] Producing elite-caliber musicians was a careful distillation process. The Music School moved slowly, graduating its first student, Sarah O. Stivers, in the spring of 1936.[16] The other possibility is that Ellison chose to put as much distance as possible between himself and the Music School, something that could have happened because of the disappearance of the Music School head. Dawson married on September 21 in Virginia; his absence from the campus during the first couple of weeks of the quarter coincided with Ellison's developing sense of entitlement. Dawson even missed Tuskegee's inaugural Sunday night Chapel talk. Instead of nationally renowned William Dawson, Mrs. Alberta Simms conducted the choir.[17] Ellison decided that college meant more than refinement and classical music. Of the six courses required by Music School juniors, by Monday, September 9, 1935, Ellison had enrolled in only one, beginning French.

Ellison's major effort went to Morteza Sprague's dearly anticipated upper-level English course on the novel, ordinarily open only to seniors. The junior intended to prove himself a better writer and reader than his freshman grades in composition had indicated. Sprague selected rigorous texts for the course and admitted only a handful of students, feeling that novel courses offered the student too much entertainment and too little mental exertion. In previous Tuskegee courses, novels had not been interpreted, analyzed, or critiqued enough; teachers spent too much energy recounting plot and theme. The English professor strove to infuse students with "an abiding love of, and thoughtful reverence for, the best literature," a high ground that students could gain only through the application of rigorous analytical tools. Sprague suggested that in order to cope with the less-than-ideal level of critical discourse on literature in the Tuskegee classroom, "we must revise and enlarge courses in English."[18] Under the candid Sprague's increasing friendship, Ralph explored Fielding, Scott, Austen, Dickens, Thackeray, Trollope, Reade, and Kingsley.

Ellison also remained interested in the social sciences, taking Ralph Davis's sociology series on black American life, The Negro in America and the Problem of Races and Nationalities. The series began with a sociology course, The Negro. Ralph also went on with his recently found passion for art with Professor Hamlin, enrolling in advanced sculpting. When he had completed his registration, Ellison had signed up for Tuskegee's most reading-intensive liberal arts courses. That fall of 1935, he submitted to his intellectual cravings and to the part of him that went limp watching the sun dip below the horizon at dusk or the moon glowing brilliantly; he was crafting himself as a humanist.

The fall of 1935 brought on another momentous change in Alabama. An aged Moton was replaced by Tuskegee's third president, Frederick D. Patterson. Fair-complexioned, tall, and well dressed, Patterson evoked the polished demeanor of Duke Ellington. Recommended by Moton and elected by the faculty, Patterson apparently had not campaigned for the post. It did not hurt his candidacy that he had married Moton's daughter Catherine in June. The new president with an impressive Ph.D. from Cornell came to the administration from the agricultural department. But with Patterson at the helm, Tuskegee began its slide from an institution of national importance in racial affairs and the education of black Americans to an isolated outpost in the semifeudal South.

The school's decline resulted from growths in American society that Washington's vision of hands-on learning and yeoman farming had been unable to anticipate, the revolution in American industrial technology and manufacturing that ended farming and small landownership as a way of life. The second wave of the great migration of black agrarian workers into the Northern industrial centers of Chicago, Detroit, Cleveland, Toledo, Pittsburgh, Philadelphia, and New York City diminished the prominence of the deep South's premier black institution. In the fall of 1935, though, Patterson focused his attention on the unremitting economic pressure of the Depression. He faced the challenge squarely, announcing to colleagues and students alike: "The institution is in need of funds; its courses of study must be reshaped to meet the needs of the new economic order."[19] Patterson immediately approved a program of economic retrenchment in all departments. The first limbs of the Tuskegee body to suffer were campus publications; the widely circulated *Messenger,* the school's official journal, now combined two months into each issue, and the print shop released no academic bulletin for the 1935–1936 school year. The Music School, always an extravagance with its richly paid faculty, lost its sponsorship from the president's office. Immediately, Hazel Harrison began to put out feelers for other teaching opportunities; by the fall of 1936, she would be on the faculty at Howard University. The downfall of the Music School was swift, and a sharp student like Ellison would have sensed jeopardy. With the power of the Music School diminished, he had no one to apologize to for his eclectic course work. After graduating five students from Ellison's year in the spring of 1937, Patterson and the trustees "discontinued" the four-year program leading to the bachelor's degree in music.[20] By the fall of 1937, the Music School had lost its autonomy and became a department. Two years after Ellison's junior year, Tuskegee would no longer graduate students with bachelor's degrees in music.

Ellison did not break completely with the Music School; in fact, oddly enough, September brought on the new responsibility of being student band conductor. The band traveled with the football team to Chicago, Jacksonville, Florida, New Orleans, and Marshall, Texas. At home games in the Tuskegee Bowl, Ellison led the band at halftime, directing with his baton from a portable podium that freshmen carried onto the field. On September 19, a Thursday evening, Ellison and his band comrades played in Montgomery on the steps of the Scottish Rite Temple to a crowd of one thousand people. The concert, conducted by Frank Drye, typified the sort of public relations work always under way by Tuskegee administrators. The Negro band members could not play inside the hall, but the success of "Greater Montgomery Trade Week," particularly the outward appearance of amiable race relations, would ultimately affect black business. So Tuskegee sent their premier music group, who expertly played classics, marches, and spirituals, then paraded down Dexter Avenue and gave a "Tiger Yell" for the local newspaper, the *Montgomery Advertiser.*[21]

Patterson's early October induction ceremony, attended by segregationist Alabama Governor Bibb Graves and educator Mary McLeod-Bethune, increased Ellison's disappointment with Tuskegee. Band members played in the rain during afternoon-long ceremonies and smiled for out-of-town visitors. Patterson took over the president's house, promising to remain within the tradition of Washington, the Founder, and Moton, the Builder; but he went on to recognize the "task of agricultural readjustment" facing the South as cotton markets became less reliable.[22]

The school's attempts to deal with challenges of the marketplace enabled a more vigorous spirit to arise on the campus. Though perhaps uninterested in the plight of Southern agriculture, Ellison became more learned about global politics and socialism, a taboo subject in the South. Tuskegee students like Ellison were introduced to radical politics by way of the Italian invasion of Ethiopia and the worldwide rise of fascism. They even had an effective symbol to rally around. In the fall of 1935, a Tuskegee graduate named Charles Robinson, class of 1920, was named the commander of the emperor Haile Selassie's small Ethiopian air force.

But band duties took precedence over course work and incipient politics, and certainly Ellison did not object to the plums that came his way. On October 19, he happily made the pilgrimage to Soldier Field in Chicago for the annual gridiron battle against Wilberforce. The band members visited the opera while in the city, Ellison's first attendance at such a gala performance.

Ellison would recall from his last year at the school not the opportunity to travel North but a distinctive Tuskegee experience. His career at the Institute mixed intellectual discovery with remedial classroom training. In Ralph Davis's fall semester sociology class, The Negro, Ellison confronted horror in an all-black college: academic justification for racial stereotypes. The class attempted to understand the habitat and conditions of blacks all over the globe and the contact of the African with other races and nationalities. Davis used the prominent sociology text in the field, one that he might have imagined almost too sophisticated for his students, written by former Washington aide de camp Robert Park. Among its other components, Park's central textbook *Introduction to the Science of Sociology* (1921) included a large number of axiomatic pronouncements on the black racial type. Ellison could have anticipated some difficulty with Park's theories had he known that the Chicago sociologist thought Kelly Miller, whom Ellison had heard pontificating pseudo-scientific racial bilge from the Tuskegee podium, to be "the most philosophical of the leaders and teachers of his race."[23] Reading Park's chapter on "Human Nature," Ellison stumbled across the following:

> The temperament of the Negro, as I conceive it, consists in a few elementary but distinctive characteristics, determined by physical organizations and transmitted biologically. These characteristics manifest themselves in a genial, sunny, social disposition, in an interest and attachment to external, physical things rather than to subjective states and objects of introspection, in a disposition for expression rather than enterprise and action.
>
> The result has been that this racial temperament has selected out of the mass of cultural materials to which it had access, such technical, mechanical, and intellectual devices as it needs at a particular period of existence. . . .

Everywhere and always it has been interested rather in expression than in action; interested in life itself rather than its reconstruction or reformation. The Negro is, by natural disposition, neither an intellectual nor an idealist, like the Jew; nor a brooding introspective, like the East Indian; nor a pioneer and a frontiersman, like the Anglo-Saxon. He is primarily an artist, loving life for its own sake. His métier is expression rather than action. He is, so to speak, the lady among the races.[24]

Ellison must have dropped his jaw after he read that sincere thesis of innate black passivity. If Tuskegee's public speeches encouraging an almost childlike obedience had not insulted him enough, Ellison again confronted facile theories describing black behavior and mental inclination. With the imprimatur of the academic community, Davis palmed off the passage without expressing even mild irony.

Ellison resented being slammed into a racial cul-de-sac that predicted his performance and appetites. It insulted him with the same severity as the jibes he had heard about the various pathologies that would befall him as a fatherless son. He had spent his summer seeing himself as the youthful protagonist in Hemingway's essays on sport and American manhood, impressed with the writer's difficult sentences that were deceptively simple in appearance. He could not stomach Park's rambling, unsubstantiated taunt. Angered and greatly disappointed, Ellison left the classroom realizing that he labored in an academic backwater.

Absurd ideas about black nature continued to sift into the classroom. Park had put a limit on black character and had offended Ellison's sense of manliness, a virility already precarious at Booker T.'s Institute. Nearly ten years later, in a skeptical review of Swedish social scientist Gunnar Myrdal's *An American Dilemma,* Ellison would still express dismay at Park's thesis: "Imagine the effect such teachings have had on Negro students alone!"[25] And the *Introduction to the Science of Sociology,* used well into the 1940s, did have a considerable effect on American students. Park's theory of social contact predicted a resolution of racial conflict at the completion of a cycle with five parts: migration, competition, conflict, accommodation, and assimilation. While the sociologist felt that his claims of racial personality were accurate, Park quietly rejected the absolute biological basis for racism and segregation by asserting that human nature was acquired through interaction with others and was not genetically predetermined. His refutation of racial and biological essences did not undermine his general thesis about the evolution of the well-segregated black race. Currently in the stage of accommodation, he said, blacks modified their habits and customs to coincide with the dominant Anglo culture. Park pointed not only to racial harmony in the South as proof of the black desire to ultimately assimilate white mores, but to books like Matthew

G. Lewis's *Journal of a West India Planter* (1834), fully reprinted in Park's book. Park claimed that Jamaican blacks saw whites as gods in the flesh.

Ellison may have been told that Park, a white man, based his conclusions about the Negro on extensive experiences in Macon County, no less. He had spent over seven years in Alabama as an adjunct to Washington and as a Tuskegee instructor. When he left the South, Park was confident in his knowledge of the Negro racial personality. Indeed, Park was so certain of his admission to black inner life and his own thorough adaptation of black Southern mannerisms that he felt himself "for all intents and purposes, for the time, a Negro."[26] Park accepted the historical thesis of the civilizing plantation that offered the African cultivation. Blacks had endured bondage with only minor rebellions because of their docile, carefree racial constitution. Park disregarded any refutation of the theme of black contentment and docility: "the Negro has uniformly shown a disposition to loyalty during slavery to his master and during freedom to the South and the country as a whole." Park saw nothing particularly abhorrent or unique about American chatteldom; it was instead "the usual method by which peoples have been incorporated into alien groups."[27] In Park's theory, the subordinate class agreeably accepted the system of unequal relationships. The mass of Southern blacks had not merely endured but prospered under bondage, an experience transformed into tutelage. In his chapter "Conflict," the third theoretical stage of group interaction, Park suggested: "In the mass the southern Negro has not bothered himself about the ballot for more than twenty years, not since his so-called political leaders have left him alone; he is not disturbed over the matter of separate schools and cars, and he neither knows nor cares anything about 'social equality.'"[28]

If less inclined than their Jamaican cousins to deify whites, Southern blacks harbored neither animosity for previous ill-treatment nor ambitions of upward social mobility. Park had swallowed whole Booker T. Washington's oft-repeated thesis.

Ellison's personal and regional history directly countered Park's ideas. Ida had always told him that his grandfather Alfred Ellison was not just a photograph on the wall, but an active Reconstruction era politician who'd fought a lynch mob in South Carolina.[29] J. D. Randolph, Inman Page, and others Ellison knew well in Oklahoma City had been born into bondage and did not in the least deify whites or easily discard their political rights. Ellison shared the campus with fellow Oklahomans who defied the worn-out stereotype of black passivity, a large number of whom came from Taft (frequently outnumbering Oklahoma City's Tuskegee matriculants), one of the Territory's all-black towns. Taft residents cherished their bold reputation. When segregation laws were put in effect in 1908, resulting in jim crow railroad cars and station waiting rooms, Taft blacks put to the torch the entire Mid-Land Valley station and attacked Lieutenant Governor George W. Bellamy's train.[30] Firm in his sense of origins, Ellison found no core of truth in Park's generalizations, presented as scientifically certified fact.

Still, Park's thousand-page thesis on human group interaction, particularly his arguments about the biological transmission of behavioral qualities, presented a formidable challenge for the twenty-two-year-old student. Beyond suggesting black passivity in the American context, the book offered scientific proof of the indelible African nature of American blacks. To find a metaphor for the permanence of racial characteristics, Park turned to the psychological analysis of Freud. The transmutation of African into Afro-American, Park said, was similar to the wish in dream life. The African cultural memory was the wish (though Park believed that virtually no concrete survivals from African culture existed among American blacks) that became clothed in the customs and traditions native to British colonial society. The two combined to form a cultural mutation whose "inner meaning, sentiment, emphasis, and emotional color" were entirely African, "the Negroes' own."[31] Park's efforts to permanently imprint Africa on the black American probably had a great deal to do with Ellison's ultimate distance from African traditions and customs.[32]

Ellison identified strongly with the New Negro tradition, and had little use for the consistent references to Africa, now a century removed from American Negro life. Nor did he care to have spectacular black achievement summarily excused as aberrant. Park's thesis, which also ventured a critique of black art, would not reward him. In 1913 (after Park had just left the comradeship of Booker T. Washington at Tuskegee), the sociologist had outlined the difficulties of black assimilation. Following the criticism of William Dean Howells, Park celebrated the work of Paul Laurence Dunbar, whose dialect verse presented the black "not as he looks, but as he feels and is." Though he recognized that educated blacks were more often than not scornful of Dunbar's dialect work (as the poet himself was suspicious of fame solely based upon his dialect verse), Park defended dialect poetry, and following that, racial essences, refuting the black elite: "The assumption seems to have been that if they had been written for Negroes it would have been impossible in his poetry to distinguish black people from white. This was sentiment which was never shared by the masses of people."

It would have been unsurprising if the instructor Davis confirmed Park's comments on black art, certain that not many students in his class had any interest, let alone expertise, in literature. Few students at Tuskegee, if any, took the sort of eclectic liberal arts load managed by Ellison in the 1935–1936 academic year—a course load that led to no degree. Whatever the case, Ellison recognized that broad swaths of black life went unaccounted for, and that the black intelligentsia, when not inadequate, had been totally ignored.

Park admitted that the "American white man knows little or nothing about the thought and opinion of the [educated] colored men and women who today largely mold and direct Negro public opinion in this country."[33] But for the sociologist's purposes, ignorance of the black educated class and the Northern and Western migrants, who had "lost the typical habit and attitude of the Negro," was a lacuna that whites could afford. After all, blacks played no significant role in the American nation, but were treated as wards, merely the "peculiar" problem of the South. Ellison knew a great deal of this black educated and striving class in the West and the South. Why had Park ignored their mobility and ambition? For the college junior from Oklahoma, Park's ideas on race were stultifying anachronisms. Ellison remained in the sociology course throughout the year, probably because of Tuskegee's credit system, which penalized students for jumping out of the yearlong course sequences. Ellison responded by learning enough to reject utterly Park's thesis and method, and even the social science tradition in general.

Then there was the question of Ralph Davis. Though in his essays Ellison ultimately exposed Park and American social science for simultaneously easing racial borders while furthering racist assumptions, he saved his special ire for the intellectually sluggish sociology professor.[34] Davis, as a teacher of sociology and anthropology and a former student of the Chicago School, probably took Park's theories as reflecting the order of the day, well in line with Washington's and Moton's public views about black personality and therefore favorable. When providing students (whom he thought of as the "children of the plantations") with paper topics, he likely went with Park's suggestions, such as "Race and Culture, and the Problem of the Relative Superiority and Inferiority of Races." In the American context, as everyone at Tuskegee was reminded by newspaper, radio broadcasts, and book-length treatises, blacks were "[r]elatively" the inferior race. Generally this was not a debate but something ceded; the mere existence of black slavery—the discussion of which educated blacks avoided like pestilence—cemented the public perception of blacks as an inferior race. An older, reserved Southerner, Davis believed in decorum in the classroom and would have been caught off guard by a serious challenge to his position and that of an internationally known textbook.[35]

For Ellison, fashionable in everything from his welt-seamed slacks and two-toned shoes to the modernist poetry he unraveled in the library, Davis's refusal to powerfully debate Park's material turned the professor into an apostate. Over the next thirty years, Ellison reserved more disgust for this classroom confrontation than any other single experience dealing with race. The scoundrel Davis "blandly" spoke such filth, without even the self-respect to "wash his hands, much less his teeth."[36] Davis led Tuskegee students like cows, "away from attitudes of aggression and courage."[37] Ellison's animus for the Tuskegee professor, whose lessons he continued to absorb for the remainder of the school year, suggests an intimidation bordering on revenge. Ellison might have engaged the professor and had his experiences of black self-determination in Oklahoma made to appear insignificant. Unable to obtain satisfaction, for two semesters he slumped in his seat in outrage.

The sociology debacle had broader consequences for Ellison's intellectual growth. He decided that he would approach intellectual issues, literature, and the arts as an individual, regardless of the artist's particular racial bias. Ellison grouped Park with the other manipulative spokespeople he had heard from the podium at Tuskegee, and decided that he would not allow them to determine what fascinated his intellect. His strategy came from the barbershop in Oklahoma City, where the black patrons absolutely demystified the rich and powerful, even John D. Rockefeller. By "abstracting desirable qualities" from the people around, "even enemies," Ellison could embrace the truth achieved in any art. After reading the Hemingway *Esquire* essays in Oklahoma City, he had discovered also the author's collection of short stories *In Our Time*. Refusing to disregard Hemingway's fiction because of unflattering descriptions of black characters (Bugs in "The Battler" had "long nigger legs," and the feminine "low soft voice of the Negro"), Ellison decided to take the "desirable qualities" from the Nick Adams story and identify himself with the protagonist.[38] He had more than cerebral sympathy for the story. Like "The Battler's" hero, Ellison too had experienced violence while hoboing on a freight train. Though the newfangled approach to ideas permitted him to gain something from Park's rather slanted remarks, after the sociology class with Davis, Ellison maintained a serious distrust of sociological studies.

At the time, Ellison found far more truth in Ernest Hemingway's technical ode to the Spanish bullfight, *Death in the Afternoon* (1932), his guidebook to the creative process during the fall of 1935.[39] Ellison's acceptance of Hemingway had to do less with any rebellion against campus wisdom than with the shared themes and life experiences that he found in the writing. Following his disappointment with sociology, he identified with the desire to reject commonly accepted formulas of convention. After so recently being subjected to Park's rehash of racial platitudes, Ellison was deeply influenced by Hemingway's words: "I found the greatest difficulty, aside from knowing truly what you really felt, rather than what you were supposed to feel, and had been taught to feel, was to put down what really happened in action; what the actual things were which produced the emotion that you experienced."[40]

Hemingway's literature of action offered far more scientific truth than the bombast of social science. Literature of action, "if you stated it purely enough," warned Hemingway, guaranteed more accurate depictions of human behavior than the social sciences, because literature was precise, specific, and individual—group representation led to sloppy generalizations. Ellison assimilated Hemingway's criteria piecemeal, in his own "naive fashion," but *Death in the*

Afternoon offered a confluence of narrative style and historical fact that exemplified well the eternal compositional ideal of *showing* instead of *telling*. Robert Park was guilty of *telling*, explaining all the nitty-gritty insider's information about blacks, a technique grossly inaccurate to Ellison because it lacked convincing descriptions *showing* the facts of the matter, as Hemingway, or even Booker T. Washington, had done.[41] With the help of Hemingway, Ellison began to develop a mature code with which to determine literary merit as well as personal integrity. Sociology teacher Davis, whose own technique of "deception and evasion" had crept into his class lectures, could not teach Ellison truth. As a junior at Tuskegee, Ellison came to appreciate writers who were unflinching and candid with their views. The stress Hemingway placed upon truth and integrity made his commitment to art a model, like those of the jazz musicians Ellison had known on Second Street.

Hemingway supported the idea that art was a completely individual pursuit, and he belittled the pupil who fulfilled the duty of his master through obeisance to a particular school of thought. The emphasis on individuality continued to drive the wedge between Ellison and Dawson, with whom the trumpeter unquestionably had an estranged relationship around the winter of 1935. As an example of the growing distance between teacher and pupil, instead of vying for position of first trumpet in the band, Ellison often worked with the percussionists, striking bells and gongs during musical programs.[42] He was moving away from strict regimens imposed by others. Certainly Hemingway's notions of originality and the process of extending the established aesthetic conventions precipitated Ellison's future debates regarding literary influences: "[T]he things, by being imitated, with the original gone, soon distort, lengthen, shorten, weaken and lose all reference to the original. All art is only done by the individual . . . all schools only serve to classify their members as failures."

Hemingway also had a great deal to say about "fakery," which produced any of the various gradations that separated mere writing from art. He trounced formulas and decoration, pushing for sincere, if meticulously stripped-down creations. "A character is a caricature," wrote Hemingway, and he demanded that the artist create "real living people," warts and all.

> Prose is architecture, not interior decoration, and the Baroque is over. For a writer to put his own intellectual musings, which he might sell for a low price as essays, into the mouths of artificially constructed characters which are more remunerative when issued as people in a novel is good economics, perhaps, but does not make literature. People in a novel, not skillfully constructed characters, must be projected from the writer's assimilated experience, from his knowledge, from his head, from his heart and from all there is of him.[43]

Ellison began to read as a writer, with Hemingway's introduction into the issues of craft.

There were other reasons that Ellison found sociological studies perpetuating notions of a mentally timid black personality to be arcane. In December at the beginning of the winter quarter, he heard fellow classical musician Cleveland Eneas and *Campus Digest* editor Major Lightfoote describe the outcome of the Morehouse College and Oxford University debate, which the two had attended in Atlanta. The Morehouse men had held their own against the oldest English-speaking university; and Tuskegee's debate team often defeated Morehouse.[44] Crass platitudes about plantation-era racial generalizations were ridiculous when modern evidence showed that in open competition, race had little to do with performance. The experience in sociology class fed Ellison's ideological break with Tuskegee, assisted by the intellectually remote faculty and the hostile surroundings. He had abandoned the symbolic guardianship of Dawson and now turned his mental efforts to resist parts of his education that more properly seemed straightforward indoctrination.

Ellison's resistance to Tuskegee dogma had sparkling results; he made some of his best marks in the fall of 1935. He submitted impressive work to Sprague and Hamlin and even earned an above-average mark from the excruciating Davis. With a strong quarter under his belt and less censure from Dawson, Ellison's sense of independence soared. His friend Carolyn Walcott, a couple of years his junior, started teaching in the Agriculture Department at the beginning of winter quarter, proving that career opportunities crept out in unlikely, unpredictable places.[45] Carolyn's new status also drove home to him the artificiality of the distinctions between students and professors. Around this time, Ellison began to harbor a new dream of venturing forth; even though he was not technically a member of the middle-class elite like Carolyn, perhaps he could make his way in one of the large Northern cities proclaimed for their racially modern lifestyles. Who knew, maybe he could even wind up in the cultural stratosphere of New York City.

Winter quarter at the Institute began early on Monday, December 2, 1935. Ellison still participated in Music School events and led the halftime student band at the Tuskegee Bowl during football games, but he kept up his eclectic course work, substituting the required Music School course in acoustics for another art class with Hamlin that winter. The class in acoustics may have been Ellison's way of not completely breaking with the Music School, but obviously the rift showed no signs of closing. Hazel Harrison's numerous nearly monthlong absences also contributed to Ellison's evolution toward literary pursuits. Sprague's winter class, English 408, worked through nineteenth century British literature including the Brontës, Stevenson, Eliot, Meredith, Hardy, Conrad, Galsworthy, Wells, and Bennett. Davis's sociology class, The Negro in America, analyzed and interpreted the problems of slavery and freedom and studied black and white relations from the viewpoint of isolation and social contact.[46] Dawson, who had never been accessible to Ellison, fretted over the eclipse of his own fame. William Grant Still's *Afro-American Symphony,* published in 1931, was performed at Carnegie Hall in New York that December.[47]

Ellison firmly made a shift in mentors and now almost exclusively sought the advice of Professor Sprague. Though not an intensely intellectual professor, Mort Sprague was compelling to students with his warmth and unassuming intelligence. For students at Tuskegee during the 1930s, Sprague combined all the heroic qualities of art and the humanities. Disdaining pretension in favor of intellectual honesty, Mort Sprague was open and comfortable with students, who in turn respected him as the new breed of professional academic. Ellison wasn't the only one who noticed the tranquil Sprague's magnificent abilities. Freshman Albert Murray gravitated immediately toward the English professor, as Murray intellectually tiptoed after Ellison's wanderings through the Hollis Frissell Library. Finding Ellison's name in all the top-rank literature in the library, Murray was inspired by the upperclassman who included Isak Dinesen, Edna St. Vincent Millay, Ezra Pound, Robinson Jeffers, and Francis Thompson among his literary explorations.[48]

During a career in the U.S. Air Force, Murray would teach English at Tuskegee in the 1940s and 1950s; and he would go on to become a superior writer and critic, publishing books on American culture, the blues and jazz, and several novels. As Sprague's colleague, he would introduce his former teacher to the latest developments in the novel and poetry.[49] While still a Tuskegee student, Al Murray connected Sprague's manner and dress to those of such internationally known intellectuals as André Malraux. Sprague erected standards of scholarship similar to Hazel Harrison's—and what was most exciting, not because he advocated cultural assimilation. In his memoir *South to a Very Old Place,* Murray remembered Sprague's creed of academically challenging the students "not because he wanted you to become a carbon copy of any white man who ever lived, not excepting Shakespeare or even Leonardo da Vinci. But because to him you were the very special vehicle through which contemporary man, and not just contemporary black man either, would inherit the experiences of all decipherable time."[50]

Ellison's active literary and artistic pursuits fit in well with his increasing sense of himself as a man of consequence. As was his custom, Ellison spent most of the Christmas break of 1935 at parties around the VA Hospital and in the suburban homes of its staff. With its broad range of talented black doctors and professionals from all over the country, the black bourgeois stronghold of Greenwood was an oasis for an artistically sensible young man like Ellison. Tuskegee students considered it a great honor to receive an invitation to the home of one of the local doctors or administrators. Ellison enjoyed the society of young people who had had the opportunity to attend prestigious preparatory schools like Phillips Academy at Andover. Beyond their well-bred and urbane tastes, the upper-middle-class black youth had access to automobiles, an unprecedented privilege. Borrowing a parent's car, the boys could make their way to the local bootlegger or to the Lion's Mouth juke joint, the arena of Pete Adams, local badman.[51] But not all of Ellison's energy went toward attempting to satisfy young adult curiosity in drink and sex. He particularly enjoyed the connections with the well-read young people, like Cornell graduate student George Carver Campbell—an opportunity to discuss the fine arts, literature, and politics.

Literature seemed to extend the ever deepening chasm between Ellison and the Music School. A few weeks after being moved by the emotional desolation of *Wuthering Heights,* perhaps in mid-January, Ellison read Thomas Hardy's *Jude the Obscure,* a book that had significant and enduring meaning for him. In Hardy's dismal and pathetic tale of a young orphan's unfulfilled search for a grail of intellectual advancement, moral rectitude, and spiritual altruism, Ellison would find echoes of his own life experiences. Misunderstood by his family and cut off from their experiences by a roiling consciousness and sense of individual purpose, Ellison plainly related to the sympathetic portrayal of Jude Fawley's isolation. And Hardy, a writer with indelible working-class roots, wrote with superior craftsmanship, honed not in the anointed halls of Oxford (Jude's "Christminster"), but by candlelight in a dank room, after a hard day of toil.

Ellison sympathized with Jude's strong desire to pursue an intellectually challenging education at Christminster; it was akin to his own wishes, and some of his friends', to study at Juilliard or Harvard. He had embraced individual advancement, and like Jude, had begun to come to grips with the disillusionment confronting even the most principled individual in the face of the grinding modern industrial world. Hardy's book broadened his perspective on the limitations of Southern life; class played as important a factor as race. The metaphor of invisibility, central to Ellison's vision of race and consciousness in the twentieth century, found elementary voice in Hardy's classic description of the hero Jude Fawley and the young men he wished to join at the college:

> [The college students saw] a young workman in a white blouse, and with stone-dust in the creases of his clothes; and in passing him they did not even see him or hear him, rather saw through him as through a pane of glass at their familiars beyond. Whatever they were to him, he to them was not on the spot at all; and yet he had fancied he would be close to their lives by coming there.[52]

Though Ellison dressed the part of the college student, in contrast to members of the black educated class who attended Howard, Fisk, and a handful of liberal white colleges, he noticed, sharply perhaps, the dust in the creases of his own working-class origins. Ellison was never confused about the identity of the real black elite at Tuskegee. Tuskegee students who appeared prosperous were in one sphere, students whose parents worked as doctors at the VA Hospital and who attended the more prestigious Northern universities inhabited another. Ellison "suffered" while reading the book.[53]

His most significant literary discovery of 1935 was T. S. Eliot's "The Waste Land." If *Jude the Obscure* had been a moving, introspective, sentimental, and intellectually engaging look in the mirror for bandleader Ellison, "The Waste Land" shattered the reflective glass. The poem by Eliot reoriented the waffling trumpeter's perspective away from the world of music and toward literary composition. Ellison veered diffidently toward "the real transition to writing," though Eliot's work seemed a sweet release from music more than a career path. Within weeks of reading it, Ellison began to write his own free verse, his first creative work since high school, hiding his attempts in books of poetry and fiction safely stacked along the walls in Hollis Frissell, where he had succumbed to the poem.[54]

After his discovery, he went to Sprague. The English Department chairman maintained his excitement in Ellison's ardent and unconventional interest. Though in composition class he hadn't allowed Ellison's disarming smile and polite manners to get in the way of giving him average marks, as an instructor he continued to be fair and honest. No, he hadn't read the mystifying poem, but he certainly knew of journals and digests that published critiques of the work.[55]

Ellison was emotionally ripe for transformation at the hands of Eliot's masterpiece. He had suffered Dawson's temper and later his success; he no longer could fuel himself with the ambition of being the first to write a symphony combining major black folk materials. But literature was a completely wide-open game. After taking in the far-ranging and engrossing poem, Ellison immediately recognized the absence of anything comparable by a modern black poet. He knew of no black literary tradition bold enough to engage unflinchingly all of the complex American heritage: white and black, European and African, elite and vernacular, classical and blues-rooted. "The Waste Land," with its ability to "seize [my] mind," upset the presumptuous order of things.[56]

Eliot's poem had unusual resonance for the young student, who'd been postponing his literary interests since he was a small boy in Oklahoma City. Ellison enjoyed the challenge of the poem's difficulty and its eeriness, the foreboding quality of the line, "I will show you fear in a handful of dust." Importantly for Ellison, the poem combined qualities of jazz and the classics, which for the black Victorians had been unbroachable dichotomies. Though marked by a sophisticated tone and furiously intellectual references, the poem also beckoned toward the raucous and jagged vernacular. Thematically "The

Waste Land" played with schemes of condescension and superiority, hierarchy and order, only to dispose of them, puzzling the trumpeter, who could not "reduce [it] to a logical system."[57] The modern style of the poem also constituted a complete break from the English Romantic poets like Wordsworth and Tennyson, and America's Victorian, Longfellow, all popular at Tuskegee. Eliot used a jazzlike method of snatching phrases from popular and classical literature, and then inserting them into unexpected places. The poem's improvisational rhythms varied and swung like Oklahoma stomp music, with a range of allusion as broad as that employed by Louis Armstrong himself.[58]

Eliot also treated modern urban and industrial themes, so he seemed in obvious dialogue with blues singers who borrowed their rhythm from the steam locomotive, and jazz players who eloquently rendered the bustle and delight of fast-paced urban life. Louis Armstrong's popular "St. James Infirmary," a lament to the sporting life, combined the bittersweet elements of the blues life, mourning death and syphilis, with a celebration of straight-laced shoes, twenty-dollar gold pieces, and sexual abandon. Ellison probably would have connected that popular melody with Eliot's own representation of the modern plight in furtive, unfulfilling sexual relationships in industrial England. The poem even had a fleeting allusion to Armstrong's "China Moon"; the references to Armstrong and also to Cole Porter unequivocally reflected Eliot's iconoclasm. And the up-front representation of abortion made Ellison feel that the poet dealt with problems facing the modern generation. The academically tough poem also provided Ellison with another angle for entrance into middle-class society, a sort of Sunday-suit that advertised intellectual rigor.[59] Unaided, he had discovered a work of art eminently valuable—artwork unknown to his middle-class Tuskegee professor.

With a prodigious expenditure of energy, Ellison stepped up his reading in order to nail down the poem's meaning. He looked up Eliot's seven pages of references, with Sprague's collegial advice informing his search, and began to unpack the layers of the poem. The explanatory footnotes juxtaposed the art of poetry more concretely with the art of music. Poetry, too, required a conscious act of creation and responded to a traditional body of work that had appeared before it. In short order, the library explorations took him into the new territories of geography and anthropology. Ellison began with Jessie Wetson's *From Ritual to Romance,* Eliot's recommended sourcebook, to "elucidate the difficulties of the poem."[60] Wetson revealed the Arthurian legend and fisher king myths directly behind Eliot's poem. George Frazer's multivolumed *The Golden Bough* provided him with an overview of human ritual and culture. Ellison revived his dusty Latin skills, drilled into him at Douglass, in order to understand a generous Ovid quote that Eliot had found indispensable; and he made use of the smattering of French that he'd learned in the fall. The exhausting research netted him intimacy with many of the major canonical Western classics not staples in the Tuskegee curriculum, such as Virgil, Ovid, Saint Augustine, Dante, Spenser, Milton, and Shakespeare. In the weeks following this historical education in literature and anthropology, he came to the works of Ford Madox Ford, Sherwood Anderson, and Gertrude Stein, and more Hemingway. Ellison, who in later years would humbly call himself "a very poor English student," had begun his "conscious education in literature."[61]

After Ellison had explored the poem's literary references, Sprague introduced his enthusiastic friend to contemporary literary criticism. Ellison learned where to find the critical efforts of Harriet Monroe, Babette Deutsch, Ezra Pound, and perhaps most important, Edmund Wilson.[62] Wilson's *Axel's Castle* (1931) provided Ellison with a chic analysis of the latest literary trends and the origins of the major literary schools. Before him were the influences and literary agendas of the most powerful living writers: not only Eliot, but W. B. Yeats, James Joyce, Gertrude Stein, and Paul Valéry. Having been encouraged to look at black writers like Douglass, Washington, and Du Bois since his earliest years in school, Ellison felt challenged and rewarded with the concerns of the European moderns. A musician who had mastered the classics and jazz, he appreciated brave writers tackling the status of human civilization and creating a new idiom for expression. Black writers confined to the generations-old concern of proving the humanity of "the race" radiated decay.

Wilson provided a reader as schematically innocent as Ellison with a framework to view post-Renaissance Western literature in terms of schools and groups. The debates over objectivity and subjectivity, scientific precision, and the power of the individual had been raging since the sixteenth century. The scientific theories of Darwin and the literary imagination of Zola produced Naturalism in letters, which was displaced at the hands of what Wilson called the "second reaction," Symbolism, led by the Frenchman Stéphane Mallarmé. Symbolists attempted to "intimate things rather than state them plainly." The Symbolist writers' artistic code called for "a complicated association of ideas represented by a medley of metaphors to communicate unique personal feelings."[63] As a musician, Ellison expected art to operate in the range of emotion and sensual enjoyment; he enjoyed learning about literature's conscious strategy to produce feeling in a reader.

Wilson continued to stress the musical nature of "The Waste Land"; Eliot had "brought a new personal rhythm into language." Ellison also learned that the music had an overriding influence on poetic development; Wagner's contribution to shaping the course of Symbolism "was as important as that of any poet."[64]

Babette Deutsch's new collection of essays, *This Modern Poetry* (1935), similarly reinforced the notion of the centrality of music to the poem: "Here the idea that the abuse of love has meant the denial of life is treated as a musician might handle it, although perhaps never as directly. It is implied rather than stated, but the suggested idea is introduced, counterpointed, repeated, complicated, transposed and developed with musicianly skill and symphonic effect."[65]

Deutsch translated Eliot's technical marvel into familiar language for Ellison. This sort of analysis of Eliot's project inspired Ellison and enabled him to make sympathetic connections between the realms of literature and his own course of study. Bridging the two camps of music and prose would not necessarily be an impossible task. The Symbolist code penetrated the depths of Ellison's artistic sensibility, fixing him permanently with the work of the era's high modernist authors.

For Ellison, the primacy of colloquial speech in the poem represented another considerable achievement of the new verse style, not only further displacing the kind of perfect couplets typical of Paul Laurence Dunbar (held in esteem at Tuskegee) but also enabling the vernacular language to reach the highest levels of European cultural sophistication. It was similar to the labors of the black jazz musician, creating work from a landscape that was underrepresented on the international scene. Seeing it laid out in such clear terms, Ellison thought it slightly odd that a Symbolist-inspired approach had not been taken to black American culture, incorporating the contributions of black music or using characters from the fullest range of black social life. Was there no Dawson lurking in African American poetry or fiction?

With a new understanding concerning the academic technique required to compose a poem, Ellison thoroughly ravished the library. He quickly outshot the depth of his class. Sprague and fellow students like Trementia Birth and Letitia Woods skirmished with him in the classroom over the merits of particular works, but he accomplished most of his literary exploration in solitude. Sprague taught a demanding load, and the other advanced students were seniors, preoccupied with graduation and beyond. For Ellison, a new world had opened its doors, and there was a proverbial closure of sorts in his "round about until we come" route back to the literary course his father had envisioned. For the time being, he was on a hiatus from the real work of music. The literary campaign required little effort, "because it involved no deadlines or credits," occurring outside of the inspection of Dawson.[66]

Ellison's intellectual growth in isolation obviously had benefits and drawbacks. His literary explorations were fun compared with the intense scrutiny he encountered in the Music School. Even though gained vicariously through literature and not through a grand tour of Europe, the innermost knowledge of elite American and British culture and taste provided an avenue to move head and shoulders above even the most pretentious of the black elite. But the isolation from other students allowed Ellison to nearly fetishize individual accomplishment and ignore how racism shaped broader group dynamics. If the entire student body had suddenly decided to use the library, the eclectic and ample book supply, a blessing to Ellison, would have been easily exhausted. Rigid campus discipline also defeated intellectual curiosity among the student body. Tuskegee's elaborate system of campus rules monitoring student behavior, a system with the very practical purpose of preventing the lynching and sexual assault of Tuskegeeans, contributed to the tepid scholastic atmosphere. Clear-cut physical and material boundaries took precedence over abstract and philosophical ones. Students experienced more physical freedom when they ambled across the street to the restricted "Block," or downtown to the flat-out dangerous town square to visit the Macon Theater, than they did by plucking books from the stacks of Hollis Frissell. Social isolation contributed to Ellison's impatience with others incapable of or uninterested in dwelling in a theoretical and almost esoteric plane. Tolerant only of comrades committed to colossal literary adventures, Ellison became a little more haughty.

For most of Tuskegee, the winter of 1936 did not bring vigorous exploration of the Western canon, but rather signaled the beginning of another year of fund-raising. While Tuskegee students remained more familiar with Dunbar than with any other black poet (Longfellow was the most popular poet overall), they were perhaps even more familiar with the white philanthropist who endowed their school.[67] Certainly the philanthropist received greater attention. In a February Chapel talk, President Patterson praised the contributions of Julius Rosenwald, a Zeus-like figure in the erection of black schools in the South. Rosenwald's $30 million fund was the bedrock of charitable gifts for rural schools, though Patterson stressed Washington's hand in the creation and distribution of the fund. But in times of economic uncertainty, appeals to philanthropists enabled Tuskegee's survival, even if only by way of invoking their names and deeds in Chapel. Though Patterson's talk was accurate enough, as Ellison learned more about racial interaction and the economic purposes of slavery, his opinions about industrialists' gifts would become ambivalent. With a waggish upperclassman's sense that the Chapel exercise was just a charade, Ellison longed for a message of courage from the school's president, particularly in the weeks following Davis's humiliating failure in the sociology class. Patterson did not quite come through: "We are grateful for Julius Rosenwald and we are thankful that our Founder, Booker T. Washington, had the rare vision to point out to him a manner in which he might so wisely administer his beneficence."[68]

For Ellison, Patterson's rhetorical stroking wore thin. He was purportedly one of the brightest and most influential black leaders of the era, but Ellison felt the Tuskegee president needed to move in a more assertive manner, less removed from the tumultuous international political scene that called into question the economic framework of the entire country.

With his thoughts on the future, Ellison continued his wide reading. Course work continued to go well, and by the end of his examinations in early March 1936, Ellison had finally earned himself a place on the dean's list.

Meanwhile, the music department had begun to fray. During finals on the first Friday in March, President Patterson and William Dawson tried to assuage the increasing dissatisfaction of the band members at Tuskegee.[69] The backbone of Tuskegee's entertainment for visitors, and consequently an integral link in the philanthropic chain, band members were very much campus employees, though entirely unpaid. Considering their demanding public schedule, they had little time to adequately prepare for classes and work other campus jobs. Patterson and Dawson attended the Friday afternoon rehearsal in the band cottage to entertain questions. As student band conductor, Ellison likely headed these negotiations between administration and students, if the afternoon pep talk could be viewed as a meeting where two parties would present grievances and hammer out differences. It seems likely that Ellison, a leader in the student band who had already bucked the Music School curriculum, was on course for a falling-out with Tuskegee's important administrators.

On Monday, March 9, 1936, Ellison began what would be his last quarter as a Tuskegee student, a week after his twenty-third birthday. Uninfluenced by whatever may have occurred in the band cottage or in Dawson's office, he signed up for another Hamlin art class, mainly watercolors and oil painting. Sprague's course that spring would discuss American and modern writers, including Cooper, Melville, Hawthorne, James, Twain, Howells, Wharton, Dreiser, and "as many others as time permits."[70] Ellison's other courses reflected his increasing interest in the American Negro. Davis's sociology class, The Race Problem, dealt specifically with conflict and adjustment between whites and Negroes. To top off the platter, Ellison took another class with Alva Hudson, this one on black education in the United States, Negro Education.

As if Eliot's work on the infertility of spring and Hemingway's celebration of killing had been some sort of harbinger, Ellison had to deal with the mortality of the young in its most devastating manifestation during the spring of 1936. His friend George Campbell, the son of a doctor from the VA Hospital, died of acute appendicitis. Campbell had been a graduate student at Cornell University, in his first year of the engineering program.[71] Ellison was genuinely hurt, and the rumors flew that a local white hospital had refused admission to a deathly ill Campbell, allowing his inflamed appendix to kill him.[72] The loss was a dear one for a tightly knit community who had little to celebrate, but who prided themselves on one as successful as Campbell. Ellison turned his morose feelings into verse, publishing his first poem in the *Campus Digest*. In his lines "Death is nothing,/ Life is nothing,/How beautiful these two nothings!"[73] he philosophically attempted to come to grips with mortality through an ambivalent and ironic Eliot-like narrator. He shunned a realist description of the jim crow policy that may have consigned Campbell to the grave.

Despite his grief at the loss of a friend and his growing disenchantment with the Music School, one surprise during the beginning of spring quarter gave him reason for cheer. In the same year that Ellison was sharply refocusing his perspective toward literature, he met perhaps the leading black critic of his era, Alain Locke. Locke, head of the philosophy department at Howard University and a former teacher of Sprague's, visited Hazel Harrison in March at Tuskegee. In an afternoon, Locke, Harrison, and a group of students discoursed on the latest trends in literature and art, particularly Locke's passion for opera singer Marian Anderson and the excellence of the world-famous Negro tenor, Roland Hayes.[74] Ellison enjoyed the slim, well-dressed, gentle professor, the shepherd to Harlem writers of the 1920s. Locke, who had just published his yearly review for *Opportunity,* exhibited an intellectual poise that was totally unique. Though Locke was not a spectacular writer himself, Ellison recognized that the Howard professor was Duke Ellington's equivalent in the classroom and conspicuously aware of the latest literary developments.

Locke warmed immediately to any conversation about modern black writing. That January, he had written in *Opportunity* that black literature for 1935 embraced "a protestant and belligerent universalism of social analysis and protest." This movement away from the Harlem Renaissance's cries of black beauty and local color toward "the literature of class protest and proletarian realism" indicated growth, though Locke predicted that "the approaching proletarian phase is not the hoped-for sea but the inescapable delta." Black writers were advancing with realism, but still had miles to go before reaching "the oceanic depths of universal art." Locke reinforced Ellison's disappointment with black poets, who instead of picking up Eliot's challenge, did not seem to notice that epoch-changing modernist poetry such as "The Waste Land" had surfaced. Locke thought black poetry that year unremarkable. Neither James Weldon Johnson nor Countee Cullen, the two prominent blacks publishing verse in 1935, had kept pace with their genre's latest developments. Drama, too, had not reached full development, and Ellison internalized Locke's critique of the cycles of black expression from renaissance to realism—"skill without courage, or courage without skill." In tweed coat and black-and-white shoes, and talking about his latest library discoveries—Eliot and Edmund Wilson—Ellison impressed the elder statesman of black letters. Locke's cry that spring inspired a new mission for younger black artists—to undertake "the most desired of all desirables—indigenous criticism on the part of the creative and articulate Negro himself."[75] Prone to mount an "academic high horse" when dealing with black audiences, Locke sensed enough potential in Ellison to remember his face. The older man, disturbed at the paucity of "very necessary soberness which so far as I can see alone makes truth-speaking possible," may have found in Ellison the "sober" black student.[76]

Invigorated with a taste of a cosmopolis beyond Alabama, Ellison donned his musician's costume to play in the band for the spring school functions. On Saturday, April 5, Dr. Emmet J. Scott of Howard University came to Tuskegee to deliver the Founder's Day address. Scott had served as Washington's personal secretary while the Wizard steered black America, and had also held a post in the Department of the Interior under President Wilson. As usual, the Music School played a central role in the elaborate Founder's Day exercise, witnessed by a "monster crowd," the *Messenger* recorded. Scott spoke of his personal relationship with the great man as they built Tuskegee in the late 1890s. His talk included a self-ascribed who's who of philanthropy in America. By the end of his tenure in Alabama, Ellison would be able to recite the names of several powerful white Americans who had committed themselves to black higher education, often in the face of adversity. But Scott's rigid path of gradualism and deference to white authority and power seemed somehow antique. Modern literature, particularly Hemingway and Eliot, had given Ellison new tools to dismantle the strictures not only of Tuskegee, but of Western civilization. As Ellison matured intellectually, he began to realize that his fight for peace of mind and quality of life, though greatly affected by race, were impinged upon principally by his status as a human being, struggling in the modern world.

The evening following the address, the orchestra and choir rendered superbly Samuel Coleridge-Taylor's *Hiawatha's Wedding Feast,* "devoid of all amateur aspects," the campus newspaper decided.[77] Having to perform that Sunday afternoon on the White Hall lawn gnawed at Ellison, as Patterson and his cronies hosted and entertained the dignitaries, sparing no expense. Throughout his years at Tuskegee, he'd always struggled to pay his university bill. He had only to recall his freshman year when he had been allowed to register only as a part-term student because of his penury. Scott symbolized the old-school system, uncritical and obsequious. Distraught over his dire need for credits to pull off a miracle and get his degree by the spring of 1937, Ellison was more interested in earning money to pay his fees than in blowing for dignitaries. Ellison witnessed the efficient marketing of black culture by Tuskegee officials. During prearranged parts of the program, the audience was led in spirituals. He could see that the black power brokers made a big deal out of the race game, while squeezing nickels and dimes out of students to live well.

Almost two weeks later, nearing examination time, Ellison enjoyed a lecture given by Professor Sprague at the local YMCA. Interested in stimulating black playwrights, in February Sprague had chaired a committee of black professors at the College English Teachers Conference (an offshoot of the then segregated Modern Language Association); and earlier in the month, on April 3, Tuskegee had hosted the Dillard University Players, who presented Randolph Edmonds's radical drama *Nat Turner*. Sprague's YMCA lecture was on theater and the Negro, in which he recommended Paul Green and Eugene O'Neill for their competent artistic representations of black life. Having returned from a trip to New Orleans with the Tuskegee drama club and responding to Willis Richardson's recently published book *Negro History in Thirteen Plays* (1935), the English department chair continued to champion the theme of racial greatness through the arts, especially literature and drama. "The Drama represents the highest development in literature of a people. The greatest plays are written during the greatest periods in the history of a people."[78] The necessary reference to Richardson and his circle of Washington, D.C., playwrights reinforced Ellison's opinions about Sprague's openness to new ideas and his position as something of the campus dissident.

A lecture praising Richardson's new collection was not for the faint of heart. The radical cultural nationalist historian Carter G. Woodson, dismissed from Howard University in 1922 for refusing to apologize to the school's white president J. Stanley Durkee for his opinions regarding the necessity of teaching black history courses, had written an unflinching introduction to Richardson's book.[79] Woodson thought *Negro History in Thirteen Plays* both salient and imperative because of the miserable artistic climate— "few worth while plays on stage." Without a "new stimulus from the proper source," the stage would become "the worst sort of evil."[80] Richardson was the ideological protégé of Professor Woodson, whose book *Miseducation of the Negro* (1933) had already scathingly exposed the intellectual and political backwardness of the black educated class in the United States. Consequently, *Negro History in Thirteen Plays* openly defied the narrow historical narratives that had been allowed blacks in the South, comprising plays that depicted such courageous and heroic blacks as the Cuban Antonio Maceo, Crispus Attucks, the Abyssinian Emperor Menelek, Nat Turner, Frederick Douglass, Harriet Tubman, and Sojourner Truth. Booker T. Washington's efforts went unrepresented. In the conclusion of his lecture, Sprague also alerted students to the recently developed Federal Works Progress Administration and its efforts to cultivate black actors and artists.[81] This information would have made a trip to Washington, D.C., or New York City, where the WPA had an extensive program, especially attractive to Ellison, recoiling from the intellectual solitude and petty bureaucrats of Macon County.

Ellison earned his best marks at Tuskegee in the spring of 1936, achieving excellence in nearly every class except sociology. Commencement exercises began on Sunday, May 24, requiring the customary parade led by the band, then an afternoon concert, concluding with a Chapel concert at evening Vespers.

Seniors took their degrees on Thursday the twenty-eighth. After an excellent academic term, Ellison perhaps thought that he might reestablish a rapport with Dawson. He spent several weeks in Alabama attempting to straighten out his course plans, degree schedule, and funding for the next term. Then in a burst of inspiration, he decided to follow Eva Hamlin's advice about studying sculpture for the summer with Augusta Savage in Harlem. He thought he could earn enough money as a porter on the Hudson River summer cruises to pay for his tuition in the fall, without Music School support. He would not return to Tuskegee for the better part of two decades.

7

One-Winged Flying

1936–1938

O N JULY 4, 1936, Ellison arrived in New York City hoping to earn enough to pay for fall tuition.[1] He collected his bags after a fatiguing bus ride from Alabama and stepped into the heat wave that gripped New York the week of his arrival. From the Dixie Terminal on West Forty-second Street, he made his way over to Times Square and the subway, and followed the route to the "Negro Mecca" described by Mike Rabb, who had worked on the Hudson River excursion cruises during his summers away from Tuskegee. The Lenox Avenue underground train whisked him uptown to the barely three-year-old Harlem YMCA at 180 135th Street, a short walk up the block in the direction of Seventh Avenue.

Ellison took in all the stature and glamour of the world's modern Negro metropolis. Besides being the home to the elite of entertainers, athletes, artists, and writers—many of whom held apartments at 409 Edgecombe, the citadel of black urban living—Harlem boasted black institutions and businesses, art galleries and literary salons, libraries and world-famous nightclubs. In Harlem, black people had first-class establishments: the Theresa Hotel, a brand new branch of the YMCA, Mt. Morris Park, and the Apollo Theater. Along the magnificent boulevards of Lenox and Seventh Avenues between 125th and 145th Streets, black American splendor ran riot in the colorful Sunday afternoon parades of churchgoers in their finery. Black newcomers moved into a geography fully captured by Claude McKay in his 1940 book, *Harlem: Negro Metropolis:*

> [Harlem] stretches from Morningside Avenue to Lexington and sweeping
> up 110th Street and skirting the Harlem River, it abruptly takes the hill and

extends to 164th Street. Then coming down Amsterdam Avenue, it embraces Convent Avenue to 141st Street and turns off, dropping down under the high terrace of the College of the City of New York. It follows the margin of Harlem-under-the-hill up to 129th Street. Then it strikes out among white houses and almost seems lost. But hard by the Lincoln school fronting the park at 123rd Street it captures Morningside Avenue and runs down under Columbia University Heights to 110th Street.[2]

It was not long however, before Ellison noticed the things that did not make front page news in the black press. Harlem in the summer of 1936 was coming to grips with its own destiny. It had been struck a damaging blow by the Depression and escalating racial tensions, evidenced by the still visible signs of the full-scale riot that had ravaged 135th Street the summer before. The former Arcadia of black migrants' hopes showed signs of despair. But none of the uneasy harbingers checked the steady migration of Southern blacks, propelled there by the devastated economy.

Harlem had one of the most dense concentrations of blacks anywhere in the world, and the numbers were still growing. A soft real estate market in 1904 and the work of realtor Philip A. Payton Jr. and the Afro-American Realty Company had opened up apartments to black tenants at 134th Street and 5th Avenue.[3] Black New Yorkers came to Harlem directly from the San Juan Hill and the Tenderloin districts in midtown Manhattan beginning at the turn of the century; but after World War I the flood of Southern-born and -reared blacks began in earnest, quickly expanding the neighborhood's boundaries. When black churches relocated to the northern reaches of Manhattan and the masses of postwar black migrants began to populate their pews, whites abandoned the community. Racial antipathy and avarice sealed the fate of America's most famous black neighborhood. With few other places available on the island to live, black Harlemites paid twice the rent of other New Yorkers. Families took to basement apartments, dungeons without windows. Black migrants coped with cracked cement floors and stone walls in order to have a roof over their heads. They slept in shifts on "hot" beds, used cans for toilets, and shared apartments with several families.[4] By the mid-1930s, the Harlem dream was losing its luster.

Ellison had left Tuskegee not for squalor, but for summertime adventure. Most spectacular to the musician was Harlem's saving grace, its still viable music scene—it was yet the dance music capital of the modern world, replete with famous ballrooms like the Savoy, and bands and composers whose sensual worldview represented a stark contrast to the neo-Puritanism Ellison had encountered at Tuskegee. But the most tangible difference from Tuskegee were the wild antics and exhortations of the soapbox orators manning the street corners. Spouting theatrical speeches covering everything from politics to religion, the soapbox shouters commanded attention. Most of them would have been jailed for declaring their views in Alabama—or taken to the mental hospital. Old-school Garveyites roamed the corner of 117th Street, but farther uptown, Carlos Cooks's hard-line black nationalists, called the "Black Shirts," held forth. Ellison was impressed, if not overwhelmed, by the strident, unapologetic militancy of their political speeches, the opposite of the public accommodationist strategies of the blacks he knew in Alabama. But militant vigor could not solve the problems facing the race. Within days, Ellison learned the Harlemites' favorite self-effacing dictum, which reflected the outlook of the fast-growing ghetto: "Harlem is nowhere," he heard.[5] For him to make the most of the summer, he would have to venture downtown. Manhattan beckoned as a place of romantic discovery, the summit of art and culture and the place of epic transformation for a young student from a Southern college. Ellison thought of New York as having the refinement and cultivation of Paris. Harlem was his Left Bank.

On his second day in Harlem, Ellison walked from the Annex, where he had his rooms, across the street to the YMCA's main building. In the lobby, he recognized Alain Locke, whom he'd warmed to in an afternoon at Tuskegee that spring. Locke was chatting with another man. No longer bound by the rigid hierarchies of Tuskegee, Ellison ambled over to the two men and introduced himself. Locke remembered him and welcomed him into the conversation with the other man, who turned out to be Langston Hughes.[6] Ironically, Locke had run into Hughes on his way to the YMCA for breakfast, after having chosen his room location specifically to avoid Hughes.[7] Locke was not openly discourteous to Hughes—the men still exchanged letters—but he felt Hughes's talent was shallow and artificial; given the opportunity, he tried to put the artist in his place. He may have allowed Ellison to enter the conversation as a means of quiet escape from an artist he found irresponsible with his gifts. Hughes gravitated to Ellison, whose combination of intelligence, genteel manners, and Southwestern drawl charmed both of the older men.

When Locke left the two men, Ellison launched straight into a discussion with Hughes on modern poetry and music, quietly dazzling the poet laureate of the Negro race. Ellison told him of all the heavyweight poetry that he had read, including "The Waste Land." He also indicated that he knew poetry criticism such as Babette Deutsch's *This Modern Poetry*. Hughes had served with Deutsch on a literary panel that spring.

In the brief encounter, Ellison impressed Hughes immensely. Educated blacks, particularly those excited about Eliot's "Waste Land," were few. Hughes told the college junior that he was working hard on plays (his *Mulatto* was at the Vanderbilt Theater) as well as music. The two men also had something in common: Hughes was preparing to leave New York for Cleveland, where his mother was ill, and Ellison's immediate family also planned to relocate to Ohio. Ellison appreciated Hughes's easygoing familiarity; the older man welcomed him as something of an intellectual peer. The well-traveled Hughes seems to have peered through Ellison's polished demeanor and recognized that his new friend from Oklahoma needed guidance in the huge city. And as they continued talking, Hughes sensed that the intellectually eager Ellison was ripe for political reorientation, and broached the topics of Marxism and communism. He found that while modernist in his aesthetic sensibility, Ellison had little exposure to socialist-influenced prose and verse. Hughes suggested that he read the British socialist poet Cecil Day Lewis, whose book he happened to have with him.

Ellison told Hughes that he had come to New York for a summer of enrichment. His art professor Eva Hamlin had written him an introductory letter to Augusta Savage. In an act of friendship, perhaps typical of the socialist climate as well as the heightened camaraderie among blacks following the Scottsboro case, Hughes offered to become an advocate for Ellison. To begin with, he offered alternatives to Savage and her well-known Harlem Community Art Center on 125th Street. If Ellison was really an intellectual, as his conversation indicated, he needed to know about the astounding Charles Seifert and his Ethiopian Art School at 313 West 137th Street, where Romare Bearden, Earl Sweeting, Robert Savion Pious, and other exciting young artists learned about African history and culture. Hughes could also recommend Charles Alston's WPA-sponsored showing room, where the debates were more intellectual, and where the young painter Jacob Lawrence flourished.[8] But Hughes went further than conversation. He either wrote out an introductory note on the spot, or agreed to telephone Richmond Barthé, a younger but well-known black sculptor. He assured Ellison that Barthé surpassed Augusta Savage in "anatomical truthfulness" and in his modernist sensibility. Hughes offered to continue their relationship on more formal terms; Ellison would become his occasional secretary. His first assignment would be to mail to Louise Thompson wrapped copies of André Malraux's *Man's Fate* and the recently published *Days of Wrath*.[9] When their conversation ended, Ellison left, spilling over with thoughts and ideas, trying to remember street names and places. Excited that Hughes was approachable, Ellison had found a man who was less a hero and more a friend.

Even with such a boon, Ellison had to face his own blues. In his room at the YMCA, he fingered his quickly diminishing $75. He had lingered in Alabama through June. Because he had started out for his summer job quite late—on the eve of July 4—he had little hope of finding work quickly as a greenhorn in the North. Ellison hoped that the introductory letters from Dawson to the composer Jacques Gordon, and perhaps another letter to the New York Philharmonic at Carnegie Hall, would lead to employment opportunities. To pay for his room and board, he took a job doing counter work over the steam tables at the Y's cafeteria. Ellison considered scalding his arms in greasy steam-table water and serving other college boys beneath him; he told himself that it would only be for a fortnight. Reasonably sure of his rent money, Ellison focused on the array of cultural activities in New York. He'd just missed the all-Negro cast perform *Turpentine* at the famous Lafayette Theater on Seventh Avenue. Harlemites had also recently produced a sensationalized version of Shakespeare—a "voodoo" *Macbeth*.[10] Freed from his trumpet, he had lectures, museums, galleries, and the architecture and geography of the largest U.S. city to titillate him. And his literary sensibility expanded. Hughes had loaned him C. Day Lewis's *A Hope for Poetry*. Lewis wrote radical left-wing poetry, including "Magic Mountain," which expressed sympathy with communism. The British poet's essay "A Hope for Poetry" was mild enough to whet Ellison's interest in art and social advocacy without wearying him with dogma. Lewis thought that "only revolutionary activity can make a revolutionary poet," but he also believed that the "poet is a sensitive instrument, not a leader."[11] This combination of an appreciation for art with a commitment to social justice seemed appropriate to Ellison.

Ellison did not linger as a student in Augusta Savage's West 143rd Street basement studio. Savage's popularity and her brash manner (she once showed Kenneth Clark her breast to stimulate his artistic abilities) did not entirely put newcomers at ease. A crusader for black civil rights, Savage had a surly side. Some even thought the sophistication of her sculpture was on the decline.[12] Relying upon Hughes's introduction, Ellison made his way to Richmond Barthé's studio in Greenwich Village, where the artist's work, and attitude, appealed to him. Impressed by Ellison's skill and self-confident deportment, Barthé, who had always been too busy sculpting to teach, took him on as his first pupil.

In 1936, Richmond Barthé was approaching the crest of his career as arguably the single greatest African American sculptor. Like Ellison, the artist had moved to New York with neither money nor contacts, but in short order had solidly established himself. The dashing thirty-five-year-old Barthé was prolific. In 1937, he received a commission from the New York Treasury Public Works of Art Project to produce two giant bas-relief panels to adorn the Harlem River Housing Project. The Whitney Museum of American Art had purchased several of his pieces.[13]

Elegant, handsome, and poised, Barthé shunned a hectic public life. Though he focused on black subjects and used African motifs in his sculpture, he avoided the "race problem" in his personal life, socializing downtown with dealers and collectors. In his works in the late 1930s, Barthé focused on fluid forms. He had moved beyond the realism of his piece "African Dancer" (1932) to more elasticity and elongation with "Feral Benga," a statue of an African man dancing with a machete, completed in 1937.[14]

Barthé's Greenwich Village studio on West 14th Street was an oasis for Ellison. Greenwich Village, with its unsegregated eateries, sockless bohemians, interracial couples, and plentiful bookstores, came to embody Ellison's early New York experience. He turned his Dawson-influenced discipline to sculpture; within four weeks he completed two heads and started work on a torso. Barthé introduced Ellison to a number of his friends, including Greenwich Village poet Edna Millay and the composer David Guions. Just twelve days in New York, and Ellison had begun to socialize with established artists in the city. He followed fellow bohemian Hughes's "formula with success"; he charmed his new acquaintances and allowed them to pay for his meals.[15] The first two weeks in the city were like freshman year at Tuskegee, an incredible assault on the senses. Ellison generally stayed up all night engrossed in conversation, gracefully meeting whites as if accustomed to adult interaction across the color line.

But even as he attended cosmopolitan affairs with Barthé and socialized with white people, Ellison still suffered his own turmoil. Much of his time he spent working at the Y, wearing a white cap and apron, shuffling his feet as he dished up portions from the hot trays. He had underestimated how tough it would be to crack the job market and had let his inner self-confidence get the best of him. Even though Macon County had its limitations, he'd mastered its system; he'd worked in Tuskegee's library, not its cafeteria. He disliked the assumptions that haughty patrons of the cafeteria made about him. He did not let on to Hughes that his connections had not gotten him an excellent summer job. Not all was perfect in the Village, either. If alone and at an unfamiliar eatery there, sometimes the waiters saturated his food with salt, then dramatically crushed his dishes in the fireplace, as if he carried tuberculosis. He revived the coping mechanism that had enabled him to survive Alabama. He refused to show disappointment in public and "assumed a mask which I conceived as that of a New Yorker."[16]

To ensure that the mask fit properly, Ellison continued to explore the city. He rode the subways and elevated trains, and spent an evening on the Staten Island Ferry, but he found his greatest satisfaction by sitting anywhere that he wanted on the bus. On Fifty-ninth Street, he located a bookstore and bought Eliot's *Collected Poems* as well as a biography of the nineteenth-century French composer Berlioz. When he reported to Hughes his reading schedule, he didn't want the poet to imagine that he had misled him about his familiarity with the most important modernist poet at their first conversation. "I feel I knew his best work before I bought this collection," Ellison assured Langston Hughes in a letter.[17] At the bookstore, Ellison had an unpleasant encounter with a Jewish City College student, reminding him that despite his freedom to sit in the front of the bus, even young intellectuals were quick to remind blacks of racial boundaries. Comparing notes on Eliot with the young man, Ellison remarked, "Boy, was my face red." The other student turned his metaphor into a snub. "What you *really* mean is ashes of roses." He had a quick temper that protected him, and in Oklahoma City he had grown up learning a "hoary formula with which to make him [the young City College student] squirm." But in New York, Ellison thought he had left alley games and taunts in childhood.[18] This time, his humor maneuvered him out of the situation, but from then on, he reserved a distance, an intellectual skepticism, about racial harmony. Generally when whites had an advantage, they pressed it. The incident also began his education about New Yorkers. "One man's cliché was another man's facile opportunity for victimage," he later recalled.[19]

Within a couple of weeks, he wrote to Langston Hughes, who had moved in with his ill mother in Cleveland. Ellison had accomplished all of Hughes's tasks. Hughes had requested that he deliver a manuscript by hand; mail two prewrapped books; then later mail a third (which he read), Lewis's work.[20] Afraid that Hughes might consider him a mere errand boy, Ellison provided evidence that he considered himself to be on equal social footing with the celebrated poet. He wanted to avoid a relationship like the one he had had with the domineering Dawson, and so, Ellison wrote to Hughes informing him of an opportunity. He had met the white composer Guions, who wanted James Weldon Johnson to write lyrics for an African ballet that he was turning into a play. If Johnson rejected the offer, Ellison wrote, would Hughes consider it? Hughes's earliest conversations with him not only had made Ellison feel absolutely comfortable, but to some degree had matured the younger man. Ellison concluded with a warning to the poet not to be shocked if he saw him on the corner of Seventh Avenue on a soapbox denouncing capitalism and white supremacy. The recently liberated homeboy from Alabama had become "decidedly interested in the left."

Ellison continued to explore the city. He frequented the Metropolitan Museum of Art, art galleries, bookstores, and the glorious library on Forty-second Street, and enjoyed many other events thanks to Barthé's connections. Then his prospects brightened. Toward the end of July, Ellison got a job as a receptionist and file clerk for the psychiatrist Harry Stack Sullivan at the doctor's office on East Sixty-fourth Street.[21] Sullivan was a liberal on racial equality and close friend to the dancer Kathleen Dunham. He took a liking to Ellison, who had learned of the job through Barthé, an avid dancer himself, who may have known the psychiatrist through Dunham. Ellison worked in Sullivan's office five days a week from nine until two. He devoted the rest of his day to sculpting. The job with Sullivan, however, had not come early enough; by late July, Ellison realized that returning to Tuskegee in the fall would be impossible, even if he could have hoped to graduate with his class.

By the late summer, he would have heard that Hazel Harrison would not be returning to Tuskegee, and he may have known that the Music School itself was on the ropes; and of course, he had no love lost for Dawson, who had either misled him about summer prospects, or delayed his journey, or both. Even Eva Hamlin had fallen out of his esteem by suggesting in a letter that, due to his talent, Barthé was a towering intellectual capable of filling Ellison with wisdom. Strongly disagreeing, he thought Hamlin's assumption a perfect example of Tuskegee professors' misinformed presumptuousness.[22] Nor had the Tuskegee connection been helpful. Neither Dawson's reputation nor that of Tuskegee's much-touted Music School had gained him serious attention. The Depression had flooded New York with high-caliber musicians whose expertise prevented him from finding easy employ. His last hope to obtain a job had been through the musicians' union, but the high cost of dues had made membership impossible.

By late August, Ellison had moved into a spare room close to Barthé's studio at 236 West Fourteenth Street. He wrote to Hughes, gushing over a letter that he had unexpectedly received from the busy poet in an age when people had time to read letters, but not to write them. Most of the letters of recommendation he had taken with him from Alabama had failed him, despite the impressive individuals they were addressed to. Hughes's friendship and counsel, on the other hand, were of great help to him during the summer. The relationship with Barthé was going smoothly, he reported to his literary friend. And Ellison never shied away from a critical judgment. He agreed with Hughes on the delightful merits of Barthé over several of the major black sculptors, then he admitted to Hughes that he had been a bit disingenuous about employment prospects; he felt sure that the Y job would sink their friendship. Hesitantly, Ellison told the truth: he worked now at the YMCA cafeteria, hating the job, but needing the money badly. He did not want Hughes to think less of him, so he quickly hit a more upbeat note. Expressing joy and fulfillment in his move to New York, he casually referred to his inability to return to Tuskegee that fall as only a minor hitch in an otherwise bright future. He optimistically if a bit pretentiously told Hughes that he planned to stay current with music by enrolling in a class or two at Juilliard. Juilliard turned out to be beyond his reach. He did take in an occasional Sunday night concert at Carnegie Hall. On September 13, Ellison would attend a concert, made possible by General Motors, to listen to Debussy and Beethoven. Stepping forward boldly and offering his ticket, he experienced not only first-class symphony, but something quite new, integration in a formal public space. The following January, when Igor Stravinsky directed the New York Philharmonic, Ellison made sure to get a ticket.[23]

Ellison encouraged Hughes to cultivate the radical literary aspect of their relationship. He reminded the writer to mail him André Malraux's *Man's Fate,* as well as John Strachey's "Literature and Dialectical Materialism" at the end of the summer. He had been consumed with sculpting, and with his job reorganizing Sullivan's files, but the young reader wrote to Hughes that he yearned to learn about the works and concerns of the literary Left. His ignorance had little to do with lack of curiosity, since radical literature rarely pene-trated the deep South in the early thirties. In the summer of 1935, communist-linked writers Nelson Algren and Jack Conroy had been arrested in Birming-ham for the possession of the *New Republic, The Nation, New Masses,* and the *Daily Worker* (Alabama state laws forbade the possession of more than two pieces of "radical" literature), then hustled out of the state by the police, gun-fire ringing in their ears.[24] Ellison could not encounter the literary "Left" in the South.

His concern about left-wing politics and radical literature, and his own steady bohemianism signified the end of childhood posturing. Ellison was searching to discover what the new fulfillment of his interests meant to his old dreams, as well as his attenuated ties to his family. In 1936 Ida, Herbert, and John had moved from Ellison's birthplace to Cleveland, Ohio. But the town on Lake Erie did not suit his mother, and so, after two weeks, she packed up and they went down to Dayton, where she discovered an overflow of relatives from Georgia. His mother's ragtag pilgrimage across the Midwest reminded Ellison of his fatherless family's treks canvassing the east side of Oklahoma City, McAlester, and Gary, Indiana. To Hughes, Ellison admitted being a little embarrassed; he thought that his mother might even return to Oklahoma City. Ida Ellison Bell was not a woman of means, and her son's casual remarks about her potential relocation hid the underlying desperation of the family's life. Ellison had few illusions about the sacrifice he would be making if he returned to Ohio or to Tuskegee in Alabama to aid his family. His gifts of musical discipline and easy literacy had earned him independence from them, an autonomy he never relinquished. Besides, he had finally reached a place where his talents, all of them, were welcomed. In contrast to the sometimes aching isolation that literacy had brought him at school in Alabama, in New York he breezily made connections with a few more of Hughes's acquaintances.

To his joy and surprise, Hughes mailed him the "Leftist literature"—André Malraux—before fall. Ellison read Chevalier's translation of *Man's Fate* (*La Conditione Humaine*) as the French author André Malraux's fame had begun to peak with American intellectuals. The novel soared, offering a real-istic portrait of the main actors in the communist revolt in China in 1927. Ellison greatly appreciated the novel's challenging series of philosophical and psychological portraits that ground the major actions in the plot. The June 24 *New Republic* had printed an interview with Malraux in which the writer, who had firsthand knowledge of the revolution in China, defined the role of the artist in relation to the Communist Party. Despite his own political advo-cacy, Malraux supported caution and distance by the artist toward politics: "I do not think . . . that he should follow the Party in its tactics and maneuvers (which are perhaps necessary in the political arena). He has everything to lose by this identification."[25] In his book, Malraux had explored the inner workings of the Communist Party from a decidedly nonutopian outlook, entirely avoiding dogmatism. His characters' actions sprang from intensive internal debates and well-established psychological convictions. In the era of routine black hate crimes, the optimistic side of Ellison easily identified with the character Kyo, a half-Japanese, half-French rebel leader, an intellectual who strove to provide other men with dignity. But Ellison's more feral instincts were drawn in by Ch'en, the Chinese assassin, bent on a heroic sacrifice, intoxicated by confronting his own mortality—an overriding theme in Malraux's work. Malraux's description of Ch'en was inspiring: "Everything had pushed him into political activity: the hope of a different world, the possibility of eating, though wretchedly (he was naturally austere, perhaps through pride), the gratification of his hatreds, his mind, his character. This activity gave meaning to his solitude."[26] The book was a sort of springboard for Ellison's nascent infatuation—which became a deep commitment—with the radical left political and aesthetic movement.

Ellison was spending less time sightseeing and was starting to concentrate on the concerns of the intellectual world. Malraux's revolutionary book familiarized him with the terms of the debate. July 17, 1936, marked Nazi-backed Franco's rebellion against the socialist government in Spain. The Spanish Civil War had begun, the epic prelude to the oncoming global conflagration. Malraux's *Days of Wrath* alerted the world to the peril of the Nazis. For Ellison, Malraux's most recent work reinforced the triumph of human spirit in his detailed examination of psychological damage. The protagonist Kassner, held in a concentration camp, struggled to maintain his sanity, and rejected the tempting solace of suicide. Ellison identified with the mental triumph. It was a victory he wished to see blacks able to advance. Malraux's work continued to explore the dynamic heritage of the communist and socialist revolutionary movements. In his mind, Ellison recast Malraux's revealing political novels in domestic terms. The profundity of the characterization enabled him to fully grasp the psychological cost paid by each Scottsboro captive, for example. Malraux's work became the indispensable cornerstone for Ellison's standard of political and artistic understanding.

The other book that Hughes gave Ellison developed the important social and political theme of the time. Strachey's published lecture, "Literature and Dialectical Materialism," brought Ellison up to speed on the politics of writers and the broad ideological strokes of the political parties. The fascists were unconscionable enemies of culture whose excessive militarism actually represented the last desperate attempts of capitalism to promote the mirage of a unified world system. Ellison had every reason to gravitate to the unsympathetic portrait of greedy monopolists as he struggled to earn a living. His home state and the word "Okie" had become national symbols for destitution. Strachey presented the concept of dialectical materialism as a formula for interpreting historical transformation, indicated by qualitative changes or "revolutionary leaps" by people in capitalist countries. Strachey emphasized the need for a dialectical critique that fastens and unhinges. He warned of "decadence" in bourgeois writers such as the brilliant Proust, who had been able to depict only a small sphere of society. Malraux's grand achievement, on the other hand, had been a fuller portrait of human interaction, and Ellison was engaged as fully by Malraux's politics as by his artistic imagination. Such writers as D. H. Lawrence and Archibald MacLeish represented the "fascist unconsciousness" and unfortunately perpetuated stereotypes beneficial only to the ruling elite. Ellison was even encouraged to reformulate his feelings about his favorite writer. Hemingway was "world-weary," a "nihilist," an emblem of a social system that had "exhausted almost all its possibilities of development."[27] While Ellison continued to deeply appreciate Hemingway's writing techniques, he paid careful attention to Strachey's critique. Strachey shocked Ellison to his core with his confident Marxism, extolling the precipitous decline and inevitable rapid transformation of society. The modern world promised only swift and violent change.

Langston Hughes's friend Louise Thompson continued Ellison's introduction to radical politics, and to Harlem life and history. Thompson possessed what perhaps no other person had, not even Langston Hughes: feet firmly planted in both the Communist Party and the black bourgeoisie. She had been a delegate, with prominent black Communist James Ford (a vice-presidential candidate in 1936), to Mayor Fiorello La Guardia's office in City Hall for the hearings following the Harlem Riot of 1935. She was in a position to offer Ellison candid information on the city's inner workings as well as on Harlem's prominent Communists. A graduate of the University of California at Berkeley, Thompson was one of the core group of artists and intellectuals who had undertaken a Renaissance in Harlem in the late 1920s and early 1930s. An attractive woman, she had served as a secretary to Hughes and Zora Neale Hurston, had married insurgent editor Wallace Thurman, and even had traveled to Russia (Hughes in tow) to make a blunt film depicting the plight of American blacks. Impressed with the young man, Louise Thompson offered her home on Convent Avenue as an oasis for Ellison, as the Walcotts' had been at Tuskegee. In her home, she cultivated a salon-like atmosphere, and there many black artists and intellectuals had found their first introduction to Marx; she had led a Marxist study group with the help of Augusta Savage.[28] Thompson's contacts were vast, her tongue was sharp, and her critical insights on celebrities and politicos fierce.

As a bona fide member of the CP, Louise Thompson familiarized Ellison with Party headquarters at 306 Lenox Avenue, just north of 125th Street. In response to the mid-1930s threat of Hitler, the Communists' perspective had shifted from seeking an exclusive alliance with working classes advocating revolution to welcoming an alliance with anyone who was avowedly anti-Nazi. It was the era of the Popular Front. In this environment, Ellison did not have to choose between enjoying modernist art as a member of the contemptible bourgeoisie, or criticizing the status quo for the current economic crisis and racial injustice as a radical. In this social and political mixture, he also found himself able to reveal a full emotional range and to experience some psychological catharsis. Among Communists, he was made to feel comfortable discussing his working-class roots; he did not have to puff up his pedigree and credentials. The Popular Front banner proudly courted all social classes.

In addition to spreading their ideas in the *Daily Worker* and the *New Masses,* Communists conveyed their messages from the available street corners. Harlem was bitterly contested political territory, and though the Communists flaunted their problack commitments in the Scottsboro and Angelo Herndon cases, when they ventured up to 135th Street—still controlled by Arthur Reid and Ira Kemp of the African Patriotic League, survivors of the old Tiger Division of the United Negro Improvement Association—they prepared for battle. Ellison learned that the Communists and the Garveyites clashed frequently and violently; in June of 1930, black Communist Alfred Levy had been killed in an altercation with the Garveyites.

But the Party was also a party, and its reputation for revelry appealed to the twenty-four-year-old Ellison. According to Young Communist League leader Howard Johnson, a member in the late 1930s:

> Party members in other parts of the country didn't have the kind of time we had in Harlem. They didn't know how to party . . . being a communist in Harlem was like being the swinging present and the swinging future simultaneously . . . you were enjoying all the boogying and boozing and everything in the present, while you had your socialist perspective to give you the inspiration to continue.[29]

Another member recalled that in Harlem, Jewish girls seeking freedom from the shelter of immigrant life in Brooklyn and the Bronx often obtained independence in the most deeply symbolic form, a romantic liaison with a young black man.[30] Harlem offered a furious-paced and sociable progressive Left.

Ellison did not completely forget his ambition to become a musician. In the spring of 1937, he signed up for selected individual instruction classes at the Downtown Music School, which offered evening classes at 68 East 12th Street, a couple of blocks from Barthé's studio. While he didn't plunk down the $12.50 or $20 required for a full term of musical instruction in the four-person classes, Ellison paid for a couple of private lessons from the classical instructor Wallingford Reigger at his West 90th Street studio. Happily, Reigger shared Ellison's devotion to the music of Duke Ellington. In his spare time, Ellison visited the revues at the Apollo on Wednesday and Sunday nights, where for fifteen cents he took in a short film, a feature movie, and then a variety of live acts, comedians, dancers, and finally a large band performance. The chorus girls at the Apollo were considered the best in New York, and the Apollo's black comedians Buck and Bubbles, Pigmeat Markham, and Dusty Fletcher performed in blackface.[31] While Ellison was interested in serious theater, the Apollo provided whatever little black drama there was in New York in the winter of 1937. New York City's Federal Theater Project, which provided affordable entertainment, was hesitant to produce even one of playwright Paul Green's interracial dramas. They would not discover black playwrights for another couple of years.

In early March 1937, Langston Hughes breezed back into town for a series of lectures and radio skits and to market his new play *When the Jack Hollers*.[32] On March 7, 1937, Hughes carried Ellison over to Brooklyn in a cab for a night of fast-paced cultural high life. Hughes and radical poet Genevieve Taggard headlined a poetry reading at the Brooklyn Academy of Arts and Sciences. While Hughes read his bluesy but proletarian verse before a racially mixed crowd, Ellison felt the same rush of excitement he had experienced the night that enthusiasm for Louis Armstrong had shattered Oklahoma City segregation laws. Hughes, who normally was casually attired, was dressed in full formal regalia; and the invigorating reading stirred visions of what Ellison had ultimately wanted Tuskegee to be. The event combined formal appearance with insurgent content. "For the first time I felt a certain sense of possibility about a life in the arts," he later recalled.[33] He hadn't known that writers—poets especially—had elegant nights; now a certain curiosity had been heightened.

On another evening, Hughes took an eager Ellison to Broadway to see Jack Kirkland's adaptation of Erskine Caldwell's *Tobacco Road*. The experience reminded Ellison of an Alabama that he had striven to forget and, in effect, was in the process of abandoning completely. In another adventure, Hughes took Ellison with him to Duke Ellington's apartment at 308 Edgecombe Avenue in the historic Sugar Hill area of Harlem.[34] By mid-March, Hughes had returned to Cleveland, but through the wheeling and dealing of his radical other half Louise Thompson, now working for the International Workers Order, he had published ten thousand copies of *A New Song*. Hughes's latest book collected all of his most radical poems and was introduced by Mike Gold, editor of the *New Masses*, which Ellison now read regularly. Openly courting blacks, the February 16 edition of the magazine had featured a lithograph of a handsome, pensive black boy on the cover, similar to the thoughtful heads sculpted by Barthé, as well as an essay on "Lincoln and Negro Youth." In less than a year, Hughes had exposed Ellison to theories of race and social evolution that had at best merely simmered in his sociology classroom at Tuskegee. In New York among the black literati, Ellison found a passionate excitement and articulate conviction about the ideas that he had always found attractive. The race, class, and gender revolution was in full throttle. But far more important was the intimate connection that the two men were able to make. Ellison was an extraordinarily sensitive young man. He had plenty of survival skills, but he also enjoyed noting that the leaves turn color in the fall. When he had observed the languid moons in the clear night skies of Alabama, Ellison had known himself to turn soft inside. Occasionally the intensity of his reveries and his desire for the dreamscapes worried him as unaffordable indolence. Especially did the dreamy undertow of his personality worry him in the spring of 1937, when he lost the cushy job in Sullivan's office and took work in a paint factory. In a long conversation, Hughes helped him to understand his sensitivity as an asset, something fulfilling, upon which he could base artistic expression. Before Hughes left to return to Cleveland, Ellison made his friend a present of a photograph, a self-portrait: "To Langston, the 'dream keeper,' in sincerity and admiration, Ralph Ellison."[35]

When Hughes's gentle counsel was unavailable, Ellison wrote letters revealing the other side of the artistic young man, the part of him pained by nine hours of work in a factory while spring broke resplendently outside the dungeon walls. "I wish I had the nerve to go on and take a boat and go until I grow tired," he wrote to his mother in the spring of 1937. The wide-open spaces of Oklahoma and the wisteria and Judas trees of Alabama called to his eyes, now stunted from the poverty of New York City's concrete gray. Ellison was wistful and dreamy, and wanting his sojourn to work out. He could impress his mother by dropping the name of the best-known black poet, with whom he was on a first-name basis, but he admitted to Ida that despite his lessons at the Downtown Music School, and the blazing confidence that his family knew as his trademark, he was a bit "bewildered." He couldn't finger precisely where his new yearnings would take him. "[T]he urge I feel within seems not to fade away but becomes more insistent for expression and I have yet to discover just what form it will take. Let us hope I shall soon find myself."[36]

Finding himself meant taking a deep look at the success of the Left in general, and New York's high-flying Communists in particular. The U.S. Supreme Court's stunning April 26 overthrow of Communist organizer Angelo Herndon's Georgia conviction further satisfied Ellison with the merits of New York Communists, including black lawyer Ben Davis, who had orchestrated Herndon's defense.[37] In a trial with the same sort of publicity and open racial hostility as the Scottsboro cases, the young black political organizer Herndon had been sentenced to the Georgia penitentiary for violating legal codes that had been written to prevent slave insurrection. The public weakening of the old regime of the South inspired and changed Ellison. When he had arrived in New York, he had had a decidedly "Southern" cast. Radical New York brought back his Southwestern temerity, a vitality he had suppressed in Alabama. He found increasing dissatisfaction with his eclectic artistic wanderings. Ellison wished for a medium that might convey swift action and dramatic results. Sculpting took on the aspects of a patient vocation more than a fulfilling hobby, and there Ellison's devoted interest in it ended. He struggled with the limitations of the form to convey the radical political and aesthetic education he was receiving.

Ellison's interaction with Hughes and Thompson had changed him. When first in New York, he had gravitated to the gaudy entertainment of the Apollo, followed by late-night jaunts for waffles. Conversations with the thirty-five-year-old Hughes had made him impatient with the Apollo's slapstick and vaudeville revues. Offering him another medium to explore artistically, Hughes generously lent him a typewriter for as long as he needed it. As Ellison became close to the older man, he confided his pains to him: his insecurity about his home life and the travails that lay ahead, his doubt about leaving his school program and being unable to find work, his frustration at having come close to getting his bachelor's degree and then having his hopes dashed by the collapse of his department and his poor relationship with Dawson.

During the spring of 1937, Hughes suggested that Ellison look through old editions of the popular Leftist journals. Hughes had been involved in the League of American Writers, and he encouraged Ellison to read the radical publications on politics and culture. Turning to the pages of the July–August 1935 *Partisan Review*, Hughes showed Ellison a poem by a young black author named Richard Wright, called "Between the World and Me."[38] Wright's poem collapsed the distance between a person who stumbles upon a lynching victim and the murdered man himself—all deeply touching to Ellison, who had brushed against deadly violence in Alabama. Wright vigorously explored a topic that few American writers seemed capable of noticing. "Between the World and Me" began its dramatic crescendo when the "dry bones stirred, rattled, lifted, melting themselves into my bones." With its uncanny images, compellingly recreating the horrific scene of a human burnt alive—"begging I clutched childlike, clutched to the hot sides of death"—Wright had succeeded in representing the universality of the barbaric experience. Lynching, brutality, white desire—all stood between a black person's apprehension of the self and individual existence in society. Ellison had been on the lookout for a poet combining T. S. Eliot's artistic experiments and black material, and he enjoyed Wright's poem enough to mention to Hughes that he was interested in meeting this remarkable writer.

He had moved on to even more comfortable terms with Hughes, whom he now affectionately called "Lang." When Hughes again departed New

York, this time for Cleveland and the West Coast, Ellison once more felt that intellectual loneliness. But it was mild compared to what else befell him. A slight throbbing in the back of his throat turned into grossly inflamed tonsils, which eventually sent him to the hospital.[39] It was of interest to Ellison that his famous friend was in Los Angeles working on a musical collaboration with William Grant Still. A musician of formidable stature, Still seemed intellectually naive to Ellison, who now scoffed at the composer's platitude that "*beauty gives birth to beauty*." Now, as his interest in sculpture completely waned, Ellison picked up his reading and became more attached to Hughes. The artist reciprocated. In the hopes of developing such a precocious talent, Hughes, always financially strapped, rewarded Ellison's friendship with an incredible gift, a set of first editions of Thomas Mann. Ellison was appropriately flabbergasted, and accepted the first editions with unconcealed delight. Tucked away in his room at Hughes's friend and "Aunt" Toy Harper's or at Louise Thompson's reading Thomas Mann, Ellison joked about his pain and intellectual loneliness. The two men with their Western frontier roots (Hughes was from Missouri) had hammered out a technique for catharsis: literature. After putting down roots in New York over the previous ten months and surviving his first Northern winter, the formula was pouring his suffering and his survival into words.

In jest, he considered himself a poet, at least when writing to one. Ellison's early poetic letters to Hughes were written during the height of their emotional intimacy and the young dilettante of sculpture, poetry, and music affected the self-conscious pose of the artist in his letters to the man who had introduced him to the literary Left. Ellison thought of his inflamed tonsils in elaborate similes, which connected to everything from the design of the carpet to the news of the latest fascist victory.[40] He was beginning to synthesize the elements of reality at his disposal and his sense of the contours of that reality, particularly concerning the arts, was always broad. Thomas Mann's writing, the delicacy of its style, enabled him to put into words his dreamy imagination. After tackling *Death in Venice and Seven Other Stories,* Ellison told Hughes that he found it impossible not to identify with protagonist Tonio Kroger, his favorite character. Mann's short story, an antecedent of Joyce's *Portrait of the Artist as a Young Man,* chronicled the life and shifting loves of a bookish, sensitive youth who becomes a writer. The story illuminated talks Ellison had had frequently with Hughes over the last couple of months, and helped him grasp the complex philosophy of writing. Was writing only cynicism? Was it the brash heroism and commitment of someone like Malraux? What exactly did writers commit themselves to do? Was all writing propaganda, as the Communists said? Ellison learned a little about patience and the double-edged sword of revealing one's thoughts on the page. It had been hard for him not to be incredulous when Hughes revealed that the brief moment of perception was ultimately unfulfilling. In the story, Kroger tells a friend, "Literature is not a calling, it is a curse . . . there is a gulf of ironic sensibility, of knowledge, skepticism, disagreement between you and others; it grows deeper and deeper, you realize that you are alone." Mann's delicate exploration of a young man's influences and pursuit of artistic goals struck home. Ellison realized that he had moved far from his days of trying to win the approval of Oklahoma City trumpeter Frank Meade, and perhaps just as far from seeking the respect of William Dawson. Mann also spoke to his clearly evident sense of alienation. Ellison was becoming bohemian, but like Hughes (who had recently reapproached the NAACP), "a bohemian who feels nostalgic yearning for respectability." Mann's *Death in Venice* reminded Ellison to bind his experiences and his innermost feelings tightly to his heart. "If you care too much about what you say, if your heart is too much in it, you can be pretty sure of making a mess."[41] This was a rule for social protest even for the sensational and unashamed Hughes. Ellison determined to lock much of the "mess" of his life, like his east side poverty, his stepfathers, and his Decatur freight yard incident, into the basement of his experience.

Hughes's unpretentious intellectualism, with its obvious roots in everyday life, had profoundly affected Ellison. His feelings of alienation and self-consciousness were growing, ruining his desires to soak up the brightly packaged commodities that 125th Street had to offer. He admitted in a letter in April the pain that came from growing into an intellectual. After his conversations with Hughes, the luster of the Apollo and Harlem's all-night eateries had dulled considerably.

The connection that he felt to Hughes did not end with Ellison's criticisms of Harlem life. Although he was intensely guarded about his home life, Ellison revealed some of his deepest anxieties regarding his family. He confided to Hughes his decision to put distance between himself and Oklahoma, Ohio, and Tuskegee. His family did not satisfy him and he thought of them and their household as something out of a Lewis Carroll fairy tale.[42] Enormous differences of opinion had not broken up the marriage between Ida and John Bell. Herbert, fully grown but far from his intellectual peer, disappointed him. The family's zany style of living lacked the regularity and normalcy that, despite his bohemian leanings, he had always craved. Their inability to help him clarify his dreams was frustrating, and he thought less of returning to their fold. Though the job market for performers was nearly closed, Ellison had gone to college to learn high-level conducting and theory, and a job teaching music in a school of any caliber, for instance, would have helped his family to survive. But by the spring, feeling less and less a musician, Ellison had ceased to mention any plans of returning South to Tuskegee or moving to Ohio to rejoin his family.

His inclination to stay in New York was further whetted by the arrival in February of André Malraux, who delivered lectures to raise money for the Loyalist forces fighting fascism valiantly in Spain. The heroic Malraux engaged audiences at the Mecca Temple. The towering figure, so fresh from the battlefields of Spain that his hands trembled as he spoke, dazzled his listeners.[43] Malraux was so passionate a speaker that he usually exhausted his interpreter. Ellison heard about Malraux as the writer felt the pressure to champion the Communists as clear adversaries to fascism. Before Malraux returned to France in April, during an interview at Random House's offices, he would dismiss Trotsky and other opponents of Stalin's Moscow Trials as being obsessed with "intellectual considerations" during the moment when "the fate of mankind is at present being decided in Spain."[44] Communism was heroic, an ideology that fought the forces of oppression not only in Alabama but all over the world. The crisis of the world did not make room for questions, only for action. Ellison was so taken with Malraux that after the writer's visit, he had his edition of *Man's Fate* bound in leather.

Before June, Ellison got a postcard from the twenty-eight-year-old Richard Wright: "Langston Hughes tells me that you'd like to meet me."[45] The poet Richard Wright had left Chicago after a deep misunderstanding with the Chicago Communist Party during the 1936 May Day parade. He later claimed that he had been bodily expelled from the march.[46] Not wishing to lose an extremely talented member of the Party—someone with literary potential, who was a magnet for attracting blacks into the Communist ranks—Wright's superior James Ford had sent the young writer to New York to placate him.[47] Wright would not be subjected to the demands of his unit, which placed importance on organizing over writing. Now he headed the Harlem bureau of the *Daily Worker* at 306 Lenox Avenue under the supervision of Benjamin Davis Jr.

Although mild-mannered, Wright took himself seriously as a writer, obsessively carrying around his current work with him at all times, storing finished stories in the bottom of his desk drawer at the *Daily Worker*. He had rejected a lucrative job at the Post Office in Chicago so that he could move to Manhattan, where he hoped to market his unpublished novel, a raw and realistic tale of black life called *Cesspool* (published after his death as *Lawd Today*). Wright's decision to leave his mother, aunt, and brother in order to pursue his career resonated with Ellison at the deepest levels. Yet, despite his ambition and drive, Wright was intensely shy, self-conscious, and suspicious of others. He had few close friends. Born in rural Mississippi, the son of a day laborer and a teacher, he had not finished high school because of nagging family problems. He distrusted middle-class blacks, but he had little in common with ordinary working folk, a difference made all the more pronounced by his passion for reading and his keen analytical mind. In December 1937, when Wright first started work on the Federal Writers Project, his colleague Ellen Tarry remembered that "he was so shy that the men in my group had told me to find out if he could talk."[48]

Ellison's meeting with Wright probably took place around Monday, May 31, 1937.[49] The rendezvous, arranged by Hughes, had one immediate and tangible effect. Ellison's encounter with Wright's committed Marxism radicalized him. He had disabused himself of his Alabama "ignorance of the left," and he had moved, with Hughes's glowing encouragement, toward street rallies and organizing, and the works of Malraux and Thomas Mann. With Wright's friendship, Ellison embarked upon relationships not only with the radical Left but with the major theoretical and literary talents of his era. Hughes had been an occasional contributor to leftist journals and causes; Wright captained a bureau of the *Daily Worker*. And their meeting was as exhilarating as Ellison had anticipated. In all respects a professional writer, Wright was even more impressive than his *Partisan Review* poetry indicated. He not only combined modernist techniques with a defiantly Negro perspective, but he pursued his artistic projects with an analysis emphasizing both the life of the mind and the influence of environment upon the human personality. Literature had a social function, Wright told Ellison, and black writers in particular had an important task. Richard Wright had just written "Joe Louis Uncovers Dynamite" for the *New Masses,* and was intellectually engaged in understanding the origins of mass consciousness and group psychology. When analyzing the mass spirit that was palpable among large groups of blacks after a Louis victory in the boxing ring, Wright wrote: "Here's that *something,* that pent-up folk consciousness. Here's a fleeting glimpse of the heart of the Negro."[50] Perhaps even more exciting, Wright was leaning toward a theory that envisioned an American class revolution with a Negro vanguard, a perspective that was heretical to strict Marxists.

His interests in revolutionary theory, black nationalism, and art afforded Wright a unique perspective. As soon as he hit the Harlem office of the *Daily Worker,* Benjamin Davis presented Wright with a task more appealing than covering local news from a racial and materialist perspective. He encouraged Wright to help revitalize the former *Challenge* magazine, implementing a more theoretical and Marxist orientation. The magazine would be called *New Challenge.* Wright would work with the journal's founding editors, the left-leaning Dorothy West and Marian Minus, whom Wright knew from his South Side Chicago Writers Group. In early June 1937 when he met Ellison, Wright was, like Langston Hughes eleven years before, about to formulate the aesthetic principles for a generation of black writers. Ellison's intuition about Wright's innovative approach to literature had been apt. Wright was expressly concerned with writing fiction specifically dealing with black themes and characters and entirely adamant about symbolically exploring an individual psychology in his characters, and whatever else modernist techniques had to offer. In the summer of 1937, after Cab Calloway, Count Basie, and Fats Waller had headlined at Carnegie Hall to spearhead a communist recruitment drive for volunteers to war-torn Spain, the latest literary perspective for black writers had to be Marxist. Early that summer in his office at the *Daily Worker,* Wright had summed up that approach for the journal *New Challenge* and called it "Blueprint for Negro Writing." He also worked furiously on four novellas, one of which, "Fire and Cloud," eventually won him a *Story* magazine prize and $500.

The essay "Blueprint for Negro Writing" thrust Richard Wright onto the national scene of black American writing and criticism. He was an outsider to the insular, well-educated community of Harlem's black writerly elite, and his hissing attack on the black art movement of the 1920s stood as a formidable watershed; instead of crying for more freedom, Wright demanded from artists more discipline and responsibility. Using the Sixth Communist International's thesis of 1928 that Negroes in the United States constituted a nation within a nation, complemented by the understanding that even if blacks wanted to move beyond petit bourgeois nationalism, they must first embrace the nationalist ethos, "Blueprint" brutally faulted black artists "curtsying to show that the Negro was not inferior, that he was human."[51] The critical essay turned Wright into an intellectual contender, someone whose ideas had to be taken into consideration.

Wright's intelligence, manic energy, and enviable self-confidence easily swept up Ellison. Their intellectual and emotional camaraderie was cemented by other fortunate circumstances. Ellison walked into Wright's office the week of the second League of American Writers Congress, which represented the major public thrust of the Communists Popular Front strategy. The Party had abandoned its former stance of promoting exclusively proletarian fiction by working-class writers, and now embraced (and was embraced by) some of the most popular and respected names in literature who currently expressed a social conscience. Apart from the political rivalries, the overarching benefit of the congress came from its talented personnel. Famous writers and intellectuals like Malcolm Cowley, Martha Gelhorn, Albert Rhys Williams, and Kenneth Burke graced the rostrum. The congress made accessible a cadre of artists and intellectuals who otherwise would have been entirely unavailable to young blacks like Ellison and Wright.

Ellison showed Wright the city subways and pointed out eateries as the two men went to Carnegie Hall on Friday evening of June 4, where they saw their hero Hemingway give the conference's keynote address. Nervous, and speaking simply, a tanned, heavyset Hemingway enjoined the audience to assist Spain, pushing writers to speak for truth.[52] Wright and Ellison had heard it said that his point of view was generally naive, that the writer was well-known for having a limited understanding of the conflict. Still, the conference afforded them an opportunity to see larger-than-life heroes in person. On Saturday, Martha Gelhorn cheered writers who were going to Spain not for the purpose of observing "local color" but instead because "they wished to bury their personalities in something worth fighting for, namely democracy."[53] The conference seemed to ache with tension over whether or not it was a Communist front. Ellison undoubtedly shared the enthusiasm generated for attendees who were joining the Abraham Lincoln Brigades to fight alongside the Loyalists in Spain—especially as the embargo on modern weapons placed by Britain and the United States almost guaranteed the defeat of the brave Republican government. The conference brought out, in glamorous and embattled fashion, the passions and commitments of a generation of writers and intellectuals. The two men both felt passionately about the work of André Malraux, the writer who spent his time leading the Loyalist air force. Ellison's new friend Wright found Malraux to be an "interpreter" of the highest order, presenting the struggle of millions the world over "trying to rise above a degraded status" with the vital literary and conceptual technique of "heroic action."[54]

More brilliant than Hemingway were the seminars held at the New School of Social Research, continuing the conference on Saturday, June 5.[55] Kenneth Burke presented his essay "The Rhetoric of Hitler's Battle," controversial to the impatiently anti-Nazi crowd.[56] Burke was considered a maverick by the pro-Communist audience. In an episode unforgivable to the Communists during the 1935 conference, Burke had caused a shouting match among CP members by suggesting that an image of "the people" replace "the workers" in Communist symbolism.[57] Burke had offered pessimism and poor sportsmanship as countering tactics to capitalist efficiency in his book *Counter-Statement* (1931). His most heretical suggestion, though, was that aesthetics preceded and ultimately dictated politics: symbols before action. In his Saturday afternoon talk, Burke urged his audience to read Hitler's just-translated autobiography *Mein Kampf,* instead of summarily dismissing it. Burke dissected the Führer's anti-Semitic ravings in plain language: "Our job is to find all available ways of making the Hitlerite distortions of religion apparent, in order that politicians of his kind in America be unable to perform a similar swindle." Burke showed how the Nazi media conflated national and religious symbols to scapegoat Jews, effectively masking the utter neglect of economic issues in Hitler's rhetoric. The analysis was unprecedented. Burke pointed to rituals of primitive society to lay bare Hitler's wily manipulation of anti-Jewish prejudice and subsequent ignoring of German economic woes: "[Hitler promoted] unification by a fictitious devil-function, gradually made convincing by the sloganizing repetitiousness of standard advertising techniques."[58] Ellison, achingly familiar with Scottsboro and the crucified Claude Neale, as well as the customarily unflattering depictions of blacks in cinema and in advertising, saw need for a Burkean analysis on his home turf.

What Ellison found particularly smart about the lecture was Burke's synthesis of insights from both Freud and Marx.[59] The combination of the two perspectives had seemed improbable. Ellison's exposure to Communist Party intellectuals had revealed them to be confident in their doctrine but rigid. They refused to recognize the insights of psychology for fear of placing primacy on individual behavior. But Burke used the unraveling individual psychology as a place to project the effect of much larger group dynamics. He quoted at length from Freud's *Totem and Taboo* to demonstrate how Hitler, like a paranoid or primitive, had cast Jews in the role of an omnipotent being that had to be destroyed. By using the latest theoretical insights, Burke illuminated Hitler's manifesto as an example of "persecution mania."

Ellison's siding with Burke, who represented to many of the League's organizers an uncomfortable hyperacademic and bourgeois presence, indicated his own Eliot-formed sensibility toward literature and political theory, except when racial matters were at issue. He enjoyed what was experimental and new, flavored by a long historical view of the preceding tradition.

The Popular Front era, when the CP played down its proletarian emphasis in order to structure a large coalition against fascism, reached its climax with the 1937 writers conference. Opposition to the Communist influence, however, was quite vocal at the congress. During Communist Party Chairman Earl Browder's speech, Claude McKay stepped off the speaker's platform and walked out of the auditorium. Poet and Trotskyite Harry Roskelenko peppered all of the question-and-answer sessions with disturbing accusations about the ongoing Soviet purges under the guise of the Moscow Trials. In the most sensational episode, Philip Rahv and William Phillips and their wing of writers from the newly reconstructed *Partisan Review* interrupted Granville Hicks, the most renowned American Communist academic critic, with shouts proclaiming Leon Trotsky's innocence.[60]

The writers congress concluded on Sunday, June 6, with a blistering denunciation by WPA Writing Project director Henry G. Alsberg of "scab . . . book reviewers or special writers who work for nothing."[61] Ellison learned that writers had a great deal in common with workers in the shipyards, factories, and fields. His association with the League of American Writers, of which he remained proud throughout the rest of his life, began for him an era of forthright political engagement. His relationship with Wright brought him into contact with the sectarian challenges of the liberal movement of the 1930s, though he entered the movement as a bourgeois liberal reformer, well to the right of his Marxist friend. Still, he did not stigmatize actual members of the Communist Party, as evidenced by his connections to their policies, the groups organized by them, and the magazines they supported. In fact, the Party ran along the center of Roosevelt's New Deal coalition, which would have pulled Ellison into its fold because of its progressive racial politics.[62]

The trials in Moscow that had begun in 1936 polarized radical circles into two camps: those who maintained faith in the Soviet Union and supported Joseph Stalin, and a minority whose stand against the corruption of Marx's and Lenin's communitarian vision brought them in line with Leon Trotsky, the most famous Communist dissident, in exile in Mexico. Many writers who, like Wright, had gained their first public exposure by being published in Party journals, became uncomfortable with the Communists' proscriptive approach to literature as their technical skills grew and they gained greater access to publication elsewhere. One of Wright's significant guides in aesthetic and theoretical matters was James T. Farrell, whose trilogy *Studs Lonigan* Wright admired. Farrell had been faithful to the Communists, but by 1937 was actively leading an insurrection against the dogma of thinkers like Granville Hicks. Farrell's 1936 *A Note on Literary Criticism* put him at the forefront of the articulate malcontents, disgusted with the Communist International's directives. By the late 1930s, Farrell had become a strong supporter of Trotsky. Also aligned with Farrell in the fight were two insurgent editors of the magazine *Partisan Review*. *Partisan,* where Wright had published his early poetry, had served as the literary organ of New York's John Reed Club. When editors Rahv and Phillips revived *Partisan Review* in December of 1937, they, too, would begin an unrelenting attack upon the communist literary practices, the Moscow Trials, and even Ellison's sacred cow, the Popular Front.

Wright leaned toward literary and intellectual freedom in this fight; he had detested the Chicago Communist Party's xenophobia and clannishness, which demanded that he receive approval for his creative and political expressions through a supervisory committee. However, in public at least, Wright stood beside the Communists and probably did not share the more pointed aspects of his life in the Party with a relative newcomer like Ellison. After knowing Ellison for a year, he was still capable of writing to close friends from the South and extolling the wisdom and vision of communism.[63] Wright well understood that there was no standing invitation from more purely academic Marxists to join their ranks. Perhaps the Party was mainly interested in him because of his color and his social class origins. But even if they were uncomfortable with his ambition and leadership drive, their publications, congresses, and conferences afforded a rare opportunity for his artistic development.[64] Ellison was not politically grounded enough to see the fullness of the interchange between Marxism and Trotskyism, and their intersections with black nationalism. Impressed that the Party had high-ranking blacks like James Ford (who ran for vice president on Party head Earl Browder's ticket), and that it had established such a commanding presence in Harlem politics (people still talked about their influence during the 1935 riot on 135th Street, which brought discussions of economic and racial exploitation to the fore), Ellison enthusiastically applauded the revolution by the workers. Marx's ideas transmuted by Lenin seemed as viable a solution for the raging Depression and putrid racism of America as anything else. By becoming fully active during the Popular Front era, he had found a solution to his Tuskegee professor Bess Wolcott's dilemma, the "panacea" seemingly capable of eradicating the "eczema" of race prejudice.

Ellison surely also appreciated the unusual friendship with Wright, who trusted him and accepted him as something of an intellectual peer. Ellison gravitated to the Harlem CP Bureau as much as prudence allowed; there simply was no more interesting place to be than at the desk of a black writer engaged in the most pressing social and intellectual questions of the moment. The office of the *Daily Worker*, which was circulating the boldest articles on the race question in New York City ("Protests Against Slugging Grow, Butcher Who Attacked Negro Boy Is Fired"), hummed like a place of consequence and radical struggle. Tuskegee's gang of contemptuous professors who herded students away from the paths of a justifiable fight smelled rank by comparison. In the Communist milieu, Ellison gained the confidence that he could abandon the poverty of his youth, even without a college degree. Wright was a man changing the world with his pen, decrying the physical and psychological injustices that Ellison knew too well, and making a living that way.

In their talks following the writers conference, Wright confidently assumed the superior role in their exchanges, wrongly intuiting that Ellison was naive about composition and completely ignorant of literary criticism.[65] Wright held forth with his interpretations of Marx, Freud, and Nietzsche. He presumed also that Ellison knew nothing of partisan literati, like Conrad and Dostoyevsky. Though Ellison was needled at first that Wright did not exactly believe him his equal, Wright's sense of his own superiority gave Ellison intellectual breathing space. Beyond their kinship regarding Malraux, he felt out Wright's strength and vigor and offered something of an intellectual "rope-a-dope" in return. He sustained challenges and thrusts without vesting enough in conversations to suffer a bruised intellectual ego. "Forget it [pride], you know what you know; so now learn what he thinks," Ellison told himself.[66] Of course, Wright also had the major advantage of believing in and speaking from the fairly organized and coherent body of literary Marxism. Ellison knew the story of the possum, so he sat back; he wasn't eager to face another "ashes of roses" experience. And soon enough, they did find something immediately to talk about, pretty much as equals. Both men had read everything by Hemingway.

Richard Wright's life was rigid and disciplined. Serious and demanding of himself, Wright structured his life around his writing; and even as he and Ellison were peers, he was a role model for Ellison. He did not have the glamour or generosity, and perhaps not the brilliant sensitivity, of Langston Hughes, who had achieved greatness in his early youth. A disciplined and systematic reader, Wright seemed comfortable with straightforward toil. Composition for him was neither pretty nor an act of divine intervention: "I sweat over my work. . . . I usually write a rough draft, then go over it page by page. It's work."[67] He took in few music events or folk arts, but relentlessly pounded the keys of his typewriter. His pace and enthusiasm manifested themselves broadly. Even such casual acquaintances as Alfred Kazin, a mildly radical socialist at the time and book reviewer for the *New Republic,* described Wright in the summer of 1937 as "relentless" and "unsatisfiable."[68]

Whatever free time he had away from an uninspiring series of odd jobs Ellison spent at the *Daily Worker* office. He often asked Wright about the writing process, and freely read the short stories that tumbled out of his friend's typewriter and lay in the bottom drawer of his desk, among them "Fire and Cloud," "Big Boy Leaves Home," and "Long Black Song." Witnessing Wright's turbulent relationships with subordinates and Communist officials while he served as chief editor of the Harlem bureau of the *Daily Worker* (where Wright tried to organize clubs for Harlem's youth, activities thought to detract from the idea of a Popular Front) enabled Ellison to observe vicious Communist infighting without officially joining. It may ultimately have been the central dynamic that kept him from becoming a member of the Communist Party. With its Popular Front tactic of actively making overtures to white elites, the CP sometimes turned a blind eye to outcroppings of white chauvinism. On the other hand, Harlem Communists kept Wright at bay, jealous that he was being groomed by central leadership to take over the Harlem bureau. Ellison's interest in Wright's excellent short stories afforded him the valuable opportunity to view from a distance the inevitable jockeying for position in a large organization.

At the very end of June, Langston Hughes, the vital public standard bearer for the black Left, came to New York briefly enough to say hello, and then shipped out on the SS *Aquitania* for Spain and the war front. Around that time, the contrast between black and white, Communist and cultural nationalist, came to a head in Harlem in a controversy that was gloriously reported in the *Amsterdam News.* Erstwhile veteran of black letters Claude McKay rejected Helen Boardman, a white Communist, from membership in his black writers' society.[69] McKay had attempted to bring together black writers in Harlem under the umbrella of a cultural nationalist movement, but his headstrong personality and desire to have the membership rolls read like a who's who among famous blacks doomed the effort. Nevertheless, though neither Ellison nor Wright was well enough established to join Harlem's writerly elite, the proximity of a famous and articulate constituency was encouraging to Ellison's "sense of opportunity." Hughes, McKay, Countee Cullen, and the honorary Manhattanites, Sterling Brown and Alain Locke, offered a "living presence . . . part of the glamour of Harlem."[70]

Ellison's relationship with Wright was not without its blemishes. Not long into their friendship, Ellison noted that besides Wright's intellectual and other obvious gifts, he was emotionally high-strung, unable to contain the kinds of pressures that Ellison had grown used to concealing. It was perhaps obvious why Richard Wright had fled the South. Toward the end of the summer, the pressure of his new environment and hand-to-mouth existence began to wear down Wright. He technically was the "director" of the Harlem branch of the *Daily Worker,* but he had no editorial staff, and he took out his frustrations by screaming at the copy boys and messengers, Wright required "opposition" and "antagonism," Ellison thought.[71] The writer's mind was also conflicted. Wright refrained from engaging fully with the CP lawyer Benjamin Davis, because he distrusted Davis's credentials as an attorney and feared that the man was an FBI spy. At the same time, he despised Harlem's other prominent Communists James Ford and Haywood Patterson (who he thought were contemptuous of him because he was a writer) for making the fairly intellectual Davis's life "hard." Willard Maas was the only person other than Ellison whom Wright spoke to fraternally in his office. Wright and Ellison frequently attempted to discuss art and politics with Abner Berry, the Harlem bureau's head of the League of Struggle for Negro Rights, and Theodore Bassett, the Harlem education director. But Wright made the two Harlem CP men uncomfortable; he was too inquisitive and independent for their taste. Unsurprisingly, Wright grew increasingly frustrated. He was fighting off black academics, calling them apathetic bourgeoisie, while at the same time resisting the dogmatic tendencies of men like Berry and Bassett and attempting to transform the CP ideological line.

Ellison appealed to Wright's sensibility, however. Ellison had been unable to maintain his chic college wardrobe as he dipped in and out of poverty. Reading the CP theoretical pamphlets by Lenin and Marx abundant at the 306 West Lenox Party office, Ellison was deeply influenced by the communist theory, which he gravitated toward as a means to explain racism.[72] He nearly joined the Party, but never committed to it, probably because cosmopolitan New York City graciously emitted no small degree of racial tolerance, just as Ellison had learned from his college reading of Johnson's *Black Manhattan.* With more avenues of interest open to a serious intellectual in the large anonymous city and thriving black metropolitan area, he had no need for membership; being a fellow traveler was adequately fulfilling.

Ellison and Wright shared more than just theoretical and artistic interests. Wright told him about the poverty he had known as a child in Mississippi and the wrenching sense of tension and psychic destabilization that moving to Chicago had caused him. Ellison had had similar experiences, wandering about in a vulnerable family in dust bowl Oklahoma. Over the course of their first several months together, Ellison frequently made mental notes about the surprising confluence of their lives. In 1941, he thought out loud to Wright in a letter regarding the coincidences and intangibles that made them "brothers," calling up the fundamental sameness of their experience that had caused them to immediately fall in with one another.

> I think it is because this past which filters through your book [*Twelve Million Black Voices*] has always been tender and aching within us. We are the ones who had no comforting amnesia of childhood, and for whom the trauma of passing from the country to the city of destruction brought no anesthesia of unconsciousness, but left our nerves peeled and quivering. We are not the numbed, but the seething.[73]

He believed that moving to New York from Alabama began his self-conscious manhood, and now Ellison sparkled at finding a suitable comrade who had similar passions and had overcome similar obstacles.

In midsummer, the chief of Harlem's *Daily Worker* bureau broached the question to Ellison of writing a book review for *New Challenge*. Ellison demurred. Reading Wright's typed copies of "Fire and Cloud" and "Long Black Song" was different from criticizing an entire published monograph. Besides, who knew whether he wanted to be a writer? Wright pressed him with the responsibility of examining contemporary black writers from the literary perspective of the radical. Ellison was smart, well-read, and critical, he said, not easily fooled by the rhetorical smokescreens put up by Party pundits and black romantics. Ellison had shown his hand by mentioning to Wright his own minor experiments with poetry and musical composition; now he faced a challenge. The natural question came up: what was he doing in New York? The review offer was a choice opportunity, even if it did not help him make ends meet. Ellison decided to try, after Wright assured him that he had a finer literary sensibility than that of many published writers.[74] Even if he didn't know exactly what he was doing, he'd stumble along. Ellison talked with Wright in earnest; Wright explained to him the principles behind the essay he had worked on for the same *New Challenge* issue, which was his "Blueprint for Negro Writing." Ellison now saw this chance to write as even more fantastic and energizing than reading on his own at Tuskegee. Now his former college instructors would be able to direct students to one of their own, a radical modernist who was publishing in distinguished company. By August, he had handed to Wright his review of Waters Turpin's novel *These Low Grounds*.

In his first published piece, Ellison clearly named two criteria for art: adherence to the regional authenticity of folk culture, and theoretical sophistication. Mainly, he gathered up his critical tools of Marxist literary theory. He knew of the effort that had gone into producing the book—the actual work involved—and mildly rewarded Turpin for his initiative in setting the story in a colorful local region, the oyster beds of Maryland's eastern shore. He liked the fact that Turpin proposed to "essay a saga," but felt unsure about whether the author had succeeded at his task. "There is a certain realism demanded by the types Turpin sought to portray. This realism which demands sincerity on the part of the writer has been missing in the work of a great many of those who have preceded Turpin." Ultimately Ellison saw in the book "undigested lumps" of characters and the flaw of "superficial motivation" which "bespeaks a certain lack of historical and political consciousness." Turpin had missed the fact that the writer's responsibility included actively engaging global politics. Didn't he know that there was another writers congress going on in war-torn Spain? Turpin had failed to "utilize yet transcend his immediate environment and grasp the historic process as a whole, and his group's relation to it." Put most simply, Turpin had not yet read Malraux and as a result had produced one-dimensional characters: "he [Turpin] might profit by a closer acquaintance with the techniques of his contemporaries, since their problems are his, and their achievements similar to those he seeks."[75] Ellison did not absolutely bury the book, but he articulated a high standard for achievement. Without fully assimilating current artistic techniques, even if only to reject them, it was impossible for Turpin's *These Low Grounds* to produce a character possessing a fully rounded consciousness.

After editing Ellison's piece, Wright requested that he make a foray into the craft of fiction. Again, Ellison at first refused: "But I've never even tried to write a story."[76] Wright advised him to stay within himself and write a story about things that interested him and that he'd experienced firsthand. Ellison asked for more detailed counsel, and Wright became precise. He recommended that Ellison read Henry James's prefaces (a new edition had come out edited by R. P. Blackmur called *The Art of Fiction*), Dostoyevsky's and Conrad's letters, and the criticism of Joseph Warren Beach.[77] In the end, Ellison was convinced to work on a short story as a portion of his commitment to the movement. During that time, he collected subscriptions to the magazine from poets and teachers, novelists, and hangers-on to the radical cause. He even encouraged a group of Swarthmore literary professors to take out the $5 subscriptions to *New Challenge*.

During the summer of 1937, Ellison began to feel the importance and necessity of the left-wing political circles he was accepted in, and of the writers he was modeling himself after. His vigorous friendship with Wright and the opportunity to publish helped convince him to associate with the Communists. When he wrote his mother toward the end of the summer from Toy Harper's house, he bitterly deplored "[t]his system which offers a poor person practically nothing but work for a low wage from birth to death." When he thought of the collectivization process that had taken place in Russia, and then of his poor family in America, where his job prospects were bleak, he lamented, "I wish we could live there." He hoped that in the coming fall he would be able to get a good job aboard one of the Hudson River cruise ships, or even better, a job on the WPA Writers Project. He no longer sought his pleasures at Carnegie Hall. He had become a man of the people. Now his enjoyment sprang from mingling in the brightly dressed crowds along Eighth Avenue, where vendors sold fried fish, hog maws, home fries, and tropical fruits, where the smells of hair grease, washed and unwashed bodies, and dogs wafted in the air, where he heard the cacophony of many languages being spoken at once. He wrote to his mother of the simple pleasures of life: "I like to walk on such streets. Life on them is right out in the open and they [people] make no pretense of being what they are not."[78] He was cutting his ties with the past.

Probably during that summer, sometime between July and September, Ellison produced his first known short story, "Hymie's Bull."[79] Using first-person narration, he strove for Hemingway's spartan employment of language and the dramatic tension of violence. But his greatest achievement in the early story was the creation of a sympathetic narrator, the result of his close reading of Henry James's preface to the *Princess of Casamassima,* where he was introduced to the concept of "economy of interest"—to grasp lightly the sympathetic qualities in his characters. He had followed Wright's suggestion and learned the rules of fiction, going so far as to repunctuate James's prose in pencil in his copy to increase its clarity. James advanced a skillful degree of characterization. He told readers that a dull cast led to boredom in fiction: "agents in any drama are only interesting in as much as they feel their respective situations." But James simultaneously counseled them to avoid the snare that might make articulate an "obviously limited vessel of consciousness." The master of the nineteenth-century American novel advised writers not to make characters "too prigishly clever or intelligent."[80]

In "Hymie's Bull," Ellison borrowed from his own experience, the train ride that yet tormented him, combining elements of his journey on the rails with his fair-skinned "uncle" Charlie and the pummeling he suffered in the Decatur freight yard. He came close to divulging his terror, but sagely maintained control of the artistic structure of the short story by refusing to fully reveal his personal feelings about the violent ride through Decatur four summers before. The protagonist of the story describes the brutality of the train ride and the punishments that black boys take at the hands of hypermasculine railroad bulls. Hoboes are brained with sticks and blackjacks and thrown off trains like rolling logs. Everybody carries a knife for protection, and "when you hear that spades are the only bums that carry knives you can just put that down as bull talk," he tells his reader.[81] Jews, like "an ofay bum named Hymie," says the narrator, carry them and are more prone to use them to deadly effect, even though this sort of retributive violence makes things difficult for black hoboes.

Ellison impressed Wright with his command of language and dramatic tension. His bold theme connected with the ongoing Scottsboro trials, and it refuted the stereotype of docile blacks herded by the detectives. Nor were most blacks as evil as cutthroats. And Ellison already showed a flair for gritty realism in metaphor: "Once a bull hit me across the bridge of the nose and I felt like I was coming apart like a cigarette in a urinal." He had accumulated great distance between himself and the harrowing experience, and he had gotten it down on paper well enough for it to be accepted for the second issue of *New Challenge*.

Despite the success of his first experience writing and the knowledge that his name would appear in print, Ellison had little to go on insofar as his own economic success was concerned. His education in literature may not have cost him much, but so far it had earned him nothing. He cautiously waited for something to happen as his funds again neared depletion. And something did.

Perhaps toward the end of the first week of October, maybe as early as late September, Ellison got word that his mother had become ill. Earlier in the summer, she had taken a nasty spill at the house in Dayton, which resulted in an annoying pain in her hip. But doctors at the segregated hospital in Dayton had dismissed the fifty-two-year-old woman as being cranky and overanxious. She merely had rheumatism or arthritis, they speculated, neglecting to perform x-rays. Not until fall did they discover that Ida had cracked her hip, and that tuberculosis had set in. She was moved closer to her sister—thirty miles south to Cincinnati—where the hospital had superior medical facilities. Upon receiving the news, Ellison set out for Ohio, and arrived in the city on the north side of the Ohio River on October 15. He made his way over to the hospital, where Ida was in so much pain that she could hardly recognize her oldest child. The next day, October 16, she died.[82]

The loss of Ida Ellison Bell was the deepest hurt he'd experienced in his life, but Ellison was a twenty-four-year-old male during an era when a man's distance from his emotions was purported to signal the depth of his masculinity. Trained to ignore pain as a three-year-old, despite his obvious sensitivity, he had to struggle to release deep despair or anguish. Now Ellison was emotionally numb. And, as when Lewis had died, he had someone else to be strong for, someone who needed him more than he needed himself. Herbert, fully grown but less in control of his emotions than his brother, was devastated. The Ellison boys were alone in the world, and Ralph stepped in to care for the brother he hadn't seen in almost three years.

Following Ida's funeral and interment at Hillcrest Cemetery, the brothers moved back up to Dayton, to their great-aunt's humble house at 742 West Fifth Street, in order to transact final business. The small black sections of Cincinnati and Dayton, the rows of wooden Negro shacks and unpaved streets, reminded Ellison of Oklahoma City, as much as being slung from house to house over a couple of weeks repeated what he had known in childhood. He had left the Manhattan of three hundred thousand big-city Negroes for Dayton and her ten thousand blacks, centered around Fifth Street, the same sort of all-black business hub he had known on Oklahoma City's Second Street. Dayton had neither the elegant brownstones of Harlem nor the skyscrapers of Manhattan. Ellison expressed his difference from his Ohio relatives and friends by asking for a typewriter within days of his arrival. Surrounded by barely literate relatives, after ten days he banged out a letter to Richard Wright, whose unique friendship and vigorous mind he now had reason to value more dearly. He apologized for not writing, and told his friend about his grief. Ellison briefly lowered his guard, and allowed himself some emotion in stoic and philosophical prose: "This is real, and the most final thing I've ever encountered." In their discussions, they had played with myth and reality, knowledge and pretentiousness, eschatology and apocalypse. But in the face of his mother's death and the collapse of family as he had known it, Ellison came to the "real" and the "most final thing." He did not expect much by way of response from Wright, because, with the help of philosophy and the voguish ideology of materialism, the two of them often had ridiculed sentimental emotion in writing and in life. Still, he acknowledged that the loss of Ida was the "end of childhood . . . I used to pretend this was so when I came to New York but now I know it was just pretense and nothing more."[83] When Wright wrote him back in dispatch-style prose, his condolences reflected his beliefs and, perhaps, the proper gauge of his emotional range: "like the sun and the rain, it [death] is an inescapable part of life."[84]

Ellison had other demons that accompanied him on his passage to adulthood. A significant emotional tension simmered in the background, emblematic of the degree to which he had distanced himself from his earliest years, and of his determination to remain distant. Ralph expected his old animosities to flare up with Herbert once the searing pain of Ida's death subsided. "We avoid talking of certain things and I see he spends much time away from me so as not to mention these painful things . . . the antagonism between us will come alive and then things will be very difficult to manage." He confided to Wright his troubles in the most general terms: "We [Ralph and Herbert] are so utterly different." The oblique characterization of his relationship with his brother hid a messier truth. Endowed with quite different gifts, Ellison was not about to abandon his career for the sake of his sibling.[85] And like Langston Hughes, Wright was an excellent confidant with whom to share the experience of family relationships failing to meet expectations. Both men had grown up in matriarchal households; both had younger brothers whose talents and life experiences were different from their own. Although Ellison would remain in contact with Herbert over the years, in terms of his other blood relatives, Ralph would become something of an orphan.

As if to symbolize his difference from the rest of his family, the *New Challenge* issue carrying his review was slated to appear within a week or two. In a state of excitement, Ellison reminded Wright to send him copies of the magazine. It was a telling moment that combined his expression of authentic grief with his newly asserted sense of adulthood. He had found a passion and wanted to hold on to it. Ellison scoured Dayton for the *Daily Worker* and *New Masses* but found communist advocacy absent from middle America. Within days, he would walk a mile from Fifth Street to downtown Dayton stores to read the *New York Times,* in particular Hemingway's field reports on the Spanish Civil War.[86] Ellison found ordinary American Negro life to be woefully lacking an international perspective. Scrambling around the region for employment, he discovered workers in Richmond, Indiana, who asked him if the CIO (Congress of Industrial Organizations) wasn't the new railroad. His inability to find any semblance of revolution in America's heartland gravely disappointed him. Ellison came to grips with the fact that American wheels turned much more slowly than did Soviet ones. He may have begun to suspect that New York, despite the brag that it held a position of cultural leadership, actually only preached to the converted. Instead of living on the edge, Ellison thought, perhaps he was really on the fringe. Dayton reminded him that for survival, he'd still need to maintain skepticism, even if it was skepticism about the holy class revolution. As if to confirm his feelings of isolation from radical writers and ideas, the local paper carried only the syndicated "tripe" writers—columnist Westbrook "Tin-drawers" Pegler and Boake Carter. Despite his hardships, or perhaps because of the difficulty of getting news, Ellison splurged and bought Hemingway's latest, *To Have and Have Not,* the story of fisherman Harry Morgan. He completed the novel the same day that he had purchased it from the bookstore and wished for more substance. A combination of three short stories, two of which Ellison had already read in *Esquire, To Have* did not sustain rereadings. But the purchase of books during hard times reflected his priorities. Wearing his coat of rags proudly, he considered himself an intellectual.

Wright wrote a letter, which Ellison, somewhat recovered from his grief after three weeks, received in the solitude and isolation of Dayton. Wright reminded him of the liabilities of New York, but Ellison, bedridden with a cold, longed for the personalities and characters of their New York literary crowd. Ellison had severed his former attachments, and now thought himself a New Yorker. With his brother, the only common ground was sexual boasting about the local girls at Cox's Drugstore on Fifth Street or at Moses Moore's, one of three downtown restaurants open to blacks. Though from his experiences all over the country, Ellison was certain he could win the affections of one of the small-town Negro girls, he felt he would be taking advantage of the situation, and either retreated or acted calculatedly repulsive to discourage amorous interest. He was a serious student of Marx; and though he did not mention it to the godless Wright, he probably was still well in touch with his A.M.E. moralism. Pious in his refusal to fake commitment in order to bed the young waitresses, he wanted to leave well enough alone. Besides, regaling girls with stories of romance and lifelong fidelity was bourgeoisie.

Telling him what he was missing out on, Wright teased him with information about local social events with the radical crowd, with whom he still remained at odds. At one fête, Benjamin Davis had invited Communist Party members over and promptly grilled Wright about the nationalist message in "Blueprint for a Negro Intellectual." Ellison and Wright quipped in their letters about the social dynamic of the Party, where the radicals' determination to reject the color bar created sexual electricity. Boasting of his own sexual drawing power in Communist Party circles, Ellison joked to Wright about the clumsy sexual innuendo and curiosity of the female Communists.[87] Sensitive to instances of sexual fetishism and exploitation, Ellison laughed loudly at the legendary freewheeling sexuality in the New York intellectual and literary circles of the Left in Greenwich Village. Shy and less comfortable with women than Ellison, Wright found the trysts with white women provocative, and enjoyed the rush of excitement when being courted because of, or in defiance of, the racial taboo. Still stuck in Dayton, Ohio, Ellison had only memories from the summer.

In Dayton, as he tried to maneuver around his mother's relatives and plan his future, winter struck. Ellison was unworried about Herbert, whose home had been in Ohio for more than a year; but Ellison, with nothing concrete to return to in New York, had no choice but to hunker down during the rough weather. To prove to his relatives that he was contributing to his room and board, since he was unable to find work, Ellison took to the fields with another local boy, a dog, and .22 caliber rifle, in search of rabbits, squirrels, and pheasant. Glorying in having a writerly friend to communicate with and dead serious about his own literary education, he crafted his hunting descriptions into doggerel for Wright: "perhaps I'll be back in New York by that time and some one else will bring these elusive dinners down to dust with metal sticks which roar and into flames do *bust*. (How's that? Me, Marvell, Eliot, Hemingway)."[88] The only person in the world who understood him and validated his need for books, and for ideas in relation to their social context, Wright helped to make a writer out of him, and Ellison cared about his approval.

Hunting was more difficult than writing poetry at first, since he hadn't hunted since he left Oklahoma. The first week, he struggled to distinguish the animals from their surroundings, but soon Ellison was bringing in enough surplus birds to sell, earning enough money to take himself, his brother, and a friend to the drugstore for sandwiches and to the Classic Theater on Fifth Street for a movie.[89] The Ellisons supplemented their fare by picking bushels of pears and gunny sacks full of walnuts and butternuts. Mildly surprised by his Thoreau-like existence, he admitted to Wright, who lacked all of the outdoor skills, "I don't hold Rousseau in very high regard but nature in fall dress is nice." The young radical had little use for Rousseau's romance of the prelapsarian natural world as mankind's cradle; Ellison was battling for his life against nature. And while he struggled gamely for survival that winter, he gained memories of his mother's kin who had struggled not so much against nature as they had against man. His great-aunt, born a slave in Virginia during the presidency of Martin Van Buren, still had vivid memories of the Civil War, which had brought cataclysmic change to her life, and where she now spent most of her mental time. Seeing that Herbert did not warm to conversation dealing with heady topics, she opened up to Ralph, who was intently reading the newspaper and plunking away at the typewriter. Millsaps talked up to the white folks and ran off to the Yankees, she wouldn't let him forget. Twelve years later, when he was writing his novel *Invisible Man*, Ellison recalled in his fiction a description of his grandfather he would have heard about that winter. In his treatment from the draft, which was later edited and removed, he called his grandfather by the name "Polk Milsaps," and has the tale told to the Invisible Man in rich Negro vernacular by an older boarder at Mary Rambo's rooming house. The Polk Milsaps tale is a trickster story, where Polk, an ornery bondsman, is trusted by his slave master during the Civil War to guard the family fortune. When Milsaps is given deliberate instructions to take the gold and silver North and out of harm's way, he takes advantage of the precision of the instructions sending him "North," and goes on to Canada.[90] However, it was a bit difficult to accept the heritage of slavery. As a modern man, Ellison equated the antebellum period with the prehistoric era as a means of increasing his emotional and intellectual distance from the bondage of his grandparents. In circles of distinguished blacks, talk of ancestry centered on relatives who had been born in freedom prior to the issuance of Lincoln's proclamation. But behind his eyes, Ellison was proud.

Somehow Ellison sniffed out the black thinkers in the town, though it had no big-city radical element. An ambitious janitor at Wright airfield talked of entering his drawings into engineering contests, but the main source of support came from Dayton's politicians.[91] The Montgomery County Republican Committee had two prominent black members, an architect named Frank Sutter and a lawyer named William O. Stokes. A pillar of Dayton's black community, Stokes began to take a liking to the young man from New York who read the *Times* every day and hunted with deadly accuracy. He allowed Ellison access to his office at 449 West Fifth Street, and more important, provided Ellison with stationery, a supply of paper so he could continue his forays into fiction.[92] Ellison had signed off his first letter to Wright with "Workers of the world must write!!!!"; now in his letters he consciously wrote of creating art. In Paul Laurence Dunbar's hometown, he began to write with the manic fury of his friend. In "Hymie's Bull," he had dramatized his flight to Tuskegee as a hobo. In the stories he wrote during the winter of 1938, he returned to childhood, minding Thomas Mann's dictum about not wallowing in heartfelt and anguishing experience while continuing to write about what he knew well. First there was "Boy On a Train," which recalled his and Ida's well-remembered struggle to find work in McAlester, Oklahoma, where Ralph had first started selling papers at 4 A.M. to help the family. He mined this early territory and cast a reflective glance at his mother, whose own ambition had been snuffed and transferred to her children.

Ida's death ended not only his childhood, but his childhood dream of becoming a musician. To soften the sting of her departure, he carefully recreated his mother's speech through the vehicle of his newfound passion. Conscious of having lost his closest connection to Lewis, he didn't want his poignant memory of her to fade. He worked hard at reproducing his mother's homespun tale of their family odyssey, the Ellison myth of origin. But most telling of his perspective during the Ohio winter of 1937 was his decision to allow the character James, based upon himself, to intuitively arrive at a communist perspective, namely the rejection of religion. After watching his mother cry, though he does not know why she is weeping, James decides to destroy the forces that bring her pain. "Yes, I'll kill it. I'll make it cry. Even if it's God, I'll make God cry, he thought. I'll kill him; I'll kill God and not be sorry."[93]

Ellison's earliest short stories combined segments of his own life with his radical political vision. A follow-up story to "Hymie's Bull" called "I Did Not Know Their Names" covered his train ride to college in even greater detail. Now he let all of himself shine through. He began by making the protagonist and narrator an articulate musician on his way from Oklahoma to Alabama to attend music school. To retain control and perspective, he did not tell of the beating he had endured and then escaped, choosing instead to leave his protagonist in a jail cell, suggestive of the inevitable violent levy accompanying incarceration. The story's overarching theme, like that of "Hymie's Bull," was the possibility for alliances across racial and class lines.

Like his mentors Wright and Hughes, Ellison wanted to take part in the proletarian struggle shaking the world. The stories poured out of him in a torrent. Beyond the autobiographical pieces, he felt especially inspired to construct a short story with immense social relevancy. Both "Boy on a Train" and "I Did Not Know Their Names" hinted at the modern social horror of lynching but did not confront it entirely. Ellison had been captivated by the power of Wright's memorable poem "Between the World and Me," and picked up on the theme of lynching in a powerful story he could never title. He strove to elaborate fictionally on Wright's vivid description of the lynching and burning of a black man, in which the protagonist's skin bubbles off. Ellison emulated Hemingway's hard-boiled realism and sparse diction; and in an approach both daring and theoretically astute, he employed a white protagonist (making him from nearby Cincinnati) who has observed a lynching, and who graphically describes the scene in all of its grotesqueness. Using a white character freed Ellison from a maudlin sermonizing about the evils of race hatred, enabling him to focus upon the actual physical horrors of the scene without assuming a tone of moral righteousness—or worse, revealing his own personal fear of the lynch rope. For his setting, he returned to the town square in downtown Tuskegee, where as a college student he had frequently encountered whites who he knew were capable of burning a black man with gasoline at the stake.[94] His protagonist narrates the most brutal details of the story in deadpan fashion.

> Well, that nigger was tough. I have to give it to that nigger; he was really tough. He had started to burn like a house afire and was making the smoke smell like hides. . . . I'll never forget it. Every time I eat barbeque I'll remember that nigger. His back was just like a barbecued hog. I could see the prints of his ribs where they start around from his backbone and curved down and around. It was a sight to see, that nigger's back.[95]

Ellison's style and narrator were similar to Hemingway's *To Have and Have Not,* one of his few books. Ellison's effort was impressive, taking on the national horror of lynching and exposing the contradictions of class politics among starving whites who lynched as one of the leading symbolic and ritualistic means of asserting their dominance. In almost a word-for-word parallel of narrator Harry Morgan's concluding remarks in the first chapter of *To Have,* admiring a black with a machine gun, Ellison's white character from Cincinnati ends the grotesque short story with an assertion of envy for the black victim: "That Bacote nigger was some nigger!"[96]

Despite the rewarding experience of writing these stories, other life issues intruded. After a couple of months at his aunt's, pride drove him and his brother away, and the boys' only friend was Republican committee chairman Stokes. The lawyer encouraged Ellison to attend events like the Bethel Baptist Church, the Republican Committee's McKinley Day Celebration, or a dinner honoring Wilberforce College. (Noting the refinement among the membership, Ellison was reminded of the fact that the scapegoated Jews were the most cultured ethnic group in Germany.)[97] Stokes assisted the wandering Ellison brothers as much as he could. In the dead of the Ohio winter, Ralph and Herbert slept in his office and one freezing night, they slept in an automobile in an open garage. Even while suffering from the severity of Ohio's winter, Ellison experienced fulfillment at writing full-time; perhaps as much as with anything that he had yet done. He spent many joyous and fertile evenings and mornings at the typewriter raking over his imagination. During those winter months, he quickly produced four short stories. When spring broke, Ellison learned that Wright's magazine had failed; but the taste of having had his own story accepted for publication tantalized him. He would find the means to return to New York. He made his peace with his ancestors and with his relatives. Leaving Herbert in Dayton, where the younger Ellison would remain until the American entry into World War II, Ellison made his way back to Manhattan.

8

Is Politics an Expression of Love?

1938–1941

ELLISON RETURNED to New York in late April 1938, penniless and without his vehicle into the world of art, politics, and criticism. Wright's *New Challenge* was finished. After a series of disagreements with Marian Minus and Dorothy West, who thought that Wright was muscling too much politics into a journal for the arts, the project had collapsed.[1] Its lack of subscriptions had not helped matters, though Ellison had methodically collected many when he lived in New York. The magazine's downfall indicated the continuing paradox of Wright's interaction with other groups of blacks. Liberals and non-Party leftists considered him too concerned with radical social change; communists labeled him both an "individualist," striving for the middle class, and a "bourgeois nationalist," splintering class solidarity by focusing on race.

When Ellison returned, Wright was renting a room at 139 West 143rd Street from a woman named Sawyer, and also dating his landlady's daughter. In the early weeks of Ellison's re-acclimation to New York, a pregnancy scare sent Wright and his girlfriend to the medical examiner, who diagnosed the girl with congenital syphilis. Wright backed out of a shotgun wedding and the household, beginning a gradual self-imposed social ostracism from Harlem.

Despite the shambles of his personal life, Wright had wonderful professional prospects. On March 23, he had published *Uncle Tom's Children,* the short stories that Ellison had read in the Harlem bureau office on Lenox Avenue. The mainstream press lauded Wright as the new black literary giant, comparing him to Hemingway and even suggesting that a first-rate Negro novelist was on the horizon.[2] Only Zora Neale Hurston, writing for the orthodox *Saturday Review of Literature,* and a first-rate novelist herself, downplayed the book's impact. She called Wright's dialect "tone deaf," and criticized him for stirring up trouble, furthering a "picture of the South that the communists have been passing around of late." However, Hurston, who had suffered from Wright's venom in "Blueprint," was most perceptive in her appraisal of Wright's psychology and the "wish-fulfillment theme": "In each story, the hero suffers but he gets his man."[3]

Ellison showed Wright his own bulging folder of stories, telling him that they were only fodder, further exercises in composition. He had made up his mind that he would write short stories—perhaps even a novel—and he gamely accepted the prospect of poverty that came with the life of the intellectual artist and political radical. The feeling of adventure and being out of bounds reminded him of his experiences hoboing. He had changed, though, from the college freshman en route to Tuskegee. He now made decisions based on a hunter's intuition—he had been able to survive in Dayton by using a gun—and he cared less, much less, what people thought of him. Some nights he slept in Harlem's St. Nicholas Park, awaiting opportunities for work, then shared a couch in a friend's living room. But soon he got work collecting material for the Federal Writers Project of New York City, thanks no doubt to Wright's Communist-union ties. Though he had been a city resident only off and on for two years, and had published only a single review, Ellison still managed to qualify for relief as a skilled writer, probably with the help of the powerful Communist lobby. The New Deal welfare state remedies of Franklin D. Roosevelt coordinated, oddly enough, with the Popular Front rubric of the Communist Party. Ellison joined the Project at a period of relative harmony, when it was not quite a contradiction for a vanguard revolutionary artist to be employed by the capitalist State.

The New York City Federal Writers Project was arguably the best place in the country for any apprentice writer, but especially a Negro. Nationwide, blacks comprised only two percent of the FWP; in Ellison's native Oklahoma, whites in the Project refused to share the water fountain with blacks; and in Mississippi, "two of the four Negroes were dropped, one 'left' to 'haul cotton' and the fourth was transferred."[4] With his duties as a "legman" for Wright and an ample salary of about $21.67 per week from the Project, Ellison was able to pursue full-time his love for reading and engaging in heated discussions with other writers interested in the craft, some neophytes like himself.

At the Project, he began work gathering information on blacks in New York alongside Ellen Tarry, Ted Poston, Waring Cuney, Abram Hill, and

Everet Beanne, under the overall direction of Roi Ottley. Ellison took a lik-
ing to the witty and affable Sterling Brown, the national editor of the Negro
Affairs department for the Project, who frequently came to New York from
Washington to check on progress.

The relative lack of racial prejudice on the Project in New York did not
eliminate all difficulties. Ottley confused his staff with his dictatorial and
secretive administrative style. He never shared his comprehensive vision with
the other writers, preferring to give several writers the same assignments,
destroying any overall sense of teamwork and breeding insecurity and jealousy. Ottley's brand of leadership also included frequent untoward advances
to women on his staff. To Ellison, Ottley was a black man with little interest
in the problems of race in American society; Ottley had limited his interests
to the bedroom and his bank account.[5] Though Ellison hung on to his job
with the New York Writers Project until 1942, Ottley and most of the other
workers were dismissed following congressional investigations of 1939.

Early on, Ellison spent most of his time collecting evidence of the black
presence in Manhattan. He would report at the New York Port Authority
Building at Forty-second Street and Eighth Avenue to discuss his material
with a supervisor. He then usually went uptown to the 135th Street Branch
of the New York Public Library or over to the mammoth Forty-second Street
Branch for an enjoyable day of research.[6] Uptown, he talked with the 135th
Street librarians, such as Jean Blackwell, a former member of the John Reed
Club, and the Ph.D. Lawrence D. Reddick, curator of the Schomburg collection. Ellison's research in black history, like his reading of Eliot's poem, led
him off "in all directions."[7] Later, after the Project folded, Ottley took the
research done on blacks in New York and used it as the basis for his own
manuscript.

The FWP work provided Ellison with firm historical grounding regarding the prominent role of blacks in New York since the seventeenth century.
His research into Manhattan's black past further secured his connection to
the city and diminished his sense of himself as a visitor. In June, he logged
hours in the early eighteenth- and nineteenth-century archives. Working under
editor Charles Cumberbatch, he read through the minutes of the 1831 First
Annual Convention of the People of Colour and turned in a brief report on
"Negro Instructors in New York of Higher Learning." The essay mainly explored the achievements of James Weldon Johnson and the socialist-minded
refugee from South Africa, Max Yergan. To enhance his American colonial
perspective, Ellison examined period journals, Hoshendon's "The Negro
Conspiracy . . . New York, 1744" and Charles Beard's first volume of the
Rise of American Civilization.

His longest project essay was "The Insurrection of 1741," about a slave
rebellion that he found inspirational, particularly because of its resounding
similarities to the black freedom struggle of the 1930s. Intent upon directing

his work to modern-day crises, Ellison traced parallels between them and the 1741 "wave of terror" in New York City: "The affair (the Insurrection of 1741) seems to parallel the Scottsboro case of our own day in some of its surface details, since both resulted in the unjustified persecution of innocent Negroes, and both as the result of the testimony of white women of doubtful character."[8] Ellison learned that the revolt in New York began over petty theft and then, fueled by white paranoia and guilt, wound up destroying black life with the same ferocity and blind vengeance that had characterized the Tulsa pogrom of 1921. Colonists left a Negro man named Caesar to rot in a cage in full public view as an example of the punishment awaiting Negro rebels.

Ellison went about his library work with a strident sense of radical purpose that was relatively absent in the other, better-known writers on the Harlem project, including Wesley Cartwright, Waring Cuney, Richard Bruce Nugent, Arthur Gray, Wilbur Young, Henry Lee Moon, Dorothy West, and Abram Hill. As a cub reporter with little journalistic experience, Ellison generally received small, single-page assignments. Ottley never really paid him close attention. However, he used his tasks on the Project as a complement to his more stimulating exchanges with literary Marxists. Ellison constructed a sort of improvised graduate school for himself, turning in regular assignments, conducting heavy research, and honing his writing skills. He benefited from the interaction with the older, more experienced journalists, though many of them frustrated him intellectually. They seemed for the most part uninterested in political discussions or fine art, his passions. Ellen Tarry, for instance, one of Ellison's fellow project writers who went on to become a regular columnist for the black press, distrusted the writers' union because it raised money for the Spanish Loyalists. She later admitted in her autobiography that "most of the talk about politics which I heard on my job flowed . . . above my thought levels."[9]

Despite the reticence of some members of the black middle class to engage in the conversation, the Federal Writers Project was a hotbed of political discussion in 1938 as Europe crept closer to total war. The political climate in the United States became less tolerant of Communists, who were seen nearly as agents of a foreign power. But many of Ellison's friends held their course. In April 1938, Wright added his name to a list of supporters who upheld Stalin's persecution of Trotsky and the Moscow Trials that had resulted in the public execution of most of the original leaders of the October Revolution. By the end of the year, Wright had helped to author a statement exonerating Soviet Russia for freeing itself from "insidious internal dangers" which threatened "peace and democracy."[10] Stalin purged the Communist Party with the dramatic trials, and the Soviet Union steadily proceeded in the direction of totalitarianism. Wright's sharp focus on the racial situation guaranteed his allegiance to the Party; Communists at the time still considered the "Negro Question" imperative in their national strategy.

Although Ellison joined the communist picket lines to demand an integrated National Maritime Union, his library jaunts kept him out of the Project office, where tension was mounting steadily. Communists, applying their proven abilities at organization, were attempting to dominate the policies and practices of the New York Writers Project. Project administrators were vulnerable to the charge that they had no blacks in leadership positions; so the Communists began agitating for a leadership position for Richard Wright. They caused a series of disturbances—they formed picket lines, elected delegates, and even cordoned off areas of the office to express their rights to sovereignty. Wright, while going along with the hardball game downtown at the Project, was playing a bit of hardball of his own in Harlem, where he was trying to wring concessions from the Communists for youth development programs. An advocate of art over doctrine, which translated into the freedom to write having priority over the necessity of political organization, Wright continued to ally himself with the political group with which he was most comfortable. In May, the Communist-backed cultural journal *New Masses* published "Bright and Morning Star," Wright's dutiful plea for interracial workers' alliances.

Ellison considered Wright heroic, and felt glad to have a job owing in part to his friend's Communist beliefs. Still assimilating doctrine and struggling to get hard-to-find translations of Marx, Ellison stuck with the pragmatic anti-imperialist politics of people like Wright and Louise Thompson. They hoped to band with groups resisting the great colonial Anglo-French empires that imposed racist practices in Africa, China, India, and Indochina. Meanwhile, the schism deepened between the Stalinists and the Trotskyite camp gathering around *Partisan Review* and Edmund Wilson. While the Communists pushed Negroes like James Ford, Harry Haywood, Angelo Herndon, and Ben Davis into high-profile positions of leadership, the highbrow Left, generally more sympathetic to Trotsky's flexible position on art and culture, was largely unable to incorporate race into their political and social theories, and seemed skeptical of any overthrow of the racist status quo. By 1940, Philip Rahv, editor of *Partisan Review,* would call for an overhaul of Marxist theory and speculate that the socialist revolution in America was "sheer romanticism."[11]

Although the Communists repeatedly championed blacks in politics, the CP organization and doctrinaire responses to complex issues alienated independent thinkers like Wright, who were maligned in Party ranks as lacking discipline. Nor did Communists approve of modernist writers, whose difficult techniques were thought alienating to readers. Several of the Communists and slackers on the Writers Project refused to turn in assignments, seeing the Project as a well-deserved arm of government welfare. In contrast, hard at work on his assignments, Ellison took his job seriously and hoped to get a short story into the second issue of *Direction,* a Writers Project journal. His aims were foiled when the CP-controlled American Writers Union scuttled this attempt by New York FWP director Alsberg to launch another vehicle for creative writers because they were disgusted with *Direction*'s editor Harold Rosenberg. Unable to secure an editor they approved of, the union claimed that the national magazine wasn't "democratic" enough.[12] Meanwhile, Wright retreated to his solitude in Brooklyn to work on his new project, and Ellison listened more closely to the words of independent liberals like Kenneth Burke, in a move that surely took him away from vocal Communists, whom he might have found more politically stimulating, but that also increased his own job security. By the fall of 1938, the House Committee on Un-American activities had begun to scrutinize the Federal Writers Project, focusing particularly on the New York division.[13]

At the gatherings at Harlem's Communist headquarters, Ellison encountered doctrine more rigid than the views of his Tuskegee professors. He was far more interested in the literature of the Writers Project and the CP's downtown headquarters. Nor was he impressed by the highest black official in the CP, whose rank seemed to indicate obedience rather than talent. James Ford was called a "Red Uncle Tom" because of his fawning personal style around whites at the Party headquarters.[14] It was thought that Ford would shift his positions on issues to retain his influence in the Party, seemingly at any cost. Ellison thought that obsequious behavior was thoroughly anachronistic; as he saw it, Harlem blacks were waiting to be organized so that they could declare their own agenda. A good example of a missed opportunity came on June 22 when Joe Louis knocked out avowed Nazi Max Schmeling in the first round at Yankee Stadium—a fight Ellison had tickets to but missed. Crowds in Harlem celebrated the victory by brandishing hand-lettered anti-Nazi slogans.[15] The fairly uncreative Harlem section organizer Abner Berry, who led the Party's day-to-day uptown activities, failed to use what could have been a powerful moment to organize the multitude of blacks who were plainly seeking political change. A newspaperman, Berry had a journalist's disregard for depth; he mainly accepted the directives of Harlem district organizer Charles Krumbein, who worked at the national CPUSA headquarters on Twelfth Street. Most of Harlem's leaders were in awe of the political maneuvering—some of it justly impressive—taking place on the ninth floor where the Party's Central Committee met. They avoided dealing with the problems of Harlem within a cultural nationalist framework since Negro self-determination in practice threatened the broad-based racial and class alliances of the Popular Front. Richard Wright, uncomfortable with the way that race was conveniently downplayed, reasserted his opinion of the power of Joe Louis as an organizing tool and rallying point for American blacks in his essay "High Tide in Harlem," published in the *New Masses* in early July.

While Party life uptown may have been stagnant, with its policies clearly influenced less by the conditions in Harlem than by international directives, other Harlem cultural activities began to come up to Ellison's new demanding standard. Uptown, Langston Hughes had been having tremendous success with his self-promoted and -directed Harlem Suitcase Theater. This avant-garde theater used free-ranging dialogue along with blues music and poetry, eliminated props and sets, and pitched its content to the masses. Hughes successfully staged his free-form blues play, "Don't You Want to Be Free," with the organizational help of the International Workers Order. During the summer of 1938, the Manhattan Council of the National Negro Congress sponsored the WPA Negro Theater performance *The Bourbons Got the Blues*—a satire of the Senate filibuster of the antilynching bill. Ellison's buddy Richard Wright visited occasionally. When not working in Brooklyn, Wright returned to Harlem for social activities with Schomburg librarian Jean Blackwell.[16] In this fertile uptown brew, Ellison met and became romantically involved with the professional actress and dancer Rose Poindexter.

Because of Ellison's sympathetic working relationships with Communists down at the WPA and his friendship with Wright, he never came to fully know Claude McKay, the best-known black literary presence on the New York Project. McKay had recently published his sensational memoir *A Long Way from Home;* like Wright, he worked on the Project largely on his own, unsupervised.[17] McKay was cantankerous, grating toward even his closest friends, and uninterested in nurturing the creative sensibilities of younger artists. He went as far as almost ending his relationship with Arthur Schomburg when the book collector encouraged young authors and admirers to visit McKay, disrupting his authorial solitude.[18] He was also arguably the foremost black prose writer of his time, a man who had known the Soviet Union firsthand, a native Jamaican who had traveled the world and offered his caustic opinion of much of it. During the summer of 1938, McKay and the black poet Countee Cullen were coediting the journal *African,* which McKay hoped to turn into a vehicle for his proposed group, the League of Negro Writers of America. McKay was interested chiefly in what he described as a "radical counter-movement sponsored by Negroes themselves" to keep them out of Communist clutches and to forcefully expose unjust racial conditions in America.[19] In the informal discussions at the Project headquarters at the Port Authority building, Ellison found the deradicalized McKay entirely dispassionate in terms of interracial alliances, as well as negligent in failing to take on a historic role as a leader in the struggle against fascism. In September 1938, McKay published "Negro Author Sees Disaster If the Communist Party Gains Control of Negro Workers" in the *New Leader.* McKay found Wright's allegiance to communism simpleminded, and probably dismissed Ellison as a naive young flunky of Wright's.[20]

For his part, as Ellison further explored the works of the popular modernist writers that the elite of the Project's young intellectual crowd were reading—Proust, Eliot, Mann, Malraux, Joyce, Gide—he thought McKay (who had opposed *New Challenge*) uninterested in the technical aspects of writing.[21] In his autobiography, *A Long Way from Home* (1937), McKay proposed a mystical, romanticized pattern for artistic creation:

> For many days I was possessed with an unusually lyrical feeling, which grew and increased into form of expression until one day . . . there was a wild buzzing in my head. The buzzing was so great that it confused and crowded out all orders, so much so that my mechanical self could not function. . . . And hurrying to the lavatory I locked myself in and wrote the stuff out on a scrap of paper.[22]

Ellison was looking for models and patterns upon which to flesh out his own experience effectively, but he found McKay's writing imprecise and vague.

The gap between the Communist-allied blacks on the Left, like Wright, and the black center staffed by the survivors of the Harlem Renaissance, like Claude McKay, was bridged only by Langston Hughes. Hughes's position as a war correspondent in Spain and his membership on the central committee of the League of American Writers plainly bespoke his political sympathies, while his commitment to a folk theater in Harlem and loyalty to the black folk idiom in his work commanded notice from even the fairly conservative Negro press. But by 1938, Ellison had grown mildly frustrated with Hughes, who admitted in closed circles that "the only thing I can do is string along with the Left until maybe someday all of us poor folk will get enough to eat."[23] Such playfulness did not comfort Ellison, who was struggling to live out his convictions and now felt intellectually equipped for more serious discussions about writing. Wright and Ellison were inclined to see McKay, Hughes, and their generation of Harlem Renaissance–era writers as anachronisms who pandered black exoticism to a white public in exchange for meager sustenance. Self-consciously shaping themselves in the manner of Hemingway and Malraux, Ellison and Wright thought the Harlem Renaissance celebrators of black folk culture soft-boiled.

For their part, Ellison and Wright may have had little need, in fact, for the professional or moral support of other black writers. Wright encouraged Ellison's reading, and with his own appointment to the editorial board of the *New Masses* in June, he was in a position to help his partner publish more book reviews.[24] Elated to appear in a widely circulated national magazine, Ellison reviewed Arthur Huff Fauset's biography *Sojourner Truth: God's Faithful Pilgrim,* which he called a "pioneering effort" that would have "wide influence upon later Negro biography." True to his radical impatience, much of the five-hundred-word essay lamented Fauset's "dated style." Fauset, he found, was no modern historian, but relied upon a "confused historical approach and a static philosophy" when he faced the task of uncovering the layers of Sojourner Truth's psyche in American religious experience:

> Fauset presupposes that man is made up of a set of fixed qualities, which allows no scope for development and change of the individual through dynamic contact with the social and economic factors constituting environment.
>
> What is so romantically called "paganism" in the American Negro is perhaps no more than the result of a badly injured conscious will actively seeking to adjust itself to an environment where the main institutionalized social outlet is a very inadequate church. It is the display of a high degree of consciousness and striving under the most unfriendly conditions that makes for the beauty and significance of Sojourner Truth.[25]

In Ellison's materialist-inflected view, a modern historian would be negligent if he failed to note that Truth triumphed when she transcended her spiritual preoccupation with mysticism to pursue a practical, "material" avenue of struggle: abolition. He had started criticizing sacred black cows with his Marxism. Not quite a full year after his mother's death, Ellison revealed in the review his convictions about African Americans' "very inadequate church." Nearing marriage to Rose, he put some distance between himself and the black church, and perhaps, also, the pious image of his mother Ida.

In the summer of 1938, Richard Wright kept a room at the home of the interracial couple Herbert and Jane Newton in Brooklyn, first at 175 Carlton Avenue, then by the fall at 522 Gates Avenue.[26] Hard at work on a manuscript that he was already calling *Native Son*, Wright immersed himself completely in his fictional world and lessened his contact with the Writers Project. He was one of four established writers allowed to remain at home and work independently on an artistic project. While his friend and landlady Jane Newton argued with Wright about his prose style, encouraging him to reconsider the approaches of Tolstoy and Dostoyevsky, his younger colleague Ellison also greatly influenced the novel. After a lengthy critical discussion between the two men in the late summer, Wright was able to complete the final third of his novel, which dealt with the ambivalent role of whites in a movement for black freedom. Ellison was one of only a few other writers with whom Wright could argue through this central ideological question, one that also appeared in Wright's revolutionary story "Bright and Morning Star." Could whites be trusted? Was there a possibility for a relationship beyond the confines of condescension, patronage, mockery, and duplicity?

The principal elements that Ellison brought to his discussions with Wright were his widely divergent life experiences; he knew an entirely different range of people than Richard Wright, from Oklahoma pioneers to the patients and doctors of Tuskegee's Veterans Hospital. Ellison and Wright discussed the variations in dialect among these divergent groups of black Americans—a consuming problem in fiction. It required a certain diligence to re-produce the complexity of black speech on the printed page without resorting to the "eye-dialect" of Renaissance writers, which promoted the idea that black speech had little in common with standard English. In their technical discussions they tried to determine consistent strategies to translate the oral sound into the visual word of the printed page.

Wright was not Ellison's only outlet for challenging literary conversation. Ellison grew as a critic by making new friends on the New York Project, par-ticularly among the younger Jewish writers.[27] It was Jewish writers and intel-lectuals on the political Left who defined the radical movement in New York during the late 1930s. For young writers like Alfred Kazin and Irving Howe, the radical socialist movement had set the tone for their educational coming of age as early as junior high school, and it continued through their matricu-lation at City College. As teenagers, they had been encouraged to take their politics seriously and to pursue critical discernment as a means of escaping the provincialism of Jewish ethnicity while at the same time shunning assim-ilation into the sterile American middle class. Leftist ideology was a crucial part of their experience, available through a veritable pageant of organizations. In his memoir *Starting Out in the Thirties,* Alfred Kazin remembered the panoply of political groups that attracted even high school students: "Norman Thomas Socialists, old-line Social Democrats, Austro-Marxists; Communists Stalinist centrists, Trotskyite leftists, Lovestoneite right-wingers, Musteites and Fieldites; Zionists who were Progressive Labor Zionists, left Social Zion-ists and Religious Zionists. . . . "[28]

In Greenwich Village on Saturday evening at the newfangled Automat cafeteria—which dispensed sandwiches and fruit from coin-operated machines and as a result, could not subscribe to segregation—these tribes of young socialists hammered out political programs. Politics was in the air and part of everyday life.[29] These radicals were different in style and approach, even beyond their obvious cultural differences, from Ellison's exceptional friends at Tuskegee and the educated blacks of Harlem. Unlike most of Harlem's radi-cal street-corner orators, these young men were steeped in modern literature and were passionately concerned about determining the value of art. The young members of the Project also pushed Ellison's politics further left, encouraging his allegiance to, or criticism of, the current ideologies, demand-ing that writers change the world.

Some of these writers decided that the sword was mightier than the pen, and in Ellison's third summer in New York, they were among the young men of the Bronx Young Communist League trooping off to join the Abraham Lincoln Brigade fighting in Spain. Participation in the war was glorified, though the poorly trained and ill-equipped Brigade ultimately suffered horri-bly; nearly half of the almost three thousand American volunteers perished.

One early episode that plucked away the veil of romanticism from the war in Spain occurred when two trucks full of New York City activists took a wrong turn on their way to the front, resulting in the massacre of all the troops.[30]

Left circles encouraged black participation in the integrated fighting units, and Negroes responded. In 1938, Oliver Law, a high-ranking African American combat soldier killed in Spain, was judged a hero in leftist and liberal political circles. Black Milton Herndon, brother of nationally renowned Communist Angelo Herndon and the namesake of the uptown branch of the CP, had died manning a machine gun post on the Aragon Front the year before.[31] Though Ellison apparently felt a good deal of pressure to live out his liberal democratic convictions on the battlefield, one of the more tangible reasons for him not joining the International Brigades was personal. On September 17, 1938, justice of the peace Charles Henebel married twenty-five-year-old Ralph Waldo Ellison to twenty-six-year-old Rose Aramita Poindexter in New Haven, Connecticut.[32] The couple had known each other only a short time and then hurried into marriage, taking an apartment at 470 West 150th Street. Rose Poindexter was an actress, dancer, and singer, and was from Edgecombe Circle, the haven of the black elite. While their careers had similarities, the young couple had disagreements with her parents, who thought struggling writers unequipped for the financial responsibility of marriage.[33]

Even though he did not engage in the shooting war, he battled on the front of literary ideals. Ellison stepped into something of a literary hornet's nest when he began working as a reviewer for the *New Masses*. The journal was closely associated with its editor of the 1920s and early 1930s, Mike Gold, a noted devotee of the proletarian school of writing, who had just written the introduction to Hughes's radical collection of poetry, *A New Song*. Gold freely attacked anything he judged to be bourgeois excess, and he was well-known for his acidic views. He dismissed the literary modernists, writing that Gertrude Stein, the godmother of American modernism (and well respected by Wright), was a "literary idiot."[34]

At the nationally circulated magazine *New Masses,* with its broad political influence and immense prestige prior to 1939, Ellison encountered an ironic form of censorship. The irony lay in the fact that the hard communist left was nurturing him in an era when to overlook race was an act of generosity; yet they could not overlook his literary wanderings. In the effort to promote justice and equality, *New Masses* had imposed something of a literary blacklist. Dostoyevsky, for example, was condemned for his flagrant anti-Semitism, and Henry James was rejected as a snob.[35] Ellison's earliest misgivings about the journal stemmed from its attempts to exclude writers whose techniques he studied. But the post as an occasional unpaid reviewer for *New Masses* augmented his work on the Writers Project and enabled him to think of himself as a legitimate professional writer. Ellison was also infatuated with the explanatory power and theoretical language of Marxism in the late 1930s; and the association with like-minded writers and thinkers among Communists pleased him. He made the most of the situation and probably got the better of the exchange. If it took enthusiastic participation at a Communist cell meeting in order to discuss Marx's ideas about history and social evolution, then it was unnecessary for the comrades to know that he was studying decadent bourgeois writers. While the tensions surrounding the artist's role were quite genuine—and already Richard Wright had begun to recoil from them— Ellison emerged from the Left as a published writer during the Popular Front years, a brief historical moment during which strict adherence to political policies was not demanded. By the time Ellison's work began to appear in 1938, the *New Masses* had softened its editorial policy in keeping with the American Communist Party's drive to form allegiances with sympathetic bourgeois writers and intellectuals. The *New Masses'* open format was not broad enough, however, to include all of New York's literary radicals. The nearly pro-Trotsky *Partisan Review* touted itself as the journal of fearless intellectuals, unbound by Communist dogma and unafraid to promote complex and illuminating literature, even if it was penned by the so-called bourgeoisie. Lead editor Philip Rahv scoffed at the *New Masses;* he squarely placed the label "totalitarian" upon the Communists and their literary organs.[36]

The dissident Trotsky, exiled in Mexico, attracted many politically committed artists and writers to his ideas. In his 1923 publication "Literature and Revolution," he had rejected any sort of government control or direction in the arts. Trotsky's letter to Harry Roskolenko qualified his beliefs about art and political parties: "The party is obliged to permit a very extensive liberty in the field of art, eliminating pitilessly only that which is directed against the revolutionary task of the proletariat; on the other hand, the party cannot assume an immediate and direct responsibility for the declarations of its various members in the field of art even when it accords them its tribune."[37]

Partisan Review and the Trotskyist side of the Marxist debate seemingly would have been a natural home for Ellison, blending his interest in politics, high art, and autonomy. In August 1938, *Partisan Review* published André Breton's manifesto "Toward a Free Revolutionary Art," decrying Soviet prohibitions and calling for complete artistic freedom. As an independent journal, it did strive to publish competing points of view. In another year or so, Ellison would read in its pages the words of the poet T. S. Eliot, who was known as something of a royalist and anti-Semite among radicals. Wright, who had been on the review board of *Partisan Review* in 1936 and had been asked to contribute to the magazine, was liked by members of the influential non-Communist left. The attraction between *Partisan's* critics and the literary elite also was stimulating. And Ellison, while he was gratified to be publishing in Communist-sponsored journals like *New Masses,* had always dreamed of appearing in the literary equivalent of opening night at Carnegie Hall. He expected to serve as an apprentice, perfecting his style of literary critique and artistic approach, until an exceptional opportunity—like the scholarship that initially had led him to Tuskegee—might present itself. Yet, despite many reasons for being sympathetic toward the journal, Ellison's position in 1938 was to reject *Partisan* as practically a fifth column attempt to undermine the united efforts of the Left. He thought of himself as challenging Trotskyite politics, which, while not overwhelmingly popular, threatened to draw off intellectuals from the Communist cause, severely weakening the Popular Front's work against very tangible American racism. To Ellison's further distaste, *Partisan* dismissed the League of American Writers, the open congress organized and supported by the Communist Party. Ellison would remain loyal to the *New Masses* and the Communist-backed League into the 1940s, going so far as to get an independent journal together to spread League views.

The de facto segregation of the WPA, where black writers worked exclusively on the black community, continued to provide Ellison with a rich, even academic, perspective on black history. He pushed deeply into the archives, possibly in the company of Dorothy West, attempting to track down Annie D'Angola's 1667 deed to the area of land in Manhattan currently called Madison Square. Princely director Ottley told him to leave the research alone if all that could be done was to resort to city hall's six-month-long trace method. Nevertheless, Ellison stayed busy on his entries regarding Colonial-era blacks, submitting several historical investigations: "The Negro as a Factor in the Surrender of New Netherlands"; "Negroes and the Leisler Insurrection"; and a review, "Woodson's *The Beginning of Miscegenation of the Whites and Blacks*." Not all of his literary discoveries were gratifying. He was greatly disappointed to find Jupiter Hammon encouraging his fellow slaves to accept bondage. But editor Cumberbatch crossed out Ellison's analysis that "Jupiter Hammon's way was not the way of his contemporaries," forcing Ellison to accent the positives. "Hammon's significance today lies in his having been the first American Negro to express himself in verse," read his final draft.[38] Reading books from Maryland and Pennsylvania that tracked slave legislation to the mid-seventeenth century, all of which crudely attempted to prohibit white women from marrying and conceiving children with black men, Ellison found examples of "hundreds of white women thus fascinated by black men."[39]

With his access to journals steadily increasing, Ellison began to operate in a grander and more intellectual artistic world. Toward the end of the year, playwright Theodore Ward came from Chicago to live in New York. Ward had participated in the South Side Writers Group with Wright; now he came to New York as a member of the New York City Federal Theater Project. Ward moved into the attic apartment at the Newtons' home in Brooklyn, providing Wright with a clique of allies. Ward helped Wright with practical stylistic matters, and helped him add to the realism of *Native Son* with his impressive collection of blues records.[40] Educated at the University of Utah and a graduate of the University of Wisconsin, Ward was an exceptional kind of black, with well-formed literary and aesthetic tastes. He was determined to go beyond the confines of contemporary black drama, which was still unable to deal complexly with racial, political, and historical issues. Ward had come to New York with the hope of producing his much-lauded play *Big White Fog* (the name taken from a line in *Uncle Tom's Children*), which explored the conjunction between Marcus Garvey and socialism in a black family. And like Ellison, Ward had elevated himself from his poor boyhood in rural Louisiana to become a discerning and literary urbanite who had traveled the country and lived in Chicago and now New York.[41] Yet, despite his education, Ward liked to think of himself as a man of the people. Though he was friendly to him, Ward's first impression of Ellison was that he was young and relatively unremarkable.[42] Nevertheless, within a year he would be reading alongside Ellison in the effort to achieve the summit of intellectual achievement for the late 1930s, what his group of writers called a "heightened consciousness."[43]

Near the end of the year, Wright's circle widened to include the brilliant Trinidadian Trotskyite C. L. R. James, a writer of novels, history, and literary criticism who had moved to the United States in November. James had recently completed a history of the black revolt in Santo Domingo, his *Black Jacobins*.[44] He would reside in the United States for the next fifteen years and pioneer the idea of an autonomous black socialist party, unfettered by white control. Talking about the problems facing socialism all over the globe, James riveted the attention of Ellison and Wright, who had read intently of revolution in China in the pages of Malraux's *Man's Fate*. James argued that the inept bureaucrat Joseph Stalin had ruined the 1925–1927 revolt in China by supporting a coalition between the proletariat and the petite bourgeoisie in the radical Chinese congress called the Kuomintang.[45] The influx of Trotskyism that came with James advanced Wright and Ellison theoretically. James greatly admired Wright's achievement; he thought Wright "a revolutionary political person, whose whole life was spent, wherever possible, aiming blows at capitalist society."[46] In the company of his dazzling and accomplished friends, Wright finished his first draft of *Native Son* sometime in early 1939.

Wright's friendship with Ellison, whom he was still trying to launch, took on less importance as Wright cemented relationships with artists and intellectuals who were at the peak of their creative powers and near the height of their public popularity. As if the relationship with James indicated that Wright's intellectual focus would shift toward empiricism, by 1939 Wright had developed a friendship with the sociologist Horace Cayton. Cayton's interest in academic sociology and public policy combined well with similarities in the two men's lifestyles. As Wright's importance increased and his inner circle widened, his ego grew; and it is possible that Ellison's accomplishment, which initially had impressed him, lost some of its brightness. Furthermore, Wright thought that Ellison had probably waited too long to become serious about writing, and that even if he was serious, he had to mature emotionally, to give his impressive strength in reading and understanding difficult concepts time to evolve into literary feeling.[47] Accustomed to some sort of distance from Wright, Ellison maintained the friendship, especially as he improved his powers of analysis and taste in literature. In any case, Ellison himself was at no loss for company. A young man involved in his first significant sexual and emotional commitment, he happily spent a great deal of his time with his new wife, Rose.

A consistent presence on bookstore shelves also managed to keep Ellison and Wright in close contact. Somewhere between late 1938 and 1939, Malraux's latest work, devoted to the war in Spain, appeared. Malraux personified the inexhaustible prophet of his generation of Western writers, exposing injustice with his mighty pen from Asia to Europe and in record time. *Man's Hope* confronted the morass of the still raging Spanish Civil War, delineating the positions of communists, socialists, anarchists, Loyalists, and even fascists. Ellison and Wright consumed Malraux's latest effort, which was far superior to them than that of any war correspondent. Malraux's optimistic book dutifully chronicled the main episodes of the bitter war, concluding with the successful spring defense of Madrid against Franco in 1938. Malraux championed the possibility of a broad political coalition to defeat fascism.

The French novelist's work continued to broaden Ellison philosophically, and to increase his impatience with the purportedly iron laws of history and human advancement endlessly recited by hard-line Communists. Malraux had the stunning ability not only to reveal the terror and necessity of war but also to argue an ideological point from a philosophical perspective. He was unafraid of contradiction, and he carefully created motive and behavior. For example, the Soviet Union was the only government to offer military assistance to the Spanish antifascists, but Malraux did not deny the complex human dynamics that prevented communism from prevailing in Spain for the sake of advancing Soviet hegemony. Most interesting to Ellison and Wright was the writer's exploration of the Spanish mentality, the tragic sense of life that enabled the citizens of Spain to survive the devastating horror of war.

Malraux also briefly presented the views of the leading Spanish writer and intellectual, Miguel Unamuno. Unamuno had initially supported the fascists because he disliked the "forcible centralisation" of the communists, then finally denounced Franco in a speech giving priority to Life and Truth over Pleasure and Intellect. Unamuno echoed the militant international feeling of

Ellison's generation: "Truth alone is justice; there is no other justice. And truth, as Sophocles said, is mightier than intellect. As life is mightier than pleasure or pain. Truth and Life, then, shall be my motto; not Intellect and Pleasure. To live in Truth, even though it means to suffer, rather than to exercise intelligence in pleasure or to take pleasure in intelligence."

Communists had little use for Unamuno. In the novel *Man's Hope*, the communist soldier Garcia feels, "What good to me are all those thoughts of yours, if you can't give my tragedy any thought." Still, for artists and intellectuals, Malraux powerfully articulated the hopeless ambiguity of reason that plagued Unamuno.

> The great intellectual is a man of subtleties, of fine shades of evaluations; he's interested in absolute truth and in the complexity of things. He is— how shall I put it?—antimanichean by definition, by nature. But all forms of action are manichean, because all action pays a tribute to the devil; that manichean element is most intense when the masses are involved. Every true revolutionary is a born manichean. The same is true of politics, all politics.

Arguing further that the intellectual's main contribution to revolution lay in explication and not in judgment, Malraux proposed in *Man's Hope* that to be an intellectual entailed accepting a tragic burden, a tragic fate, if the intellectual concurred with violent resistance:

> But once we've agreed on the vital point—that we've *got* to put up resistance, we've taken up a line of action which commits us once [and] for all to a programme, with all its inevitable consequences. In certain cases, the choice is a tragic one. For the intellectual, it's almost always so, above all for the artist. Yet, even so, wasn't it up to him to resist?
>
> For a thinker, the revolution's a tragedy. But for such a man, life, too, is tragic. And if he is counting on the revolution to abolish his private tragedy, he's making a mistake. . . . [48]

It was a point upon which Ellison never waffled.

Keeping up with what Wright was reading and taking research assignments from the Writers Project afforded Ellison a range of material that was so broad, it almost amounted to postgraduate level course work. In January 1939, Ellison investigated the Colonial-era history of blacks in the printing industry and learned of a Negro man, curiously called Primus, who had worked in the trade and lived in Boston and Portsmouth until he was past ninety.[49] Then, Ellison's work with editor Charles Alexander returned him to archival research, where he learned about New York's famous Free African School of the late 1700s, which led him to his most extensively researched assignment on the Project, a study of the 1830 edition of the *History of the African Free School* by Charles Andrews.

Wright, meanwhile, was preparing to leave the New York Writers Project. Wright's work and conversation were maturing as he grew increasingly independent of the Communist Party and the FWP; and Ellison's attraction continued toward the man who seemed a beacon of intellectual and artistic thought. In contrast, Ellison's relationship had cooled with Hughes, the man who had initially introduced him to leftist politics, modern art, and the New York panorama. He did regularly keep in touch with the recently married Louise Thompson-Patterson, who now lived at 530 Manhattan Avenue, and was still the leader of the radical salon in Harlem.[50] From her, Ellison learned that Langston Hughes was about to return to New York from the West Coast.

A generous literary correspondence had been the trademark of their early relationship, but now Hughes owed him a letter. Ellison no longer expected the busy author, who had recently collaborated with Wright to dramatize the short story "Fire and Cloud," to make an overture. Ellison wrote to Hughes at the end of January 1939, playful and intimate and jokingly anointing himself with the titles of Eastern and African noblemen: Mohammed and Ras.[51] Now almost twenty-six, Ellison still wanted to defer to Hughes, whose most recent work, collected in A New Song—"Ballad of Lenin," "Let America Be America Again," "Letter to the Academy," and "Elderly Race Leader"— reflected the impatience of the radical mood. And yet, Ellison saw himself as a bit more radical than merely an Islamic or Ethiopian lord. In fact, Ellison wanted something more from Hughes, something that the poet who had offered such generous and unstinting friendship could not provide.

He acknowledged to Hughes that while his good friend Wright was aiming for a publisher's March deadline, he spent his time going about the difficult business of turning himself into a writer. At his apartment at 470 West 150th Street, Ellison was working hard on the novel he had decided to call Slick. Wright's novel Native Son, which Ellison had been reading as it came off the typewriter, was phenomenal in its impressiveness. However, a Congressional budget cut engineered by the American bourbons—whom Ellison's crowd called "torries"—threatened his own longevity on the Writers Project. Negroes were especially vulnerable to dismissal, but they had organized and lost only four jobs. Aside from political talk, Ellison was flush enough to be able to attend the theater, and he thought highly of dramatist Clifford Odet's Rocket to the Moon, chiefly because of the outstanding performance of star Luther Adler, even though the play suffered from what Ellison liked to call "conceptional" problems. He was not beyond offering advice. Perhaps the magnificent Ethel Waters, lauded by the press for her performance in Mamba's Daughters, would help to revive Hughes's Suitcase Theater? And as if to proclaim the distance growing between the two men, he had secured enough money to buy his own literary weapon, a Remington Noiseless. He would return to Hughes's brother Kit a typewriter that had been on loan so long that it was physically disorienting to use another machine.

Ellison had referred to himself in his letter as "Mohammed Ras De Terror," playfully reminding Hughes of professional black chauvinism. His sense of humor was important in sustaining his political commitments. During the spring of 1939, the optimism of the Left was shattered. First the Federal Writers Project fell under a cloud. The House Committee on Un-American Activities, spearheaded by Texas Congressman Martin Dies, viciously attacked the arts, blacks, and the political Left. When the hearings had begun in late 1938, Dies had singled out Wright's heartfelt autobiographical essay "Ethics of Living Jim Crow" as "one of the most filthy things I have seen."[52] By spring, the Dies Committee had pruned the WPA to make it right-wing and lily-white. Ellison barely clung to his job. Then Loyalist forces capitulated to the fascists in Spain, and in April, Franco declared himself the victor.

Spring ended with the 1939 League of American Writers Congress. Opening on Friday, June 2, the conference featured deposed Czechoslovak President Edouard Benes, whose capital had been occupied since March by the Nazis. More than 5,500 people attended the keynote address, and Langston Hughes sat prominently on the governing board.[53] At the New School of Social Research at 66 West 12th Street, the sessions got under way. The congress was an exceptional gathering of black literati and notables, including Hughes, Alain Locke, Sterling Brown, and the celebrated new immigrant to New York City, Angelo Herndon. On Friday afternoon, professor Melville Herskovits delivered a paper, "The Negro in American Literature, Past and Future." During a Saturday afternoon session on literary criticism, Ellison introduced himself to Margaret Walker, one of Richard Wright's friends, fresh from Chicago.[54] Ellison lunched with Walker and the two showed each other their work. Later Saturday sessions included offerings on folklore from the New York Writers Project, concluding with a moving film that emphasized the continued racial brutality in America. The picture climaxed with a depiction of the 1935 lynching of Joseph Shoemaker in Tampa, Florida. At the conclusion of the writers' congress on Sunday, Langston Hughes somberly read the names of forty-five writers who had been murdered in the struggle against fascism the world over. The audience bowed their heads in silence.[55]

During the meeting, Ellison met a young white woman novelist originally from Oklahoma but then living in California named Sanora Babb. Babb and Ellison were drawn to each other during the weekend, and at some point that fall they became lovers. Ellison apparently was estranged from his wife Rose, and while living in the same apartment, the two were nearing a separation. Ellison was also at the time suffering from liver problems, which led to jaundice. He would joke with Sanora that she had become attracted to him at a time when he was "yellow." When the League determined to publish a writers magazine with a New York and a Hollywood editor, these two, both contributors to the *New Masses,* were delighted to help develop the project. The affair continued into the 1940s, when Babb visited New York. She lodged at the St. Moritz Hotel, where the manager informed her that he did not allow entertaining. To avoid confrontations, Ellison took the rear stairs to her room.[56] The racially mixed couple were limited in their entertainment to a walk in Central Park or a trip to the Museum of Modern Art, sometimes as much by penury as by jim crow. But Babb hardly minded. She was nearly in love with the serious black writer who spoke so reverently of his own parents that she assumed they were alive. For his part, Ellison cherished the intimate connection with the attractive brown-haired woman who went on to become a successful short story writer. The lovers remained close throughout the 1940s. While he was honest about his feelings of resentment and betrayal toward successful black men who married white women as their symbol of success and freedom, Ellison treasured his own private intimacies across the color line.

After the congress, Ellison enjoyed following up on the many artistic and intellectual contacts he had made; and around that time, he found the theme for his first novel. At the end of the summer—and likely with a word of favor from Wright, who served on the journal's editorial board—Ellison published a chapter from his novel in progress in *Direction* as a short story entitled "Slick Gonna Learn." Ellison was joyous over having a piece of fiction in the issue, which was devoted to writers on the Project. He wrote the story based not upon his own experiences, but instead, emulating the realism of Wright, he tried to use the proletarian approach advocated by the Communists, giving voice to the common man in the streets—at least what he imagined him to be. His protagonist Slick Williams was a black migrant to New York, out of work because of discrimination and with a large family to support. In a two-hundred-word synopsis used as a header to the story, Ellison reinforced the theoretical backbone of his fiction with urgent political imperatives. Marx and Freud leapt out: "The Negro," "a condition," "the stereotype situation," "denies him Callie's [Slick's wife] humanity," "rigidly enforced taboos," "the psychological barrier," "the power to act."

With the story of Slick Williams, Ellison tried to toe the mark of the proletarian school, but also to interpolate his own distinctive sense of the unpredictability of the natural environment. The short story actually displayed his inchoate antirealism, because unlike Wright with his relatively static and rigidly Manichean interactions between races, Ellison stretched to reveal the subterranean layers in the relationship between blacks and whites. White brutality alone did not define Slick Williams's life. In the story, Slick's near fatal encounter with violence occurs after a black pimp insults his wife—an event that Ellison interpreted as denying Callie her humanity. In the ensuing melee, the pimp knocks Slick unconscious. When the protagonist regains his senses, he finds a white policeman staring at him, whom he promptly knocks out. The act of defying white authority so profoundly upsets Slick Williams that he falls into a paralytic stupor until the policeman awakes.

At his arraignment, cruel fate appears to turn in Slick's favor. Instead of being sentenced to jail for assaulting a police officer as charged, Slick is released by the corrupt judge because "we cain't afford any more publicity just now." On the steps of the courthouse, an emboldened Slick verbally challenges the arresting officer. Within an hour, a squad of vigilante police take Slick into the country to lynch him, aborting their mission only when they are recalled to put down a factory riot. Slick's terrifying day ends as a white truck driver insists on giving him a ride back to town despite his hesitant fear. "He did not trust the white man and he did not wish to have to say too much to him." The story concludes as Slick tries to reconcile his dealings with whites that day; he tries to mesh the brutality and callous lethality of the police officers with the unsolicited friendship from the Irish truck driver. "He turned and watched the man bent over the steering wheel, studying his face and tried to connect him with the experiences of the day."[57] Ellison's first major effort suggested that despite a corrupt system, racial collaboration among common classes was possible. Slick ran into different kinds of whites: some who judged him on the ground of his color, some who looked at him as a political symbol, and others who treated him as a fellow human being.

In his political approach to his fiction, Ellison never let the Communists hold the trump cards. In this he differed from Wright, who had been given a push into writing by the John Reed Clubs and overtly Communist literary organs; in Wright's fiction, white allies were Communists. There was a five-year age gap between the two writers; and consequently, they had entered Communist literary circles during fundamentally different periods, which had significant implications for their work. Wright had known the slogans of the proletarian literature movement; Ellison, the banners of the Popular Front.[58] Ellison saw the WPA, with all of its shifting political ground, contested hallways, and cross-purposes, as a model for interracial antagonistic democracy in cooperative action. His job on Forty-second Street, and the appearance of his first short story in a journal published under the auspices of the Project, cemented his allegiance to it. The League of American Writers represented a similar sort of free-wheeling democracy for Ellison. Though he hesitated to form permanent ties with any group or ideology, Ellison would never reject the groups and organs that had promoted his earliest fiction.

But despite their different orientations, Ellison stuck with Wright and remained outside the mainstream in his approach to politics. In late August 1939, Stalin announced a nonaggression pact with Germany, giving Hitler free rein to blitz Poland. A wave of intellectuals and writers shook free from the Communists and the League, while the faithful defended Stalin as a brilliant tactician who had made a splendid bargain that would keep the USSR out of the "second" imperialist war. Wright had no place to turn, and angled through the political mess with the Communists. Other important critics such as Granville Hicks and Malcolm Cowley, who had stuck with the Party during the crisis of the Moscow Trials, the attacks on Trotsky, and the accommodating Popular Front, viewed the Stalin-Hitler pact as the swan song of their Communist commitments.

Further evidence of Wright's alienation from the conservative values of the black bourgeoisie and white America was his marriage in the beginning of August to a white dancer and CP member, Dheema Meidman. Ellison served as the best man at the couple's wedding at the Episcopalian Church on Convent Avenue.[59] In some respects, Wright had made a stereotypical black New York Communist move. Black male Communists in Harlem were so notorious for focusing their amorous affections exclusively on white women that in the early 1930s, black women in the Harlem CP demanded a ban of interracial marriages.[60] Secretary Abner Berry, Theodore Bassett, Herbert Newton, and Jim Ford all married white women (as would C. L. R. James, George Padmore, Horace Cayton, and St. Clair Drake). That several black men, though equipped with the critical tools with which to analyze the psychological effect of racism, pursued white women indicates the extreme degree of incompatibility that these men felt with black middle-class circles, which still were stratified according to skin color and access to privilege. In their pursuit of intellectual freedom, they also allied themselves with the cultural symbol of freedom in one's personal life—marriage across the color line. The choice to marry a white woman had another significant connotation. After such a marriage, these writers and intellectuals would never move to the South; the die was cast for a Northern, urban, and generally integrated life experience.

In the month before full-out European war erupted, Ellison, too, strengthened his ties to the Communists by publishing again in *New Masses*. With a flair for identifying what Kenneth Burke had called the "scapegoat mechanism," his August 1939 article took an unpopular tack and pointed to fascistic tendencies in the United States. Ellison's essay "Judge Lynch in New York" was an attack on the growing racist brutality in New York City. His target was the notorious Catholic priest and radio personality Father Coughlin. Using understatement and dialogue to his advantage, Ellison blasted the openly anti-Semitic and racist priest by telling the story of the hopeful migration north of Negro college boys, a story that turned into tragedy—one especially poignant to Ellison because the tale was so similar to his own migratory experiences:

> The boys hadn't heard about such things in the North. All year they had attended a Southern college located at least forty miles from any neighboring towns. It was a Negro school and since it was so isolated they saw few

white faces during the year except those visitors from the North, who were said to give large sums of money to the school and for whom they were made to parade about the campus to the music of the school band. At the close of the term . . . there had been no work. . . .

So the boys, Edward Meggs, Harry Smith, and Marvin Jackson, decided to go North, to New York . . . though they found no work and saw relief lines and heard about Congress and the WPA, they did not become discouraged.[61]

In his twenty-six-year-old hands, the story of the three young black men became the story of the black Everyman. True, most blacks couldn't attend college in the Depression, but lack of education stopped few from coming north for work. In the North, blacks lost "a certain tension that they had known." The North provided a space of utopian refuge. "Free from Jim Crow" ran the essay's subheading; but that freedom was destroyed by the ground troops of Negro repression, "the cops." Walking along the Hudson River on Harlem's west side, the three black collegians had been set upon by the police: "You, nigger! You got a knife on you?" After this introduction to the ritualized black nightmare, the young men then fell prey to an Irish mob that had been incited by Coughlin's Christian Front rhetoric. Two of the black students spent the night in the hospital. Ellison obviously had enormous sympathy with the young men; he'd experienced both white brutality and the trek north, and the young victims now lived across the street from Ellison's apartment on 150th Street.[62] The piece showed that even though he rejected facile optimism about life in the North for blacks, Ellison increasingly was determined to use writing as a tool for freedom.

Editors Samuel Sillen and Joe North of the *New Masses* revised the piece to conform to the journal's political agenda. Ellison's original essay had contained the brewing tension and understatement of a novel, relying heavily on description and dialogue. He had concentrated his energies on lyrical passages, emphasizing the pastoral Hudson River, the bounty that the young black men were denied. Sillen and North found the work too much like fiction and too racial. *New Masses* and the Popular Front promoted coalitions. In his original typescript, Ellison had concluded his essay with a bitter decrescendo:

"As soon as Edward Meggs recovers from a concussion of the brain the boys plan to return South; where if there's a section where you are not supposed to go you know it; even if you're told by a sign that says 'No Dogs and niggers allowed.' The only difference between the North and South, one of them says, is that they're beating the Jews as well as the Negroes."[63]

The accepted form of response in radical New York circles to such an attack was committee and protest. Instead of wondering where the black gangs were for retributive punishment and turf boundary reenforcement, *New Masses* had him emphasize the potential for success through nonviolence. "The Negroes, however, *are* fighting back, but in a democratic way," the published version concluded.[64]

It was the first time his work had undergone editorial revision for tone. The editors had removed much of the work's original cynicism and diluted the narrative style. Because he admired their commitment to the Party and their willingness to help a young black, Ellison accepted their advice. He was not uncomfortable with his *New Masses* mentors, but rather, he was eager to learn from them and to master the ideas of Marxism.

In the early fall, as he brought the novel *Slick* to its climax, he worked on sections where the protagonist gets his proper introduction to Marx. Ellison used the character Booker Smalls to begin Slick's technical introduction to Marxism, a group of concepts that Slick understands intuitively. Shortly after meeting Slick, Booker warns him that he frequently quotes Marx; Ellison was revealing his own imperative concerns.[65]

The publication of his fiction and social commentary started transforming Ellison into an influential voice representing black concerns throughout the city. Even Richard Wright was impressed. While working on a project assignment entitled "Katy Ferguson," an essay about the first black founder of a Sabbath School in New York City, Ellison strengthened his connections with editors Samuel Sillen and Joe North at *New Masses*. A few months later, he landed a job as a regular reviewer at their magazine, partly because more-established writers wanted to put the maximum distance between themselves and the pro-Stalinist left after the Nazi-Soviet pact, the Soviet occupation of Poland, and in November, the violent attack on Finland. Ellison, however, tied himself firmly to the *New Masses* during late 1939 and 1940, the journal's most unpopular period. Certain of his convictions and delighted by new success, he felt strongly enough about his beliefs to stride against the mainstream: he lived in a country that was racist and corrupt and he tacitly aligned himself with a different system. Likewise, Wright (as did Langston Hughes) believed in the Soviet operation.[66] In the Sunday, February 11, 1940, *Worker*, Wright again voiced the opinion of those who had stuck with the USSR, arguing that "the Soviet-German pact threw panic and fear into the British and French ruling circles and upset the balance of power . . . the Soviet Union struck a blow against imperialist war intrigues of Chamberlain on the continent."[67] In contrast to the American Revolution and the Civil War, in which blacks had fought nobly for good purpose, Wright saw American blacks being duped into fighting to protect "the vast colonial holdings" of England and France, who "oppress more Negroes and colonial peoples than all the Empires of the world combined."

That winter of the first year of the Second World War was a good time for purity of thought, and Wright dug up a copy of *The Tragic Sense of Life* by Unamuno, Malraux's philosopher hero. Fascinated, Ellison scoured book-stores until he turned up a waterlogged copy at Dauber and Pine bookseller.[68] The reigning Spanish philosopher, whose epic life spanned both the nine-teenth and twentieth centuries, Unamuno had died a few months into the Spanish Civil War. Known to advertise the fact of his Moorish blood, he was a series of contradictions. In his main philosophical work, Unamuno did not offer the theory of the communist "end of history" that would be achieved by the effortless exchange of goods and services. Instead, he proposed the men-tal primacy of individual consciousness—a perpetually ascending spiral of thought always considering and reconsidering the conscious thought that has preceded it. In Unamuno's theory, the cycle of thought extends to and be-comes immortality.

Promoting the idea that consciousness (the soul in action) was actually a virus or sickness, Unamuno called for heroism as the strategy to overcome the human condition. Consciousness for Unamuno perpetually disturbed man and was the source of his suffering, of his feelings of futility. Paradoxically, he said, the recognition of such negative feelings became the raw materials for man's ultimate success. Heroism enabled man to overcome his fear, through the deep suffering that became despair, allowing man to feel inadequate enough to attempt the impossible or absurd—the essence of heroic behavior. For Ellison and Wright, who jointly studied and discussed the book, a theory heralding individual action was timely as they increasingly faced fundamental differences with other artists and thinkers. Unamuno's philosophy had great potential for explaining the American Negro experience—an experience imbued, as both men felt, with epic tragedy. The struggle of black people in the face of overwhelming odds, time and again, was not merely tragic, but also heroic. Unamuno thought that the true hero was properly a gadfly to his community: "Charity does not mean rocking and lulling our brothers to sleep in the inertia and drowsiness of matter, but rather to awaken them to the anxiety and torment of the spirit."[69] As politically conscious artists, Ellison and Wright had a vocational interest in rejecting orthodoxies and stirring passionate discussion. And the theory neatly complemented Ellison's concept of the "New York mentality." Moreover, in Unamuno's theory, Ellison's father's life of dreams and struggle against the odds resurfaced in invigorating fashion.

Notwithstanding such an act of friendship as sharing a favorite author, the relationship between Ellison and Wright did not always strike a balance. With more than two hundred pages of his novel written, Ellison was indeed holding true to his goal and turning the dedication he had had to music into a career in writing. But he thought that his narrative drive in *Slick* was not working effectively. He accepted the slowness with which he should approach the mastery of his form, practicing his craft as he had once performed solfeg-gio drills in college, using accepted models and working on his effects. He went to Wright with drafts of the story and asked for his opinion. After a considerable delay, Wright reacted sharply to the portion that Ellison had given him, a vignette about a waiter in an Oklahoma City men's club. Like so much of *Slick,* the section was autobiographical, based on Ellison's experiences as an occasional waiter in Nichols Hill and with the Oklahoma City Diner's Club. His hero Slick loses a job at the Monroy Club after a violent fight where Slick slams a heavy silver pitcher on the patron's head.[70] In the experimental piece, Ellison was also trying out the stream of consciousness style of narration, and having Slick speak an especially flexible black dialect.

It was not the best time to seek Wright's opinion. Fraught with anxieties over the publication of his new book, the Nazi-Soviet pact, and increasing tension with his new bride, Wright was becoming mildly estranged from his friends. Earlier that winter, he had intimated to playwright Ted Ward that Ward had more promise as an actor than as a playwright. Wright had recently dismissed his former close friend from Chicago, nervous and chatty Margaret Walker.[71] Wright could be irascible and even jealous of good friends. Ellison pressed him about the story, "Well, what *about* it? What *about* it?" Claiming ownership, and stepping into an area of competition, with an authority reminiscent of Bill Dawson, Wright reprimanded Ellison: "That's my stuff."[72] Ellison told him, perhaps a bit disingenuously, that he did not intend to publish the material. He was not completely surprised by Wright's suspicious and territorial reaction. But the occasion sobered him enough to resolve to no longer show Wright his fiction. Ellison had a wife of his own and a fairly secure job, and he, too, figured to write a magnificent novel.

If artistic temperament stood in the way of their relationship, the two men still had similar artistic and political criteria. Ellison was far along in fitting Freud's ideas neatly into Marxist theory. In the December *New Masses,* he continued to carry the torch of the class struggle. Reviewing the novel *Boss Man* by Louis Cochran, he found the author guilty of missing the connections between the class struggle and the psychological alienation experienced by the novel's protagonist: "The South's condition is not due to alienated individuals, for no matter how powerful an individual may become, he is dependent upon others with similar interests; it is this group's consciousness of itself as a class—and its links lead to Wall Street—that is responsible."[73]

Ellison hoped for artistic representations that moved beyond one-dimensional stereotypes and that were capable of contributing to "American writing and to democracy." Two weeks later, he broke down Gene Fowler's *Illusion of Java* with the same analytical tools. In a naive anthropological story of Tahiti and Bali, Fowler celebrated the Tahitian culture grandly, but left out politics. Ellison doubted that the "highly lyrical" style of the "escapist fiction" accurately captured the reality of "almost forty million people living under the colonial rule of the Dutch." "Folklore, even when most charming," he lectured the reader, "reveals a contradictory, bitter-sweet quality when something is known of the conditions that give it birth. Here is the sweet with the bitter extracted."[74] Three-and-a-half years after he had jokingly warned Hughes that he might step up on a soapbox on 136th Street, Ellison had found his own special bully pulpit.

Despite his prominent reviews, in 1940 Ellison still had to hustle to make ends meet. He worked full-time at the Project, which had been renamed the New York Writers Project after Roosevelt took federal support entirely out of the arts business in the early summer of 1939.[75] Despite the fact that his professional home base was in one of their journals, Ellison felt bitter toward the Communists, whose militancy and disruptive tactics continued to bring the entire national writers program under hostile scrutiny. The jobs of black writers, who were still categorically rejected by major newspapers and magazines because of their race, were in constant jeopardy. Project director Alsberg retained the powerful union-supported Communists, whose presence was exaggerated by the press and the Dies Committee. Concerned about keeping his job on the Project, Ellison thought carefully about his connections with the Communists, signing petitions, and carrying a picket sign. Between December and January, though, his Project work had few apparent political overtones. During the two months, he collected mounds of children's short stories, gags, counting games, rhymes, tall tales, folklore, and the like, mainly by scouting out the playground of P.S. 89 at 135th Street and Lenox Avenue. Asking people whether they had been born in New York or in the South, Ellison sought the roots of the divergent folklore of Harlem. The job of petty anthropology was fun. "I hung around the playgrounds. I hung around the streets, the bars. I went into hundreds of apartment buildings and just knocked on doors. I would tell some stories to get people going and then I'd sit back and try to get it down as accurately as I could," he later recalled.[76] The most impressive tale he collected was from a street vendor on Seventh Avenue, who knocked him off his feet laughing with the tale of "Sweet the Monkey," a folktale of a black man in antebellum South Carolina who could turn himself invisible.

Perhaps as a result of the distressing episode with Wright, and probably in part because he was incensed with the "Judge Lynch" activities of the Christian Right and the Irish hatred at his back door in Harlem, Ellison initiated some new experiments in fiction. Interacting with ten-year-olds for a few weeks allowed him to escape the pressing politics of the New York Writers Project and return to his youth, a particularly fecund creative source for him. In his fiction, he had dealt in some fashion with the wounds from his train ride to Tuskegee; his Slick Williams saga explored the life of an uneducated colored man his own age struggling to make a living in the North. But engaging the bright and energetic kids from Convent Temple at 141st Street and Eighth Avenue, the Utopia Children's House, and P.S. 89 took him back to his own years in Oklahoma City, tapping into a vital stream of memory. He remembered being nine and learning the taunt "Eenny Meany Minny Moe/ Catch a White Peck By the Toe," and reciting rhymes at Douglass.[77] He recognized considerable sophistication in the children's rhymes, noticing how they were used ritualistically to inculcate morality, to ward off danger, and to lay the framework for a philosophical view of life such as those fleshed out in the lyrics of blues songs. Like the ethically ambiguous stories of Br'er Rabbit, the playground taunts and toasts emphasized the unpredictable and erratic course of childhood and later adult life. Sifting through his Oklahoma City childhood, he uncovered a new fictional direction awaiting his attention when he returned after work to his apartment. Ellison experienced something of an epiphany, and began to envision stories celebrating his own childhood adventures in the alleys and backyards of Deep Second. But these sagas of youth would not leave the terrain of radical politics behind. He saw connections between his earliest folk knowledge and the beginnings of a political ideology, in a manner that emphasized artistic form. If Wright was so touchy about his fiction experiments, perhaps Ellison would explore his own childhood, indirectly connecting his experiences to larger adult psychological and artistic concerns.

So instead of continuing his project of social relevancy and hard-hitting realism that seemed similar to *Native Son* in style, Ellison recalled his youth, beginning a series of stories he would continue working on through the summer of 1943 (with a coda, "A Coupla Scalped Indians," published in 1956). His stories were set in Oklahoma City and were reminiscent of his earliest writing efforts in Dayton, though for these he returned to his childhood adventures with Frank Meade. By the end of the year, his short story "Afternoon" had been accepted for publication in *American Writing 1940,* a WPA publication that was suspicious of the military, critical of the causes of the Depression, and fiercely emblematic of the social realist concerns of the staff and the nation.[78]

"Afternoon" captured an idle day of the athlete Riley and his slightly younger friend Buster. Both boys possess qualities reminiscent of the youthful Ellison. Keeping pace with his skillful friend, Buster encounters his stern mother, an Ida Ellison figure, driven into an antagonistic attitude because of her painful encounters with whites. Ellison experimented with dialect and folklore in the story and explored the quotidian in black life. In an obvious break with Wright, he showed that while black life was inflected by race, any honest discussion of human interaction and behavior needed to focus on more than the color line. For Ellison, regional contrasts, and especially the effects of expanding technology and industry in American cities, became important avenues for creative development. Hearing the nursery and grammar-school rhymes as he wrote, he wove folklore into a story for the first time, deepening the significance and texture of black life. Negro Americans were not merely lampblacked Anglo-Saxons; nor, on the other hand, was their culture somehow foreign to the American experience. Accordingly, "Afternoon" is something of an urban pastoral. The youngsters walk along a glass-strewn alleyway in their bare feet, throwing rocks and apples, imitating their favorite baseball player, Lou Gehrig. The short piece ends with Riley delivering one of the most popular early-twentieth-century prideful black folk toasts: "If it hadnt a been/ for the referee/ Jack Johnson woulda killed/ Jim Jefferie."[79]

Meanwhile, the pace at the Project slowed considerably; many of the personnel had been replaced by stooges for the Dies committee. Ellison was working on a manuscript entitled "Famous New York Trials," under the guidance of project director Frederick Clayton. In February, Ellison published two reviews and one essay in the *New Masses*. "Camp Lost Colony" gave an explanation of the modern-day proletarian movement, revealing how the farm combines exploited both blacks and whites. In "The 'Good Life,'" Ellison reviewed J. B. Priestley's *Let the People Sing,* a book that attempted to show class struggle in England as played out in a feud over the use of a local town hall. In Priestley's story, Tories wanted to turn the workers' hall into a museum, only to find resistance from the industrialists, who proposed to convert the hall into a showroom. Without tackling the "fundamental" crisis, the novel proposed comedy and wine as remedies. Turning his own classical education with Breaux and Dawson on its head, Ellison sneered at the gentry's plan for social equality: "let 'em (the workers) eat Bach, Beethoven, Mozart, and Brahms."[80] He was reconsidering his own years spent consuming the celebrated composers.

Later in February, Ellison went to see his estranged wife Rose perform in Cabaret TAC's *Saturday Night in Harlem,* the first black revue to separate itself completely from the minstrel tradition. Gone was the grease-painted end man who had marked the regular revues showcased at the Apollo. Ellison found especially pleasing the satire of the movie *Gone With the Wind* (fully taken to task in the January issues of *New Masses*), in which Negroes played the plantation owners, combining political satire and burlesque to effect "the quality of the unreal." The overthrow of the minstrel act left Ellison with high standards for comedy: "[It] is achieved only when there is as much understanding and emotion as is required of tragedy."[81]

By March, he had distilled his reviews down to a formula: a brief overview and plot summary; an investigation in dialogue form of a curiosity he had found in the piece; and a brief assertion of his politics. In his review of Conrad Richter's *The Trees,* the story of the early nineteenth-century settlement of Ohio, Ellison gravely counseled nonintervention in the warfare among the Germans, the Belgians, and the French. Richter's characters symbolized not merely the domination of Canada by American colonialists, but the pursuit of "civil equality and justice." Ellison warned that the book had more than local or merely artistic ramifications: "Words which might well be said now to those who would place our frontiers across the Atlantic."[82] Ellison would remain isolationist as long as the USSR was out of the war. In April, the Germans took Paris.

Despite many views that jibed with the Communists', his work at the Project began to take on the cause of American self-defense. John D. Newsom, the director of the national advisory board of the newly named Federal Works Project Administration, thought that the state Projects could be of great value in this time of international crisis. Newsom advised superiors that writers could make major contributions in case of national emergency. The director suggested the WPA's first goal be to "survey and report upon racial minority groups with particular reference to their geographic distribution and degree of integration."[83] Working on the New York Project, Ellison was ambivalent about his own position, since his efforts could be taken advantage of by reactionaries like Newsom for the war effort. His critical antennae were up, keen to find work to replace his job on the Project.

Ellison reached a watershed moment on his twenty-seventh birthday, March 1, 1940. It was the day that Richard Wright's long-awaited novel *Native Son* arrived at the bookstores. Wright's novel, chosen by the Book-of-the-Month Club as the March selection, rocketed straight into the stratosphere. Within three weeks it sold two hundred thousand copies, and Wright was hailed as the "Sepia Steinbeck," the creator of "*Grapes of Wrath* 1940" and "a black *American Tragedy*."[84] Glowing in the splendor of such phenomenal success, Wright moved with his wife to Mexico. He was fast at work on his next thriller, tentatively entitled *Little Sister*. Wright had decided to devote himself to the story of black working-class women and the time-tested theme of blacks passing for white. He asked Ellison to send him articles about black domestics.

While Wright worked frantically on his new novel in pleasant Mexico, reaction to his volcanic novel *Native Son* erupted in the States. Ellison soon wrote to Wright verifying that *Native Son* had indeed brought to the surface the troubling contradictions peculiar to black leftists. They were threatened by the book because it demanded that they do their own thinking.[85] Mainly, Ellison meant Benjamin Davis Jr.'s review of *Native Son* in the *Worker*. Sticking maddeningly within Party guidelines, Davis praised Wright for his politics— "The book is a terrific indictment of capitalist America"—and he proposed that when revealing the "mechanics of the state machinery," the writing was "magnificent." But Davis was clearly disappointed by Wright's dark pessimism concerning the process of revolutionary change. Davis characterized Wright's portrait of Bigger's family as a betrayal, "utterly devoid of a smattering of the progressive development." Wright had erred in drawing symbolic connections between masses of blacks and Bigger, he said. Black Americans did not suffer from a subnormal or psychotic disposition—which were the terms that reviewers used to refer to the mind-set of Bigger Thomas. Instead, the "book could have, for example, made of Bigger's mother a strong woman typical of Negro womanhood today," opined Davis. And most unforgivably, Wright had erred in his presentation of the CP. In dramatic, nearly gothic prose, Davis wrote that "the Communist Party is the only organization which can give the ray of light to penetrate the swamp of degradation into which the Negro people have been hurled."[86] Wright's intimation that Jan could and did patronize Bigger was blasphemy: "in life, [the Communist Party] ruthlessly burns out such chauvinist ideas." Davis finished with an overall suggestion that black communists should have been featured in the novel because only the combined pressure of "Negro and white masses" under communist leadership would have produced Bigger Thomas's acquittal.

Ellison thought that the Harvard-trained Davis, who came from a prosperous Atlanta family, knew little of ordinary Negro misfortune and less of the artist's commitment to truth and freedom of expression. Surprisingly enough, Davis's perspective actually paralleled W. E. B. Du Bois's *Crisis* editorials of the 1920s, which clamored for artistic representations of blacks in ascots and dinner jackets. Davis's lieutenants, Abner Berry and Theodore Bassett, echoed his opinions at local meetings in Harlem. The gap widened considerably between the iron rules of class revolution advanced by the card-carrying Communists and the necessity of indignant black masses talked up by Wright and Ellison. Within weeks of the novel's release, it became a focal point for activism and erudition, education and indoctrination. The liberal Sender Garlin defended the novel to small groups in Harlem, countering Berry's smug and violent denunciations. In a fit of desperation, one evening in March, Ellison and Ted Ward sat Berry and Bassett down for six hours, explaining the nature of fiction and the arts, Ellison told Wright. Berry replied that he accepted Wright's "Blueprint for Negro Writing," but remained convinced that *Native Son* had not lived up to it. Berry asked the writers for their favorite metaphors for the black condition. In his work, Wright had compared black life to living in a steel cage; for Ward, Negro life meant being veiled in a white fog; Ellison proposed the never-ending road, fraught with danger.[87] Berry apparently had no image of his own, at least none independent enough to satisfy Ellison. When speaking to large groups, the Communist leader generally rehashed the opinions of the cautious Baltimore *Afro-American.* Try as they might, black Communist radicals were so worried about the Communist International and downtown bureaucracy that they were unable to take the initiative to change conditions in Harlem. Despite the controversy accompanying the novel as it filtered into increasingly diverse American circles, black Communists would fail to use the novel's publication as a galvanizing moment to interest neutral blacks in radical politics.

The grand success of such a close friend guaranteed Ellison a new role in their circle of friends and activists. He found himself talking about, explaining, and defending Wright's *Native Son* until he was exhausted. Love him or hate him, everyone was listening to or taking the measure of Richard Wright. As an insider who was extremely knowledgeable about Wright's creative process, Ellison defended the author in public discussions. He spoke to groups in the Village, in Harlem, wherever he could gain a hearing, explaining Wright's use of realism, his Marxist analysis, as well as the political importance of literature. *Native Son* was not only something that he had helped to create but a part of the life that he had lived. Wright had treated an inflammatory issue with courage, intelligence, and discipline, and it had opened doors. Ellison continued to deeply admire Wright, and felt that Wright's method of struggling for social justice in the artistic realm made more sense than any other tactic. Wright was helping to educate, at a very fast rate, the leadership cadre of the radicals.

Ellison, too, was being educated by the process. Scolding Wright's critics led him to explore the fine points of Marx's oeuvre. To speak competently before groups, he read whatever translated sections were available from the *Holy Family* and the *German Ideology*.[88] "[T]he only thing to do is to study until I can quote Marx till I'm blue in the face" he wrote to Wright in April of 1940. In the *Holy Family,* he found the current mélée over *Native Son* presaged in Marx's analysis of Eugene Sue's gothic novel *The Mysteries of Paris.* His labors brought constraints along with understanding. Questioning Wright, whom he considered his superior on theoretical issues, he wrote: "How far can the Marxist writer go in presenting a personalized, humanist version of his ideology? . . . Then again, does the writer who accepts Marxism have the freedom to expound a personalized philosophy?"[89] Still recalling the changes he'd made to his essays and reviews in the name of conforming to orthodoxy, Ellison wanted the authority to follow his own insight. He sensed real limits in Marxism's application to the problem of the individual, but had not solved the problem. Ellison finished his letter "Am I shooting up a blind alley in this?"

At his different talks, Ellison found exasperating the inability of black Communists to understand Wright's protagonist Bigger Thomas. Disgruntled with the lack of analytic powers of Lenox Avenue, Ellison closed another letter to Wright, "No one here seems aware of how really nationalistic NS [*Native Son*] happens to be. It is NEGRO American lit."[90] Party members formulated facile arguments that demanded bourgeois respectability in fictional proletarian characters; they were unable to accept the theoretical possibility that, due to the exigencies of the current historical moment, black culture might produce an unrespectable consciousness. Bigger was no scion of the bourgeoisie, but instead was loaded with "revolutionary significance"; and as Kenneth Burke had suggested, was the oppositional antidote to capitalist efficacy. Ben Davis's demand that Bigger Thomas act like a Young Communist League member caused Ellison to agree with Richard Wright, his fellow young Turk, that theoretical consciousness in Harlem was low. Building on their marvelous discussions, Ellison articulated and theorized for Wright. He tried to counter naysayers with the explanation that Wright was playing with the Hegelian notions of spirit and consciousness—that the blend of Hegel's ideas about the unconscious with Marx's dialectical materialism explained Bigger's character in ultimate terms:

> They fail to see that what's *bad* in Bigger from the point of view of bourgeois society is *good* from our point of view. He, Bigger, has what Hegel called the "indignant consciousness" and because of this he is more human than those who sent him to his death; for it was they, not he who fostered the dehumanizing conditions which shaped his personality. When the "indignant consciousness" becomes the "theoretical consciousness" indignant man is aware of his historical destiny and fights to achieve it. Would that *all* Negroes were psychologically free as Bigger and as capable of positive action!

He recognized that Bigger represented not simply a diametric opposition but an important evolution in dialectical terms. Ellison was attacked by dilettantes for his defense of Wright's work; and he was impatient with blacks and whites who posed as radicals but were actually uninterested in the new theoretical possibilities revealed by the novel. He wanted to examine the theoretical fountainhead of Marx's own framework in order to take the philosophical reasoning that undergirded the theories of dialectical materialism and class struggle and apply it to the evolution of the individual consciousness. He asked Wright about a book he was searching for: Hegel's *Phenomenology of the Mind*.[91]

Ellison was on the verge of moving beyond his circle, and he found a vehicle compatible with his own ideas of radical struggle. During the first week in May, Ellison and several friends drove down to Washington, D.C., to attend the third National Negro Congress. The NNC was a broad-based umbrella organization headed by John P. Davis (well respected for publicly upbraiding Congressman Martin Dies) that pushed for black civil rights, protested the arms-race hysteria while advocating for New Deal social welfare programs, and carried Communists in key organizational positions. Unlike the social protest organizations of the black middle class, the NNC was not necessarily focused on the overthrow of segregation, the bane of black middle-class identity; nor was it their tactic to seek racial uplift. They proposed to tackle the underlying economic issues of the poor. Attendees to the congress were incensed mainly by the crushing poverty and debt peonage facing rural blacks, part of their reason for joining a united front with Communists. Using as a rallying point the recent fire in Natchez, Mississippi, that had killed 250 blacks, the National Negro Congress took Washington by storm.

Ellison would make his first front-page byline in the *New Masses* for his article "A Congress Jim Crow Didn't Attend." The essay's title was ironic: although "jim crow" did not attend the multiracial conference, Washington was a furiously jim crow city. The carload of New Yorkers had entered the South on their best behavior, noting the troops of U.S. cavalry who flanked the highway as they motored through Maryland. A few months before, D.C.'s Little Theater had held a film festival called "Art Knows No Boundaries," and even featured Robeson's *The Emperor Jones*, while still refusing to admit Negroes into the theater.[92] For the congress, the delegates were housed in open tents near the Washington monument, a situation that Ellison likened to Steinbeck's fictional landscapes teeming with squatters. There were no public facilities for large numbers of blacks in the District.

Ellison maintained a distinctive idealism toward the congress and its Pollyannish goals. Since he had not experienced the repression of civil liberties following the First World War, he was capable of bright optimism. He recognized the collective spirit of the NNC as a will toward freedom and "the best guarantee of America's future":

> For years Negroes have struggled for that unity, seeking to find their allies; sometimes gaining, and sometimes losing ground. And in all Negroes at some period of their lives there is that yearning for a sense of group unity that is the yearning of men for a flag: for a unity that cannot be compromised, that cannot be bought; that is conscious of itself, of its strength that is militant. I had come to realize that such a unity is a unity of a class. I had not thought of the Congress in such terms, but it was more like a hope to be realized.[93]

He noticed a singular determination in the people he met and interviewed during the three-day conference. In fact, everyone seemed to him thoroughly progressive, except for Harlem's black Communists. Ellison was amused and embarrassed by the likes of Abner Berry, denouncing *Native Son* in the same language as the black bourgeois newspapers, failing to see the clear enthusiasm that the novel elicited from young people and how well it articulated their struggles. In an otherwise ebullient May letter to Wright about the congress, he could not escape a lengthy commentary on the imbecility of black Communist leaders.

At a panel discussion, a particularly enthusiastic young woman expressed dismay at the consistent resistance to *Native Son*, and she spoke forcefully of the need to defend the novel. Mainly, she felt that the book put well her experiences and feelings as an American Negro. After the panel, Ellison struck up a conversation with her and found that she had already had a serious row with New Yorkers Berry and Carlton Moss, who had echoed the sentiment of the black middle class, that writers the caliber of Richard Wright were in short supply, but that books like *Native Son* were obscene and repulsive. When another young woman joined the conversation and remarked that the reluctance of Communists to accept the novel only proved that whites were fundamentally incapable of understanding the striving of the Negro toward freedom, Ellison had to explain delicately that the Communists in question were black. He took heart from the discussion though; blacks outside of Harlem's fog were taking from the novel its most salient and remarkable features and were using it to bolster the radical struggle.[94]

Ellison's frustration was born of the fact that he was deeply committed to the potential of the Communist coalition with the NNC. His focus, as well as his training, was on art and human beings, and he misunderstood the political disaster taking place at the conference. To Ellison's mind, the major disappointment at the congress was A. Philip Randolph, former head of the Brotherhood of Sleeping Car Porters and now editor of the socialist *Messenger*.

Randolph took the dais after Congress of Industrial Organizations head John L. Lewis and spoke abstractly about power politics and alignments for black civil rights. To Ellison's ears, Randolph, heckled by Communists during the speech, was a "red-baiter," calling for distance between blacks and the Communist-run CIO. In later years, Ellison fully recognized the irony that in New York's racist unions "one seldom saw a skilled Negro workman," but that in the South "there were scores [of skilled Negro workers] to be seen."[95] But during that summer, anyone pointing up the contradictions of the unions, or the Communists running some of them, met with his disapproval: "I [had] sat through the address with a feeling of betrayal," he wrote in his *New Masses* account. Randolph's speech precipitated his famous March on Washington Movement that eventually opened up war industries to blacks, a cause that the Communists never supported. Ellison was still struggling with his own feelings of indignation, not unlike Bigger Thomas, which made compromise seem like cowardice. "I have seen many of my friends frustrated in their effort to create themselves. They are boys full of protest and indignation which has no social outlet. They are unhappy working at jobs they hate, living under restrictions they hate." But in spite of his protest, he was missing a key shift in the civil rights movement. Instead of seeing the NNC's leadership replaced by factions more loyal to Communists than to black interests, Ellison saw in Randolph "a scramble to raise the Booker T. Washington symbol anew in Negro life."

Trying to combine his concerns about both race and class, Ellison during this period was as close rhetorically to the proletarian movement as he ever got. He met a worker at the congress named Hank Johnson from Chicago, and promptly transformed him into a vision that would have made even Mike Gold proud: "When he spoke all the violence that America has made our Negro heritage was flowing from him transformed into a will to change a civilization." After seeing the broad-based enthusiasm and discipline of participants from all over the country who challenged their local governments to recognize their equality, Ellison called the congress "the most exciting thing to happen to me . . . the first real basis for faith in our revolutionary potentialities."[96] This blending of race and class issues also made Marxism work for him. He could now picture blacks as the vanguard group, capable of outstripping their proscribed role in the sequential development of the class struggle. He had tapped into the welled-up folk spirit, the consciousness of a will to change shared experiences, which overflowed like a swollen river.

Ellison's optimism about the National Negro Congress remained strong for the congress's next couple of years of existence, as its leadership passed into the hands of Communist Max Yergan. In the middle of November 1940, the congress held a conference for the New York region at the Park Palace on 110th Street, and now openly advocated nonparticipation in the global conflict: "[T]he National Negro Congress . . . has repeatedly affirmed it to be to the best interest of the Negro people in America that our country stay out of the war."[97] Flush with earnest enthusiasm toward the Congress, Ellison noted to himself a confident martial spirit among the attendees, "a resiliency, a reserve, a feeling of controlled energy. They might bend in the attacks to come but they will not break." The meeting of three hundred delegates proposed a list of demands for Mayor LaGuardia and Governor Lehman, aimed at bringing Negroes on board for the lucrative building contracts in New York City, particularly to construct schools in Harlem, where students had to receive instruction in staggered shifts because of a shortage of classroom space.

The discussion of grievances brought up some of his more poignant memories. He recalled living in Dayton; his mother Ida's toughness when the guard turned them away from the Oklahoma City zoo; hunting in Ohio; hearing about the Tulsa riots, and witnessing the aftermath as a boy when his family passed through the city. But as time went on, NNC activities slowed, and like the Writers League, the congress made a rightward swing toward American intervention once the Nazis invaded the Soviet Union in 1941. Though the congress was still in existence, promoting a cultural program from its office at 307 Lenox Avenue (the CP Harlem bureau was at 306 Lenox) and headed by Yergan and black Communist Edward Strong, it no longer sustained the sort of mass organizing capacity it had exhibited in 1940.[98] The momentum now swept toward Randolph and his March on Washington

Movement, which started brokering deals with Roosevelt. Yergan soon left the shell of the congress for a more lucrative position on Adam Clayton Powell's *People's Voice* newspaper.

Despite his consciousness about rural folk and his profound feeling of communal heritage with the heavily Southern Congress, New York, with its confident ultra-urban swagger, remained Ellison's home. His work was going well. *New Masses* editors Sillen and North offered him greater freedom to explore all aspects of the Negro Question. Ellison had the idea of bringing on board the writers E. Franklin Frazier, Sterling Brown, Ralph Bunche, and Eugene Holmes as contributors to *New Masses,* so it would fully reflect the intricacies of black life in America. In the meantime, he would continue as a steady reviewer for the *New Masses.*

After writing two brief essays, one on Walter D. Edmonds's antebellum novel *Chad Hannah,* and the other on Herbert Lewis's tale of the current European war, *Spring Offensive,* Ellison published his third short story in July 1940, "The Birthmark." The source for this gripping and realistic story about a lynching may well have come out of conversations that Ellison had at the congress; most notably, he met Kentuckian James McMillian, who had survived a lynching. But the timing of the story and its appearance in the *New Masses* coincided with the Senate vote on the perennially filibustered lynching bill, which had passed the House in January. In "The Birthmark," Clara and Matt's brother Willie has been lynched. The body has been obliterated to such an extent (the actual carnage duplicates the injuries done to Claude Neal in 1934) that Matt can determine the identity of his brother only by "the mark . . . just below Willie's navel." When he eventually does look for his brother's birthmark, Matt finds "only a bloody mound of torn flesh and hair." This description hints at Ellison's awakening to the powers of symbolism: black men are shorn of phallic manhood; castration is their American birthmark.

Ellison paid close attention to details: a body lying covered with newspapers, a sizzling concrete highway, and a menacing highway patrolman whose refrain is, "We don't allow no lynching round here no more!" He built dramatic tension by focusing on the middle ground occupied by Matt, who seeks to placate both the threatening whites and his own strong-willed and assertive sister. Clara demands to see the body, and despite her brother's gentle refusals, she observes how he was brutalized and then refuses to be silenced, uttering aloud the unspeakable in the story's commanding denouement—"They lynched Willie." As the story concludes, the body of her brother is visible only between the legs of the white patrolman. The destroyed black body enforces the symbol of the white man's generative power.

The title "The Birthmark" connotes the ambiguous natal heritage of African Americans and connects easily to its precursor *Native Son.* Though by 1940

Wright was loosening his ties to the Communist Party, Ellison continued to propose that the best chances for black humanity lay in a considered analysis of Marxism, folk spirit, and self-determination. He determinedly explored the brutal physical confrontation still common in the Southern world of debt peonage and minimal labor organization—the points of focus for the National Negro Congress. In the story, Clara says accusingly to her surviving brother, "They asked us last month to sign a piece of paper saying we wanted things like this to stop and you was afraid. Now look at my brother, he's laying there looking like something ain't even human."[99] "The Birthmark" remains the most violent foray into the horrors of race relations that Ellison ever made public during his lifetime. He also had shifted his perspective on rendering black speech. He now emphasized Negro idiom by verbal repetition and omission, rather than the extreme visual and aural contrasts he had used in *Slick*. After the short story's publication, Ellison abandoned completely the less-than-fully articulate "proletarian" protagonist, making symbolism a more central weapon in his fictional arsenal.

Over the summer, Langston Hughes's autobiography *The Big Sea* appeared, and in the September *New Masses* "Review and Comment" column, Ellison analyzed Hughes's latest contribution. He set his review, titled "Stormy Weather," in motion by dismissing the Harlem Renaissance. Wright's "Blueprint for Negro Writing" had described the movement sensationally as a "liaison between inferiority complexed Negro 'geniuses' and burnt-out white Bohemians with money."[100] According to Wright's formula, the educated black writers of the 1920s had betrayed the interest of the black nation. Ellison stepped beyond Wright's idea of an inferiority complex; instead, he thought that the black elites could never fully represent the interests of the black masses.

> In a pathetic attempt to reconcile unreconcilables, these writers sought to wed the passive philosophy of the Negro middle class to the militant racial protest of the Negro masses. Thus, since the black masses had evolved no writers of their own, the energy of the whole people became perverted to the ends of a class which had grown conscious of itself through the economic alliances it made when it supported the war.[101]

Hughes was an important figure in this reinterpretation of the 1920s, and Ellison cheered him for what *The Big Sea* did provide on the issues of class and race: "It offers a valuable picture of the class divisions within the Negro group, shows their tradition and folkways and the effects of an expanding industrial capitalism upon several generations of a Negro family." While he granted that the story was told "in evocative prose of the personal experiences of a sensitive Negro in the modern world," in the end Ellison chastised Hughes for his literary—and intellectual—irresponsibility. Hughes's carefree descriptions were pleasant, but superficial. "In his next book, however, we hope that besides the colorful incidents, the word pictures, the feel, the taste, and smell of his experiences, Langston Hughes will tell us more of how he felt and thought about them." In the review, Ellison signaled a rupture with black dabblers in artistic theory. The discussions he had had with Hughes concerning emotional sensitivity now seemed pale in comparison with the talks of philosophy and psychology he was having with Richard Wright. In a letter to Wright in the spring, he had already sniped at Hughes. Ellison suggested that Wright do an investigative piece on race and class in Mexico; he was cross that Hughes, who had also lived in Mexico and spoke Spanish, had never analyzed critically the features of Central America.[102] Always impatient with leaders and authority figures, Ellison had little time for an internationally known black writer who refused to show "the processes by which a sensitive Negro attains a heightened consciousness of a world in which most of the odds are against his doing so."[103]

Ellison went with his heart, which generally traveled the intellectual high road. At one end was a Hughes-like approach: artful and well described, but theoretically vapid. At the other extreme was the propaganda of the CPUSA—of Abner Berry, for instance, who had called Ellison's lively first-person essay on the third Negro National Congress "too individualistic."[104] And Ellison had good reason to be wary of Wright, still an intellectual and artistic mentor, but one who could be catty and underhanded with friends. Before the year ended, Ellison abandoned proletarian fiction altogether. His decision to reject Slick Williams and Matt as appropriate narrators signaled a growing artistic distance from Wright. As his fame grew in 1940, Wright indulged in petty tests of fidelity with members of his close circle. One of his favorite ploys was to tell Ellison a secret, supposedly held in utter confidence. Ellison would later find out that Ted Ward or Herbert Newton had been given precisely the same tidbit of information with the same proscription. "Dick was in his conspiratorial mood," he said about it.[105]

Their personal lives were deeply intertwined. Both men were in difficult marriages with glamorous, independent, high-profile women, pursuing artistic careers. Rose Poindexter had married Ellison after a fair career in motion pictures in Europe. In his letters to friends, Ellison bemoaned that his wife was salty and a bit caustic. After less than a year of marriage, Wright was dissatisfied with the prima donna Dheema, who wielded an almost tyrannical power over him. Wright was emotionally more interested in Ellen Poplar, a member of the same Communist cell as the Newtons. Ellison had run into Poplar at the congress in Washington, where she asked for Wright's address and made specific queries about the quality of his marriage with Dheema. Ellison wrote to Wright in late May that he had seen a tense and nervous Ellen Poplar at the Washington, D.C., conference. Ellison did not want to be in the middle of Wright's contentious personal life, and he stated as candidly as he could that he had no bias against Ellen. But Ellison wanted Wright to stay with Dheema, whom he admired and who resembled in some ways his own wife—a woman whose stature was equal to that of her husband. Ellison thought that Wright had made a coup by marrying Dheema. When Wright invited him out to purchase clothes with his windfall from the novel's sales, for instance, Ellison was often surprised at the lack of cultivation in his taste; he felt that Dheema might offer him refinement.[106] Dheema returned from Mexico several months in advance of Richard, and when the Ellisons moved into a large apartment next door to jazz musician Teddy Wilson at 25 Hamilton Terrace, Dheema moved in as well. Tree-lined Hamilton Terrace with its yellow brick town homes was home to Harlem's chichi art community. Ralph and Rose hoped to promote a reconciliation for the Wrights, perhaps hoping it would bring new life into their marriage as well.

Wright returned to New York from Mexico by way of Mississippi, where he visited with his father and uncles, seeing his relatives for the first time in twenty years. After the open hostility toward educated blacks that he had experienced in the South, he came back to New York with little patience for Dheema's sophisticated attitude and aloof behavior. And Wright often felt that even his close friends were laughing at him, and he tended to be suspicious of them. He assumed that Ellison and his wife had invited Dheema into their apartment so that he would be forced to pay half of the rent. By the end of the summer, he had started living with Ellen Poplar in the Newtons' home in Brooklyn, and he did not even give his address to Ellison. The sanguine relationship between the men, their peak of intimacy and fraternity, had come to an end.

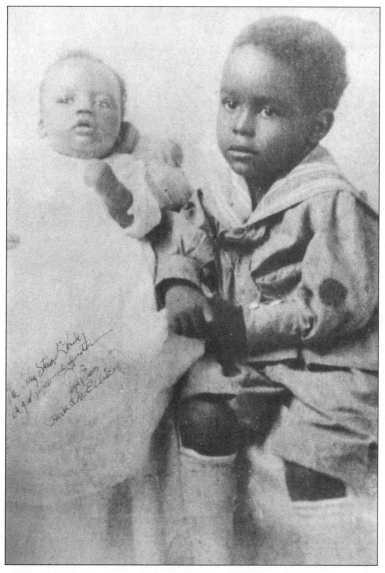

Ralph and Herbert Ellison, ca. 1916. (Courtesy of Jimmie Lewis Franklin Jr.)

Ralph Ellison (second boy kneeling from left) and classmates from the Frederick Douglass School, Oklahoma City, ca. 1919. (Courtesy of *Oklahoma City Black Dispatch*)

Oklahoma University Hospital, as it looked when Lewis Ellison died in 1916. (Courtesy of Jim Edwards and Hal Ottaway, *The Vanished Splendor: Postcard Views of Early Oklahoma City.* Oklahoma City: Abalche Book Shop, 1984)

Second Street, Oklahoma City, ca. 1920. (Courtesy of Jim Edwards and Hal Ottaway, *The Vanished Splendor: Postcard Views of Early Oklahoma City.* Oklahoma City: Abalche Book Shop, 1984)

Inman Page, Principal of Douglass School and former president of Langston Colored Agricultural and Normal Institute. (Courtesy of Oklahoma State Historical Society)

Frederick Douglass School teachers and classroom. Johnson Whittaker, former West Point cadet, is standing in rear. (Courtesy of Jim Edwards and Hal Ottaway, *The Vanished Splendor: Postcard Views of Early Oklahoma City.* Oklahoma City: Abalche Book Shop, 1984)

Zelia N. Breaux, superintendent of music for Oklahoma City Colored Schools. (Courtesy of Oklahoma State Historical Society)

Roscoe Dunjee, editor-in-chief of *Oklahoma City Black Dispatch*. (Courtesy of Oklahoma State Historical Society)

Douglass High School Graduation, 1931. Ralph Ellison is standing in the last row, fourth from the left, underneath the "R" and "A" in the word "GRADUATING." (Courtesy of *Oklahoma City Black Dispatch*)

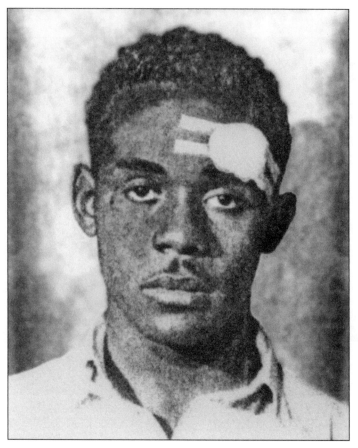

Ralph Ellison on arrival at Tuskegee, July 1933. (Courtesy of Tuskegee University)

Robert Russa Moton, president of Tuskegee, 1915–1935.

Morteza Sprague, professor of English and director of library services, Tuskegee Institute and University.

Tuskegee Music School Faculty, ca. 1933. William L. Dawson is in the center in tails; Hazel Harrison is immediately to his left; Frank Drye is on his far right. (Courtesy of Jean E. Cazort and Constance Hobson, *Born to Play.* Westport, Conn.: Greenwood Press, 1983)

Tuskegee Music School Classroom, Andrew F. Rosemond in center and Frank Drye, seated with French horn. Ellison may be sitting in front row, first chair to Rosemond's right. (Courtesy of Mrs. Elwyn Welch)

Black History Week Performance at Tuskegee, February 1934. Ralph Ellison wears overalls and has his hands on a broom, in the center of the photograph. (Courtesy of *Tuskegee Messenger* and Avon Kirkland)

Ralph Ellison, 1942.
(Courtesy of *New Masses* and Reference Center for Marxist Studies, New York)

Richard and Ellen Wright, ca. 1944. (Courtesy of estate of Ellen Wright and Michel Fabre; Yale Collection of American Literature, Beinecke Rare Book and Manuscript Library)

Richard Wright, mid-1940s. (Courtesy of estate of Ellen Wright and Michel Fabre; Yale Collection of American Literature, Beinecke Rare Book and Manuscript Library)

Langston Hughes, ca. 1945. (Courtesy of estate of Ralph Ellison; Yale Collection of American Literature, Beinecke Rare Book and Manuscript Library)

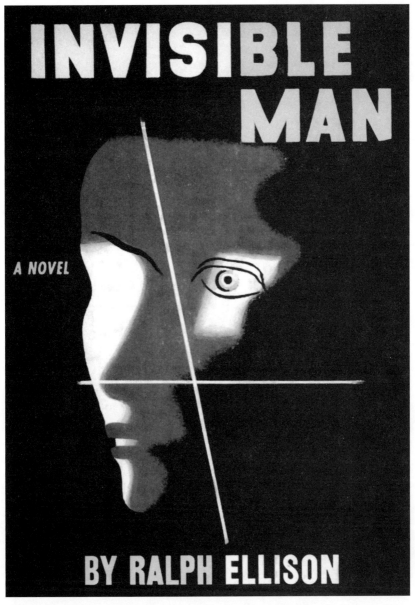

The jacket for *Invisible Man*. (Courtesy of Random House; photograph courtesy of Moorland-Spingarn Library, Howard University)

Ralph Ellison, book jacket photo for *Invisible Man*. (Courtesy of estate of Gordon Parks and the Schomburg Center for Research in Black Culture, New York Public Library)

9

New Negro at
Negro Quarterly

1941–1942

THE EVENTS OF the summer of 1941 made his association with the *New Masses* magazine uncomfortable for Ellison. He contributed two more book reviews, hewing to the basic political agenda of communists and fellow travelers, but felt keenly a growing uneasiness. On June 22, counter to conventional military wisdom, the Germans opened a second military front, using their tactic of lightning war. Nazi panzers took only six weeks to surge several hundred miles into the Soviet Union and to capture Kiev. Soviet communiqués made plain to the U.S. Communist hierarchy that the imperatives for the military survival of the USSR demanded complete cooperation with the American war industry—an utter about-face for Communist strategy in the United States. All programs that could be construed as hampering or diverting energy from American war readiness were swiftly discarded. This fundamental alteration in policy translated into the loss of support for the National Negro Congress, and most significant, a hard line against activism promoting racial equality within the war industry and armed forces. Before the end of the year, it became obvious that A. Philip Randolph's crusade for black rights would far outstrip any Communist-backed campaigns for Negroes. Ellison had some egg on his face.

The League of American Writers, which initially had been mobilized to fight fascist warmongering, was now completely without Communist support and was nearing the end of its days. Especially shocking to those who remained of the critical black Left was the unselfconscious manner in which the pro-Negro programs were abandoned and even opposed. Communist-influenced organs like the *Worker* and the *New Masses* no longer emphasized disparity in America, but sought to unify classes and races against the Nazis. Sometimes the adherence to new policies seemed so partisan as to be neurotic. In September 1941, Harlem Communist leader Benjamin Davis Jr. would claim that "the CP is disturbed by the increasing struggle of Negroes for jobs in defense plants."[1] Four years later, he shrilly supported the Army's persecution of black WACs at Fort Devens who had protested the military's maltreatment of wounded black GI's. The dissolution of Southern branches of the CP was not far off. In a 1945 letter to Richard Wright, Ellison signaled his final disgust at the American Communist Party's decision to abandon black rights, a move that led to its loss of political viability. Disparaging the leader of the American Communist Party, Earl Browder, Ellison compared him to that other American icon whose vision matched his ability to think on his feet: Herbert Hoover.[2]

At work at the *New Masses*, Samuel Sillen and other editors told Ellison that it was time to "soft-pedal this Negro thing. We've got to get production going."[3] Although the magazine did not entirely abandon its critical treatment of black American life, editorial censorship of a substantive sort—dictating the subject matter and angle for an essay or a review—was a source first of irritation, and later of increasing resentment, for Ellison, who offered the maverick opinion that war production efforts would actually improve with racial equality. Though he did not always keep his opinions to himself, Ellison took advantage of his strengths—intelligence, energy, high-profile friends—and instead of letting his bruised ego dispirit him, he worked himself into positions of leadership outside of the CP. He became a key figure at the New York League of American Writers and began to build a professional reputation—and to help others to do the same. Ellison's career would benefit from the war.

At the same time, Ellison was experimenting with his prose. Over the previous year, he had consolidated his position as a professional writer for the *New Masses*. He had published eight book reviews, four assorted reviews of theater and public entertainment, and the short story based on his Oklahoma childhood, "Mister Toussan." His literary efforts had culminated in his dramatic treatment of the National Negro Congress, "A Congress Jim Crow Didn't Attend." His *New Masses* essays had reflected the primary concern laid out in Richard Wright's "Blueprint for Negro Writing": the black writer's necessary immersion in the nationalist context of the Negro Question.

Before the middle of 1941, Ellison would articulate a fairly coherent literary agenda, reworking his cogent "Stormy Weather" review from 1940, his response to the two artistic bombshells of that year, written by members of his own circle: Richard Wright's *Native Son* and the New York performance of Ted Ward's play *Big White Fog.* In the midst of a renaissance of black artistic production, Ellison would follow the leftist trail away from its Communist center, in the direction of the periphery.

Ellison's relationship with the Communist Richard Wright continued to be tainted by his friend's cunning and manipulation. In February 1941, during casting for the stage version of *Native Son,* which starred Canada Lee and was directed by Orson Welles, Ellison hoped that his wife, Rose, would have a chance at an important role. Wright claimed that he had telegrammed them with an audition date, but somehow the wire did not get through. Ellison connected this snub to Wright's secretive marriage to Ellen Poplar. And Wright still believed that Ellison and Rose had somehow wangled a couple of months of free rent out of him when he was leaving his former wife Dheema. Wright's popularity among writers and intellectuals, his prominence in New York, and his ability to reach an audience had something to do with the fact that Ellison was more surprised than angry and more hurt than embarrassed at the affront. He figured he would have to put up with Wright's inconsideration.

In June 1941, the League of American Writers sponsored the Fourth American Writers Congress. Langston Hughes declined to continue in a leadership position, resigning as the vice president, and on May 26 he recommended Ellison, along with Richard Wright, Sterling Brown, Jesse Fauset, and Eugene Holmes, as likely candidates to fill his post.[4] While the League selected the iron man Richard Wright, by September Ellison would be elected into its upper ranks, to the Executive Committee and the Negro Literature Committee.[5]

The title of the June conference, which was held scant weeks prior to the German invasion of the Soviet Union, was "In Defense of Culture." The Communist-backed League, whose president was the detective writer Dashiell Hammett, "opposed economic royalists, their wars and their fascism."[6] At the conference's opening on the evening of Friday, June 6, at the Manhattan Center, Wright gave a speech entitled "What We Think of Their War." The Yanks with pens and brushes were not coming to save Europe, Wright told the crowd, reversing the popular slogan of Anglo-American and European cooperation. The next two days featured seminars and panels filled with Ellison's comrades and friends; nearly everyone was connected to the *New Masses.* A Saturday afternoon critics panel, chaired by Samuel Sillen, featured Mike Gold, Edwin Burgum, and the Columbia University history graduate student Herbert Aptheker, who presented a paper on Negro contributions to

American culture. Ellison expressed his growing interest in the art form of the blues lyric—particularly his sense of it as dramatic tragedy. He had begun to notice a connection between the formal artistic properties of tragedy and the psychological and thematic structure of blues lyrics. But the editors on the panel, committed to a wooden Marxist approach with its poor understanding of cultural dynamics—especially those of the Negro—disagreed with him. He was to hear again from authority figures that he was high-strung, nervous, and seeing something that wasn't there. Politely they reminded him of the iron economic laws that dictated the progress of civilization; eons if not epochs separated the postbellum creators of the blues from the bards of Elizabethan tragedy. He was told gently that he was way off-base, despite the fact that Negro folk singers Leadbelly and Josh White were scheduled to sing in the East Ballroom on the next evening. Ellison felt that their remarks were condescending. He was hurt, but also took into consideration his opinion that the *New Masses* editors rejected the hard task of thinking for themselves.[7] While he recognized organized political Marxism, he was finding its rigid patterns of thought inadequate to explain his observations of the world. It helped matters little that the Communists wanted him to close ranks and join a segregated army to defeat Hitler.

Ellison thought that the blues and the art forms and artifacts associated with the Negro lower class were vital and fundamentally important to an analysis of African American culture. He trusted his own instincts and observations, and worked as a powerful advocate for what later came to be termed a "Blues School" of literature. Ellison reached out to literary publications that were better known for their catholicity of taste than their political partisanship. He published "Richard Wright and Recent Negro Fiction," his first long critical assessment of black writers, in the summer issue of *Direction,* a Federal Writers Project organ edited by the well-regarded but mildly obscurantist thinker Kenneth Burke. Burke's iconoclastic work, such as the essay "The Philosophy of Literary Form," managed to make both literary Marxist and Aristotelian formalists wince. Burke had intrigued Ellison ever since his 1937 League of American Writers speech "The Rhetoric of Hitler's Battle," which had applied the theories of psychology and the understanding of primitive ritual to expose the inner workings of Hitler's deadly propaganda machine.

In his essay, Ellison offered a polished dispute with black writers, one that he would abbreviate and republish in *New Masses* at the end of the summer. "Richard Wright and Recent Negro Fiction" continued to upbraid black writers of the 1920s by comparing their work to the colossal epic *Native Son:*

> [Negro fiction of the 1920s] grew out of the post-war prosperity and the rise of the conscious Negro middle class. Usually their work was apologetic and an expression of middle class ideology rather than the point of view of Negro workers or farmers. Except for the work of Langston Hughes it ig-

nored the existence of Negro folklore and perceived no connection between its efforts and the symbols and images of Negro folk forms; it avoided psychology; was unconscious of politics; and most of the deeper problems arising out of the relationship of the Negro group to the American whole, were avoided.[8]

Using Wright's *Native Son* as a shining example of "maturity" and "high artistry," Ellison deplored the disjunction between the "theme" and the "technique" employed by the majority of black writers. Negroes either delved into socially and racially revolutionary themes with inadequate technical expertise or they avoided the charged world of contemporary social and racial politics altogether. Artistic quality depended upon blacks enjoying "freedom of association with advanced white writers"—difficult to achieve, considering the prejudice of white society, but which inevitably would lead to "the merging of the imaginative depiction of Negro life into the broad stream of American literature." Ellison was mindful that *Huckleberry Finn* included the Negro Jim as Huck's mentor. In a sense, Negro life was already a part of a broader American culture, and the job of the critic was to make the connections that seemed invisible more apparent.

In "Richard Wright and Recent Negro Fiction," he pointed to the work of the next generation of writers: "There can be no stepping back from the artistic and social achievements of *Native Son*. The Negro writer must toe this mark if he is to be effective." In the progression of black literature from the isolated voice of a minority into the broad mainstream of American and international writing and thinking, Wright's work would serve as a "take-off in a leap which promises to carry over a whole tradition." While *Native Son* had eclipsed Harlem Renaissance writers, Ellison could see room for an improved and vitalized vision of black life and culture in the future. Ellison's arguments simultaneously advocated on the one hand, greater black cultural consciousness, and on the other hand, the transcendence of that consciousness with universalism.

In August, shortly after the German invasion of the USSR, Ellison reissued his cry for quickened black literary development in an essay in *New Masses*. The magazine included a subtitle, using terminology that it would soon repudiate: "Ralph Ellison discusses the growing achievements of Negro novelists in depicting the consciousness of an oppressed nation." The Negro nation thesis, formulated first by editor Cyril Briggs of the socialist *Messenger* in Harlem in 1917, argued that Negroes constituted an independent nation living in the so-called Black Belt of the Southern U.S.[9] After the 1941 attack on the Soviets by the Nazis, the Communist Party's Stalin-allied information sources discarded that idea in favor of promoting the unity, not the splintering, of American experience. Yet Ellison was able to express his independent opinion in his review in the Communist magazine. His essay in *Direction* had alluded to an implicit rift between classes, and an evolution in consciousness which he desired to advance his own utopian vision. In the *New Masses* essay "Recent Negro Fiction," he was explicit. The writers of the 1920s (again, save Hughes) had failed, he said; Zora Neale Hurston wasted her technical gifts on "calculated burlesque"; and most of the younger writers still groped to match complex themes with quality technique. Much of the lack of technical precision was due to "the Jim Crow retardation of the natural flow of the Negro folk consciousness into the machines and institutions which constitute the organism of North American society." In a vein remarkably similar to the Trinidadian Trotskyite C. L. R. James,[10] Ellison thought that blacks must recognize their potential as a vanguard class, and entirely move beyond mimicking white elites.

> This will mean of course far more than attaining the consciousness of the American bourgeois, for the institutional support of bourgeois consciousness is rapidly disintegrating under the pressure of capitalism's decay. The new Negro consciousness must of necessity go beyond the highest point of bourgeois consciousness and work towards the creation of conditions in which it might integrate and stabilize itself; it demands new institutions, a new society.[11]

Ellison's radical program held the writer to be a vital articulator of the new vision of society. He was convinced of the moral duty of the writer, and ultimately the creative artist's prophetic office. Without the John Reed Clubs and League of American Writers, it was impossible for blacks to overcome the limitations of segregation that thwarted the development of their artistic vision. Only with increased contacts would black people "overcome this handicap and possess the conscious meaning of their lives." Taking his cue from Lenin's ideas about the vanguard's role in spearheading the revolution, he envisioned an intellectual revolutionary movement in which the avant garde would theoretically exceed and then displace the structures of bourgeois dominance. Insofar as artists prepared the consciousness of the radical elite, the work of the black writer in preparing the advanced cadres was critical.

Ellison's theoretical understanding of the black artists' frontline role in developing the consciousness of the elites signaled the direction of his own work. He realized the importance of an art that not only invoked the theme of struggle, but also located itself in a formal structure that was adequate to convey its nationalist implications. The essence of all of this was the important psychological feat of possessing self-identity, a sort of gestalt in which an individual's concept of history and understanding of the present cohered as "the conscious meaning" of one's life. For Ellison, who refined his ideas of consciousness through readings of James Joyce's *Portrait of the Artist as a Young Man*, this was hard-won intellectual turf.

At more than five thousand words, "Recent Negro Fiction" was the longest essay Ralph Ellison ever had published in *New Masses*. If his tour de force had been printed in the *Saturday Review* or the *New Yorker,* he would have been well paid. The *New Masses* editors, now vigorously involved in shaping the consciousness of their readers for an all-out shooting war, wanted to marshal black labor toward the war industry and into the military. Aware of his value to the editors, Ellison told them that he wanted more than exposure; he wanted income. Ellison, the *New Masses'* "young Negro writer," who had published his earliest pieces for free, demanded payment from the pro-Stalin journal. To his great surprise, editors Sillen and North agreed. Sometimes he received as much as $15 for an article.[12] He would no longer be *New Masses'* at-large voice of the Negro people; they would have to treat him like a salaried writer.

The desire for consistent pay reflected not only the changing times but also Ellison's advancing maturity and frustration with his progress relative to his peers. Wright lived off a salary guaranteed by the enormous sales of *Native Son.* His largesse was such that on January 31 (perhaps as a way of endearing himself to the radicals once more as he moved further from the Communists), Wright threw a party for the cast of *Salute to Negro Troops* in the Village, an interracial success that the *Amsterdam News* said "brought out the town's better knowns from up and downtown."[13] Ellison's Tuskegee buddy Mike Rabb visited him, reminding him of the good life available to the quiet black Southern bourgeoisie. Teddy Wilson was, in his circle of musicians, a superstar. He had broken segregation barriers and played with the nationally renowned Benny Goodman, and had himself helped to make famous another black migrant to New York with a past she had tried to outgrow, the sultry blues singer and heartthrob Billie Holiday. If Wilson's masterful piano playing wasn't enough, his innovative harmonic changes and fluid style were beginning to interest a whole new group of pianists who were inventing a musical genre that people were already calling "bop." Ellison, too, wanted something to show for having successfully passed his apprenticeship, and with his persistent criticism of social realist fiction, he would not find professional rewards at *New Masses.*

He became more involved with the League of American Writers, taking advantage of the leadership vacuum after the mass resignations of 1939 in protest of the Russo-German pact. A National League board member by the fall of 1941, Ellison helped to edit a statement for the League's Hollywood journal, the *Clipper,* probably at the request of his close friend Sanora Babb. He was also on the *Clipper's* editorial board, a post that he shared with Dorothy Brewster and Myra Page. Their statement pointed out that the literary situation was disagreeable for fiction writers: "Twelve years of depression have added new restrictions and formulas to the editorial censorship, and now there is war. . . . Generations ago, in the days of small circulation and relatively numerous mediums, there was more scope for the writer . . . even when the marketplace was less avid for propaganda than it is now."[14] Ellison stood for artistic freedom and opportunity in a time when the artistic opportunities for him were few.

Having a venue for his new ideas was becoming quite important to him. Although he had worked his way into the *New Masses* and the League with his critiques of Negro art and life, Ellison wanted his critical work to have a broad range. Around the middle of 1941 he decided to deal with the work of Ernest Hemingway, who in the *Green Hills of Africa* had argued that all of modern American literature had grown out of Twain's *Huckleberry Finn.* The idea of the moral play between Huck and the Nigger Jim being the center-piece of American literature deeply intrigued Ellison. Hemingway was now considered irrelevant by Communists, at least in part because of his descrip-tion of Communist failings in *For Whom the Bell Tolls,* but Ellison thought the writer's significance too broad to be ignored. He also felt it necessary to make a literary evaluation that addressed the formidable problem of the Marx-ist literary critic. Ellison's ideas were radical because he claimed that artistic mastery would inevitably prove that fine art and the most strident Marxist class criticism were in concord. Hemingway was of importance for the Left be-cause he had distilled his prose and his ideas, but wrote with bright clarity.[15] Ellison never published the essay on Hemingway, which collected his earliest notions about the sources and expressive tendencies of American literature.

By November, Ellison's marriage with Rose had soured to the point where he moved out of their apartment and into a flat on 140th Street. Not long after, he sent Wright a long letter reestablishing their friendship. In it he praised the publication of *Twelve Million Black Voices.* Wright's new book, a blend of photography and essay, had struck at Ellison's core and left him cry-ing in the afternoon sun in his apartment. It chronicled the rags-to-rags story of the black Everyman, running from the Southern cotton fields to the equally ruinous urban ghetto. Ellison thought of his own mother's trek across the country in search of work and decent housing. Ellison commended the book as a timely device to create black unity and self-conscious identity. The book channeled the suffering and degradation of American Negroes in a manner that proved that a black writer owned those horrors, rather than was ashamed of them. He admitted to being so pleased with the volume that he placed it upon the mantelpiece for his visitors to see.

As perceptive of the book's necessity and impact as he was desirous of mending fences, Ellison admiringly recognized that he and Wright were "brothers." "I felt so intensely the fire of our common experience. . . . When experiences such as ours are organized as you have done it here, there is noth-ing left for a man to do but fight." But despite his desire to recapture his and Wright's special bond of friendship, he hinted at the oak that was in his will concerning his own distinctive artistic understanding. He had neither forgotten their disagreement over his short story or Wright's reaction. In Wright's future works, Ellison said, he expected more individuality and less of the pursuit of mythic figures and archetypes, the black Everyman. He wrote to him that even though it was the time for stressing the themes which made them brothers and of necessity transcended the individual experience, in the future, when Wright wrote his autobiographies he had a sacred obligation to stress the specific individual contours of his life.[16]

As an intimate friend of Richard Wright and Langston Hughes, Ellison attracted the attention of the League and the Communist upper crust. Toward the end of November, the celebrity black Communist Angelo Herndon wrote to Ralph "Ellerson" from his position as the secretary of the Negro Publication Society of America. Herndon wrote that he was in charge of a quarterly journal devoted to Negroes, and that he wanted it available by Negro History Week in February.[17] From Ralph Ellison he wanted a contribution. A fund-raiser without peer, in no small reason because of his good looks and his celebrity status among leftists as a living man who had nearly been martyred and faced the odds with a great deal of courage, Herndon carried an air of high seriousness. And while the board of the Negro Publication Society were all leftists and included many of the members of the League of American Writers, it was not dominated by the Communist party.

Herndon was not alone in seeking Ellison's participation. League-sponsored events offered him the chance to speak and debate in public. On November 27, Ellison was the interpolating critical voice between the *New Masses'* Samuel Sillen and NAACP *Crisis* magazine editor Roy Wilkins at the 124th Street Library for Harlem librarian Lawrence Reddick's "Evenings with Negro Authors" series.[18] The critics devoted themselves to a discussion of William Attaway, author of that year's sensational piece of naturalist fiction, *Blood on the Forge.* Attaway's novel had been a hard and pessimistic scrutiny of black migration from the rural South to the industrial North. Like Wright, Attaway relied heavily on mythic and symbolic characters to represent not merely Negroes, but the Negro. Representing the League of American Writers, Ellison strove for a position between Sillen and Wilkins and the powerful constituencies that they represented. Ellison understood that Wilkins's real constituency was the Negro elite, while Sillen's attitude toward the current movement for civil rights for blacks was to subdue its thunder in order to benefit the world proletariat. Ellison was in a position to correct Sillen, an English professor, for diminishing the dramatic range of black culture, or Wilkins for his politician's approach to art-as-public-relations.

Ellison was on his way to earning a reputation as a penetrating critic comfortable not only with Marxism, but also with sociology and psychology. His written assessment of Attaway's novel saw print the first week in December in a long *New Masses* "Review and Comment" piece. Ellison challenged Attaway to fulfill the historic role of the black realist writer. While approving of the writer's efforts—"easily one of the season's best novels" with its important "contribution of new themes"—Ellison sorrowfully noted that the novel could not grasp the historic change afoot. "Conceptionally, Attaway grasped the destruction of the folk, but missed its rebirth at a higher level."[19] The realistic writer, he said, could not merely content himself with the perception of the destructive forces of nature and industry that threatened Negroes migrating to the urban North, because to do so would be to limit his scope merely to naturalism. The writer of realistic fiction, Ellison argued, had a sacred duty, such as that displayed by the heroic André Malraux, to detail emergent forms of liberating social consciousness.

Sensing the extremely tendentious approaches of the organizations linked to the production of black art, Ellison pushed for greater artistic freedom and independence. On December 12, he was the League's "recognized expert" commentator on Millen Brand's Harlem-based novel-in-progress. The reading and the commentary were a feature of the Friday Night Reading series which took place at 237 East Sixty-first Street. The next week, Wright read a passage from his novel-in-progress on black domestic life, the one Ellison had helped him research the previous spring. At the end of January 1942, Ellison would comment on another work-in-progress, Lillian Gilkes's sharecropping novel set in Arkansas. Ellison's duties as a public intellectual, explaining the function of the novel to audiences with varying levels of academic preparation, added to his sense that art was poorly explained by political slogans, and was impoverished generally when constructed for political ends. He had in mind the tightrope Richard Wright was walking between trying to create a representative mythic black experience and chronicling his own life in *Twelve Million Black Voices*. In some fashion, it was becoming as simple for Ellison as the difference between telling the truth and telling a lie.

And Ellison continued to harbor a resentment toward the *New Masses* crowd for their inability to accept the blues lyric as a valid dramatic expression of tragedy. His feelings about the novel as a piece of art caused Ellison to lose patience with well-known artists who openly worked closely with the Communists—people like Theodore Ward. Ellison now gravitated toward a more selective breed, who perhaps offered fewer answers to pertinent social and political questions, but who recognized the writer's need for imaginative freedom. The freedom that Ellison sought in the early 1940s was mainly the freedom to criticize. More frequently at Harlem literary parties and public discussions, squabbles broke out. Some thought his dissenting attitude petty and undemocratic, while others took offense at his criticisms of Attaway, a popular raconteur of black life. Ellison had been sharp-tongued in his review of *Blood on the Forge*. He thought the renditions of black language ordinary—

"his ear sometimes plays him false"—and he compared the effort to that of the sorcerer's apprentice "who has released powerful forces but does not know the key word for keeping them under control."[20]

Two days after the publication of his review on Attaway, the stigma attached to artists stringing along in Communist circles diminished considerably. Japanese warplanes attacked the U.S. naval fleet stationed in Hawaii, precipitating a declaration of war by the United States against Japan and Germany. Despite the reprieve from appearing overly partisan toward the Soviet war machine, Ellison was in no hurry to don the uniform of the Army, repelled by further examples of the viciousness and absurdity of American racism. In December, the Red Cross had rejected blood donations from blacks; then later accepted the blood only if it was labeled and set aside for Negroes. Such events caused Ellison to do more than tolerate a black national outlook. By the spring of 1942, he would be working side by side with Angelo Herndon in the publication of the journal *Negro Quarterly*.

On January 11, the eve of the magazine's first issue, a "Salute to Negro Troops" pageant was held at Mecca Temple and attended by such luminaries as Paul Robeson, Marian Anderson, and Eleanor Roosevelt. Written by Carlton Moss and publicized by John Velasco, the theatrical show dwelt on the fundamental Negro ambivalence about participation in the U.S. armed forces. With a smart crowd of three thousand in attendance, Herndon applauded the heightened consciousness of the moment, banking on the creation of a large, aggressive-minded body of Americans prepared to tackle some of the nagging issues inside the American racial closet of demons.

Herndon had given over the first issue of *Negro Quarterly* to criticism and history from the pens of Sterling Brown, Doxey Wilkerson, and Herbert Aptheker, devoting almost thirty pages to Aptheker's "Slaveocracy's System of Control." (When Richard Wright had been introduced to Aptheker at the office of the *New Masses,* he was rumored to have deferentially kissed Aptheker's book *Negro Slave Revolts*.)[21] Herndon solicited the strongest work from Ellison's circle of writers, critics, and academics, accepting articles and poetry from Langston Hughes, Waring Cuney, and Owen Dodson (with whom he was familiar from their days at *New Challenge*), and Association of Negro Life and History member Harcourt Tynes. Brown's "The Negro Author and His Publisher" and Wilkerson's "Negro Education and the War" carried the torch of the contemporary black in need of a victory at home and abroad. Brown explored the manner in which the boundaries of segregation had inflicted caste status upon black writers, while Wilkerson revealed the imbecility of a national war effort that, as in the Civil War, failed to make use of one of its richest resources—highly motivated black soldiers. Also included was a down-home dose of Negro satire—Jourdon Anderson's dictated letter to his former slavemaster. Full of bravery, wit, and self determination, the ex-slave's letter candidly confronted the former master as a greedy thief who had stolen labor, failed to honor his word, and violated the chastity of the vulnerable. *Negro Quarterly* aimed for the Frederick Douglass style of black pride.

"It means ending affirmatively the myth of quiescent Negro slaves," Herndon told his Mecca Temple audience. With such a sizable chunk of the magazine given over to Communists Wilkerson and Aptheker, there was the inevitable spate of queries regarding the journal's backers. Finally the New York State CP issued a declaration denying any connection whatsoever with the editorial policies of the journal. One of the tangible benefits of bringing Ellison on board was to secure someone who was decidedly on the Left, but was not exclusively a Communist partisan.

Negro Quarterly was intelligent and distinctive, describing itself as "a review of Negro thought and opinion." It catered to the need for an independent publication providing political and cultural reviews far more sophisticated than journalism and focusing on issues facing American Negroes and colonial nations. It filled a void in the discussion of weighty contemporary issues with significance to blacks, but it was different from the *Journal of Negro History,* for instance, published by the Association for the Study of Negro Life and History. *Negro Quarterly* did not hold itself to any particular association or thematic approach, nor was its editorial policy shaped by middle-aged conservatives from quasi-civil-rights organizations or Negro colleges. The support for the journal stemmed from a critical mass of people centered around several popular Harlem institutions: the Harlem Branch of the New York Public Library (now located at 135th Street), headed by Lawrence Reddick and Jean Blackwell; the Association for the Study of Negro Life and History; the Harlem branch of the Communist Party; the Interracial Club; the Committee for Cultural Freedom; various loosely knit Harlem writers groups; the American Negro Theater; the Urban League; the NAACP; and the remnants of the League of American Writers. At the center was Herndon, a nationally famous radical, then Ellison, the quick-minded critic with his feet in two cultural worlds—worlds with few intersecting points.

On March 8, 1942, the magazine was formally launched at Harry Levine's home at 13 Gramercy Park. The journal *Negro Quarterly* sought support from left-leaning liberals and pursued its own autonomy. Lawrence Reddick of the 135th Street Branch of the New York Public Library, the poet Gwendolyn Bennett, Alice Ware, the frequent *New Masses* reviewer William Blake, and of course Herndon, held forth at the founding soirée. By the end of the winter and the United States's official entry into World War II, the editorial board had been shuffled a bit and now included the famous Negro stalwarts Alain Locke and Arthur Huff Fauset. The journal, unlike the Communist Party, was "Double V" for all of its four issues—victory against fascism and victory against jim crow. The impressive early events attracted celebrities and showed the promise of an interracial organization on the Left with something of a Negro cultural nationalist perspective. Herndon touted his fund-raising capabilities and guaranteed Ellison a salary comparable to the money he had earned on the New York Writers Project.[22] By April, Ellison had come on board as the managing editor.

Ellison's shedding of the organized, Stalin-backed Left would take about a year and a half, and would coincide with Richard Wright rescinding his membership in the Communist Party. His would be a more precarious move than Wright's. But while Ellison was certainly in danger of losing his early supporters among the Communists, and he could count on few journals to publish his work, Wright, the embattled public icon, also paid a price for his decision. The established writer was politically embarrassed as he moved out from the Communist camp and soon became a target of steady Communist attack. Wright's embarrassment was not confined to his choice of political party. In 1941, he had petitioned New Jersey's governor for the release of a convicted murderer named Clinton Brewer; shortly after the man was paroled, he killed again.[23] Ellison reckoned that fiction writers were less than adequate as politicians and social reformers; the only real thing they had to cling to was their craft.

For a critic poised to spread his intellectual wings, Herndon's offer was timely. Ellison had felt increasingly claustrophobic around the *New Masses* crowd, and the Communists had adopted a policy that caused them to lose the allegiance of many of their most steadfast supporters, among them their golden boy Richard Wright. His embroiled relationship with them had come to a head when the Central Committee refused to endorse A. Philip Randolph's March on Washington Movement. In late spring of 1941, Randolph had threatened President Roosevelt with a march of a hundred thousand on Washington to protest the practice of racial discrimination in the war services industries. Randolph had kept his movement alive as a viable civil rights entity. The CP balked at providing its legal support, organizational finesse, or endorsement, wanting the March to reject the planned demonstration altogether; and with that Wright determined he had had enough. He quietly withdrew his membership around the middle of 1942.[24]

Ellison's position at the helm of a radical magazine of culture and politics was the inevitable apotheosis of his critical vision. He was also fulfilling his determination not to join in the ranks of hapless war conscripts. As he had said in a letter to Richard Wright in 1940, he would "write" against Hitler, not fight him. Nor did he need the patriotism of the country to help ground his own identity; he was not in the position his father had been in fifty years earlier, of having to run off on a gunboat for Uncle Sam.

Negro Quarterly struggled through a year and a half of publication, pushing the limit of the censor's envelope and bordering on the seditious with its cries for black rights, understood within a broad international context of Asian and African anticolonial movements. Herndon's brainchild and the events that he sponsored were actively monitored by the Federal Bureau of Investigation.[25] The journal blended social commentary, sociological and economic analyses of literature, contemporary fiction and poetry, book reviews, and historically influenced political briefs. If the journal seemed to lack a readership or to have no business plan, the events of the day spurred them on and built their confidence.

Herndon had wooed Ellison away from the League and the *New Masses* because he was the most decently qualified black in New York, with the intellect and commitment to manage such a serious and difficult project. While Herndon was the figurehead, Ellison had the duty of running the quarterly, which at first brought him immense joy, as he sat on the other side of the editor's desk. Certainly the prospect of satisfaction in his first critical independence must have ranked with the promise of money to have persuaded him to join forces with Herndon. Ellison liked and respected the black Communist who had faced death row, but did not consider him an intellectual powerhouse. The new job gave him prestige; now he could write to critics he admired and offer to send them the latest books for review. But mainly, the source of his pleasure was the opportunity to hammer away at a better version of American democracy. Although the journal did not have a large subscription base, its existence was justified by the glaring ideological racism of the day.

Toward the end of 1941, the cream of the New York press, the *Times* and *Herald Tribune,* had begun to instigate hysteria after two well-publicized attacks had occurred on whites. In reaction, not too long after he joined the journal, Ellison began a never published short essay called "Let Us Consider the Harlem Crime Wave," designed to detail the manner in which the news media scapegoated Negro crime while obscuring the real social ills contributing to the viciousness of black urban life. As the editor of a Negro journal, Ellison was the black voice of social conscience. Comparing the pathetic lifestyles of many Harlemites to a fetus going through stages of development, Ellison refused to consider Negro identity as separable from the larger American republic. He was emulating the language and logic of Richard Wright's hard-hitting *Twelve Million Black Voices*.

And while a denial of a separate existence for American blacks and whites coincided with the new Stalinist party line, Ellison had arrived at this view after considerable contemplation, a process of self- and group examination. He had grown capable of accepting certain important truths from Marx, while at the same time admitting to the flaws of communism as it was practiced in Russia. Negroes were not a separate nation, he thought, but actually a minority group who had to develop a self-conscious identity out of their American experience. Perhaps what was most important, he understood that the group characteristics of Negro Americans which made them distinct were inextricably tied to the geography of North America. Indeed, he had heard the same idea at Tuskegee nearly ten years before.

Like a tiger, Ellison fought paternalism and the scapegoating of black Americans, a people who had made their existence on society's margins palatable. Harlemites' lives were bathed in crime, according to the reports in the mainstream press: they bought their expensive clothes on the black market from the "hot stuff man," smoked illegal reefers to fight the caffeine-nicotine driven American society, and broke social customs. Point by point, he showed in the essay how black Americans defied Western tastes and standards of beauty, a defiance that made blacks appear criminal to whites. But even in his trenchant social commentary, Ellison's playful sense of the irony of life (for which he was well known in League circles) was dominant. He developed in his essay observations on the importance of obtaining electric light that he would later recreate in the famous prologue to *Invisible Man.*

Harlem had solved the problem of satisfying the expensive rates of Consolidated Edison by routinely short-circuiting their electric meters.[26] Light to brighten meager apartments and power to operate radios and phonographs were the invaluable antidotes to what Ellison thought of as America's daily psychological violence against black people.

His language in the essay owed its cadence to the rhythms he had recalled in his Oklahoma-based stories, a reflection of the sermons he had heard in his youth at Avery Chapel and as a student at Tuskegee. But while the sermons he had heard as a child and young adult had encouraged conservatism and gradualism, Ellison had channeled them through his irony and had produced a vision of wry dissent in his essay.

Within weeks of setting up offices at 1 West 125th Street, at the corner of Lenox Avenue, *Negro Quarterly*'s editors, along with librarians Lawrence Reddick and Ernest Kaiser, incorporated the Negro Publication Society of America. It was a collective that planned to offer immediate publication to worthy artists, particularly those whose material was too incendiary for the mainstream press. In the late 1930s when she served as secretary of the International Workers Organization (IWO), Louise Thompson-Patterson had wanted to bring out a collection of Langston Hughes's poems. In the spring of 1942, the Negro Publication Society published a twenty-five-cent pamphlet of Hughes's most radical verse, "Jim Crow's Last Stand." By the fall, they would publish Peter Still's 1856 slave narrative told to Kate Pickard, *The Kidnapped and the Ransomed,* as well as distribute *Native Son* and the anthology of black writing, *Negro Caravan.* Ellison had tried dissent as a voice crying in the wilderness, now he would put on the togs of the managerial class and make available to the public black writers and black lives.

He began his task as managing editor with vigor, and contacted important critical thinkers. In a draft of a letter to Horace Cayton, Ellison broached the difficult problem of black leadership. He began by distinguishing between critical intellectuals and credentialed sycophants, but he could not resolve his shock at Negro leadership's ineffectiveness and rejection of Marxist theories that Ellison found compelling and accurate to dismantle American racism. In his view, the purpose of black leadership was to organize the masses, uplift their thinking, and provide them with a sense of historical destiny. He wanted to join forces with Cayton and produce an analysis of the black community from its economic and political base up to its superstructure of churches, fraternities, and entertainers. Ellison also continued to work on the concept of black national identity. His tone was radical and his perspective was global. He saw the end point of the intellectuals' work as developing the characteristics of the "oppressed" Negro nation, and using these qualities as the ground for renewed attack on injustice.[27]

Not long after he tried to form his letter to Cayton, he caught a train down to Howard University to visit with the Negro brain trust residing there. Ellison sought to solicit manuscripts and ideas from the established intellectual leadership. In particular he wanted to talk to Marxists Eugene Holmes and Doxey Wilkerson, cultural nationalists Sterling Brown, Arthur P. Davis, Rayford Logan, and Alain Locke, and sociologist E. Franklin Frazier. These scholars were his critical peers, and not only did Ellison need them to develop his own ideas, he felt that most of the professional intellectuals could benefit from *Negro Quarterly* to shake off their own mental torpor. Ellison had begun to think of his own theoretical strategy for eradicating race prejudice and for complicating American identity as the "critical" approach, distinct from the dogma of the Communists but built from the conceptual tools available, especially Marxist theory. Ellison worried that few writers or thinkers were moving as far. By May he would write to Gene Holmes that the reviews submitted to *Negro Quarterly* were theoretically naive. The writers either cheerily promoted black life or gave in to simplistic generalizations that did not see the broad interrelationships among races and social classes. Typical of the failure of critical perspective, in his view, was the introduction to *Negro Caravan,* the black American literature anthology published by Brown, which Ellison believed could have been significantly improved. Ellison also found fault with Alain Locke's popular ideas about black culture, which perhaps to him smacked of too many African origins, a perspective made broadly popular with the publication of Melville Herskovitz's *The Myth of the Negro Past* in 1941. To the young editor, Locke had badly interpreted the foundations of Negro art, but of course, there was no public opposition to his view.[28]

The stridently independent Ellison was firing shots over the bow at the established black elites, the monied white voyeurs, and the rigid Marxists. As editor, he initiated literary exchanges with the "little magazines" and journals, seeking publishing slots in the radical journals of art and commentary for his friends and for his own works as well. He wrote to editors of *Accent, Fantasy,* and the University of Chicago's *Trend,* requesting an exchange of subscriptions in the short term to keep his journal afloat and to spread its recognition. *Negro Quarterly* and the Negro Publication Society were ardent supporters of Richard Wright's work; and in Ellison's letter to Kirker Quinn of *Accent* he lauded them for publishing sections of Wright's "The Man Who Lived Underground." Ellison let everyone know that he was fashionably ahead of the curve with his tastes and that his journal was not merely a pamphlet promoting civil rights, but a serious publication really grappling with the issues of modern literature. Speaking of Wright's latest work, Ellison pitched its potential high. He felt that "The Man Who Lived Underground" presented the only important portrait of black religious conversion and that it compared favorably to Kafka.[29] But Ellison faced the brick wall of disinterest from fellow blacks in a journal aiming to run with the white academic and literary group and the counter-feeling among whites that nothing black could be quite good enough. It was a difficult balancing act to cultivate and stroke both groups. He reminded John Barnes of *Trend* that he was wide-ranging in his interest when he requested critical articles that examined the Negro American in all his horror and glory. These connections were not merely window-dressing. For Ellison, the publication of black critics and artists in white journals and vice versa was imperative, since integration was the profound fulfillment of the potential of democracy.[30] He wanted *Negro Quarterly* to move beyond the traditional lines of American racial demarcation.

As the shooting war increased in intensity in the South Pacific, Ellison confronted his own ideas about mortality. In the first week of March, the young jazz guitar virtuoso Charlie Christian had died in New York of tuberculosis at Sea View Hospital.[31] To Ellison, Christian was more than an extraordinarily vivid example of spectacular professional and creative success. Charlie Christian was an Oklahoma City homeboy from Deep Deuce, whose exodus from the sandy floors of the slums by the Canadian River confirmed part of Ellison's identity, and helped him to see his own dreams as realizable. While the jazz world mourned the loss of one of its premier craftsmen and innovators, Ellison thought of Christian's origins and the desperate nature of black life and its apparently unavoidable and crushing tragedy. He believed that Christian had picked up the fatal disease in the slum not far from the old Douglass High School (which had moved by 1942). Musicians rumored of another story: that Christian had been on his way to full recovery but had backslid with alcohol, sex, and drugs while in the hospital, causing his final relapse. But Ellison didn't have to go even that far for the deep tragedy of everyday living blues. Next door to his old apartment, his buddy Teddy Wilson's estranged mistress tried to take her own life by turning on the gas jets of 27 Hamilton Terrace.[32]

Continuing to involve himself across the color line, Ellison organized League engagements in the spring, as the congress, founded initially out of the popular front strategies of the Communists to prevent war, began to wind down its activities.[33] In its last months of existence, though, Ellison found the opportunity for significant leadership and the chance to carry out the agenda of racial equity. He was consulted about the applications of new members like the cartoonist Ollie Stewart (who was approved) and Carl Ruthven Offord. He could derive particular satisfaction from his own publishing efforts when program director Louis Mally asked Ellison if Offord had enough publications to merit membership in the League.[34] In March, Nan Golden wrote to him to ask his advice on the point of departure in Harry Slochower's essay, which examined "the chaos of standards in the post-war period." She wanted Ellison to provide a public commentary along with a couple of German writers at a Friday Series discussion on March 27. Ellison so impressed Slochower that after the panel, the critic dug up an extra copy of one of Kafka's works and sent it to him.[35] The next month, on April 17, he chaired a panel with New York University professors Bernard Meyers and V. J. McGill, who commented on Edwin Burgum's "The Propaganda Value of Art in Time of War." Ellison now sat in judgment of influential editors who not long before had judged his work.

As an editor, Ellison had more than one occasion to offer artistic advice. When the young writer Julia Brice, convinced of the originality of her novice script and hesitant to show it around lest her opus be stolen from her, pressed him for help publishing and advertising, Ellison rebuked her for the conviction that her authentic suffering made her tale unique and interesting. Scheduled as a paid lecturer for the League of American Writers School that winter, the *Negro Quarterly* editor told her not merely to stop wasting his time with fantasies of becoming a celebrity but what was more important, to develop a serious relationship with her craft.[36]

He refused to let his friendships stand in the way of frank criticism. In September, he would write to Langston Hughes after Hughes had been upbraided in the summer *Negro Quarterly* for letting his publishers advertise his book *Shakespeare in Harlem* with insulting caricatures of Negroes on the cover. Ellison took the opportunity to slyly put Hughes in his place. He split his letter to the man who had loaned him his first typewriter by also addressing the writer Carson McCullers, who shared a place at the writers colony at Yaddo with Hughes that summer. Although he was only twenty-nine, Ellison's position as managing editor gave him some new boots to fill. He took on a parent's demeanor with the affable Hughes, warning him from the rain, but to McCullers, he made a somber plea to ensure that Hughes at least took constitutional walks around the grounds.[37] In fact, Ellison worked on a longer letter to McCullers, the author of the haunting and famous *The Heart Is a Lonely Hunter,* telling the young Southern gothicist that *Negro Quarterly* greatly enjoyed her work. Ellison approved of her portrayal of the South and of the Negro, and hoped that she would publish something in *Negro Quarterly*.[38] Effortlessly comfortable with his celebrity friends, Ralph Ellison was now clearly on the make. He had come to the point where he was confident in his views; and although he was working as a professional editor, he knew who he was, exactly: a writer.

But though he did not shy away from the rarefied ground of criticism, he also reached out with humility. He recognized that there was much for him to learn, and that his criticism and his fiction needed to grow. Ellison cultivated relationships with critics and writers whom he admired and whom he wanted to contribute free book reviews to *Negro Quarterly*. One of these was twenty-three-year-old Stanley Edgar Hyman, a new member of the *New Yorker* staff. Courting Hyman as a prospective contributor to *Negro Quarterly*, in August 1942 Ellison lauded his work on John Steinbeck's recent war novel and encouraged Hyman to lay into a review of James Street's *Tap Roots*. He wrote to the young critic that the essay, "Some Notes on John Steinbeck" from the June *Antioch Review*, had presented lucidly, for the first time, the theme of ecology in Steinbeck's work. A close reader of Harry Slochower's essay on the structure of Nazi psychology, Ellison had initially disapproved of Steinbeck's latest work, a novel on the German occupation of Scandinavia, *The Moon Is Down;* but after reading Hyman's "Some Notes on John Steinbeck," which had come out in the *Antioch Review*, he was reconsidering: "I think your article did a lot to clear the air."[39]

A young Jewish writer and Syracuse University graduate, Hyman was boldly pursuing a full-fledged career in literary criticism in conjunction with his wife, the fiction writer Shirley Jackson. Hyman had abandoned his undergraduate major of journalism in favor of English after meeting Ellison's hero Kenneth Burke. With artistic comrades like Hyman, Ellison could fulfill his own dictum "for Negro writers to establish contact with white writers." Interracial relationships were necessary if the black writer was to acquire "the techniques and discipline of [his] art . . . usually the heritage and privilege of those who control the nation's wealth."[40] Foremost among Ellison's thoughts was how a literary approach such as the one Hyman took to Steinbeck might invigorate black writers in Harlem, especially if the analysis candidly evaluated Richard Wright's work: "I cannot help but reflect on how useful your notes would be to a group of young writers here in Harlem; it would be an education in the writers' strategy and in the art of the critic. And should you do such a job on Richard Wright it would produce no less than a leap in Negro literary craftsmanship."[41] The Harlem crowd of writers had never overwhelmed Ellison with their intellectualism or artistry; indeed, he hoped for a promised land that might be achieved by "a leap in Negro literary craftsmanship." If there was a means of surpassing the boundaries imposed by craft, Ellison was keen to explore them.

A relationship between the two men blossomed also because Hyman had a great interest in the blues and in black folklore. But Ellison's friendly overtures to Hyman belied the weakness of his own position. It was difficult to get established white critics to take seriously the status of the Negro in America. As the bills challenging Southern poll taxes were consistently defeated in Congress, Ellison had to contend with a public climate in which the problems of the Negro minority were viewed with disdain. The indulgent white liberal response ran the gamut, from Librarian of Congress Archibald MacLeish's dour February address to the National Urban League Conference demanding that Negroes suppress all claims for racial justice until after the war, to Pearl Buck's open "Letter to Colored Americans." Published in the *New York Times* and *Opportunity* simultaneously, Buck's letter was a ceremonial gesture capable of having real meaning only to the most supercilious and vain of the black elites. She entreated Negroes to behave with "honesty, magnanimity and dignity," essential characteristics if they wished to gain human rights concessions from whites who were on a "difficult and unfamiliar road" in their current movement "toward the meaning of freedom and human equality."[42] In other words, blacks could either ignore the race problem or they could act like angelic martyrs.

Despite his tendency to pick apart blandishments, or to set people's teeth on edge by pointing to the most ironic contradiction of an opinion touted as "liberal," Ellison tried to bring groups together during a year that saw no small measure of misunderstanding and pain. Writers League president Dashiell Hammett asked him to set up a meeting in Harlem on March 31 with fifty prominent writers and artists to engage in a dialogue with Buck, which he agreed to do.[43] Sometimes it was impossible to talk politics at meetings in Harlem, but Ellison consistently tried to bring together divergent groups, and for more than just smiling photographs and cocktails.

Ellison and *Negro Quarterly* were setting the agenda for intellectual discussions on race in New York. For his journal, he wanted an eclectic mix of articles, ranging broadly over the issue of imperialism and concerning themselves particularly with the psychological ramifications of racism on blacks and whites. Even the *Daily Worker* offered its approval by way of an article titled "'The Negro Quarterly' A Vigorous Journal," by black Communist Abner Berry, though he did not even mention Ellison by name. Berry granted that the editors had uncovered "many new facets of Negro thought" but he faulted them for eschewing the bread-and-butter issues of the Communist literary agenda. The poetry of the journal, Berry wrote, was far too abstract, and in need of declarative statements "simple, strong and moving in a way that can be instantly understood. . . [I]t seems that the editors should have in mind the audience to be reached and seek to keep the poetry within the limits of the Quarterly's 'personality.'" The other consequential flaw, from the

Communist close-ranks perspective, was to "slur over the dignified role of Negro heroes."[44] Ellison, who had written to Owen Dodson for poems because he felt that the work in the first couple of editions did not inspire, actually found some points of agreement with Berry. However, he thought that it was typical of Berry as a Communist to completely misunderstand the aim, or "personality," of the journal. *Negro Quarterly* promoted an "intellectual democracy," and the intellectuals were an elite group.

Ellison's dissatisfaction with the state of black art came through in his own contribution to the journal. In a lengthy review, Ellison once again brought William Attaway's *Blood on the Forge* into focus. He stressed the consistency of his literary judgments, wanting his audience to understand that he had found flaws with Attaway even when his reviews had appeared in journals uncontrolled by the Communist Party. The core problem with *Blood on the Forge,* he felt, was its failure to distinguish between fascist and democratic whites. Failing to recognize the utopian possibility of transracial alliances, the book, Ellison wrote, lacked a place where black people were "free to build a philosophy, a political structure and hope that leads toward peace. . . . A true work of art is at the same time an encounter with the past and a challenge to the future. The blood spilled at Pearl Harbor has emphasized the demand that works like *Blood On The Forge* be more than a summation of phases of the Negro people's aching past: they must be a guide and discipline for the future."[45]

Part of Ellison's critical perspective stemmed from what he saw as the inadequacy of the techniques of literary realism to properly treat the situation at hand. For example, the understatement that characterized Hemingway's style seemed impossible to pull off; whites and blacks had little basis for the shared cultural assumptions that made understatement effective. Ellison's continued exposure to radical artists and critics and his contempt for the Communists' manipulation of the black rights movement greatly reduced his appreciation for the social protest fiction of writers like Attaway. It seems likely that Attaway, who had joined the Navy, felt oddly persecuted by Ellison, who had three times identified the weakness of his novel. Not long after Ellison's sharp-toned review, Attaway's and Ted Ward's friendships with him and Wright collapsed.

In contrast to Ellison's critical approach to Attaway, Herndon's review of Wright's *Twelve Million Black Voices,* which liberally quoted from the book, read like a promotional advertisement. Wright was the figurehead of their movement to spur black literacy and quicken intellectual life; if readers agreed to join the society and receive issues of the quarterly and discounted books, they would be sent Modern Library's new printing of *Native Son.* Although it was necessary to cast Wright as a hero to advance the aims of the Negro Publication Society, Ellison promoted essays with broader applications than racism or the problems exclusively confronting the American Negro. Harry Slochower's "In the Fascist Styx," printed in the fall issue (and which Ellison had publicly commented on in a League forum), concentrated almost exclusively on international writers dealing with fascism: Remarque, Zweig, and Toller, with only a portion of the essay devoted to Wright.

Ellison's demanding criticism appeared at a time when his own fictional efforts were lagging. Editing *Negro Quarterly* from the journal's home office on Lenox Avenue and 125th Street consumed all his efforts—when he was not daydreaming and gazing out of the huge plate glass window separating him from the Harlem crowds. Ellison read voraciously but lost his writing time to managing technical details, increasing subscriptions, editing manuscripts, and writing to publishers for books to send reviewers. Yet the news that he read daily in the Harlem papers—Kafkaesque in its absurdity—was certainly enough to suggest the dramatic structures and tensions of fiction. In one incident in April a casino manager was brutally beaten by robbers, then was refused treatment at two hospitals. When the man determined to press charges against the nurse and police officer who refused him aid at Harlem Hospital, the police officer had the man straitjacketed and sent to Bellevue's psychiatric ward for observation.[46] In another surreal episode of the violence meted out to Negroes, a well-known mental patient was shot by a police officer as Harlemites looked on. A crowd of two thousand nearly broke into violent protest.[47]

Racial injustice wounded Ellison. He was deeply troubled by the mounting homicides of the youth gangs and the violence between the sexes. He understood that the cause of the worst in human behavior in Harlem—where the crimes were different from those in other areas of New York, and the deadly violence was out of proportion to the actual number of Negroes—lay in an inadequate social environment, and the fact that the fundamentally agrarian values of the group had not had the opportunity to catch up with the industrial and vocational requirements of urban life. While his own fiction lay in a desk drawer, he could get some sense of self-worth from his editorial work, which, given the shortage of independent intellectuals, amounted to an important *engagée* position.

On the occasions when he would put aside his copy of reading (*Shakespeare's Imagery* in late spring of 1942), Ellison enjoyed attending the local dance clubs with friends (the Apollo or Savoy), or being a guest of Teddy Wilson at the Café Society Downtown. It was arguably the most chic on Ellison's list of places to visit, partly because it was an integrated hangout downtown that attracted intellectuals, and partly because it showcased premier music talent. Located in Greenwich Village's Sheridan Square, Café Society was the swing pianist Wilson's headquarters; Billie Holiday had started her Manhattan career there. Richard Wright liked to visit in the company of Paul Robeson.[48] Since it had opened its doors in 1938, Café Society Downtown had been one of the first places in New York outside of Harlem to publicly endorse interracial crowds and interracial dancing. The club became so successful that after a year the owner had opened Café Society Uptown at East Fifty-eighth Street. Count Basie, featuring Holiday and the Oklahoman Jimmie Rushing, played before some of the first mixed crowds in New York City at these two premier nightspots popular with the Left and liberals. But, while he enjoyed meeting his WPA and literary-minded friends in the Village, for dancing Ellison preferred Harlem's Rhythm Club, Savoy, and Clark Monroe's Uptown House at 138th Street, where he could resuscitate his Apollo dancing legs.

And if the war and *Negro Quarterly* did not offer enough excitement, a sea change in music was taking place as well, some of the music initiated by Tuskegee- and Juilliard-trained Teddy Wilson himself, a profound stylist in his own right, even if he did not possess an extraordinary musical charisma.[49] But the real sources were the young musicians playing in the bands of Cab Calloway, Earl Hines, and Billy Eckstine, who jammed at the Hotel Cecil on 118th Street in a spot called Minton's Playhouse. Minton's Playhouse was run by Teddy Hill and featured the drummer Kenny Clark, whom musicians called "Klook Mop," and the trumpeter John Gillespie, known as "Dizzy." Hill threw open his doors on Mondays for "Celebrity Nights" and invited all musicians to come and take part. The music, called variously "bop," "rebop," and "bebop," was a signal departure from the big band swing music of Duke Ellington, Jimmy Lunceford, Fletcher Henderson, Cab Calloway, and Count Basie. Bop emphasized surprising melodic injections, dramatic chord changes, and breakaway quick tempos. The music struck Ellison as conspicuously urban, though aside from Max Roach and Minton's house pianist Thelonius Sphere Monk, it was purveyed by men born and bred in the South and West. Bop music suggested a new creed and lifestyle. Whereas big bands had demanded conformity in dress and playing style, and the suppression of personal creativity, the standard bop combo worked in almost the opposite register. In fact, the band's energy and approach seemed a direct descendant of the "cutting contest," the ritualistic series of aggressive musical statements followed by a flood of responses, some complimentary, others critical. These musical ripostes, assertions, defenses, and counterattacks constituted the classroom of modern American jazz. The almost subcultural quality of this activity with its elaborate and meaningful rituals appealed to Ellison, who was still trying to make sense of his Music School experience at Tuskegee. Where he had been taught sublimation through harmony, soloing was now the center attraction; and the beat, once dominated by the bass drum, now had "bombs" dropped in—snare and bass accents—and time was maintained rigorously only on the hi-hat cymbal.

Although attracted to bop, Ellison favored the more lyrical music, such as the kind sung by Apollo debutante Sarah Vaughan blowing the lid off Tadd Dameron's "If You Could See Me Now." Like Lester Young, whose sound was shaped by the marching bands and spirituals of his childhood years in the deep South, Ellison preferred the omnibus version of black culture with its roots clearly in vaudeville, variety shows, and the blues, art forms still widely available throughout Harlem during the 1940s. One performing group, for example, might carry with it a dance band that played two sets per performance, a male and female singer, a tandem of dancers, several comedians, and a blackface performer. For Ellison, who was a friend to theater producers Carlton Moss and John Velasco, the theatrical energy and drama of black music had a natural gravitational pull. Besides, on Monday nights Teddy Hill had an open invitation to the current performers at the Apollo to join a sumptuous feast of fried chicken, Southern seasoned vegetables, and hot rolls, all of which could be washed down with copious amounts of gratis whiskey.

Boppers' onstage dramatics were minimal; and while several of the men whose names would become synonymous with the bop movement thought little of performing while floating in a cloud of narcotics, the young jazz players reacted sharply against anything that hinted at the comic tradition of black performers. Louis Armstrong was not an idol. Bop tended to take shape with smaller urban combos, as the jazzmen refused to travel in the South and play to segregated audiences or to endure segregated travel and hotel accommodations. Even such up-and-coming white performers as Gene Krupa canceled lucrative Southern trips because the places where their bands were booked refused to allow an integrated band to perform. In spite of the musicians' pretensions to be politically engaged, Ellison found himself disconnected from their struggle. As an ex-musician whose dedication to writing reflected steady patience, Ellison had less tolerance for the style of the impetuous young musicians who wanted to end segregation—chiefly the indignity of the black middle class—when it inconvenienced them. Ellison found the men as a group uninterested in battling the deeper economic structure of racism in the United States. When he really wanted to hear bop experimentations, he frequented Sidney Bechet's club on Seventh Avenue, where Art Tatum and Teddy Wilson jammed. But true to his Oklahoma City roots, Ellison tended to enjoy the swing-boppish sounds of Count Basie's band, not only because Basie employed Rushing, known to Ellison from their days in Oklahoma City, but also because of Basie's featured trumpeter, Clark Terry, who Ellison thought was technically more perfect than Dizzy Gillespie.[50]

For someone like Ellison with serious musical training, the bop experiments were curious but harsh on the ear, at least at first. The new music was grating; listeners, even musicians, often thought that the new players were deliberately sounding wrong notes—that in some fashion, conceptually, this new art was merely one that rejected formal standards, a kind of musical dadaism. Ellison was not entirely comfortable with what he would describe in his 1957 essay "The Golden Age, Time Past" as the "texture of fragments" that sounded to the uninitiated like noise: "repetitive, nervous, not fully formed . . . secret and taunting . . . flat or shrill. . . . Its rhythms were out of stride and seemingly arbitrary." Instead of looking at it as evidence of conceptual genius, as a musical form that would be pondered and celebrated for generations, Ellison saw it in the short term: "the revolutionary rumpus sounding like a series of flubbed notes."[51]

The music was "frantic" and "hectic" and "mad" in the argot of 1940s Harlem. The art form's purveyors acknowledged that for nearly everyone, save the musicians engaged in it, bebop would sound like cacophony.[52] What further distanced Ellison from the innovations of the young jazz legends in the making was the utter disdain the performers seemed to hold for the dancing pleasure of the audience—the single criterion for the big band. His Marxist-influenced sensibility, though undergoing what he termed "deflation" at the time, remained strong enough to warn him about the danger of removing the artistic form from the arena of its creation. What would happen to the dynamic interplay between performers and dancers, particularly since so many musicians exclusively crafted their styles based upon repeated listening to recorded solos? Ellison could see the musical shift as indicative of another change in Harlem, a settled sense of despair, a situation in which machine technology superseded human beings in importance. On the one hand, an unpopular war overseas awaited young men, while on the other, New York City afforded them few opportunities for advancement and education. At the corner of 133rd Street and Seventh Avenue, the Nomads and the Celtics engaged in deadly warfare and frisked passersby for their wallets. The term "mugging" entered the popular lexicon, and Harlem turned into the dream deferred.

The transformation in musical aesthetics reflected deeper social movements. The summer of 1942 represented a worsening crisis for black Americans who intended to change the social framework of a country now vigorously at war. A crisis had occurred earlier in the year in Detroit at the Sojourner Truth Homes. White mobs had blocked the passage of black families into a new housing development, indicating the reluctance of white workers to abandon what could no longer be dismissed as an exclusively Southern prejudice against the Negro. On June 26, Ellison's Negro Publication Society held a town hall meeting in New York to address the brewing grievances of blacks. With his cadre of writers and intellectuals masterfully influencing the dialogue, Ellison's public visibility increased; and his sense of himself sharpened as a man whose writing was an articulate voice for "the Negro." Earl Robinson and Richard Wright lent their names to the program, called "Folk Songs on the Firing Line," featuring groups of singers steeped in the pantheon of collaborative folk music: folk songs from World War I and the current conflict; traditional work songs like "John Henry"; and then divergent offerings from Chinese, Australian, and of course, Soviet soldiers. The next day, four hundred delegates attended a trade union and Negro People's Conference at the Fraternal Clubhouse, followed on Sunday by a gala event at the Golden Gate Ballroom, a six-thousand-person Unity for Victory mass rally. The weekend's events resoundingly echoed the push for the inclusion of blacks in war-related industries and for the granting of criminal prosecution powers to the Fair Employment Practices Committee. But the unflagging insistence on black rights, and the ultimately quixotic aims of the Negro Labor Victory Committee, were underscored by its "Thirteen Point Program" of the summer of 1942. The final point of the committee, working in concert with the Negro Publication Society, was "Full freedom now for the colonial peoples of Asia, Africa, Latin America and the West Indies."[53] Their aims were unrealistic, but they stuck to the principle of freedom.

That fall, Ellison and Herndon put an edge on black participation in the war effort. In the *Quarterly*'s editorial, they argued for a keen, fully conscious attitude on the part of blacks and the allies of black rights:

> This attitude holds that any action which is advantageous to the United Nations must also be advantageous to the Negro and colonial peoples. Programs which would sacrifice the Negro or any other people are considered dangerous for the United Nations; and the only honorable course for Negroes to take is first to protest and then to fight against them. And while willing to give and take in the interest of national unity, it rejects that old pattern of American thought that regards any Negro demand for justice as treasonable, or any Negro act of self-defense as an assault against the state.[54] [The term "United Nations" grew out of Roosevelt's and Churchill's Atlantic Charter Treaty of 1941.]

The editorial bordered on advocating armed rebellion in the face of an implacable government, in testy defiance of the Smith Act, a law that had essentially made public political dissent the equivalent of treason. Ellison's objective was to clearly raise the bar for the aims of the New Negro during World War II several notches higher than simply the rejection of racial stereotypes and the determination to leave the rural South—the goals for New Negroes that Alain Locke had identified in 1924. Ellison wanted to link the success of black freedom to the stability of the allied Western world. Several of the journal's other, lengthier essays advocated a similar vision. The Nigerian writer Kweku Gardiner pushed for the abolition of colonial exploitation in Africa. Kumar Goshal, a lecturer at the School for Democracy, detailed the extraordinarily volatile situation in India between the British and the Ghandi/Nehru camps, set in motion by the British delegate Stafford Cripps's insulting rejection of India's plea for a new constitution and democratic elections.

Even the fiction in the *Negro Quarterly* uttered tones of defiance. J. Saunders Redding's "Rosalie," published that fall, roundly disparaged the American way of life. Redding brought the much-touted black middle class into focus with a psychological portrait of the grotesque Rosalie, a young adult incapable of human warmth and integrity because of her discomfort with her medium-tone skin color. Exhibiting a more gross pathology alive in the black psyche than even Wallace Thurman's 1929 novel *The Blacker the Berry,* the character Rosalie feels that her life's worth has been lost over a shade or two in skin tone to her lighter-skinned and thus advantaged brothers. Her character vacillates between two emotional extremes. She expects the world to submit to her every whim because she is a member of the caste-elect, or she emotionally disintegrates whenever she glimpses her own physical appearance within the context of her fair-skinned family. The emotional turmoil leads the young woman to alcoholism, maternal rejection, and, Redding hints, much worse. What hope was there when black elites, even black women with long hair and finely chiseled features, those champion pinups of the *Crisis* and *Opportunity,* found in the ordinary contradictions of society the route to their own destruction?

Despite their intensity, *Negro Quarterly*'s essays did not reach a wide audience. Herndon hoped to promote large public events in order to build up steam for a mass movement, and for him the journal tended to take a backseat. He devoted most of his time to arranging public events, and left the journal to Ellison. However, Herndon's efforts as publicist were costly, and within a couple of months he had nearly squandered the joint bank account between the *Quarterly* and the Publication Society. In October, both groups sank the entirety of their funds into another Golden Gate rally. Within several months, the journal would go bankrupt. Ellison responded to the financial roller-coaster by keeping some of his options open. *New Masses,* for example, still carried Ellison as a contributor. In this capacity he may have ghostwritten a few unsigned editorials.[55] Samuel Sillen and Edwin Burgum needed Ralph Ellison in the fall of 1942. Not that other young Negro writers would have been unwilling to work for a nationally distributed journal of literature and politics for minimal pay, but the fact was that there were very few young men of such promise and intellectual poise as the twenty-nine-year-old Ellison, who took the Left seriously enough as a source of valuable information that he thought it necessary to read through and understand the position of Communists, even if only to argue them down.

Ellison's work raising consciousness had hit a stride. His efforts to keep race in the forefront of the agenda at the *New Masses,* where he was a guest editor, were rewarded that October: the magazine devoted a fairly balanced issue to Negroes in the war effort. The cover of the *New Masses* October 20 edition carried the picture of a sweating black man in a construction helmet with the caption "War Worker." Inside, nearly every article discussed some aspect of the Negro and the war, whether as a victim of discrimination in the service, or the inability of the Fair Employment Practices Commission to secure employment for colored workers. Several other authors who had agreed to write for this issue of *New Masses,* including Reddick, Wilkerson, and Redding, had already published articles in *Negro Quarterly*. Ellison's journalistic essay, "The Way It Is," provided a real human component to the more academic pieces of sociology and political science (and outright propaganda) in the magazine. Alongside a handsome snapshot of himself (an innovation at *New Masses*) and a paragraph of his accomplishments, "The Way It Is" described the peculiar despondency of Harlem life at the opening of the war. He used the plight of Mrs. Jackson, a black matriarch raising her family alone, to invoke the necessity of extending the powers of government to freeze rents, to control prices, and to expand the jurisdiction of the FEPC. Dispossessed and with a son in the Army, a widow, a steady domestic, Mrs. Jackson wanted mainly, like W. E. B. Du Bois, for black young people to be trained according to their ability. Her tragedy was personal; her nephew, a natural mechanic whose talents would have been best used in stateside industries, died as a messman on a Merchant Marine ship.

Ellison's interview with Mrs. Jackson was interesting from another vantage point: it marked another moment in his steady climb out of the pit of black working-class consciousness and into the American middle class. During his interview, Mrs. Jackson assumed that he lived on Sugar Hill with the pretentious Negroes. Ellison was able-bodied and had escaped the Army. How did he come along speaking polite English and wearing a suit? Ellison had begun to strike people with a subtle eminence and a confident air of success. When the *New Masses* editors put his age in the brief biographical paragraph, Ellison took a year off his birth date and told them he was twenty-eight. For the remainder of his life, he stuck to the birth year of 1914. The literary editor and "young Negro" writer had recreated himself.

His focus on the humanity of Harlem always won new friends and stimulated old ones. Langston Hughes, still working at the artist colony at Yaddo in Saratoga Springs, sent Ellison a brief but ecstatic note of praise for the article on Harlemites' day-to-day struggles.[56] Hughes also sent greetings to Rosie, a sad tiding because the couple's split was permanent. Before the end of October, Ellison had moved again to another apartment, the top floor of 306 West 141st Street, a building owned by the Macedonia Baptist Church. At $35 per month, he likely selected the apartment on the basis of its technical merits, such as those he had pointed out in his essay on the Harlem crime wave. The significant criterion to base a decision to rent an apartment was the presence or absence of the electric meter inside of the room.[57] With his paychecks in jeopardy because of Herndon's impecunious habits, Ellison needed help keeping the bills down, and he was not above jiggling the gauge of the light meter to do it.

But he had other pressing concerns toward the end of the year, even greater than paying his electric bill. Separated and without children, Ellison could count on a 1-A draft classification. The crises of his marriage breaking up and the threat of impending induction into a jim crow Army—the same military that had deeply wounded his own father—apparently had no small effect on Ellison. Throughout the fall of 1942 and into early 1943, he would suffer weeklong bouts of a mysterious illness and severe stomach irritation. It seems that around this time, Ellison, known to some of his friends as a tee-totaler, picked up the habits of both alcohol and tobacco.

In December, Ellison sat on the *New Masses'* "Words Can Be Bullets" panel and banquet with National Negro Congress president Max Yergan and the poet Alfred Kreymbourg.[58] The panel presentation would become something of an anomaly for Ellison, who continued to be frustrated with the *New Masses* crowd and the direction of the National Negro Congress, and was continually unhappy with the efforts of fiction writers to directly intervene in the political realm. However, as managing editor at *Negro Quarterly,* Ellison had finally arrived at a public position to criticize some the inadequacies of the Left, even if not in print. In November, peers like Molly Moon of the Urban League sponsored interracial gatherings and cocktail-sips, designed to bring blacks and whites together to "Strike a Match for Victory."[59] For Ellison these showcases were frustrating and time-consuming, though he had a certain duty to attend public functions if he wanted to generate support for his magazine. The bourgeois groups attracted to the glitzy functions were pretentious and seemingly concerned with only their high status. Though Ralph Ellison had outgrown the anxiety over his unfinished collegiate education, whether or not he had adequate shoe leather, or even if his aim to become a writer was too far-flung, the self-involved trifles of the black elite nearly always made him feel that he was wasting his breath. People tended to accuse him of being overly ambitious. Ellison was disappointed because most of the intellectual conversations could not move beyond the accepted ranges of polite discourse. But soon enough, the dilemma of editing the journal and steering a path for the black leftist artist in the war lost importance. He was drafted.

10

Labor of Love

1943–1944

DESPITE HIS personal qualms and political differences with the Communists, Ellison used his clout in Communist-influenced union circles to quickly muster into the National Maritime Union. In February, he carried a personal note from his friend Add Bates to Bill Campbell, one of the Maritime Union heads, to enable him to go to sea as a third cook. Ellison was able to sidestep some of the bureaucratic problems with Bates's brief handwritten letter of recommendation.[1] Campbell endorsed the letter and sent Ellison on to the dispatcher. Getting a berth on board a Merchant Marine ship kept him out of the Army.

Ellison would not clamber aboard his first Merchant Marine vessel headed for the North Atlantic until September 1943, around the time that his review of Bucklin Moon's book *Darker Brother* appeared in that month's issue of *Tomorrow*. In spite of his attendance in June 1943 at Jacob Lawrence's "Test Tribunal," a workshop for "racial objectors" on 138th Street, Ellison did not try to evade the draft. He would have to fight and write against Hitler. He might not have been exactly a black Yank, but he was coming. Ellison followed the example of people like black Communist Harry Haywood and went with his ship into dangerous ports of call, ferrying raw materials, troops, and arms in the service of the Allied war industries. The ships were organized in convoys to bring war matériel to Britain and the Soviet Union. Most convoys journeyed in large groups of fifty, sometimes spread over nine miles of ocean, with the help of naval warships to ward off the enemy U-boats. The voyages were perilous for the merchant fleet—a hodgepodge of hastily converted tankers to carry liquid material and freighters for hauling dried goods. They had to overcome bad weather, Nazi submarines, and piloting errors in the convoy—all equally lethal.

The merchant ships were more democratically administered than military vessels. Some were even captained by blacks, and one was christened the *James Weldon Johnson*. Although seamen had to undergo the rigorous discipline of the ship when they were onboard and when visiting different ports of call, the Merchant Marine offered considerable freedom outside of the parameters of the voyages. Once the ship returned to its port of origin, the sailors had considerable leeway and autonomy before they shipped out again. Only if they waited too many months to ship out once more for duty did the draft board hunt them down. And although the merchant seamen suffered casualties at a rate higher than in any other branch of the military, when Ellison went to sea the danger was decreasing for the convoys. The battle for Atlantic sea lanes, when the German assault on the cargo ships was strongest, had occurred in 1942 and the first half of 1943; from August 1943, Nazi attacks tapered off until the end of the war.[2]

Ellison's physical condition had deteriorated during the first months of 1943 as he faced the pressure of impending military service. When he met with Richard Wright that winter, Wright thought he was afflicted with nervous exhaustion, fatigue, and perhaps even a recurrence of the jaundice he had suffered in 1939. Ellison stumbled on in his managerial capacity at the *Negro Quarterly*. The magazine's depleted finances and shaky future had forced Herndon and Ellison to move the office again, this time to 308 Lenox Avenue, and accept the generosity of the Harlem Communist bureau, whose headquarters were next door. He had lost his fire for turning the journal into the standard-bearer for radical Negro thought. However, he remained concerned about the artist and setting aesthetic standards for black art, or art about blacks.

Ellison took the work of mentoring young writers seriously; he edited their work and provided evaluations of their prose. He revealed his literary criteria in a powerful and generous piece of explanatory critical prose, a letter to a young poet whose work had been rejected by *Negro Quarterly*. The problem with Lloyd Mallan's "Mulatto Mama," he wrote, began with the poem's assumption of a common shared experience and historical understanding between blacks and whites. Without the necessary grounding, the poem's irony could be badly misunderstood; it seemed more like ridicule. Ellison counseled Mallan firmly to shore up the description of the black characters so that stereotypes could not enter a reader's mind. Ellison tried to carefully redirect the poet, a translator of Guillen and other Spanish poets, to a more accurate perspective on American prejudice and race in the arts. Here, it was as if Ellison was having a conversation with himself as he told the writer of the precarious balancing act between black life and culture and the larger American version of the Western intellectual and artistic heritage. The volatility of global war coupled with the shifting ideologies of so many trusted friends had helped make Ellison's own mind firm about his cultural position. He felt that Mallan needed assistance so that the poem, poised to serve as a gate between white and black, did not appear to blacks as an unyielding barrier.

In his letter, Ellison reflected upon the layers of Negro vernacular, and despite the earlier discouragement from his Marxist friends, continued his deep exploration into the blues. He identified Mallan's poem as having similar qualities to the blues, and he wanted to make sure that the unskilled poet had the proper definition. Ellison had found increasing validity in the blues as an art form because the lyrics demystified the agony of black life with laughter. In their ritualistic use among the black lower class, the blues offered a challenge, and sometimes a repudiation, of Western aesthetics. Knowledge of how the blues operated was important if one, such as Mallan, wanted to write a poem with black characters like "Mulatto Mama." In fact, Ellison faulted Mallan's overreliance upon the modernist techniques of Eliot and Joyce, because the world of the descendants of slaves could not exactly be revealed by the fin de siècle art movement or post–World War I avant garde techniques.[3]

Ellison's understanding of cultural dynamics lay on a foundation of materialist principles, and if the characters in "Mulatto Mama" had helped to sustain Western society, the benefit that they took from it was ambiguous at best. Ellison argued for the necessary conjunction between dramatic structure and philosophy of history in exactly the terms that Richard Wright would use in his upcoming autobiography, *Black Boy*. "Negroes had never been able to catch the full spirit of Western civilization, they lived somehow in it but not of it," Wright wrote in the summer of 1944.[4]

As the months wore on, Ellison held to a less rigid understanding of artistic cycles and historic phases; and perhaps his old animosities toward Communists like Abner Berry and Ben Davis, whom he now saw on a regular basis, made him feel uncomfortable with the possible inference that, if Mulatto Mama were defined as residing on the outskirts of Western culture, then Negroes inevitably would be thought of as primitive.

To conserve resources, he and Herndon decided to join their winter and spring issues into a combined final volume. In the *Quarterly*'s last searching editorial, Ellison looked at the Negroes' attitude toward participation in the war, and subsequently, the core of Negro identity. "Unqualified acceptance," or participation in the American military on jim crow terms, Ellison thought "psychopathic." On the other hand, "unqualified rejection" of the war asserted empty heroism, "inadequate to deal with complex problems." The only course available for adults was "critical participation," capable of affirming the justice of the Allied cause while advocating the "Negro peoples' stake in the struggle." But to get a toehold on exactly what Negro people wanted, one had to figure out what the Negro people were. Ellison called for the black political leadership to immerse itself in the lives of the people it purported to represent. Without learning the "myths and symbols which abound among the Negro masses," the leadership program would fail. The symbol of the disjunction between the masses and the leadership for Ellison was sartorial: "perhaps the zoot-suit conceals profound political meaning."[5] Ellison wrote that the neglected backyards and alleys of Negro culture deserved further scrutiny. For the artist, the struggle to identify the features of Negro life and culture centered on the discovery of methods by which to offer the kernel of truth of the black experience in terms that might broadly be understood.

He kept busy with his editorial duties, which included preparing public remarks on J. Saunders Redding's recent autobiography *No Day of Triumph* at a forum sponsored by Henrietta Buckmaster on March 7. In April, the *Amsterdam News* sent their left-wing reporter Marvel Cooke, a devotee of Paul Robeson, to interview Ellison and Herndon. Cooke later would say that she believed Ellison was one of the most arrogant and snide black artists coming out of Harlem. Yet in the second week of April 1943, she thought he and Herndon were cutting-edge. Advancing the notion that "the basis of freedom is self-knowledge," in the interview Ellison described his campaign at *Negro Quarterly* and the Negro Publication Society as a sophisticated political struggle. He told the newspaper his reasons for working on the twin ventures:

> Negroes have sprung up so fast in a complicated world that they have had no time to develop a critical attitude towards themselves and their relationship towards the rest of society. In other words the technique of critical self-analysis to affect greater unity among peoples is the adult way to see ourselves in relationship with others. Otherwise we constantly function on the other fellow's terms.[6]

Ellison was advancing a program of "critical self-analysis" and working to uncover the "terms" for proper group self-examination. The project was smart and high-profile, and the men of *Negro Quarterly* seemed on the verge of going somewhere. But not for long.

Creditors were hounding Ellison for the funds to cover the Negro Publication Society's unpaid debts. To individuals or organizations to whom he owed money, Herndon was keeping a low profile. An editor from Dryden Press, who offered to accept payment in the form of unsold copies of *Negro Caravan,* had personally guaranteed a loan to the Negro Publication Society for $400. She came to Ellison to resolve a bounced check of Herndon's.[7] The leftist writer Henrietta Buckmaster had given her Ellison's home address. A week later, Ellison's own financial situation was put in doubt when Louis Katz of the Harlem Check Cashing Corporation threatened him with a lawsuit over another bounced Negro Publication Society check.[8] Ellison later described the time as one where "sometimes you got paid, and sometimes you didn't";[9] but after the spring of 1943, there would be no more paydays. *Negro Quarterly* had been timely, though maybe a tad haughty at the beginning of its run; it went to dust before the middle of 1943.

Nimble if anything following his three years at Tuskegee, Ellison landed on his feet. In the summer of 1943, not long after the demise of *Negro Quarterly*, the new journal *Common Ground* published Ellison's "That I Had Wings," a short story set in Oklahoma and a follow-up to "Mister Toussan." Borrowing his central motif of flight from the thwarted dream of Wright's antihero Bigger Thomas, Ellison made it an extended analogy about the Negro's desire for full participation in American life. He dramatized the confrontation of values between the older and younger generation of black Americans, represented by the young character Riley and Riley's aged Aunt Kate. In the story, the older black woman from the slave era invokes the Christian ethos as a means of experiencing a fulfilling life and avoiding the wrathful white world. This approach is entirely inadequate for Riley, who bucks Christian salvation in favor of a destiny based on understanding nature and manipulating technology. Ellison indicated the boy's extreme distance from his theologically bound forebear by his impetuous and repeated iteration of blues songs and bawdy tales. The story had clear racial overtones, but was told artistically enough to avoid the narrow parochialism of a black chauvinist approach. The Ellison-like narrator Riley and his comrade Buster learn about their own dreams by observing the trial of a young robin learning the rudiments of flight. Riley is inspired enough by the robin's flight to try to make chicks fly, or at least descend gracefully in a homemade parachute. But the chaos of the adult world impinges upon Riley's fantasy of flying chickens, and the birds perish.

The New Negroes were on their own and reflecting on ways to dramatically advance their condition and fly. More robust than Langston Hughes's 1934 treatment of Midwestern boyhood in *Not Without Laughter,* Ellison's story was also important evidence that "New Negroness" was not merely a phenomenon of the Northern metropolis. The combination of classic ambition and the indignant refusal to submit to the older patterns of conformity to jim crow percolated freely through the black Southwest of Riley and Buster.

Ellison's motif of flying, soloing, extending oneself experimentally into the unknown and up against traditional boundaries, emphasized the status of his own career, which had progressed to a new level but was not at a peak. And so did the story's publication in a different literary journal, which he felt was a career advancement. A complete departure from the Communist-backed *New Masses, Common Ground* boasted celebrity supporters and represented a broader political coalition than the American Writers League and the New York Writers Project. Backed by the Common Council for American Unity, the magazine deliberately pursued creative and historical analyses of "the racial-cultural situation and its problems."[10] It was a liberal-minded effort to breach the gaping chasm of race conflict during a shooting war, a time when national interest demanded a coherent and fraternal American identity. In keeping with the journal's purpose—and perhaps with its underlying skepticism at the long-term possibility of meeting those goals—*Common Ground* had as regular black contributors Zora Neale Hurston and George Schuyler, whose biracial daughter Philippa, featured frequently and prominently in the pages of *Crisis* and *Opportunity,* was practically an advertisement for the merit of interracial marriages. These two self-styled iconoclasts were known for both their reluctance to condemn jim crow outright and their outright phobia of communism. But Ellison welcomed the move beyond the Left-dominated circle of influence, especially since, now that he had piloted his own literary journal, the Left had much less to offer him as a fulfilling reward.

Around the time that *Common Ground* began to filter into the salons of those urbane intellectuals who had an interest in American ethnic groups, and Ellison's thoughts were turning seriously to the question of the independent nature of black culture, a new acquaintance entered his circle named Ida Guggenheimer. For his changing fictional approach and expanding vision of America, Ida Guggenheimer, the wife of the independently wealthy J. Caesar Guggenheimer, was a good tonic. Ellison began spending afternoons with the middle-aged woman, who deeply favored and was influenced by the men running the Communist Party, whom she considered heroes. After a while, Ellison became a sort of mentor, explaining to Guggenheimer the speciousness and duplicity that was rife in Party life as it attempted to deal adequately with the race question. Guggenheimer was at first nonplussed; her wealth had generally made her comfortable giving instructions and making commanding analyses of issues. As a friend of Richard Wright's, the nation's leading colored writer, she expected her thoughts on racial problems to have weight. However, within a few months, she came to rely greatly on Ellison's advice. Guggenheimer became, in effect, a repository for Ellison's evolving articulation of his distance from the Communists. Ellison's conversations with Guggenheimer were a necessary part of his determination to be independent.

Now that *Negro Quarterly* was no longer publishing, he could concentrate fully on his fiction, interrupted only occasionally by business for the Negro Publication Society. When he had sold "That I Had Wings," he considered it apprentice work and out of step with his newer writing efforts, but he had badly needed the money, and clearly it had a certain polish. The story's publication, while it evidenced an excellent application of the twin contrasting themes of growth and limitation, also represented the end of something. The short story closed the book on Ellison's childhood memories of Oklahoma for the next decade. He had resolved his dilemma by depicting an embattled but dynamic ego, besieged by overbearing adults bent upon silencing a precocious child and by contemporaries who lacked his sense of daring and ingenuity. While the story was not a literal re-creation of his childhood, it enabled him to stop his incessant wading through the terrain of memory. Ellison decided to seal away the material he had collected while gathering children's rhymes for the WPA and return to the adult protagonist of his work from 1939, *Slick*.

His new friend Stanley Hyman of the *New Yorker* kept in touch, and Ellison didn't mind taking lessons from the young professional critic. Through their stimulating relationship, Ellison was personally introduced to the critic Kenneth Burke, a rustic man who lived with his family on a New Jersey farm without electricity. Soon after meeting him, Ellison found his own escape from the demanding pace of city life in the serenity of the countryside. In May 1943, Ellison left the war rallies and bill collectors of New York and holed up at the farm of John Bates in Waitsfield, Vermont, trying to disengage emotionally from the prospect of the draft or the live-fire shipping zones and recuperating from a sick spell. To get better, he pitched hay in the barn and did other farm chores. In quieter moments, he perused a copy of Kenneth Burke's 1931 *Counterstatement*. Ellison had written to Burke personally to order the hard-to-find book. He relished Burke's accumulated observations toward a theory of literary and cultural symbols. *Counterstatement* described the difference between artistic and political engagement. And while Ellison admitted the depth of what he read, he was impatiently awaiting the next installment in Burke's oeuvre. He thought that the iconoclastic literary and social theorist, heavily indebted to Marxism, provided a firm bedrock for belief during their era of crisis.[11] Burke had recently advanced a notion concerning the dramatic explanation for motive in human behavior with a pentad of terms: act, scene, agent, agency, purpose. Ellison's relationship with Burke's work would revive his interest in French Symbolism which had started in college when he read Edmund Wilson's *Axel's Castle*, and would give him a new perspective with which to assess the Kafka rage that was taking place. Reading Burke and talking to Hyman did something to his fiction during the early 1940s. Ellison began to find social realism a senseless limiting of technical and moral range when compared to, among other things, experiments with surrealism and abstract symbolism. Especially since, as he had discussed in his letter to the young poet Mallan, the power of "hard-boiled" realism, which relied heavily on understatement and irony, came from a body of shared assumptions. Without a deep understanding of Negro American history and cultural forms (like the blues), the assumptions upon which literary techniques such as understatement or irony operated proved too narrow for the sustenance of the art. He wanted to add depth to his fictional toolbox.

Ellison wanted his fiction to explain and explore the violence and despair rifling through the United States during the late spring and summer of 1943. Whites from Detroit remained insulted by the habitation of the Sojourner Truth Housing Project by Negroes, who remained in the houses often under the protection of police and government troops. At Fort Bragg, North Carolina, and Fort Dix, New Jersey, and in Arkansas, Houston, and Virginia, white civilians and military police killed Negro troopers under suspicious circumstances and with few consequences. At Fort Dix, forty black soldiers fired on the military police in retaliation for the killings. Riots broke out at shipyards and steel mills, airplane factories and munitions yards, wherever blacks attempted to take jobs alongside whites. But violence on the government run installations could be contained, and hid a messier civilian truth. During a June 20 picnic at Belle Isle on the Detroit River, a resort mutually shared by the races, tempers flared over a car accident, resulting in vicious rumors of wrongdoing. Within hours, mobs of whites were combing theaters and public shops for Negroes, pulling them off streetcars, and setting fires. A week later, more than a score of Detroiters were dead and hundreds wounded. The majority of the dead were unarmed Negroes shot down by police. In addition to the human casualties, the war industries took a blow. During one of the crucial moments of the Second World War, more than a million hours of wartime production were lost at the nation's largest war products manufacturing center. At the same time as the Detroit tumult, the city of Los Angeles erupted into conflagration. Mexican pachucos in zoot suits and similarly attired blacks from South Central were set upon by sailors (the Navy was well-known for racial antipathy), provoking running battles over the city. The *Worker* ran stories that blamed a Nazi-sympathizing fifth column for the violence.

Negro New York wryly asked itself not if, but when, the turmoil would come to its streets. Harlem had been on edge with a palpable tension since the newspapers had reported the "Negro crime wave," and the police had been trying to keep whites from coming above 112th Street. In 1942, military authorities had begun a campaign of removing white women from Harlem, the rationale being to protect servicemen's morale. Such enforcement of rigid racial segregation and harassment had predictable consequences. There was little surprise, then, on the evening of August 1, 1943, when a shocking but credible rumor raced along 125th Street, the lifeblood corridor of Harlem, that a black serviceman named Bandy had been shot and killed while defending his mother and his wife from a white policeman in the Braddock Hotel. Sheer pandemonium resulted. The uproar, similar to the riot of 1935, was directed almost exclusively at the small shops and businesses owned by whites on the main commercial thoroughfares of 125th Street and sections of Seventh and Eighth Avenues from 110th up to 145th Street. It was a time to settle grievances, and observers could make out the revenge-minded mentality of the largely Southern-immigrant population of the city within a city.

While almost all Harlemites were angry, a significant segment—those who lived on the neighborhood's fringes, nearer to Central Park than to 135th Street, or closer to City College than Lenox Avenue, skirting the ridge of Edgecombe Avenue and the Polo Grounds—would have none of the outpouring of frustration and enmity that took the form of public looting. Second-generation blacks in Harlem felt a distinctive pride in calling themselves New Yorkers; some felt that the race prejudice and harassment were aimed only at the unrestrained Southern migrants, who were pouring into New York in search of work. Some blacks read the *New York Times* more than the sensational *Amsterdam-Star News* and sympathized with conservative whites about the infectious sartorial disease called the zoot suit—an infection which, of course, came from the Southerners. Just as galling to this group was the proliferation of the unintelligible argot known as "jive," which was popularized by Cab Calloway's performances that blared forth from the radio, and even was printed in the newspaper.

The migrants from the South, and also adolescents from the overcrowded tenements, could not see themselves as part of this self-appointed elect. Many of the recent arrivals to Harlem were impoverished educationally and financially, and found it difficult to get a job in the defense industries. For them the riot offered both vengeance and high-fueled excitement. It was a spectacular event, where the everyday, indiscriminate, anonymous abuse at the hands of whites could be resolved. And that is what took place.

Back in New York after a couple of weeks in Vermont, Ellison was returning from an evening at the Woodside home of Stanley Hyman and Shirley Jackson.[12] As he exited the A train subway station at 145th and St. Nicholas Avenue, he heard the sound of bagpipes in the distance. Bagpipes in Harlem struck him as odd, or eerily celebratory. When he reached his apartment, he received a message from the *New York Post*, probably through regular columnist Dorothy Norman, a mutual friend of his and Richard Wright's; or Ted Poston, another staff worker whom Ellison knew from the Federal Writers Project. The *Post*, a tabloid filled with the essential news of New York City events, wanted him to cover the riot for the paper. It could be excellent exposure, a chance to do a solid piece of work that he could show to an editor, apart from the book reviews he had done for the Marxist journals. Ellison jotted down deadline and submission information and hastened out of his apartment into the early morning of August 2 to cover the story, catching the subway down to 127th Street and Eighth Avenue.

When Ellison filed his account of the civil disturbance, Harlem's biggest in the twentieth century, he was decamping from his Marxist cloister, but he still had a well-known public commitment to the cause of Negro liberation. Ellison approached his paid assignment professionally and with a great deal of objectivity. He understood that the newspaper would require a narrative of human interest and personal experience; his was not to be the lead story designed to provide facts and simply describe the experience for the majority of white readers. But he also could appreciate that his perspective was vital: this uprising, like the riot in 1935, was taking place in the new context that Harlem provided for African Americans.

Riots in America's industrial age, beginning with the New York Draft Riot of 1863 and brought into the twentieth century with the Atlanta Riot of 1906, had always involved white mobs murdering and brutalizing any Negroes they could get their hands on. The recent Detroit violence had exemplified that model very well. Ellison was a migrant to Manhattan and correctly understood that New York City was the summit of freedom for large groups of Negroes in the United States. For that reason, he wanted to assuage white fears, which had been simmering for more than a year about a menacing black presence in the city. While acknowledging the evidence of violence among the black rioters, Ellison also strove to acknowledge the rioters' similarity, where he could, with other white New Yorkers. He opened the essay with twin themes, which must have seemed a dramatic contradiction: "When I came out, there was the sound of gunfire and the shouting as of a great celebration." The Harlem riot had a deadly component to be sure (as in Detroit, most of the dead were black men shot by police), but for Harlemites, homicide was not the intent. At three-thirty in the morning, groups of Harlemites could be seen hauling gaudy linoleum and coffee tables and chairs rapidly through the streets, calling out to one another to determine which stores were black-owned. They wanted to direct their rage against specific pawnshops and groceries on Eighth Avenue. In Ellison's informed view, "this whole incident was a naive, peasant-like act of revenge." As they were breaking windows, rioters could be heard saying to one another, "I'm doing this for revenge." By daybreak, the crowd began to disperse: but since the rumor of Bandy's death had been only the spark that ignited long-smoldering racial tensions, Ellison foresaw little likelihood of an end to the pressures he had explored in his 1942 article "The Way It Is." He could root his prediction in the litany of abuses suffered by Negroes; the dangerous situation would not just pass like a summer thunderstorm. The next evening the mob continued ravaging, which Ellison ascribed to causes other than the shooting of an unarmed soldier by the police: "I get the impression that they were giving way to resentment over the price of food and other necessities, police brutality and the general indignation borne by Negro soldiers."[13]

While the *Post* article provided him more name recognition and put some change in his pocket, the effort did not satisfy completely his need to engage in critical analysis. The next day he wrote another essay, which he intended to publish, but perhaps the less-than-sensational title, "Harlem Twenty-four Hours After—Peace and Quiet Reign," held little interest for the papers. Without his editor's post at *Negro Quarterly,* he no longer had a dependable outlet for work beyond the parameters of the literary quarterlies; his pride (and integrity) wouldn't let him return to *New Masses.* Ellison faced the professional challenge by turning inward, and resolving the problem with further reading and practice writing. To Harlemites John Clarke and Marvel Cooke, and others in the heat of radical struggle for the first time, Ellison seemed a bright but aloof loner, uninterested in participating in the vital discussions of the YMCA black history club or at the Harlem Communist headquarters.[14]

With the danger of riot just beneath the surface of everyday life and ambivalence the main characteristic of Harlem's attitude toward the war, Ellison had many reasons shortly after August 1943 to revisit Slick Williams, his version of the Black Everyman. The fundamental innovation he brought to the character was to concentrate on the dangerous interiors of the mind, and to show how his protagonist bore the complicated psychological dilemmas of the modern man. He also wanted to treat the surging passion and potential for violence he had witnessed in Harlem's streets, while he embarked upon new experiments with the power of symbols.

The result was "King of the Bingo Game," a short story that compared favorably with the works of his contemporaries, like Wright and the young Chicago writer Saul Bellow. Though it covered some of the same rich thematic terrain, his story was artistically different than Wright's latest effort, "The Man Who Lived Underground." Ellison achieved the contrast by orienting the story around his protagonist's investment in bingo, a symbol of possibility, fortune, and ritual. With his short work, Ellison shaped the vanguard aesthetic criteria he had developed over the previous six years into imaginative form. Now the question was whether he had the stamina and discipline to erect a novel on the foundation of a handful of slim stories and reviews. His instinct about the value of the story was strong enough for him to rescind his self-imposed rule against showing his fiction to Wright. Recognizing the deft use of symbols for group ritual and psychological desire and the pungency of the writing, Wright praised the work in casual but significant fashion, "You've written some kind of crazy thing there man!"[15] Freed from anxiety about imitating the work of his friend, Ellison stepped away from his years as Wright's apprentice.

The story explored a black migrant's dizzying afternoon in a bingo parlor, where the "King" of bingo hopes to win money to pay his wife's medical bills. The nameless hero laments the absence of kinship among blacks in the North, realizing painfully that he can no longer count on physical and emotional sustenance from these brown strangers. "[U]p here it was different. Ask somebody for something, and they'd think you were crazy."[16] The repudiation of ethnic kinship is a severe emotional trial for him, and when the King winds up with the winning bingo number and a chance at the jackpot, he is already unsettled. For Ellison's protagonist, whose luck literally runs out on the stage, the only means to negotiate the destructive element of chaotic life is by focusing on a symbol for possibility. The hero imputes powers of omniscience and interpretation to the bingo wheel. He chooses and sanctifies the bingo wheel as a totem, so that subconsciously he can shape and develop his own life. The crisis reaches its absurd climax only when, in the course of events, policemen beat the hero unconscious and remove the button that controls the wheel from his hand.

In the story, Ellison created a feeling of feverish tension, partially by the use of mildly absurd dramatic situations within the natural development of his character and plot. He also was beginning to express a profound ambivalence about the fundamental nature of the human condition—about success, freedom, and the coherence of relationships. The King of Bingo becomes more and more berserk in an effort to cling to a rational sense of reality and possibility. The hero maddeningly pursues a unified self-image in the face of his own disfigured and fragmented identity.

Ellison considered "King of the Bingo Game" to be the achievement of his distinctive fictional voice. In October he sold the story to *Tomorrow;*[17] that same month a story by Saul Bellow was appearing for the second time in *Partisan Review*. The two writers had a great deal in common; Bellow's ruminating and pessimistic characters arose from the same types of urban ethnic American pockets that Ellison struggled to portray. Bellow's short story "The Dangling Man" captured the tense months before the draft board sent its somber greetings to one of the Army's prospective inductees. *Partisan Review* liked the short story well enough to publish it as a first novel, *The Dangling Man*, the next year.[18] In fact, Bellow's 1941 short story "Two Morning Monologues" had probably given Ellison something to aim at as he developed his material. "Two Morning Monologues" bears a close resemblance to "King of the Bingo Game"; like the King of Bingo, Bellow's working-class protagonist feels displaced and alienated from his social surroundings, and is confident only that further misery will befall him. He leaves his house every morning at nine, accepting the ritual of order established by his parents, and goes to look for work—the theme of the first monologue. By 11:30 A.M., the protagonist's search for work is abandoned in favor of a card game—beginning the second monologue entitled "The Gambler," and introducing the themes of chaos and chance. Bellow's hero ends the story accepting defeat: "What does it amount to? Close my eyes and pick, I may as well. It turns out the same; mostly sour loss."[19] The two young American writers had survived a Depression in their childhood, and now as adults they faced the conflagration of war. It was difficult for them to hold an optimistic view.

Despite the fact that much of literary New York considered *Partisan Review* the elite carrier of fiction and criticism, Ellison had been too close with the Communists during the era of the Moscow trials and the Nazi-Soviet pact to feel utterly compelled by the circle associated with the journal. There was a cattiness about *Partisan*'s exclusivity, an aura of in-group self-promotion and preening show-off attitude. It sometimes amounted to a refusal to consider works of outsiders; and certainly no black critics were published for more than ten years of the magazine's history until Anatole Broyard surreptitiously broke the color barrier in 1948, followed a few months later in a more open lowering of the barrier with James Baldwin. Ellison's mentor Kenneth Burke called the journal "Fartisan" in his letters, to express his feeling of disagreement with the review.[20] Ellison regularly read the journal, cultivating his familiarity with the material with the same devotion he had once applied to practicing musical scales. Despite the value of the work it published, he retained an intense dislike for the journal's editors, and yet, like it or not, in his own political views he never seriously digressed from the major trends of Philip Rahv, the figure most associated with *Partisan Review*.[21]

Not long after he sold "King of the Bingo Game," Ellison renewed a project he had been taking notes on and which was stirring considerable conflict in the news: the plight of black flyers, or as they came to be known, the Tuskegee Airmen. In 1942, the U.S. Army Air Corps had opened a flying school at Tuskegee. Ellison felt some pride that Tuskegee was singled out for recognition and for the training of advanced troops, the all-black Ninety-ninth Pursuit Squadron. Even Brigadier General Benjamin O. Davis's son Colonel Benjamin Davis Jr. was sent down to Macon County to learn flying. But the creation of the flight school was not without controversy, and by 1943 Ellison was calling the entire affair "window dressing" that had been "palmed off on the American people as the real thing."[22] Initially the Army balked at training the Negroes as airmen at all; then the Army determined to have the fighters trained as pursuit pilots, the most difficult sort of flying assignment, and to train them in this assignment without fighter aircraft. The air cadets were being set up for failure. Despite the controversy, however, the fliers represented a kind of glorious ambition for black people. Harlem saw the Negro airman, in an age when vendors in pony carts could still be found on the streets, as the confirmation of freedom in America and the arrival of the technological age. The Ninety-ninth's eventual distinguished record in the European theater only reinforced the irony and absurdity of American racist practices.

Ellison created a short story that dramatized the difficult position of the African American serviceman in the figure of a flier whose vocation nearly erased the boundaries between machine and man, and myth and history. The flier was a Negro Icarus who had surged dangerously beyond the confines of the realistic world. As a fictional character the black flier was decidedly liberating for Ellison, because here was a protagonist who, as an articulate cosmopolitan adult, could finally voice the complex social and psychological problems of Negro identity. (Saul Bellow and the writer Delmore Schwartz had created similar characters.) The title of Ellison's story paid homage to the recently deceased friend of his boyhood, Charlie Christian, the Oklahoma jazz innovator who had soloed with phenomenal acuity in Benny Goodman's group on the popular tune "Flying Home."

"Flying Home," a tale that brings a college-educated Tuskegee Airman into contact with a black Alabama sharecropper, carried the theme, the protagonist, and the dramatic situation of Ellison's mature life's work. The airman, named Todd, struggles against the racial assumptions that automatically link him to the poor black sharecropper, Jefferson. Yet is painfully obvious that Todd must overcome his reluctance to connect himself with Jefferson, because the sharecropper possesses the folk wisdom to transcend the racial enmity that threatens to keep Todd on the ground. Ellison was pointing to the gap between America's urban and rural Negroes as the key to the badly understood black identity, and thus, the key to black destiny. The field hand Jefferson understands airman Todd's deepest impulses and flight-school struggles and gives expression to them through an elaborate flying folktale, linking the folk mass with the black elite and offering folk remedies for earthly predicaments.

Ellison both exaggerates and relieves the mounting tension of his realistic portrait with aspects of the carnival and burlesque. He brings his Tuskegee flier to earth with a lowly buzzard, a bird reduced to a spray of blackness and blood as it covers the plane's windshield. (After the story's publication, Tuskegee alum Albert Murray, then teaching in Tuskegee's English department, told Ellison on one of his regular trips up to New York City that a B-25 from Tuskegee's airfield was actually struck on the windshield by a buzzard. Ellison told him that life was imitating art.[23]) Ellison stretched the comic absurdity of the short story to include other singular events from the Harlem news, such as the incident when police had ordered a wounded casino manager straitjacketed and sent off for psychological observation.[24] In the story, instead of finding a doctor for the wounded black flier, the local white landowning despot sends for attendants from an asylum with straitjackets. Only Jefferson's humorous tall tale, offering blues-tinged laughter at pain and confusion, appears as a method of coping for the young airman, who must "fly home" to the sharecropper for psychological survival. Although Wright had snatches of the same themes and techniques in his writing, Ellison here pioneered a vision of a deranged modern social landscape where the potential for liberation lay in grasping slave-tale allegories and deep cultural structures like the blues. To accommodate all of his ideas inside a frame that had more in common with art than social philosophy, Ellison experimented with an elastic literary style that went far beyond the tightly wound realism of the so-called hard-boiled school.

Ellison finished "Flying Home" in Stanley Hyman's living room on 36 Grove Street in the late fall of 1943, literally hours before shipping out for the North Atlantic.[25] The two men had grown closer after a year or so of friendship. Hyman and his wife, Shirley Jackson, enormous supporters of Ellison's talent, pushed him to finish the story, which had been languishing. Ralph had received editor Edwin Seaver's notice announcing that an upcoming anthology called *Cross Section* was seeking unpublished fiction from writers in the States during the summer. But the work that had begun purposefully had tapered off into the fall of 1943. Despondent and melancholy on the eve of his first Atlantic crossing, Ellison had had difficulty concentrating on his fiction. But among his published friends, he managed to regain his focus and raise the mark of his achievement. In the published collection that appeared in 1944, his closest artistic comrades appeared alongside him in print: Richard Wright, Stanley Hyman, Shirley Jackson, and Langston Hughes. Wright's entire novella "The Man Who Lived Underground" was presented in the book, probably eclipsing the attention that readers gave to Ellison's short story. But he had received recognition on the same footing as Wright, and he seemed poised to surpass Hughes—a significant accomplishment. In fact, Seaver gave his two younger Negro contributors elaborate praise. Predictably, Wright was called "probably the outstanding Negro writer in the United States today," but Ellison was not many marks behind as a "leading Negro writer."[26] Including "Flying Home," Seaver pointed out, Ellison had published exactly seven short stories. Hughes's biography mentioned his publications but said nothing of his historic stature. None of the other writers in the collection were given any sort of laudatory preludes to their efforts, not even the twenty-one-year-old Harvard graduate Norman Mailer, who had a thirty-six-page story accepted.

The literary world took notice. On November 1, the literary agent Henry Volkening, of the Russell and Volkening Literary Agency, who represented Bucklin Moon and who had shopped the work of Ted Poston and Bill Attaway, wrote to Ellison and offered to take him on as a client. Impressed by Volkening's clients, Ellison engaged the agent to represent him. Volkening's office was on Fifth Avenue; Ellison was living up to his billing now as a member of the revolutionary "Blues School" of literature. Within a year, he would show the literary community precisely what recognition as a blues man meant.

He turned his experiences overseas, where he had served mainly as a third cook on the S.S. *Sun Yat Sen* of the North Atlantic and Gulf Steamship Company, into a short story called "In a Strange Country." His work now included increasingly complex narrative voices and also a new insight. While at *Negro Quarterly,* he had worked hard to offer space to critics of British and American imperialism, but his trips with the convoy to Wales, France, and the banks of the Rhine had forcibly shown him the impact of his American nativity, and also something of its inescapability. For while the hero Parker of "In a Strange Country" is violently attacked by white American GIs in Wales because of his skin color, Parker's deepest impulses are not racial, but individual. When describing his vanquishment to foreigners, he recalls the melee with the soldiers as a "family quarrel." And to cement his American heritage, after Parker hears a ringing series of patriotic Welsh anthems—a scene in which the absence of similarly emotionally rousing epic material from his own cultural chest causes him to suffer—the Welshmen salute him with the "Star Spangled Banner." The generous gesture by the Welsh singers drives home Parker's ambivalent national identity so poignantly that he is moved to tears.

The themes that were to consume Ellison over the next seven years were now close at hand. "In a Strange Country" borrowed from the ancient dramatic situation that developed heroism: the stranger making his way into the village. Ellison had also begun to evolve an idea out of his bull sessions with the well-known artists and intellectuals Lawrence Reddick, Richard Wright, John Velasco, Carlton Moss, and Angelo Herndon. In the past they had mocked the sociological reports that glibly attributed lynching to the Negro's "high visibility."[27] Now Ellison began to discuss racial complexity in terms of the observation of blackness. American soldiers set upon his hero Parker after they had first cut through the darkness with a flashlight. The mechanism prohibiting Parker's potential acceptance—the problem with his American identity—can be reduced to the white soldiers' optical gaze, artificially enhanced by means of a flashlight. Nothing is wrong with Parker; rather, it is a case of how others see him. Parker is not different from other Americans, and in some cases, white Americans do not even see him as being different; they need the help of technology to impose racial differences. But the ensuing violence blinds Parker to the sight of his own identity. Entering a club with Welsh friends, the protagonist finds that "When the light struck his injured eye, it was as though it were being peeled by an invisible hand." Ellison also enjoyed playing with Parker's tragic moment through Negro America's practice of laughter in the face of adversity. Nor did he limit the comic coping device of his hero to homespun tales. Wondering to himself what further aberration to expect after being set upon by fellow Americans and befriended by foreigners who revere Negro spirituals, Parker is beset by self-mocking thoughts when he agrees to attend a Welsh choral concert: "Maybe, he thought, you'll hear that old 'spiritual' classic *Massa's in de-Massa's in de Old Cold Masochism!*"[28] The hero's doubt, wit, and self-conscious intellect represented new directions for the author.

Seaman Ellison returned to New York during the spring of 1944 and was greeted with good news. Volkening had been working to sell his stories, and while he had been turned down at *New Yorker* and *Harpers,* the journal *Tomorrow* had snapped up "In a Strange Country" for $100, the most he had ever been paid for his fiction. The story would be published that summer. More exciting, though, than being published in a magazine was the possibility of a contract for a novel. On May 19, Volkening wrote to say that he had an offer on the table from Frank Taylor of Reynal and Hitchcock. Taylor promised a $1,200 advance against royalties in return for a novel in twelve months.[29] Ellison's concern was to complete the work; he had several ideas and many, many themes, but no concrete topic.

Having been a bachelor for about three years, Ellison resumed his romantic life in the spring of 1944. Langston Hughes, who knew of the collapse of Ellison's marriage, might have bragged to his friend Fanny Buford (now using her maiden name, McConnell) that he had a friend with an incredible library.[30] Glamorous and sophisticated, Fanny McConnell worked for the Urban League, and had known Hughes when she and her husband John Buford ran the Negro Peoples' Theater company in Chicago in the 1930s. The slender and attractive fair-skinned woman was a writer who had worked as James Weldon Johnson's secretary while an undergraduate at Fisk, and who held an advanced degree from the University of Iowa. The two of them talked on the phone and made an informal arrangement for her to see the magnificent library. Fanny McConnell was mildly impressed with Ellison's large collection of books; but was more profoundly moved by the confident and brilliant man who discussed the works lovingly. They met in mid-June, and had one of their earliest dates with another friend as chaperone. Fanny agreed to meet him again, at Frank's restaurant on 125th Street, where she ordered chicken à la king out of consideration for his wallet. Ellison was as delighted with this accomplished woman as she was with him. He had conserved his resources, and was prepared to spend some money on the date, but when the waiter turned to him for his order, to spare her embarrassment, he asked for the same dish. Their conversation about books was so intriguing that before the end of the month, Fanny McConnell was tracking down Malraux's *Man's Fate* and *Days of Wrath.*[31]

Besides the fast bloom of romance, the connection had another meaning for Fanny McConnell. She decided to scale back her own impulses toward writing fiction. Her intimate connection with a dedicated writer showed her that to succeed, a level of allegiance to the craft was called for that she did not possess: "I had begun to think, before I met Ralph, that I wasn't a writer. After I met him I was convinced I wasn't."[32] Politically, however, they had a great deal in common. While she had not been closely allied with the radical Left, her sentiments against enormous capitalist machines, entrenched nepotism, and racial exploitation agreed with his. Within a year of meeting, they would be living together, which was not considered too outrageous for two divorcées past thirty, especially given the wartime erosion of strict morality and Ellison's participation in the military looming over their intimacy. Fanny McConnell's accomplishment and intelligence enriched his perspective. Fanny reviewed Philip Yourdan's play *Anna Lucasta,* the surprising Broadway hit with the black cast, in *Opportunity.* She was anxious to celebrate "theater history" with a work that she said had moved beyond "clown school" stereotypes of religious fervor and dice shooting licentiousness.[33] In short order, Fanny became an integral component of Ellison's composition process, typing out his longhand notes, usually after he read the passages aloud to her.

Toward the end of the summer, Harcourt Brace also offered Ellison a contract on the book. On August 22, the publisher told his agent that they would pay $250 for the first fifty pages of his novel, and if it met with their editorial approval, offer a contract for the completed work. Frank Taylor of Reynal and Hitchcock took his initial offer up an additional $300, making a final offer of $1,500.[34] Ellison was mildly amused to be courted by the major publishers before they had even so much as seen a proposal.[35] Edwin Seaver, the editor of *Cross Section,* recalled that toward the end of the war "publishers were ready to offer a promising young author a thousand dollar advance at the drop of a hat."[36] Seaver's commentary was prescient, at least for Ellison. The contracts available to writers also suggest that the international ascendancy of the American novel in the 1950s relied upon the country's firm economic footing.

Ellison decided to go with Reynal and Hitchcock's "bird-in-hand" offer, and Volkening supplied him with a contract to look over. Ellison mailed the agreement to Richard Wright, on holiday in Ottawa, Canada, for a professional's assessment. Wright was impressed with the advance, the percentage of the royalty, and the retention of foreign rights. "It is a very good first contract. . . . You can consider yourself lucky."[37] His one word of advice was to postpone delivery of the manuscript for more than a year; the contract stipulated delivery in about six months. Ellison signed the contract sometime after September 5, after changing the date of delivery to September 1, 1945. The contract was apparently backdated for August 28.[38] Reynal and Hitchcock paid him $250 when he signed, and then $250 at the first of every month until the advance was paid out. Ellison vowed to begin work immediately. This new relationship with publisher and agent defined him as a professional writer; as for a topic for the novel, he decided to develop the rich character he had first explored in "Flying Home."

The contract with Reynal and Hitchcock (who would publish Hughes's translation of the Haitian Jacques Roumain's brilliant novel *Masters of the Dew*) validated this new literary voice. Ellison was tickled to be received as a partner in the professional literary community. He was no longer window-shopping along the boulevards of Oklahoma City, but sipping cognac on Fifth Avenue. Volkening threw a "clients only" party at his house on October 6, and Ellison was tantalized with the air of exclusivity and refinement that came with being a member of the club. "Would you like to come to the Volkenings for cocktails, Friday the 6th? No wives, no husbands, no editors. Clients only . . . Helen Eustis was in here today, asking whether you'd like to go to Yaddo. Told her damned if I knew. She'll be writing you. She'll also be at the party."[39] Ellison had written letters to the cream of fiction writers at Yaddo; now a billet was dangled in front of him. Deals were made and futures decided over the cocktail hour, and he was on the guest list.

The publishing contract came at a good time. Ellison needed professional recognition outside of his own group of writers in Harlem and outside of the Left. He was reminded of Wright's spectacular power as a writer when "I Tried to Be a Communist" was published in the *Atlantic Monthly* in installments that August and September. Wright's public break (and Ellison's too) with the American Communist Party had the effect of maddening blacks and sympathetic whites who traveled in leftist circles. The essay sent the two men's joint friend and patron Ida Guggenheimer into a tailspin. Ellison spent several days patiently explaining Wright's essay to her at her hotel, as he had done four years earlier in Communist circles after the publication of *Native Son.*

Ellison made the rounds of literary parties, debating William Attaway at a September 4 soirée at the home of *New Yorker* cartoonist William Steig. Ellison took seriously his role as Wright's defender, seeing the embattled author as a Malreauxean purveyor of "morality in action." Naturally, the other writers did not share Ellison's estimate of a man they all knew personally; it was easier to label Ellison a brazen sycophant. Many of the writers, like Attaway, were suspicious of Wright's success and resentful of the criticisms that the self-supportive duo of Wright and Ellison so confidently levied against lesser works. And while they granted that Ralph Ellison had an extremely perceptive intelligence, they also wanted to keep him well within their ranks. It was bad enough that Richard Wright had exceeded the expectations—commercial and artistic—that had limited black writers' performances for generations, but who wanted another iconoclast increasing levels of anxiety about writers' talents? During the party, Attaway began to malign Wright's work, using the tactics of Ben Davis and Sam Sillen by calling Wright anti-Semitic. Everyone knew that Wright had married a Jew. The author of *Blood on the Forge* tried first to flatter Ellison by telling him that he was twice the intellectual that

Wright was; then he tried to frighten him by claiming that Ellison knew nothing about any other author. It was a crude ploy, and when the gaggle of literati went on to label Wright deranged, Ellison countered the charge. In a world of surreal contradictions, such as blacks in the United States were subjected to, he responded that any sensitive artist inevitably showed some form of neurotic behavior.[40] The group rapidly quieted.

At another party, a woman recoiled when Ellison delivered his by now patented unorthodox opinion about the position of the writer in society and the necessity of mastering craft and interracial alliances for the black writer. "How do you come talking like that?" the woman asked. "I never even heard of you."[41] In some camps, Ellison's refusal to gain easy notoriety by condemning Wright as a Communist, or as an anticommunist, or both, made him seem equal parts incorrigible and unpleasant. While Wright's renunciation of the Communists caused a storm uptown (he was attacked as a "sadist" scoring the black Left) and was perfunctorily countered by Ben Davis in an essay called "New Times: A Few Words on Richard Wright and 'New Ideas,'" Wright's article hit its mark. In December 1944, *Negro Digest* would sponsor a symposium in New York with Horace Cayton, and Communists William Patterson, Ben Davis, and James Ford (who had been satirized mercilessly in Wright's essay) with the title "Have Communists Quit Fighting For Negro Rights." Even though Ben Davis would still serve as Harlem's representative to the New York City Council, after 1944 the power of the Communists in black politics quickly disappeared.

Now that he had a decent book contract, Ellison did not have to tolerate the prattle of Wright's enemies. At social gatherings that fall, he let people know that he had been awarded a generous advance to publish a novel. He also applied his exuberant intellectual spirits to helping the "Conference of Psychologists and Writers" get off the ground, inviting all of the local talent: Richard Wright, Langston Hughes, Harry Overstreet, and Fanny McConnell. Ellison led a seminar on the novel. In the meantime Richard Wright, too, had significant plans. He intended to form a journal of his own with the help of a stunning group of black critics, writers, and social scientists.

With an agent pounding the bricks for him, Ellison sold his story of the merchant marine in Wales to *Negro Digest,* his first publication in the black surrogate of "Reader's Digest." "Black Yank in Britain" was published in September.[42] In terms of original criticism, Ellison polished off several reviews in the second half of the year. He gave pleasant if fairly ordinary evaluations of James Porter's *Modern Negro Art* in *Tomorrow*'s November edition, followed the next month with analyses of Jean Stafford's *Boston Adventure* and Frank Goodwin's *The Magic of Limping John.* His most condemning review, unsurprisingly, evaluated Roi Ottley's *New World A-Coming* in the same *Tomorrow* December issue. In comments about his fellow craftsmen, like William

Attaway and Ted Ward, he would praise them for their strengths while revealing their shortcomings. His Ottley review showed what could happen when Ralph Ellison was on the warpath with legitimate grievances combined with personal enmity. Ellison had reason to bristle when dealing with Ottley beyond the two men's personal distaste for each other. Ottley had taken works done by writers employed with the Writers Project and was now publishing them under his own name. The review of his book went to the quick and laid the blame squarely on Ottley's attitude, not his craftsmanship. Ellison despaired of the view, fashionable among some blacks, that their lives as Negroes prepared them to answer with authority all questions regarding black life. Ottley's omnibus was "neither scholarly nor responsible journalism," was "distorted," and tended to "blur[s] even the obvious meaning of Negro experience." In Ellison's view, Ottley sensationalized black life where possible, and mistakenly saw Harlem as a microcosm of Negro America. Finally, Ellison saw in Ottley the attitude of the racial coward, a sentiment rejected by the younger generation. "*New World A-Comin* belongs with those recent movies which, after promising to depict Negroes honestly, slip back into the blackface of traditional burlesque. One profound implication of Negro activity today is the rejection, even unto death, of the attitude behind Ottley's stylistic clowning."[43] Ottley's perfidy contributed to the polished facade of black life that the wartime propaganda machine churned out. His book complemented the release of the short film *The Negro Soldier*, directed by Carlton Moss, showing cheery black Army life without the insults of segregation, contrary to the graphic accounts of the Negro press. Since Communist spokesmen like Ben Davis glibly sanctioned such blithe representations of Negro life, Ellison was basically alone in his criticisms. Richard Wright wrote to him during the late summer that Canadian film critics were disturbed by the "blatant lie about Negro army conditions." As usual, Wright was battling: "I had to tell the Canadians here in Ottawa that I had no connections whatever with that film, so that I could keep my self-respect."[44]

Ellison's most consequential analytical work for 1944, however, was not published, probably because he had to ship out to sea in the wake of the opening of a second theater of warfare off the coast of France in June. While biding his time and waiting for the last possible minute to go, he had developed ties with *Antioch Review*, a young intellectual and academic journal published in Yellow Springs, Ohio, since the beginning of the 1940s. Through the pages of *Antioch* he had first gotten to know Stanley Hyman and seen the work published of his *New Masses* colleague Edwin Berry Burgum, along with such critics as Granville Hicks. The editorial staff arranged for Ellison to review *An American Dilemma*, the book that had piqued the American public's conscience, still blistering after the 1943 race riots.

Ellison found the study by the Swedish social scientist Gunnar Myrdal (aided by Ralph Bunche and Sterling Brown) dangerously flawed. Instead of devoting volumes to prove that Negro society suffered at the hands of white racism, what was called for, Ellison said, in his famous paraphrase of Joyce, was Negro cultural self-determination: "What is needed are Negroes to take it [Negro culture] and create of it 'the uncreated consciousness of their race.'" More interesting than the tragedy of Negro life in America, he said, should have been an analysis of the cultural forms and rituals that Negroes had actively chosen in the face of the "higher values" of white America. And he had not given up his interest in the class dynamic or the wielding of power, which he said Myrdal misunderstood. "All of this, of course, avoids the question of power *and* the question of who manipulates that power."[45] He was reminded of his college days and the white philanthropist who came to Tuskegee to be entertained and to dictate the future of the black race. Ellison saw condescension in the Carnegie Commission's decision to hire a Swede, instead of any number of qualified black researchers, to study the important question of racism. His review was a little too hot for *Antioch,* which begged off publication. Ralph Ellison would grow accustomed to confining the acid of his views to literature.

11

Portrait of the Artist as a Young Critic

1945

EARLY 1945 found Ellison without a place to publish a sharp review of Gunnar Myrdal's book, another indication of the power of the segregation of the word. He had completed working on his lengthy review of *American Dilemma* in the face of his own dilemma—the draft board's urgent summons after he had prolonged heading off to sea again. The messages from the board compelling his appearance dashed his optimism about escaping the military. The question of personal danger aside, the Merchant Marine, regardless of its merits, did not fulfill his intellectual and personal passion for racial and social justice. In New York, he had become an increasingly important voice at meetings and public lectures, and he was reckoned a formidable member of Harlem's writerly elite. His position as public social critic and draft-age Negro tested his emotional balance.

His first voyage on a ship, in mid-1943, had supported his feelings that in the face of danger, the obstacle of race could be overcome. Later voyages filled him with considerable disgust and pessimism. He went out again, more than a year later in the winter of 1945, close to the final German counterattack in the Battle of the Bulge. Before he even stepped on board ship, he heard disturbing accounts from men who had sailed on previous trips of open racial warfare as their ships had edged their way into war zones. Naval gun crews had trained their weapons on blacks and whites who were on the verge of rioting over shipboard insults and disagreements.[1]

304

Ellison's evasion of military service not only reflected his political views, but also jibed with the perspective of Harlem's new breed of spirited street-corner hipsters, whose music and dress were being discovered downtown, first in the Village, and then in Manhattan's nightclub district. Zoot-suited men and boys professed a surprisingly regimented social and political ideology, one that Ellison and Herndon had commented on as editors of *Negro Quarterly,* and which they thought imperative to the construction of a "New Deal" for African Americans. The hipsters and sharpies who colored Harlem exhibited a unique savoir faire that distinguished the black bohemians of the under-world. Their defiance was visually symbolic. It was illegal to wear the "drape-shape" zoot suit, with its broad padded shoulders, long jacket, and pants bal-looning at the knee but tapered for snugness at the ankle, because it violated clothes rationing ordinances. These nattily dressed men and boys were known for their epicurean tastes in food as well as their extravagant consumption of jazz music. The streetwise actors defied the color line in their romantic pur-suits. They had an obvious passion for leisure and indulged in their pleasures—food, sex, intoxicants—in wanton displays of abundance—a conscious repu-diation of the American middle-class ethos of hard work, thrift, and sobriety. Hipsters flaunted their outrageous behavior, rejecting the cautious sentiment of the only recently past Prohibition and Depression. And they conspicuously disregarded the all-out shooting war.

But if hipsters indifferently crossed the color line and adapted quickly to and enjoyed modern technology, they strongly resisted appropriation from the mainstream.[2] When Ralph Ellison took an evening at Minton's to enjoy the world of the knowledgeable jazz elite, he encountered zoot-suited musi-cians full of disdain for the organized homogenous world of downtown.

Disgust with jim crow, with the war, and with something that was becom-ing more and more obvious to Ellison—the disintegration of rural black folk values in the urban industrialized North—deeply affected the musician's art form. If the players of the 1920s had been embittered by tangible, obvious racial insults, the later generation—who were one step further removed from chattel slavery—creatively expressed their bitterness with innovative musical forms. In their after-hours jam sessions, the jazzmen and their zoot-suited fans showed their resentment toward the commercial success of imitative white swing bands. In concert with the steely attitude on the street, the music re-jected any allegiance to white America. Bop, even in its technical composition—with its difficult to follow transitions, accents on the off-beat, and rapid chord and progression changes—represented a rejection of cultural exploitation and assimilation. When whites still flocked to see the performers, some players adopted an almost contemptuous attitude toward the audience, refusing to face their listeners or provide them with danceable music. Ellison thought the hipsters' leisure-based rebellions were important, calling to mind Kenneth Burke's *Counterstatement,* which had proposed the bohemian as an antidote to the capitalist bourgeoisie, and named the "aesthetic" approach as being more capable than economic forces of solving the problem of fairness in a democracy.

The decline in technique of Ellison's jazz hero Lester Young after he was released by the U.S. military seemed to confirm the negative opinions about the military held by musicians and the Harlem cultural elite. For hipsters like Malcolm X, known then as Detroit Red, and bop-blowing trumpeter Dizzy Gillespie, the Army induction medical exam was the place to wear the most outrageous zoot suit and to banter in the most incomprehensible jive. After concluding their Army psychiatric interviews by detailing their plans to kill whites once they were trained as riflemen, both Harlemites were rewarded with 4-F status.[3]

Ellison not only felt considerable solidarity with the young men on Harlem's streets, but with his intellectual credentials and myriad political contacts, he felt a political responsibility to resist the draft. The jim crow Army promised to break those who did not conform.

If the author Malraux was committed enough to be leading fighters in the Maquis—the French resistance—how then should Ellison be reacting against Harlem's puppet regime, propped up by white business and political interests, and rallying Negroes for war?

At Seventh Avenue at 125th Street, the draft-age men called each other "Daddy-o," and wore sunglasses and wide-brimmed hats. These men had been seasoned by riot, and Ellison knew that the hipsters were prepared to face death squarely but not in the Army, as he had already alerted readers in his editorials at *Negro Quarterly,* as well as in his review of Roi Ottley's *New World A-Coming.* (As counterpoint, Harlem men also signed up for a suicide squad which had been organized to battle the Japanese kamikazes.) Cognizant of the brewing resentment and discontent, Ellison thought ruefully of black politicians whose opportunism prevented them from accurately gauging the evolution of a new mass movement. And on a national level, he thought of the missed opportunity for the advance of racial equality when the black Democratic Party machines had closed solidly behind Roosevelt after the president, under pressure from Dixiecrats, had in the 1944 presidential campaign dismissed his liberal vice president Henry Wallace in favor of the more domestically conservative Missourian Harry S Truman. Roosevelt in 1944 had few if any of the original New Deal architects left in his cabinet.

Of course, when it came to serious discussion about race and politics, Ellison had no friend on a par with Richard Wright to relieve his frustrations about draft notices from a segregated military or a racially troubled Merchant Marine. Toward the end of January 1945, Ellison confessed to Wright his agonies over the induction papers he'd received from the draft board. Apparently he had not served enough time on board ship to suit them. In early January, he visited a social worker to find out how he could get a draft exemption based on the stomach ailments that had increased in severity since his previous voyage. The consultation led to an appointment with a psychiatrist, who refused him a deferment after diagnosing the cause of Ellison's high blood pressure, racing pulse, and erratically beating heart: the doctor told the professional writer to stop "thinking too much and too hard." Ellison fought down the desire to smack him. On the morning of January 22, Ellison called Wright, deeply troubled about possibly having to serve. Wright recorded in his diary later that day: "Ralph called; his voice was husky. He says that the pressure upon him, despite his bad stomach, by his draft board and the merchant marine is so much that he'll have to leave soon, either for the sea or the army."[4] Ellison talked of going to jail rather than serving in the military. Taking on a role somewhere between older brother and psychoanalyst—the attitude he adopted when counseling Ellison on most things—Wright said he thought Ellison had started late in searching for a way to avoid the draft.

As Wright had become increasingly famous, his sense of himself as a man of consequence had grown. In January 1945, he was on the verge of another major literary success with his autobiography *Black Boy,* another Book-of-the-Month Club selection. Important, powerful people, the heads of companies, news and philanthropic organizations, vied for Wright's time. His personality, as well as his connection to Ellison, began to change. Wright also began to settle domestically, even more so after his first child, Julia, was born. In the early weeks of January, he told Ellison of his plans to purchase a home in Greenwich Village. Ellison was experiencing a sort of rootlessness because of the war, his political views, an uncertain artistic career, and even the anxieties and unknowns of his early romantic relationship with Fanny McConnell. Wright now saw Ellison as fitting into a pattern not too different from his other friends; a mind-set in which racial oppression was the governing subject of their lives. Because so much of their relationship had revolved around examining race in American society, Ellison kept to the topics of the men's well-established conversations, which inevitably fed into Wright's contrived views. Wright especially used the trouble with the draft board to question Ellison's decision to become a writer; in some form, Wright cast Ellison as disillusioned artist, pulled toward a medium that might allow the best expression of protest against the racial conditions that beset him. In his journal, Wright thought candidly about Ellison and his motivation. In the diary's longest uninterrupted account of Ellison's character, Wright decided finally that while the two men were very close, Ellison was limited in his range:

> Pending Ralph's visit, I keep thinking of him and of the fact that almost every act of a Negro is partly or wholly conditioned by his being a Negro. Ralph did not want to join the army because it is a Jim Crow army and he went into the merchant marine. He writes because he is a Negro; he really

wanted to be a sculpture [sic], but he found he could not say what was hotly in him to say with stone and marble. Now again he [is] making decisions based solely on his racial identity. He has no choice.[5]

Wright, who knew authentic stories of Negroes going berserk under racial pressure, wanted to distance himself from Ellison's potentially futile attempts to avoid the draft. On January 23, 1945, Wright suggested that Ellison try a visit to Dr. Frederic Wertham, a psychiatrist who might write a psychological evaluation that he was unfit to serve. According to Wright's diary, Ellison had already scheduled an appointment with a different doctor, and planned to see Wertham to hedge his bets against the possibility that the other doctor wouldn't help him. Wertham agreed to psychoanalyze Ellison, but only if the examination was exclusive. Wright, whose status as head of household precluded him from the draft, explained to Ellison "coldly" that it would be "dangerous" to keep both appointments. He confessed in the journal that even after their seven years of friendship, he was afraid that Ellison would "double-cross" him to escape the draft.[6]

Wright's account of the weeks leading up to Ellison's final Merchant Marine voyage, an account that Ellison refuted in interviews later in his life,[7] is probably accurate at least so far as indicating the turmoil and deep conflict of the moment. But Wright's anxiety indicated nothing. On January 26, Wertham called him and said that he planned to help Ellison evade the draft. The doctor based his profile of Ellison on the fact that his brother Herbert had enlisted in the Army and had not been heard from. Two days after Wright's conversation with Wertham, Ellison went over to Wright's Brooklyn house at 89 Lefferts Place to show him Wertham's letter, mistakenly addressed to "Robert Ellison." Their conversation was stirring and deeply personal, reminiscent of the closeness they had known around the time in 1941 when Wright had published *Twelve Million Black Voices.* In a rare personal revelation, Ellison told Wright a portion of what had been tearing him apart during the previous weeks, other than his brother's disappearance. He admitted to a hidden personal wound: his father Lewis Ellison had been dishonorably discharged by the U.S. Army.[8]

However, Wertham's evaluation did not satisfy the military officials. On Monday, January 29, the draft board rejected the doctor's diagnosis of neurosis. Ellison could not change their minds by arguing that he had paid good money for the psychiatrist's evaluation, or that Wertham had a sterling reputation.[9] Facing the minimum of five years in prison, Ellison began to make arrangements to ship out to sea. For a couple of days, he kept his head in a bottle of whiskey and called on friends. On Friday, February 2, he told Wright that he had heard of seventy-one Negroes sentenced to twenty to thirty years for refusing to join the Army. He stood fast in his rejection of the jim crow military, and thought that perhaps it was better to take a prison term.[10] But ultimately he decided he might do better with the Merchant Marine than with Fort Leavenworth. Ellison jumped aboard a merchant ship near Valentine's Day to escape the MPs coming for him. By February 17, he was aboard a supply ship headed for Le Havre, France. Fanny successfully intervened with the draft board to nullify the standing orders for his capture as soon as he returned to the States. To compound matters, Ellison had to notify his publishers Reynal and Hitchcock that his military duties required him to postpone submitting his manuscript. Ellison would not return to New York until April 1945, about a month before the German surrender.

While Ellison was gone, Wright would bring into his confidence several other young writers, among them the savvy young New Yorker James Baldwin. If Ellison had accepted the occasional condescending assumptions that went along with Wright's friendship, Baldwin did the opposite. Though he was a younger man than Ellison had been when he had initially met Wright, Baldwin took the position of co-craftsman and never yielded ground. A child preacher whose father's funeral was held the week of Harlem's 1943 riot, Baldwin had grown used to scolding his peers and offering worldly advice to much older adults. Unlike most of the people writing about Harlem life, he did not have a scientific or clinical view, but rather one of personal authority, a strength that he recognized and never conceded. He effected a pose of importance in his bearing toward Wright, who was appropriately impressed with the steady confidence of the young man who so clearly was a bohemian. Wright's strong recommendation in July obtained Baldwin the Saxton Fellowship in November, an act of generosity that Ellison mildly resented; he saw Wright as failing him yet again.[11] In the summer, he would go to Kenneth Burke of *Direction,* rather than Richard Wright, for a recommendation for the Rosenwald Fellowship.

Later that year another man entered the circle of New York's articulate black literati. Chester Himes's novel *If He Hollers Let Him Go* appeared in the spring of 1945. The book detailed prejudice in the defense industries in Los Angeles. Himes had developed his craft during a seven-year stint in prison. A nomad until he settled in Paris in the 1950s, Himes had left Ohio, where he had gone to college and later been sentenced to the penitentiary; and he had moved East after several years in California. With the help of his cousin's wife Molly Moon (a connection that had perhaps also enabled his regular contributions to *Crisis* and *Opportunity*), he landed a Rosenwald Fellowship and came to New York to celebrate a book contract with Doubleday. Himes was a loaded pistol. Despite his satisfying marriage, New York City's bacchanalian interracial feast enthralled him. He wrote of his adventures there: "In New York at that time there were many white women who wanted to give me their bodies and I took them. . . . I lost myself in sex and drunkenness."[12] Himes, who had been published by *Esquire* and never shied away from racial themes, fit in fairly easily with Wright, whom he admired, and Ellison, with whom he became close friends. That summer Himes would invite Ellison and Fanny to the vacationing Moon's apartment on St. Nicholas Place for a party.

While he was at sea, Ellison took notes for his airman novel and continued to write criticism. In March, *Tomorrow* published his review of *Escape Thunder* by Lonnie Coleman. Ellison used the review to remind everyone of the inadequate treatment generally accorded to African Americans by Southern novelists, a theme of increasing importance for him. Throughout the year, he compiled notes on the poor treatment of the Negro by American writers, and thought anew about Hemingway's meager treatment of blacks. He also picked up psychological works that helped him understand how the subconscious desires of white writers were satisfied by inadequate portraits of Negroes. Erich Fromm's *Escape from Freedom* and works by Wilhelm Reich were revealing. Reading Reich's psychological studies of libidinal theory and the psychic gratification of fascism, Ellison hoped to track down the subterfuge in the mysterious psychological organization of the white American. As he increasingly understood the dynamics of repression and the transference of complex emotions onto scapegoat groups, Ellison considered the ridiculous images purveyed as authentic reality in the motion picture industry as a window into the probable sort of psychic trauma that demanded the distortion of the black image. He also strongly suspected that Negroes had not been as absent from the American landscape as a cursory glance at American literature proposed. Few white writers were as courageous as Gertrude Stein, who in "Melanctha" had treated a black protagonist with complexity. If white writers as a whole had resisted creating complex African American characters, the idea of the black American, Ellison found, actually thrived in literature priding itself on its absence.

When the March issue of *Tomorrow* appeared bearing his latest review, Ellison was at sea in the North Atlantic. His ship was crossing waters that increasingly had become safe as the Third Reich teetered on collapse (made possible very much by pressure of the Soviet Army, an irony that would not have been lost on Ellison). While he helped in the bakery or prepared meals, Ellison scribbled notes on Red Cross ship's menus. He made notes from Malraux's latest article in *Verve* on the back of cards describing proper procedure if the ship was torpedoed. Docking in bomb-devastated Le Havre, France, and drinking ship water the color and consistency of tomato soup, Ellison had reason to contemplate the nature of mortality and will. He worked conscientiously if not compulsively on his novel about a Tuskegee flyer, scraping together random ideas and thoughts, some of which might not have seemed germane to the project but which greatly sharpened his ideas about his own life and the psychosocial conditioning of the Negro. "When a child he had lived in a storefront glass house on edge of a white neighborhood. Returns to a hole in order to seek relief as that had been his life in a show window."[13] The theme of the man who went underground had surfaced.

On April 6, 1945, Ellison returned from the war zone. He had sailed down the Rhine on an ammunition ship close enough to live fire to watch the enormous hulls of German Tiger Tanks burning out of control near the Cathedral of Rouen. On his nighttime journey overland back down the Le Havre road, GIs had nearly run him over in their Army jeeps.[14] Stateside, he quickly visited Wright with Fanny in Brooklyn on April 8. Although he had returned unscathed, the conversation was dry and uneventful: Ellison was exhausted and Wright was consumed by the upcoming publication of *Black Boy*. Tired and recovering from a stomach illness brought on by the ship's water, Ellison was still worried about the draft board. In the next couple of weeks, he would again have extraordinary difficulty finding work. He was an ex-musician and a former reporter with links to every New York City radical and fringe group, and he had publicly criticized black bourgeois leadership and written scathing reviews of popular Negro writers. Indicative of his exclusion from mainstream events were the successes of his personal whipping boys. Roi Ottley's book *New World A-Coming* was being turned into a motion picture.

The tumult stateside was comparable in some ways to the violent conflict winding down in Europe. That April Jacques Duclos, the secretary of the French Communist Party, wrote a letter vilifying American Communist Party chief Earl Browder. Under Browder's leadership, the CP had advanced the slogan "Communism is twentieth century Americanism." Now major Party theorists rejected the compatible coexistence of socialism and capitalism, and by July, Browder would be ousted.

While he had begun working on a review of Wright's *Black Boy*, which promised to become another blockbuster, Ellison had little to do to make ends meet. His love for Fanny had deepened, and the two began thinking about marriage; in the spring Ellison's divorce from Rose Poindexter went through. But the jobs open to Ellison, still without college credentials, were limited. He turned for work to his friend Add Bates, installing high-fidelity stereo systems, wiring components together and building cabinets.

Ellison's best hope to relieve his financial pressures was to get a Julius Rosenwald Fellowship. At the Hotel Theresa, he had run into Wright's buddy Horace Cayton, the head of the Parkway Community Center and a regular columnist for the black newspaper the *Chicago Defender*. With his encouragement, Ellison completed the application for the Rosenwald funding. Cayton, a friend of grant administrator Edwin Embree, had told Ellison he was likely to get the award. Originally designed to prepare teachers for careers at Southern Negro colleges, the fund had been broadened to afford creative writers an independent year of work. By 1944, the writers Owen Dodson, Waters Turpin,

Langston Hughes, Margaret Walker, and Chester Himes had received monies from the fund.[15] As he typed up his application, Ellison had the chance to think broadly about the future of his career. He hoped first to produce a novel—his book about the Tuskegee-trained airman who, like his character Todd from "Flying Home," struggles to deal with racial caste and identity as the ranking American officer in a prisoner of war camp in Germany. But Ellison also predicted that he had three other books in him—enough, he thought, to make a fulfilling career. He wanted to devote a novel to the study of black leadership, write a book of criticism or "studies in [the] esthetics of Negro art forms," and collect his short stories.[16]

For the first several weeks after his return to New York, Ellison devoted himself to an essay on Wright's new autobiographical work. While most critics had praised it (R. L. Duffus of the *New York Times* called *Black Boy* "poignant and disturbing," authored by "one of the most gifted of America's younger writers"; Lionel Trilling, writing for the *Nation,* called the book "remarkably fine"),[17] W. E. B. Du Bois's review in the March 4 *Herald Tribune* Weekly Book Review had called Wright's undeniably bleak view of black life "unconvincing" as autobiography. At best, Wright had offered a "fictionalized autobiography," rent by its basic "misjudgment of black folk," Du Bois wrote. "But if the book is meant to be a creative picture and a warning, even then, it misses its possible effectiveness because it is a work of art so patently and terribly overdrawn."[18] In part, Ellison wanted to rescue Wright's book from interpretations like Du Bois's, which mischaracterized the intent of the work. Ellison and Wright both believed in the importance of unveiling the inner psyche as a necessary component of black freedom, a theme that Wright had explored fictionally with "The Man Who Lived Underground."

His critique of Richard Wright's *Black Boy,* published in the summer 1945 issue of *Antioch Review,* changed Ellison's career. He brilliantly pitched Wright's work well beyond the crusty Edwardian logic of Du Bois. He delicately showed how Wright had produced a work that surpassed previous standards of honesty and craft for the black writer.

Ellison wrote "Richard Wright's Blues" as an expert and an insider—which is to say as a superbly well educated literary critic who could hold his own against the college professors. In the essay he managed to do two things exceedingly well. He praised Wright's work, as he had always done; but he also advanced a new and uncommon notion: blues lyrics specifically, and the tradition of exaggerative black pessimism in art in general, were the critical entry point to an understanding of black culture on Negro terms. His essay carried on the tradition of Hughes's "Negro Artist and the Racial Mountain" and Wright's "Blueprint for Negro Writing"—artistic manifestos that had carved out spaces for creative movements. One of Ellison's important contributions was to meticulously identify Negro secular and vernacular culture as producing a profound philosophical statement.

"Richard Wright's Blues" showcased Ellison's remarkable mental strength as well as his broad intellectual range. The essay also formally introduced his concept of the role of a blues ideology that was implicit in black life—a historically based collective subconscious that enabled blacks to face and triumph over adversity. Instead of admonishing Wright for expressing a negative perspective of black life, as Ellison had done with realistic writers like William Attaway, he instead focused on the elements of "blues" implicit in Wright's tale as a source of value. "He [Wright] has converted the American Negro impulse toward self-annihilation and the 'going-underground' impulse into a will to confront the world." For the two men, versed in the psychological theories of confrontation and concealment—the axis for both the revolutionary theory and the dramatic tension in their work—the individual's ability to emerge from an indulgence with nurturing cultural rites ("going-underground") in favor of engaging in adult resistance against oppressive forces epitomized freedom. Ellison particularly defended the most controversial passage in Wright's autobiographical narrative, controversial because Wright had stingingly announced the "essential bleakness of black life." In his essay, Ellison almost celebrated Wright's approach: "But far from implying that Negroes have no capacity for culture, as one critic interprets it, this is the strongest affirmation they have. Wright is pointing out what should be obvious (especially to his Marxist critics) that Negro sensibility is socially and historically conditioned."

Ellison found Wright's harsh portrayal daring because he had exposed the baleful influence of environment in shaping black life. Wright wrote in the time-tested vein guaranteed to *épater le bourgeois,* or shake the status quo, even the bourgeois wolves who cloaked themselves in the garments of Marxist sheep. The book obviously had an even more direct impact upon the world of politics. Wright's work erected the popular framework that enabled black social scientists to argue for government intervention in black life on the basis of the damage wrought by slavery and nearly a century of discrimination and segregation. Du Bois's generation had argued against the jim crow railroad car because it forced together blacks of distinction and refinement with those of the lowest class. The argument had shifted following the migration of large numbers of blacks to the urban North. Wright's example of himself violently rejected the Southern stereotype of contented, docile, and affable blacks. But his well-crafted and shocking hostility was meant to be understood also as the creation of the segregated society. With racial integration and social equality, Wright would be mild-mannered, and black people would be in no danger of missing the benefits of Western civilization. Ellison thought that his friend's language was caustic, but his logic foolproof: "Wright learned that it is not enough merely to reject the white South, but that he had to reject that part of the South that lay within. As a rebel, he formulated that rejection negatively." Ellison reasoned that Wright's decision to present the "cultural barrenness of black life" was actually black culture's "strongest affirmation."[19] Wright was heroic because he stressed the process of dissolution, even if *Black Boy*'s final diagnosis was negative.

Leading the chorus lauding the essay was Richard Wright, who would even suggest that Ellison abandon his fictional efforts and become a critic and essayist: "It is the best writing you've done to date. Indeed I'm tempted to feel that you write better prose in non-fiction than in fiction. I'd say that if your novel does not pan out as you plan it, then switch without blinking to non-fiction. I don't think I've read any sharper non-fiction prose by a Negro than was contained in that article."[20]

Writing from Canada, Wright was not overstating the case for the sake of puffing up a friend's ego. Nor did Ellison take him seriously about abandoning his aim at a novel: "I want to give myself as much of a break as you gave *you*rself when you continued to wrestle with the form even after LAWD TODAY and TARBABY'S DAWN."[21] Close behind Wright in their praise were the editorial staff of the *New Republic,* who would offer Ellison a chance to publish in their magazine, an opportunity that became the review-essay "Beating That Boy."

Ellison's support of Wright's dark vision of African American life contradicted his earlier criticisms of black social realist writers. But by advancing the new idea of the blues, he escaped the disciple's snare. The celebratory tenor of the review hid at least one underlying quarrel. Ellison had warned Wright in 1941 that his autobiography would need to reflect deeply on the power of Wright's individual experience. Since he found Wright trying to speak in the broadest terms possible, Ellison spent a good portion of the essay discussing the blues as a philosophical point of departure by which to appreciate fully Wright's book. He knew that Wright, a devoted materialist, found little of interest in the vague theoretical interplay of African American culture. Wright believed that Ellison had "over-rated" the concept of the blues, and perhaps as well, the depth of African American folk life. While praising Ellison's mastery of psychoanalytic concepts, Wright told him that "the blues concept; I do see it, but only very slightly. And surely not enough to play such an important role as you assigned it."[22] Even though Wright had collaborated with Paul Robeson and Count Basie to write the "King Joe Blues" in 1941, he distrusted the elastic folk concept and felt infinitely more at home wielding the explanatory tools of political science and sociology to repair the African American lifestyle, which Wright considered a damaged form of civilization. Certainly he did not believe that black folks were able to overcome the despair of their lives by producing a tragic art form.

Ellison did. He thought of the blues as a folk product performing an emotional and psychological catharsis: "to transcend it [painful details and episodes of a tragic experience], not by consolation of philosophy but by squeezing from it a near-tragic, near-comic lyricism."[23] And here, despite their profound political agreements, the different shaping of the two men's artistic sensibilities came into play. Ellison gravitated toward a description of black cultural behavior that emphasized the power of art. He could do little else. He had emerged from an artistic tradition that began with William Haywood of Avery Chapel A.M.E., went on to Zelia Breaux who cultivated his talent, and was burnished in the fire of William Dawson and Hazel Harrison at Tuskegee. Wright may have known something of black middle-class pretensions toward classical music, as he certainly knew something of the honky-tonk and nightclub; but for him, the art of life lay in the power, not the music, of the word. Though in his review Ellison deliberately downplayed their divergence, the two writers' different perceptions of the horizons and purposes of African American folk life and folk culture gained coherence in the essay. In private, Ellison thought *Black Boy* a deliberate regression in artistic form—almost a kind of propaganda, which Wright had pursued to comment upon the turmoil of his age, not necessarily because he lacked aesthetic appreciation. Most satisfying for Ellison were his telephone conversations with Wright after the essay was published. Wright not only approved of the act of critical friendship, but admitted the essay had "gone way beyond the book."[24]

Wright's words inspired Ellison and restored the two men's allegiance in the short term; after all, the man who had withheld praise in 1940 now extended it. But in the coming months, these feelings would cause a dramatic shift in Ellison's perspective on their relationship. Freed from his reliance upon Wright for intellectual recognition, and given Wright's first acknowledgment of him as an intellectual peer, he felt capable of constructing his own artistic framework. For a man who had for many years been guided by the work and opinions of another, it was an act of liberation, and to a degree, an acceptance of the insecurity and vulnerability that came with freedom.

In November, Ellison wrote a detailed letter to Kenneth Burke, both defending Wright and distinguishing his own approach to art. While he agreed with Burke that there were richer forms of expression at hand, Ellison remained a steadfast adherent to Wright's clarion call denouncing racial injustice. He admitted that Wright's aesthetic tastes were inconsiderable and, using a metaphor from his years as a composer, Ellison thought of his own work as employing the full range of the musical scale, while Wright deliberately had limited his efforts to the blue notes. Also, Ellison understood that his essay "Richard Wright's Blues" had cast the autobiography up against a broader frame of reference and allusion than Wright had originally envisioned. However, Wright's hardboiled prose and searing experiences emphasized an essence of Negro life that black people had usually been too ashamed to admit. By destroying the mechanisms of repression and fear, which previously had held back black frustration, Wright had triumphed.

Speaking freely to Burke, whose achievements Ellison more than admired, he offered his candid and enduring evaluation of Wright's work. In 1945, he saw little room to move beyond a parochial cultural nationalism and into the universal. Awash in the liquid of Wright's expression of black anger, Ellison used Burke's semiotics to steer a course: "The one stable thing I have in this sea of uncertainty is the raft of [Burke's] concepts on which I lie as I paddle my way towards the shore."[25] Ellison still saw the crux of his artistic conundrum as constructing, as he had written in 1944, "the uncreated consciousness of [the black] race."

Along with his emergence in the relationship from the position of subordinate came Ellison's understanding that more and more he would be joined inextricably to Wright. The two men were the frontline intellectual troops of the independent Negro freedom movement, both of them already dreaming of a way to gather an at-large group of public critics who would bring theoretical rigor to the existing knowledge on Negroes in the West and shape the institutions taking that knowledge into the future.

Ellison had been preparing for this role when he took his job with Herndon. *Negro Quarterly* had been quickly recognized as a leader in analyzing race in a global context. After his return from the Merchant Marine, Ellison was an important figure to be consulted on questions concerning art and politics. His friend and patron Ida Guggenheimer strongly recommended Ellison to local politicians as a new and important voice. These included John Connolly, head of the American Labor Party, who requested a briefing from Ellison to learn specifics on Ben Davis (whom the ALP refused to back for New York City Council) and Adam Clayton Powell. Guggenheimer thought so highly of Ellison that she introduced his *Antioch Review* article to Howard University sociologist E. Franklin Frazier.

The *Antioch Review* essay enabled him to share in Wright's glory as *Black Boy* soared onto the best-sellers' list. Ellison was recognized as the leading interpreter of Wright's work. During the summer, he talked with writer and *Pittsburgh Courier* columnist J. A. Rogers about his recent sympathetic review of *Black Boy*. Rogers, too, had defended Wright from Du Bois's condemnation. Ellison now stood at the head of the group of writers, artists, and public intellectuals who demanded an invigorated discussion of race. One time, when passing the West Indian Garveyite Richard B. Moore's bookshop, Ellison smiled happily to himself at the growing crowds glancing curiously at the *Life* magazine photographs of Wright promoting *Black Boy*. Here was part of the equation—public excitement—which might carry over into a more sustained social consciousness.

In late July, he stumbled upon Howard University professor and Communist official Gene Holmes at the Hotel Teresa. Ellison no longer cozied up to Holmes as he had when he was editor at *Negro Quarterly*. After the debacle following Wright's "I Tried to Be a Communist," Ellison was less interested in dialogue; in "Richard Wright's Blues" he had made clear his own decision to part ways with the Communists. Trying to provoke him into a debate, Holmes attempted to pigeonhole Ellison in an artistic camp, if not with the Marxist journal *Science and Society* or the patriotic and multiethnic *Common Ground,* then with Richard Wright. Ellison rebuffed him with a statement that hinted at the new philosophical tendency he would shortly embrace: existentialism. "Wright is by himself. I am by myself. We are individuals."[26]

Not all of the connections he made pertained to his relationship with Wright. Other writers sought Ellison's opinion, including William Melvin B. Tolson, who probably had first met Ellison in 1940 when writing his Columbia master's thesis, which had investigated Harlem's writers. Tolson's book *Rendezvous with America* had just come out toward the end of 1944, and the writer, teaching at Wiley College in Texas, expected Harlem's intelligentsia to have a healthy interest in the poetry, written in the elevated modernist style. But during a conversation in the mid-1940s, Ellison refused him the shelter of naive hope concerning Harlem's progressive artistic community. Tolson wanted to blame the stagnation of black intellectual life on the class dynamic. At the time, he was digesting his first large bites of abstract Marxism, easy to swallow in the sole company of other students at the New York universities. Tolson was intrigued by the Communists and felt uncomfortable connecting them to the low level of intellectual sophistication in Harlem. Ellison responded candidly and with ease, drawing from his own intimate knowledge of the Communists' failures to promote the interests of black workers. Ellison advanced the notion that what was needed was the austerity of mental independence rather than the comforting blindness of obedience to a hierarchical order. Ellison focused upon free will and mastering freedom, even if he had to appropriate the concepts and techniques of reactionary artists or thinkers to produce a model for human existence. Certainly the systems and orders that claimed to offer absolute answers to the problem of human existence through "History," "Science," and "God" were dead. Ellison later commented to Wright that Tolson, who at the meeting had belittled the importance of the modernist poets Eliot and Auden, was in the phase of adulatory Marxism. His tempering of Tolson's enthusiasm afforded Ellison a new perspective on older writers and academics such as Langston Hughes, Morteza Sprague at Tuskegee, and Claude McKay from the Federal Writers Project. Confident and daring, he and Wright now fathered their older peers.[27]

Another episode of discounting the pieties of their elders came shortly after the publication of "Richard Wright's Blues." Ellison's articulation of a subtle philosophy within the black American cultural idiom was a response to the recurring notions among segments of the black intelligentsia of a sort of Jungian racial unconscious. While Ellison was more interested than Wright in the approaches to existence that found expression throughout the blues, Ellison also felt the need to identify a tangible cultural form upon which to base the philosophical claim. This marked him in some manner as an empiricist. The socialist and ex-League of American Writers member William Blake shared with Ellison the most recent outcropping of spirit-like racial chauvinism. Paul Robeson was advocating among his circle that blacks, from either America or Africa, possessed a mystical sensibility for rhythm, music, and art, from which whites were excluded. Ellison and Blake chuckled about the appearance of neo-Garveyism from a wealthy singer, heralded for his academic achievements. Here was a growth that Ellison was bound to reject, even if its proponent was Paul Robeson, and he scoffed at the idea in his regular contact with Wright. "And as for the Davises, Fords, Wilkersons, Yergans, yes, and Robesons, we can laugh those clowns to death."[28]

Near the end of the summer of 1945, when it may have seemed that the bottom was about to fall out of his finances, Ellison received the happy news from the Rosenwald Committee that he had been awarded $1,800 for a fellowship to work on his novel. Fanny had moved into the apartment rented to him by Macedonia Baptist Church around the time he settled back into his life in New York. Now that they had something of a nest egg, in August, Ellison and Fanny McConnell returned to the Bates farm in Waitsfield, Vermont. In theory at least, Ellison went away from the city to recover his health. The escape also offered some solitude and inner self-preservation, and it was a vacation of sorts for the couple, one of their first trips away together. Ellison had tender moments alone with his sweetheart, the woman whom he had introduced to everyone that he knew and respected. On August 6, the dangerous war in Japan neared its bloody finale. A single atomic bomb incinerated tens of thousands of civilians in Hiroshima. Neighbors brought the news of the war developments to the Vermont farmhouse. Three days later, Truman ordered another bomb dropped on Nagasaki, with the Japanese high command left to infer that bombs would next fall on Tokyo. Within a week, the Japanese declared a cease-fire; and in September, they fully surrendered. Ellison's days of running from his draft board had ended, and America emerged from the Second World War as the unquestioned victor.

Ellison labored over his writing pad on the Bates farm near the barn door, observing the Bates children's wild play and marveling at the four-thousand-foot peaks of the Green Mountain range ringing the flawless skyline. The clean air of late summertime in the Vermont hills brought on some salubrious feelings for him and Fanny. Taking dips in the brisk creek for their baths, and munching on fresh cucumbers, potatoes, and wild blackberries (they had no meat), the couple enjoyed deeply the tranquillity of country life. Fanny joked with Ellison that they had to find a helicopter so that they might continue their getaways unimpeded. As casual visitors, they imagined themselves to be Romantic impressionists, like Gauguin, in some exotic locale. When the couple peered more closely, however, they noticed a certain cultural poverty in the furthest outreach of New England. They took in a square dance at a public fair one evening, and Ellison thought the people of Washington County looked bleached-out and anemic, with the numerous small children wearing glasses, an indication of declining community health. Ellison saw this as practically a judgment against the standards of cultural and racial purity. When he and Fanny won the quilt in the raffle and outperformed the locals in square dances that were native to the town, Ellison felt very proud about his own ancestry with its hopelessly tangled racial and cultural roots—a mixture that seemed to him to suggest something quite vibrant and uniquely American.

Farm life in the hills refreshed and inspired Ellison after a couple of days. He was convinced that city life in Harlem was detrimental to the creation of serious literature because politics and people—especially friends like Ida Guggenheimer—constantly interfered. Early in the summer when he was working on the airman novel in his apartment, he enjoyed an interruption or two from a colleague like Stanley Hyman, but Guggenheimer, Henrietta Buckmaster, and other cronies from his League and Communist days left him feeling drained and irritable. Before his Vermont sabbatical, Ellison had changed his telephone number in an effort to curb the distractions, and when Hyman casually shared the number during that summer, an annoyed Ellison gave him both barrels, and again changed his telephone number. Henrietta Buckmaster had been the culprit.[29]

And if the pressure from his wide acquaintanceship was not enough to derail his writing schedule, his escalating travails with the Macedonia Baptist Church's rented property—the second floor of 306 West 141st Street—promised to swallow him completely. At first, the apartment had seemed affordable and decent, resting on the hill off of Seventh Avenue, three blocks north of Striver's Row. Soon enough, though, Macedonia began to make problems for the couple, and that factor combined with the grotesque cries and shouts of Harlem street life made conditions less hospitable to writing fiction. Now the church threatened both a lawsuit and to have the Edison company cancel his electrical service in order to get him out of the apartment. When he returned from Vermont, Ellison would have the bothersome predicament once again of putting a roof over his head in overcrowded Harlem. Moving elsewhere, except perhaps to sections of Brownsville and Bedford-Stuyvesant in Brooklyn, was either unaffordable or made impossible by segregation. Postwar Greenwich Village, once a haven to bohemians and jazz musicians of all races, had lost its tolerance for blacks. Now roving bands of Italian toughs made dangerous the sort of fraternization and ease that had been the area's hallmark during the late 1930s, when Ellison had lived there and studied with Richmond Barthé.

One morning, sitting in the open barn, Ellison eased his pen across the paper and wrote out the lines "I am an invisible man." He often doodled on his writing pads, drawing profiles as if still in Eva Hamlin's art class, and playing free-association games. But these words lingered, and haunted him. In a briefcase, he carried an outline, a sheaf of notes and a couple of typed pages of the novel he had been working on. His hero was a sentient young black pilot who had the mixed fortune to outrank all of the other American officers at a German prison camp. He was even reading Lord Raglan's *The Hero* as research to help him structure the mythic dimensions of his character. But despite the appealing heroism of his character and the timeliness of a war story (Ellison had noted young private Norman Mailer's long story, which became *The Naked and the Dead*), the lines he had just written about invisibility, and the dilemma of existence as a black American, wormed their way into him. Within a couple of days he had the germ of a story, one that resonated most deeply for him, in part because it was his own.

Ellison had encountered the idea of invisibility that summer while reading James Joyce to prepare a lecture that Stanley Hyman had invited him to give at Bennington College, where Hyman had recently gained an appointment. In *Ulysses*, when Stephen Daedelus thinks of his mother, he imagines her hearing a pantomime of *Turko the Terrible*. "I am the boy/That can enjoy/Invisibility."[30] The idea he had encountered in Joyce and the prospect of creating the "uncreated conscience" of his race, combined with the tranquillity he enjoyed in the Green Mountains of Vermont, prompted Ellison to hear and respond to an insistent and demanding fictional voice.

A vault of charged emotions was opened when Ellison embraced the theme of his masterwork. He experienced a cathartic moment, in which he could safely divulge the deep-seated pain that he had carried with him over the years. Dramatic scenes crept into his mind that summer, homegrown and rooted in Ellison's most trying personal moments, in Oklahoma City and at Tuskegee. As was his tendency, he recalled the most poignant and painful memories with humor and irony. He remembered having dogs set upon him walking down the roads—the spectacles, insults, and burlesques of a poor black teenager's life in Oklahoma City. He recalled the dangers he faced onboard the train to college and the violence that almost incapacitated him for his music school audition. He thought most bitterly of losing his scholarship and the charades he endured in the campus Chapel.

Writing the earliest chapters of the novel that bubbled out of him, Ellison could derive satisfaction from the sense that his work was markedly different from Wright's. Although his theme was similar to Wright's, particularly in Wright's *Black Boy* and "The Man Who Lived Underground"—the journey of a black male toward self-conscious possession of his identity in a hostile or indifferent world—Ellison's approach was unique. His work did not necessarily confine itself to protest or struggle, but instead, exaggerated and made spectacular the conjunctions of black and white life, always tuning to a fine pitch the distinction between the misery and the comedy of these episodes. Blending elements of the comic, the tragic, and the absurd, he made it impossible to simply pity the protagonist, and subsequently increased the reader's ability to see beyond racial identity. The narrator was already making his entrance as an ambitious and bright college boy, capable, at points at least, of recognizing and articulating his conundrum. In fact, the narrator was so bright that he would erase Ellison's personal shame; instead of graduating high school at twenty, the narrator is a college junior at nineteen.

The development of the outline occurred fairly rapidly, though it would take Ellison roughly six years to complete the novel, which became his most significant work. After a year he had outlined the first half of the project, and before the end of 1947 he had a fairly coherent idea of how the story should end. Before the end of 1945, he had sketched out versions of the first section, in which an underhanded college president named Bledsoe expels the hero from school. Ellison chose to explore the contradiction of black identity, the idea of a competing and opposite reality that is submerged but rides alongside of popularly recognized poses of existence. The humble Bledsoe was a tyrant; the hero's accommodating grandfather a revolutionary. Here was part of the twelve-toned musical scale he hoped to use in his fictional orchestrations. In Wright's *Black Boy,* the protagonist says, "Negroes too sometimes have those dreams," an understatement that ironically suggests the common humanity of blacks and whites. Ellison took the next step, the assumption of shared dreams among black and white, and made his hero's quest an unflagging pursuit of individual discovery. The strategy was a gamble in an anti-black world.

When Ellison returned to New York in September, he got an assignment from the left-leaning magazine the *New Republic.* It was a coup. On the basis of "Richard Wright's Blues," Ellison was being asked to review books for the important and well-circulated national magazine. The editors for *New Republic* historically were intellectual writers with strong academic interests. The literary historians Malcolm Cowley and Alfred Kazin both had edited portions of the journal. Ellison's October 22 *New Republic* essay-review of Bucklin Moon's anthology *A Primer for White Folks,* called "Beating That Boy," signaled his arrival as a new public figure. At thirty-two, Zelia Breaux's Oklahoma City protégé had become a major success and his attitude was blasé. Of the other black writers even peripherally connected to *New Masses,* not even a handful—mainly those with academic connections—would be able to move onward to reach a broad audience after their *New Masses* days. Ellison had broken with his former comrades over an ideological point, and now he was being courted by what was regarded as one of the heavyweight journals of American politics and literature. Of course, he followed Wright, who earlier had reviewed Carson McCullers's 1940 novel *The Heart Is a Lonely Hunter* for the journal.

Since *A Primer for White Folks* reprinted already published essays on race in America, Ellison's *New Republic* essay was less a review of the work itself than a commentary full of fresh insights on American society. Ellison's essay had little in common with work he had done for *Tomorrow*. He took his title from a popular colloquialism used by blacks and whites to refer to intimate discussions of the racial problem. But despite the use of a vernacular title to establish himself as an insider, at best the racial problem served only as a backdrop to his life. He refused, with the examples of Wright and Himes in his peripheral view, to allow the concern with racial identity to stand in and for itself as a proper spirit of the age.

His tone was that of a singular kind of black writer: humorous, familiar with the Western liberal arts canon, witty, prone to elaborate metaphor, yet swift with his fists. Ellison unseated the voice of social science from its place of primacy in the discourse on American racial policy. He introduced an articulation of the race struggle that was leagues different from Wright's work, which always stressed the punishment meted out to blacks by racism. To move to a deeper level than the concerns of the social worker and sociologist, Ellison called up the traditional dialectical formula for race relations in America: the thesis of white American pioneerism combined with the antithesis of Negro slavery. The union had failed, however, to produce a synthesis of mulatto democracy, due to an ongoing psychological repression in the white unconscious mind. Ellison had satisfactorily meshed the theories of Hegel and Freud, and his self-confidence showed. In the wake of reams of American propaganda celebrating the triumph of democracy over fascism, Ellison looked the hypocrisy of democracy squarely in the eye: "This unwillingness to resolve the conflict in keeping with his democratic ideal has compelled the white American, figuratively, to force the Negro down into the deeper levels of his consciousness, into the inner world." He explored the ideological constraints that kept the acknowledgment of black American oppression from reaching the surface of white America's moral consciousness: "[T]he 'Negro Problem' is actually a guilt problem charged with pain. Just how painful might be judged from the ceaseless effort expended to dull its throbbing with the anesthesia of legend, myth, hypnotic ritual and narcotic modes of thinking . . . even our social sciences and serious literature have been conscripted . . . to drown out the persistent voice of outraged conscience."

The artist's dilemma was greatly magnified in such a cauldron of social self-deception. Just as it was necessary to free blacks, so, too, was it the duty of the responsible artist to come to terms with the processes drowning the "outraged conscience" of white Americans. Instead of giving accurate portrayals, white writers tended to ignore powerful racial material, which consequently became distorted as it was forced down into the deep regions of the mind. Ellison briefly sketched a profile of white American psychological life in a passage for which he would become famous:

> For imprisoned in the deepest drives in human society, it is practically impossible for the white American to think of sex, economics, his children or womenfolk, or of sweeping socio-political changes, without summoning into consciousness fear-flecked images of black men. Indeed, it seems that the Negro has become identified with those unpleasant aspects of conscience and consciousness which it is part of the American's character to avoid.[31]

Ellison here reversed Wright's famous dictum that black life had been grossly limited by white racism. In Ellison's reformulation, instead of blacks being malformed, it was whites who showed the greatest amount of long-term stunted psychological growth. White America, in the pursuit of its lily-white totems of purity, actually exhibited an obsessive-compulsive personality disorder. Ellison offered one of his most trenchant observations, that whites' racial obsession revealed more about themselves than about the object of their obsession.

Stanley Hyman's summer invitation to Ellison to deliver the Bennington College fall lecture further secured his place as a recognized intellectual, a battler for ideas on the American scene. Ellison knew that City College professors had attended Hubert Harrison's Harlem street-corner orations, and he of course had witnessed some of Wright's public debates, radio programs, and disputes with the Communists; but there were few opportunities for black writers and intellectuals to offer public talks at American colleges and universities. He would be speaking as a part of the same series that included the psychologist Erich Fromm and a U.S. Supreme Court Justice. Ellison decided to address Bennington's students on the topic of James Joyce's modern classic *Portrait of the Artist As a Young Man,* while at the same time exploring the work of the genius and enfant terrible Richard Wright. He was also eager to say in public things about the Negro that he had been unable to publish—his opinion of Gunnar Myrdal's *American Dilemma,* for example. He prepared his talk throughout October, enjoying the pressure and amassing more research than he could deliver.

Comfortable with an arsenal of weapons—literary criticism, psychology, sociology, anthropology—Ellison could devastate, when he wanted. He disliked

Edmund Wilson's flip dismissal of Malraux, who in *Twice a Year* had recommended a process of intellectualization for American literature. Ellison let fly his new weight in a letter to Hyman and chastised the doyen of pedigreed American critics and artists who had cast their lot with the Left after the First World War. To Ellison's mind, Wilson had in his career ranged from artist, to critic, to Freudian convert, and had finally, in effect, lost all bearing on judgments of art and politics. Ellison's growing temerity caused him to examine coherently his relationship with Communists, whose public flagellation of *Black Boy* was countered by private words of approval and praise. Ellison told Hyman in the letter that Sam Sillen and Isadore Schneider—men whose critical minds Ellison had admired—had disgraced themselves by faulting Wright's work. Their duplicity was so open that he had a difficult time seeing anything positive in the relationship with these men, which had stretched on for nearly eight years. In fact, he thought of himself as one who had bargained with a mob of lynchers, whose perversion of socialism had disfigured the philosophy as awfully as Nazi crematoriums had incinerated European Jewry. During the years Browder transformed the Communist Party USA into the Communist Political Association, and dissolved the party in the rapidly industrializing South, Ellison determined he had been witness to a slick job of political deception. "Browder ran the nag down a cliff, broke its legs and left it moaning in the shallow water; Forster has told it the bones have mended, shot it full of dope and God knows what'll happen now."[32]

On Thursday, November 1, at 7:30 P.M., at the Bennington College Theater, after a daylong train ride, Ellison walked onto the stage of the all-women campus to give his talk, "American Negro Writing: A Problem of Identity."[33] It was his first large public lecture; and writing afterward for the Associated Negro Press, Marjorie Green made news of the lecture, heralding Ellison as a "brilliant young Negro writer . . . fast becoming one of the outstanding reviewers on the American literary scene."[34] Ellison touched on the main currents of black literature beginning with Phillis Wheatley, and he detailed the ideological choices or affinities of each generation of writers. His main point was to rebuke the Harlem Renaissance generation for their excessive primitivism, and to propose that Wright was "the most important thing to happen to Negro writing since the days of Douglass."[35] Negro writing now concerned itself with the psychological, which was the proper avenue for "defining the true nature of Negro personality and Negro culture." He emphasized the importance of Wright's autobiographical turn because it emphasized self-consciousness in black writing and the tendency toward greater artistic achievement. Wright's work prepared the stage for the modern black writer, who doubled as something of a prophet. Ellison saw writers as people "for whom all stable values have become fluid . . . faced with manifold possibilities"; their task was to crystallize those values.

Fanny had accompanied him to Bennington, and the couple were housed in the Guest Suite of the Commons. The next afternoon, Ellison took over Hyman's class and offered a discussion of Joyce's *Portrait of the Artist* and Wright's *Black Boy.* Fanny took shorthand notes. While Ellison's work was interesting enough to gain him a student or two whose theses now included Wright, faculty member Leonard Brown also sat in on this early foray of Ellison's into the academic world. Ellison spoke convincingly of the repressive force that had formed each writer—the Catholic Church and the feudal South—and the subsequent images that were meaningful to both men as symbols of freedom. Especially important were both writers' decisions to encase themselves within their national ethnic identities as the first step toward transcending those identities.

In the December edition of *New Republic,* Ellison received more public recognition. It was clear that the ideas he had put forth in his October essay were powerful and stimulating. The editor and literary critic Thomas Sancton gave him due credit. Speaking of "Beating That Boy," Sancton wrote, "Ralph Ellison's two page review . . . seems a little high-powered to this reader, but the second page is as profound a passage of literary criticism as I have seen in the New Republic."[36] Sancton elaborated on Ellison's use of Hemingway as an example of botched values and mores, and pointed to writers who were as driven by their commitment to values as they were to technique. While he appreciated the praise, Ellison thought to himself after reading Sancton's piece that if he wasn't careful and speedy, he might lose his important theme. In a letter to Hyman in mid-December, he downplayed the threat, fastening to himself the armor of understatement. Sancton had had only an empathetic insight into "Beating That Boy." However, Ellison allowed to Hyman that seeing his ideas used by another critic had turned up the heat; it was time for him to polish off his book of cultural criticism.[37] He wanted dearly to assert himself as an intellectual, as a critic—but essays took time away from novels. Ellison could be tenacious—as he was on December 11 when he disputed his rent payments with Macedonia Baptist at the Office of Price Control—and the same gritty tenacity added weight to his criticism and literacy theory. Still, that month when he viewed Leni Riefenstahl's film *Triumph of the Will,* a Nazi masterpiece in the examination of ritual, ceremony, and mass psychology, the movie drove home for him the power of the patiently derived artistic effort. In 1946, Ellison would try to stand equally in the camps of the artists and the critics.

12

African American Thoreau

1946

By THE END OF 1946, Ralph Ellison had pulled further away from the Harlem community of writers and intellectuals, a parallel to the departure of his friend Richard Wright, who moved temporarily, and then permanently, away from the United States. Ellison did not return to Waitsfield, Vermont, where he had summered in 1944 and 1945, but he did regularly leave New York City for the pastoral Long Island retreat of Westhampton. His physical distance from Harlem concretized a pivotal decision. It amounted to determining who was the important audience for his work. He had told Kenneth Burke in November of 1943 that the important artistic achievement lay in demolishing the stereotypes and caricatures that white Americans used to keep the humanity of black Americans at bay.[1] At the end of World War II, after viewing the rubble of Europe firsthand and experiencing the collapse of the American communist movement at home, Ellison had decided to leave the protective walls of his familiar community. Like Thoreau, who had decided a hundred years earlier to leave Walden Pond to take up the fight for abolition, Ellison left the cloister of Harlem, the Communist Party, and his critic's post at the liberal and leftist journals where he had been successful.

In 1946, Ralph Ellison would change his vocation from art critic to artist. He would be reborn in the broadest possible terms as a fiction writer consumed by the great artistic and philosophical issues of his era, and the year 1947 would celebrate his international arrival as the fiction writer sensation of his generation. Having left behind the Communist-inspired literary magazines, Ellison made his way into the social mainstream, where, despite the temptation to continue with his early success as a critic, he decided that he could flourish as an artist. Contributing to widely circulated magazines and popular book publishing houses was, he had increasingly rationalized, the only way to assure their transformation. Entering the prime of his adult years, Ellison also listened for guidance more closely with his childhood ear, and respected his own craving for polite society and high artistic achievement. While he had not the resources to display quite chesterfieldean elegance, Ellison's days among the déclassé were close to an end, not too coincidentally, with the formal end of the Depression. Ellison was ready to move beyond his earlier roles as assistant to Angelo Herndon and Richard Wright, black men who had become celebrities by corralling liberal support. Ellison hoped for a different sort of triumph: a success that while not necessarily refusing liberal largesse, would enable him to stand as an independent artist and not the icon of a social movement.

Ellison's postwar transformation was not accomplished in isolation, but rather was made possible by a consolidation in his life. Arguably the single greatest event that occurred in Ralph Ellison's life in 1946 had nothing whatsoever to do with literature—unusual for a man who had committed his life, in the face of unrelenting pressures, to fine arts and scholarship. In late August of that year, he married his live-in partner Fanny McConnell Buford. His connection to Fanny—a connection whose intimacy reached the highest intellectual and emotional planes—catapulted his art to a higher level. For one thing, she was a partner and a sounding board for his composition; she was concerned with his interests and was astute and polished enough to promote them well. After he had written out his chapters in flourishing cursive longhand, Fanny typed the manuscripts. Her steady income was as responsible for the creation of the novel *Invisible Man* as Ellison's artistic genius and his determined ambition. During the 1940s, she worked as a secretary at the Astoria Press, the Parish Press, and the Liberal Press. Convinced of her husband's talent, she kept regular business hours while Ellison embraced the uneven process of creation. Perhaps one element contributing to their harmony during these lean years when they defied conventional gender roles was the fact that they remained childless.

Fanny also was not white; she had none of the blindness that came from white privilege, nor did she have the notion to placate a man she felt had been unjustly disturbed by race. And unlike Ellison's writer friends—his agent Volkening or friend Stanley Hyman or Richard Wright—she didn't display the petty jealousy or carping that came from unconscious competition with another writer. In fact, Fanny was deeply impressed by her new husband. She thought he was one of the most talented men she had ever met. Her words and her encouragement emerged from Fanny Ellison's own desires to see her confident friend and lover succeed, and perhaps also to see his own personal sufferings relieved. She saw a side of him that was hidden from the world, and this gave Ellison the kind of emotional shelter necessary to achieve proper artistic distance from his work. Ellison's marriage to Fanny—a woman so familiar with his literary world and tendencies that she took over much of his literary correspondence by the mid-1960s—sealed an emotional and intellectual connection of primal importance.

An early sign of Ellison's revitalized feelings about the nature of his American experience came with a follow-up in *New Republic* to his praised review "Beating That Boy." Ellison landed again in America's premier weekly of art and politics on February 18, 1946, with a short piece called "The Booker T.," a review of John Beecher's book on the Merchant Marine. Always keeping a sharp eye on the violent racial tensions underneath the surface of American public life, Ellison called for an end to the repression of conflict in books about black and white life. He faulted Beecher for "omitting even that normal interracial conflict which at this stage of historical development is the dynamic health of American democratic institutions."[2]

In the couple's apartment on 141st Street, Ellison wrote drafts of an ultraviolent "Battle Royal" short story, a fight to the finish where his hero is brutalized by whites for their own entertainment. For the writer who had experienced explosive racial tension aboard Merchant Marine craft, suppressing the subject of physical violence was an attempt to give a false picture of health to Americans while burying deeply the cancerous tumor.

With the publication of this new review, Ellison had reason to be impressed with himself. Now his name appeared in the list of contributors alongside those of other professional craftsmen: the famous "New Critic" John Crowe Ransom, a Bennington English professor, and a fellow writer contracted by Reynal and Hitchcock.

Ellison's movement toward such mainstream publications as the *New Republic* was fortuitous. The week prior to his review, the novelist Albert Maltz had written in *New Masses* that the tortured conscience of the artists who wanted their art to perform political miracles resulted in "wasted writing or bad art." Maltz, a confirmed radical, laid the blame for the poor work of many of his generation on the "intellectual atmosphere of the left wing,"[3] one indication among many that postwar America would soon end its flirtation with the Left.

If Harlem was Ellison's ironic Walden Pond—the nagging, contentious home ground that fueled his critical abilities—then his Harlem reviews of 1945, "Richard Wright's Blues" and "Beating That Boy," had been, like Thoreau's *Civil Disobedience,* direct critical attempts to combat the contemporary order of things. His interventions had redeemed Wright's blistering work from some of its critics by elevating it theoretically. He had transformed the understanding of Bucklin Moon's anthology, *A Primer for White Folks,* by way of a delicate exposure of white American subconscious motive.

Ellison was advancing his artistic theories in the face of deplorable American race relations, which reached a midcentury nadir with the return of black troops to the South. Ellison's enduring pessimism throughout the war about the life chances of black veterans had been prescient. He and Wright had commiserated over the situation throughout the hostilities. Before the end of the summer, he could update Wright, abroad in France, that the lynchings of black American servicemen had broken out all over the South.[4] In North Carolina, for daring to wear the uniform of Uncle Sam, one veteran sergeant had his eyes gouged out by police wielding nightsticks. Riots, beatings, maimings, and lynchings shook the country, but they were not met with the organized black resistance that had marked the troopers' return from World War I in the late 1910s. In the South, as a group, black veterans encountered the same grim determination to uphold white supremacy that had greeted their fathers' generation more than twenty-five years earlier—the same racial supremacy that the vets had risked their lives to defeat in Germany and Japan. The irony of the situation increased its tragedy and bared America's unique racial myopia.

While he and Wright used each other as sounding boards to properly "beat the boy," Ellison kept racial bitterness out of his conversations with whites. His ability to engage whites both intellectually and as fellow writers without contempt or hostility had an effect. Increasingly, Ellison began to see "that boy" as a personal struggle against chaos and social isolation. Whites took him more seriously when he articulated the primary problem of existence as an individual dilemma, and when he told personal anecdotes emphasizing his own triumphs and the contradictions of existence—tales which in effect served to pierce their shield of stereotypes. And he was turned to as a voice of wisdom and intelligence for his catholic perspective. In the early winter of 1946, through an arrangement by Ida Guggenheimer, Ellison gave a series of lectures on literature and Negro American identity as part of a larger program involving Harlem's most prestigious public intellectual, the librarian and lone Negro City College professor of history L. D. Reddick, and the increasingly renowned Howard University sociologist E. Franklin Frazier.[5] In such company, Ellison concluded that racism was a primitive social ritual designed to establish group identity. He saw man's persecution of the scapegoat as a simple attempt to control, completely, one element of the environment because so much else of the natural world was chaotic and feral.

His evolving approach to the interlocking set of values and beliefs that constituted racial oppression stemmed not only from his associations with a handful of black Ph.D.s. The flower of Europe's intellectual class had come to New York, many of them German Jewish refugees, and the word of the day was psychoanalysis as a response to human pain and suffering. The New School of Social Research in Greenwich Village featured many well-known left-leaning professors, including Erich Fromm, whom Ellison may have met the previous fall at Bennington. The newly created college's real strength was in the comparatively new field of psychology, and among the faculty were people who had known Freud.

The postwar vogue for psychoanalysis originated with refugee academics desirous of curing the Western mind by exposing humanity's inability to confront the challenge of freedom. While German-Jewish refugee academics like Theodore Adorno and Max Horkheimer, traveling around Hollywood in the middle of 1945, were skeptical about the ability of scientific and philosophical rationalism to heal the breach in Western humanism exposed by war and the concentration camps, the order of the day for such intellectuals as the brilliant Hannah Arendt was to use their work to stamp out vestiges of authoritarianism and to uphold America as a land of freedom and possibility. Before the end of the decade, former liberal allies of the Communists were shifting to a pro-American stance. Arendt's and other respected thinkers' complete repudiation of Stalin's purged Soviet Union forcefully linked Nazi Germany and the USSR; they were different sides of the same totalitarian coin. After experiencing the American Communist Party's chicanery and Janus-faced maneuvers, culminating in its dissolution in 1945, Ellison found vital the psychological analyses of the human pursuit of punishing social orders and rigid racial hierarchies. He also was observing firsthand an important model of cultural assimilation with the increasing predominance and public acceptance of a circle of Jewish intellectuals whose ties to the Old World—obliterated in the war (and the gas chambers)—stamped them with a sense of purpose and agency, and gave them a culture of writing and thinking unmatched in the middle of the twentieth century.

Ellison observed this group scaling the heights of American culture, achieving a success that did not necessarily include him, and with which he did not feel entirely comfortable. Saul Bellow—regarded by even his successful peers as a singular prodigy[6]—would publish *The Adventures of Augie March*, a novel whose concluding anthem compared the protagonist to Christopher Columbus, around the same time as Ellison's *Invisible Man*. The self-taught Chicagoan Augie March's ambition to see a valuable comparison between himself and Columbus stood for a gritty vernacular optimism that Ellison might have craved, but one which he saw as foolish to adapt. Ellison determined to make his own novel a political allegory, with the same trenchant power of any of the fiction published or reviewed in *Partisan Review,* and layered with the depth and richness of Negro American culture. To remain optimistic and to keep his standards high required fortitude. That winter, Ellison braved the cold and haunted Dick Moore's bookshop in Harlem or the Gotham Book-mart, reading the latest literary journals—the *Partisan, Antioch, Kenyon,* and *Sewanee.* As he picked his way through the latest adventures in art, craft, and criticism, Ellison had reason for more than just ordinary anxiety. Most press-ing was the fact he had signed a contract to submit the airman manuscript by the end of 1945, and instead he had focused his energies on his new project called *Invisible Man.*

Ambling up and down Seventh Avenue in 1946, Ellison noticed many other young men who seemed to be on the outskirts of American society. The blatant resistance of the bebop generation to the draft reflected the dismissal of aspirations toward middle-class respectability. The movement's iconogra-phy—zoot suit, sunglasses, wide-brimmed hat, knob-toed shoes, and distinc-tive argot—became so forceful that it transcended the exclusive nature of bop music and African American culture and began to stand for something of broader social significance, American counterculture. The urban hipster move-ment was an early and articulate in-group voice disparaging the blind pursuit of the middle-class dream for blacks in urban America; certainly it was the first coherent group of styles and ideas to emerge from the black urban land-scape. But most of the city did not read the refulgent symbolism of the youth as a profound social statement on the nature of urban Negro identity. The most penetrating analyses viewed the hipster style as indicative only of the degree of alienation among Harlem's young—that and something else. The cultural distance evoked by the hipster style became a convenient explanation for the astronomical rates of black juvenile delinquency. Constituting less than ten percent of the population, African American youth accounted for more than fifty percent of all juvenile offenders in New York City.

Ellison and Richard Wright still had the 1943 newspaper headlines label-ing Harlem the denizen of hoodlums fresh in their minds, and they talked about novel approaches to curb delinquency, with terms like "free-floating hostility," "personality disorganization" and "metaphysical wholeness" pep-pering their conversations. They needed a way to broadcast the real problem, which they saw as the collapse of traditional rural values among black migrants once they arrived in the urban North. To effectively combat the problem—which was difficult even to diagnose properly given a public climate rife with discussions of black genetic predisposition to criminality—the two writers determined to use their intellectual insights and other resources to help pre-vent juvenile waywardness. Wright lent his considerable prestige and Ellison his legwork to founding an institution. Psychoanalysis was in vogue at the time, and Wright's gambit to help open a psychiatric clinic was a natural step, after all. The lifelong theme of his work was black youth traumatized by prejudice. Wright's friend, the progressive psychiatrist Dr. Frederic Wertham, expressed interest in offering his psychoanalytic skills to Harlem, and with the help of Earl Brown, an *Amsterdam News* reporter, the men established a free psychiatric center under Wertham's leadership.

The LaFargue Mental Hygiene Clinic opened its doors on March 8, 1946. Ellison had asked Episcopal Bishop Shelton Hale for permission to use the basement of the parish house of St. Philips Church at 215 West 133rd Street, two damp rooms accessible only through a dingy, refuse-strewn alleyway. There was simply no other space in overcrowded rent-exploiting Harlem to house a free clinic. The LaFargue's aims reflected the ambition of psychoanalysis during the 1940s. The modestly begun clinic featured Wertham and several of his former students as well as Andre Tweed, one of only eight black American psychologists in the United States. They operated two nights a week out of the parish basement, ministering to the needs of old and young, black and white, charging twenty-five cents to those who could afford it (fifty cents if the patient required a court appearance) and nothing to those who could not. Psychoanalysis was considered a scientifically verifiable advancement in the study and cure of the mind, and like a college education, it was not yet available to the general public. Wertham hoped to use the clinic to deter juvenile delinquency—one of his broad aims, as attested to by *Dark Legend,* his monograph-length study of one wayward young person. Psychiatric techniques and the study of the mind promised an understanding of the nebulous subconscious, an advance for human social interactions, and a solid plank in a progressivist future. Finally, here was a tool that might combine the objective findings of the biologist and neurologist with a perspective that accounted for environment and social orientation.

Paul LaFargue was a nineteenth-century Afro-Cuban physician who had married into the family of Karl Marx. LaFargue had valiantly crusaded against injustice, and the Harlem clinic named for him treated mental health disorders in order to heal the wounds created by a racist society. As Wright and Ellison reached artistic maturity, justice meant not only destroying the forces of oppression, but healing psychic wounds, especially those suffered by the black poor. The basement clinic attempted to address the psychosocial problems that were being neglected by the American psychological community. Most white psychiatrists and psychologists, whatever their personal beliefs about Negroes, refused to offer services to blacks for fear of losing other white clients. For Ellison, the existence of LaFargue, the need for it to operate in a democratic society, signaled America's ongoing incapacity to redress racial injustice. He began to term racism "ethical schizophrenia." The pathology did not limit itself to whites. Following the war, Ellison noted that the streets of Harlem were filled with "free-floating hostility," a new psychological term for a near-predatorial attitude that was foreign to the black American South, where black relationships had always been marked by gregariousness and amiability—even when that custom was self-serving and designed to ensure conformity.

The rest of New York soon looked to the clinic as a form of salvation. The press, previously silent on the paucity of mental health care options available to black Americans, loudly applauded the effort as a success. Wright's liberal friend and supporter Dorothy Norman gave the clinic high praise in her *New York Post* column "Help for the Troubled in Harlem," writing that the clinic gave proof that "the impossible is still possible."[7] Even the mainstream press accepted the value of the clinic: "One month's intensive operation has proved that Harlem's high rates of delinquency and nervous breakdown stem not from biological predilections toward crime existing in Negroes, but from an almost total lack of community services to cope with the problems of Harlem's individuals."[8]

In early April, Wright asked Ellison to write up a page-long treatment of the history and aims of the clinic as envisioned by the founders. Wright himself was working on a longer piece describing the purpose of the clinic. Ellison thought by 1946 of "urgent action"—his solution for the dire situation in Harlem—as the direct application of a social science technique like psychiatry. Whereas political protest may have been his mantra during the first half of the decade, now he saw the direct treatment of actual wounds as also important.

Even though he was involved in the important work of the clinic, the business of writing continued to demand Ellison's best efforts. Every year presented him with another competitor, and Ellison felt keenly the inroads upon his time caused by his activism. In January, Doubleday threw a book party to celebrate Chester Himes's new novel about segregation in the war industries, *If He Hollers Let Him Go.* The success of newcomer Himes spurred Ellison's efforts on his own book.

Not too far into the year, Ellison and Fanny moved from Macedonia Baptist's contested apartment to the ground floor of 749 St. Nicholas Avenue, a place with a backyard large enough to accommodate dogs. The couple started raising a couple of Scotch terriers. The apartment complemented Ellison's vision of the black world; from his steps he could look down into the valley of Harlem and check the pulse of the black United States, while immediately to the east he could see the rise of City College. It was the quintessence of urban living, but over the years it exacted a high price. From the mid- through the late 1940s it became increasingly difficult for him to perform his daily labors at the typewriter when he had to wage war with berserk drunks who crowded the alleyway and rear of the ground-floor apartment. His midday reverie at the typewriter was constantly interrupted by loud arguments, singing, and crying, that ricocheted off the tall apartment building to the east and lingered in the air. By 1949, when the noise from a second floor soprano practicing overhead became unbearable, he would turn up the stereo full blast to drown her out, selecting records for the duel that would demonstrate the flaws of the upstairs soloist.[9] Ralph Ellison walked Harlem now with his dogs, and there were times when he'd come in and besotted neighbors, idling on the adjacent stoop, would inspect him for faults. One woman, eyes cloudy with grog, wondered aloud if he was not a sweetback living off "jellyroll."[10] Though amused, he began sequestering himself further, as it became plain that the task of writing penetrating intellectual fiction required the life of a recluse.

While his successful buddies seemed capable of conceiving and executing book-length works, Ellison worried over his entire project, to the point where he became reticent about even discussing it. He wrote quickly, and ideas popped into his consciousness with such speed that he frequently scribbled his notes while on the subway or at a lunch counter, tearing off the end of an envelope or a receipt, to keep the freshest ideas from fleeing. After collecting notes, he'd write them out on sheets of legal paper and sometimes transfer these ideas to the typed page.

At the time, Ellison's publisher, Reynal and Hitchcock, was experiencing some internal dissension that eventually would lead to the departure of editor Albert Erskine and promotional agent Frank Taylor. As a result, Ellison escaped editorial supervision; in fact, the publishers almost forgot him entirely. In early March, his literary agent Henry Volkening wrote to him requesting to be let in on the "little secret" of Ellison's feelings about his relationship with his publishers, and perhaps as well, the little secret of how his novel would end. The truth behind the matter, which Ellison may not have shared with Volkening, was that Ellison considered Erskine and Taylor valuable enough to his project to follow their move to Random House. After all, so few people understood what he was attempting to do with *Invisible Man,* anyway. When Peggy Hitchcock from Reynal and Hitchcock wrote to him requesting basic biographical information and a sense of the forthcoming chapters, he mailed her a detailed note sharing his vision of the novel. Ellison believed that he was writing an allegory of black American life that would resonate chiefly in the realm of politics. The Invisible Man's plight would show the maddening inconsistency of black politicians and the general crisis of black leadership. Since Ellison gravely doubted the ability of a typical white reader to accept certain obvious inferences regarding Negro characters, he explained to Hitchcock, he hoped to have the novel operating on enough different levels— psychological, literary, ritualistic, mythic, historical, and so on—"as to make it difficult for the reader to escape my meaning." And though he had generated a theory for the novel, he was unsure what it would resemble on the page.

In the conclusion of the letter he admitted that he had only come but so far: "the end, the climax, evades me."[11] But if Ellison needed fuel to rekindle his creative imagination, the success of other writers known to him spurred him on. By May 17, when he attended the American Academy of Arts and Letters ceremony honoring Langston Hughes, Richmond Barthé, Kenneth Burke, and Negro America's young poetic sensation Gwendolyn Brooks, Ellison could impress Hughes with the sheer intellectual ambition of his project. Certainly seeing the recognition given to old friends like Hughes and Barthé, and his intellectual beacon Burke, made the fulfillment of his own artistic goals imperative and within reach. Even if no one at the prestigious American Academy knew the Oklahoma City boy's name, or if they didn't care for his pointed opinions, there was no doubt that he was one among a group of recognized artists and achievers. If Ellison himself needed tangible proof, he got it when Hughes invited him to speak at a series of lectures at the New School in the spring of 1947, regretting that he couldn't arrange for Ellison to speak that fall at a lecture series called "Invitation to Learning."[12]

By June 1946, the *New Republic* had run a piece on the clinic (after rejecting the article Richard Wright had been working on) and had created the idea of a "Wertham Circle." Reporter Ralph Martin cheekily implied that Ellison and Wright were involved in a social and artistic movement that was headed, of course, by the clinic's leading white figure, Wertham. Ellison had always been suspicious of people who were quick to make him a disciple of Richard Wright's, and in a letter to his friend Stanley Hyman he repudiated the idea of a group, and of any special association with the psychiatrist. Ellison thought his connection peripheral; as for Wertham, he called the good doctor a friend of Wright's.[13]

Ellison nevertheless took advantage of the significant resource, frequently wandering over to the LaFargue to engage Wertham in speculative conversations about psychoanalysis. He wondered aloud to Wertham about "what effect the removal of sympathetic nervous system would have on personality."[14] The psychiatrist, on the other hand, suggested taking a close look at urban populations for problems in coping with racism: "The psychiatric problems of Negroes are much more serious in the North than in the South. Why not face it right here? It is the contrast between the rural and urban civilization again. The exploitation of Negroes in the South is a very direct and brutal one. In the North, it is very insidious—half concealed—and in the long run really much more ruthless and deadly."[15]

Wertham's insight into the effects of Northern race prejudice on blacks brought him into the discussions with Ellison's theoretically inclined friends, who now gathered at the clinic on occasion for talks. Part of Wertham's appeal to the writers was his modesty and frankness. Instead of holding himself up as a modern-day abolitionist wielding the progressivist sword of psychoanalysis, he saw contemporary psychiatry as "over glamorized and over-publicized at a time when actually it is at a low ebb with respect to both scientific progress and humane application."[16]

The photographers' bulbs were still flashing around the clinic when Ellison hid himself in the village of Quogue, Long Island, in the middle of May. Ellison had left New York to accomplish serious writing a few weeks after Richard Wright's first departure for France. Wright had gone to Paris as a guest of the French government in the last week of April, and his departure had all the air of a clandestine operation by a foreign power. Having received minimal assistance from the U.S. State Department, Wright had to make an eleventh-hour journey to Washington, D.C., for his passport. He communicated with no friends or supporters until his announcement of the pier from which his ship would sail, and he indulged in his favorite game of testing of friends with purportedly secret information. While the causes of Wright's anxiety were real—his movements were monitored by the F.B.I.—friendship with Wright was not particularly easy, and could be emotionally unsettling. And Ellison found Wright's behavior contradictory for someone who was upset over the system of racial abuses. One afternoon in New York they had been roughly jostled by a passing cab while making their way to the Gotham Book-mart. Ellison's reaction was to get the driver out of the car and into the street; Wright hung back, giving Ellison pause to wonder about the Mississippian's courage.[17] While Ellison believed in the truth of Wright's work and found him especially well-read and interested in psychology, during Wright's last full year in the United States, Ellison had become reluctant not only to share fiction but even to discuss popular books and social theories with Wright. Ellison now was more comfortable with others for intellectual discussions.

If he was prepared in some respect to distance himself from Richard Wright, Ellison had even more reason to see a gap between himself and other former colleagues. The staff of the *New Masses,* the Communist-run journal where he had learned the writer's trade, tried to lure him back into the fold. They were on the verge of a major transformation into *Masses and Mainstream*—an overt attempt by the Party to assimilate into the main currents of American public thought—but Ellison rejected them less on the basis of their desire to ingratiate themselves into Truman-era politics and society than on their public abandonment of black rights, a move for which he would never forgive the American Communists. When his former comrades from the *New Masses* made overtures to republish his early work, he snubbed them.[18] His triumphs with the *New Republic* and at Bennington proved that he might slip the yoke of racial limitations without the continued assistance of the hard Left. And Ellison's place in elite writing circles continued to improve by increments. By June, he could justify somewhat his self-imposed austerity at his Long Island retreat. With his first appearance in *Saturday Review of Literature,* reviewing Era Thompson's memoir *American Daughter,* he had achieved the seal of public respectability.

Thompson's book had been well promoted, a signal that modern America was prepared to ease racial boundaries for those blacks who denied the legacy of racial injustice. Ellison torpedoed the Midwestern black woman's autobiography, which was almost a point-by-point refutation of Wright's *Black Boy:* "It would be a mistake to take 'American Daughter' as a serious contribution either to American biography or to the rising discussion over the damaging effect of our system of race relations upon Negro personality and our democratic health. It should be read as one Negro's point of view, not as a refutation of the validity of the view held by others."[19]

Thompson had authored not a compelling version of race and American culture, Ellison wrote, but only a "stepchild fantasy." His article scratched the surface of an underlying problem. The speedy publication of a work that countered Wright's politics also served as a reminder of the ambivalence of art as a means of social protest. The real power of Wright's work lay in its ability to evoke the coarse and easy emotion of pity. But Wright's narratives of black suffering were neutralized by the black heroes like Thompson or George Washington Carver, whose documented lives fundamentally contradicted the notion of a racially punitive society and appealed to the easy-to-reach and equally coarse white American vanity and self-congratulation. The futile seesaw between black critics of and adherents to the "American way," however, supported Ellison's own theories on the purpose of art. The successful high artistic achievement, because it penetrated the layers of simple emotional defenses and reached the core of belief, remained one of the few means to sustain a lasting critique, or to change fundamentally the manner in which an idea or social value was understood.

Not long after Wright's May departure, at the Hotel Theresa Ellison ran into the playwright Ted Ward, who, like other Chicago black artists, had turned bitterly against Richard Wright. Still a member of the Communist Party, Ward had not seen Ellison in years. Ward and others judged Wright a pariah, partly on the basis of his publication in the Hearst-owned media of "I Tried to Be a Communist." Early in their conversation, Ellison found his former political ally and artistic mentor to be smug and blazing with the predictable rhetoric of the Communist Party. Within a couple of minutes, however, Ward cooled his guns. With their feet on the brass rail, and after Ward downed several whiskeys, his tough veneer faded and he slowed his jousting with the younger man. In a letter to Wright, Ellison described Ward's messy confession. Ward admitted that he had been alienated from the party's wartime policy of minimizing racial injustice. But he had seen no other choice than to resign himself to the sometimes uncomfortable transformations in communist ideology, even if the shifts threatened him with personal and financial ruin. Doubting himself now, Ward had decided to leave his thinking to the party bureaucrats. Then it was Ellison's turn to be hard. Ward's capitulation made Ellison think less of him; he suggested to Wright that Ward's physical dishevelment—everything from the obvious effects of booze to his rapid aging—were examples of a suicide attempt. If ever a fraternity of black leftwing political actors and artists had undertaken a unique mission in Manhattan in the late 1930s and early 1940s, that group's day had passed. But mainly Ellison saw the encounter with Ward as another example of his successful arrival as an artist to be reckoned with. Ward's views had shifted, signaling the changing of the guard. When they finally put their drinks down he had shown careful regard and consideration of Ellison's ideas.[20]

Ellison tried to spend his weekends in New York with Fanny, leaving behind the solitude of Long Island. In an occasional letter from Wright, he heard descriptions of the state of French literary and intellectual affairs. In Paris, Wright had met Sylvia Beach of the famous bookstore *Shakespeare and Company,* and he had lunched with his hero Gertrude Stein. Ellison competed against Wright's descriptions of French heritage and legacy with his own expositions of American efficiency and mechanical progress. He mentioned to Wright the gems of America's emerging postindustrial society: indoor light switches and toilets that operated without any annoying noise and the wonders of the electric refrigerator. Curiously enough, in Ellison's increasing distance from Wright's disparaging view of the United States, one of the sources of independence developed around Ellison's fondness for the technological advancements of American culture.

His relationship with Wright was almost always on his mind, since accusations, hearsay, and humble queries about Wright were rampant among literary New Yorkers. In July at a party with his editors from Reynal and Hitchcock, rumors circulated freely that Wright had left his wife Ellen and was living in France alone. He ended the speculation by loudly denouncing the slander and cocktail party gossip. Later that summer, members of the music and theater crowd suggested that Wright had gone off to the USSR or Mexico, or that he was in France with Jacques Duclos, the French Communist whose letter had brought down American Communist Party head Earl Browder. Ellison maintained an amused silence, more curious about the tendency of his crowd to imagine fanciful scenarios of political intrigue than he was concerned about defending Wright's reputation.

Ellison continued to benefit from his friendship with Wright, who quickly made the most of France's literary traditions. Something of vital importance to Ellison before the end of the war had been the emergence of a new stream of thought in France. The existential philosophy of the newly visible writers Jean Paul Sartre and Albert Camus was grounded in the ideas of the Danish theologian Søren Kierkegaard and made important links to the absurd in life. Ellison's exposure to existentialism had come through the novelist André Malraux, particularly the scenes in *Man's Hope* that fictionalized the historical figure Miguel de Unamuno, the pioneering Spanish philosopher of the *Tragic Sense of Life*. Unamuno characterized the profound personal tragedy of the human mind with the notable metaphor "consciousness is a virus."

Ellison's delving into existentialism fed his need to confront and triumph over the absurdities and chaos of the world that he lived in. In a philosophical sense, it offered an escape from worry over the distortion or the omission of the Negro from Western history and literature. By dealing with the problem of being rather than the problem of epistemology, Ellison could attempt the construction of an optimum philosophical model of existence for himself and for his fictional characters. Existentialism also offered Ellison new terms with which to understand his own artistic career, as he tried to form more greatly fulfilling friendships and relationships with fellow artists and critics. Increasingly he saw an artistic success of the loftiest aesthetic standards as a conscious act of defiance and confrontation that was ultimately redemptive. This theoretical position moved him away from writers like Richard Wright, Langston Hughes, and Chester Himes. Traditionally, black writers were prone to use art as a means of confrontation—chiefly to express indignity at racism. The struggle of the black writer for recognition made the simple act of publishing redemptive regardless of the reception of the book. Ellison had set his own standard for achievement where it meant something distinctive for him, and his expectations were high. He hoped to write an intellectual novel of the highest magnitude, one tightly stretched between comedy and tragedy and thus capable of transcending the limits of his particular experience in order to achieve universal significance. Ellison wanted to abandon completely the world of sloganing in favor of the universally recognized artistic endeavor. As he encountered the existentialist movement overtaking scholars and intellectuals, Ellison began to perceive more black writers as sloganeers, using race as the chief engine of their literary locomotives.

At the center point of the significant postwar intellectual movement, Richard Wright solidified his own position (and self-importance) by discounting the philosophical and aesthetic directions of French writers. He told Ellison that the French were naive. Ellison, too, did not expect to take leadership from war torn France, a nation bracing its society for industrialization, American-style. But more important than the effect of great technological change on human beings was the conceptual advantage of existence as an American Negro, a subjectivity that Ellison increasingly had come to believe was one of the most redoubtable and enviable things to have in a world with fast-changing values, where old societies were blasted away like dynamite bursting. He agreed with Wright about the inherent weaknesses of the Continental culture, especially when compared to the vigor of American Negro life. His sense of the historical and philosophical significance of African American life came from its intimacy with the somber experience of tragedy. Ellison wrote to Wright in France that American blacks, living with the tension of horror and chaos enjoined to their most significant emotions and experiences, had a philosophical advantage over the French existentialists. The French had to dive from the height of their philosophy into the deep pool of reality; black Americans spent their day-to-day lives underneath the surface of the water. Black life inevitably combined both the abstraction and pensiveness of philosophy with the urgency of action in order to navigate real-life conditions. Ellison's digestion of the credo of the existentialist, that being precedes essence, that action becomes meaning, and that human beings make conscious choices that shape their lives in the face of the absurd, enabled him to mount more optimistically his own fictional investigations.[21]

For his 1946 Long Island sojourns, he and Fanny rented a beach house from a family named Johnson two doors from Wright's friend, the newsreporter Earl Brown. His neighbors were impressed with his determination to write a novel. Stationed on Long Island, Ellison found some comfort in the routines of the sea and the resort town. But despite his intentions to replicate Thoreau's existence on Walden Pond, not all was tranquil. In fact, when in the midst of an artistic retreat and generating the first several sections of the novel—"Battle Royal" and "Trueblood" and "Golden Day"—he felt gravely the ambiguity of his position: "Here the nerves may relax their tension, but the troubled heart finds peace only in spiritual suicide."[22]

With an uncluttered schedule on Long Island, Ellison comfortably wrote out his chapters. Ellison had conceived the basic structure of his novel during the late winter and early spring, gathering episodes from Oklahoma and Tuskegee and basing the Invisible Man's plight in the urban North on the topsy-turvy careers of Angelo Herndon and Richard Wright in the Communist Party.

When he wasn't writing, his personal contacts flowered more and more across the color line. These relationships were vital to him because of the historic moment; open black and white artistic and intellectual fraternity simply had not occurred before. Ellison had already noted what prejudice often did to American friendships: "situations which might make for friendships undergo quicksilver transformations into their opposite when they occur between blacks and whites."[23]

The interracial friendships were important to Ralph and Fanny Ellison, but sometimes they came at a price. One memorable incident that summer at the beach house with Fanny and their friends etches the Ellisons' intense desire to make interracial contacts successful. After a day's work, the crowd of local intellectuals, writers, war correspondents, and artists would often amble over to the Ellisons with whiskey and rum. The adults played games of make-believe, transforming their identities and genders. But for the Ellisons, the game of transformation went on throughout an entire week. For the sake of preserving the sensibilities of one of the children, a young girl from the deep South who was greatly intrigued by the fair-skinned Fanny, Ellison and his wife were referred to by the crowd as "Spaniards." His experience of racial passing was memorable enough for Ellison to leave a dramatic record of the episode in his notes.[24] He and his wife tried to ease the artificial tensions created by race, and acted out their role during a week that was as tragic as it was comic in its moments of living room theater. It seemed odd that as if by magic the two adults were disguised sufficiently to be unknown as Americans even, although they spoke the same language as the other guests, and were less different in speech and appearance than several. Ellison noticed the incredible irony that in psychological terms, he and Fanny were more symbolically distant to Americans than Spanish or even African people; they were from that remote continent of Harlem. He thought the event painful, but rationalized that the ruse was merely another element of discomfort in an excruciating world. His willingness to engage in an ethnic masquerade for the preservation of American custom reflected the tenor of his own beliefs. His integrity had no mechanical spring, such as a Garveyite's race pride; rather, he thought out his allegiances as an individual and in terms of his own individual obligation and benefit. A larger transformation was also taking place. Ellison was less interested in using his work for the wholesale remedy of the injuries black people had suffered within a social order of racial and social class domination. Instead, he wanted to describe the patterns and ritualistic behavior, and the utter paradox of the American racial logic that defined both master and slave, both dominant and subordinate. His insight placed him on a tightrope.

He chose to consider the positive benefit of the masquerade, believing that the child, who greatly admired and imitated his wife Fanny, would ultimately combine the experience with her future exposure to American Negroes in a worthwhile manner. In spite of his acceptance of individual responsibility, he still held to the power of truth to overcome psychological repression. Expecting truth to appear seems to have been both reassuring and almost a force of neurosis in his life. Ellison's optimism was capable of blinding him to the notion that white Americans might lack subtler psychological feelings like indebtedness, guilt, or remorse when it came to their relationship with the culturally fertile yet politically powerless American Negro. But Ellison saw his work, as well as his masquerade, as contributing to a recipe for repair.

Not all of the summer's interracial gatherings were fun. At the country home of the electric-shock therapy proponent, psychiatrist Harold Ellis, Ellison was appalled by the wanton consumption and crude flirtation engaged in by his professionally trained and well-regarded host, whom he compared to members of the mechanical Washington petit-bourgeoisie.[25] Without the prestige of a title or credential or a high-paying job, Ellison found solace in the rigorous maintenance of values.

There was also more than a little tension between Ellison and one black friend whom he would see on Long Island, the important writer and power broker sociologist Horace Cayton, a regular columnist for the *Pittsburgh Courier*. That summer, Cayton had continued to defend Wright's autobiography *Black Boy* in a series of articles in the *Courier* in which he counterpunched those who dismissed Wright, drawing a distinction between the "hard-boiled" realists and the "sweetness and light crowd." Cayton saw Ellison as a disciple of Wright, naming Ellison and Wright along with Chester Himes as members of the "blues school" of literature, a group committed to probing the "dark inner landscape of emotional conflict which is raging in the heart of all Americans."[26]

The two men had frequent conversations during free moments on Long Island. Cayton's conversation was both humble and arrogant, though Ellison was usually impressed by his candor and unceasing self-examination. Cayton sometimes viewed Ellison as only a well-read dilettante, who cumbersomely appropriated different disciplines and was unable to complete a book-length project. Ellison likewise had reservations about Cayton, and disagreed sharply with his fear-hate-fear complex, used to explain blacks' psychological reactions to whites. Ellison probably connected the theory with the fact that its creator admitted that he had fallen into deep depression and was then undergoing extensive sessions of psychoanalysis. When their conversations moved to their mutual friend Richard Wright, Cayton delivered a harangue that accused Wright either of returning to the Communist Party or joining the orthodox Church. Cayton bragged to Ellison, telling him that July that he planned a long lecture tour in England, a regimen that the less than emotionally fit man seemed incapable of fulfilling. In a note he scribbled on the back of an envelope, Ellison later dismissed the idea that he belonged to a literary clique with Himes and Wright: "There is no 'Blues' school."[27]

The circumstances that bred insecurity and professional failure, however—the closing of avenues for artistic creation that crippled Ted Ward, Bill Attaway, Chester Himes, and a host of lesser-known writers—did not particularly trouble Ellison. In the middle of 1946, he seemed on the verge of gaining major critical acceptance, on a level unknown to even W. E. B. Du Bois. On the basis of his three well-regarded and widely read reviews that had appeared in about a year's time—"Richard Wright's Blues," "Beating That Boy," and "Stepchild Fantasy"—Ellison received a request (care of Bucklin Moon) to write an essay from the Mississippi-based editor Thomas Sancton. With significant connections to the writing community, Sancton had agreed to edit a special edition of *Survey Graphic*; he probably wanted it to rival the important *Survey* issue of twenty years before, guest edited by Alain Locke, which had grandly announced the Harlem Renaissance, and then been republished as Locke's *New Negro*. Sancton had first met Ellison in 1942 in his capacity as managing editor of *Negro Quarterly*. At the time, Ellison and Herndon had convinced Sancton to produce a treatment on race, which result in Sancton's article "A Southern View of the Race Question." Ellison's editorial freedom from set remedies for the race problem had enabled Sancton's essay to go beyond ordinary justifications of racial bitterness and stereotype. Since then, Sancton had come increasingly to admire of Ellison "the things you have written, said, or done, and which have been reported to me."[28] And then there had been Sancton's effusive praise of "Beating That Boy" in the December 1945 *New Republic*. In Sancton's mind, Ellison was the sturdiest black critic available.

The ensuing drama that unfolded over the next six months, between Sancton's pursuit of Ellison and Ellison's final rejection of any association with *Survey Graphic*, appears as a bitter saga that drove Ellison from the ranks of the critics to the reclusive autonomy of the world of the fiction writer. Sancton initially wanted Ellison to write a five-thousand-word essay to be called "Imprisoned in Words" (he had generously suggested the title to his writer). He was looking for, in essence, a hatchet job on the leading Southern writers, William Faulkner and Eudora Welty. For Sancton, Faulkner's prose had done well to explore the disintegration of the planter society, but he argued that because Faulkner "has never outgrown the planter mythology about Negroes . . . [his] criticisms of white degeneracy is in the long run nullified." Ellison shared Sancton's reasoning that the ruling Southern elite's perpetuation of black myths was indeed a force in orchestrating black submission and poor white apathy. However, in his examination of American culture, Ellison did not indict only the South; he understood as early as his piece about Father Coughlin and Irish lynch mobs that to argue only against Southern attitudes was to advocate a kind of neglect of the causes and patterns of racial discrimination in the United States as a whole. Ellison felt that the American writers' neglect of the Negro had less to do with region and more to do with generation and technique.

Ellison's theoretical beliefs were a little ahead of their time. Among the celebrated critics of his era—Edmund Wilson, Malcolm Cowley, Granville Hicks, F. O. Matthiesen, the new literary historian of Ellison's generation Alfred Kazin, the reigning critic of the elite radical left movement Philip Rahv, and the emerging academic superstar Lionel Trilling—none had produced a compelling analysis of the connection between race and values in the evolution of American society and culture. Most of the critics ignored the Negro presence in art and literature; and the more current, like Kazin (who undoubtedly crossed paths with Ellison while shored up for five years in the open reading room of the New York Public Library), included Richard

Wright's work in literary analysis but thought that the "Sepia Steinbeck" was essentially a headline-grabbing sensationalist whose blend of naturalism and realism lagged far behind the train of the literary modernists. Rahv's work on American literature, especially the essay "Palefaces and Redskins," did indicate a sensitivity toward the notion of a harmful bifurcation in American literature between highbrow and lowbrow, but the Russian immigrant who had taught himself to read in several languages saw little of artistic complexity in the American idiom; he did not possess a nuanced perspective on the entire culture or its many constituents. Not until Leslie Fiedler's work began to appear in 1948 would an academic critic treat seriously the complex intertwining of American literature and culture with the question of race and the Negro.

Ellison theorized that white fiction writers, far from rejecting the Negro, had long been obsessed by Negroes, whose blackness they had consciously and deliberately connected with sin in order to rationalize the injustice and cruelty of slavery. By condemning the Africans and their descendants to the paradoxically powerful cultural role as the antithesis of right and good, the ruling elites—as contemporary psychology of the 1940s demanded that they must—found some means of excising their rampaging guilt. To accomplish this feat, a series of myths and taboos had been created, and finally, rituals of sacrifice and atonement.

Sancton imagined that Ellison would write a lively critical piece. Anticipating a reproof because he requested the essay in four weeks, Sancton reminded Ellison that "I once did that piece for you, under similar circumstances." Ellison responded with alacrity and enthusiasm on June 16. While his writing schedule would not permit immediate interruption, he hastened to add that "I like the idea of the article which you suggest." Ellison was fast at work on the college scene of *Invisible Man,* tightening his descriptions of college president Bledsoe, which he had drafted as early as April.[29] Probably during that summer, when he tried to press out about sixteen pages per day, he constructed his protagonist's conversations with Professor Woodridge, a daring and outrageous Tuskegee professor who offers advice prior to the Invisible Man's dismissal.

For the piece for Sancton, in order not to disrupt his own work rhythms, a deadline in early October seemed suitable to Ellison. As for the theme, Ellison would build off of a paper he likely had presented at the 1945 Conference of Psychologists and Writers, which had featured sessions such as "The Role of the Novel in the Creation of the American Experience," "A Definition of the Slave's Vision of American Reality," "Early Twentieth Century Negro Writing as a Search for Identity," and "The 1940's: Negro Fiction and the Crisis of Sensibility."[30] Ellison thought of the essay as symbolizing his chosen vocation as surgeon of the American cultural psyche. Convinced that the Negro had been connected at the deepest level of American culture with fear, evil, and chaos, Ellison wanted the essay to explore the subconscious motive of American novelists, who sometimes had presented a Negro caricature, and in other instances, erased the Negro character entirely. In his mind, the best of American fiction had failed to produce authentic tragedy because of the flaw.[31] When Ellison published the essay in 1953 with the title "Twentieth Century Fiction and the Black Mask of Humanity," he argued the inadequacy of writers who scapegoated the black image either by its presence or absence. "It is not accidental that the disappearance of the human Negro from our fiction coincides with the disappearance of deep-probing doubt and a sense of evil. Not that doubt in some form was not always present . . . But it is a shallow doubt, which seldom turns inwards upon the writer's own values."[32]

At the end of July, Sancton mailed a hard-writing Ellison a letter accepting the terms and the outlined proposal. Sancton understood that what Ellison had offered to write was different from Sancton's original request. He was flush with praise, however, for the anticipated Ellison original: "I have the feeling that you are developing the first profound literary interpretation of the influence of the Negro in American letters."[33] Sancton accepted Ellison's request and extended the deadline to the middle of December, sending on a word of encouragement from Lester Granger, the Urban League chief.

The early fall of 1946 proved to be something of a watershed for Ellison's comrades in the radical American Left. A large CP purge, in part brought on by the major shake-up in the Party generated by the Duclos letter, sounded a warning to all the fence straddlers. The entire United States became increasingly polarized as the USSR was propped up as the new national enemy. By the fall, the best-known liberal figure in the country, New Deal reformer Henry Wallace, had been ousted from Truman's cabinet. For Ellison, Angelo Herndon's abandonment of the radical Left signaled the end of the era of radical involvement. In September, Herndon dropped in on the Ellisons at 749 St. Nicholas Avenue, regaling Ralph and Fanny with stories of his exploits as an insurance broker and retail merchandiser. Sounding a bit like a perverse snippet of Richard Wright's autobiography, Herndon amused himself by revealing the profits he made by selling furs on installment to poor women. With Wright in France and Herndon in the chips in Chicago, Ellison saw his own mature artistry as a steadying course. His early guides had left him to steer by himself.

The public climate bearing down on the Left seemed appropriate for the creation of new critics, who might become heroes. A black writer's sweeping analysis of American culture and symbolic life was an extraordinary rarity in the mid-1940s; certainly of the potential candidates to offer critiques for national consumption—Du Bois, Cayton, Wright, Reddick, Redding, or Brown—only Cayton and Reddick were well versed in psychological texts, and neither man had extensive experience with literature. In fact, September 1946 was marked by the publication of the white psychologist Harry A. Overstreet's perspective on black fiction in *Saturday Review,* "The Negro Writer as Spokesman." Overstreet worked out of the classifications of his profession and remedied black literature (and thus, black life) by way of the construction of artistic stereotypes (Tragic Negro, Brave Negro, Genius Negro, Negro Organizer, Negro Integrationist). Overstreet's work also suggested that psychology might learn a great deal from a literary examination of the symbols of American life. The essay renewed interest in racial issues on the domestic front, during a moment of tension nationwide as returning black veterans continued to receive abuse at the hands of white mobs. While the words were hollow for Ellison, the publication of a position like Overstreet's in such a widely distributed journal tended to impose a limiting critical model. Ellison hoped to use criticism as a means of pushing boundaries open, and he realized that in a reactionary and conformist publishing industry, black writers might be expected to stick to the successful models established by white writers. By October, Sancton praised Ellison's potential, but had pushed up his submission date by six weeks.

Ellison looked at the contemporary critical situation as unimaginative and bent his talents to the creation of a new critical idiom. Late in October, he and Fanny took a couple of days and went out to Wading River, Long Island, at the invitation of Chester Himes and his wife Jean. Himes was completing his new project, *The Lonely Crusade.*[34] What most significantly impressed Himes that fall were Ellison's social views, frequently expressed with frosty independence if not acerbity. When their conversation veered toward the nature of black family life or other social crises, Ellison fired off salvos that were completely uncharacteristic of any bourgeois intellectual striving for acceptance in white America. He argued that the black family was matriarchal, at least in the lower class, but refused to admit that the assumption of matriarchy conformed to popular notions of Negro social disorganization or pathology. So affected by Ellison was Himes that he immortalized one of their disagreements in his novel published a year later. Recreating Ellison as John Elsworth, a Tuskegee graduate in architecture, Himes characterized Elsworth as "the Negro scholar who not only was convinced, himself, of his own inferiority, but went to great scholastic lengths to prove why it was so."[35]

In the second week of November 1946, Sancton, after receiving Ellison's essay, telegrammed him with a vital message: "I talked to the New Republic today. I suggest you telephone Pat Patterson their personnel chief. Immediately. Mention that I asked you to do so. Regards."[36] If Ellison was being considered for a post at the *New Republic,* which then was under the editorial leadership of Henry Wallace, it would have been extraordinary. A post as staff writer or editor would have meant the kind of exposure for a black writer that was unheard of in midcentury America, and carried with it an assumption of thorough competence and high aesthetics that even Richard Wright, despite his celebrity and kudos, would forever be denied. The idea of it all must have tantalized Ellison, writing in a cluttered apartment on noisy St. Nicholas Avenue. The job and steady income could send him and Fanny to a quiet, tree-lined street in Harlem, or into a newer apartment with all of the modern amenities.

It is possible that the *New Republic*'s Patterson balked at making such an outrageous gesture in 1946, prior to the desegregation of the U.S. Armed Forces and in the same year that Jackie Robinson joined the Brooklyn Dodgers and broke the color barrier in major league baseball. On the other hand, Ellison may have rejected the concept of a permanent post out-of-hand. He may have felt that a secure job was fool's gold that might only atrophy his art and cloud his writer's vision, kept precise and sharp by his poverty and his social ambiguity. Living close to the vest with holes in his shoes was not succumbing completely to the sentimental idea of the poet and artist, but the more obvious characteristics of the bohemian style enforced a necessary distance from the stilted bourgeoisie. Most likely it was some combination of the two, with Ellison reasoning away the dangerous racism of the former with the sentiment of the latter. Whatever the case, Ellison was not employed at *New Republic*. And his brief review "The Booker T.," published in early 1946, was his last ever to appear in *New Republic*. Nor did he ever publish in *Survey Graphic*.

The crushing blow to the relationship between Ellison and the literary Left—and really, the break between Ellison's definition of himself as a critic and as a writer of prose fiction—came sometime during the month of December, as *Survey* proceeded toward its January press deadline. In December the editorial board returned a stern decision on his manuscript, along with comments from Sancton, telling him that the essay was too long. It was one of his enduring problems as a critic and a writer; there was too much to say. Two days before Christmas, Paul Kellog, *Survey*'s general editor, wrote to Ellison, returning the original manuscript, which Ellison had revised in early December, along with Thomas Sancton's seven-page rewrite of the essay and Kellog's own copy editing. About a week before, Kellog had phoned him to say that his revised essay as it stood had been rejected by Sancton and himself. Sancton had thought the piece too anecdotal and fluffy, without the concentrated punch of a deliberate thinker. In a show of good faith, Sancton had attempted an Olympian rewrite of almost the entire essay, hoping to have it in time for publication. Kellog had agreed with Sancton's considerate request that Ellison be paid the $100 fee and still offered gratis copies of the forthcoming issue. "We appreciate the time and creative work you put in on the assignment . . . and we shall be ever so happy if you are game to tackle a revision for a later general issue of Survey Graphic with elbow room on all counts."[37]

Ellison wrote to Kellog within a week and through him to Sancton, and his blood boiled. His letter was a rebuttal, written in the pointed style he had developed from his earliest correspondences dealing with any unpleasantness, especially when his reputation, even tangentially, was at stake. He had reason for dismay and venom; he had sacrificed valuable time, only to finish the contest empty-handed. Mainly Ellison bristled at Sancton's quotidian editorial suggestions. Sancton had trotted in verbatim passages from "Beating That Boy," unnecessary additions that Ellison thought insipid to repeat. By greatly simplifying and arithmetically ordering the essay, Sancton had yoked Ellison's essay not only to Sterling Brown's early work, but the recently published essay by psychologist Harry A. Overstreet, "The Negro Writer as Spokesman," even more central to the white reader's opinion. Ellison did not stop with rhetoric but put his money where his mouth was, returning the check for $100 to make certain that there was no misunderstanding. He didn't want to see the essay published.[38]

Ellison's early career as a critic had come to a close. He would publish the nucleus of the work he had done for *Survey* under the title "Twentieth Century Fiction and the Black Mask of Humanity" in the journal *Confluence* almost eight years later, when, as a celebrity fiction writer, he did not have to endure editorial imperatives. If he understood his time spent as a critic as a sort of Thoreau-like hibernation away from his destiny as a novelist, he now had reason to bring out his favored self. One morning he jotted Thoreau's words on a piece of stationery, telling the story: "I left the woods for as good a reason as I went there. Perhaps it seemed to me that I had several lives to live, and could not spend any more time for that one."[39]

13

Absurdly, an Invisible Man

1947

I N 1947, Ellison would publish the first section of his classic, *Invisible Man*, knowing only that he had triumphed and had put the unpleasantness with *Survey Graphic* and the *New Republic* crowd behind him. The first chapter of his novel would appear in Cyril Connolly's British journal *Horizon*, and American critics would take notice of Ellison's work in a way that its publication in any U.S. journal—arguably even *Partisan Review*—never would have aroused. Ellison's appearance in *Horizon* was pivotal. In fact, by the end of the year, the editors at *Partisan Review* would be asking him for some of his work, which he dithered over submitting, because of his earlier disagreements with them. He remembered vividly their speedy turn to anti-Stalinism, which blended seamlessly into a defense of the status quo under the Marshall Plan, and the policy that became known as the Truman Doctrine. As postwar America was beginning to accept the mutually exclusive polarity of "freedom" under capitalism in contrast with "tyranny" under communism, Ellison continued to struggle for recognition of the fundamental humanity of the Negro.

Ellison's work came into sharper focus. It was his third year on the same project, and he was able to exert more control over his writing. Around this time, Ellison melded aspects of his professional approach to literature and criticism into a style that later came to be known as "Ellisonianism." With a domestic relationship that did not require him to keep a steady job, he felt prepared to fulfill his deepest felt artistic longings.

Seeking cultivation in a world quick to stereotype him as a bohemian or a down-and-out scribbler caused a kind of defensiveness that took the appearance of conceit. His bearing grew more formal and he suffered fools less gladly. In the late 1940s, he assumed more of the bearing of a gentleman, and adjectives like "rather" crept into his speech. Along with his ongoing research in psychology and the latest essays on modernism, Ellison steeped himself in the rites and rituals of British culture and history. He read work on the Victorians and Romantics, flew off briefly into Coleridge, and then explored criticism of the Elizabethan period. Ellison developed his own conception of an "Elizabethan manner," a metaphor for practiced ritual and ceremony—which he loved to apply to extreme Negro behavior. To some degree this was armor, an affectation that he used to protect himself. Since he signified for his white friends an immutable blackness that could not be stripped away, he had no thought of losing his ethnic identity as different tony mannerisms filtered into his speech and behavior. Besides, a broad range of African American men, from the Communist Abner Berry to *PM* magazine's up-and-coming photographer James Baldwin, readily adopted a linguistic mode that distinguished them from rural peasants and urbanites who lacked formal education. While he shouted blasts for democracy, Ellison was feeling more and more like that rare bird, the successful Negro American.

In January 1947, Richard Wright returned to the United States, brimming with enthusiasm over the lack of race prejudice in France.[1] Ralph and Fanny Ellison told Richard and Ellen that they planned to visit France as soon as things were settled, which probably meant whenever Ellison finished his novel. Despite the separation of eight months and the inevitable chill that distance had brought to their friendship, Ellison and Wright had a history together. The men enjoyed each other's company and were again covering similar philosophical and political terrain, chiefly French existentialism and the effect of American industries on the postwar globe. But despite their promise of travel, the Ellisons were not in a position to consider going abroad. In fact, the suggestion could have stirred resentment in Ellison, a writer having a difficult time making an independent living by his craft, certainly compared to Wright. Ellison and Wright began to socialize in different circles. Part of this had to do with the fact that Wright quickly told people that he would return to France permanently and leave behind America's crude attitude toward African Americans. And Wright's complaints were far from imaginary; in fact, racism was still conspicuous enough to again be one of the major factors attracting a young generation of blacks to the Communist Party, after the Party was reconstituted. Wright's friend the Communist writer Howard Fast observed that in the late 1940s African Americans rarely received service in the better class of New York City restaurants.[2] For someone as suddenly affluent as Wright, this became a crushing indignity; for Ellison, living in uptown's genteel poverty, it was less of a concern.

But even if their philosophical and political interests converged, in terms of their circumstances and outlooks Ellison and Wright were at opposite poles during Wright's several months in New York. Wright felt secure enough in his identity to leave the United States, and though Ellison had by then completed an early draft of the chapter "Invisible Man" (which he did not share with Wright), he was known chiefly as Wright's artful spokesman. Ellison brooded upon one episode that indicated the gap in their relationship—a gap that would close when Ellison achieved a measure of fame and critical success and no longer had Wright as a mark to topple. Wright returned to the United States after having met with the leading French writers Albert Camus, Simone de Beauvoir, and André Gide, a fact that pulled the American intellectual cluster to him like a magnet. One afternoon, Ellison went to Wright's Charles Street home, where Wright and Lionel Abel, a knowledgeable francophile and *Partisan Review* critic, sat immersed in discussion. Ellison approached the two men, who were deeply engaged in a conversation about sacrifice and negation in Japanese culture. Wright intimated that the Japanese, renowned for spectacular kamikaze attacks on American ships and banzai suicide charges against impossible odds, had little ability to experience humor or pleasure. Ellison, who had seen a bit more of the war than Wright, replied that the capacity for humor and pleasure were implicit in the biology of man. The chastised Wright, in the presence of Abel, whom he had expected to leave with a commanding impression, seemed wounded to Ellison, as if Ellison "had broken up a nice little game."[3] He had become impatient with Wright's tactic of presenting an authoritative but obviously subjective view of the world and historical situations as if it were impartial—as he had done in *Black Boy*. Ellison was more convinced of the truth of his own ideas. When Richard and Ellen Wright prepared in late July for their voyage back to France, it's probable that Ellison felt if not relief, then at least indifference.

To compound the strain between the two men, Ellison was undaunted in his assessment of his friend's work. He had to be. He was now publicly associating with internationally recognized writers who operated with few signs of overt racial prejudice. When prejudice appeared in these circles, it usually came out as ignorance or neglect, a willful amnesia of the black presence in America. Ellison's friendships and exchanges with critics Kenneth Burke, Stanley Hyman, and Alfred Kazin, his conversations with literary agents and editors Thomas Sancton, Paul Kellog, Frank Taylor, Albert Erskine, and Henry Volkening, and Random House publishers Bennett Cerf and Robert Haas, all disposed him to defend passionately the unique vision of the individual writer rather than the political aims of the propagandist. Few of the literati were likely to advocate any sort of political rebellion. Ellison no longer operated in an insurrectionary group like the League of American Writers or the *New Masses,* where one could earn esteem for one's revolutionary vitriol or derive authority from the darkness of one's skin tone. His new associates would not ask him to head any panel discussions on racial issues, or feature him as a "leading Negro writer." Because of their similarities, and Ellison's defense of his friend's work, he was inevitably compared to Wright. Their judgments of Wright as an artist were harsh, as were their judgments of most black writers. Despite the commercial and social power of Wright, it is unlikely that Ellison's editors and friends wanted to see the same kind of public persona in Ellison—defiant, arrogant, and stunningly successful. While Wright's celebrity and charm ironically brought favor to the United States, the country that had produced him—and even to the South—it would have been difficult for Ellison's literary peers to enjoy up close the same sort of success and defiance. Also, Wright's international reputation considerably raised the bar of political advocacy for the writers of his generation.

Ellison's acquaintances would often tell him that he had experienced far too much racial pain to be able to effectively express himself as a novelist. He rejected that conclusion. His goal was not simply to craft a novel that was stylistically superior to *Native Son,* but to fashion the conceptual next step, to reach a new artistic level, which he had skillfully bruised Bill Attaway and others for failing to grasp. He wanted to do more than show the devastation of the black psyche by racism, or merely reverse the terms and present a nurturing pro-Negro environment. He hoped to portray the complex interaction between devastation and the potential for fulfillment, while the Negro, whose mulatto ancestry made him quintessentially American, struck a path for freedom, democracy, and human equality.

There were clear drawbacks to sticking too closely to Wright, regardless of the like sinews of their intellectual endeavors and imaginative energies. America's elite writing community might have published, but was not quite prepared to accept, the Mississippian and ex-Communist whose every printed word had repudiated his country. Along with polishing up his own manners, Ellison was determined to delineate the differences between their two upbringings. Malcolm Cowley, a pillar of the *New Republic* in the 1930s and 1940s and a figure of influence in the literary community, considered Richard Wright a "man of strong and rather Christian instincts" who "hasn't very clear ideas about philosophical meaning."[4] The critic Kenneth Burke shared Cowley's estimate, finding Wright's artistic aesthetic somewhat meager and deficient. Whereas Ellison once was concerned with defending Wright from Communist Party attacks, now as he reached the upper strata of the American writing community, he wished to disentangle himself from a particularly strong association with Wright.

Ellison's relationship to Kenneth Burke and his assimilation of Burke's philosophy during the mid-1940s represented a new level of intellectual and artistic growth. The kinship with Burke, certainly a maverick among literary critics, was perhaps a logical choice for Ellison, whose commitment to Marxism was dwindling, and who was still guarding himself from what may have seemed the royalism of the *Partisan Review* crowd. Malcolm Cowley thought of Burke as a speculative thinker in the tradition of William James and mainly Thorstein Veblen, with whom Burke shared "a concern with hidden social motives."[5] Burke, who saw as much value in linguistics and semantics as he did in any philosophy or literary theory, had a unique vocabulary for his own quirky critical method that he called "perspective by incongruity." He promoted his radical literary and social agenda by juxtaposing unusual and unfamiliar terms alongside language that was more common and ordinarily accepted. In 1947, Burke's tour de force work, the book *A Grammar of Motives,* had been out for a year.

Burke's writings provided Ellison with two schematic outlines to structure the dramatic pace of his novel and to tap in best to the reader's emotions. In the 1941 essay "The Philosophy of Literary Form," Burke proposed three terms as capable of defining the scope of dramatic action in art: purpose, passion, and perception. In *Grammar of Motives,* he offered a pentad of "dramatistic" terms that he argued were the fundamental keys to any sort of explanation of human behavior: scene, act, agent, agency, and purpose. Working through this framework in early 1947, Ellison drafted an outline of the first two parts of his book. Using the triad proposed in "The Philosophy of Literary Form," he constructed each section of the book to move the hero toward enlightenment—from passion to purpose and finally arriving at perception. Not only would the internal action of the individual chapters unfold according to the three-part pattern, in the larger scheme of the project (much like *Native Son*) each individual section and its collection of experiences were to duplicate the same sort of tragic rhythm: purpose, passion, and perception.

Ellison had begun his relationship with Burke as a member of the audience at a conference, and then as editor at *Negro Quarterly* he continued his contact with the critic, who had a reputation for being difficult. In the early years of the relationship, Ellison was trying both to impress a mentor and to present himself as a well-studied intellectual of superior tastes. In his letter thanking Burke for helping him win the 1945 Rosenwald grant, Ellison decided that the letter recommending him for the grant was an insignificant favor when compared to what he owed for the concepts and ideas he had learned—and continued to glean—from Burke's published work.[6] While Ellison spoke and wrote with a confident assertiveness and avoided an overly fawning attitude, he was wooing Burke. Burke's essays on the philosophy of language and symbolic action provided Ellison with important intellectual material, and the relationship that he cultivated with one of America's foremost thinkers who was not a snob provided Ellison with new social outlets and contacts. Ellison wrote to Burke requesting that they meet, and he made himself available to continue their conversations on other terms—a friendship. Ellison could offer in the friendship principally a deep intimacy with Negro American life and culture, which, scant years after the publication of the landmark *An American Dilemma* and months before Truman desegregated the U.S. armed forces and federal workplaces, constituted an increasingly important piece of an intellectual's weaponry.

Fanny Ellison first visited Burke's Andover, New Jersey, home during the summers after the war. In the company of R. P. and Helen Blackmur, and Stanley Hyman and Shirley Jackson, Fanny felt herself mildly awed. By her own account, she felt a bit of fright in the prestigious company.[7] Burke's wife Libby noticed Fanny's embarrassment at the group's sometimes opaque conversation and paid special attention to Fanny, offering her compliments and pulling her into the orbit of conversation by introducing comfortable topics. For Ralph Ellison, this summer of picnics and highball soirees was an opportunity to prove himself and to impress these famous critics and literary figures. He probably trotted out his latest ideas for fiction. Ellison's thoughts were filled with images of sewers, bowels, and other hints of the depths of humankind, the subterranean images of the world. This crowd of intellectual writers would have been impressed by the connection of black life to these metaphors for the expulsion of social wastes—a creative concept in keeping with Ellison's ideas about why white writers need caricatures of Negroes. All of this also meant, of course, working through and rewriting Wright's "The Man Who Lived Underground." Ellison was delighted when one of his new friends gave him a call or suggested he drop by for a visit; on other occasions, he extended some invitations on his own. The friendships with the critics who had at first caused his wife apprehension had deeply satisfying consequences for Ellison. In the main, they served as stunning proof that the racism and rejection he had experienced his entire life, the enforced alienation from a considerable portion of his American heritage, had been an egregious lie. Absurd as had been some of the means that kept him at bay, from segregation's nearly innocuous subtle "super fry" effects to the most violent reminders of race, his skeptic's faith that he belonged had been vindicated.

Still bristling from the *Survey Graphic* rejection, Ellison sent off his version of "Imprisoned in Words" to his agent, Henry Volkening. On February 1, Volkening wrote back to him with a negative report, one that was shared by others, and which shed light for Ellison on the real limitations facing him as a working critic. Calling the piece "rather amorphous and wordy," Volkening now thought that the entire episode had been too costly: "The mistake I guess was that you undertook to do it at all."[8] While it was not fundamentally flawed, Volkening told him that the twenty-page essay needed to be either shortened or expanded. Ellison understood that despite his new status, in a public climate growing intolerant of both the old Left and any ideas that could be considered tarnishing the "American" way of life, he would not find an outlet that would publish his essays hinting that the "Negro problem" was actually a "white problem." Ellison was caught in the middle of a historic flux that rapidly eliminated radical and unorthodox ideas from public debate. On March 12, 1947, Truman delivered a speech plainly stating his determination to oppose, with the military if necessary, the growth of communism and the USSR, the policy that became known as the Truman Doctrine. Less than a fortnight later, Truman announced the use of investigations and loyalty oaths for all federal employees. Within months, Secretary of State George Marshall put American money behind the military agenda and devoted tens of billions of dollars to the rebuilding of Europe, the generous Marshall Plan with its caveat of anticommunism.[9] These international strategies fueled the domestic persecution of dissent, turning up the heat under fellow travelers, parlor pinks, Reds, and Communists to a roaring flame, a fire that would burn for the next forty years and become America's legacy for half a century.

The collapse of the Left indicated for Ellison an inevitable rapprochement with the *Partisan Review* crowd, in part because of the growing prominence of the New Critical approach to literature, which continued to push for a separation between art and politics, a set of assumptions that was growing in its appeal to editors like Rahv and William Philips. As he increasingly embraced the Aristotelian logic espoused by Kenneth Burke, and further left behind his Communist associations, Ellison, too, accommodated the separation. His ideas about politics were also mellowing.

In her jaunty 1949 roman à clef *The Oasis,* the writer and intellectual Mary McCarthy, personally committed to the cultural wing of the Truman Doctrine, articulated the broad position that the anti-Stalinist Left had lost its coherence as a viable social force:

> They had accepted as their historic mission the awakening of the left to the dangers of Red totalitarianism, and this task, with the aid of actual developments, they had accomplished with credit, but history itself (surely their real enemy) had superseded them, taking matters into its own hands, while the ungrateful left had failed to reward them with the unquestioning trust and obedience which they felt to be the logical sequel and kept demanding. . . . [O]thers, more reckless than they, hurried on ahead of them to rediscover the blessings of capitalism; still others remained obstinately true to the axioms of the socialist textbook—protection for minorities, opposition to wars and

governments—and a third group, most recusant, tried to reject the whole materialist doctrine or to assert, in small groups outside the main current, man's power to dwell in relative harmony and justice.[10]

McCarthy captured the kind of splintering that was happening among Ellison's comrades and the complexity of his position when he was writing *Invisible Man*. Confronted with difficulty in finding publication outlets for his critical work, Ellison had few allies. He had remained with the Communists into World War II, a loyalty that stirred the ire of the self-appointed critics of Stalin. But then he had dropped the Party, and the adherents to social realist fiction, before the end of the war. Still, Ellison had published in *New Republic* scant months prior to Henry Wallace's tenure as its editor; his intellectual and philosophical sentiments were on the Left. However, at the time close to Ellison's *Survey Graphic* rejection, it would have been difficult for even Richard Wright, a bankable writer, to publish ardent critical work in the United States. After the demise of *Negro Quarterly*, there were few journals friendly to the idea of a black writer's lengthy or vanguard criticism. To continue as a writer, Ellison responded to marketplace and literary pressures, and decided to keep mainly to his fictional work.

Ellison responded instead to a call from Cyril Connolly, editor of the British *Horizon* magazine, sending him a chunk from the polished section of *Invisible Man,* the first chapter, called "Invisible Man." Connolly was well-known to America's literary circle as the heir to the British small journal. He had started *Horizon* in 1939, when war threatened the established periodicals like T. S. Eliot's *Criterion*; by 1947, the literary magazine's circulation was over ten thousand, with several thousand American readers. The year before, Connolly had been featured on the cover of the *Saturday Review of Literature;* he was described in *Atlantic Monthly* as a "representative modern mind."[11]

Connolly showed his brass by accepting "Invisible Man" for publication. The short story made American culture seem anything but a compliment to the American industrial might that was redefining the globe. It was a searing tale of a black high school valedictorian in the Deep South presenting himself before the town's refined whites, only to be forced into a humiliating boxing match, and it became Ellison's best-known work.

Ellison's real artistry in the short story lay in his ability to raise the dramatic intensity by revealing a deeper human crisis at each turn of the plot. The hero starts out with a naive desire for successful assimilation, a desire that draws him into a series of overwhelming challenges: a naked blonde's dance, a flaunting of the primeval sexual taboo; the spectacular sadomasochistic brutality of the boxing ring and electrified rug; a public speech before an angry white mob. The valedictorian's nightmarish predicament regains a semblance of calm as he gives his address, only to become an utter and complete farce. Things are not what they seem, and much lies beneath the surface. Ellison's descriptions of the naked blonde, the electrified rug, and the hero's gargling of bloody saliva while accidentally advancing "social . . . equality" struck the same notes of timelessness and breadth as other central American literary symbols: images of bullfighting, the green light, the Mississippi, and the white whale. The central haunting theme of his absurd and macabre tale came from a recurring American drama that derived fascinated amusement at punishing Negroes. The manipulation of black Americans, the stunning haze of confusion they faced, was summed up in the story's concluding aphorism, "keep that nigger boy moving." Less benign than the manipulation was the public spectacle of terrorizing Negroes, indicated by his battle royal and its aftermath. Ellison's chapter was a fresh modernist look at the rituals underlying lynching, though he did not evoke the ultimate symbolic destruction of the Negro scapegoat, as he had in his earlier story "The Birthmark." These currents channeled through his thinking consistently, but they were illustrated especially by the day-to-day world of 1940s America. Ellison had experienced several of the components of his traumatic short story in his boyhood; and of course, Wright's *Black Boy* depicted a crucial battle royal, immediately before the teenage Richard escapes Memphis. And if the images had waned in his memory, in 1946 the *Amsterdam News* ran a photograph that Ellison saved, showing blindfolded black boys in a ring in the Bahamas, battling it out, then forced to pick up their prize money—silver coins—while still encumbered by oversized boxing gloves. Most of the boys used their teeth to collect their wages.

With a couple of chapters in his desk and one slated for summertime publication, writing seemed to be going well for the newly minted fiction expert, but the business side of his work hit a few bumps. When his team of editors Erskine and Taylor departed Reynal and Hitchcock unamicably sometime that spring, Ellison tried to avoid being left in the lurch. He politicked with Random House to see if they would be interested in buying out his contract, and showed them a lengthy outline of his project, which detailed the psychological explorations he thought were necessary to trace the narrator's movement from disembodiment to wholeness. These exercises were helpful to Ellison. Near the time of his earliest meetings with Random House, he was still largely experimenting with the second two-thirds of the book. Ellison took his early drafts in many directions. His method was to outline the movement of each chapter using the Burkeian schemata, then to write a textured summary. After he wrote out a final draft in longhand, Fanny would type it up. In his earliest versions, he developed certain absurd notions that appealed to him; for instance indigestion would send the Invisible Man to the hospital, not the factory explosion that occurred in the published novel. There would be a torrid interracial affair, and the protagonist would force his white girlfriend to tan her skin to look like a mulatto, only to betray her. In a scenario similar to Angelo Herndon's incredible early life, the Invisible Man would go South, avoid prison, and become friends with a conciliatory Southern Negro leader. The novel was to end as the Invisible Man returned North and, following a riot, moved to another part of the city and announced himself a reformed criminal who then wanted to open up a storefront church full of electric gadgets: guitars, sound recordings, and a broadcast system.[12]

Ellison maintained an iron discipline when plotting out his narrative improvisations, subjecting the elements of plot to his dramatic framework, and then demanding from himself a complex psychological analysis from the characters and situations. His investment was not small; nor was the act of writing out the words always emotionally safe. As he trod close to personal ground, Ellison undoubtedly came to recognize that Richard Wright, even in his autobiographies, had refused consistently—arguably at the cost of his artistry—to bridge the distance between his private emotional life and those of his characters. The process of capturing these symbolically charged episodes and then thinking of the best way to mine fully their dramatic and ritualistic potential had disquieting moments. Sitting at his typewriter and choosing between a tension-fraught moment in the narrative or a dangerous dose of writer's block, Ellison would ponder the crushing anxieties that came from working on the race theme and imbuing his work with the charged electricity of his own lived experience: "(Now it's coming close to home. I feel my composure going. I want to scream. I can no longer strive to achieve 'objectivity,' to present those times and those selves with proper literary effects.)"[13] Sometimes satirizing or even analyzing deeply the stereotypes of black Americans, especially those he knew not to be true but could not disprove given the scientific rules of the Western world, threatened his mental balance. Ellison's finest artistic tool—his sensitive temperament—occasionally menaced him.

In April, Reynal and Hitchcock editor Peggy Hitchcock requested a meeting with Ellison to discuss the project, which still didn't have a conclusion. Ellison prepared by jotting down notes, excavating the archives of his memory, and asking friends for literary suggestions. Stanley Hyman provided him with a shopping list of literary critics and necessary texts, mainly touching upon aesthetics: Christopher Cauldwell, Benedetto Croce, I. A. Richards, William Empson, Van Wyck Brooks, Caroline Spurgeon, and G. Wilson Knight.[14]

After the war Ellison continued to make ends meet by planning elaborate stereo-component sound systems. He anticipated the coming ubiquity of electricity. Fashionable Harlem preachers brought the electric guitar into the pulpit and shouted the word of God onto Seventh Avenue and 125th Street by way of a public address system. Black popular music, the blues, and gospel met up with electrified instruments and amplified voices, and were changed. The urbanized blues sounds picked up rolling electric guitar chords and the rocking new accents of the jazz drum, producing a new music that was vibrant even if it did not require much artistic mastery. Mainly it was loud.

Bop music underwent another sort of metamorphosis when under the influence of Dizzy Gillespie it was infused with Latin American rhythms. During a September performance at Carnegie Hall, Gillespie featured Chano Pozo, a Cuban conga player.[15] Ellison felt as uncomfortable with the new hybrid as he had with the original departure from swing melodies, though he recognized the popularity of the music, especially with the urban generation. In this, despite his own forceful identification with city life, he was becoming in mentality more like a commuter. Ellison craved the opportunities, the art galleries, the magnetism that pulled in the entire Western world to New York, but he also coveted the solace of the country for his work; and in the increasingly dense African American jazz music he found less and less that spoke artistically to his sensibilities. He thought that the city of promise perhaps had succumbed to overindulgence and torpor. Ellison saw the meshing with the Afro-Cuban rhythm as a strategic mistake, indicative of a quintessentially American form of ethical schizophrenia, which black Americans suffered from as fully as their white countrymen did. Musicians chose the folk-peasant music of the exotic Latin countries while they consciously and dramatically rejected the homegrown idiom of the Negro American South and West, an idiom whose customs and rituals they were initiates of.

The music blaring out of radios and from the bandstands pulled him away from his experiments on the narrative structure of his novel. Ellison filled his notebooks with cultural commentaries, which he intended to publish. He wrote that he found the prominence of bop deeply ironic: "Bebopers search in Latin American music for folk content which it has rejected in Jazz."[16] The rejection of the heritage of the deep South, the blues, and the Dixieland jazz band style by the purveyors of urbanized African American culture, who then pursued a foreign musical idiom, struck Ellison as slightly absurd. When he heard boppers playing rhumbas, he understood that the music expressed the same cultural impurity and borrowing and free-floating and chaotic blending that in part reflected his own life and artistic approach. But it also exposed the sad truth of denial, the abandonment of a vital and creative field. In some form, it represented one of the chief dangers to the black artist, and one that Ellison himself would not entirely escape.

His editors figured he spent all of his time listening to bop and twiddling his thumbs. Richard Wright had written the blockbuster novel *Native Son* between 1938 and 1939. Ellison had been at work for two years and still had not conceived the conclusion to a first novel, a project the publishers already considered risky because it was experimental. In May 1947, Volkening encouraged Ellison to send preliminary chapters to Reynal and Hitchcock, detailing the book. Relations with the publisher were not going smoothly, and Volk-ening hoped to placate them. He also tossed Ellison a bone. Volkening had lunched with Dwight McDonald, recently departed from *Partisan Review,* and had talked of submitting Ellison's "Imprisoned" essay in McDonald's new journal, *Politics.* If he liked it, McDonald would pay half a cent a word. Ellison may have been less than excited about the possibility of meager remu-neration, and while he headed in that direction, he still bore a grudge toward anybody connected to the *Partisan* crowd. Also, McDonald was zealously anticommunist by 1947, seeing no difference between Nazi fascism and the USSR's protectionist strategies. While Ellison was no longer a *New Masses* partisan, publishing in McDonald's journal would be a form of betrayal of his formative years. In the years to come, he never renounced Marxism in his critical works, and he probably was not as ready as Wright had been to repu-diate the Communists by appearing in a staunchly anticommunist publica-tion. Volkening knew as much, and even as he suggested the arrangement, he added slyly that he only brought up the matter in innocent ignorance of Ellison's current politics: "I hardly know any more, these days, who loves or hates anything."[17] Volkening's quip hid real sentiment. In June, Howard Fast, the Communist and best-selling novelist and friend of Wright's, would be tried and sentenced to prison for contempt of the Georgian Representative John Wood's House Committee on Un-American Activities. America was filled with anticommunist hysteria; in Manhattan, Catholic schoolchildren held signs "Kill a Commie for Christ" when marchers in the annual May Day Parade filed past.[18] Of course, Volkening's remark, which implied a closer relationship with the Left than Ellison had had in a couple of years, indicated that by the late 1940s Ellison had almost completely eschewed any public mention of politics.

Ellison wanted to move from Hitchcock to Random House, where Frank Taylor and Albert Erskine had been since early April,[19] and in early June, he met with Random House publishers and editors to discuss the possibility. He liked the atmosphere at the publishing house, which had braved litigation to bring out James Joyce's *Ulysses,* as well as the fact that they were impressed enough with his work to offer to buy out his old contract and pay him an additional $500 advance. Ellison's fear that spring was that the publishing house Reynal and Hitchcock, hostile after an ugly breach with Taylor and Erskine, might hold up his release in order to frustrate their former employ-ees. He need not have worried. On July 18, Bennett Cerf and Frank Taylor signed him on to Random House, buying him out of his contract at Reynal and Hitchcock. He agreed to submit his novel before April 30, 1948.[20]

Ellison may have used the move to Random House to reinvigorate his efforts on the project. It seems possible that his business difficulties had diminished his energy that spring. Under the stress of landing the new contract, and the pace of his work, and his ideas, he began to seem neurotic to some people who knew him. His agent Volkening wrote gently to him as the switch was about to occur, "I'm very happy indeed that all this has worked out . . . [f]or I know it will ease your mind a great deal, and ultimately make what started out to be a very very fine novel, even better.[21] Fanny Ellison, typing up a draft for him in her spare time, became consumed enough by the nature of his passion and that of the troubled narrator in the book that she accidentally would write in "Ralph" for the Invisible Man in the drafts.[22] Pressure on all fronts increased when he was offered a spot at the writers' colony at Yaddo. In the rush and jumble of changing publishing houses, Ellison failed to receive the galley proofs for "Invisible Man" from *Horizon* in time to check them before the magazine went to press. He mailed back the corrections to Connolly, but not in time for all of his emendations to take effect.[23]

Near the end of the summer, Ellison reflected mainly on the publication of his short story and his acceptance into the ranks of an elite journal. When he wrote to Kenneth Burke in late August from Vermont that he had finally defeated the "psychological ice-jam"—a bout of crippling writer's block—he dripped with the heady confidence of having advanced a rank: "Connolly . . . threw out two pieces to make space for it ['Invisible Man']." The vision of success was, however, not entirely one of untrammeled progress. Ellison could feel the ground of literature shifting under his feet; he was anxious to take on new projects: "I only wish the damn thing was completely finished, agonized over, learned from, and forgotten in the enthusiasm for my next."

And though Ellison wanted to ingratiate himself with the older man whom he genuinely liked (he concluded his letter by challenging Burke, his wife, and his sons, to visit his cramped Harlem apartment on St. Nicholas Avenue), he came close to revealing the high cost of writing on his emotional and psychological life in a letter he wrote to Burke extolling the virtues of the South Londonberry farmhouse where he was staying: "In Harlem I live out my horrors during the day; here I have my nightmares at night and by eight in the morning. . . . I've achieved enough of a precarious tranquillity to turn in a rather successful day of writing." Harlem life was not conducive to artistic fulfillment. "When your nose is bumped against your life too consistently and in too short an arch, there's no perspective in which the imagination can come into focus."[24] In his letter, Ellison offered to Burke what the young creole writer Anatole Broyard offered to *Partisan Review* critics Milton Klonsky and Delmore Schwartz—the inside of jazz, black life, and Harlem, still quivering from aftershocks of the 1943 riot.

Ellison's description of life in Harlem could easily have been applied to all of Manhattan. New York City life in the postwar 1940s—even if the city was an international mecca for intellectuals and artists—rivaled the dissipation and anomie rendered by the early twentieth century realists: Theodore

Dreiser's *Sister Carrie,* Paul Laurence Dunbar's *Sport of the Gods,* and James Weldon Johnson's *Autobiography of an Ex-Colored Man.* Ellison's intimates during this period created few sanguine pictures of Manhattan. That summer, Ellison helped to edit Shirley Jackson's novel *The Road Through the Wall;* Ellison also congratulated her on selling a short story, "Pillar of Salt."[25] Spending her days in the fresh air of Bennington, Vermont, and raising her young children, Jackson had written a story describing the deterioration and brutal anonymity of life and death in urban New York, culminating with the inability of the story's heroine, visiting Manhattan for a pleasurable vacation, to successfully cross the busy urban street in the face of hostile and indifferent crowds and careening automobiles.

> The light changed before she was ready and in the minute before she collected herself traffic turning the corner overwhelmed her and she shrank back against the curb. She looked longingly at the cigar store on the opposite corner, with her apartment house beyond; she wondered, How do people ever manage to get there, and knew that by admitting a doubt, she was lost. The light changed and she looked back at it with hatred, a dumb thing, turning back and forth, back and forth, with no purpose and no meaning.[26]

Ellison was able to give Jackson helpful criticisms for her novel, in part because they used similar themes and tonal techniques. Both writers wanted to show gradual and ironic social alienation and spiritual emptiness. And if he gave a bit more than he got during their summertime conversations, Ellison still had reason to envy Hyman and Jackson. Noting his colleagues' serene and bucolic life in Vermont, Ellison became further convinced that he needed isolation in order to do justice to his own epic theme of empty values and alienation.

For Ellison, the quiet and serene joy of a cottage, his wife, and close friends appealed decisively over Harlem. It also won out over prestige. He turned down the Yaddo offer to spend August and September in Vermont. For a couple of months, he was able to obtain the quiet and isolation that had become more necessary. He and Fanny packed off with friends for a Vermont cottage, larger than their apartment, but more importantly, lacking disagreeable noise. He mailed a letter to Hughes celebrating the rhythm of composition he had gained in his Vermont nook without cats—feline or Negro—singing of love and sex, or shouting and playing the dozens with their homeboys in the morning's wee hours.[27]

In October, Cyril Connolly's special American issue "Art on the American *Horizon*" devoted fifteen pages to "Invisible Man," publishing the section that ultimately became the first chapter and the "Battle Royal" scene of the novel *Invisible Man.* Frank Taylor had connected with the Englishman probably during his visit to the United States in the fall of 1946, when Connolly was hunting his own contract at Macmillan. For Ellison, being published in

Britain's leading highbrow art and literature journal meant additional connections, but it also may have been the medicine he needed to heal any inadequacies he felt during his long competitive relationship with Richard Wright. Wright's essay on the indignity of jim crow in Texas rail cars had been rejected by *Horizon* in October of 1946.[28]

Now that he had a short story in *Horizon,* the literary world took notice of Ellison as an elite craftsman; his peers in the edition included not only the *Partisan Review* editorial board (William Phillips, Clement Greenberg, and William Barrett), but also John Berryman, Christopher Isherwood, E. E. Cummings, and Wallace Stevens. Ellison's story's sharp telescoping of the epic blues-tinged dilemma of the American black had an internal unity and decided intelligence that overtly linked it to modernist artistic efforts to depict human experience.

And though the narrow bands of ethnic logic generally prevented the story from being viewed as representative of the modern American condition, with its publication overseas Ellison could legitimately think of his project as an exploration into the meaning of American individualism, which was being spread rapidly throughout the globe under the Marshall Plan. In fact, Connolly's decision to devote a 1947 issue to America made perfect sense, given the politics of the era. President Truman had undertaken to restore authoritarian dictatorships in Europe as long as they opposed the Soviets, which former Vice President Henry Wallace in the pages of the *New Republic* characterized as "a global Monroe Doctrine." Under the Truman Doctrine, America pledged assistance to the British in Greece, inaugurating what the Progressive Citizens of America (the group that eventually became Henry Wallace's Progressive Party) came to think of as "American imperialism which will take over the policies, methods and failures of the British Empire."[29] Ellison's theme of the American hero naively pursuing conformity, only to be repeatedly defined by others, sharply contrasted America's international declaration of independent democratic values capable of mending world crises.

Of course, it would take a gigantic psychological and philosophical leap for most readers to see Ellison's noisy, flaring, volatile, and conceptually ambitious short story as anything more than a plaintive cry for the amelioration of U.S. racial conditions. His readers were devastated by the interior glimpse of the ruminating black personality. The metaphor of invisibility—the idea that whites actually did not see a human being when they saw a Negro—was new, Du Bois's notion of double-consciousness notwithstanding. One of the comments he received from a reader in Britain surprised him enough that he retyped part of it in his notes:

> Your short piece in Horizon. God, its frightening. Their hicks in the South must be a hard, ignorant, cruel set of rotten bastards—How ugly a country America must be, how bloody ugly their world is.

> I was very much moved by your story. It frightened me. Reading your piece is like the horrible empty feeling you get when you haven't eaten for five or six days.[30]

Still anxiously trying to finish his first novel, Ellison treasured the compliments he received. But he also knew that this ground had already been covered explicitly by Wright's *Black Boy,* which Ellison had thought simultaneously an example of "truth" in the struggle for justice and a step backward in the creation of art. Here was an emotional and professional crossroads. He was creating a fictional world with a sentient protagonist who occasionally glimpsed the web of thought and deed, history, tradition, and science that controlled the quest for adult individuality and freedom. Yet people might still read his book as simply another addendum to Wright, or to other chroniclers of black oppression, a group whose principal texts had to be rewritten every generation.

Many of Ellison's friends and admirers picked up on the sensational display of talent. Stanley Hyman was quick to express his joy over the project. In June 1948, he sent along a clipping by another admirer. Reviewer Donat O'Donnell of Dublin's *Irish Times* had found Connolly's exploration of America, regrettably, to be an advertisement for the *Partisan Review* literary crowd. O'Donnell saw little "hope for the future" with the editorial group at the review—William Phillips, Clement Greenberg, and William Barrett—"as guardians of a tradition these men are incompetent." While he thought the work by the increasingly prominent critics at *Partisan* was dissatisfying, O'Donnell saw one gem in Connolly's collection of essays and fiction:

> It is interesting enough and probably of no general significance, that by far the most remarkable piece of writing in the collection is by a Negro, Mr. Ralph Ellison. This is part of a first novel, "The Invisible Man," and describes the initiation of a black boy into adult life in the white world. . . . If the rest of Mr. Ellison's novel comes up to the level of the fragment published here by Mr. Connolly it will be one of the most important pieces of fiction for years.[31]

Ellison thought the praise exhorbitant. He did not miss the irony that his work was considered worthy of praise precisely because the established critics and writers had so little to offer. Yet here was his ambition revealed to the world, to write "one of the most important pieces of fiction for years." His talent was becoming known, and with Connolly's journal, he had seen his work appear in the company of an elite New York group. Saul Bellow called the edition of *Horizon* "dreary and better forgotten," but he read "Invisible Man" with "great excitement" and decided that Ellison's short story "might well be the high point of an excellent novel."[32] From its earliest inception, Ellison had great ambition for his project. The narrative of "Invisible Man" spliced scenes drawn from his own life with characters based on people he knew well, and it flowed thematically from him more naturally than had his airman project. But the appearance of his short chapter in *Horizon* raised the expectations for his entire work. And like any good craftsman, he began, more consciously than before, to seek out the people who might properly weigh his achievement, those who would see in his work more than just a coda to *Black Boy*.

Not everyone read the Irish critic O'Donnell. The New York literary world did not seek him out; in the fall of 1947, it celebrated literary newcomers Jean Stafford, Robert Lowell, and Truman Capote. While Ellison made the circuit of lectures and art gallery shows, he still was overlooked and remained on the outskirts of the liberal intelligentsia. Certainly the failure of Christopher Isherwood and Clement Greenberg, both of whom had been published in *Horizon,* to take note of an important black writer, made Ellison feel invisible. Isherwood felt that only Connolly's travelogue-style introduction stood out as worthwhile, and Greenberg claimed the *Horizon* issue was uneven, "the fault of the people who failed to write for it."[33] *Time* magazine—whose pages reported the increasingly grim tenor of America with its Marshall Plan and atomic bomb test—saw little extraordinary about the issue, in fact justifying its negative review because the "esthete Editor Cyril Connolly" was a heretic who had written that the American way "assumes a world without God."[34] For American popular news journals, the Brits, whose London was still in ruins, were not optimistic enough.

But in those last warm days of fall 1947, the kindest praise came from John Hersey, who phoned Volkening on October 6 and asked to run the *Horizon* story, which everyone was now calling the "smoker" section of Ellison's novel, in the journal *47: Magazine of the Year* at ten cents per word.[35] Frank Taylor had mentioned the possibility of a fruitful union with Hersey's magazine in late August or early September, and Ellison, rushing off to Vermont to guarantee a productive writing period, mailed to Taylor the "smoker" section for Hersey.[36] Wondering to his agent Volkening the reason why the magazine wanted to reprint the short story, Ellison did not know quite what to make of *47*'s sudden interest in his prose.[37] Initially he had considered writing a new piece of fiction for the collection, unwilling to do what Malcolm Cowley had done in his recent book on Faulkner—tear off chunks of a large manuscript and seed them out to the journals and magazines. For the American reissue of his work, though, he hoped to polish up the story completely. With his feet into the big lake of publishing, Ellison kept an eye on perfection. Taylor, however, had an ulterior motive beyond feeding his client and creating a desire in the public for the prose. He wanted to commit Ellison so that the writer would hurry and complete the novel.

As the temperature dipped in the evenings to seventeen degrees, Ellison longed for the comforts—Harlem being what it was—of home. Volkening responded to him that Hersey's magazine wanted to run about thirty-five hundred words of "Invisible Man." When Ellison returned to Manhattan around October 23, he learned to his severe disappointment that Random House was struggling with a copyright problem. Apparently the publication of the section in Connolly's *Horizon* entitled the British publisher to exclusive ownership of the story. When Hersey's *47* requested to run it, Random House initially had problems releasing the story, to which it did not have exclusive proprietary rights. Ellison phoned his agent Volkening, greatly concerned about the possibility of losing the copyright. Volkening felt that the blame and responsibility lay with Random House; he had had no contact with Connolly, though he was negotiating with Hersey: "the whole thing was done, as I remember, at Frank's initiative, and with his encouragement."[38] Ellison, while he was not inclined to extended moments of self-doubt, might have rethought his decision to publish internationally. American publishers indirectly punished anyone who jumped outside of the fold. The tensions over the publication and the lack of support that Ellison perceived from Volkening caused a simmering hostility. Despite Ellison's cosmopolitanism, his reputed and desired ability to interact with ease across the color line, here he undoubtedly felt snubs that may have been difficult to explain except by color prejudice. Volkening consoled him with words that Ellison was to hear frequently over the years, and that would haunt his career: "Lord knows, I don't want you to be distracted from your work."[39]

Ellison, Frank Taylor at Random House, and the literary agent Henry Volkening ultimately were able to come to effective terms about the copyright to the story "Invisible Man." In January 1948, John Hersey's *48: Magazine of the Year* would publish the "smoker." The story skirted some copyright issues with a new title: "Battle Royal." Ellison also made minor changes, modifications he had wanted for the first edition of Connolly's *Horizon.* Instead of the grandfather telling his grandson at the conclusion of the short story that the seals and envelopes are "your's," he used a word indicating perpetual confusion: "years." Censorship took the electricity out of his eroticized and violent narrator's description of the stripper and the young black fighter, deleting such passages as: "[h]er breasts," "erected buds of her nipples," "a compulsive desire to spit upon her," "to feel the soft thighs," "to stroke . . . where her thighs formed a clear, inverted v," "the erection which projected from him."

A significant addition to the *48* magazine edition of the story were illustrations by William Gropper. If Ellison and L. D. Reddick had protested Langston Hughes's *Shakespeare in Harlem* in the early 1940s for its demeaning stereotypes on the cover, now Gropper's illustrations were proof positive of the high price of earning 10 cents per word for prose. Though the first drawing expertly captured the story's raucous atmosphere—the terrified and blindfolded black youth and the white power brokers—the second and third drawings depicted black figures that would comfort a mainstream white audience: Negro caricatures. The illustration of the famous scramble for the naked blonde (she was not pictured) showed wide-eyed black boys with mouths agape.[40] The final drawing featured the protagonist, described as "ginger-colored" in the narrative, as a barefoot pickaninny sitting at a child's desk. The drawings rejected the text's portrait of a bright and sensitive hero preparing for college in favor of a silhouette that might have appeared on an advertisement for tobacco or dry goods. If he felt embarrassed in private, in public Ellison rarely let down his aura of confident self-made man. When he ran into former colleagues from the Negro Publication Society, like Ernest Kaiser, he was quick to tell them he knew exactly how to make a living from writing.[41]

After his success in October, Ellison heard from the truant Wright, who had been abroad in France since the end of the summer. Wright had had considerable difficulty in becoming settled, only finding an apartment at 166 Avenue de Neuilly after three solid weeks of hunting in the car he'd come back to America to purchase. He had seen *Horizon,* which likely is what prompted him to write, and he told Ellison he considered the story an achievement: "damn good, clear, hard and straight, and yet with that poetic bloom which is so essential."[42] Of course, in his inimitable fashion, Wright, who had seen very little if anything of *Invisible Man,* asked nothing about the work in detail other than the perennial "How goes your book? Finished yet?" The two of them couldn't talk to each other about their fiction; and it is likely that by fall of 1947, neither man felt any particular distress over the fact.

Wright had a very different agenda. He had just overseen the translations of *Native Son* and *Black Boy,* which were then making an appearance in French bookstores. He was enjoying his life in France, met regularly with fellow writers and intellectuals, and was delighted with his ability to provide a world for his family beyond the harsh racial milieu of America. For one thing, he was meeting blacks who had spurned the Communist Party. And he had run into and liked several "striking Africans," and decided to help them put together a small journal for African youth called *Presénce Africaine.*

Ellison, too, spurned the Communist-backed Left and along with it, many of the younger critical-minded blacks attempting to gain their social and literary education. In December, Charles Humboldt, a friend who had served on the staff of *New Masses* with Ellison, approached him to ask if *New Masses* could republish "Mister Toussan"—possibly a symbolic gesture. He did not ask for Ellison's new fiction, reckoning that even if contracts and copyright did not prohibit it, Ellison would have felt the magazine a bit plebeian for his latest thrust at the heart of the modernist canon. Since "Toussan" originally had come out in *New Masses,* he hoped that Ellison would allow the magazine to run it again and to use it to remind the literate community that *New Masses* had offered Ellison his start. But for Ralph Ellison, that sort of renewed association with the Communists, in the days leading to Henry Wallace's impaired third-party candidacy for president, was out of the question. In fact, he responded to Humboldt's inquiry as if insulted; and as he said to Wright in a letter, he had only grudgingly heard out the request from a person he no longer considered a friend. In his letter to *New Masses* editor A. B. Magil at the end of December, Ellison left no ambivalence about his attitude. He used exactly the same language that he reproduced in a February letter to Richard Wright. He admitted that he had been closely allied to the magazine, but that in 1942 he had been forced to "change the direction of [his] fictional efforts at the expense of much wrenching of emotions and intellectual convictions." After enduring the artistic and ideological trial, he had no reason to revive old allegiances; Ellison refused their fellowship and never looked back.[43] Five years later, and after the magazine was recreated as *Masses and Mainstream,* his work was not courted by them, but savaged. At the end of 1947, with his short story accepted for publication in an important mainstream journal, Ellison officially closed the door on the Left.

14

Progressive Isolation

1948

W HEN RALPH ELLISON wrote to Richard Wright in early January 1948, he was hidden away in Bea and Francis Steegmuller's cottage in Vermont, a cottage rifled by gusts of wind that got him out of bed early in the morning. He took breaks from the novel, where he was working on the hero's involvement with the mysterious brotherhood, by coaching a Bennington student in the finer points of Richard Wright's work. The bracing cold kept the writer on edge and productive, an agreeable situation after a bout of writer's block in the late fall of 1947. While there was slight irony in the fact that it took the cold air to thaw his creative gifts, Vermont had as good an effect upon his work as Quogue had. It was peaceful, and the lack of distractions afforded him a sense of well-being, a feeling he had gained since he had begun his working retreats from New York City beginning in the early 1940s. He considered his penury and occasional sneezing as the sacrifice the artist must make for the sake of his craft. When he returned to Manhattan that winter, he had to spray his tonsils with penicillin to fight off a nasty infection.

After the hardship of these years was behind, Ellison loved to tell an interviewer who pegged him as either a dandy or a silver-spoon: "During the late forties when I was walking around with holes in my shoes, I was spending $25 a volume for Malraux's *The Psychology of Art*. Why? Because trying to grasp his blending of art history, philosophy, and politics was more important than having dry feet."[1] And while he didn't mind a little exaggeration (the two-volume set of *Museum Without Walls* and *The Creative Act* cost $25; the *Psychology of Art* was $12.50), Ellison had shifted his priorities. His identity as

369

a professional writer was paramount, though his desire for the comfort and status of the bourgeois life was not far below.

In February when he returned to Manhattan, he accepted another assignment from *48: Magazine of the Year*. Since his successful publication of "Battle Royal" in the January issue, Ellison's work had been talk of the town. He had learned from watching Wright escape New York for a breather whenever a book of his was published. Now it was Ellison's turn to hear the gossip about his own work. The knot of literate Harlem society had had no idea that Ellison would actually pull off his creative work, and certainly not at the level of mastery his story had shown. Now Ellison was able to thumb his nose at them. If they could digest the first peek he had given them, his next publications would raise the bar even higher; he planned the next segments of the novel to increase in complexity.[2]

At Harlem cocktail parties, he was dismissed by Roi Ottley, his former supervisor at the Federal Writers Project who had ripped off the writers working under him, as being only an acolyte of Richard Wright. William Attaway initially applauded his story. Despite his favorable estimate, Attaway concluded that Ellison had been able to generate the powerful episode "Battle Royal" only by sticking to autobiographical experience. No black writer—not Jean Toomer or Zora Neale Hurston, and certainly not Richard Wright (whose autobiography included a "battle royal")—had been able to produce such a compelling and symbolically vibrant scenario purely out of their imagination, Attaway said. While Ottley and others could accept the idea that he had tried to achieve catharsis through a public portrayal of repressed experience, Ellison believed that they refused to concede that he had the artistic discipline necessary to elaborate a vast fictional structure upon the kernel of an autobiographical truth. Ellison perceived the sniping for what it was, and became accustomed to the inability of readers to grant that he had any authorial distance from his work.

Attaway's imprecise criticism did not emanate entirely from jealousy; American readers in general assumed that black writers had only their own story to tell. The misunderstandings became regular enough that by May, Ellison had to publish a rejoinder in *48*, four months after "Battle Royal" appeared, attesting to the imaginative and fictional nature of his work.

> I believe the story to be an imaginative re-creation of certain aspects of our American life and the effect these have upon our personality. As such, it is to be read as a near allegory or an extended metaphor. . . . The facts themselves are of no moment, are, for me, even amusing. The aim is realism dilated to deal with the almost surreal state of our everyday American life. . . . *Battle Royal* is only a short section from a full length novel in which I am attempting to create a character who possesses both the eloquence and the

insight into the interconnections between his own personality and the world about him to make a judgment upon our culture.[3]

Ellison was gaining recognition for his depth; he was determined a thinker and writer of the first magnitude. His *48* letter, replete with the critical jargon and bored self-confidence of a writer immersed in a technical project, was not necessarily directed at the layman. Terms like "surreal," "extended metaphor," and "near allegory" were almost as challenging to the ordinary reader as his fiction, a fact for which he did not apologize. He was aiming for his peers among the literary intelligentsia.

One reader, whose political and cultural obligations caused him to use sparingly terms like allegory and metaphor, was Langston Hughes. During the winter holidays, Hughes had dropped in on Ralph and Fanny, and instead of getting into an in-depth conversation analyzing Ellison's triumph, he supplied Harlem's intellectual couple with the latest gossip. Molly Moon, the creator of the Urban League's Guild, had adopted a baby. He continued with amusing stories of Horace Cayton's gratuitous feats of intellectualism at the writers' colony at Yaddo in Saratoga Springs. While Ellison was fascinated by the intellectual proclivities of the educated black elites, he was confused by Hughes's behavior. After "Invisible Man" had appeared in *Horizon*, Hughes had trooped over in a show of bonhomie, and had been welcomed; but he had never told Ellison what he thought of the story. Ellison was stung by such negligence from the world-renowned writer, the person who had sparked his own affinity for Malraux, the friend who had loaned him a typewriter and to whom Ellison had however briefly poured out his dreams and deep-felt desires. Now for the second time he was denied a fully competent evaluation of his work; and though he certainly desired commendation, he would have been gratified to hear a spirited critique.

Ellison was also driven to resolve the relationship with Hughes, which had been less than adequate since the 1940 publication of Hughes's *The Big Sea*. Ellison felt that he had surpassed Hughes's achievement, and he awaited acknowledgment of this from Hughes. Instead, Ellison heard only polite encouragement and glib approbation, only a trifling recognition, which exasperated him. In fact, Hughes's only expression of his growing confidence in the phenomenal Harlem writer was to ask him to edit his upcoming collection of columns from the *Chicago Defender,* named after the lead character Jesse B. Semple, in what became Hughes's most popular and seemingly innocuous work. Ellison saw the offer as demeaning, even though it indicated that Hughes thought of him as an artistic equal. Disgusted, he vented to Wright about Hughes's failure to take on the intellectual responsibility of a writer and public figure. Trying to get even dear friends to take his work seriously, Ellison bristled at the insinuation that he had any time to spare. In the letter to

Wright he sighed, "What does one do with people like that?"[4] It was curious, the moment of confidence with Wright made possible by finding fault with Hughes. There was considerable irony in Ellison's appealing to Wright for solace, since in 1940 Ellison had had to swear off sharing his fiction with Wright to avoid professional jealousy and manipulation. And of course, Wright himself had offered no exceptionally candid reading of the short story. In effect, Ellison's pleas hinted at the Harlemite's bind: he had no black peers.

Ellison felt himself closing in on the novel, which had become something like a piece of radioactive uranium whose energy he had to harness before another talented writer learned how to split the atom. Nevertheless, though he had turned down Hughes, he continued to pursue stimulating writing assignments. Hersey's *48* magazine of the year offered him ten cents per word for a serious essay on Harlem's LaFargue psychiatric clinic, which had been open for about eighteen months. *Life* magazine approached him to author a photojournalism essay on the clinic and the desperate need for psychiatry in Harlem. Ellison agreed to *48,* and seriously considered the offer from *Life.* Wright's earlier essay on the clinic had been rejected by *New Republic;* now Ellison had the chance to shape public debate. Gordon Parks, who had just begun his tenure at *Life* magazine, agreed to shoot photographs to help Ellison transform his theories about Harlem's schizophrenia and day-to-day psychoses into visual images for the *48* essay. Ellison started the project by researching official crime records and court dockets. In the files of court cases for juveniles and adults whose lives had been skewed by racism's devastating effects, Ellison encountered nothing that he hadn't conceived of himself. But seeing the products of his imagination actually reflected in officially documented lives invigorated him and lent to his fiction the same sort of political urgency and savvy he had found in the work of André Malraux. Of course, it also indicated that if Ellison wanted his work to remain in the modernist front rank, as a true synthesis of the emerging ideas and artistic techniques, he'd have to complete his novel before the steady accumulation of social events caught up with, and then moved beyond, the scope of his vision.

After collecting material on the clinic, he interviewed the local intelligentsia who were in a position to comment upon the necessity of psychology in Harlem. Ellison visited Lawrence Reddick's library office and asked him frankly about his opinion of Wertham's work. Reddick dismissed the clinic as a social scientist's laboratory experiment that would last only as long as it took to write a book. Ellison used the opportunity to make several visits to Wertham, whom he had seen only sporadically since the war. The psychologist asked after Wright, worried that he had not heard from the writer who had been so instrumental in founding the clinic. Later in the month, Ellison again conversed with Wertham and mentioned, in the presence of Reddick's former secretary, the chief librarian's skeptical opinion about the clinic.[5]

Within days, Reddick telephoned him, reprimanding Ellison angrily for his indiscretion. Even Harlem's power brokers scurried when white liberals found out exactly what was on their minds.

Though both he and Fanny had their doubts about the editorial treatment *Life* might give to his work, Ellison moved ahead with the *48* photographs with Parks. Ellison planned to layer his observations of frantic movement, depression, guile, and isolation in the essay, which he thought would be "something new in photo journalism." Since the riot of 1943, Ellison had grown more pessimistic about Harlem life. Less and less did he feel that black life was a journey, as he had believed in the early 1940s when discussing metaphors for Negro life with Abner Berry, Richard Wright, and Ted Ward. Now his comparisons took him more toward Franz Kafka and less toward Robert Frost; Ellison thought of black life as a maze. Living the redoubtable maze of Harlem life had easily identifiable destructive consequences, which Ellison noted with a specific eye to males: "adolescents become cynical, furtive, violent; men in their prime resigned, bewildered." Ellison intended his piece to appeal to the art world as much as to writers and intellectuals. He developed a shooting script with shots of stairways from extreme angles that might suggest a mugger's crouched position. It was important to show crowded areaways and tunnel-like passages overflowing with garbage, peopled by figures hustling through doorways and streaking across the picture frame. Women and children would appear to fall down the stairs of tenements in a blur of clothing and motion challenging the most basic notions of survival. In addition to illustrating the purpose and pursuits of the clinic, Ellison wanted his *48* piece and Parks's camera work to capture the irony of the situation. He intended the camera to emphasize the "maze-like aspect of ghetto living" remedied by the clinic:

> I shall play upon the irony of its being located in a basement which the patient can reach only by threading his way through a disturbingly narrow maze-like series of halls and stairways, before he comes to the brightly lighted rooms of the clinic with their screened cubicles, behind which he finds friendly social workers and psychiatrists—who themselves had to go "underground" to conduct their work. Thus we shall try to begin with the "maze" of psychological dispossession, and end with the "maze" (the clinic) through which the individual is helped to rediscover himself; the "maze" through which he is given the courage to live in a hostile world.[6]

By the winter of 1948, he had developed a detachment and precision exceeding those of the trained scientist when it came to analyzing the black condition in Harlem, in particular the life of the migrants who had left the feudal South clinging to archaic values but making a life in the industrial giant of a city. He was fascinated by the juxtaposition of past and present: "men whose grandparents still believe in magic prepare optimistically to become atomic scientists."[7] Ellison had been yearning for several years to answer the question, "What happens to personality when there is no institutional guidance?"[8] It nestled at the heart of his fiction, his criticism, and his social essays on the riots, black servicemen, and urban life. By what procedure might the self take on a homegrown form?

Ellison's essay advanced the argument that black people had been psychologically disfigured—temporarily—by white racism. In this, he was involved in an intellectual movement along with fiction writers Richard Wright, Chester Himes, Ann Petry, and the social scientists Horace Cayton, St. Clair Drake, and E. Franklin Frazier, which aimed to overcome segregation by demonstrating its deleterious effects. The solution to the problem—from psychiatry and from literature—was a heightened consciousness that might enable black people to transcend the limits of local conditions. Paradoxically, at this critical moment for Ellison's fiction and future career, and simultaneous with his efforts to advance the agenda of overcoming segregation, he was becoming increasingly frustrated with Harlem—distant from its people, its institutions, and finally from the geographical terrain of St. Nicholas Avenue. Perhaps it was more satisfying to have discussions with Wertham, whose serious writing and commitment to the clinic were a tangible contribution to the struggle for racial equality, than it was to pop in on his old friend Langston Hughes, living with Toy Harper at 127th Street, a woman who continued to argue for the greatness of Paul Robeson and the need for black people to champion folk art over high art and favor unity over dissent. Ellison wanted his public voice to offer another perspective, one that rejected racial provinces. He felt that he had worked through the ground of black nationalism, and had emerged.

In the final version of his essay, Ellison remained distinctly a postwar humanist, fighting for black rights and alert to the encroachments on the human personality made by heavy industry and technology. In his understanding of the world, he saw the achievement of Negro Americans potentially best reflected in a patriotic U.S. tapestry. Unlike Robeson, his was still the classic battle for inclusion, not revolution. Ellison indicated a wish for patriotism, a "bulwark[s] which men place between themselves and the constant threat of chaos," a form of "therapy" denied African Americans. But if the industrial giant (the same one that crushes possibility in the last scenes of *Invisible Man*) were to surge forward, the fine textures of culture would be unable to perform their important work. In a similar vein, the therapeutic theme or melody of early jazz was giving way under the pressures of bebop's "near-themeless technical virtuosity . . . a further triumph of technology over humanism." This American-brewed social environment overtly threatened individual stability: "one's identity drifts in capricious reality in which even the most commonly held assumptions are questionable."[9]

Ellison advanced the idea, in sync with Richard Wright, that American Negro life teetered on unreality, and that white Americans had to make the key sacrifice in order to restore to health an ailing portion of American citizenry. His allegiance to the techniques of absurdism and clusters of symbols capable of implying the subconscious were also supported by his research of the LaFargue clinic and his exposure to life stories of African Americans beset by an absurdly punitive day-to-day reality. Ellison justified his surrealist literary technique in the reality of Harlem life, and he combined with his stylistic approach the project of moral accountability, always at the core of nineteenth-century American realism.

Around the beginning of February, John H. Johnson, publisher of the widely circulated *Negro Digest,* wrote to Ellison in care of Volkening and asked for permission to reprint the chapter published in *48*'s "Battle Royal." Volkening was polite in his response and noted that he and his author were "anxious" to publish with the most widely circulated black journal, but he was also clear that he regarded Johnson's outfit as sandlot ball and that Ellison was in the big leagues. Johnson was rebuffed because "with all the good-will in the world, we still can't jeopardize a financially much larger possibility." Random House thought that *Omnibook* or another large-circulation magazine might reprint the short story, affording "a very advantageous and enriching sale." Frank Taylor called to alert Ellison to Johnson's offer. His agent reminded him that "it might be unwise, particularly for the small sum obtainable."[10] However, the story was never reprinted. Far more exciting to Ellison was the chance that John Hersey might publish another section of his manuscript, either the "Golden Day" or the "Trueblood" episode, which he had shown to his agents.

Ellison probably followed Taylor's advice regarding the *Negro Digest* offer with little objection. While serious white artists regularly published portions of their work in *Negro Digest,* and Wright had released a portion of *Black Boy* to them, the magazine took seriously white America's accusations and slander against Negroes. Were segregated schools unfair? Had blacks fought well in the war? Ellison, who found some truth in Frederic Wertham's association of comic books with juvenile delinquency, resisted certain forms of popular culture. In fact, Ellison may have been reminded of Roi Ottley and thought little of the mainstream black publishing industry, with its penchant for lurid headlines and stories spiced with Hollywood-style sexual theatrics. Whatever the case may have been, his focus during the month of February was on preparing his essay about the clinic and working with Gordon Parks to set up photographs. Parks delivered an advance of $100 on February 9, which turned out to be all of the money that Ellison would receive from the endeavor.

Ellison admired the rough-hewn Parks, who was making a name for himself with *Life*'s editors. Parks was like Ellison, skilled at several disciplines: a photographer, a competent musician, and a featured singer with an orchestra who had knocked about on his own since he was fifteen. Parks had made his way in Harlem by initially hustling reefers, then had started reading seriously and visiting art galleries while working as a waiter. Like Ellison, he was from the West—he had been born in Fort Scott, Kansas; and like Ellison and Wright, he had many experiences hoboing and in resisting white violence. Parks openly refused to knuckle under to white bigotry or jim crow, once nearly losing a finger during fisticuffs with a bunch of white toughs. As Ellison got to know him, he began to model a character in his novel after Parks, a black nationalist named "Ras," which was an Eastern title of nobility and wisdom that Ellison had joked about in a letter to Hughes.[11]

From the beginning of February through the end of March, the two men met every couple of days, shooting street scenes and making prints. Photography was one of Ellison's accomplishments; he had taken book jacket photos in 1946 for Francis Steegmuller. In his date book, Fanny wrote that with Ellison's combination of expertise and curiosity in the field of photography, and his formidable work ethic, in a way her husband had outperformed the paid photographer. On February 19, Fanny Ellison entered, "Ralph developed. Parks slept."[12] Parks, whom Ellison also thought a bit of a character and an indefatigable go-getter, had made a name for himself first as a fashion photographer at *Glamour* and *Vogue*. After his productive initial assignment with Ellison, for which he secured his fees immediately following completion of the photographs, Parks went on to conduct a famous series of portraits for *Life* on the Harlem Midtowner's gang leader, Red Jackson.[13] In October, Parks published the important series of photographs on homicidal gang life in Harlem, capturing the tone of urban youth violence for the next fifty years.

Ellison had his hands full keeping his fingers on Harlem's pulse that winter. Wright's young protégé James Baldwin, a book reviewer for Eliot Cohen's *Commentary,* entered the public consciousness with his February essay "The Harlem Ghetto." A Harlem native, Baldwin dropped Ellison's *Antioch Review* style of intellectualism for exceptionally clean, honest prose. His essay reveled in the art of the subtle exposure of the interior of Harlem life: the black press, the black church; and he even offered criticisms of the liberal coalition, the relationship between blacks and Jews. Two elements marked Baldwin as a member of the next generation: he was suspicious and critical of Communists, and he looked to Richard Wright as a source of authority. But with Wright in France, a new authority on Negro affairs was in the making.

Early in 1948, Harlem's hopeful politicos on the Left had begun to rally for the upcoming presidential election. The defeat that year of the Progressive Party and its candidate, former Vice President (under Roosevelt) Henry Wallace, ushered in the age of conformity and conservatism, and an American economy growing from its war preparations with the Soviets. Wallace's third-party campaign to become president sought to remobilize the leftist Popular Front constituency that had pushed America to the brink of socialism in the 1930s, but which had collapsed with the Nazi-Soviet pact. And in 1948, again the Communists were at the eye of the storm. Once valued for their organizational talents, which Wallace needed desperately, Communists now were viewed as agents of a foreign and totalitarian power. Wallace rejected their important capabilities and was still slandered as "soft" on Reds. Even ex-Communists who were not artful and vocal critics of their former Party were seen as liabilities. The claims of the political Left for human justice seemed secondary in the aftermath of the hugely popular war ending the Depression.

Unwilling to straddle the fence as he had after the Nazi-Soviet pact in 1939, Ellison had grown tired of the liberal crowd. High-profile Max Lerner and the Partisan Review circle known for their sweeping political opinions now seemed to him to move with fear. But in spite of his bitterness toward them, he was correct; the impending failure of the Progressives left little to hold steadily to in the raging wind of political conservatism, complete with a peacetime draft, a tangible enemy, and an economy whose industries flourished by creating products for the military. In a move more futile than Wallace's campaign, *PM* editor Lerner backed the old socialist Norman Thomas for president. However, there were few desirable options as Truman's hold on the presidency stiffened and pushed the country sharply to the right in the political contest that would shape American society and its struggle with the Soviet Union for decades to come. *PM* provided some of the little positive publicity that the Wallace campaign received. Lerner cast the former vice president's socialist-sounding concerns as influenced less by communism than by native American populism.[14]

Predictably, Robeson and Du Bois came out in favor of Wallace, while the heads of the mainstream bourgeois groups—Walter White at the NAACP and Lester Granger of the Urban League—backed Truman, who desegregated the armed forces to much fanfare and presented a civil rights speech in Harlem. However, Truman gained the momentum necessary to defeat Governor Dewey of New York by ingratiating himself to congressional hawks. In the newly elected Congress, the standing Senate Committee on Un-American Activities was taken over by a little-known Wisconsin Senator named Joseph McCarthy. As if to signal the futility of principled resistance, Wallace ultimately received fewer votes than the arch-segregationist governor of South Carolina, Strom Thurmond. The days of open liberalism, of the sort that countenanced friendly relations with socialists or the USSR, had come to an end.

Artists and blacks on the Left felt the tension as politics began to dissolve their fragile alliances. One of the first casualties was the Council on African Affairs, the group that brought together Harlem's traditional anti-imperialist

Left. The bickering among the Left-Communist-nationalist intelligentsia in Harlem also scuttled the newspaper the *People's Voice,* Harlem's militant left-wing newspaper and forum for such black leftist writers as Marvel Cooke, St. Clair Bourne, and Ann Petry. The Council and the *People's Voice* failed chiefly because of the realignment of the well-known Harlemite, South African Max Yergan, former National Negro Congress president, who had shared the dais with Ellison at a *New Masses* promotion in 1942. Yergan managed to break the paper, which he published, as well as the council, where he had been director. Robeson and Yergan, the cochairs of the Council, battled for control of the important organization, gaining court orders and injunctions, until the Council passed from existence. In public, Yergan claimed now that his effort was to thwart communism, a surprising turnabout from his earlier communist convictions. The *Daily Worker* ran essays by Doxey Wilkerson, the former editor of the *People's Voice,* attacking and bitterly criticizing Yergan. With these attacks, Ellison noted that the Communists had lost control of the *People's Voice,* originally the bully pulpit of Adam Clayton Powell Jr., which Powell had left in 1946 claiming that it was too Red for his tastes. Ellison suspected that the well-publicized disagreements were some sort of Communist ploy, designed to silence Harlem's dissent in order to promote unrelated Communist interest. The venues for adult criticism, principled activism, and public discourse by blacks were drying up.

Contributing to the strain among New York's black Left, a major national scandal occurred at the end of March when A. Philip Randolph, calling on the necessity of subordination to a "higher law," testified before the Senate Armed Services Committee that "I personally will advise Negroes to refuse to fight as slaves for a democracy they cannot possess and cannot enjoy."[15] Randolph was branded a traitor by the right and a reckless extremist by the black professional core, the *Pittsburgh Courier, Amsterdam News,* and *Urban League,* regardless of whether he had hit upon the true temper of the disgruntled black veterans returning home. He had, however, spoken Ellison's conscience, though as Ellison entered his thirty-fifth year, he could reasonably doubt that he would be called to bear arms against the Soviets, who took on the role of aggressor after orchestrating a February coup in Czechoslovakia. When Ellison returned to Harlem from Vermont, he saw Randolph, the dignified head of black labor for thirty years, warning young men to resist the draft from a soapbox on 125th Street and Seventh Avenue. When Harlem's eighteen-year-olds were polled by *PM* magazine in regard to their willingness to serve in a jim crow army, seventy-one percent said that they would favor Randolph's tactic of civil disobedience against the draft. Politics and the national scene had an unslakable thirst for tumult, and offered very little reward.

Communicating as if they were back in their old rhythm, Wright posted a letter not two weeks into the new year. After recounting his adventures in Paris, he asked Ellison for Fanny's help in securing information documenting the somewhat obscene American wartime practice of segregating blood banks, a practice inconceivable to many scientists in Europe. Wright's buddy Dr. Julian Huxley had promised to get the story of the black doctor Charles Drew's development of plasma and the United States government's segregation of Negro blood to "every reader in the civilized world."[16] Wright acknowledged the tenuousness of his standing; he had no right to expect any favors: "Ralph, I know that you are too busy, but could Fanny, in the interest of the world Negro, get together all the dope on this stuff that can be found and air mail it to me? I'd pay any and all expenses involved." Ellison complied, once again consigned to the role of errand runner for a Wright enterprise. Wright carried on in the role of black liberator; he had spent most of January and February helping *Presénce Africain.* The fledgling magazine, which had introduced the works of the outstanding Senegalese Alioune Diop and Leopold Senghor, also presented to an international audience the works of Horace Cayton and Frank Marshall Davis, Wright's Chicago cohort. Fearing a negative estimate of the journal ("please don't think that I agree with all that is printed there") and admitting a couple of "soft spots" in it, instead of offering to print one of Ellison's many essays, Wright instructed the group to fire off an issue to Ellison as soon as the journal came off of the press. In his own way, Wright was acknowledging the arrival of an equal.

One of the pleasant rewards of publishing and being well respected were the new bragging rights Ellison had in his relationship with Wright. *48* had asked him to write a piece; he was an accepted member of the critical community, not merely some fringe radical writing anonymous reports and trying to huckster them past reviewers. With his new authority came a more elite sense of himself. Now Ellison voiced disagreements with Wright's admirers and friends. When, for example, Wright asked about the value of Chester Himes's latest novel *The Lonely Crusade* (1947), Ellison held nothing back from his critique. He thought the book "dishonest" and "false"; but worse, Ellison did not find the work an example of artistic craftsmanship. Instead of well-digested political and social theories functioning implicitly within a story that expertly maneuvered the reader toward a dramatic climax, Ellison saw Lenin's political terms from *Materialism in Empirio-Criticism* haphazardly strewn about as if by a new convert to the faith. "If a writer is serious about his politics and its relationship to man, then he should at least attempt to master the ideas (artistic, technical, philosophical, metaphysical) which that political position embodies explicitly."[17]

Ellison's attitudes toward his colleagues were changing. He no longer needed the nurturing relationships of an intellectual fraternity, but instead, the higher moral ground of his own intellectual truth. Himes earlier had been put off by what he considered Ellison's high-handed treatment, and retreated from the friendship, characterizing Ellison as an aloof intellectual. Ellison speculated that Himes, who had returned to New York in late 1947 and sent a

Christmas card but neglected to drop by St. Nicholas Avenue, worried about writerly retribution. He reminded Wright of the depth of their ten-year camaraderie in a jest about Himes's reluctance to remain on intimate artistic, and personal, terms: "Could he fear I might put *him* in my book?" Then he joked to Wright that Himes, who had spent seven years in jail and caroused obsessively with white women though married, had already starred in a fiction—as Bigger Thomas of *Native Son*. In spite of what Ellison may have thought about him, Himes led a charmed life in 1948. In May, he was offered a two-month respite at the writers' colony at Yaddo, where he read Faulkner, Joyce, and Rimbaud. The next month, fellow Yaddo alum Horace Cayton arranged for Himes to deliver a lecture at the University of Chicago called "The Dilemma of the Negro Writer." Intoxicated by benzedrine and champagne, Himes emphasized in all of its glory the effects of racism on the black mind:

> If this plumbing for truth reveals within the Negro personality homicidal mania, lust for white women, a pathetic sense of inferiority, paradoxical anti-Semitism, arrogance, Uncle Tomism, hate and fear and self-hate, this then is the effect of oppression on the human personality. These are the daily horrors, the daily realities, the daily experiences of an oppressed minority.[18]

The speech received national attention. But Ellison thought that Himes's embarrassing declarations were a weak substitute for formal literary analysis and philosophical precision. Himes had pitched a speech that was nearly the opposite of Ellison's academic and dispassionate Bennington address. Part of this difference seems to have come from the manner in which the literary men were training themselves. Ellison fundamentally accepted, as a bedrock principle, specific Aristotelian concepts (which he first had been introduced to in less static form in the work of Kenneth Burke); namely, the transhistorical nature of literary form and the importance of mastery of the form in creating a fully dramatic work of art.

His pursuit of unflinching honesty in his estimates of contemporary Negro art obviously had further ramifications. Mainly, Ellison's judgments of Himes could be applied to the work Wright had done in the past. Ellison's negative estimate of Himes's application of philosophical theory would become his overriding criticism of Wright's work into the future, especially *The Outsider* (1953). Their correspondence of February 1948, one of the last deeply personal and revealing letters between Ellison and Wright, showed almost a symbolic break between the formerly close friends and their artistic projects. Wright (and Himes, who would soon join him in Paris as an expatriate) evidently felt more urgency about the international domination of blacks by white imperialism and chose to present his complex ideas as accessibly as possible. Wright also liked Himes's *The Lonely Crusade,* which he wrote an introduction for when the French edition of the novel appeared. He likened the novel's power to Gunnar Myrdal's *An American Dilemma* and applauded Himes's use of "rich images and sensual prose" to explore "the schism existing between America's ideals and her practices."[19] It is possible that Richard Wright thought of Ellison's criticisms of Himes as a gloved slap at his own work.

Himes, who wore his emotions on his sleeves, never resolved the distance between his own self-definition and how white America of the 1940s designated black men as a group. The series of menial jobs he accepted to earn a living while he wrote fiction humiliated him. With his consciousness finely tuned to pick up the mildest vibration in the human being, Himes's sensitivity was routinely assaulted by casual prejudice while he worked as a janitor, a porter, a stencil operator, and any of the other jobs that brought him in contact with the white public. To add to his sense of indignation, Himes felt threatened by his wife's professional career and the gracious treatment she tended to receive from whites. Ellison had formulated a strategy early on to avoid this anxiety, beyond repressing or dismissing any threat that Fanny's steady income may have posed to his sense of dignity. Also, his mother Ida Ellison's determination to raise her son with a sense of entitlement had a great deal to do with his internal sense of security. He already had something of a part-time job when he linked up with Add Bates to produce and repair stereo cabinets and audio amplifiers. While it wasn't steady, his work helped him maintain an air of independent self-importance, which lessened the public insults of mid-twentieth-century racial prejudice: the waiter's salt in the coffee, the doorman's refusal to acknowledge, the never-ending assumption of idiocy and incompetence. Another venture that he took to, which offered the same sort of freedom and technical expertise, was photography. During that year he attended regular meetings of a photographic league and took them seriously as an opportunity to develop his craft. His interests bespoke his decision to maintain his identity as sort of an urban artisan. He knew something of electricity, photography, audioelectronics, and moving pictures. In an era when these developments were just coming into widespread use, and were thought unusual or even odd, Ellison's technological know-how enabled him to feel like a new breed.

Ellison kept up his major social commitment to the eighty-two-year-old Ida Guggenheimer, his patron. In February and March, he met with Guggenheimer, escorting her to lunch from her home at the Hotel Ansonia at Seventy-fourth and Broadway, or having dinner with her at a restaurant, like Frank's in Harlem, willing to serve an interracial party. This ritualistic interaction between artist and patron took place on a different ground than that of the Harlem Renaissance writers and their benefactors of twenty years before, if under circumstances that Ellison did not entirely dictate. In her letters to Richard Wright and E. Franklin Frazier, Guggenheimer consistently championed Ellison, treating his opinions with the kind of reverence and esteem generally reserved for very well-established writers and intellectuals. She had thought Ellison's review of *Black Boy* "superb." "It moved me so deeply, it is so understanding and written with such a fine insight into the whole complicated case of injustice and wickedness and inhumanness."[20] (In fact, following the publication of *Invisible Man,* Frazier suspended his correspondence with Guggenheimer until he had completed the novel.[21]) Ellison merited this estimate in part because he took the relationship seriously and did not speak loosely with Guggenheimer, favoring an almost tutorial approach in their interactions.

While working on the second section of the book and pulling together the *48* article, Ellison could not keep out of his mind the essay he had written for *Survey Graphic* on American fiction and black characters, which he had worked on so diligently in the fall of 1946. He finally had conceived a proper coda for the piece, which would center on the connections among Twain, Hemingway, and Faulkner; the closing would show a "fuller discussion of Faulkner and his seeking for forms of Negro humanity," in particular the transference of "worthy human actions values ideals" that the character Dilsey expects to receive in the story from Reverend Sheegog.[22] He had begun to think more competitively with Wright; he had led Wright to believe he had "almost finished" the novel, and he wanted Wright to expect significantly more complex prose as the work went on.

In the middle of March, Ellison and Parks worked hard on the layout for the *48* photo essay. For a breather he watched the Humphrey Bogart film *Treasure of the Sierra Madre* and shot portraits of his close friend Albert Murray. Toward the end of that month an intellectual celebrity and hero of Ellison's came to town, Arthur Koestler, the Hungarian Jewish writer known for his 1941 book disavowing communism, *Darkness at Noon.* Koestler spoke to a packed Carnegie Hall audience, sitting on a table and swinging his legs in collegial fashion (according to his biographer David Cesarani because of a faulty microphone; Ellison thought the mannerisms staged and condescending).[23] Koestler castigated "adolescent" American audiences for being soft on communism in a speech called the "Seven Fallacies." Ellison was impressed chiefly by Koestler's estimate of the French existentialist Sartre and the French political scene; in the wake of the Duclos affair, it was fascinating to see someone dispense with French Communists. He meshed Koestler's talk with the firsthand information he received from Wright to come up with a grasp of world events. Despite the turmoil facing the French, who had called on the military's General Charles de Gaulle to restore order, knowledgeable Americans looked to France as the cutting edge for representative democracies. France combined in its legislative houses representatives of democratic capitalists, socialists, and communists; as a nation it dealt with severe political tensions. And since the Duclos letter had had such a definitive impact on the American Communist Party, there was reason to look to that country, which had had much of the war fought on its soil, to determine what Western life might look like for the second half of the century.

The evening following Koestler's Carnegie Hall debut, Ellison went to Dorothy Norman's house for a cocktail party with Koestler and the British poet Stephen Spender. Koestler, known for excessive drinking and womanizing, had befriended Langston Hughes during a visit to Turkmenistan in the early 1930s. Koestler longed to experience Harlem from the insider's perspective. If Ellison had revealed the insider's Harlem to the Hungarian—the LaFargue Clinic, black urban poverty, the bebop generation's rejection of rural culture and values—he might have caused Koestler to reevaluate his endorsement of America.

Not long after the lecture, Ellison spent an afternoon with his former lover and literary comrade Sanora Babb. In early April, he went alone to the museum with Gordon and Sally Parks to see the photography exhibit "In and Out of Focus"; in a month, he would introduce Parks to Ida Guggenheimer and visit the Parks's White Plains home. Ellison settled into a routine, working during the day and meeting friends and supporters for lunch and dinner. Shortly after the nineteenth, he received the galleys and photo captions for his *48* essay.[24] He went to the magazine's office to finish writing the captions and to approve the photographic sequences. That month, he also lunched with Ida Guggenheimer and attended a party for John Lehman and met Pearl Kazin at the home of Knopf editor Harry Ford on April 23, where he dined again exactly a week later. Ford became a close friend and important confidant, who also read a considerable portion of the manuscript and gave Ellison detailed comments on copyediting and conciseness.

His polish made Ellison an attractive houseguest, and he became fond friends and intimates of many New Yorkers, including Francis Steegmuller, a regular companion. Steegmuller, who was translating Flaubert, was Ellison's intellectual peer. A critic, translator, and biographer (he went on to win a National Book Award in 1971 for *Cocteau: A Biography*), Steegmuller wrote witty essays on travel and culture for the *New Yorker*. In 1946, he had collected these essays into a book called *French Follies and Other Follies: Twenty Stories from the* New Yorker. While Steegmuller and his wife Bea provided Ellison with hospitality and occasional work (he took the book jacket photos probably for *Blue Harpsichord* and *Maupassant: A Lion in the Path*), on the eve of their overseas travel in the spring of 1948, they provided him with something even more important: an office at 608 Fifth Avenue, on the eighth floor, in a jeweler's boutique.[25] In a letter to Wright he voiced his enthusiasm for the new location. In an office distant from home, Ellison felt completely invigorated, and wondered why he hadn't moved earlier.[26] While Ellison found the location important for composition—it was imperative to abandon briefly the concerns of home and Harlem—he also experienced the existential confusion of living what for him was a thoroughgoing and philosophically complex relationship to modernity, while being conscripted into whites' feudalistic fantasies because of his skin color. He wrote to Stanley Edgar Hyman that when visitors to the luxurious roof gardens of the office building across Fifth Avenue spotted him, they tended to gawk with extraordinary surprise at an African American typing away in a posh office, as if his presence signaled the violation of an ancient law of social hygiene.[27] While jotting notes on his wife's stationery, Ellison continued to come to terms with the dense implications of the metaphor of invisibility. His consistent experiences of whites and blacks refusing certain aspects of his identity reinforced the odd truth of his concept.

Ellison gained a considerable amount of confidence and ease in the company of increasingly polite society. With the near swagger he had adopted early on when making his way in New York, a posture more typical of Texans, he thrust himself into conversations and places that had precluded Negroes, and he did so without apology. In his letters and conversations to intimates and acquaintances he could be brash and salty. He was rewarded for his panache, however, and his intelligence often overwhelmed skeptics. He had little time to pine over making enemies, anyway, but instead used his freedom to continue to educate himself and cultivate his interests. He went to Philadelphia to take in the Matisse exhibit, another of photographer Alfred Stieglitz's philanthropic contributions to the American public. Ellison's various acquaintanceships with New Yorkers, such as Dorothy Norman, Stieglitz's student and lover, enabled him to feel that he was a part owner of the evolving American cosmopolitan sensibility. His own application of the Burkeian "perspective by incongruity" theory decidedly worked. On May 11, he met the eccentric young Southerner and literary prizewinner Truman Capote at dinner at Francis Steegmuller's house. Capote's collection of short stories *Other Voices, Other Rooms* would be published that year. A week later, he and Steegmuller talked photography and commiserated over the latest mishap in his career.

Ellison had spent most of the winter and spring working on his *48* article, only to learn that the magazine now was in serious financial difficulty. Ellison received a letter dated May 17 revealing the sad story that the editorial board had decided to suspend publication—they hoped "temporarily."[28] Regarding his essay, the magazine's lawyers had advised against the withdrawal of manuscripts by artists. His hoped-for fee of more than $350 went by the board. When Ellison called editor Dick Lauterbach, Lauterbach begged his patience, telling him that his essay was one of the strongest arguments that the board had for continuing publication when they negotiated with the banks.

At the end of May, Ellison entertained two friends of Wright's. Remi and Colette Dreyfuss, who had been French resistance fighters in the war, were taking holiday in the United States. The Dreyfusses had written to Ellison when they arrived in New York, but he had been in Philadelphia for the Matisse show and unable to make the connection. Then he waited for a week for Fanny's check to come in so that Harlem's intellectual couple would have enough money to entertain properly their European guests. On Tuesday, he stumbled into the French couple at the LaFargue Clinic, a day before they were due to make their way out to Chicago to see Cayton. Ellison invited them back to St. Nicholas Avenue, sorry that he had waited for money to entertain the couple. The next morning he spent several hours with the Dreyfusses before they took a train out of New York. With the help of his guidance, the French radicals had begun to see through the veneer of the American dream.

He was invited to the May 27 Joyce Society lecture, one of a series that was highly regarded in the literary world, followed by cocktails at a tony Gramercy Park residence with Stanley Hyman and his wife Shirley Jackson. Hyman and Jackson expressed their optimism about his essay on the Harlem clinic. As an apparent harbinger of good things to come, the June issue of *48* included a caption advertising Ellison's work: "'A thousand clinics could not cure the sense of unreality that haunts Harlem as it haunts the world.' A brilliant writer and a distinguished photographer, with a sensitive comprehension of their own people, examine New York's troubled Negro city as a laboratory for universal problems."[29]

While more and more of Ellison's close intimates were increasingly white professional writers, he enjoyed considerably his friendship with Albert Murray, who had graduated from Tuskegee in 1939. Ellison and Murray had been introduced by Mike Rabb in 1940, and Murray, like many in Harlem, was greatly impressed by Ellison's collection of books. When he had a chance, Ellison would spend an afternoon in Central Park with Murray and his family. The two men became close friends during the fall of 1947 and the spring of 1948, when Murray, an English instructor at Tuskegee, completed a master's degree in English at New York University.[30]

Awaiting the publication of his work on the LaFargue Clinic, Ellison noticed two essays in the pages of *Partisan Review*. Although he disliked that crowd, whom he considered snobs with their conspicuous elitism and anti-Stalinism, and he faulted them for never seriously adopting the struggle for black rights, Ellison viewed the articles as competition in his own intellectual province. One essay, by the English professor Leslie Fiedler, "Come Back to the Raft Ag'in, Huck Honey," argued for a connection between homosexuality and blackness at the core of American novels. The other, by a young

Army veteran and newcomer to New York literary circles, the writer Anatole Broyard, detailed the philosophical life of Harlem's black hipsters. Ellison disliked, as was his tendency, anything that intruded on his own turf, and here certainly were two things: an essay unveiling the same elements of American literature to which he had devoted himself, and a chic, intimate portrait of uptown's hepcats, sharp like a switchblade knife and burnished with the theoretical jargon of Erich Fromm, the Marxist Sidney Hook, and analogies from Meyer Schapiro's famous art lectures. Ellison had been undercut with his own essay on blackness in American literature. The troubles at *48* had kept Ellison's "Harlem Is Nowhere"—his own offering on the texture and inner detail of that world—out of the public eye. He could see the changing times, when white scholars (Broyard, when pushed, defined himself as "creole") would have full possession of black material, as had the likes of Octavus Roy Cohen, Julia Peterkin, and Carl Van Vechten twenty years before.

Ellison had grown steely in his determination to fend off competitors, and in his correspondence to Hyman, he dismissed the other writers. Fiedler's exploration was based on premises similar to Ellison's own thesis of American cultural immaturity and psychological repression, he said. American culture exhibited "no resources (no tradition of courtesy, no honored mode of cynicism) for dealing with a contradiction between principle and practice," that might allow it to deal more effectively with the consequences of racism. Instead, at its heart was a juvenile innocent's wish for atonement: "[the white American] dreams of his acceptance at the breast he has most utterly offended."[31] Since it only used in more elaborate form Ellison's ideas from "Beating That Boy," he found the Fiedler essay dancing on the surface. Broyard, on the other hand, offered a great deal of new materials and considerable detail. But he had failed to recognize the Negro hipster's hybrid lineage, partly from the American Lost Generation of the 1920s, and thus misunderstood the general cultural ambiguity of hipster origins.

Ellison's dismissal of Broyard was on the mark; Broyard became a reviewer for the *New York Times,* but never published an extended work of consequence. Fiedler, however, who went on to use the essay in his more comprehensive work *Love and Death in the American Novel,* revitalized Ellison's interest in broad American themes and contributed to his thinking about the structure of American myth. Fiedler's connection between the Negro and homosexuality sent Ellison back to Walt Whitman.[32] For one thing, he was eager to look at Whitman's works in order to pinpoint the appearance of concerns with race and sexuality. What were the links between the early portraits of blacks in the epic *Leaves of Grass,* and in Whitman's tour de force work on sexual identity "Calamus"? Fiedler's essay helped Ellison to produce the "Emerson" scene of his novel, where the frustrated narrator loses the dream of returning to college. "Emerson is a messenger who brings news which destroys 'IM' changing him from believer into questioner."[33] In his typed notes, he wondered about the construction of the tension between the blind hero and young Emerson, a secondary character who assists in the hero's sight. Ellison thought it apt to make Emerson a student of American literature, potentially even interested in writing Whitman's biography, and, of course, homosexual. These characteristics were important to produce a character who would move outside of at least some of the textures and patterns of normative behavior to help the Invisible Man.

Ellison also wanted Emerson's appearance strategically to pinpoint another of his discoveries of American writers. He continued to see white American writers using Negroes as a means to escape the confrontation with evil and injustice, and he thought he could prove that Whitman's incorporation of black material in his poetry corresponded to the poet's struggle to render homosexuality.[34] When American writers were faced with the challenges of difficult material, Negroes seemed to pop up in their work. As he concluded the first third of the novel with his hero in the young industrialist Emerson's office—the section that Burke had identified as the "purpose" segment of the dramatic act—he looked for a metaphor adequate to explain the tangled lines of blood and filiation for his young Negro character. In his notes he analogized the hero to Sophocles's Oedipus. While his hero would read the contents of Bledsoe's letters, Ellison wanted to temper the tragic revelation with the hero's dense pride; his dramatic analogy derived from Oedipus's self-blinding.

Confidently knocking about with the literary upper-crust, Ellison ran into *Partisan Review*'s editor William Phillips at a literary party. As Ellison talked up Kenneth Burke to two young coeds, Phillips butted in, saying that Burke was incomprehensible. Ellison deferred to the older critic, avoiding a row, but in his pocket was the Irish critic Donat O'Donnell's favorable estimate of his *Horizon* short story. O'Donnell had also lambasted the *Partisan Review* critical establishment. Restraining himself from passing the review around as proof of Phillips's own abusive and obscure language, Ellison again came away with a negative view of the *Partisan* circle. Speaking of Phillips, he wrote to Hyman that he believed the editor a bit rude and presumptuous. Ellison, however, needed influential editors. At the end of June, *48* declared bankruptcy and stopped its publication.

Ellison's increasing remoteness from the ground floor of Harlem life coincided with his inability to publish in-depth essays on local conditions and the slowing of Harlem's radicals. Ben Davis lost his City Council seat amidst the rising chorus against communism. Keeping his distance was the artist's prerogative, and Ellison clearly enjoyed his right to isolation. But he also saw more accurately the weaknesses of black intellectuals and black audiences, who could neither sustain critical discussions nor consume high art. When he walked out of his apartment on St. Nicholas Avenue, he frequently ran into the famous blues composer W. C. Handy. Ellison was grimly amused over the irony of having casual access to the renowned "Father of the Blues," who now shuttled around Harlem's streets blind.[35] But rubbing shoulders with history in the form of Handy reminded him of the fickleness of celebrity, the speed with which an important innovator could be forgotten and abandoned. He and Fanny painted their own apartment to simulate the appearance of the good life, but without his significant financial contribution, or the eradication of segregated housing guidelines, it was impossible to find a better place to live.

Ellison continued to bear down on his work as the summer sun increased in its intensity. At the office, without the telephone ringing or the jukeboxes blaring, he wrote about twenty-five finished pages of the novel per week. When Langston Hughes called his apartment, he received no answer. July brought renewed success for Ellison's friends Stanley Hyman and Shirley Jackson. Hyman's first book of criticism, *The Armed Vision,* was published by Knopf and reviewed for the *New York Times* by Harvey Breit. Hyman's study examined the works of ten critics and their methods, with some favor toward the work of Kenneth Burke. The book described Hyman as "awesomely well read" and "extremely bright," whose writing technique reflected "scientific purposiveness."[36] The same month, Shirley Jackson published her short story "The Lottery," which became something of a cult favorite and secured her place among modern writers. That year her collection of short stories *The Road Through the Wall* appeared. All three writers were deeply invested in folklore and mythology, and Jackson's short story, a contemporary account of an ancient sacrifice ritual, deeply horrified her readers. While Ellison enjoyed Hyman's book, by August he found himself uncomfortable with some of Hyman's latest perspectives on folklore. In his usual encyclopedic fashion, Hyman had reviewed *Adventures of a Ballad Hunter, The Child's Book of Folklore, Folksongs U.S.A., The Folktale, A Treasury of New England Folklore, Mexican Folkways,* and *Legends of Paul Bunyan,* among many others. Ellison felt positively about Hyman's work, which analyzed the material according to a Burkeian triad of origin, structure, and function. But he was not completely satisfied with the effort. In a disagreement that would reach its most eloquent formulation in a 1957 essay called "Change the Joke and Slip the Yoke," Ellison identified in Hyman a tendency to concentrate on origin in folklore evolution, a concern with linear development that Ellison thought was futile. Because of the natural tendency of the collectors of the material to carry unrecognized prejudices, and for others to take merely a sentimental view of folklore without seeing its deep philosophical meaning, Ellison did not investigate questions of cultural origin. Hyman had announced himself interested in the terms "structure," "function," and "origin," and Ellison devoted his interest to the first two. He cared for origin only when he viewed it more broadly in the sense of myth and ritual, mainly because he rejected both the possibility of art coinciding with a completely rational function as well as the ability to confine artistic expression to a pure source.

Hyman was not discerning enough about the implicit bias in the collections upon which he relied, Ellison thought. He was also quite critical of American's premier collector of vernacular and African American folklore, Alan Lomax, whom Ellison thought an innocent in the world of the theory of cultural origin and also a carrier of fairly base racial assumptions.[37] Nine years later, when Hyman continued in this vein of thinking and applied the same idea to the novel *Invisible Man,* namely, that the grandfather and his riddle were essentially borrowed without alteration from the trickster figure of black folklore, Ellison lamented in a letter to Albert Murray, "I really thought I'd raised that boy better than that."[38]

Ellison also offered his opinion of Shirley Jackson's much celebrated "The Lottery," which he did not find "as successful as most of her stories." He objected to the understatement of tragedy in the conclusion of the short story, whose climax is reached with the stoning death of the scapegoat character Tessie Hutchinson.

> . . . the villagers moved in on her. "It isn't fair," she said. A stone hit her on the side of the head.
>
> Old Man Warner was saying, "Come on, come on, everyone." Steve Adams was in the front of the crowd of villagers, with Mrs. Graves beside him.
>
> "It isn't fair, it isn't right," Mrs. Hutchinson screamed, and then they were upon her.[39]

Ellison felt that Jackson's story, symbolizing war, the infancy of humanity, and the burial rituals that complete the cycle of human life, had not developed the ancient rituals fully enough to afford it an urgent contemporary meaning, thus violating Aristotle's principle of proper scope for tragedy.[40] He objected to the understated treatment of the ritual at the story's core, feeling that Jackson had obscured the tragic action at the center. Ellison did not take lightly exploring serious themes with scant pages, a technique he saw as the surviving influence of "hard-boiled" realism. Part of his reaction, if not caused by envy from the kudos Jackson had received, came from the acknowledgment that he and Jackson were working on the same rich materials and striving to have similar psychological impacts on their audiences.

Meanwhile, he and his agent held on to the rights of "Battle Royal," again rebuffing John Johnson's *Negro Digest* on September 29, still holding out hope that *Omnibook* might make him rich. Ellison struggled to retain his critical credibility with few publications to show and little money to go on (most of the Random House advance had been used to pay off the contract with Reynal and Hitchcock). But while *48* had suspended publication and *Horizon* was in England, his friend Shirley Jackson had ably cracked the *New Yorker* circuit, as had John Hersey and the reigning king of contemporary Southern gothic horror, Truman Capote. Ellison, on the other hand, had missed yet another publisher's deadline to submit his manuscript. He may have felt that he had to work twice as hard for far fewer rewards. He now entered a phase of legal action against *48*. Before the end of the summer, he had filed a claim as a "creditor" of *48 Magazine*, the suit referenced under the name "Associated Magazine Contributors, Inc." He had given up any hope of being paid, and now mainly wanted his manuscript and photographs returned. In September, he was asked by a law firm to turn in copies of his invoices, in preparation for a bankruptcy claim. Before the end of the month, he authored a detailed description of his entire association with the LaFargue project, beginning in early 1947, and the unsatisfactory submission of the essay. He hoped that within thirty days, the copyright would return to the artist so that he might shop his piece elsewhere in time to make enough money to escape the city for a couple of weeks. He sent the lawyers a formal plea for the rights to his work, a long letter to document his suffering.[41] It would take until the end of October before a trustee could be appointed in the case of the bankruptcy to rule on the status of artistic materials. The results were ultimately less than encouraging, and seem to have been enduring enough to outlive the days of legal racial segregation, which initially made the clinic a necessity. The LaFargue Clinic closed its doors in 1959. Ellison published the essay "Harlem is Nowhere" in 1964, in his collection of critical essays *Shadow and Act*.

Ellison was also on the verge of seeking new sources for ideas for his own artistic growth. Even Burke's work had become less compelling. *Hudson Review* carried an essay by Burke on Milton's poem "Samson Agonistes," called "The Imagery of Killing." Ellison hoped that his own work, involved in sacrifice and ritualistic killing, would offer more complexity, "the kind that giveth life and light." The assertion of a life-giving principle was important in the wake of an increasingly reactionary public climate. He would essentially receive no more queries from independent journals, those that could survive the changing American political climate and conformity of the emerging Cold War. The Urban League president Lester Granger, flush with enthusiasm for Harry Truman, declared now that the progressive candidate Wallace's campaign was entirely a Communist front. That October, the young critic James Baldwin published another feature essay, this time in the *New Leader*, charging that Wallace's movement in the South was basically a fraud. Black Communists and leftists could content themselves only with Truman's overtures to the mainstream black establishment. Richard Wright's residence in Paris, the city where there was an intellectual and artistic community on the Left distinct from the Communists, afforded him a wider range of political options. Toward the end of the decade, many of the most sensitive and competent U.S. writers, black and white, would feel compelled to join him. Ralph Ellison did not.

15

Time Stands Still

1949

THE SUCCESS OF the short story "Invisible Man" and its republication as "Battle Royal" had afforded Ellison breathing space with his publishers, but their patience was not limitless. By the middle of February 1949, Ellison was putting in long stretches at his desk, trying to close in on the work that brought him equal parts of satisfaction and challenge. In those months he was at war with the typewriter and the novel's third section that dealt with contemporary politics. To Stanley Hyman he described the process as trying to toss around enormous formations of rock with the hopes that he could produce a house.[1] He aimed for his house to be strong like granite.

As he pushed chunks of the work that had grown into an enormous novel into place, Ellison joined the major dialogue of his generation of writers, the confrontation between communism and capitalism, the debate between a socialist society that claimed to ameliorate human want and a democratic society that purported to guarantee individual freedom. In 1949 he imaginatively reconstructed the differences between the left-wing political organization identified in his novel as the "Brotherhood" and the Harlem black nationalist groups symbolized by the character Ras the Exhorter. While he intended for his terms to be broadly allegorical for the politics of the 1930s and 1940s, and general enough to apply to any political situation, the richness of his description closely approximated what he had seen. His perspective on those decades in Harlem—terrain he knew firsthand—especially his bitterness over the Communist Party shifting its agenda by fiat and without any qualms concerning the human beings involved, came through in brilliant

392

writing. During the months he worked on depicting the sophistry and deception of the Brotherhood, he had as a colorful illustration the trial of New York Communist leaders accused of violating the Smith Act, which began on January 17. One of the primary defendants was Benjamin Davis, a man Ellison thought had lost his integrity defending the notorious Communist Party "line" shifts. In the novel he satirized black defenders of the faith like Ben Davis, Abner Berry, Theodore Bassett, and James Ford by creating the characters Brother Twobit and Brother Wrestrum, black yes-men. Ellison's distressing conclusion to the final third of his novel, a scene in which the hero, serving the disinterested Brotherhood, leads black Harlem into a futile riot, reflected the tenor of academic thinking on the manipulation of blacks by the Communist Party. In 1949, the historian Wilson Record, in close communication with Horace Cayton, was writing *The Negro and the Communist Party*, a study whose final chapter indicated the book's conclusion with the title: "Red and Black: Unblending Colors." Harold Cruse borrowed heavily from the work of both Record and Ellison when he revisited the same terrain and reached even more severe conclusions in 1967 with his *Crisis of the Negro Intellectual*. For most of his professional life, Ellison would be seen as the jury foreman who read the verdict that Negroes connected to the Communist Party were its pawns and that the Communist Party never became an organic part of Harlem life.

In the late 1940s and early 1950s, American writers of the New York intellectual scene were avidly questioning their political beliefs. Mary McCarthy's 1949 novel *The Oasis* and Norman Mailer's 1951 *Barbary Shore* were just two of many attempts by well-known, articulate, political progressives to publicly challenge and examine the flaws of the American radical movement, in particular the Communists' loss of moral and intellectual authority. McCarthy's roman à clef satirized prominent New York intellectuals as either "purist" adherents to radical social transformation (symbolized by the charismatic Italian anarchist Niccola Chiaramonte and his American ambassador Dwight McDonald), or as "realist" upholders of Marxism, who wanted mainly cultural authority in America and the deposing of Stalin (Philip Rahv and *Partisan Review*). In a similar vein portraying the competing sects of the leftists, Mailer's protagonist wanted to swim to the purer Neoplatonic world, or "Barbary Shore," through the putrid ocean of communist betrayal, totalitarian plots, and sleazy American patriots.

Ellison faced an imposing task as he planned to join the battle. Certainly based upon "Battle Royal," few critics could guess where he was really heading. At their most generous, they might have credited him with attempting to expose Southern Bourbon aristocrats and their ruthless manipulations of blacks; at worst, they may have deemed Ellison simply another protest writer, wrapped in the shroud of Richard Wright. Yet any novel that put race at its center alongside intellectual social and political philosophy would have been distinct, if not distinguished, since black life was still something fairly unknown, just beginning to creep into the domain of America's critical elites. Ellison felt challenged to finish his novel amid the increasing tension of political fighting inside the United States, culminating in the decision to invade Korea in 1950. It marked a crucial turning point in his career as an artist. His hope soared for his novel, and his ambition increased: he wanted to reveal the crisis that modernism had laid at America's feet, which had been addressed inadequately in the novels of pessimism and moral leanness that preceded his. Columbia University's Lionel Trilling, whose elevation to the post of leading critic in the United States indicated the rise of the American academy, had described the instability of contemporary novels in an essay "Freud and the Crisis of Our Culture." Trilling proposed the problem as the "progressive deterioration of accurate knowledge of the self and of the right relation between the self and the culture."[2] While determined to explore the mind of an individual character and to enable that consciousness to ramble freely, Ellison intended to avoid a complete turn inward to awareness of only oneself. He wanted to reveal convincingly the inner working of the psyche and the emotions without forsaking broader social themes.

Ellison understood that if America engaged the Soviet Union in armed conflict—which looked almost certain after the Communists roared to victory in China in the fall of 1949—a novel concerned with domestic social life would be poorly received. The country made preparations for violent conflict. As it had in the early 1940s, the wartime atmosphere occasioned a quieting of the pursuit for racial rights in favor of a unified patriotic national front. With Du Bois unmoored from the NAACP (and the *Crisis*) for disagreeing with Walter White's advocacy of Truman, it had become clear that dissent—and sometimes even intellectual opinions plainly stated—would not be tolerated. The intellectuals' and writers' colony at Yaddo came under increasing fire as a haven for communists and art once again seemed on the verge of succumbing to politics.

Indeed, within the next couple of weeks, precisely that took place. On February 20 the Library of Congress Bollingen Foundation Committee, whose members were all Fellows in American Letters at the Library of Congress and included such luminaries as W. H. Auden, T. S. Eliot, Allen Tate, Robert Penn Warren, Katherine Anne Porter, and Robert Lowell, awarded its first prize in poetry to the impaired Ezra Pound. The poet was an inmate at St. Elizabeth's Hospital in Washington, D.C., having been remanded to the mental institution after his trial for high treason against the government of the United States. The former voice of Rome, who had delivered propaganda broadcasts for Mussolini's Italy, and who had written openly anti-Semitic poems, had earned the award for his *Pisan Cantos*. Aware that their selection was bound to set off a firestorm, the committee delivered a prepared statement. Pound's verse had influenced his contemporaries and the field of poets had not shown spectacular strength, thought the important governing board. The Pound controversy brought to the forefront of public consciousness the issue of racial justice and fairness vis-à-vis artistic creativity and critical autonomy. American writers and intellectuals, who routinely were scolded for their insufficient irony and complexity, their distaste for fundamentally ambivalent situations, recoiled from the awarding of the prize to an anti-Semite and hatemonger. New York intellectuals on the Left, from *Partisan Review*'s William Barrett to *Masses and Mainstream*'s Samuel Sillen, took issue with the choice.[3] Barrett noted with wryness that in the same week that Pound won the Bollingen, the American Nazi Fritz Kuhn was granted an honorable discharge by the military. The committee's failure to disqualify Pound's work on the basis of its profascist sentiment spoke to another agenda: the rehabilitation of anticommunists, even if they had at one time espoused fascism. For the moment, fascism in Italy and Germany had been defeated, and the U.S. State Department was cultivating ex-fascists in their attempts to safeguard wartorn Europe from communism. The anticommunist Pound might be excused for his fascism and awarded the Bollingen prize, but as Hannah Arendt's linkage of the defeated Hitler to the thriving Stalin in *The Origins of Totalitarianism* would make clear by 1951, leftist writing could gain no audience in the United States.

As vociferous as the accusations of prejudice was the committee's defense. The Bollingen committee did not idly accept disputations of their decision. They responded directly to criticism, sending a prepared statement to the press, which was ultimately lauded as an example of freedom, an example of the ability to choose and judge that was not allowed in the USSR. (Dwight McDonald, whose journal *Politics* was near collapse, applauded the decision as a healthy sign of American democratic life.) But the rapid exchange of letters and ripostes became legendary mainly because of poet and professor Allen Tate's famous challenge to William Barrett. Tate took the accusation of bias from the *Partisan Review* critic as a slander upon his honor, a slight he refused to tolerate: "Courage and honor are not subjects of a literary controversy, but occasions of action," he rebutted, and actually challenged Barrett to a duel.[4]

The Pound controversy tended to illuminate the poles of America's critical elites. One group was New York–based, heavily Jewish, and gleaned their insights at least in part from Marx and Freud. The other camp tended to have Southern and WASP origins, and to base their intellectual principles on Aristotelian formalism. Ellison had educated himself mainly among the New York Jewish group, though he was mending his own fences with white Southern critics, who held Kenneth Burke, a heavyweight in philosophy, in fairly high regard. Ellison also wanted to surmount what the philosopher and ex-Communist Sidney Hook called the "failure of nerve," the charge facing critics who dismissed the considerable evidence against the Soviets because of their sentimental longings for a communist utopia. Ellison also began to accept the works of Southern writers, like William Faulkner and Robert Penn Warren, which despite their murky race politics, strode against the emotional leanness of Hemingway. His friendships outside the insular world of academic journals and relatively highbrow magazines helped to protect his ego, and nurture his own feelings of autonomy and self-definition. Most satisfying for Ellison was his friendship with Albert Murray, to whom he wrote that February, insisting that Murray secure a copy of Kenneth Burke's "The Philosophy of Literary Form."[5] Living in the deep South, Murray suffered no conflicting "failure of nerve" when it came to selecting an artistically superior literary tradition.

After a birthday party for Langston Hughes in the beginning of February, Ellison prepared a lecture for the Women's Conference of the Society for Ethical Culture. He brought together again his interest in Melville, Twain, and Hemingway, determined to use the concept of the "black mask of humanity" to steer his lecture away from sociological treatments of race. The "black mask of humanity" reversed the Du Boisian notion of a veil separating blacks from whites and malforming the blacks. Instead, Ellison shifted the gaze toward black strength and essential humanity. He also examined white sickness, chiefly in the form of a psychological repression that cemented onto the image of the Negro taboo desires and fears. Around the time that he prepared the lecture, he picked up Herman Melville's *Confidence Man* and was stunned to find Melville's protagonist resonant with Rinehart, one of the characters from his own novel's concluding section.

The confluence with Melville proved splendid. When he showed his manuscript-in-progress to Albert Erskine the evidence of artistic devotion consoled the higher-ups at Random House. Ellison's work impressed Erskine, who encouraged him to push for a fall 1949 publication. While Ellison couldn't be sure how much of his work was making sense to his editor, he thought well of Erskine's easy mannerisms, in particular, his confidence in Ellison's ability to write.[6] While Fanny organized for an art auction, Ellison let the phone ring off the hook, content to shut himself away from the world's distractions and bear down on the first full draft.

Seclusion served him well, even while the arts community, particularly writers, saw the need to act in the months following the collapse of Wallace's presidential campaign, of which Pound's Bollingen Prize had been a sign. Three thousand people attended the March "Cultural and Scientific Conference for World Peace" at the Waldorf-Astoria, put on with backing from the Soviet Union and featuring several prominent apologists for the communist repression in Eastern Europe. *Partisan Review* decried the entire premise of the conference, calling the speakers "intellectual fly-weights." In fact, famous writers T. S. Eliot, Ignazio Silone, and Arthur Koestler aligned themselves with the opposition group Americans for Intellectual Freedom, whose main efforts were designed to expose the Soviet power behind the conference. But not all writers were ready to line up behind the committee's artistic Marshall Plan.[7] The doomed F. O. Matthiesen spoke glowingly of Melville's "common man," but within months he would find the pressures of anticommunism coursing through the academy so powerful that he would take his own life.

At the Waldorf-Astoria Conference, the left wing of American artists tried to estimate its strength, but was unable to operate as a group or identify a coherent agenda without first silencing the criticisms, from the Left and the Right, that they were a Communist front. The older leftist writers who had endorsed the Moscow Trials and been passionately committed to literary realism gave way to a new generation. Younger voices like Norman Mailer, Saul Bellow, and Ralph Ellison were bringing out a new tier of intellectual literature to confront an increasingly complex world where the possibility of liberty seemed to lead to frustration. The new mantra was a near categorical rejection of the earlier era's laconic realism with its serene confidence and pruned self-exploration. The twenty-six-year-old Mailer, whose novel *The Naked and the Dead* was among the most able literary representation of World War II, spoke at the conference and forecast the inevitability of war between the United States and the Soviet Union and their varieties of state-sponsored capitalism. Mailer, whose political education came from French Trotskyite Jean Malaquais, denounced the conference as a fraud.[8]

A month later and across the Atlantic, Paris hosted the 1949 World Peace Congress, where Richard Wright refused to speak before the body of delegates because of the Communist influence in the congress. As head of the leadership of the brand-new Rassemblement Démocratique Révolutionnaire with Sartre and Merleau-Ponty, he rejected both the Warsaw Pact and the Atlantic Pact (NATO). Formally rebuking the non-Communist Left, Wright had stepped out further from the shelter of traditional political groups. Du Bois headed the American delegation, but the attention focused largely on another American star. At the conference, Paul Robeson, the public symbol of black intellectual radicalism, called for a "fight for peace" and objected to making "war on anyone." His words were corrupted by the Associated Press into a fierce denunciation of the United States, which became the basis for the revocation of Robeson's passport and subsequently the crippling of his professional life.[9] When the famous singer and performing star returned to the United States in June, the *New York Times* headline read "Loves Soviet Best, Robeson Declares." Ellison probably thought that Robeson was somewhat naive about Communists—viewing them from his vantage at the heights of international fame—as well as opportunistic for making remarks in

France that he did not ordinarily utter in the United States. Nor did Ellison accept too readily Richard Wright's latest position to the right of the Communists and yet left of center. Ellison's keen eye told him that abroad it was necessary for a black artist to make flamboyant political pronouncements to earn venues for art. He saw Robeson and Wright consistently cast as international politicos, a role for which Ellison increasingly thought neither man was sufficiently equipped. And worse, he thought that their art suffered. Ellison did not feel that either of the men—both the inheritors of prodigious artistic gifts—had improved artistically as the 1940s wore on and their international prominence increased.

As America stepped into the leadership role for international democracy in postwar years, her need for evidence of a sunny domestic life increased. Among Soviet Prime Minister Molotov's rebuttals to Western cries in the UN against Soviet brutality was the deplorable treatment of African Americans in the South. As a result, in the late 1940s an increasingly complex understanding of black American culture emerged, first in the pages of Jewish magazines and journals, striving to portray America as a viable vessel for the cultivation of human values, an antidote to the authoritarian regimes that had taken so many lives. Identifying black culture as worthy of criticism implicitly suggested its richness and obviously changed the quality about black Americans that had appeared foreign to Henry James at the turn of the century. That April, Milton Klonsky, another house writer for *Partisan Review,* would publish "Along the Midway of Mass Culture." Essays like Klonsky's began to bring black culture into the arena of criticism formerly reserved for high art, moving it from the street corner and barbershop and amateur pages of *Negro Digest* to more elite venues and the audiences of professional critics.

The public interest in critical explorations of Negro American life—music, literature, sociology, and psychology—opened doors for a new generation of critics. The newly minted race "experts," many of whom were white, wrote their way onto the pages of magazines and periodicals in very different terms than had such writers as Wright, brought into the writing profession by Communist agitation during the depths of the Depression. The new breed appeared during an era of nascent prosperity, when even something like the largesse of the Federal Works Project was looked at as unseemly, un-American. Ellison noted the new writers but did not doff his cap; he thought some of them parasites, arrivistes, and facile opportunists. Besides, he was still unable to publish his writings about the schizophrenic nature of American society.

Part of his distance was also geographic. He lived in Harlem, away from the Fourth Street bookstores and bars in Greenwich Village that were home base to writers for *Partisan Review* and *Commentary.* Anatole Broyard, ten years younger than Ellison and a "comer" on the New York literary scene, a compadre of the celebrated poet and *PR* editor Delmore Schwartz, had a different perspective on the slowness of *PR* to include the occasional article with black content. Broyard's youth caused him to look differently at editors Philip Rahv and William Phillips; to his younger eyes, their journal was the pinnacle of artistic achievement. He had not witnessed the journal's quest for identity during the 1930s, when it changed its name from the Communist-backed *New Anvil,* and abandoned its interest in black rights well ahead of the Nazi-Soviet pact. Broyard considered it a distinction to be connected to the influential circle.

> Milton Klonsky asked me to collaborate with him on a piece he had been asked to write for *Partisan Review.* The piece was on modern jazz, a subject neither Milton nor the editors of *Partisan* knew anything about. Since I had always been interested in jazz, Milton suggested that I write the first draft and he would rewrite it. What he meant was that I'd supply the facts and he'd turn them into prose. It never occurred to me to resent this arrangement—I was awed by *Partisan Review* and flattered by Milton's offer.[10]

In the resulting essay, Klonsky accepted the age-old stereotype of the fecund black body with small capacity for thought. According to the *PR* crowd, jazz music had gone untreated "in any detail so far" by responsible critics. Commenting that jazz music was not individually distinct—the important compositions were "often anonymous"—Klonsky appropriately lamented that many of the virtuoso jazzmen "are yet unable to read even the simplest score." The music, however, had significance. It was the "prototype of all the mass arts. For in no other are ideas and feelings presented for their immediate effect at the moment of conception." However, the faces of jazz (and the blues)—Louis Armstrong and Bessie Smith, Duke Ellington and Count Basie—had gone unacknowledged. Despite the fact that they had pioneered the form, black Americans themselves failed to appear as tangible icons in American culture. Klonsky further argued that the tragic deficiency of the musicians was doubled by the uncritical (and distinctly American) vacuity of the black audience. "By some absurd double irony, however, the great majority of the Negro population penned in the Northern and Midwestern ghettos actually prefer bleached imitations of commercial jazz or even the white varieties themselves—driven by the same leveling pressure of the Boss culture that makes them straighten their hair or value lighter colored women as more sexually desirable."[11] Even Richard Wright, at the height of his paranoia and rage, had not described African American life as being so empty. To Ellison, Klonsky's were fighting words, narrow half-truths perpetuated by writers who had not thought through the issues sufficiently to rightfully stake the claim. The prominent philosopher Donald Davidson's work justifying segregation had not been any more arrogant or—depending upon the nature of one's sensitivity—any more cruel.

Klonsky's ranking of jazz music as anonymous, and black audiences as uncritical and bland, suggested a decided inertia and unoriginality in black

American culture. The essay's tone was one of presumptive confidence, which piqued Ellison as the sociological declarations by Robert Park had at Tuskegee. And if journals like *PR* had now begun to adopt Wright's blistering perspective on black life, they had little intention of bringing his art into the magic circle. In June, the real boundaries of an argument over the nature of black art and life were defined with the first sortie in *Partisan Review* aimed at bringing the political and artistic project of Richard Wright into focus. Written by James Baldwin, the young writer whose photographic work had appeared in *PM* but who now was slumming around Paris, the essay "Everybody's Protest Novel" indicated the changing of the guard. Reprinted from *Zero* magazine, Baldwin's critique of realism dismissed Harriet Beecher Stowe's classic *Uncle Tom's Cabin,* and briefly examined *Native Son.* A brilliant if somewhat shrill New York native, Baldwin had not had to put in the kind of apprenticeship years Ellison and Wright had. Baldwin had gained admission into the elite journals not long after his days as Countee Cullen's student at DeWitt Clinton High School. His high literary standards were conspicuous, and his essay came to stand for the heart of the criticism of social realist writing; Baldwin pilloried Wright for his membership in the "protest school":

> Below the surface of this novel [*Native Son*] there lies, it seems to me, a continuation, a complement of that monstrous legend it was written to destroy. . . . Bigger's tragedy [is that] he has accepted the theology which denies him life, that he admits the possibility of being sub-human. . . . The failure in the protest novel lies in its rejection of life, the human being, the denial of his beauty, dread, power, in its insistence that it is his categorization alone which is real and cannot be transcended.[12]

Writing as one of the newest members of the community of American writers in Paris, Baldwin argued that protest writers were inferior craftsmen and deeply flawed theorists, incapable of permanently eliminating the forces of race and class oppression. Baldwin characterized the propaganda tactics of protest writers as being cheap and sentimental, capable only of reinforcing the most crude stereotypes of human behavior. He connected Wright's effort to sway society with the same passion—and limitation—of Harriet Beecher Stowe's best-selling *Uncle Tom's Cabin,* which he called in the essay a "very bad novel." Baldwin's argument illustrated his keen understanding of dialectics, and moreover reflected the changing face of America's new Left in the age of the Cold War. The young essayist's arguments had weaknesses—another critic, for example, might have invoked the momentous social movements stirred by *Uncle Tom's Cabin* and *Native Son*—but there was no Ellison writing a "Richard Wright's Blues" to give a different perspective. Instead, Baldwin's promotion of high aesthetics stood alone as the most important critique of Wright's work for more than thirty years. A riot later that summer countered the expatriate Baldwin's pithy recipe for American art. Two months following Baldwin's importuning about artistic freedom and the irrelevance of social protest fiction, a violent mob of veterans fueled by anticommunism and racism attacked Paul Robeson's August concert at Peekskill, New York.

"Everybody's Protest Novel" started the erosion of the public standing of Richard Wright in America. It chastised in skillful and dismissive fashion a writer who had taken easily the central role in the international movement against domestic racism, imperialism, and the war gains of American industries. Wright had anticipated that the Marshall Plan in Europe would be accompanied by less benign forms of sponsorship and aid in other parts of the world. He continued to consolidate his international reputation for combating racism and American institutions. That he was also known as a former member of the Communist Party added to his notoriety. (Wright's biographer Michel Fabre suspects that the U.S. State Department, which prohibited the filming of *Native Son* in France because it threatened America's global image, was greatly pleased at the arrival of another black writer who condemned the author of *Native Son*. That Baldwin's essay, after appearing simultaneously in France and the United States, was reprinted two years later in *Perspectives USA,* a journal that was intended for international distribution in 1951 and was supported by the Ford Foundation, is perhaps evidence of the sort of ideological value that the essay came to possess in the late 1940s and early 1950s.)

Baldwin's work had other appeals besides its congruence with American State Department policy. His essay showed the shift in prominence from the confrontational dialectical ethos of Hegel to the introspective and moral philosophy of Kierkegaard. Wright's character Bigger Thomas could possess his humanity only through the catharsis of murder. Baldwin's brilliant essay supposed that this confrontation was not only unnecessary, but meaningless. In its place Baldwin proposed a more intimate confrontation with chaos; an encounter with the Self. For Baldwin in the 1940s and 1950s, protest was not enough.

Wright's work was destined for steady condemnation, even though he was by far the American most obviously linked to the vogue existential movement of Sartre, Camus, de Beauvoir, and Merleu-Ponty. But in spite of his solid connection to the chic philosophy, Wright was given little recognition during the Cold War in the U.S. In a September analysis of Sartre's *What Is Literature,* William Barrett wrote that the French existentialist's belief in the term "*littérature engagée*" and his reliance upon Wright as a significant writer in that tradition indicated the definite weakness of art. Wright's international reputation represented "a deliberate abnegation from the great ambitions of modern literature." In Barrett's view, the "abnegation" reflected the "end of a whole literary period."[13] Literature—the novel specifically—was in great jeopardy.

Though the developments of French intellectuals fascinated Ellison, contacts with Wright grew increasingly rare. Wright returned briefly to the United States in August to select actors and film the Chicago scenes for the movie *Native Son*. It is unclear if, as he quickly made his way through New York, he contacted Ellison; Wright was now a citizen of the world and had little time for even loyal friends. In any event, the world's leading black writer and existentialist wired Ellison around the time he returned to America to film in Chicago, probably toward the end of September. As usual, Wright had an assignment for Ellison. He had completed the lyrics for his gentle satire "FB Eye Blues" and wanted them set to music. Wright asked Ellison to hunt down Harlem's elite composers and arrangers, Count Basie or Teddy Wilson, and to see to it that his lyrical critique of the American anticommunist hysteria was set to music.

> Woke up this morning
> FB eye under my bed
> Said I woke up this morning
> FB eye under my bed
> Told me all I dreamed last night, every word I said.[14]

Ellison wrote back and puffed Wright up, recounting a conversation where Teddy Wilson had felt that even in simple blues lyrics, Wright's genius was evident. It was necessary to build up Wright's ego for the bruising that was in store, for in the fall of 1949, Ellison saw the noncommunist Left as finished. The political vulnerability of Negroes prevented Wright from securing a famous composer for his lyric. Ellison wrote back to him that Negro musicians would lose their jobs if they endorsed sentiment critical of the government. The noncommunist black Left no longer existed.[15] In his letter, Ellison took care not to mention even the names of the artists whom he tracked down for Wright, in case Wright's mail was being read. When Wright dropped a line at the end of October attempting to find out who might become available for the job, Fanny Ellison wrote in response, saying that her husband was "terribly swamped at the moment."[16] She told Wright that the folk singer Josh White, who had been active in the radical movement during the late 1930s and early 1940s, would set the lyrics to music. Within about a year, Josh White's public radicalism also reached its end. After Robeson denounced the war in Korea as imperialism, White would join the far more conservative baseball hero Jackie Robinson and Urban League chief Lester Granger in publicly denouncing the most popular African American still publicly connected to the Communists.

When blacks abandoned the left wing, Ellison discovered that he could countenance increasing doses of the centrist "New Liberal" movement, intellectuals and artists who hotly rejected Communists while claiming to work for democratic and liberal goals in the United States. He occupied a position somewhere between the *Partisan Review* group of intellectuals, committed anticommunists, and black radicals who abhorred any vestige of racial chauvinism and accepted the communists principally as a movement promoting the elimination of prejudice. Offering up liberalism as a confrontational pragmatism, intellectuals like Arthur Schlesinger Jr. saw it as high time that "bubble of false optimism of the 19th century"—when Marx had theorized the communist utopia—was broken, an act of recognition that one signaled by admitting that the USSR was a totalitarian regime.[17] The New Liberals were bent upon smashing the omnipotent and determining "ideologies" of communism and fascism (as Daniel Bell's book later captured in its title *The End of Ideology*). New Liberals based their ideas on the moral theories of theologian Reinhold Niebuhr, who believed that the utilitarian thinkers of the eighteenth and nineteenth centuries had underestimated the flaws of human character, defects that made utopian societies impossible. The popular Niebuhr proposed that to even consider utopia was "the stupidity of the children of light in its most vivid form." The liberal community envisioned literature as capable of bringing human nature—its possibility and its limits—into important focus. The leading literary critics were involved intimately with designing the orthodoxy of New Liberalism. Lionel Trilling's 1949 collection of essays *The Liberal Imagination* offered the theological responsibilities of literature; the "human activity that takes the fullest and most precise account of variousness, possibility, complexity, and difficulty."[18] Literature was primed to take up the vacuum left by ideology.

Ellison's intense frustration with the Communists and the weakness of the other left-wing clusters had the effect of dampening his cherished disputes with *Partisan Review*'s editorial board. The ground shifted for Ellison as literature became the new religion of the intellectuals. Among the influential journals promoting the new sensibility—Sewanee, Kenyon, Hudson, Western—*Partisan Review* provided the most space for liberal dissent and for politics. *Partisan Review*'s importance in dictating public taste during the late 1940s was so important that the journal came out as a monthly in 1948 and 1949, then shifted to a bimonthly format in 1950. It was a time when people went not only to their psychoanalysts with their troubles, but also to their literary critics.

The reconfigured *Masses and Mainstream* surprisingly had a great deal in common with *Partisan Review*. Ellison's former quarters had become home to an interracial group of radical castaways whose more strident (and pedantic) politics and tastes often replicated those of their better-respected peers. *Masses and Mainstream* boasted an editorial board that included Samuel Sillen, W. E. B. Du Bois, Herbert Aptheker, Ted Ward, and a relative newcomer to left publishing, the black journalist Lloyd Brown.

In 1949, the survivors of the Communist Left at *Masses and Mainstream* made it clear that it had no room for Richard Wright. Doxey Wilkerson's

criticism of Wright in "Negro Culture: Heritage and Weapon" rehashed earlier attacks, finding him guilty of too great a concern with individual behavior. Wright had made a cardinal error by revealing a "tendency to see the
problems of the Negro people as deeply rooted in unfathomable psychological mysteries, not basically in the class struggle." Ellison, trying hard not to
have his prose look as if he had applied psychological case studies to his characters, had little interest in the *Masses*' hapless writer. Wilkerson's attempts to
understand the distinctions of black culture from within the framework of
communism did not lead to clarity: "Negro culture is much more than a
mere reflection of the liberation struggles of an oppressed people; it is a social
force which can do much to advance the freedom struggles of which it is an
integral part." The essay's devotion to the language of social struggle repeated
a traditional dogma in basic terms that Ellison had outgrown and would
never return to. Wilkerson and the Stalinist Left still promoted artistic purity,
and wished to censure artists "who succumb to decadent and irrational tendencies so generally characteristic of our moribund capitalist civilization."[19]
These sorts of words stuck in Ellison's throat as the cant of ideology. Wilkerson's hissing cry, "Let him try to isolate himself from the social foundations
that are his very being and his art will inevitably reveal the distortions of any
uprooted thing," seemed comic from the man who had been deposed from
the *People's Voice*. Ellison had known for years that the "social foundations"
of the black urban world were detracting from his art. His rejection of his former comrades had been final. When Ben Davis and other Communist leaders were convicted of conspiring to overthrow the U.S. government in October and sentenced to five years in prison, they would receive little sympathy
from Ralph Ellison.

In the fall of 1949, *Reporter* magazine offered Ellison an opportunity to
write a review essay on the recent spate of popular cinema featuring black
themes. The *Reporter*, founded by Italian émigré academic Max Ascoli, was
progressive and offered a vision of democratic liberalism and a welfare state.
From the time he was a child in Oklahoma City, Ellison had warmed to the
notion of a darkened movie theater with a screen filled with apparitions of
reality. Thematically, a cinematic perspective dominated his post–*Invisible
Man* fiction. Ellison reviewed three movies, among them Hollywood's version
of Faulkner's first novel to win wide popularity, *Intruder in the Dust*. Another,
Home of the Brave, was a military picture that detailed the hysteria experienced by a young and intelligent Negro soldier named Moss (after Harlemite
Carlton Moss) who becomes paralyzed after watching a friend die in combat.
The movie, with a scene almost directly from Ellison's *Invisible Man* episode
set in a paint factory hospital, climaxes when a white psychiatrist snaps the
black soldier Moss out of his guilt-induced paralysis by shocking him, calling
him a "dirty nigger," and then diagnosing Moss's psychological problem as

rooted in racial hypersensitivity and shame. The black soldier is cured when he can reject his racial sensitivity. Black theatergoers in Harlem had greeted the improbable responses of the black and white actors with derisive laughter. Ellison found the white audiences observing these dramas unprepared to analyze the films critically, chiefly because of "an inner psychological need to see Negroes as less than men." Instead of engaging in critical thinking about the origin of racial tensions and their own part in perpetuating them, whites were moved to maudlin sentiment. "[I]n predominantly white audiences is the profuse flow of tears and sighs of profound emotional catharsis."[20] Ellison thought these responses as false as the reaction Baldwin had noticed from the audiences of Richard Wright's novels. He thought that *Intruder in the Dust* was the only film of the recent group that might be seen in Harlem and not greeted with chortles of laughter at its poignant moments. Unlike *Home of the Brave,* or *Lost Boundaries,* films that both promoted assimilation, the movie adapted from Faulkner's novel concluded with the white lawyer John Stevens telling his nephew Chick Mallison that black Lucas Beauchamp is "the keeper of my conscience, the keeper of our conscience."[21] Ellison estimated that black moviegoers' scorn of Hollywood portraits of black life were the best tonic for democratic health: "Perhaps this is what Faulkner means about Negroes keeping the white man's conscience." Ellison noted the impossibility of shared assumptions among callused black Americans and liberal whites. And even the best of the lot, *Intruder,* was not without its imperfections. In a letter to his buddy Albert Murray, he felt nearly humiliated by what the two friends termed an unheroic and inauthentic portrait of the character Aleck Sander, played by Elzie Emanuel. His essay for *Reporter* was not long, but he actually liked his treatment from the editorial staff, and recommended to Murray that he send in some work to the journal.

Ellison continued to appear and work in the court of the elites, though he staunchly refused to let his life be completely determined by the idiosyncratic whim of their judgment. Shortly after accepting the movie review assignment, Ellison stumbled across the usual crowd when he ventured to hear India's renegade prime minister Jawaharlal Nehru at a New York reception for the leader of the two-year-old independent state. When Alfred Kazin asked a stunningly naive question about the influence of twentieth-century religious movements on Indian socialists, Nehru answered him that Gandhi's movement was a twentieth-century religious movement. Ellison chalked it up to an additional blindness among the liberal humanists in literary New York. Ellison never ceased to be amazed by the cocky assumptions of professing liberals when they confronted nonwhites. Kazin seemed not to have read Kierkegaard, Ellison moaned to Stanley Hyman, lamenting the lack of an existentialist perspective, the unwillingness to see Gandhi's movement as involved in shaping the religious strategies of the modern world.

Ellison's ambivalence and tentative judgments about the shifting political and artistic world around him could not be held at bay in his novel, but rather, began to take it over. He pushed his hero from the bosom of a Southern college and into the arms of urban New York. He had as real-life examples for his hero, of course, the brilliant careers of Angelo Herndon and Richard Wright, and he could read of and listen to the multitude of well-known public repudiations of communism. In November, Wright's pieces from *Atlantic Monthly* appeared alongside essays by André Gide, Arthur Koestler, Ignazio Silone, Stephen Spender, and Louis Fischer in *The God That Failed,* an anthology of prominent ex-Communists.

The anticommunist movement spread throughout the artistic and intellectual community. From his house in New Jersey, Kenneth Burke reproved the Communists and began to disentangle himself from his earlier association with them. In the 1950s, when his work from the 1930s was reprinted, especially *Permanence and Change* and *Attitudes Towards History,* Burke purged most of the earlier important connections to the communist movement, going so far as to remove his concluding pages.[22] Ellison probably had initially been compelled by these works because of Burke's clarity and openness about being stimulated by communist utopian ideas, but now both men had gone through the processes of disillusion, growth, and rebirth.

Along with the Communists, certain elements of the novel had grown less enchanting with age. Around the middle of fall, he began to remove from the novel the long sections devoted to the Invisible Man's tragic relationship with Louise, the hero's white girlfriend. Ellison told friends that he had removed the "Othello theme" from the book.[23] After striking the "Othello" parts, he realized increasingly that as far as thematic material was concerned, the novel was an embarrassment of riches. He didn't have to rely on the power of piercing America's favorite taboos. The removal of the interracial love affair allowed other sections to feature more prominently, and the somewhat playful black and white romance may have seemed inappropriate in the months surrounding the trial and death sentence of Willie McGee in Mississippi for engaging in a consensual romantic relationship with a white woman. Instead, Ellison intensified the symbolism of one of the novel's villains, Brother Jack. He asked Stanley Hyman, whose latest *Kenyon Review* essay, "Myth, Ritual and Nonsense," had covered a host of Shakespeare criticism, for references from *King Lear,* ranging from the removal of an eye to a bloody sun.

Communist and liberal bickering left little room for fledgling black writers to emerge toward the end of 1949. Ellison observed the developments of the next cadre of Negro writers in Harlem with a mixture of hope and pity. In 1949, a short-lived periodical called the *Harlem Quarterly* crept through the ruins of *Negro Quarterly* and the Negro Publication Society. Under the editorial leadership of Benjamin Brown, *Harlem Quarterly* was made up of members of the Harlem Writers Club, which had included Harold Cruse, Julian Fast (Howard Fast's younger brother), his wife Barbara Fast, Jim Williams, John Hudson Jones, Walter Christmas, Willard Moore, and Ernest Kaiser.[24] The journal and the club strove to advance the construction of a cultural commission "to oversee the complicated and aggravated situation in the community," Cruse later wrote.[25] Beyond learning their craft and battling racism, the young writers had to jostle with the Communist-backed Committee for Negroes in the Arts (which went on to sponsor the rival Harlem Writers Guild). The predictable aesthetic and political disagreements among competing writing clubs erupted at a conference at the Jefferson School of Social Science. Kaiser, who had criticized both Doxey Wilkerson and Herbert Aptheker in his essay "Racial Dialectics—the Aptheker-Myrdal Controversy," was branded a Trotskyite, which seemed to effectively end the importance of the *Harlem Quarterly* group, so powerful a derogation was the label. Many of the writers scattered by the feuds and controversies, including the twenty-year-old Lorraine Hansberry, would gather around Paul Robeson's journal *Freedom* in 1950. Harlem would soon have many groups and collectives, but their power to create an independent arts movement would not cohere until the cries of "black power" broke out in the 1960s. Ellison spoke to Brown and the other men of the writers' club and found the group already split along the traditional axis between beginning writers and political opportunists. To Wright, he candidly and bitterly described the situation that had characterized the years of his own earliest efforts. The tensions unique to black writers trying to grapple with the implications of politics in Harlem were still suffocating.[26]

16

Cold War and Inauthentic Blacks

1950

Ellison was approaching his thirty-seventh year at the plumb middle of what media mogul Henry Luce called the "American Century," and his confidence in the unique importance of his artistic vision and the acuity of his novel was high, not inconsequentially from the fact that his manuscript had grown to almost eight hundred pages. He split his days between composition and revision, winnowing his expansive thoughts and ideas. He was wrestling with the ending of the novel, where he had decided his protagonist would reject political organizing, like the real-life Angelo Herndon, in favor of crass individual pursuits. The Invisible Man was to finish his career as master of electronic gadgets and leader of a Harlem storefront church. But the ending did not seem as difficult to confront as the sheer volume of the novel, which he anticipated would have to be cut. Many of the editorial waterloos he had suffered in his career stemmed from the nature of his writing, his own rhetorical tendency to delay the force of his arguments until a powerful climax. Trying to stave off the inevitable emendations by Erskine and Taylor, he revised the manuscript systematically, line by line, trying to condense; by the end of the year he had cut its length by a quarter.

From the beginning, he had been determined to apply a strict dramatic structure to his work that would "take the maximum advantage of those psychological and emotional currents within myself and in the reader which endow the prose with meaning and . . . make prose magical," as he had written to Richard Wright in the summer of 1945.[1] But as he verged on fulfilling his artistic criteria—the very criteria he had faulted Himes for being unable to master—more and more he felt the need to perfect his expression. Ellison's deliberateness was also probably prompted by the increasing number of critical sharpshooters—like James Baldwin—afield. His devotion to thoroughness became legendary among the Harlem crowd, many of whom regarded his intensity as self-absorption.

That year brought not only a resumption of the McCarthy hearings but also, in June, a shooting war in Korea. Langston Hughes, when he was in New York at his home on 127th Street, felt keenly the tensions the writer of *Invisible Man* endured as he poured himself into his serious work on race and politics. Hughes felt mildly wounded, as the two writers were still social acquaintances but not quite kinsmen. Ellison no longer seemed delighted by the achievement of the older man. He had become frustrated by the limitations of his intimates, as he readied himself for another period of hibernation to complete the novel. He desired fulfilling friendships that might reflect his core motives and beliefs. He found his white friends often naive about the fundamental nature of black life, and some refused to believe that he had not been overbrutalized by the conditions of race. Wright did not extend himself intellectually in letters unless the men talked politics, while Hughes cared little for the complexity of either politics or literary form. A couple of years later, Ellison would lament to Wright the almost total impossibility of finding friends with whom he could share the weight of his intellect and his experience. He no longer had fellow Negro writers with whom he might discuss technical matters.[2] Hughes, noting Ellison's reluctance to banter, his growing preference for books over people, and his increasingly abstract references, in later years would write to his steadfast friend Arna Bontemps with a friendly jest, hinting at both the former intimacy of his friendship with Ellison and the frost that cooled it in the 1950s: "Ralphie is getting real baldheaded—further proof that he is an intellectual."[3]

Former mentors could look to him as a serious intellect, but his scholastic endeavors failed to bring him financial success. In January, Ellison was still trying to make some money plotting out electrical diagrams for transmitters and audio components and building stereo amplifiers and speaker cabinets, while Fanny continued to earn the lion's share of their income. Ida Guggenheimer and Stanley Hyman remained his stalwart supporters as he neared completion of his final draft. He was also beginning to connect regularly with New York's premier writers and critics. A week into the new year, he met with Alfred Kazin, who had returned recently from the American literature seminar in Salzburg, Austria, and was busy editing Hannah Arendt's massive book *Origins of Totalitarianism.* The men both had friends undergoing the discomforting scrutiny by the McCarthy committee (Mark Van Doren and Langston Hughes). And even if Ellison was critical of Kazin's insights, there was little denying Kazin's stature in the New York literary world.

One of his friends outshone the others. On January 24, he mailed to Albert Murray a copy of his *Reporter* movie review, "The Shadow and the Act," and also let his buddy know that he was considering writing an essay for the magazine about jazz music's Southwestern origins. Ellison took seriously his position as a contributor to the American public record, and his steady contact with Murray, who also had survived a Tuskegee education, revived Ellison's feelings that his work might do more than just shape the minds of white liberals. If in the past he had hoped his project *Invisible Man* would pierce the shield of stereotypes protecting white America, then in 1950 he had an inkling that cultivating the liberal reader might not actually change the status quo. Ellison let drop his guard when he wrote to Murray, "I get the feeling that most times the stuff is seen only by whites and that, I'm afraid, doesn't mean much in the long run."[4] By reaching black readers, Ellison hoped to invigorate and shape upcoming writers like Murray, and ultimately form a cadre of artists and intellectuals. He felt that one viable antidote to the ineffectuality of the Left was the addition of new voices, and he encouraged Murray to mail the *Reporter* a review. Appealing to his optimism about the potential of new black thinkers that winter was a meeting with a recent Columbia University graduate, the black psychology Ph.D. Kenneth Clark. Clark would go on to clinically elaborate on Wertham's theories about the effect of segregation on black children with his influential doll studies, which were entered as evidence in the landmark 1954 *Brown v. Board of Education* Supreme Court decision on school segregation. Murray and Clark represented a new breed of Negro, tough-minded, capable of handling ambivalence, and not likely to lose their principles in the glitter of limelight.

Ellison's closeness with and confidence in Albert Murray satisfied him and compensated for the loss of regular intimacy with Wright. His connection to Murray was stronger than with Tuskegee buddies they had in common. And their friendship was based on more than their mutual admiration for the special sort of education and encouragement they had received at Tuskegee from people like Morteza Sprague. With Murray, Ellison perhaps came closest to revealing the deep interiors and vulnerability of his personality. The college men spoke the same language, which Ellison valued, as he was able to share his gut reaction alongside his artistic philosophy. Murray had been reared in the briar patch of Nokomis, Alabama, and was as saturated in the vernacular culture of the black South as he was in the refined academicism of the literary and artistic journal. His active intelligence flourished at challenges, and the spirited Murray boasted of his hardiness and ability to overcome them. The men did not talk politics, which was all right with Ellison, whose weighty political statements decrying Gunnar Myrdal, the Harlem riots, or World War II were six years behind him. For Negroes without power or public notoriety, it had become a time of quietude. In September, the McCarran Act would pass Congress, legalizing the detention of "subversives" and strongly equating public dissent with treason. Although Ellison's activities as a writer and dissenter would not be recorded by the FBI until June 1958 (when the Bureau opened an inactive file on Ellison as part of their monitoring of the purported infiltration of the NAACP by Communists),[5] he could smell punishment in the air. Despite considerable provocation, Ellison would never rescind his former protest against social conditions. He was comfortable with hibernation, and then with emerging from it under a different guise. Another appealing feature about Murray, a former U.S. Air Force officer, was his martial bearing and confident masculine assertiveness, the Hemingway-like quality that Ellison found infrequently in educated black men from the South or the bookish Jews he knew from New York. Murray was a fitting comrade, a warlike Telemachus to match the heroism of Ellison's own inner Odysseus.

Ellison's desire for the same professional success he had observed among his friends sometimes complemented his struggles over Cold War alliances and the duties of black writer. His 1950 review of J. Saunders Redding's book *Stranger and Alone* appeared in the *New York Times* Sunday *Book Review*. Having an article in the Sunday *Times* was a flaring indication of Ellison's success as a fairly well recognized writer. And though the *Times* edited his review to condense it and make his style more accessible, it was exceedingly rare for them to print a review by a black critic. Redding, the irascible book reviewer for the *Afro-American* newspaper and a Hampton University professor, had written a novel with a plot nearly the same as Ellison's: a poor black boy makes it to college only to be taken advantage of and become disillusioned. *Stranger* portrayed the moral descent of a Southern mulatto from virtuous striver to immoral capitulationist. Both men had taken inspiration from the modern chronicle of African American experience, James Weldon Johnson's *Autobiography of an Ex-Colored Man*. Compelling as a document of conditions for black advancement in the South, Ellison noted that Redding's novel did not quite achieve artistic excellence. But on the verge of publishing his first novel, Ellison put aside the strident critical vocabulary he had used in *New Challenge* and *Negro Quarterly*. In an easygoing review, he praised the novel's sociological value. "The first thing to be said is that *Stranger and Alone* is sociologically important." Ellison saw in the novel an attempt to come to terms with the abuse of power in the black leadership class, an effort that he believed was important: "[*Stranger and Alone*] is actually about treason and that complex of mixed motives, snarled emotions and allegiances found in the collaborator." While he could not hide all of the book's flaws, he linked the work of the black novelist to broader social and psychological dynamics that had bearing on the American cultural identity.

> And if in his first novel Mr. Redding has selected a protagonist too limited in personal appeal, and if his writing lacks the high quality that marked his autobiographical "No Day of Triumph," he has done, nevertheless, a vastly important job of reporting the little known role of those Negro leaders who by collaborating with the despoilers of the South do insidious damage to us all.[6]

In private, the book's lack of artistry disturbed Ellison. Again, it was Murray, an educator at a black college, with whom he shared his full opinion: "[I]f my own nightmare of a book didn't touch some of the same material, I might have handled him a bit roughly. But hell, it's easy to knife a guy, the creative and difficult thing is to make him aware of the implicit richness of the material as you see it."[7]

Noting that Redding's writing suffered from a subconscious ambivalence concerning skin color, Ellison sensed in some of the author's depictions of dark-skinned black men a comfort with Negrophobic stereotypes. Redding appeared to make a scapegoat for the race's problems of the dark-complexioned, knife-wielding, college student Inky Spillman. Talking to editors at Harcourt and Brace, Redding's publisher, Ellison learned that in the original draft, Redding's protagonist, the treason-prone Shelton Howden, also had been a dark-skinned black man. Ellison thought that Redding was confused about the symbols in his "battle of color." It appeared difficult for intellectuals of the card-carrying black middle-class to rid themselves of the skin-color caste hierarchy. Despite its inadequacies, however, *Stranger* offered a glimpse of the next step for black writers: "at last we're going to have a group of writers who are aware that their task is not that of pleading Negro humanity, but of examining and depicting the forms and rituals of that humanity."

Redding's book gave Ellison more than a moment of reflection and humility about his own work. He had a single major scene to finish, and he was becoming anxious enough to call the novel that he had labored on for so long his "you-know-what." "Is it a rock around my neck; a dream, a nasty compulsive dream . . . a ritual of regression . . . or is it a kind of death and dying?" he wrote to Murray that January.[8] Insofar as his own depictions of "the forms and rituals of humanity" were concerned, Ellison noted that in the exploration of one's humanity that was required to produce a novel, eventually one struck the ore of the psychological base. The novel, of course, was both a rock and a dream, neither of them, and much more. Surely it seemed like a dream when he met with Oklahoma friend Virgil Branam and Tuskegee-bred jazz maestro Teddy Wilson in early February. As they spent a couple of evenings talking about music and the old Territory, he noticed that Wilson was increasingly paranoid about being associated with anyone identifiably procommunist. Then Ellison went in the other direction—socially and politically—when he dined with Ida Guggenheimer. On February 14, Francis Steegmuller, Guggenheimer's son-in-law, sailed for France. Ellison's relationship with the family, particularly the fiercely loyal matron, was deep enough that he determined not too long thereafter to dedicate his book to her; of course, a dedication bearing the name "Ida" also handily included his own mother.[9]

The regular correspondence with Murray helped him feel less isolated. Murray's warm, folksy, and highly technical letters reminded Ellison of college and home and kept Ellison aware of a valuable audience immersed in both the vernacular tradition he worked out of and the formal heritage through which he crafted his art. By March, Murray saw the film Ellison had reviewed in his *Reporter* article. In colorful language, the Tuskegee English professor offered a candid assessment of the Hollywood-promoted black male image, especially as it played in the South: "Boy, that little sonofabitch playing Alex Sander almost threw the whole thing out of focus here. In the first place he tended to sound like a black Yankee." Murray felt betrayed by the film's version of Alex Sander and in portions of the letter that still remain unpublished he unleashed a scathing attack on the acting style that he thought left black men emasculated. In American cinema, black men seemed to bring to life a combined image of brainless subhuman, eunuch, and buffoon.[10] And while he did not meet with the same labels, Ellison too encountered the stereotype as he entered and became a frequenter of literary society. If Hollywood was most comfortable projecting the image of a black sissy and sambo, in real life the assumptions were reversed, a notion that Ellison had articulated in "Beating That Boy" and to which he was not personally immune. In 1953, for example, at a Princeton party following the Christian Gauss seminars, the poet Delmore Schwartz was convinced that Ellison was flirting dangerously with his wife Elizabeth.[11] Ellison would also represent a form of phallic masculinity for Saul Bellow, who after treating Schwartz's doomed life and career in *Herzog*, immortalized Ellison in the character of a penis-wielding pickpocket in the novel *Mr. Sammler's Planet*. And at this time, Norman Mailer was beginning to experiment in his writing with interracial relationships; he would produce by the end of the decade the sensational essay "The White Negro," which caused a major controversy with William Faulkner. Ellison might have been unable to silence the belief cherished among many whites that the Negro male's experience of racial injustice was utterly reversed at night. But with Murray, Ellison had a comfortable friend to whom he might cathartically voice his naked reactions to situations he was powerless to change. It was doubly satisfying that in their correspondence, the men could fall back into the warm and appealing deep Southern vernacular.

But Ellison's reply in kind about the film *Intruder* also revealed his occasional bias in critical judgment, when he exposed his own human flaws and identified a scapegoat for his troubles: "As for Alex Sander, he is a bit of a bitch all right, and a eunuch, and a denier-of-his-balls. But hell, what use has he of balls when he knows that his roly-poly eyes are enough to get him in movies?"[12] Obviously the actor Elzie Emanuel read the Ben Maddow screenplay according to director Clarence Brown's specifications. Both Ellison and Murray knew it, but to criticize the movies from actor to producer would be to acknowledge their impotence. Instead, it was the actor's fault. By donning the mask of self-determined individual responsibility, Ellison let show his contempt for "a guy who denied his manhood." He believed in the necessity of proud manhood. The identification of a scapegoat also obscured, however briefly, the lack of opportunity these very talented men faced. But the locker-room talk and the castigation of the black actor (which Ellison quietly diluted by suggesting that, like his own character Trueblood, Emanuel plied the stereotypes chiefly for his own gain) enabled a candor, and a relaxing of Ellison's liberal demeanor and athletic intelligence that was rare and perhaps he could not display in the company of other writers. Writing as chums, the two men were close. Within the next couple of weeks, Ellison would take Murray's novel of black Alabama life to Erskine and Taylor.

Ellison's editorial team was more concerned that he finish the huge novel, which still lacked a finale. Besides finishing the project, Ellison began to eliminate excess heft from the manuscript; significant tightening of the novel took place in 1950. Ellison entrusted his manuscript to a couple of friends during his editing process: Stanley Hyman was one; the editor Harry Ford of Knopf was another. Ford read the 868-page manuscript and sent Ellison back two typed pages recommending cuts and tightened dialogue to speed the pace of the narrative, a significant concern of Ellison's throughout the novel. Ford mainly dropped secondary characters and episodes. While he disagreed with an occasional point on Ford's list, Ellison accepted most of the suggestions. He revised and clipped the second section, dramatically reducing the number of pages by simplifying his factory hospital scene. Ellison would publish the full treatment of this episode in 1963 as "Out of the Hospital and Under the Bar." One of the most polished segments he eventually dropped showed the hero as a day waiter at the home of a rich white liberal who is confined to a wheelchair. After a series of humiliations and slights, the hero seizes the wheelchair-bound heiress and, in what came to be described as Ellison's trademark "hysteria," he forces the woman to confront her patronizing attitude and thus to climb out of her chair and walk. He had developed more than a hundred pages of the novel detailing his hero's life at the Harlem men's house and also developed key scenes dealing with boarders at the rooming house operated by Mary Rambo, Ellison's most crucial female character. Among Rambo's boarders, the most important character is a dead merchant marine named Leroy, whom the protagonist knows only through a journal.

In perhaps his most notable editorial decision, Ellison cut from the manuscript all of the sections dealing with Leroy's journal, a kind of scripture that offered the hero guidance and insight throughout the second half of the novel. Leroy's journal of philosophical guerrilla warfare was the Invisible Man's prized possession. As late as Ellison's original typed draft of the novel in 1951, Leroy's journal was to survive the burning of the paper contents of the hero's briefcase in the novel's final dramatic statement regarding the necessity of an individually constructed identity. Wandering the darkened sewer, the hero ignites his high school diploma, Tod Clifton's Sambo doll, his Brotherhood name, and the note from Brother Jack. "There were plenty of pages in Leroy's journal but somehow I couldn't destroy it and let it slip back. . . . I burned everything except Leroy's journal."[13]

An articulate combination of the novel's heroic black male characters—the incestuous farmer Jim Trueblood, the insane veteran-physician, Brother Tarp, Brotherhood organizer Tod Clifton, and preacher-pimp Rinehart—Leroy wrote his journal "like a criminal." Calling Frederick Douglass (the hero admired by the narrator's grandfather) a mistaken idealist, Leroy as the philosopher of history believed that Douglass's life would have been better spent as a Nat Turner. Initially, Ellison aimed to reproduce a more complicated stratum of black nationalism, to expose deliberately Ras's inadequacy and, as he had written to Murray, to take issue with the "non-violence boys" of the civil rights movement. Leroy wanted Douglass to teach Negro slaves to commit acts of violence, thereby teaching them "a tradition of responsible civic action . . . a living force in our national life." The extracted journal also included what came to be one of Ellison's favorite radical philosophies about the martyrdom of blacks in the process of obtaining a coherent national American identity: "To designate one as evil is to place oneself in his power. Especially is this dangerous for puritans, for puritans are fascinated by evil, obsessed by it. They have unwittingly obsessed themselves with us. They cannot really destroy us but that they destroy themselves." The Invisible Man reads these ideas as he prepares to join the Brotherhood, and though he fears the words written on the page, he also derives a cathartic pleasure from them.

Ellison saw the perpetuation of injustice due to race and class as flaws in the practice of democracy. Important for him were moments of great struggle for justice, the crest of democratic spirit, such as were produced during the American Civil War, and also during the socialist movement of the 1930s. After his final cuts, only a portion from the journal was salvaged and made its way into Ellison's epilogue, when the Invisible Man, writing his memoirs, in essence becomes the dead marine philosopher. One of his concluding aphorisms came unfiltered from Leroy's journal: "Without the possibility of action, all knowledge comes to one labeled 'file and forget'. I can neither file *or* forget. Nor will certain ideas forget me, they keep filing away at my lethargy, my complacency. Why should I be the one to dream this nightmare."[14]

Ellison's sense of the necessity of militancy and courage and the texture of "this nightmare" had especial salience during the middle of 1950, as interest in black nationalism peaked mainly with religious sects like the Nation of Islam. In late June, communist North Korea invaded the American-backed South Korean Republic, capturing Seoul. President Truman promised that America would retaliate, and in September, U.S. amphibious divisions landed at Inchon, taking the North Korean peninsula by November.[15] With the hero of the Pacific General Douglas MacArthur urging on his troops, the United States pushed toward the Yalu River in Manchuria, mainland China, escalating the possibility of war between East and West. Since the U.S. Army was now fielding integrated combat units, African Americans as a group—as eager to take advantage of the GI Bill as their white counterparts, to gain access to the middle class benefits of college education and home ownership—favored Truman's policies on civil rights at home and anticommunism abroad. Even intellectual interest in the process of black cultural and national formation had fallen out of favor, and in response Ellison shifted the emphasis of his book. Calling the excerpts from Leroy's journal "[p]rolix, didactic and inimical to the narrative," Harry Ford advised that the "diary should be dropped entirely."[16] Ellison considered Ford's advice about Leroy's journal timely and accurate.

But while U.S. domestic life trudged along the path of trying to end racial segregation by law, black Americans still found themselves living in a culture that was quick to identify their most simple differences as evidence of a base degradation, an exotic sensuality, or an atavistic return to primitive society. Ellison had created many black male characters who offered his protagonist guidance because he wanted to correct the increasingly complex American public sensibility that yet misperceived fundamental aspects of black life. The publication of Anatole Broyard's essay "The Inauthentic Negro" in *Commentary*'s July issue proved the electricity of the topic. *Commentary* was the American Jewish Committee's anticommunist journal of art and politics. Edited by the maverick Elliot Cohen, the journal featured the cream of the prominent intellectual writers in New York, and specifically proposed to explore Jewish identity with a candor that had not before existed. Ethnic distinction was on the decline for black Americans (Wright's *Black Boy* had almost completely abandoned dialect), but a slew of fine novelists and writers, including Bernard Malamud, Philip Roth, and Saul Bellow, were at the beginning of an extraordinary and sustained reflection on the particular ingredients of the American Jewish identity. Occasionally African Americans would be given similarly frank treatment in the magazine's pages. Editor Cohen liked to talk about his journal as moving between the distinction of highbrow and middlebrow. *Commentary* was a magazine for the "consumers" of ideas, whereas *Partisan Review* was a journal for the "producers."[17] And it was among the first to publish articles by Negroes such as Broyard.

Conspicuously borrowing from the formula of Sartre's *Anti-Semite and Jew* and making his piece more readable for the *Commentary* audience, Broyard used the traditional categories of normative personality types to suggest that black people frequently exhibited "inauthentic" behavior. "Authenticity, as I take it," Broyard coolly began, "would mean a stubborn adherence to one's essential self, in spite of the distorting pressures of one's situation. By the Negro's essential self, I mean his innate qualities and developed characteristics as an individual, as distinguished from his preponderantly defensive reactions as a member of an embattled minority." Less than fifteen years earlier, Sterling Brown had written of Negro stereotypes exploited by popular culture: sambos, zip coons, primitives, exotics, giants, and showboats. Broyard, however, proposed that Negroes actually exhibited these stereotypical qualities. He offered multiple categories: minstrels who sought white approval; romantics who attempted to make an identity out of victimhood; rebels; wallowers in bestiality; and finally, "inverts," the 1950s euphemism for homosexuality.

To illustrate his theory, Broyard personally documented episodes of startling black behavior. Broyard did not offer a percentage of "inauthentic blacks," but his implication was that Harlem (and Brooklyn) teemed with them. However, despite the listing of black pathologies, Broyard collared a new enemy: the white liberal. "[O]ur contemporary liberals have emancipated the Negro from responsibility and self-determination," he thundered as the essay reached its peak. The problem of the age was one of consciousness and modeling. "Until the Negro defines his self, then, he's not going to get very far in formulating a program for living." African American refugees had left a tangible Southern culture that included hardship and inequality, for a far less stable, and perhaps more insidious, environment in the urban North. "[T]oday the anti-Negro is a secondary problem; their [Negroes'] first problem is their individual selves, their own authenticity."[18]

Ellison did not want to escape the struggle for individuality. However, he saw Broyard's piece as a setup, a formulaic exposé tendered by the native informant. While the work lived up to academic standards, and even approached the whole truth, in Ellison's view, he still aimed to offer insights in his own work about the Negro condition which, while not understating the despair, bridged gaps between blacks and whites. Broyard's faux psychoanalytic essays not only exaggerated the conditions to melodramatic levels—an effort at titillation—but neglected the notion that there was a common ground.

The tension between Ellison and the next group of black writers arose partly from his connection to the 1930s radical movements. Ellison's most committed moments with the Communists in the late 1930s had been times of great optimism about the possibility of transcending the limits of prejudice to develop the human networks necessary to eradicate inequality. Although Ellison's political commitments were essentially cerebral by 1950, his having worked through the cadre of the political radicals had shaped his artistic "armed vision." The fair-skinned Broyard, unconnected to the political movement for black rights, could afford to think of himself exclusively as an artist. He rejected the radical struggle and mainly seems to have used his early essays on Negroes and jazz as a way of getting inside the New York literary world. "When I was going to Brooklyn College, everyone urged me to join the communist party, but I refused because I thought it was an uninteresting quarrel with the real. Modern art, though, was a quarrel that appealed to me." But Broyard's flip tone and lack of existentialist anguish were indicative of the real cleavage between the two writers' sensibilities. While Ellison approved of the direction of *Commentary* for printing the work, he reserved his judgment of Broyard.[19] Ellison's essays and fiction came at a higher emotional cost; they were self-consciously and scrupulously honest.

In New York's literary circles, however, the bar had been raised in the debate concerning the inclusion of African Americans into the society, and in particular, their fitness to serve an active role. This swirl of ideas counterbalanced for Ellison the natural attractiveness of an extended visit to France. His friend Richard Wright certainly could not understand why he had not made the journey, and may have even felt snubbed. To Wright, it seemed a natural next step: from Tuskegee (and Ohio) to New York; then from New York to France, to the land of intellectual freedom. Wright by December 1950 had helped to found the French-American Fellowship, a group of politically committed artists and writers, an extension of the narrow breathing space between Right and Left in Europe. But because political tensions remained at such a peak of volatility Wright bought tickets to get his family out of France if war came. Popular belief held that if the Marshall Plan were not in place then Stalin would drive to the English Channel.

The conflicts that were hypothetical or impending in Europe involved real carnage and loss of life in Korea. In November 1950, the Chinese, making good on promises to defend themselves if encroached upon, used hidden staging areas on the Korean side of the Yalu River and launched a determined counterattack into North Korea, pushing U.S. and United Nations troops well past the Thirty-eighth Parallel by January. While Russian envoys attempted to get a truce signed, General MacArthur scoffed publicly at Truman's idea of limited war. MacArthur promised to hasten victory by bombing military bases in mainland China. In April 1951, Truman had to relieve the outspoken general of his command. Politicians on the Right such as Senator Joseph McCarthy and Congressman Richard Nixon denounced Truman's decision and called for the president's removal; polls recorded Americans as overwhelmingly in favor of General MacArthur.[20] Americans allowed no quarter for Communists. The Smith and McCarran Acts not only had teeth in the law, but had popular support.

The open rancor toward Communists emboldened the radicals among the white supremacists. Ellison noted with displeasure the spate of bombings and lynchings in the South, especially the Florida bombing-murders of NAACP leaders, but no longer did he stop working on his fiction to write fiery essays. Ellison had chosen to live in Manhattan, the most international of America's cities, and arguably the most tolerant of racial diversity. And while politics always extracted an emotional cost from him, he spent his time in literary pursuits, reading the *Idea of Theater* and dining with Sinclair Lewis, the aging author of *Main Street* and early mentor of Hemingway. Indeed, as if to accent the changing face of American letters, James Baldwin's essay "The Negro in Paris," published in the June *Reporter*, dramatized blacks' struggle for identity when confronted by white Americans in a foreign country. Baldwin's edgy, though still tourist-oriented, account of foreign travel hinted at the assimilationist priorities—and opportunities—of black writers in the so-called American Century. The tendency of the most privileged to cry out seemed specious to Ellison. He sensed that the black writers flocking to France to escape racial slights had obscenely reduced the terms of humanity to being able to order a cup of coffee. Ellison had time only for his novel. For him, more enduring than the most brilliant essay was an artistic production that erected aesthetic standards and guideposts, the pivotal activity which, according to Kenneth Burke, preceded political action.

On December 27, Langston Hughes called Ellison to tell him that he had dedicated his book *Montage of a Dream Deferred* to Ralph and Fanny. Hughes needed his friends. Within the previous two years, the embattled poet had been connected in print and in various U.S. Senate deliberations to more than ninety Communist groups. In the early 1950s, he would have awards rescinded and would be driven from lucrative radio, film, and publishing contracts. Hughes even toned down his views on racial justice so as not to lose his lecture circuit at the Southern, largely state-supported, black colleges and universities where he made his living. Ellison confided to Hughes at the end of the year that despite valiant efforts, he had not finished his manuscript. Hughes may have been playful, but he was ultimately supportive. When writing to Arna Bontemps, Hughes looked favorably on the mysterious efforts of his former protégé, carefully considering his own position. "I was just talking to Ralph Ellison on the phone and he has not finished his book YET. So if he can take that long, why can't I"?[21] Their circumstances were different. Ellison could unreservedly seek out the fulfillment of his artistic vision despite his financial needs because of his working wife, Fanny Ellison.

But for his part, Ellison still saw Hughes's great flaw as an evasion of the intellectual's responsibility. Hughes had known Koestler, Nicolás Guillén, Garcia Lorca, and Hemingway, but not enough of his writing reflected these associations. His autobiography had been merely a "chitchat" book, Ellison had let him know in 1940. From the distance of about thirty-five years, Ellison would later recall the dedication and his relationship with Hughes in a caring but thin estimate that revealed a recurring compulsion to repudiate the famous teachers in his life. Hughes not only didn't consider himself a literary lion but was content to be a literary operator—a perspective that Ellison found appalling: "Langston said to me, 'If I wrote the book you wanted me to write, people wouldn't buy it and I would have to take a job.'" This reply was in keeping with Hughes's studied avoidance of a serious response to the publication of "The Battle Royal" in *Horizon*. In an interview with Hughes's biographer Arnold Rampersad, Ellison said he thought the dedication of the book was Hughes's way of paying a debt. "I had called his attention to what was happening in the vernacular—be-bop and so on. [Hughes] used his emotions and his sensibility more than his intellect . . . [he] was very easy going. He would not think, and during that period I was trying very hard to deal consciously both with writing and with politics."[22] Part of Hughes's resistance, however, to consciously responding to the crises of art and politics stemmed from his racial vulnerability, the same condition that ruined Robeson and Du Bois, the leading black American figures who wrestled in public with art and politics. No matter how principled his disagreements may have been with these older men, one of the differences between Ellison and Hughes was quite practical. The artist who had, in a sense, fathered himself by selecting his own birthdate, did not wish to share the fate of the three best-known black leftist figures in art and politics, public figures whose homeland had so deliberately hobbled their careers.

17

The Black Kafka and
the Fight against Reality

1951

WHILE THE BROAD CONDITION of the artist and literature always was of central interest to Ellison, the special situation of the black writer was Ellison's home. Early in the decade, that home was accommodating new members. Ellison picked up the *Kenyon Review* in early 1951 to see Richard Gibson's commentary "A No to Nothing." Gibson, a black writer just out of undergraduate school at Kenyon College, had enlarged upon James Baldwin's vilification of Richard Wright, and also included in his condemnation the public scapegoat Langston Hughes, under congressional scrutiny for affiliating with the Communist Party.

Gibson's cries for artistic freedom were typical of the younger generation challenging the old; what was new was placing these ideas in elite academic journals. Twenty-five years before, Langston Hughes had published his artistic manifesto "The Negro Artist and the Racial Mountain" in *The Nation*. Ten years after Hughes, Richard Wright's "Blueprint for Negro Writing" appeared almost unnoticed in *New Challenge*. But Gibson and Baldwin were published by *Kenyon Review* and *Partisan Review* at a time not only when those journals were widely read among nonspecialists, but also when the academic professions gained prestige and became the important conveyors of value to intellectual works and intellectuals themselves.

Essays diminishing the impact of black writers had long histories, and Gibson, who had use for neither protest nor romantic sentiment, seemed affronted by all black writers. He viewed the now fifty-year-old Hughes, the best-recognized African American writer, as something of an apostate. The attack on Hughes was furious. In his article, Gibson blamed Hughes for creating "the black hands, black faces, black Christs leering up at him from these sordid pages . . . the incompetence, the sentimentality, the hypocrisy, the intellectual irresponsibility, in sum, the entire minstrel psychology." Gibson disparaged artworks produced by African Americans: "there is not yet a single work of literature by an American Negro which, when judged without bias, stands out as a masterpiece." One was better off taking in the comparatively "rewarding" social uplift pamphlets of the NAACP or Urban League. And going in the direction that Baldwin would take in many of his future works, and which Broyard already had successfully identified in "The Inauthentic Negro," Gibson reproached the "Professional Liberal" who controlled publishing, encouraged black mediocrity in the arts, and rewarded only works that dealt with "Jim Crow, sharecropping, slum ghettoes, Georgia crackers, and the sting of his humiliation, his unending ordeal, his blackness."[1] Gibson somewhat haughtily told his readers that a black writer, instead of recalling that he was publishing at the same time as Chester Himes, should remember that he was a contemporary of Gide and Valery, Kafka, Mann, and Eliot. The essay became so popular that it was reprinted alongside James Baldwin's "Everybody's Protest Novel"—as a one-two punch for the second number of the American journal *Perspectives U.S.A.,* distributed abroad.

Although Ellison agreed on many levels with Gibson's aesthetic and intellectual opinions, he was profoundly offended by the critique. Gibson had taken full advantage of the reactionary climate to strike at ex-Communist Wright and fellow traveler Hughes, the vulnerable members of Ellison's literary family. In letters to Albert Murray, Ellison flashed his anger: "I'm sick to my guts of reading stuff like the piece by Richard Gibson in *Kenyon Review.* He's complaining that Negro writers are expected to write like Wright, Himes, and Hughes; which he thinks is unfair, by God, *he's* read Gide!" Only a couple of months before turning in his own novel, Ellison could see what would be coming from upstart young writers: public condemnation for literature dealing with themes of racial injustice.

The real word on Gibson was that he had tried to land a book contract with his personal contacts alone, having no track record in publishing and nothing to show of a manuscript. Ellison was blunt: "If he thinks he's the black Gide, why doesn't he write and prove it?"[2] Filled with the hubris of youth, which Ellison himself had had at the outset of his career, Gibson had set out to build his reputation on the carcasses of the black writers who had preceded him. Gibson, a well-regarded student at Kenyon (and obviously by John Crowe Ransom), had peeked into the elite circles of the New Critics. Ellison's umbrage at Gibson's views was due in part to his rapid success. First there was Baldwin, then Broyard (just out of his twenties), and now there appeared another black wunderkind, threatening editors and artists with elite standards and superior prose. And though Ellison took pride in resisting the temptation throughout his career to publish his work in the formalist strongholds *Kenyon Review, Sewanee Review,* or *Southern Review,* it still galled him how quickly a Negro writer with no credentials could be propped up to ridicule other Negroes.

Ellison had considerably less patience with the unpublished, represented by Gibson, clamoring for a place among the elite. By the time he had nearly finished *Invisible Man,* Ellison was intellectually and artistically muscular, confident in publicly affirming his views and enjoying the status derived from his many artistic, intellectual, and publishing contacts. He emerged more elitist, more capable of believing that inevitably genius and hard work won out. Nor did Ellison take the opportunity to castigate white liberals, as did Broyard, Gibson, and Baldwin. He saw those who had been good to him—Ida Guggenheimer and Stanley Hyman in particular—as a rare breed who, when they did not kowtow to an ideological position (such as communism) were invaluable as friends and supporters. Their friendships had proved his early theoretical arguments: with the help of whites in positions of influence, a Negro writer could advance. And of course, he noticed in the rapid ascent of the younger black writers an absence of the courage born of struggle. He saw in them something of the tendency to shirk in the face of danger, to duck before they could see the blow coming. Ellison would never totally relinquish his sense of himself as a boy from a tough neighborhood, one who conceded nothing and who took winning seriously.

Not far into spring, Ellison decamped to Westport, Connecticut, to Stanley Hyman's house, where he finished the first complete draft of the *Invisible Man* manuscript. In the house on Indian Hill Road alongside Hyman, his wife Shirley Jackson, and their young children, Ellison relaxed and overcame his anxiety about his novel. He realized that he was agonizing too much over the transitions, and he worked to gracefully move from paragraph to paragraph, chapter to chapter. Originally he had envisioned a grand operatic scheme to emphatically promote as fluid language in the book. However, it was now clear that more practical devices were necessary. Shirley Jackson was editing the page proofs of her novel *Hangsaman* dealing with the mental disintegration of a young college student; and she counseled Ellison to forgo elaborate transitional schemas. After Ellison looked at her manuscripts, he agreed to sprinkle ordinary transitions—"that," "and," "therefore," "so," and "then"—confident that plainness would not ruin the artistry of his work. In reflective moments he thought that the hesitation to submit the finished novel came from the process of distilling raw experience through his imagination, which frequently produced a chaotic blend: "I had chosen to recreate the world, but, like a self-doubting god, was uncertain that I could make the pieces fit smoothly together."[3] He also recognized that the critical world of the *New Yorker,* the home base for Hyman and Jackson and well thought of writers like John Cheever, actually applied less stringent standards than his own.

Four years after *Horizon* had published the short story "Invisible Man," Ellison completed the first draft of his novel. He submitted the manuscript to his editors in April, having trimmed 780 pages down to a leaner 612 pages. He had been groping for an experimental style in his novel that would convey the importance of the black vernacular idiom; and during the same time, the idiom of experimentation, Negro jazz, was utterly transforming. In New York, intellectuals had taken notice of Charlie Parker and the young Miles Davis. Anatole Broyard scored another piece in *Commentary,* commenting on the ascension of bebop's "cool" music and its complex emotional attitude of denial. The music and the terms of Ellison's youth—stomp, jump, swing, and jazz—were disappearing. Parker, with his blistering alto saxophone, had erased Louis Armstrong, now considered a grinning Uncle Tom. Broyard charted the music from an origin of black authenticity and fertility to the contemporary diluted and impotent hybrid. He called the current bebop music "an increasingly miscegenated ritual which was gradually losing its original identity and cathartic quality." Probably because the review so closely held to analyses of twentieth-century literature, which was considered to have completely lost its vitality after Joyce and Hemingway, Ellison was never deeply impressed with the feted Broyard. But Ellison saw a dangerous implication in the undeniably smart review, that the effect of urbanization on the Negro had been an unmitigated disaster. Broyard concluded the essay with a flair for dramatic overstatement that rivaled prosegregationists like Cole Blease: "The cool Negro is a case of social gangrene caused by frozen members. He has put his situation on ice; ostensibly, he does not wish to melt in American society. The Negro fiddles while Rome burns. But as we watch him we see the rub: in his withdrawn abstraction, the cool Negro suggests the *stunned* Negro of slavery. The irony is that coolness is self-enslavement."[4] Urban blacks were being blamed for their attitudes of alienation, an observation that Ellison believed should have a broader context.

Ellison's analysis of the passing of the swing era and the triumph of bebop and "cool" was the subject of several conversations with Langston Hughes. On May 1, Ellison rewarded himself for completing the novel by dropping in on the "poet of Negro America" at his home at 20 East 127th Street to spread the grand news that the novel was finally complete; or rather that his original draft was completed to his satisfaction.[5] He may also have indulged in some mild gloating, if not with Hughes, who kidded Ellison about working on something akin to *Moby Dick* or *Paradise Lost,* then with Hughes's housemate and adopted relative Toy Harper, a stalwart Robesonite who thought Ellison had disappeared from the vanguard after the promise of his *Negro Quarterly* days. Years earlier, he had spent a couple of nights on her couch when he was new to Manhattan, and getting his bearings, and his phenomenal growth from college kid in the late 1930s to highly respected writer in the early 1950s startled her. Hughes's friends and supporters never quite saw Ellison apart from Richard Wright, the aloof outsider who they thought had won fame by meretriciously sensationalizing the race theme. Wright was not considered a premier artist like Hughes.

To his credit, Langston Hughes had a remarkable talent for rising above base jealousies and injuries, and he remained an unambiguous and steadfast advancer of Ellison's career. In a letter to his closest friend Arna Bontemps, Hughes was impressed enough with Ellison's draft to compare the book to Negro writer Willard Motley's massive and popular *Knock on Any Door* (1947), a blockbuster novel that did not feature a Negro protagonist, and which was turned into a motion picture by Columbia in 1949. Motley's success with the "raceless" novel had been either a harbinger or an impetus for what was to come. In the late 1940s and 1950s, some of the ablest blacks writing fiction produced novels without Negro characters: Ann Petry, *The Country Place* (1947); Zora Neale Hurston, *Seraph on the Sewanee* (1948); William Gardner Smith, *Anger at Innocence* (1950); Richard Wright, *Savage Holiday* (1954); and James Baldwin, *Giovanni's Room* (1956).

A writer and Fisk College professor who also took pride in Ellison's achievements, Bontemps endorsed Hughes's warm praise of *Invisible Man,* and also identified the underlying circumstances that had enabled the creation: "His book will surely be a solid sender, after such sustained work. Gives me a notion to take 2 or 3 more years on the big one above [a never completed book on Douglass-Washington-Du Bois] and try to make it a s[olid]-s[ender] too, but I fear my gang here would come to the end of patience. They should learn a lesson from Fanny."[6] Indeed, Ellison's novel was a testament to the patience, endurance, generosity, and faith from Fanny. After considering the years spent prior to the first draft, Bontemps believed that Ellison was "making this one novel his life's work."[7]

Certainly Ellison hoped that his "life's work," as Bontemps had called it, would prove worthwhile. But artists working to transform the policies of racial injustice in the United States suffered a considerable setback that called into question the nature of a high-modernist project such as Ellison's, in comparison with the protesting realism for which Wright was known. Conditions in the South were perhaps more primitive than even Ellison at his most pessimistic had considered. Before the end of May, the state of Mississippi, calling the Negro Willie McGee's love affair with a local white woman an obvious case of "rape," carried out his death sentence. Wright fired off from France an editorial protesting the execution. But at home, the publicized killing was met by stony silence from most of America's intellectuals, who were capable of fury over Soviet influence in Czechoslovakia but were unable to recognize despotism at home.

Around June, Ellison went for an appointment with his editor to Random House's brownstone mansion at 457 Madison Avenue. Ellison and the courteous editor Albert Erskine (who often invited writers to his house for extended stays while they prepared their manuscripts for publication) devised a schedule to read the manuscript aloud, editing and revising as they went along. Ellison found the technique valuable enough to read future manuscripts aloud into a tape recorder, to hear the rhythm of the sound. The Tennessee-born Erskine was only two years older than Ellison, and was a hard worker, not a silver-spoon prodigy. He had been an intimate of most of the influential Southern writers, save Faulkner; and he enjoyed the life of a man of letters. Erskine was thought to have a "dreamy" personality—some might say excessively imaginative: at twenty-six he had married the nearly fifty-year-old Katherine Anne Porter.[8] But the range of his travels and experiences, his familiarity with the South and broad ease with differing literary approaches, and ultimately his saturation in the New Criticism, made him an apt match for Ellison's project. Their goal was to turn the book over to the printer no later than August.

With Erskine helping, in a relaxed manner they pruned the manuscript. Some of the deletions were easy to part with. They knocked off Ellison's slighter effects: all of his throwaway symbols to the radical movement were stricken from the text. The Invisible Man no longer cried "She's ofay! She's ofay" when encountering a white woman, and Brother Jack no longer sipped "Cuba Libre" beer at a Harlem bar. The references that might have made the text an advertisement for the revolutionaries were left on the cutting room floor.

Other changes had to do with making the work less of a novel aimed for the knowledgeable elite—even if it made the book more popular and less unique. During his conversations with Erskine, Ellison decided to replace Buddy Bolden, the mysterious founder of modern jazz, with the better-known Louis Armstrong. With Armstrong (a well-known "pot-head") as a standard-bearer for African American culture, Ellison treated in detail the hipsters' favorite ritual to defy public values, smoking marijuana. He had intended to reveal fully to impetuous critics like Broyard the interior ambivalence of black hipster and jazz culture. His editor worried less about reeling in wayward critics than about aligning Ellison with the aesthetic currents of the coming era.

The decision to eliminate Leroy's journal removed chunks of the novel that would have reflected the international scope of Ellison's earliest intentions. It was difficult for him to shave his global perspective, in the era of decolonization movements and formidable anticolonial analyses, such as Franz Fanon's 1952 *Peau Noire, Masques Blancs* (*Black Skin, White Masks*). Some of these early sections read like entries from Ellison's working journals, but they reflected an international political consciousness that made the hero decidedly less naive. The hero, for example, embraces the Brotherhood hoping to learn the best method of fighting colonialism. Shortly before the Invisible Man becomes the section organizer for the Harlem branch of the Brotherhood, he rereads Leroy's journal, the orienting text for the second half of the novel. In some of the diary's long exploratory passages, Leroy also writes about the nature of global color prejudice and the European domination of nonwhites. The journal persistently investigates divergent strains of utopian politics and deliberately grounds the potential victory of the oppressed outside of a Christian-based concept of justice. The coloreds of the non-European globe will triumph not because the last shall be first, but because the colonizer's brutal enforcement of alienation upon the colonized creates in the victims a degree of objectivity that makes them less vulnerable to greed and immorality. The ethical arguments advanced in the diary are philosophical wanderings trying to imagine a global shift in power, and a new ideal of justice. "If this were a world of justice we would inherit the state through sheer default. Not because the humble ever inherit anything, but because we are alienated and forced into a position which makes us less susceptible to corruption."[9]

While Ellison's deletion of such passages quickened the plot, they not only eliminated the temporal urgency he had intended for the book, but also made him even more vulnerable to the criticisms of the radicals. High seriousness in literature and accessibility for the white audience came at a price. And if it required removing insightful portions, the second read-through also netted gems. Penciled above a typed line from the journal, Ellison inserted words that captured the ironic and paradoxical nature of his novel: "For a moment I thought of my grandfather, but quickly dismissed him. What had an old slave to do with humanity?"[10] The thematic punch of the novel offered a domestic reconciliation between the Invisible Man and his slave grandfather, not the hero's pursuit of citizenship in the "non-European world."

Ellison also dropped many of the passages that, while perhaps conforming factually to the interracial reality of the Communist Party during the 1930s, made the book appear overly sensationalistic. Before submitting the final revision of his manuscript, his most remarkable editorial change was to reverse the Invisible Man's impetus for going underground. In his initial draft, Ellison's hero flees from the character Louise, the white liberal whom he has fallen in love with. Making his last major structural change, he decided to remove entirely the hero's paramour Louise, the "woman of woman," as a character.[11] In the final draft, the hero, fleeing bat-toting white toughs who interfere with his mission to assassinate Brother Jack, falls into a sewer. (To add to the confusion, in the novel's prologue, the narrator remembers fleeing Ras the Destroyer.)

As Ellison neared completion of the revised manuscript, memories of his past began to break over him; his dream-nightmare broke out in full. He remembered, sometimes quite bitterly, his defeats at Tuskegee; and he began to dream of high school in Oklahoma. There was also a sense of pride in producing a work of art that was well beyond what the Carnegies and Rockefellers had intended when they donated money to Booker T. Washington. Ellison felt that his life was redeemed, and he was finally letting go of the notion of failure that had haunted him. With his destiny as a writer at hand, he wrote a searching letter to Murray in Alabama: "I only wish I had known consciously that I was preparing myself to become something called a writer, rather than the aborted composer that I am." He thought of his thwarted music career with a characteristic mixture of bitterness and pride: "The bastards defeated me there, but I think they might have let well enough alone. Nimble is the word, they taught me to be many things in order to be myself. So I thank them although I don't forgive them." And if he had become nimble, he had also learned to focus his diverse interests for the sake of one project. Ellison asked himself the real question of his self-worth as he closed in on his fortieth birthday. Foes were quick to remind him of his thinning hair and the fact that his wife was supporting him. Albert Murray's friendship, as he came into the home stretch of the project—which seemed to take off and fly without his control—was essential. He regaled Murray with his hope that the book was "[j]ust a big fat ole Negro lie, meant to be told during cotton picking time over a water bucket full of corn, with a dipper passing back and forth at a good fast clip so that no one, not even the narrator himself, will realize how utterly preposterous the lie actually is."[12]

Ellison confided his deepest hope to Murray, that his work might contain the best that the vernacular storytelling tradition had to offer, and that it would strike a chord so true and deeply embedded in the mythic structure of the community that it would seem nearly anonymous. To the rest of the world, he was confident that he had a major success on his hands that would fulfill the high aesthetic mission he had put forth for himself and other writers.

He needed to believe so, because by late 1951, another shovelful of dirt fell upon the tomb of the American reputation of Richard Wright. Baldwin's more openly confrontational essay "Many Thousands Gone" came out. In "Everybody's Protest Novel" he had only briefly touched on Wright's *Native Son* (Baldwin had originally hoped to treat only the slew of postwar protest fiction); "Many Thousands Gone," the title taken from the Negro spiritual, devoted itself to *Native Son*. This time the Harlem-bred literary sensation not only had extended his range to deal with the nature of black stereotype in fiction, but also had appropriated a powerful rhetorical technique. Instead of criticizing whites for ignorance or negligence, or settling into a natural opposition with himself as the informed cultural insider detailing important events to *Partisan*'s audience, Baldwin made himself one with his educated middle-class readers, dispersing his own authority but raising also the intelligence and commitment of his group. Baldwin's essays were replete with "we's" and "our's," cementing him to his white liberal audience and making the material accessible to them as few black writers had before. Wright, who would in 1957 publish a book emphatically titled *White Man Listen!,* could not be more passé.

In the essay, Baldwin moved—with a confidence and steadiness and still without the appearance of contrivance—to the position of cultural leadership for the Negro, a post that would be secure by the end of the decade. Leaving aside his shrewd tactic of coupling himself to the reader, Baldwin still bore the cudgel against protest fiction and the forces of environmental determinism: "The reality of man as a social being is not his only reality and the artist is strangled who is forced to deal with human beings solely in social terms." While the contradiction that Baldwin wrote these essays in France because he could not surmount the physical conditions and psychological assumptions that threatened his identity in the United States was perhaps lost on the critics who read his work, his objective was clear-cut: "Negroes are Americans and their destiny is the country's destiny."[13]

After "Many Thousands," it was immediately clear to Ellison that the Invisible Man's journal, glowing with its theoretical affinity between Negroes and the "non-European" world, could only beg scorn. Besides decisive differences in temperament and background, Ellison was a watershed moment away from the new breed of black critics. If Broyard saw *PR* as the pinnacle of an artist's achievement, Baldwin saw the magazine, and the other New York literary journals, as an even greater means of sustenance—a lifeline. Indeed, to James Baldwin, even younger than Broyard, the journals *Commentary, New Leader,* and *Partisan Review,* and their editors, including Philip Rahv, "were all very important to my life. It is not too much to say that they helped save my life."[14] The favor worked both ways; now the critical elites had reflective black essayists who championed New Liberal ideals.

It was becoming apparent that the critical world would accept some redefinition, but not an outright repudiation, of the American identity. It was probably in that spirit that Erskine and Ellison approached the final work on the manuscript, a revision of the epilogue; the prologue was sent to a hungry *Partisan Review* for the January-February issue. By the early 1950s, *Partisan* was a journal more of cultural stewardship than artistic dissent. Advancing a cosmopolitan elitism, *Partisan* also decried the moribund status of the contemporary novel. Ellison was awarded a rather dubious artistic promotion.

In his final draft, Ellison improved the impact of his novel by discarding the philosophical education of the Invisible Man, which had been designed to lead him to an enlightenment. This change made the narrator more of a literary character and less of a mouthpiece for philosophical discussions. For example, Ellison cut from the prologue a reversal of Kierkegaard's book entitled *The Sickness unto Death*. "All sickness is not unto death, neither is invisibility." Ellison wanted to make explicit his rejection of the notion (which was also rejected by Sartre and Camus) of despair as steady detractor from a satisfying life.

Among the changes—some minor and others not so minor—the technical decision to transfer most of the prologue into the epilogue was the most weighty. It complicated the structure of the novel because ostensibly, due to the back and forth chronology of *Invisible Man*, the hero achieved enlightenment at the novel's first pages. The prologue had stored Ellison's meditations on Kierkegaard's ideas about human anguish and Henri Bergson's concept of the élan vital, blended through with Fromm and Reich's warnings about man's inability or tendency to reject the responsibility of freedom. He decided to split his efforts in the intellectually robust prologue in half and shuttle most of the insight to the end.

The ideas that spurred Baldwin's critique of Wright seemed to have been taken into consideration in some of the last decisions about structuring the prologue. Baldwin had reached his crescendo in his powerful "Many Thousands Gone" through the idea that part of what made the Negro so inviolably American was the fact of his blood relationship to white Americans: "the most profound reality of the American experience." Baldwin urged more than a biological understanding of the consanguinity between American whites and blacks. "[W]e cannot begin to unlock it until we accept how very much it contains of the force and anguish and terror of love."[15] It was natural, if not deeply necessary, for James Baldwin to speak of love. His youthful background as a child preacher in the storefront evangelical Christian Church greatly exceeded the influence of the Young People's Socialist League he joined at nineteen and abandoned as soon as Sol Levitas of the *New Leader* started publishing his reviews.[16] For Ellison, however, the notion of "love" was fairly unprecedented, in spite of his saturation in Kierkegaard. But the final draft of the prologue contained love where it had not been before: "I have been hurt to the point of abysmal pain, hurt to the point of invisibility. And I defend because of all that I find that I love. In order to get some of it down I *have* to love. I sell you no phony forgiveness, I'm a desperate man— but too much of your life will be lost, its meaning lost, unless you approach it as much through love as through hate. So I approach it through division. So I denounce and I defend and I hate and I love."[17]

Toward the end of the 1951, he turned over the final corrected version of his manuscript, filled with pencil markings, to Random House for them to produce their typescript edition. His was not the only artwork in the making.

In December, Albert Murray excitedly mailed him a copy of the novel he had completed, the same work he had just shown to Morteza Sprague. "You said maybe we both would have books coming out the same year; I'm leaving it up to you to decide," Murray wrote. Murray's estimate of his young novel jibed perfectly with the ambivalence with which Ellison described his own emotions and feelings: "Maybe it'll be a nine-pounder, and maybe we'll have to put it in an oxygen tent."[18]

18

The Briar Patch

1952–1953

ON FEBRUARY 4, 1952, Ellison turned in the corrected proofs of *Invisible Man* to Albert Erskine. Just about two months later, on April 12, Random House would bring out the novel to considerable fanfare and publicity. Erskine mailed a special note to anyone receiving an advance copy of the novel stating, "[I]t is a book of great richness and power—a book one can with complete confidence call *important*."[1]

When Ralph Ellison ran into Langston Hughes, who queried him about the work, he told the dean of Negro poets that he had written what amounted to a blues tale. Working himself mainly on the uncomplicated blues-tinged character Jesse B. Simple, Hughes did not quite believe the man who had become a towering intellectual. Unburdened by his labor of nearly seven years, if not feeling mildly bereft without the book to work on, Ellison had closed a chapter of his life in those pages. Finishing the book mellowed him, and he dearly wanted to include Hughes in whatever recognition followed. The week prior to the novel's publication, Fanny Ellison wrote to Langston Hughes on behalf of her husband as much as herself: "We feel these days as if we are about to be catapulted into something unknown—of which we are both hopeful and afraid. . . . Now on the threshold of this new and looming thing which awaits (whether only in our minds or really outside the closed door) we want and beg you to share with us the good parts of it."[2]

Indeed, Ellison was enjoying himself and felt quite relaxed. With the hefty project no longer on his desk, he had more time for talks with Saul Bellow, who was busy teasing out the nuances of his own mammoth novel *The*

Adventures of Augie March, sections of which had been published in *Partisan Review.* In earlier conversations that winter, the two men had a chance to discuss a friend in common: Albert Murray. Bellow mentioned to Ellison that he had had an unusually pleasant meeting with Murray recently in Paris. Ellison told an impressed Bellow that Murray had sectioned off the whole world as his briar patch. Ellison wrote to Murray that Bellow had been "amazed and amused over your [Murray's] ease of operation." There was admiration and even a tingle of jealousy at the maneuvering of his younger literary comrade: "You have taken that low-down Southern cullud jive of yours and spread it all over western civilization," Ellison reported to Murray after hearing Murray's trademark expressions turn up, of all places, at the home of confirmed Greenwich Village avant gardist and Haitiphile Maya Deren.

Murray's ranging from Paris with Bellow to Greenwich Village confirmed the underlying intent of the novel *Invisible Man;* Murray's traipsing hit on both the higher and lower frequencies, elite culture and the blues. Because of Murray's broad sensibility, Ellison could joke with him about the cuts that Erskine and Taylor had demanded so his novel would get past the censor's magnifying glass: "I managed to keep in everything but that sour cream in the vagina that Ras the Exhorter talks about." With Murray, Ellison could laugh in a carefree and unselfconscious manner. He told him he was satisfied with his labor and that he had kept to the creed of masculine assertiveness: "[A]ll the stuff that really counts is still there, and I didn't dodge before they drew back to strike."[3] The friendship had helped Ellison to prevail over much of his past and the episodes that had pained and angered him. While his relationship with Wright had been that of a talented younger child to an equally talented and publicly praised older sibling, with Murray, who had no public reputation to speak of or to compete against, it was peerage without rivalry. Both men had also taken their college education seriously and were completely saturated in jazz music. It was a relationship in which Ellison did not have to apologize for his views and beliefs; instead, his deepest experiences were confirmed and his sentiments shared. When Murray wrote to Ellison concerning the ability of one of their friends to acquire an authentic or pure African culture, to move closer to the purest source of black expression, Murray's intellectual reflexes about the profundity of American Negro culture were Ellison's: "I say goddamn a motherfucking Haitian. My kick is the local nitty gritty."[4]

The philosophy that he shared with Murray of not flinching in the presence of danger before the opposition had taken concrete shape had other implications for Ellison. For one thing, as the momentum surrounding the novel built up, Ellison wanted more prestige. He allowed *Partisan Review* to publish the prologue in 1952—a reversal of policy for Ellison. Possibly his growing reputation, his new contacts and friendships with well-regarded writers and celebrities, closed the breech that once had been so important to him. The prologue itself was a vintage Ellison symphony of philosophy: humanism's ability for the individual to make choices affecting destiny, the role of the unconscious in decision making, and perhaps above all, the necessity of physical struggle. The move to publish it in the journal reflected vanity more than money; *Partisan Review* notoriously underpaid writers. What he needed was publicity and the imprimatur of high art. Few might have remembered that the novel was connected to the short story published in *Horizon* in 1947, or a few months later in *48* magazine, now defunct. A glossy setup in *Partisan* would ensure that the New York intellectual and artistic crowd would take notice of his work, the group that increasingly mattered to Ellison.

The day he turned in his manuscript to Random House, he wrote to Murray in Tuskegee, to the place where his dream of a music career had taken wings as a vision of liberatory art and self-definition. At the place Ellison credited with the construction of his own lofty ideals stood their present quintessence, Albert Murray, producing new fiction. Ellison told Murray he was pleased with his book. He was having a vision of black Faulkners and Robert Penn Warrens emerging out of the old South. Ellison let his trumpet sound about the books they both had completed: "We've taken on in our first books the task of defining reality which none of the other boys had the equipment to handle—except Wright, and he could never bring himself to conceive a character as complicated as himself. I guess he was too profoundly dissatisfied with his life, his past life, to look too long in the mirror." This was his most generous, and perhaps most honest, statement about Richard Wright. Ellison's own novel had involved a long look in the mirror, as much as he could sustain. He had confronted a philosophical and emotional battle amid an artistic climate that cherished understatement and clipped speech; he had bared his soul. In the letter to Murray he celebrated their colorful refusal to limit diversity. "But you, hell, you'd eat chittlings at the Waldorf! Not because you want to brag or be different, because you know they're as good a food for the gut and poetry as any other, and I would too. More power to you."[5] And despite the fact that he was almost famous—his stomach was upset and his heart racing most of the time in anticipation of his publication date—when an old friend from Tuskegee, Adaa Peters, came to town, he sat her down for an entire afternoon to try to make her appreciate the fundamentals of Wright's artistic vision. She clung to the gloomy assessment that Wright was hopelessly askew because he had married a white woman, and could not be consoled. It aroused in Ellison the same old turmoil and anxiety about wasting time on people who had little commitment or equipment with which to approach the larger issues of art, but it was also a relief to indulge in a frivolous afternoon, as the big bear neared its final run.

With favorable comments abounding after the publication of "Invisible Man: Prologue to a Novel" in the January-February *Partisan Review,* Ellison fielded requests from *Commentary* magazine to write a series of jazz reviews (most of them were ultimately published by *Saturday Review*). *Partisan*'s Philip Rahv asked him if he wanted to contribute to a symposium on American culture in the magazine. Ellison thought that perhaps the journal had begun to take issue with the approach to black culture of James Baldwin and Anatole Broyard, to the extent that the magazine might even have room for a column or two from Albert Murray.

Neither Ellison nor Murray published in *Commentary;* it continued to be the forum for the expatriate James Baldwin. But during the spring of 1952, Ellison had more than enough public exposure; his novel was lauded immediately by the critical establishment. Its currency and vanguard intellectualism could be gleaned immediately from the E. McKnight Kauffer jacket design. A silhouette and a mask of a human face competed for visibility but were barely discernible due to the dramatic chiaroscuro effects of their composition. The book jacket suggested the fairly new frontier of abstract expressionist art— and appropriately so. Ellison shared with the new generation of visual artists the concerns with motion, fluidity, conflict, chaos, optimism and with portraying the enduring totems and rituals of human behavior.[6] On the back cover was perhaps Ellison's most sympathetic and calculatedly youthful photograph, a portrait by Gordon Parks. He looked away from the camera, with deep concern in his eyes, but the effect of foreboding was offset by the rounded freshness of his face.

The much heralded novel with its impressive covering did not disappoint. After three weeks, Ellison made the *New York Times* best-seller list at number fourteen, and by June 22 had risen to number eight, his highest position. The event was noteworthy. Rarely did a novel featured in *Partisan Review* make the best-seller list. In his story Ellison had uniquely joined the intelligence and style of the highbrow with an incredibly important theme that drew in middlebrow readers. New York literary circles congratulated him. When Random House publicist Jean Ennis wrote to Ellison at the beginning of the summer giving him a list of the advertisements Random House had placed in the *Times, Times Book Review,* and *Herald Tribune,* she could commend his success by way of the copies of the positive reviews she had received: "Here's an extra *New Yorker* and a good one (aren't they all!) from *The Cincinnati Enquirer.*"[7]

The reviews—at least those that counted—were excellent. The vehicle to convey such approval was *Partisan Review,* and convey it they did. Editor Delmore Schwartz called the book "overwhelming," "genuine," and "controlled by Ellison's critical *intellectual* intelligence, and his natural spontaneous eloquence." Ellison had scored technically by expertly dilating "a kind of controlled hysteria, a hysteria which transcends itself because it is justified by actuality." *Invisible Man,* in fact, seemed tailor-made for the critical establishment, which had touted the young literary lion James Baldwin. For Schwartz, as inevitably for much of the liberal circle who read the book, the episodes and the form of narrating the tale were interesting but decisively secondary to Ellison's hero, who resonated for the group because he took his abuse equally from blacks and whites. "But, and this is perhaps the most important thing about Ellison's book, *Invisible Man* is not merely a story about being a Negro, unless we are willing to call it everybody's protest novel, to use James Baldwin's phrase," Schwartz wrote. Though it dealt head-on with race, the novel completely rejected a one-to-one mechanical notion of white blame. Acknowledging his own limitations to properly review the book—"the language of literary criticism seems shallow and patronizing when one has to speak of a book like this"—Schwartz suggested that really only one writer had the qualifications to offer a deep estimate of Ellison's value: William Faulkner.[8]

William Barrett, writing for the *American Mercury,* enthusiastically compared Ellison's effort—"the first considerable step forward in Negro literature"—to Céline's long poem "Journey to the End of the Night." Barrett's estimate of Ellison's artistic potential continued until Ellison's death. "I do not see that we can set any limits now to how far Ellison may yet go in the novel. He has already done a book which just misses greatness."[9]

Nor were his peers silent. Saul Bellow in *Commentary* noted that Ellison had "the very strongest sort of creative intelligence," and had scored a "brilliant individual victory" by nobly resisting determining powers and "heavy influences" in order to successfully "rescue what is important."[10] Bellow properly recognized Ellison's book as a smashing blow against the severe constraints of American identity then in literary vogue. And if Ellison had escaped the limitations of racial categorization, at least one reviewer did not seek to entirely preclude the Negroness of the expression. From the far Left, Irving Howe wrote, "But of course 'Invisible Man' is a Negro novel—what white man could ever have written it? . . . To deny that this is a Negro novel is to deprive Negroes of their one basic right: the right to cry out difference."[11] Ellison's fundamental differences with Howe over the "Negroness" of his book and his expression would seriously widen in the years to come, mainly because Howe's description was ambiguous: it bordered on ignoring the well-wrought artistry of the novel and favoring the magic power of inviolable racial essences. Ellison thought it was preposterous that his "blackness," cultural or biological, had anything to do with his ability to write novels. But Howe was one of a few to pick up on the bitterness and the defiance and swift social transformation at the novel's core.

Gratifying to Ellison was news from the home front. It was perhaps most therapeutic to Ellison to have his work taken seriously at Tuskegee, where

Murray told him there was a waiting list of ninety people at the library. He learned that Tuskegee President Frederick Douglass Patterson and William Dawson were preparing statements of congratulation, while some people on the campus read the novel as straight autobiography and claimed to have remembered the entire drama of him being kicked out of school by Moton himself. He received civilized letters from the culprits in his own drama of being unable to finish his college degree, and he could still get good and angry just thinking about it: "The bastards defeated me there. . . . So I thank them although I don't forgive them and one of these days I intend to get hold of that kind of false artist, false teacher, for which Dawson stands. Just thinking about it all makes me mad all over again."[12] Ellison, who had edited from the novel a section favorably describing Frank Drye's trumpet class, still felt bitter over the Tuskegee Music School head Dawson's rigid focus. But the private thoughts he expressed to Murray would not stop him from presenting a gracious lecture at Tuskegee in 1953; nor would it stop him from kindling a satisfying relationship with Dawson that lasted for the next twenty years. Both men had softened.

The least generous reviews of the book came from black readers and from the committed left-wing activists. Failing to find the confirmation of experience or the affirmation of life, Saunders Redding, writing for the *Baltimore Afro-American* newspaper, called the book overblown. "The book's fault is that a writer of power has put all his power into describing the diurnal life of gnats."[13] Irving Howe had taken Ellison seriously but had indicated that he was less than convinced by the hero's solution of unlimited possibility and politics as love, a solution that he recognized from the pages of "little magazine[s]" and journals. "[T]he unqualified assertion of individuality is at the moment a favorite notion of literary people." From Lloyd Brown at *Masses and Mainstream* and John Oliver Killens at Paul Robeson's *Freedomways* he got pretty much what he expected. Using Marxism-Leninism to clothe their own Puritanism, they upbraided Ellison for peddling an obscenity that coincided with the "formula for literary success in today's market."[14] Brown allowed that Ellison was a "Judas" alienated from Negro masses and obsequiously squirming his way into the elite canon. Ellison couldn't have been surprised, even though *Masses and Mainstream* had tried to reprint "Mr. Toussan"; these were typical Communist tactics. Killens called the book a "vicious distortion of Negro life," citing the Trueblood episode as perverse, accusing Ellison of using distinctly Negro material to cater to a public demanding barbaric and sexual behavior from Negroes.[15] His old nemesis Abner Berry wrote in the *Daily Worker* that Ellison had rejected accuracy in favor of an "affected pretentious and other worldly style to suit the kingpins of world white supremacy."[16] Ten years after publishing his last piece in the *New Masses,* Ellison joined the likes of Max Eastman, James Rorty, and John Dos Passos as "enemies of the people."[17]

The negative reviews were dismissable. Ellison relaxed and bought a few books from Brentano's, among them Bernard De Voto's combination of literature and psychology, *The World of Fiction*. Alongside him that June while he shopped and added to his formidable library was Albert Murray, making a visit in order to congratulate his friend. Other writers also noticed him. Ellison hosted the literary sensation James Baldwin in September, while the young writer made a short sojourn to the United States to turn in a manuscript. Ellison felt at ease and uncompetitive with Baldwin in the meeting, which was surprisingly lacking in tension, considering the fact that the writer, still in his twenties, had neatly snipped the professional distance between the two. Baldwin was already a major essayist, and his first novel was in galleys. Ellison sensed something of Baldwin's inner conflict, a conflict not remote from his sexual core, and judged him with a mixture of compassion and sternness. In his letter to Wright mentioning the meeting with Wright's "protégé," Ellison thought after talking to Baldwin about France and the writer's craft that he was smart but a bit conflicted. Having read Knopf's galleys of Baldwin's book, Ellison called the tour de force *Go Tell It on the Mountain* a superior book on Negro religious conversion; nor did he miss the novel's allusion to the grapple with homosexual identity. But, sadly, he found the erudite and polished Harlemite divorced from the idiom of black language. When Baldwin's book was reviewed in 1953, the *New Yorker*'s Anthony West would find it humorless and stilted, and would point to *Invisible Man* as a better example of the use of the same material. The use of Ellison as the hallmark for black writers had begun. Still, Ellison was puzzled about Baldwin's distance from his roots. He thought that the younger writer might have better suited himself to his material by finding a more elastic and authentic narrative vernacular, and losing the formidable prose style of Henry James.[18]

Later that fall, Ellison tried to renew some old friendships at a cocktail party given by Chester Himes and his white girlfriend Vandi Haygood, a socialite, a former Rosenwald Fellowship officer, and then an executive with the International Institute on Education. Himes's raucous eighteen-month affair with Haygood became a public spectacle. After having lost his wife because of his crushing anxieties about race and manhood, the drunken Himes had few qualms about placing his guests in the position of observers of his ritualistic excoriations with Haygood on matters of racial guilt. Ellison had outgrown such discussions in the 1930s. During the party, as Himes liberally poured the scotch, he became insulting and threatening. About the affair, Himes admitted in his autobiography *The Quality of Hurt* that his relationship with Haygood had descended into physical abuse, and that "I hurt her seriously."[19] Himes tended to scapegoat his white paramours for his inability to thrive in the teeth of prejudice. After Himes told his party guests that his next novel would surpass Ellison and be on par with Shakespeare, Ellison sobered him with sardonic approval, "Great, great." When Haygood sat on the arm of Ellison's chair, Himes took her into the kitchen and threatened her with a butcher's knife.[20] Ellison intervened in a confrontational manner and responded to Himes's insults measure for measure with promises of physical violence. After their tempers cooled, Ellison feared that he had permanently rented the friendship. To Himes's friend Wright he wrote with pity and feelings of the anguish he experienced when confronting a gifted writer bent upon self-destruction. But Ellison was done with Himes as a fellow craftsman. He decided that Himes's latest fiction, a prison melodrama called *Cast the First Stone,* did not reach the mark of serious literature.[21]

Himes, admitting to his drunkenness, recalled the episodes and his relationship to Haygood in the 1955 fiction *The End of a Primitive* with a bit more humor and a bit more pain than Ellison. In the novel, the love affair between the frustrated black novelist Jesse Robinson (Himes) and the foundation officer Kriss (Haygood) ends in murder. The novel features a cocktail party that becomes a near violent confrontation between the hero Jesse and an arrogant and successful black editor named Walter Martin, apparently based on Ellison. The Ellison character possesses an "aggressive personality like the mighty Richard Coeur de Lion . . . knew everything knowable within the realm of human knowledge and much that was without it," and physically was "a handsome man with a handsome mustache." The sarcastic description captured Ellison's trademark qualities: courage, intelligence, and elegance. In the novel Himes's counterpart Robinson brutalizes his white lover because she is the stereotype of the contemptuous white liberal. The Ellison character, who is a cutthroat beneath his polished exterior, defends the white woman because of a subconscious lust for white flesh. The confrontation begins because of Walter Martin's "olympian" remarks; Jesse cannot get a novel published until he accepts the reigning critical standards of the day, "when niggers learn to behave themselves." In response, Himes's hero begins to slap his white lover, and the drama reaches its climax: " 'Listen, son—' Jesse began in a patronizing tone, and before he'd finished Walter leaped to his feet and snapped open a switchblade knife. 'I'll cut your motherfuckin' throat!' he threatened, advancing dangerously."

The confrontation between the two men is quickly defused in Himes's account, but by the novel's conclusion, Jesse has murdered the white woman. Curiously, while Himes saw the bitterness ending with fraternal gestures— "he was patting Walter on the shoulder, saying with great benevolence, 'I like you, man, hell, I'm only too glad you found the combination,' "—Ellison never again bridged the distance between the two men.[22] Even after Himes cooled down, they seemed to have had no contact whatsoever after Himes left the United States for Paris in 1953. When they spoke of each other, they tended to deliberately center on their differences rather than their friendship and literary similarities.

Ellison's magnetism in the literary community inevitably attracted some shrapnel, even among people who respected his talent. One of the humbler assessments came in a letter from Arna Bontemps to Langston Hughes, who suggested that if Baldwin was being published by Harper's, then Hughes should be able to benefit from the renewed interest in black literature. "Why don't you (as a suggestion) pick out a few of the *ideas* previously used, ideas which seem to catch the fancy of the ofays," Bontemps wrote to Hughes, and continued, "For example, the idea of elevating one Negro (like Ralph) while neglecting or closing the eyes to the millions."[23] While they were gratified at his success, many black writers did give credence to the Communist reviews; Ellison's work was being deliberately embraced by the book industry while other writers were being ignored.

The book sold briskly—more than 6,000 copies had been sold at the end of April at the retail price of $3.50, and almost another 7,500 copies by the end of October. With greater sales came increased profits, since his contract had stipulated that after sales of more than 5,000, his royalties would escalate from 12.5 percent to 15 percent. After his advance of $5,500, Ellison cleared a profit $3,092.91 for the year of 1952.[24] He sold another five thousand hardcover copies through the end of spring in 1953, after which the Signet paperback edition accounted for most of the sales. Whenever he gave a talk, he sold many copies. In April 1953, while he and Fanny were guests at Fisk College, Arna Bontemps wrote, "Every copy of *Invisible Man* in Nashville was sold."[25] Clearly Ellison was not then rich; nor would he ever become rich. He wouldn't even become financially comfortable until he began steadily working at New York University, and paperback editions of *Shadow and Act* had been contracted in the late 1960s. But he had done well enough with his novel that he startled Langston Hughes in September 1953 by saying that he was thinking about teaching.[26] Lauded professional writers wrote; they did not teach.

With a best-seller in print, Ellison had new duties. He was no longer merely the writer of an important novel, but also publicist and salesman. But not all of the exposure and celebrity benefited him. When asked by reporter Hugh McGovern from the *Denver Post* to respond to a questionnaire in June, Ellison thought it prudent to mail back a detailed response, and it took him several days to prepare. He could look out over the years and recall his youthful trip to Denver for the Elks battle of bands and was flattered to receive Western publicity for the book. But after sending in the time-consuming, ten-page response, he heard nothing about it. Ellison wrote McGovern in October, sounding a plaintive note of frustration.[27] The reporter wrote back, admitting that he had no idea when the piece, which had been cut significantly, would appear. Professional acclaim unmistakably had its pitfalls. So, protecting himself from intrusions upon his time and talent, Ellison wisely took the winter off. If he was hounded by any demons about the originality of his work, a brief letter from Richard Wright put them to rest. Wright, who had in May begged off from commenting about the novel before he had time to give it a thorough analysis, had perhaps deliberately missed some of Ellison's intention. He was convinced that his own work-in-progress, the novel *The Outsider,* was distinguished because it "waded right into the question of the Negro's relationship to the Western world." Wright's ego made it difficult for him to imagine that a writer whom he had helped learn the craft had mastered subjects that he still struggled to convey. But his judgment of Ellison's book was positive: "I think you can be proud of what you turned in, Ralph. You entered the ranks of literature with your book, and there is no doubt about it."[28]

Grateful for Wright's recognition, Ellison contented himself by cashing in on his status as something of a celebrity author. He attended Princeton's prestigious Christian Gauss Seminar in Criticism, mainly the six lectures beginning December 11 with Edmund Wilson presiding. (Also lecturing that term were theologian Paul Tillich, biographer Leon Edel, and critic Irving Howe.) Wilson included Harriet Beecher Stowe in his "The Literature of the Civil War," judging the novel by the woman Lincoln had joked was responsible for the Civil War "voluminous and about fifty percent terrible."[29] Stammering and groaning through his lecture, Wilson offered the rehabilitation of a period that was immensely important to Ellison, especially after Baldwin had dismissed the importance of *Uncle Tom's Cabin.* In the company of serious writers including Saul Bellow, John Berryman, R. W. B. Lewis, and Delmore Schwartz, Wilson probed the Civil War era in the hopes of retrieving the psychic energy of that era to remedy the current failure of the novel.[30] Throughout 1952, the critics had watched as American technological culture assumed global prominence; during the same period, they convinced themselves that the novel had died.

But if the novel was thought to be in danger, Ellison's work bespoke its vigor. Good things were brewing for him. On January 7, he received a telegram from Chicago, notifying him that he had been elected to the Chicago Defender Honor Roll of Democracy for 1953, an achievement on a par with winning the NAACP Spingarn Medal. Ellison accepted the award with a charm that became legendary. In a note of compliment to editor John Sengstacke of the *Defender,* Ellison stated that he had written, not to break down white stereotypes, but to address his book to Negroes.[31] In April, the National Newspaper Publishers Association, made up of the black weekly papers, would award him the John B. Russwurm Award, named to honor the founder of the first black newspaper and aimed at congratulating "the development of a more effective democracy in our United States."[32]

But these were, for Ellison, and the rest of the country, the prologue and epilogue, respectively. If the black media and publishing industry did acknowledge his efforts, it was the elite American reading public that made him a literary celebrity. On January 27, 1953, Ralph Ellison gained the high ground. He was presented the National Book Award Gold Medal for fiction at the Commodore Hotel in New York City, joining previous winners James Jones, Nelson Algren, and William Faulkner. Notified of the award in time to begin a schedule of engagements, radio and television interviews, and press conferences, Ellison recorded part of his acceptance speech for the Jack Fern news broadcast on Monday, January 26. On the Tuesday of the presentation of the award, he taped an interview with the *Today* show for NBC, then headed over to Random House for a photography session. At the Random House mansion, Ellison met, for the first time, William Faulkner. Ellison noted Faulkner's fine clothes, putting to rest the legends about the famous Mississippian's dishevelment. But mainly he was awed. In Random House executive Saxe Commins's office, he declared his debts: "Well Mr. Faulkner, this really completes the day for me. . . . You know . . . you have children all around. You won't be proud of all of them, just the same they're around."[33]

Before he was Faulkner's unclaimed son, though, he was his own. Saul Bellow, Martha Foley, Irving Howe, Howard Mumford Jones, and Alfred Kazin had voted Ellison the prize and had written: "With a positive exuberance of narrative gifts, he has broken away from the conventions and patterns of the tight well-made novel. Mr. Ellison has had the courage to take many literary risks, and he has succeeded with them."[34] He beat out Ernest Hemingway's tight and well-made *The Old Man and the Sea*. Ellison's winning the National Book Award was fitting, especially since it was from a committee of people he knew well and some of whom he admired. The award had been created by the National Book Publisher's Council, the American Bookseller's Association, and the Book Manufacturers Institute, to ensure a more equitable prize recognizing excellence in writing by an American citizen, an award not under the auspices of the frequently tainted and secretive deliberations involved with the Pulitzer Prizes administered by Columbia University.[35] In contrast to the Pulitzer's central literary criterion of "wholesomeness," the National Book Award aimed to accurately reflect the state of American art and writing and generally made its deliberations (as well as the names of its judges) open to the public.

Ellison stepped to the dais in a dark-blue suit that hung gracefully from his shoulders and emphasized his trim and athletic build. His style that evening bore his trademark elegance. He wore a starched white shirt and kept his tie in close with a collar pin; his hair was cut closely at the sides and brushed over the top to cover his bare pate. He told the audience with feeling and deference that his was a "not quite fully achieved attempt at a major novel." Comfortable with his audience from the literary upper crust, he let them understand his struggle to accept the name Ralph Waldo, and how that trek from musician to writer has been guided by the brief influence of his unforgotten father Lewis.

He segued in the speech from his personal struggle for identity into the broader problem of the writer. He hoped that with his novel he had accomplished the same goal that Frederick Douglass and Herman Melville had: "to return to the mood of personal moral responsibility for democracy which typified our best nineteenth century fiction." By referring to Frederick Douglass's fight, Ellison felt that he was proposing, in a most unsensational but deliberately confrontational manner, the necessity for determined action in the face of injustice. And at that time, more than ever, he saw the injustice in the literary arts as being the asphyxiation of ethnic pluralism. Receiving the award represented the culmination of a dream, administered by friends whom he respected. Given the opportunity to say it, Ellison told the audience that "except for the work of William Faulkner something vital had gone out of American prose after Mark Twain." He finished his remarks on an upbeat note, cognizant of the utter singularity of his position: "[T]here must be possible a fiction which, leaving sociology to the scientists, can arrive at the truth about the human condition, here and now, with all the bright magic of a fairy tale."[36]

He returned to his seat, and he and Fanny sat through an address from liberal Associate Supreme Court Justice William O. Douglas, whose speech obviously had less to do with art than politics. American casualties in Korea were making the paper every day, and the Justice issued a severe warning about the days ahead. "A new cohesive force must be found to hold this region together, least it become easy prey for the Soviets."[37] The hot Cold War was not to be escaped.

When photographers captured Ellison on his dream day with nonfiction winner Bernard De Voto and poetry victor Archibald MacLeish, Ellison squared his shoulders and leaned back coolly in the flash of the camera bulbs. He savored the precious moment. The sheer remarkableness of receiving the award with not only proven craftspeople, but with men like MacLeish, with whom Ellison had profoundly disagreed, inspired his hopes for democratic freedom. While the essence of his talk—a return to personal responsibility for moral democratic health—seemed conservative, it was not. The sense of moral responsibility that had undergirded the decision of many Americans to participate in the Civil War was now considered fantastic, if not perhaps fanatical. It was fitting, Ellison said, that he had risen to prominence in the company of artists whom he had challenged.

For Ellison, part of the fairy tale was the $1,000 cash prize that went with the award. Finally he and Fanny could move to a quiet apartment off Riverside Drive facing the Hudson River. In his last letter to Richard Wright, which he had started to write before he received the award, he reported his commendation in a handwritten addendum at the letter's bottom: "[P]erhaps you've heard by now that lightning struck me, leaving me standing amazed with the 1952 National Book Award for Fiction." While Ellison's award did not signal the end of the relationship with Wright, he had attained a success that the Mississippian never would. For the most part, however, Ellison never lost his humility when dealing with Wright, or his sense of the magnitude of the author of *Native Son*. He mailed to Wright a copy of the acceptance speech, which Ellison saw as revealing his own limitations. In the speech he wanted to open a new vista for American literature and language by resisting the arid and "overpraised style of writing that had gripped me for years." He was not alone in the breakout, but had outfitted himself with new comrades who shared his literary ideals. "Watch out for Bellow's novel [*The Adventures of Augie March*], by the way. It is the first real novel by an American Jew, full of variety, sharp characterization and sheer magical prose."[38] Ellison moved to accept the literary challenges in the company of creatively exuberant fellow American writers like Saul Bellow, who triumphed that year with *The Adventures of Augie March*. While Ellison thought Wright decisive as a writer and intellectual figure, Richard Wright had left the curse and the challenge of America; and though it was a cheery letter, Ellison apparently never again wrote him another.

Indeed, it was Albert Murray with whom Ellison continued to correspond vibrantly. When Murray saw the pictures of the award ceremony in the *New York Times,* his praise was effusive and his feelings bubbled over for a comrade from the same briar patch who had climbed to the heights of American culture. Murray saw Ellison, dapperly arrayed and sandwiched between De Voto and MacLeish, in mystical terms. He had begun his own explorations of modern literature with MacLeish's poetry in the late 1930s; the last time he had been with Ellison in the summer of 1952, Ellison had purchased De Voto's *The World of Fiction.* Seeing his friend in the photograph with two authors who had framed his own literary experience delighted Murray: "Boy, I got a hell of a charge out of seeing you standing there in that picture," he applauded his friend.[39] Ellison had capped his career with a life work.

Notes

Abbreviations to the Notes

The following is a list of abbreviations for books that are cited frequently in this work. The list also includes the complete publication information for interviews and essays cited here that were published prior to their collection in *Conversations with Ralph Ellison* (1995), *Going to the Territory* (1986), or *Shadow and Act* (1964).

CERE Ralph Ellison, *The Collected Essays of Ralph Ellison,* ed. John F. Callahan (New York: Modern Library, 1995).
"The Alain Locke Symposium," *Harvard Advocate* (Spring 1974): 9–28.
"Bearden," Callaloo 36.3 (1988): 416–419.
"On Being the Target of Discrimination," *New York Times Magazine* 16 Apr. 1989, 6–9.
"Introduction," *Invisible Man,* 30th anniversary edition (New York: Vintage, 1982), v–xx.

CRE *Conversations with Ralph Ellison,* Maryemma Graham and Amritjit Singh, eds. (Jackson: University of Mississippi Press, 1995).
Alfred Chester and Vilma Howard, "The Art of Fiction: An Interview," *Paris Review* 8 (Spring 1955): 55–71.
Harold Isaacs, "Five Writers and Their African Ancestors," *Phylon* (Winter 1960): 317–336.
Allen Geller, "An Interview with Ralph Ellison," 1963; *Tamarack Review* (Summer 1964): 3–24.
Richard Kostelanetz, "An Interview with Ralph Ellison," 1965; *Iowa Review* (Fall 1989): 1–10.
Steve Cannon, Lennox Raphael, and James Thompson, "A Very Stern Discipline," *Harper's,* Mar. 1967, 76–95.
James A. McPherson, "Indivisible Man," 1969; *Atlantic Monthly,* Dec. 1970, 45–60.
David L. Carson, "Ralph Ellison: Twenty Years After," 1971; *Studies in American Fiction* 1 (Spring 1973): 1–23.
Hollie I. West, "Ellison: Exploring the Life of a Not So Visible Man," *Washington Post,* 19 Aug. 1973, G1–G3.

445

Hollie I. West, "Travels with Ralph Ellison Through Time and Thought," *Washington Post,* 20 Aug. 1973, B1, B3.

Hollie I. West, "Through a Writer's Eyes" and "Growing Up Black in Frontier Oklahoma . . . From an Ellison Perspective," *Washington Post,* 21 Aug. 1973, B1, B3.

Arlene Crewdson and Rita Thomson, "Interview with Ralph Ellison" (Master's thesis, Loyola University, 1974).

John Hersey, "A Completion of Personality: A Talk With Ralph Ellison," *Ralph Ellison, a Collection of Critical Essays* (Englewood, N.J.: Prentice-Hall, 1974), 1–19.

Ron Welburn, "Ralph Ellison's Territorial Vantage," 1976; *The Grackle* 4 (1977–78): 5–15.

Steve Cannon, Ishmael Reed, and Quincy Troupe, "The Essential Ellison," *Y-Bird Reader* 1 (Fall 1977): 126–159.

Michael S. Harper and Robert B. Stepto, "Study and Experience. An Interview with Ralph Ellison," 1976; *Massachusetts Review* 18 (Fall 1977): 417–435.

Walter Lowe, "Book Essay: Invisible Man Ralph Ellison," *Playboy,* Oct. 1982, 42.

David Remnick, "Visible Man," *New Yorker,* 14 Mar. 1994, 34–38.

GTT   Ralph Ellison, *Going to the Territory* (1986; New York: Vintage, 1987).

"What These Children Are Like," *Education of the Deprived and Segregated* (Dedham, Mass.: Bank St. College, 1965), 44–51.

"The Myth of the Flawed White Southerner," *To Heal and To Build; Programs of President Lyndon B. Johnson,* ed. James B. MacGregor (New York: McGraw-Hill, 1968), 207–216.

"Homage to Duke Ellington," *Washington Star,* 27 Apr. 1969.

"On Initiation Rites and Power: Ralph Ellison Speaks at West Point," *Contemporary Literature* 15 (Spring 1974): 165–186.

"The Little Man at Chehaw Station," *American Scholar* 47 (Winter 1977–78): 25–48.

"Perspective of Literature," *American Law: The Third Century,* ed. Bernard Schwartz (Hackensack: N.J.: Rotham, 1976), 391–406.

"Going to the Territory" and "Portrait of Inman Page," *Carleton Miscellany* 18 (Winter 1980): 9–26, 18–32.

"Remembering Richard Wright," *Delta* 18 (Apr. 1984): 1–13.

SA   Ralph Ellison, *Shadow and Act* (New York: Random House, 1964).

"The Way It Is," *New Masses,* 20 Oct. 1942, 9–11.

"Richard Wright's Blues," *Antioch Review* 3 (Summer 1945): 198–211.

"Beating That Boy," *New Republic,* 22 Oct. 1945, 535–536.

"The Shadow and the Act," *Reporter,* Dec. 1949, 17–19.

"Twentieth Century Fiction and the Black Mask of Humanity," *Confluence,* Dec. 1953, 3–21.

"Living with the Music," *High Fidelity,* Dec. 1955, 60 ff.

"Change the Joke and Slip the Yoke," *Partisan Review* 35 (Spring 1958): 212–222.

"The Charlie Christian Story," *Saturday Review,* 17 May 1958, 42–43, 46.

"Remembering Jimmy," *Saturday Review,* 12 July 1958, 36–37.

"The Golden Age, Time Past," *Esquire,* Jan. 1959, 107–110.

"That Same Pain, That Same Pleasure: An Interview," Richard G. Stern, *December* 3.2 (Winter 1961): 30–32, 37–46.

"The World and the Jug," *New Leader,* 9 Dec. 1963, 22–26.

"A Rejoinder," *New Leader,* 3 Feb. 1964, 15–22. [Published in *Shadow and Act* as the single essay "The World and the Jug."]

"Hidden Name and Complex Fate," *The Writer's Experience* (Washington, D.C.: Library of Congress, 1964), 1–15.

TT   Ralph Ellison and Albert Murray, *Trading Twelves: The Selected Letters of Ralph Ellison and Albert Murray,* eds. Albert Murray and John F. Callahan (New York: Modern Library, 2000).

The following is a list of abbreviations for Papers Collections.

KBP   Kenneth Burke Papers, Pennsylvania State University Library

LHP   Langston Hughes Papers, James Weldon Johnson Collection, Beinecke Library, Yale University

MSRC   Moorland-Spingarn Research Center, Howard University

OSHS   Oklahoma State Historical Society, Oklahoma City, Oklahoma

REP   Ralph Ellison Papers, Manuscript Division, Library of Congress (mainly organizational folders, literary correspondence, *Invisible Man* manuscript, and notes)

RWP   Richard Wright Papers, James Weldon Johnson Collection, Beinecke Library, Yale University

SHP   Stanley Edgar Hyman Papers, Manuscript Division, Library of Congress

SCRBC   Schomburg Center for Research in Black Life and Black Culture, New York Public Library

Chapter 1. Geography Is Fate: 1913–1916

1. Ralph W. Ellison's father's name was alternately spelled "Louis" and "Lewis" throughout his life. In all of the census records, which probably conformed to the spelling standards of local enumerators, the senior Ellison's name was spelled "Louis." In his military enlistment records, where Ellison signed his name, he wrote it very close to "Loewis"; and whenever written by military officials, the name was spelled "Lewis." On Ellison's death certificate, the name given to the coroner was "Louis." Since Ralph Ellison spelled his father's name "Lewis," I have respected that preference in the text of this book and I have left my notations of the documents with their alternate spellings.

2. Ralph Ellison, "Hidden Name and Complex Fate," *SA*, 151.

3. Ralph Waldo Ellison's birthdate is traditionally recorded as March 1, 1914. Oklahoma City did not certify live births in the early part of the twentieth century, so there is no birth certificate. The earliest known record of the 1914 birthdate is a signed affidavit from a family friend, which Ellison used to make an application for the Merchant Marine during World War II. In all other formal records prior to 1943, Ellison and his family listed either his birth year as 1913 or his age as commensurate with a birthdate of 1913: 1920 Census of Oklahoma, Douglass School Transcript, Tuskegee Application and Transcript, 1938 Connecticut Certificate of Marriage. In addition, Ellison consistently remarked that he was three years old when his father died, and Lewis Ellison died in July 1916. Due to the absence of any available synchronic evidence contradicting the earliest known records of Ellison's birthdate, I have used the 1913 birthdate throughout this work.

4. Ralph Ellison and John Hersey, "A Completion of Personality: A Talk With Ralph Ellison," *CRE*, 273; Ralph Ellison, letter to Albert Murray, 24 July 1953, *TT*, 52.

5. Oklahoma State Certificate of Death No. C526. Louis Albert Ellison, date of death: 19 July 1916. Oklahoma State Board of Health, Bureau of Vital Statistics.

6. Michael P. Johnson and James L. Roark, *Black Masters* (New York: W. W. Norton, 1984), 349; Ralph Ellison, "Address at the Whiting Foundation," *CERE*, 854. There is some confusion over the facts. Ellison, following Lowery Ware's *Old Abbeville: Scenes of the Past of*

a Town Where Old Times Are Not Forgotten, thought that "M. A. Ellison," a pastor with the First Presbyterian Church in Abbeville, had owned Alfred and "his brother" William Ellison. Johnson and Roark are more reliable. Apparently Mary Ann ("M. A.") Ellison moved (with some of her slaves) to Abbeville Court House in 1855, where she lived with her granddaughter Mary A. Hoyt, married to Presbyterian minister Thomas Hoyt.

7. Allen B. Ballard, *One More Day's Journey* (New York: McGraw-Hill, 1984), 136.

8. Ballard, *One More,* 139.

9. Johnson and Roark, *Black Masters,* 349; Lowery Ware, *Old Abbeville: Scenes of the Past of a Town Where Old Times Are Not Forgotten* (Columbia, S.C.: SCMAR, 1992), 118; Tenth Census of the United States: 1880—Population; Abbeville Township, Abbeville County, South Carolina, Enumeration District 1, Sheet 9, "Alfred Ellison," Bureau of the Census.

10. Ellison, "Address at the Whiting," *CERE,* 854–855; Ware, *Abbeville,* 118–119.

11. Ballard, *One More,* 142–144.

12. Ware, *Abbeville,* 119; Ellison, "Address at the Whiting," *CERE,* 855.

13. Ballard, *One More,* 148.

14. Ware, *Abbeville,* 145–147.

15. Quoted in C. Vann Woodward, *The Strange Career of Jim Crow* (1957; New York: Oxford University Press, 1963), 21.

16. Ballard, *One More,* 152–153.

17. Recruitment Papers, 25th U.S. Infantry (Lewis Ellison), National Archives, Washington, D.C.

18. Regular U.S. Army Muster Rolls, 25th U.S. Infantry, Company F, Sept. 31-Oct. 1898, National Archives, Washington, D.C.

19. Record of Events, Regimental Returns, 25th U.S. Infantry, July 1898, National Archives, Washington, D.C.

20. Monroe Lee Billington, *New Mexico's Buffalo Soldiers, 1866–1900* (Boulder: University of Colorado Press, 1991), 161–163, 205.

21. Enlistment Card (Lewis Ellison), Regimental Returns, 25th U.S. Infantry, Mar.-Apr. 1899 and May-June 1899.

22. Historical Report of Activities of 25th U.S. Infantry Regiment in Philippine Insurrection, Nov. 1903, National Archives, Washington, D.C.

23. Stanley Karno, *In Our Image: America's Empire in the Philippines* (New York: Ballantine, 1989), 146.

24. Regimental Returns, 25th Infantry, Sept.-Oct. 1899.

25. Regimental Returns, 25th Infantry, Nov.-Dec. 1900.

26. Proceedings of the General Court Martial of Lewis Ellison, San Marcelino, Zambales Province, Philippine Islands, 9 Apr. 1901, National Archives, Washington, D.C., 12, 13, 14, np. Handwritten note underneath last official processing of the General Court Martial Order: "Received Sep 24 1901 Copy furnished Lewis A. Ellison Jan. 17-1902. B.M.M."

27. Jervis Anderson, "Going to the Territory," *New Yorker,* 22 Nov. 1976, 74; Ellison and Hersey, "A Completion," *CRE,* 275. In the 1974 interview with Hersey, Ellison said that Lewis ran "a candy kitchen in Chattanooga," apparently the same kind of enterprise as the Abbeville confectionery Anderson learned of in 1976.

28. George A. Devlin, *South Carolina and Black Migration, 1865–1940* (New York: Garland Publishing, 1989), 172–188.

29. Ralph Ellison, Michael S. Harper, and Robert B. Stepto, "Study and Experience: An Interview with Ralph Ellison," *CRE,* 339.

30. Jere W. Roberson, "Edward P. McCabe and the Langston Experiment," *Chronicles of Oklahoma* 51.3 (1973): 344, 354–355.

31. Howard R. Meredith and George H. Shirk, "Oklahoma City: Growth and Reconstruction, 1889–1939," *Chronicles of Oklahoma* 55.3 (1977): 293.

32. R. Halliburton Jr., "Black Slavery among the Cherokees," *Chronicles of Oklahoma* 52.4 (1974–1975): 483.

33. Jimmie Lewis Franklin, *Journey toward Hope* (Norman: University of Oklahoma Press, 1982), 4.

34. Norman L. Crockett, "Booker T. Washington Visits Boley," *Chronicles of Oklahoma* 57.4 (Winter 1989–1990): 384; George Carney, "All-Black Towns," *Chronicles of Oklahoma* 59.2 (1991): 118.

35. Meredith and Shirk, "Oklahoma City," 299.

36. Thirteenth Census of the United States: 1910–Population; Oklahoma City, Oklahoma, Enumeration District 224, Sheet 20, "Louis and Ida Ellison," Bureau of the Census. Taken in April, the 1910 U.S. Census finds the Ellisons married not even one month.

37. Twelfth Census of the United States: 1900–Population; Walton County, Georgia, Enumeration District 97, Sheet 12, "Ida Millsaps," Bureau of the Census, State of Ohio Standard Certificate of Death No. 62948. Ida Bell, date of death: 16 Oct. 1937. State Department of Health Division of Vital Statistics. These two documents offer different names for Ellison's maternal grandfather: "Pope" on the 1900 Census, and "Poke" on Ida Ellison's death certificate, filled out by Ralph Ellison. Census records also vary the spelling of the last name: "Millsap," "Millsaps," "Millsapses." "Milsap" is Ellison's spelling from his mother's 1937 death certificate. In the late 1940s, when he drafted a scene for the novel *Invisible Man* with his maternal grandfather as a character, Ellison typed the name "Polk Millsaps." I am using "Polk" for Ida Ellison's father's first name because it is a homonym of "Poke," and the last name of the eleventh President of the United States, who was in office near the time of Ellison's maternal grandfather's birth. For simplicity and some continuity, I have used "Millsap" for the last name.

38. Ellison and Hersey, "A Completion," *CRE*, 275; Robert O'Meally, *The Craft of Ralph Ellison* (Cambridge: Harvard University Press, 1980), 7.

39. Mills Lane, ed., *Standing upon the Mouth of a Volcano: New South Georgia* (Savannah: Beehive Press, 1993), 222–230.

40. Anderson, "Going to the Territory," 70.

41. J. D. Randolph, interview, 3 Feb. 1939, in Mildred McCracken Crossley, "A History of the Negro Schools of Oklahoma City, Oklahoma" (Master's thesis, University of Oklahoma, 1939), 79.

42. Crossley, "Negro Schools of Oklahoma City," 7; Henry Hawkins, "From the Wagon Yard to the Fairgrounds: The History of Douglass" (manuscript, possession of the author), ch. 2, 3.

43. Thirteenth Census of the United States: 1910—Population; Oklahoma County, Oklahoma Enumeration District 224, Sheet 20, "Louis Ellison," Bureau of the Census.

44. Charles Colcord, *The Autobiography of Charles Francis Colcord* (Oklahoma City: C.C. Helmreich, 1970), 208–220.

45. R. Bruce Shepard, "North to the Promised Land: Black Migration to the Canadian Plains," *Chronicles of Oklahoma* 66.3 (1988): 306.

46. Wilson Moses, *The Golden Age of Black Nationalism* (New York: Oxford University Press, 1978), 202–203.

47. Ralph Ellison, "The World and the Jug," *SA,* 141.

48. Von Russell Creel, "Socialists in the House: The Oklahoma Experience, Part I," *Chronicles of Oklahoma* 50.2 (1992): 148.

49. "Introductory," *Directory of Oklahoma City U.S.A. 1916,* compiled by R.L. Polk (Oklahoma City: Worley-Friss, 1916), np.

50. Ellison and Hersey, "A Completion," *CRE,* 274.

51. Ralph Ellison and Jim Lutz, interview KOCO-TV, 23 June 1975, Oklahoma Historical Society.

52. Saretta Finley, personal interview, 23 Apr. 1996.

53. Ralph Ellison and Ron Welburn, "Ralph Ellison's Territorial Vantage," *CRE*, 303.

54. Ralph Ellison and David L. Carson, "Ralph Ellison: Twenty Years After," *CRE*, 209.

55. John F. Callahan, "Frequencies of Memory," *Callaloo*, 18.2 (1995): 302.

56. Ralph Ellison, "Tell It Like It Is, Baby," *CERE*, 35.

57. Oklahoma State Certificate of Death No. C526. Louis Albert Ellison, date of death: 19 July 1916. Oklahoma State Board of Health, Bureau of Vital Statistics.

58. Mary E. Riker, Fairlawn Cemetery Association, letter to author, 20 Aug. 1996.

59. Ralph Ellison, "On Being the Target of Discrimination," *CERE*, 823.

60. Ellison, letter to Murray, 23 Oct. 1953, *TT*, 60–61.

61. Ellison and Carson, "Twenty Years After," *CRE*, 209.

62. Ellison, "Tell It," *CERE*, 42.

63. Ellison, "Hidden Name," *SA*, 151.

Chapter 2. Renaissance Man: 1916–1925

1. Herbert Ellison, personal interview, 18 May 1996; Jervis Anderson, "Going to the Territory," *New Yorker*, Nov. 22, 1976, 82.

2. Saretta Finley, personal interview, 16 Apr. 1996.

3. Ralph Ellison, letter to Albert Murray, 24 July 1953, *TT*, 52.

4. Ralph Ellison, "On Being the Target of Discrimination," *CERE*, 821; Oklahoma City fire map, vol. 1 (New York: Sanborn, 1906 and 1922); *Oklahoma City Directory*, "Ellison, Ida," (Kansas City, Mo.: R.L. Polk, 1916–1920). Ellison seems to have combined a couple of experiences. In 1919 when Ralph was six, he lived at 218 North Stiles or the Avery Chapel parsonage at 207 Geary. According to available Oklahoma City Directories, at no time does the family appear to have lived near a newly constructed elementary school. There is no way of knowing if Ida lived in North Town, nearer to the Opportunity or Wilson elementary schools, both opened around 1919. The family always had an address on the East side of Oklahoma City. The Bryant School, directly across the street from 314 (and 406) Byers, is the logical choice. The family seems to have lived on Byers from the time Ralph was past two until he was nearly five. The school was torn down and rebuilt between 1916 and 1917.

5. Juanita Harris, personal interview, 26 Apr. 1996.

6. Jervis Anderson, "Going to the Territory," *New Yorker*, 22 Nov. 1976, 82.

7. Ellison, "That Same Pain, That Same Pleasure," *SA*, 7.

8. Ellison, "That Same Pain," *SA*, 36; Ellison and Carson, "Twenty Years After," *CRE*, 196.

9. Ralph Ellison and John Hersey, "A Completion of Personality: A Talk With Ralph Ellison," *CRE*, 276.

10. Mary C. Moon, "Frederick Douglass Moon: A Study of Black Education in Oklahoma" (Ph.D. diss., University of Oklahoma, 1978), 61.

11. Ellison and Hersey, "A Completion," *CRE*, 275. Ida is the source of Lewis's elaborate and sometimes conflicting deeds.

12. See Wesley Gaines, *African Methodism in the South: or Twenty Five Years of Freedom* (1890; Chicago: Afro-Am Press, 1969); Stephen W. Angell, *Bishop Henry McNeal Turner and African-American Religion in the South* (Knoxville: University of Tennessee Press, 1992); George A. Singleton, *The Romance of African Methodism* (New York: Exposition Press, 1952); Clarence Walker, *A Rock in a Weary Land: The African Methodist Episcopal Church in the Civil War and Reconstruction* (Baton Rouge: Louisiana State University Press, 1982).

13. Walker, *A Rock*, 126.

14. Mrs. Tommie Williams, personal interview, 16 Apr. 1996; Ellison and Welburn, "Territorial Vantage," *CRE*, 303.

15. Ralph Ellison, "Living with the Music," *SA*, 197.

16. Williams, interview.

17. Ralph Ellison and Hollie I. West, "Ellison: Exploring the Life of a Not So Visible Man," *CRE,* 257.

18. Oklahoma City fire map; Ralph Ellison, "Conditions in Black Harlem," Congressional Committee, 26 Oct. 1966, Pacifica radio archives.

19. Ellison and West, "Ellison: Exploring the Life," *CRE, 257.*

20. Ralph Ellison, "Hidden Name and Complex Fate,"*SA,* 152.

21. Ellison, "On Being the Target," *CERE,* 821. In Ellison's memory of his entry to the school, he and his family were living somewhere near Ida's work, but most pivotally, across the street from a freshly built schoolhouse. Little archival evidence remains to elaborate his recollection. The Oklahoma City Directory lists his mother at either 218 North Stiles or the parsonage on Geary, residences within a block of each other and in the Oklahoma City black belt. No new elementary schools were constructed in Oklahoma City during 1919, though Irving Senior High School seems to have opened its doors at Third and Central about 1919. It seems most likely that Ralph was referring to the whites-only Bryant School, which had undergone such grand transformations during the late teens, some of which happened when Ellison lived on Byers. No matter where the actual school was that Ellison drew the anecdote from, the outcome was the same. Oklahoma segregated its schools, and did not build or refurbish new buildings for black students.

22. James R. Scales and Danney Goble, *Oklahoma Politics: A History* (Norman: University of Oklahoma Press, 1982), 36.

23. Ellison, "On Being the Target," *CERE,* 822.

24. James D. Anderson, *The Education of Blacks in the South, 1860–1935* (Chapel Hill: University of North Carolina Press, 1988), 193; Henry Allen Bullock, *A History of Negro Education in the South* (Cambridge: Harvard University Press, 1967), 177–180.

25. Anderson, *Education,* 203.

26. "Needs of Separate Schools in Oklahoma City School District," *Black Dispatch,* 5 Apr. 1918; 1.

27. "Negroes Use Wheeler Park," Oklahoma WPA Records, Box 3 "Blacks," Folder 81.105, OSHS.

28. Ellison, "On Being the Target," *CERE,* 823–824.

29. Ralph Ellison and Hollie I. West, "Growing Up Black in Frontier Oklahoma," *CRE,* 255; Jimmie Lewis Franklin, *Journey Toward Hope* (Norman: University of Oklahoma Press, 1982), 136. Ellison perhaps combined two incidents, the lynching of Chandler in Oklahoma City in 1920 and the lynching of Henry Argo in Chicasha in 1930. He recalled especially that Mayor Jack Walton came out to support black defense groups who protected the body of a man "lynched in Chicasha." Walton was mayor from 1920 to 1922, and from 1923 to 1924 was a well-known anti–Ku Klux Klan governor.

30. Albert McRill, *And Satan Came Also: An Inside Story of a City's Social and Political History* (Oklahoma City: Britton Publishing, 1955), 192.

31. Charles C. Alexander, *The Ku Klux Klan in the Southwest* (Louisville: University of Kentucky Press, 1965), 129–130.

32. Ralph Ellison, "An Extravagance of Laughter," *GTT,* 166.

33. Ralph Ellison, "The Myth of the Flawed White Southerner," *GTT,* 81.

34. Inscription of copy of *Invisible Man* to Zelia N. Breaux following novel's publication, courtesy of Mrs. Elwyn Welch.

35. Ralph Ellison, "Going to the Territory," *GTT,* 135.

36. "Pictorial Review of Judge Albert Alexander," *Black Dispatch,* 10 Jan. 1974: B2.

37. Ellison, "That Same Pain," *SA,* 11. In a 1976 interview with Ron Welburn, "Ralph Ellison's Territorial Vantage," Ellison suggests that he joined the band at eight, contradicting "That Same Pain, That Same Pleasure." However, the later entry is more plausible. According

to the best available sources, he learned to play the horn between ten and eleven, when Joseph Mead taught him the E flat instrument.

38. Ellison, "Living with the Music," *SA,* 191.

39. Finley, interview.

40. Ralph Ellison, "Roscoe Dunjee and the American Language,"*CERE,* 451.

41. Scott Ellsworth, *Death in the Promised Land* (Baton Rouge: Louisiana State Press, 1982).

42. Ralph Ellison, letter to Richard Wright, 3 Nov. 1941. Box 97, Folder "Ellison, Ralph," RWP.

43. Ellison,"On Being the Target," *CERE,* 825.

44. Ellison, "That Same Pain," *SA,* 11.

45. Oklahoma City fire map; *Oklahoma City Directory,* "Ellison, Ida," 1921, 1922.

46. O. O. McIntyre, *Another "Odd" Book* (New York: Cosmopolitan Magazine, 1932).

47. Ellison, "That Same Pain," *SA,* 5.

48. Ellison, "That Same Pain," *SA,* 6.

49. John Thompson, *Closing the Frontier* (Norman: Oklahoma University Press, 1986), 24, 26.

50. Ellison and Hersey, "A Completion," *CRE,* 276.

51. Herbert Ellison, interview.

52. Ralph Ellison, "The Charlie Christian Story," *SA,* 235, 238.

53. Ellison, "On Being the Target," *CERE,* 825.

54. Fourteenth Census of the United States: 1920—Population; Oklahoma County, Oklahoma, Enumeration District 162, Sheet 3, "Franklin Davis," Bureau of the Census.

55. Ralph Ellison, "Perspective of Literature," *GTT,* 323–324; Ray W. Lucke, ed., *Who's Who in Oklahoma City: A Biographical and Genealogical Record of Prominent and Representative Citizens* (Oklahoma City: Mid-Continent Press, 1931), 94.

56. Ellison, "That Same Pain," *SA,* 50.

57. Ellison, "On Being the Target," *CERE,* 825.

58. Ralph Ellison, "Dedication of Ralph Ellison Library," 21 June 1975, Oral History Project, OSHS.

59. Ralph Ellison, "On Initiation Rites and Power," *GTT,* 55; Ralph Ellison, "Going to the Territory," *GTT,* 133–135.

60. Harris, interview; Carla Hinton, "Great Injustice Acknowledged," *Daily Oklahoma/ Oklahoma City Times,* 4 Aug. 1996: 5.

61. Ralph Ellison and David L. Carson, "Ralph Ellison: Twenty Years After," *CRE,* 203.

62. Jacqueline Jones, "Between the Cotton Field and the Ghetto," *Labor of Love, Labor of Sorrow* (New York: Basic Books, 1985), 394, n56; Katzman, *Seven Days a Week,* 303–314; Clair Brown, *American Standards of Living* (Cambridge, England: Blackwell Press, 1994), 43.

63. Fourteenth Census of the United States: 1920—Population; Oklahoma County, Oklahoma, Enumeration District 139, Sheet 8 B, "Ida Ellison," Bureau of the Census. Ida's occupation is listed as "janitress."

64. Herbert Ellison, personal interview, 17 May 1996; Tracy McCleary, personal interview, 8 July 1997.

65. Ralph Ellison, "Bearden," *CERE,* 832.

66. Worth J. Hadley, "Roscoe Dunjee on Education: The Improvement of Black Education In Oklahoma 1930–1955" (Ph.D. diss., University of Oklahoma, 1981), 45–46.

67. Ralph Ellison, untitled note ["KKK memories . . ."], Box 52, Folder 2 "*Invisible Man* Draft's Notes," REP.

68. Jimmie Stewart, personal interview, 13 Apr. 1996.

69. Finley, interview.

70. Herbert Ellison, personal interview, 18 May 1996.

71. Ellison and Hersey, "A Completion," *CRE,* 277.

72. Ralph Ellison, "That I Had Wings," *Common Ground* 3.4 (1943): 30.

73. Ralph Ellison, "Boy on a Train," *New Yorker,* 29 Apr.–6 May 1996, 111.

74. John F. Callahan, "The Unpublished Ellison," *New Yorker,* 29 Apr.–6 May 1996, 110.

75. Ellison, "Boy on a Train," 113.

76. Ellison, letter to Wright, 3 Nov. 1941.

77. Ellison and West, "Exploring the Life," *CRE,* 247; Ralph Ellison and Arlene Crewdson and Rita Thomson, "Interview with Ralph Ellison," *CRE,* 265.

78. Ellison and Hersey, "A Completion," *CRE,* 273.

79. Oklahoma County Marriage License Record, Application for Marriage License, Marriage License and Marriage Certificate. Ida Ellison and James Amons, 8 July 1924. County Clerk's Office, Oklahoma City. On the Oklahoma application for marriage, Amons's age is recorded as "29"; on the marriage license it is recorded as "59." The Amons surname is spelled variably with both a single and double "m."

80. Ellison, "Tell It," *CERE,* 42.

81. Ralph Ellison, *Slick* manuscript, Box 55, Folder "Original Typescripts I," RWP.

82. Ralph Ellison and Michael S. Harper and Robert B. Stepto, "Study and Experience: An Interview with Ralph Ellison," *CRE,* 328; *Oklahoma City Directory,* "Ammons, Jas and Ida," 1925; *Oklahoma City Directory,* "Ellison, Ida," 1926.

83. Ellison and Carson, "Twenty Years After," *CRE,* 208.

84. Ellison, introduction to *SA,* xiii, xvii, xvi; McCleary, interview.

85. Lamonia McFarland, "Brazil and the Negro," nd., unpublished document in the author's possession, courtesy of Charles Morgan.

86. Ellison, "Hidden Name," *SA,* 151; Harris interview.

87. Robert Penn Warren and Ralph Ellison, "Leadership from the Periphery," *Who Speaks for the Negro* (New York: Vintage, 1966), 325; Herbert Ellison, interview.

88. Stewart, interview; Finley, interview; Anderson, "Going to the Territory," 60.

89. Ralph Ellison, "Portrait of Inman Page," *GTT,* 117.

90. "Conditions at Negro School Bring Inquiry," Oklahoma WPA Records, Box 3 "Blacks," Folder 81.105, OSHS.

91. Ellison, "Portrait of Inman Page," *GTT,* 117, 118.

Chapter 3. *The Horn of Plenty: 1925–1932*

1. William Savage Jr., *Singing Cowboys and All That Jazz* (Norman: Oklahoma University Press, 1983), 21.

2. Ralph Ellison and Ron Welburn, "Ralph Ellison's Territorial Vantage," *CRE,* 316; Eileen Southern, *The Music of Black Americans: A History,* 2nd ed. (New York: Norton, 1983), 361–395; Albert Murray, *Stomping the Blues* (New York: Vintage, 1976).

3. Ralph Ellison, "Hidden Name and Complex Fate," *SA,* 153.

4. Currie Ballard, telephone interview, 17 Apr. 1996; Henry Hawkins, "From the Wagon Yard to the Fair Ground: The History of Douglass" (manuscript, possession of the author).

5. Ralph Ellison and John Hersey, "A Completion of Personality: An Interview with Ralph Ellison," *CRE,* 277; Ralph Ellison, "Bearden," *CERE,* 832.

6. Zelia N. Breaux, "The Development of Instrumental Music in Negro Secondary Schools and Colleges" (Master's thesis, Northwestern University, 1939), 44.

7. Zelia Breaux, "Teacher Recommendation," Ralph Ellison's Tuskegee Institute Application, 21 June 1933, Tuskegee University Registrar.

8. Breaux, "Development," 13; Ralph Ellison, "Living with the Music," *SA,* 190–191.

9. Ralph Ellison, "Going to the Territory," *GTT,* 135.

10. Ralph Ellison, "Dedication of Ralph Ellison Library," 21 June 1975, Oral History Project, OSHS.

11. Breaux, "Development," 8.

12. Mildred McCracken Crossley, "A History of the Negro Schools of Oklahoma City, Oklahoma" (Master's thesis, University of Oklahoma, 1939), 34.

13. Nathan Pearson Jr., *Goin' to Kansas City* (Urbana: University of Illinois Press, 1987), 43–45.

14. John Perry, "Deep Second Still Lives in Dreams," *Daily Oklahoman/Oklahoma City Times*, 8 Jan. 1993, morning ed.: V1.

15. Ralph Ellison, untitled note ["KKK memories . . ."], Box 52, Folder 2, "*Invisible Man* Draft's Notes," REP.

16. Ellison, "Living with the Music," *SA*, 191–192.

17. Ellison and Hersey, "A Completion," *CRE*, 274.

18. Ralph Ellison, letter to Albert Murray, 24 July 1953, *TT*, 52.

19. Ellison and Hersey, "A Completion," *CRE*, 275.

20. Tracy McCleary, personal interview, 8 July 1997.

21. Ralph Ellison, "That Same Pain, That Same Pleasure: An Interview," *SA*, 11.

22. Ellison, "Living with the Music," *SA*, 191, 192.

23. James Collier, *Duke Ellington* (New York: Oxford University Press, 1987), 93.

24. Ellison, "Hidden Name, " *SA*, 157; Jimmie Lewis Franklin, *Journey toward Hope* (Norman: University of Oklahoma Press, 1982), 31.

25. "Some Folk Belief of Oklahoma Negroes," Oklahoma WPA Records, Box 3 "Blacks," Folder 81.105, OSHS.

26. "Early Occupational Life of the Negro: Jim Noble," Oklahoma WPA Records, Box 3 "Blacks," Folder 81.105, OSHS; Ellison, "Dedication of Ralph Ellison Library."

27. James R. Scales and Danney Goble, *Oklahoma Politics: A History* (Norman: Oklahoma University Press, 1982), 48.

28. "Early Occupational Life of the Negro: Emmitt Carruthers," Oklahoma WPA Records, Box 3 "Blacks," Folder 81.105, OSHS.

29. Saretta Finley, personal interview, 16 Apr. 1996.

30. Crossley, "Negro Schools of Oklahoma City," 80.

31. Ralph Ellison, "Perspective of Literature," *GTT*, 322.

32. Hawkins, "From the Wagon Yard," 3.1.

33. "Man Charged With Killing Street Car Conductor, To Be Buried Here," *Black Dispatch*, 26 Apr. 1928, 1.

34. Ellison, "Perspective of Literature," *GTT*, 323.

35. "Celebrating One Hundred Years of Excellence," Frederick Douglass High School brochure, 4–11 Aug. 1991, 10.

36. Gunther Schuller, *The Swing Era: The Development of Jazz, 1930–1945* (New York: Oxford University Press, 1989), 240.

37. Pearson, *Goin'*, 66, 68.

38. Ellison, "That Same Pain," *SA*, 9.

39. Ellison, "Living with the Music," *SA*, 189.

40. Ellison, "That Same Pain," *SA*, 13.

41. "Wins Music Degree," *Black Dispatch*, 18 June 1931, 1.

42. Ellison and Welburn, "Territorial Vantage," *CRE*, 307.

43. Ellison, "That Same Pain," *SA*, 13.

44. Ellison and Welburn, "Territorial Vantage," *CRE*, 304.

45. Hawkins, "From the Wagon Yard," 3.19, 5.1; Crossley, "Negro Schools of Oklahoma City," 29.

46. Ellison, "Hidden Name," *SA*, 156; Ralph Ellison and Richard Kostelanetz, "An Interview with Ralph Ellison," *CRE*, 89; Ellison and West, "Exploring the Life," *CRE*, 247.

47. Ellison and West, "Exploring the Life," *CRE*, 247.

48. Elnora Decker, personal interview, 23 Apr. 1996.

49. Harris, interview.

50. Ellison and Kostelanetz, "An Interview with Ralph Ellison," *CRE,* 89; Albion Torgeé, "Hargrove's Quarter," *Our Continent* 2.7 (1882): 215.

51. Oklahoma City Senior High School, Permanent Record, "Ralph Ellison," May 1932, Department of Education, Oklahoma City.

52. Count Basie and Albert Murray, *Good Morning Blues: The Autobiography of Count Basie as told to Albert Murray* (New York: Da Capo, 1995), 10–11, 21.

53. Ralph Ellison, "The Golden Age, Time Past," *SA,* 208.

54. Ellison and Welburn, "Territorial Vantage," *CRE,* 307–308, 311, 314.

55. Pearson, *Goin',* 40–41.

56. "Avery Chapel AME Church," *Black Dispatch,* 1 Mar. 1928, 4.

57. "Bells of Cornville," *Black Dispatch,* 16 May 1929, 5.

58. Fourteenth Census of the United States: 1920—Population; Oklahoma County, Oklahoma, Enumeration District 245, Sheet 7, "John Bell," Bureau of the Census.

59. Herbert Ellison, personal interview, 18 May 1996.

60. Ralph Ellison, "Remembering Jimmy," *SA,* 242, 243.

61. Oklahoma County Marriage License Record, Application for Marriage License, Marriage License and Marriage Certificate. John Bell and Lucy Ida Ammons, 9 Dec. 1929. County Clerk's Office, Oklahoma City.

62. Ralph Ellison and Michael S. Harper and Robert B. Stepto, "Study and Experience: An Interview with Ralph Ellison," *CRE,* 323.

63. Ellison, "That Same Pain," *SA,* 11.

64. Ralph Ellison, "The Charlie Christian Story," *SA,* 235–236; Prentiss Nolan, personal interview, 4 Jan. 1997.

65. Ralph Ellison, "Homage to Duke Ellington on His Birthday," *GTT,* 220.

66. Editorial, "The Constitution of the United States," *Black Dispatch,* 2 May 1929, 4; Ellison and West, "Exploring the Life," *CRE,* 258.

67. Ellison and Carson, "Twenty Years After," *CRE,* 199.

68. Oklahoma City Senior High School, Permanent Record, "Ralph Ellison."

69. Currie Ballard, telephone interview, 17 Apr. 1996.

70. Ellison and Carson, "Twenty Years After," *CRE,* 197.

71. "Avery Chapel Hosts Debate Between Wiley and Oklahoma City University," *Black Dispatch,* 12 Mar. 1931, 1; Ralph Ellison and Steve Cannon, Ishmael Reed, and Quincy Troupe, "The Essential Ellison," *CRE,* 369–370.

72. " 'Sonia,' Regarded as Biggest Hit of Year," *Black Dispatch,* 21 May 1931, 5.

73. Harris, interview; High School, Permanent Record; "1931–1932 Douglass High School Class Reunion," 20–22 June 1975, "Class Roll 1931" and "Class Roll 1932." Harris recalled that Ralph may have had to make up a class in 1932. Ellison started Douglass Senior High School in January 1927 and was awarded his degree in May 1932. It is unclear exactly what happened. There were frequent examples of students allowed to participate in the ceremonies who had not completed the requirements for the degree. The school transcript is indecipherable, written in script, and lists grades under ten headings "9A, 9B, 1, 2, 3, 4, 5, 6, 7, 8." It is not a ninth grade report card, since it lists both the date he entered school and the date of his graduation. Ellison is photographed with both the class of 1931 and the class of 1932.

74. Ellison and Welburn, "Territorial Vantage," *CRE,* 306.

75. "Cooperation and the Band Fund," *Black Dispatch,* 28 May 1931, 4.

76. "Band Fund Now $604.81; $96 More To Reach Goal," *Black Dispatch,* 18 June 1931, 1.

77. Ralph Ellison, letter to Albert Murray, Aug. 1959, *TT,* 216.

78. "Wins Scholarship," *Black Dispatch,* 2 July 1931, 1.

79. "Trailing the Douglass High Band to Denver," *Black Dispatch*, 2 July 1931, 1–2.

80. Ralph Ellison, "On Initiation Rites and Power," *GTT*, 57; *Oklahoma City Directory*, "Greenlease-Moore Used Cars," 1932.

81. Jimmy Stewart, personal interview, 13 Apr. 1996.

82. Ralph Ellison, "An Extravagance," *GTT*, 196; "Former Douglass High School Student Dies," *Black Dispatch*, 18 June 1931, 5.

83. "Miss McMurray Honors Miss Randolph," *Black Dispatch*, 18 June 1931, 4; "New Social Club Formed," *Black Dispatch*, 18 June 1931, 4.

84. "Miss Randolph Entertains Club," *Black Dispatch*, 23 July 1931, 5.

85. Ralph Ellison, "Homage to Duke Ellington," *GTT*, 218, 220.

86. Finley, interview.

87. Herbert Ellison, interview.

88. Zella J. Black Patterson, *Langston University: A History* (Norman: University of Oklahoma Press, 1979), 42–44.

89. Ellison, Harper, and Stepto, "Study and Experience," *CRE*, 325–326; "Oklahoma Negro High Schools In Big Song Festival," *Black Dispatch*, 18 Apr. 1929, 5.

90. John F. Callahan, personal interview, 1 May 1996.

Chapter 4. Down South: 1932–1933

1. Ralph Ellison and Richard Kostelanetz, "An Interview with Ralph Ellison," *CRE*, 88; "Radio City Premiere Is a Notable Event," *New York Times*, 28 Dec. 1932, 1,14; Brooks Atkinson, "The Play," *New York Times*, 28 Dec. 1932, 14. Ellison remembered incorrectly that the "Tuskegee choir opened Radio City Music Hall when I was in high school." He had been graduated from Douglass for six months when Dawson took the choir to New York to sing for the December 27, 1932, opening of the music hall.

2. Ellison and Kostelanetz, "An Interview," *CRE*, 88.

3. Eileen Southern, *The Music of Black Americans*, 2nd ed. (New York: Norton, 1983), 274, 420.

4. Louis Harlan, *Booker T. Washington: The Wizard of Tuskegee* (New York: Oxford University Press, 1983), 149.

5. Langston Hughes, *I Wonder As I Wander* (1956; New York: Thunder's Mouth Press, 1989), 61.

6. Manning Marable, "Tuskegee Institute in the 1920's," *Negro History Bulletin* 40 (1977): 768.

7. *Tuskegee Catalog* (1881–1882): 8–9.

8. Louis R. Harlan, *Booker T. Washington: The Making of a Black Leader, 1856–1901* (New York: Oxford, 1972), 57; Robert R. Moton, *Finding a Way Out* (Garden City, N.Y.: Doubleday, Page and Co., 1922), 60–61, 154–155.

9. David L. Johnson, "The Contributions of William L. Dawson to the School of Music at Tuskegee Institute and to Choral Music" (Ph.D. diss., University of Illinois, 1987), 52; "Tuskegee Organizes School of Music," *Tuskegee Messenger* 8.9 (1932): 6.

10. Johnson, "The Contributions," 137.

11. *Tuskegee Institute Bulletin* 27.3 (1934): 21.

12. Tuskegee Normal and Industrial Institute, Application, "Ralph Ellison," Office of the Registrar.

13. *Tuskegee Institute Bulletin* 27.3 (1934): 26, 156.

14. Receipt, May Brothers Men's Store, Box 76, Folder "Receipts," REP.

15. Jervis Anderson, "Going to the Territory," *New Yorker*, 22 Nov. (1976): 86; Payment Book, Jenkins Music Company, Box 76, Folder "Receipts," REP.

16. Ralph Ellison, "Perspective of Literature," *GTT*, 324; Johnson, "The Contributions," 140.

17. Anderson, "Going to the Territory," 86.

18. Herbert Ellison, personal interview, 18 May 1996.

19. Anderson, "Going to the Territory," 88; Saretta Finley, personal interview, 16 Apr. 1996.

20. Mike Schafer, *Classic American Railroads* (Osceola, Wis.: Motorbooks International, 1996), 69.

21. James R. Chiles, "Hallelujah, I'm a Bum," *Smithsonian* 29.5 (Aug. 1998): 68.

22. Ralph Ellison and Hollie I. West, "Exploring the Life of a Not So Visible Man," *CRE,* 248.

23. Anderson, "Going to the Territory," 88.

24. Ellison and West, "Exploring the Life," *CRE,* 250; Anderson, "Going to the Territory," 88.

25. Ralph Ellison, "I Did Not Learn Their Names," *New Yorker,* 29 Apr.–6 May 1996, 114.

26. Sean Cashman, *African-Americans and the Quest for Civil Rights: 1900–1990* (New York: New York University Press, 1991), 61.

27. Dan T. Carter, *Scottsboro: A Tragedy of the American South,* rev. ed. (Baton Rouge: Louisiana State Press, 1979), 235–240.

28. Carter, *Scottsboro,* n320–n321; Ellison, "Perspective of Literature," *GTT,* 325.

29. Jimmie Lewis Franklin, *Journey Toward Hope* (Norman: University of Oklahoma Press, 1982), 132–135.

30. Ralph Ellison, "Hymie's Bull," *Flying Home and Other Stories* (New York: Random House, 1996), 82.

31. Ellison, "Perspective of Literature," *GTT,* 325; Ellison, "I Did Not Learn," 115; Tuskegee Normal and Industrial Institute Student Record, Ralph Ellison's photo on entering; Ralph Ellison, letter to Richard Wright, 3 Nov. 1941, Box 97, Folder "Ellison, Ralph," RWP.

32. Ralph Ellison, R. W. B. Lewis, James Baldwin, William Styron, "Writers on Writing," Sept. 1967, panel discussion, Pacifica radio archives.

33. Tuskegee Normal and Industrial Institute Student Record, "Ralph Ellison," Office of the Registrar. The student records from Tuskegee of the period included pictures upon entrance and graduation.

34. Mike Rabb, personal interview, 21 Nov. 1995.

35. Cleveland W. Eneas, *Tuskegee Ra! Ra!: An Autobiography of My Youth* (Nassau, Bahamas: Commercial Print Works, 1986); Rabb, interview.

36. *Tuskegee Institute Bulletin* 27.3 (1934–1935): 27.

37. Tuskegee Institute, Application, "Ellison."

38. Ralph Ellison and Ron Welburn, "Ralph Ellison's Territorial Vantage," *CRE,* 308, 309, 313; Horace Porter, personal interview, 3 Nov. 1995.

39. *Tuskegee Institute Bulletin* 27.3 (1934): 171–201.

40. Carolyn Walcott Ford, personal interview, 15 Nov. 1995.

41. Frederick Jackson Turner, "The Significance of the Frontier," *Rereading Frederick Jackson Turner* (New York: Henry Holt, 1994), 53.

42. Daniel Singal, *The War Within: From Victorian to Modernist Thought in the South, 1919–1945* (Chapel Hill: University of North Carolina Press, 1982), 18.

Chapter 5. The Trumpet and a Barrel of Crabs: 1933–1935

1. Etheldra Robinson, personal interview, 14 Mar. 1996.

2. David L. Johnson, "The Contributions of William L. Dawson to the School of Music at Tuskegee Institute and to Choral Music" (Ph.D. diss., University of Illinois Press, 1987), 125.

3. Jean E. Carzot and Constance Hobson, *Born to Play* (Westport, Conn.: Greenwood Press, 1983), 96.

4. Manning Marable, "Tuskegee Institute in the 1920's," *Negro History Bulletin* 40 (1977): 768.

5. Ralph Ellison and Michael S. Harper and Robert B. Stepto, "Study and Experience: An Interview with Ralph Ellison," *CRE,* 337.

6. "Tuskegee Football Team at World's Fair," *Tuskegee Messenger* 9.9 (1933): 6.

7. Ralph Ellison and David L. Carson, "Ralph Ellison: Twenty Years After," *CRE,* 199.

8. Mike Rabb, personal interview, 21 Nov. 1995.

9. Ellison and Hersey, "A Completion," *CRE,* 293–294.

10. Ralph Ellison, "Jazz Scene," *Invisible Man* draft, Box 145, Folder "Jazz Music," REP.

11. Robert R. Moton, *Finding a Way Out* (Garden City, N.Y.: Doubleday, 1922), 3–15.

12. Laly Charleton Washington, personal interview, 21 Nov. 1995.

13. Moton, *Finding,* 59–61, 144–145.

14. Washington, interview; Moton, "Believing in Yourself," *Tuskegee Messenger* 9.9 (1933): 4.

15. Cleveland Eneas, *Tuskegee Ra! Ra!, An Autobiography of My Youth* (Nassau, Bahamas: Commercial Print Works, 1986), 112–113; Robert G. O'Meally, "Keeping the Faith: A Study of Ralph Ellison's Early Life and Works" (Ph.D. diss., Harvard University, 1975), 78.

16. Dr. Daniel Williams, personal interview, 20 Nov. 1995; Washington, interview.

17. "About the Campus," *Tuskegee Messenger* 9.12 (1933): 8.

18. Ralph Ellison, "Homage to William L. Dawson," *CERE,* 436.

19. Washington, interview.

20. "Morteza Drexel Sprague," *Who's Who In America* vol. 33 (Chicago: Marquis, 1964), 1902.

21. Sterling Brown, introduction to *Negro Caravan,* eds. Sterling Brown, Arthur Davis, and Ulysses Lee (New York: Dryden Press, 1941), 5.

22. *Howard University Bulletin* 9.5 (June 1930): 204; Brown, introduction, *Negro,* 7.

23. Carolyn Walcott Ford, personal interview, 15 Nov. 1995.

24. Bess B. Walcott, "Among the New Books," *Tuskegee Messenger* 9.12 (1933): 6; Ellison and Welburn, "Territorial Vantage," *CRE,* 309.

25. James Weldon Johnson, *Black Manhattan* (New York: Da Capo, 1991), 157–158, 103, 72.

26. Ford, interview.

27. "With the Clubs," *Campus Digest,* 21 Oct. 1933: 3.

28. Robert R. Moton, "The Force that Wins," *Tuskegee Messenger* 9.11 (1933): 4.

29. "Tuskegee Normal and Industrial Institute: An Evaluation," *Tuskegee Messenger* 9.11 (1933): 3.

30. Tuskegee Institute, Student Record, "Ralph Ellison."

31. *Tuskegee Institute Bulletin* 27.3 (1934–1935): 179.

32. Rabb, interview.

33. Tuskegee Institute, Student Record, "Ralph Ellison."

34. "With the Clubs," *Campus Digest,* 12 Jan. 1935: 3.

35. *Tuskegee Institute Bulletin* 27.3 (1934–1935): 106.

36. N. F. Herriford, "Transforming Calibans into Ciceros," *Tuskegee Messenger* 9.12 (1933): 7.

37. Rayford Logan, "The Fascination of the Study of Negro History," *Tuskegee Messenger* 10.4 (1934): 2.

38. Bernard L. Peterson, "Willis Richardson: Pioneer Playwright," *The Theater of Black Americans,* ed. Errol Hill (Englewood Cliffs, N.J.: Prentice-Hall, 1980), 113–114.

39. "Negro History at Tuskegee," *Tuskegee Messenger* 10.3 (1934): 2, 7.

40. Zora Lee Barnes, "Drum Beats," *Campus Digest,* 24 Feb. 1934: 3.

41. "Famous 'Maestro' Coming," *Campus Digest,* 24 Feb. 1934: 1; Ollie Stewart, "Negro Music in the Modern Mode," *Tuskegee Messenger* 10.4 (1934): 3.

42. "Founder's Day Exercises," *Tuskegee Messenger* 10.6 (1934): 1.

43. Ruth Stewart, *Portia* (Garden City, N.Y.: Doubleday, 1977), 103.

44. Ethel Edwards, *Carver of Tuskegee* (Cincinnati: Psyche Press, 1971), 124.

45. "Student Activities," *Tuskegee Messenger* 10.6 (1934): 9.

46. Ralph Ellison, "Commencement Address at the Curtis Institute of Music, 1975," Hazel Harrison Papers, Box 139-2, Folder 2, MSRC, Ralph Ellison, "Little Man at the Chehaw Station," *GTT,* 3.

47. Joel Williamson, *The Crucible of Race: Black White Relations in the American South since Emancipation* (New York: Oxford University Press, 1984), 111–115.

48. Arnold Rampersad, *The Life of Langston Hughes* vol. 1 (New York: Oxford University Press, 1986), 231.

49. Ellison, "Little Man," 4.

50. Tuskegee Institute, Student Record, "Ralph Ellison."

51. Nannie Burroughs, "The Challenge of the New Day," *Tuskegee Messenger* 10.6 (1934): 2, 11.

52. Robert R. Moton, "President's Sunday Evening Address," *Tuskegee Messenger* 10.6 (1934): 4.

53. Walter Williams, "Is Tuskegee Just Another College," *Tuskegee Messenger* 11.2 (1935): 5; "Student Activities," *Tuskegee Messenger* 10.8 (1934): 6.

54. Ralph Ellison, "Ralph Ellison Questionnaire," nd. (ca. July 1952), Box 74, Folder "Speeches, Lectures," REP.

55. Ellison and Kostelanetz, "An Interview," *CRE,* 89; George Bernard Shaw, preface to *Plays Pleasant and Unpleasant* (New York: William H. Wise, 1931), vii–xix.

56. Ralph Ellison, "The World and the Jug," *SA,* 136.

57. Ellison, "An Extravagance," *GTT,* 166; Ellison and West, "Exploring the Life," *CRE,* 242.

58. Ellison, "An Extravagance," *GTT,* 166–167.

59. Ellison, "World and the Jug," *SA,* 128.

60. Horace Porter, personal interview, 3 Nov. 1995.

61. Rabb, interview; Marable, "Tuskegee," 767.

62. Ellison, "An Extravagance," *GTT,* 172.

63. "Student Activities," *Tuskegee Messenger* 10.9 (1934): 7.

64. Washington, interview.

65. *Tuskegee Institute Bulletin* 28 (Mar. 1935): 109.

66. *Tuskegee Institute Bulletin* 28 (Mar. 1935): 159.

67. Johnson, "Contributions," 143.

68. Ellison and Kostelanetz, "An Interview," *CRE,* 88; Ellison, "Homage to William Dawson," *CERE,* 436.

69. Leonard Liebling, "Negro Symphony Proves Outstanding Work," *Tuskegee Messenger* 11.8–9 (1935): 2.

70. Leonard Liebling, "Native Musical Movement Stamped with the Strong Influence of Europe," *Tuskegee Messenger* 11.8–9 (1935): 12.

71. "Press Comment on the Negro Symphony," *Tuskegee Messenger* 11.8–9 (1935): 8.

72. Ralph Ellison and James Alan McPherson, "Indivisible Man," *CRE,* 181.

73. Ralph Ellison, "What These Children Are Like," *GTT,* 65.

74. Eneas, *Tuskegee Ra! Ra!,* 96.

75. Ellison, "What These Children," *GTT,* 70.

76. Horace Cayton, *Long Old Road* (Seattle: Washington University Press, 1963), 198.

77. "With the Faculty," *Tuskegee Messenger* 11.3 (1935): 6.

78. Charles Johnson, *The Negro College Graduate* (Chapel Hill: University of North Carolina Press, 1938), 309.

79. Ellison and West, "Exploring the Life," *CRE*, 240.

80. Ellison and McPherson, "Indivisible Man," *CRE*, 181.

81. Ralph Ellison and Harold Isaacs, "Five Writers and Their African Ancestors," *CRE*, 67.

82. Robert R. Moton, "President's Sunday Evening Address," *Tuskegee Messenger* 10.9 (1934): 4.

83. George Brown Tindall, *The Emergence of the New South* (Louisiana State Press and the Littlefield Fund, 1967), 551–552.

84. Raymond Wolters, "Tuskegee Veterans Hospital," *The New Negro on Campus: Black College Rebellions of the 1920s* (Princeton: Princeton University Press, 1975), 167–191.

85. "Negro Achievement Week at Tuskegee," *Tuskegee Messenger* 10:11 (1934): 6.

86. "Noted Poet Lectures in Chapel," *Campus Digest,* 1 Dec. 1934: 1.

87. "Morteza Drexel Sprague," *Who's Who In America* vol. 33 (Chicago: Marquis, 1964), 1902; *Howard University Bulletin* 9.5 (June 1930): 204.

88. William Stanley Braithwaite, "The Negro in American Literature," *The New Negro* (1925; New York: MacMillan, 1992), 29–30, 37–38, 41.

89. "Books-Art-Music," *Tuskegee Messenger* 11.4-5 (1935): 13.

90. Sterling Brown, "Imitation of Life: Once a Pancake," *Opportunity,* 1 Mar. 1935, 87–88.

91. "About the Campus," *Tuskegee Messenger* 10.12 (1934): 6; Ford, interview.

92. Tuskegee Institute Student Record, "Ralph Ellison."

93. "With the Faculty," *Tuskegee Messenger* 11.3 (1935): 6.

94. Washington, interview.

95. "Stop! Look! Listen!," *Campus Digest,* 12 Jan. 1935: 3.

96. "Ki Yi Anniversary Dance," *Campus Digest,* 9 Mar. 1935: 3.

97. Tuskegee Institute, Student Record, "Ralph Ellison."

Chapter 6. The Wasteland: 1935–1936

1. "Artist Meets Artist," *Campus Digest,* 9 Mar. 1935: 3.

2. Ralph Ellison, "That Same Pain, That Same Pleasure: An Interview," *SA,* 19.

3. Ralph Ellison, and Steve Cannon, Ishmael Reed, and Quincy Troupe, "The Essential Ellison," *CRE,* 346.

4. Kelly Miller, "Booker T. Washington: Race Statesman," *Tuskegee Messenger* 11.4–5 (1935): 3.

5. Miller, "Booker T.," 3.

6. James Collier, *Duke Ellington* (New York: Oxford University Press, 1987), 165–167.

7. "Duke Ellington and His Orchestra Thrill Four Thousand," *Campus Digest,* 20 Apr. 1935: 1; Ralph Ellison, "Homage to Duke Ellington," *GTT,* 221.

8. Columbia University, letter to author, 6 Dec. 1995.

9. Albert Murray, personal interview, 1 Dec. 1995.

10. Cleveland Eneas, *Tuskegee Ra! Ra!: An Autobiography of My Youth* (Nassau, Bahamas: Commercial Print Works, 1986), 81.

11. "Governor Murray Designates City Negro Zone," *Daily Oklahoman,* 2 May 1933, 9.

12. Ralph Ellison and John Corry, "An American Novelist Who Sometimes Teaches," *CRE,* 102; Ralph Ellison, "Society, Morality and the Novel," *GTT,* 259.

13. Ernest Hemingway, "Remembering Shooting-Flying," *Esquire* 3.2 (1935): 21.

14. Langston Hughes, "The Folks at Home," *Esquire* 1.6 (1934): 56.

15. Ruth Ann Stewart, *Portia* (New York: Doubleday, 1977), 104.

16. Tuskegee Annual Commencement Program, 28 May 1936, 6.

17. "First Year of Third Administration of Tuskegee Institute Has Auspicious Opening," *Tuskegee Messenger* 11.8–9 (1935): 1.

18. M. D. Sprague, "Literary Likes and Dislikes of College Students," *Tuskegee Messenger* 10.2 (1934): 3.

19. Frederick D. Patterson, "Looking Forward with Education," *Tuskegee Messenger* 11.6–7 (1935): 12.

20. Minutes of the Spring Meeting of the Board of Trustees, Tuskegee Institute, 7 Apr. 1937: 7.

21. "Band Gives Concert In Montgomery," *Campus Digest,* 28 Sept. 1935: 1.

22. "The Inaugural Address," *Tuskegee Messenger* 11.11–12 (1935): 5.

23. Robert E. Park and Ernest W. Burgess, *Introduction to the Science of Sociology* 3rd. rev. ed. (1921; Chicago: University of Chicago Press, 1969), 140.

24. Park, *Introduction,* 138–139.

25. Ralph Ellison, introduction to *SA,* xx.

26. Fred J. Baker, "The Life Histories of W.I. Thomas and Robert E. Park," *American Journal of Sociology* (Sept. 1973), 258; Fred H. Matthews, *Quest for an American Sociology: Robert E. Park and the Chicago School* (Montreal: McGill-Queen's University Press, 1977), 62.

27. Park, *Introduction,* 140, 761–762; Dorothy Ross, *The Origins of American Social Science* (New York: Cambridge University Press, 1991), 22–50.

28. Park, *Introduction,* 639.

29. Ralph Ellison and Michael S. Harper and Robert B. Stepto, "Study and Experience: An Interview with Ralph Ellison," *CRE,* 339.

30. *Tuskegee Bulletin 1934–1935* 28.3 (1935): 172–186; James R. Scales and Danney Goble, *Oklahoma Politics: A History* (Norman: Oklahoma University Press, 1982), 36.

31. Park, *Introduction,* 139.

32. Harold R. Isaacs, "Five Writers and Their African Ancestors," *CRE,* 67.

33. Robert E. Park, "Racial Assimilation in Secondary Groups: with Particular Reference to the Negro," *Race and Culture* (Glencoe, Ill: Free Press, 1950), 216.

34. Ralph Ellison, "*An American Dilemma*: A Review," *SA,* 307–308.

35. Horace Cayton, *Long Old Road* (Seattle: University of Washington Press, 1963), 198.

36. Ralph Ellison, introduction, *SA,* xx.

37. Ralph Ellison, "What These Children Are Like," *GTT,* 70.

38. Ernest Hemingway, "The Battler," *In Our Time* (New York: Scribner's, 1931), 72, 79.

39. Ellison, introduction, *SA,* xxi.

40. Ernest Hemingway, *Death in the Afternoon* (New York: Scribner's, 1932), 2.

41. Ellison, introduction, *SA,* xxi.

42. Robert O'Meally, personal interview, 31 Nov. 1995.

43. Hemingway, *Death,* 99; Ralph Ellison, "The World and the Jug," *SA,* 14.

44. "Institute Debaters Hear Oxford Contest Morehouse Team," *Campus Digest,* 21 Dec. 1935: 1.

45. "Faculty Notes," *Tuskegee Messenger* 12.3–4 (1936): 30.

46. *Tuskegee Institute Bulletin* 28.3 (1935): 109, 145.

47. Eileen Southern, *Music of Black Americans,* 2nd ed. (New York: W.W. Norton, 1983), 424–425.

48. Albert Murray, *South to a Very Old Place* (New York: Vintage, 1991), 113.

49. Murray, interview.

50. Murray, *South,* 131–132.

51. Murray, interview.

52. Thomas Hardy, *Jude the Obscure* (1895; New York: Alfred A. Knopf, 1985), 102.

53. Ralph Ellison, "What's Wrong with the American Novel?" *CRE,* 44.

54. Murray, *South,* 113; Ralph Ellison and John Hersey, "A Completion of Personality: A Talk With Ralph Ellison," *CRE,* 292.

55. Ralph Ellison and Richard Kostelanetz, "An Interview with Ralph Ellison," *CRE*, 87–88. Ellison says that when he went to Sprague about Eliot and other modernists, "he told me he hadn't given much attention to them. . . . But he told me what to do about it: the places to find discussions and criticism." This account of Sprague seems quite likely, though Ellison's earlier remark in the interview that he studied the novel under Sprague as a freshman is erroneous.

56. Ralph Ellison, "Hidden Name and Complex Fate," *SA*, 159.

57. Ralph Ellison, "Initiation Rites," *GTT*, 39.

58. Ellison, "Hidden Name," *SA*, 160.

59. Ellison and Kostelanetz, "An Interview," *CRE*, 91.

60. T. S. Eliot, *The Waste Land and Other Poems* (New York: Harcourt, Brace, 1930), 47.

61. Ralph Ellison, "Ralph Ellison Questionnaire," nd. (ca. July 1952), Box 74, Folder "Speeches, Lectures," REP; Ellison, "Hidden Name," *SA*, 163.

62. Ellison and Kostelanetz, "An Interview," *CRE*, 90.

63. Edmund Wilson, *Axel's Castle* (New York: Scribner's, 1931), 21.

64. Wilson, *Castle*, 99, 112, 19.

65. Babette Deutsch, *This Modern Poetry* (New York: W.W. Norton, 1935), 124–125.

66. Ellison, "Hidden Name," *SA*, 160.

67. M. D. Sprague, "Literary Likes and Dislikes of College Students," *Tuskegee Messenger* 10.2 (1934): 3.

68. "Julius Rosenwald: A Tribute by President Patterson," Tuskegee *Messenger* 12.1–2 (1936): 4.

69. "President Patterson Speaks to Band," *Campus Digest*, 14 March 1936: 1.

70. *Tuskegee Institute Bulletin* 28.3 (1935): 96, 110.

71. "Funeral Services for George Carver Campbell," *Tuskegee Messenger* 12.3–4 (1936): 14.

72. Ellison and Hersey, "A Completion," *CRE*, 293.

73. Murray, *South*, 113; Ralph Ellison and David Remnick, "Visible Man," *CRE*, 401.

74. Ellison and Hersey, "A Completion," 292; Alain Locke, letter to Charlotte O. Mason, 29 Feb. 1936 and 22 Apr. 1936, Alain Locke Papers, Box 164-71, Folder 9, MSRC.

75. Alain Locke, "Deep River: Deeper Sea," *Opportunity*, Jan. 1936, 7–9.

76. Locke, letter to Mason, 22 Apr. 1936.

77. "Hiawatha's Wedding Feast Outstanding Feature," *Campus Digest*, 11 Apr. 1936: 1.

78. "Conference of Dramatics and Speech Activities," *Tuskegee Messenger* 12.3–4 (1936): 32.

79. Christine R. Gray, introduction to *Plays and Pageants from the Life of the Negro*, ed. Willis Richardson (1930; Jackson: University of Mississippi Press, 1993), xi.

80. Carter G. Woodson, introduction to *Negro History in Thirteen Plays*, by Willis Richardson and May Miller (Washington, D.C.: Associated Publishers, 1935), iii.

81. "Mr. M. D. Sprague Addresses Y.M.C.A.," *Campus Digest*, 25 Apr. 1936: 1.

Chapter 7. One-Winged Flying: 1936–1938

1. Ralph Ellison, "Remembering Richard Wright," *GTT*, 199.

2. Claude McKay, *Harlem: Negro Metropolis* (New York: E.P. Dutton, 1940), 21.

3. McKay, *Harlem*, 16–20; Gilbert Osofsky, *Harlem: The Making of a Ghetto*, 2nd ed. (1963; New York: Harper and Row, 1971), xvii, 92–104; James Weldon Johnson, *Black Manhattan* (1930; New York: Da Capo, 1991).

4. Roi Ottley and Frank Weatherby, eds., *The Negro in New York* (New York: New York Public Libraries, 1967), 268; Nat Brandt, *Harlem at War: The Black Experience in W.W.II* (Syracuse: Syracuse University Press, 1996), 39.

5. Ralph Ellison, "An Extravagance," *GTT*, 157.

6. Ralph Ellison, "Hidden Name and Complex Fate," *SA*, 162; Ralph Ellison and John Hersey, "A Completion of Personality: A Talk With Ralph Ellison," *CRE*, 292; Ellison, "Remem-

bering Richard Wright," *GTT,* 199–200; Ralph Ellison, "Alain Locke," *CERE,* 441. Ellison offers several versions of how the important meeting actually took place. In the essay "Remembering Richard Wright," Ellison said that the meeting took place in the YMCA lobby; in his interview with John Hersey, he recalled that it took place across the street in front of a restaurant. In the talk at the Harvard Symposium, Ellison said that he met Locke in 1935 and that he ran into the two men on 125th Street, and also that he was introduced very briefly to Hughes. The restaurant lobby meeting seems the most likely for the principal reason that Locke and Hughes were not close. It is unlikely that they would have ventured as far as 125th Street together; and the conversation simply must have been extensive for Hughes to have entrusted Ellison with Louise Thompson's books and written him an introduction to see Richmond Barthé.

7. Alain Locke, letter to Charlotte O. Mason, 14 June 1936 and 25 June 1936, Alain Locke Papers, Box 164-71, Folder 10, MSRC.

8. Romare Bearden and Harry Henderson, *A History of African-American Artists: From 1792 to the Present* (New York: Pantheon, 1993), 247–249, 297.

9. Ralph Ellison, letter to Langston Hughes, 17 July 1936 and 24 Aug. 1936, Box 54, Folder "Ellison, Ralph," LHP.

10. Rena Fraden, *Blueprint for a Black Federal Theatre, 1935–1939* (New York: Cambridge University Press, 1994), 97–99, 193–194.

11. C. Day Lewis, *Collected Poems and a Hope for Poetry* (New York: Random House, 1935), 220.

12. Bearden and Henderson, *A History of African-American Artists,* 170–173.

13. Daniel Lang, "The Landlady Who Created a Sculptor," *New York Post,* 26 May 1942, 7, Clipping File "Richmond Barthé," SCRBC.

14. Bearden and Henderson, *A History of African-American Artists,* 136–146; Samella Lewis, *African American Art and Artists* (Berkeley: University of California Press, 1990), 86–87; Alain Locke, ed., *The Negro in Art* (1940; New York: Hacker Art, 1968), 70–75.

15. Ellison, letter to Hughes, 17 July 1936.

16. Ellison, "An Extravagance," *GTT,* 158, 165.

17. Ellison, letter to Hughes, 24 Aug. 1936.

18. Ralph Ellison, "Folklore, Harlem Children's Rhymes," 15 Dec. 1939, WPA New York Folklore, Box A648, Folder "Ralph Ellison and Frank Byrd," Manuscripts Division, Library of Congress.

19. Ellison, "An Extravagance," *GTT,* 160–161, 163.

20. Ellison, letter to Hughes, 17 July 1936; Ellison, letter to Hughes, 24 Aug. 1936.

21. Ellison, letter to Hughes, 24 Aug. 1936; A. H. Chapman, *Harry Stack Sullivan: His Life and Work* (New York: G.P. Putnam's Sons, 1976), 57–60.

22. Ralph Ellison and Michael S. Harper and Robert B. Stepto, "Study and Experience: An Interview with Ralph Ellison," *CRE,* 322–323.

23. Concert Program, The Philharmonic-Symphony Society of New York, Box 76, Folder "Programs," REP.

24. Daniel Aaron, *Writers on the Left* (New York: Harcourt, Brace, 1961), 304.

25. "Writers in Politics: Conversations with André Malraux," *New Republic,* 24 June 1936, 218.

26. André Malraux, *Man's Fate,* trans. Haakon Chevalier (1934; New York: Vintage, 1961), 64.

27. John Strachey, *Literature and Dialectical Materialism* (New York: Covici, Friede, 1934), 43.

28. Mark Naison, *Communists in Harlem During the Depression* (New York: Grove Press, 1983), 43, 100.

29. Quoted in Gerald Horne, *Black Liberation/Red Scare: Ben Davis and the Communist Party* (Newark: University of Delaware Press, 1994), 53–54.

30. Sanora Babb, personal interview, 15 June 1999.

31. Ted Fox, *Showtime at the Apollo* (New York: Holt, Rinehart and Winston, 1983), 78; Ellison, letter to Hughes, 27 Apr. 1937.

32. Arna Bontemps, letter to Langston Hughes, 28 Mar. 1937, *Arna Bontemps—Langston Hughes: Letters 1925–1967,* ed. Charles H. Nichols (New York: Paragon House, 1990), 26.

33. Ralph Ellison, "Address at the Langston Hughes Festival," City College of New York, 11 Apr. 1984, quoted in Arnold Rampersad, *The Life of Langston Hughes,* vol. 1 (New York: Oxford, 1986), 335.

34. Ralph Ellison, "Homage to Duke Ellington," *GTT,* 222.

35. Faith Berry, *Langston Hughes: Before and Beyond Harlem* (1983; New York: Wings Books, 1995), 253.

36. Ralph Ellison, letter to Ida Bell, 20 Apr. 1937, "'American Culture Is of a Whole': From the Letters of Ralph Ellison," *New Republic,* 1 Mar. 1999: 36.

37. Charles Martin, *The Angelo Herndon Case and Southern Justice* (Baton Rouge: Louisiana State University Press, 1976), 182.

38. Michel Fabre, *The Unfinished Quest of Richard Wright,* trans. Isabel Barzun (New York: William Morrow, 1973), 145, n550; Keith Kinnamon, *The Emergence of Richard Wright* (Urbana: University of Illinois Press, 1972), 71. Fabre cites interviews with Ellison in 1963 and 1970 for the specific poems "I Have Seen Black Hands," published in *New Masses* 26 June 1934, and *Partisan Review*'s "Between the World and Me." However, it is unlikely that Ellison would have been impressed with "I Have Seen Black Hands," Wright's first publication, a formulaic proletarian racial solidarity poem. Based upon his own conjecture, Kinnamon believes that Ellison had read "We of the Streets," published in *New Masses,* 13 Apr. 1937.

39. Ralph Ellison, "That Same Pain, That Same Pleasure: An Interview," *SA,* 14.

40. Ellison, letter to Hughes, 27 Apr. 1937.

41. Thomas Mann, *Death in Venice and Seven Other Stories,* trans. H. T. Lowe-Porter (1936; New York: Vintage, 1954), 99, 133, 98.

42. Ellison, letter to Hughes, 27 Apr. 1937.

43. Mary McCarthy, *Intellectual Memoirs: New York 1936–1938* (New York: Harcourt Brace Jovanovich, 1992), 73.

44. Curtis Cate, *André Malraux* (New York: Fromm International, 1995), 256.

45. Ellison, "Remembering Richard Wright," *GTT,* 201; Ellison and Harper and Stepto, "Study and Experience," *CRE,* 324; Ellison, "That Same Pain," *SA,* 15. In his 1971 lecture that became the essay "Going to the Territory," Ellison remembered meeting Wright "the day after his arrival in New York in July of 1937"—impossible because the two both remembered attending the June American Writers Congress. In a 1976 interview with Robert Stepto and Michael Harper, Ellison thought "Wright had come to New York in June 1937 and I met him the day after," which is likely more accurate. The Wright biographies are inconclusive on when Wright arrived in Manhattan; Webb and Fabre both suggest sometime in May, well before the writers congress.

46. Richard Wright, *American Hunger* (1944; New York: Harper and Row, 1977), 131–133.

47. Fabre, *Unfinished Quest,* 136–137; Constance Webb, *Richard Wright: A Biography* (New York: G.P. Putnam's Sons, 1968), 136–137, 142–143.

48. Ellen Tarry, *The Third Door: The Autobiography of an American Negro Woman* (1955; Westport, Conn.: Negro Universities Press, 1971), 149.

49. Margaret Walker, *Richard Wright Daemonic Genius* (New York: Amistad, 1988), 103.

50. Richard Wright, "Joe Louis Uncovers Dynamite," *New Masses,* 8 Oct. 1935, reprinted in *Richard Wright Reader,* eds. Ellen Wright and Michel Fabre (New York: Da Capo, 1997) 35.

51. Richard Wright, "Blueprint for Negro Writing," *New Challenge* 2.1 (1937), 5.

52. Franklin Folsom, *Days of Anger, Days of Hope: A Memoir of the League of American Writers, 1937–1942* (Niwot, Colo.: University of Colorado Press, 1994), 9.

53. "Writers Spurred to Fight Fascism," *New York Times,* 6 June 1937, sect 2: 8.

54. Richard Wright, Harry L. Shaw, Donald Thompson, James Magraw, "An Editorial Conference" (1938), Box 81, Folder 914, RWP.

55. John F. Callahan, personal interview, 1 May 1996; Fabre, *Unfinished Quest,* 141.

56. Aaron, *Writers on the Left,* 288; Ralph Ellison and Steve Cannon, Ismael Reed, and Quincy Troupe, "The Essential Ellison," *CRE* 364.

57. Judy Kutulas, "Becoming 'More Liberal': The League of American Writers, The Communist Party, and The Literary People's Front," *Journal of American Culture,* 13 (1990), 71.

58. Kenneth Burke, "The Rhetoric of Hitler's Battle," *The Philosophy of Literary Form,* 2nd ed. (Baton Rouge: Louisiana State Press, 1967), 218, 219.

59. Ellison et al., "The Essential Ellison," 364.

60. Kutulas, "Becoming 'More Liberal,'" 73; William Phillips, *A Partisan View* (New York: Stein and Day, 1983), 49–50; McCarthy, *Intellectual Memoirs,* 72–73.

61. "Writers' Vote Spurns 'Gone With The Wind'," *New York Times,* 7 June 1937, 21.

62. Malcolm Sylvers, "American Communist in the Popular Front Period," *Journal of American Studies* 23 (Dec. 1989): 377.

63. Richard Wright, *Richard Wright: Letters to Joe C. Brown,* ed. Thomas Knipp (Kent, Ohio: Kent State University Press, 1968), 7.

64. See James D. Bloom, *Left Letters: The Culture Wars of Mike Gold and Joseph Freeman* (New York: Columbia University Press, 1992); Barbara Foley, *Radical Representations: Politics and Form in U.S. Proletarian Fiction, 1929–1941* (Durham, N.C.: Duke University Press, 1993); and James F. Murphy, *The Proletarian Moment: The Controversy over Leftism in Literature* (Urbana: University of Illinois Press, 1991), for projects that celebrate the Communist influence on American fiction writers.

65. Ellison et al., "The Essential Ellison," *CRE,* 361.

66. Ralph Ellison and Michael S. Harper and Robert B. Stepto, "Study and Experience: An Interview with Ralph Ellison," *CRE,* 323.

67. "Negro Hailed as Writer" (1938), *Conversations with Richard Wright,* eds. Keith Kinnamon and Michel Fabre (Jackson: University of Mississippi Press, 1993), 28.

68. Alfred Kazin, *Starting Out in the Thirties* (Boston: Little, Brown, 1962), 106.

69. Wayne F. Cooper, *Claude McKay: Rebel Sojourner in the Harlem Renaissance* (New York: Schocken, 1987), 323.

70. Ellison et al., "The Essential Ellison," *CRE,* 346.

71. Ralph Ellison, letter to Constance Webb Pearlstein, 7 July 1967, Richard Wright Papers, SCRBC.

72. Ellison, introduction, *SA,* xxi.

73. Ralph Ellison, letter to Richard Wright, 3 Nov. 1941, Box 97, Folder "Ellison, Ralph," RWP.

74. Webb, *Richard Wright,* 145–147. Constance Webb provides the most detailed description of this event. Though purportedly based upon interviews, it is difficult to believe Webb's final account of Ellison's evolution as a writer with the help of Richard Wright. Webb's sloppiness in mistaking the twenty-four-year-old Ellison, who knew a great deal more about New York City than the twenty-eight-year-old Wright, for a teen of nineteen, makes her star-struck and sycophantic rendition of Ellison suspect. She also condenses an involved literary relationship into two paragraphs, truncating three years into three months.

75. Ralph Ellison, "Creative and Cultural Lag," *New Challenge* 2.1 (1937): 90.

76. Ellison, "Remembering Richard Wright," 203.

77. Ellison and Hersey, "A Completion," *CRE,* 295.

78. Ralph Ellison, letter to Ida Bell, 30 Aug. 1937, *New Republic,* 36.

79. Ellison, "Remembering Richard Wright," *SA,* 203; John F. Callahan, introduction to *Flying Home and Other Stories,* by Ralph Ellison (New York: Random House, 1996), x. Callahan has found typescripts of "Hymie's Bull" with the year 1937 written on them.

80. Henry James, "Preface to the Princess of Casamassima," *The Art of the Novel: Critical Prefaces,* ed. R. P. Blackmur (New York: Charles Scribners, 1934), 62–64; Ellison and Hersey, "A Completion," *CRE,* 295.

81. Ellison, "Hymie's Bull," *Flying Home and Other Stories,* 83.

82. Ralph Ellison, letter to Richard Wright, 27 Oct. 1937; State of Ohio Certificate of Death No. 62948. Ida Bell, date of death: 16 Oct. 1937. State of Ohio Department of Health, Division of Vital Statistics.

83. Ellison, letter to Wright, 27 Oct. 1937.

84. Richard Wright, letter to Ralph Ellison, 2 Nov. 1937, Box 76, Folder "Richard Wright," REP.

85. Herbert Ellison, letter to Langston Hughes, 21 Oct. 1945, Box 54, Folder "Ellison, Ralph," LHP. Herbert Ellison wrote to Langston Hughes in 1945 because he had lost his brother's address and had had only minimal contact with his older sibling.

86. Callahan, interview.

87. Ellison, letter to Wright, 8 Nov. 1937.

88. Ellison, letter to Wright, 27 Oct. 1936.

89. Herbert Ellison, personal interview, 16 May 1996.

90. Ralph Ellison, *Invisible Man* draft, Box 145, Folder "Leroy's Journal," REP, 244–245.

91. Ralph Ellison and Steve Cannon, Lennox Raphael, and James Thompson, "A Very Stern Discipline," *CRE,* 133.

92. Callahan, interview; Margaret Peters, *Dayton's African American Heritage* (Virginia Beach: Donning, 1995), 61.

93. Ellison, "Boy on a Train," *Flying Home and Other Stories,* 20.

94. Ralph Ellison, "Conditions in Black Harlem," Congressional Hearing, 26 Oct. 1966, Pacifica radio archives.

95. Ralph Ellison, "Party Down at the Square," *Flying Home and Other Stories,* 7; Callahan, introduction, *Flying Home,* xxii.

96. Ellison, "Party," 11.

97. Program, 24th Annual McKinley Day Dinner, 9 Feb. 1938, Box 76, Folder "Programs," REP.

Chapter 8. *Is Politics an Expression of Love?: 1938–1941*

1. Ralph Ellison, interview for Constance Webb, 3 Feb. 1963, Richard Wright Papers, SCRBC.

2. "White Fog," *Time,* 28 Mar. 1938, 4; Robert Van Gelder, "Four Tragic Tales," *New York Times Book Review,* 3 Apr. 1938, 11; reprinted in *Richard Wright: The Critical Reception,* ed. and intro. John M. Reilly (New York: Burt Franklin & Co., 1978), 4–5, 11–12.

3. Zora Neale Hurston, "Stories of Conflict," *Saturday Review of Literature* (2 Apr. 1938): 32, reprinted in *Richard Wright: The Critical Reception,* 9–10.

4. Jere Mangione, *The Dream and the Deal* (Boston: Little, Brown and Co., 1972), 258; Joanne V. Gabinn, *Sterling A. Brown: Building the Black Aesthetic Tradition* (Westport, Conn.: Greenwood Press, 1985), 70–71.

5. Ralph Ellison, letter to Richard Wright, 18 Aug. 1945, Box 97, Folder "Ellison, Ralph," RWP.

6. Ellen Tarry, "How the History Was Assembled," *The Negro in New York,* eds. Roi Ottley and William Weatherby (New York: New York Public Library, 1967), x–xii.

7. Mangione, *Dream,* 256.

8. Ralph Ellison, "The Insurrection of 1741," New York Writers' Project: Harlem Section 1936–1941, Reel 2 "History and Historical Questions," SCRBC.

9. Ellen Tarry, *The Third Door: The Autobiography of an American Negro Woman* (1955; Westport, Conn.: Negro Universities Press, 1971), 140.

10. Keith Kinnamon, *The Emergence of Richard Wright* (Urbana: University of Illinois Press, 1972), 117; Richard Wright, et al., "Statement of American Intellectuals," *International Literature* 7 (1938): 104.

11. Terry A. Cooney, *The Rise of New York Intellectuals: Partisan Review and Its Circle* (Madison: University of Wisconsin Press, 1986), 187.

12. Monty Penkower, *The Federal Writers' Project: A Study in Government Patronage of the Arts* (Urbana: University of Illinois Press, 1977), 175.

13. Mangione, *Dream,* 254–255.

14. Wilson Record, *The Negro and the Communist Party* (New York: Atheneum, 1971), 181.

15. George Charney, *A Long Journey* (Chicago: Quadrangle Books, 1968), 104; Michael Harper, personal interview, 7 Oct. 1996.

16. Michel Fabre, *The Unfinished Quest of Richard Wright,* trans. Isabel Barzun (New York: William Morrow, 1973), 197.

17. Mangione, *Dream,* 245.

18. Wayne Cooper, *Claude McKay: Rebel Sojourner in the Harlem Renaissance* (New York: Schocken Books, 1987), 312.

19. Eugene Levy, *James Weldon Johnson* (Chicago: University of Chicago Press, 1973), 344.

20. Cooper, *Claude McKay,* 338; Tyrone Tillery, *Claude McKay: A Black Poet's Struggle for Identity* (Amherst: University of Massachusetts Press, 1992), 155–162.

21. Ralph Ellison and John Hersey, "A Completion of Personality: A Talk With Ralph Ellison," *CRE,* 294–295.

22. Claude McKay, *A Long Way From Home* (1937; San Diego: Harcourt Brace Jovanovich, 1970), 30; Richard Wright, letter to Alain Locke, 8 July 1937, Alain Locke Papers, Box 164-96, folder "Wright, Richard," MSRC.

23. Langston Hughes, letter to Noel Sullivan, 29 Jan. 1936, quoted in Arnold Rampersad, *The Life of Langston Hughes,* vol. 1 (New York: Oxford University Press, 1986), 323.

24. Kinnamon, *Emergence,* 117; "Richard Wright Given Literary Post for Work," *New York Amsterdam News,* 25 June 1938, 6.

25. Ralph Ellison, "Practical Mystic," *New Masses,* 16 Aug. 1938, 26.

26. Fabre, *Unfinished Quest,* 169–175; Kinnamon, *Emergence,* 115.

27. Ralph Ellison and Steve Cannon, Ismael Reed, and Quincy Troupe, "The Essential Ellison," *CRE,* 347.

28. Alfred Kazin, *Starting Out in the Thirties* (Boston: Little, Brown, 1962), 5.

29. Irving Howe, *A Margin of Hope* (New York: Harcourt Brace Jovanovich, 1982), 42.

30. Cecil Eby, *Between the Bullet and the Lie* (New York: Holt, Rinehart and Winston, 1969), 59–64; Howe, *Margin,* 76; See also Carl Geiser, *Prisoner of the Good Fight* (Westport, Conn.: Lawrence Hill, 1986).

31. James Yates, *Mississippi to Madrid* (Seattle: Shamal Books, 1986), 102; Ralph Ellison, "The World and the Jug," *SA,* 142.

32. Connecticut State Department of Health. Certificate of Marriage. 17 Sept. 1938. Ralph Ellison and Rose Poindexter.

33. Sanora Babb, personal interview, 15 June 1999; Ralph Ellison and James A. McPherson, "Indivisible Man," *CRE,* 181.

34. "Negro Hailed as New Writer," *Conversations with Richard Wright,* eds. Keith Kinnamon and Michel Fabre (Jackson: University of Mississippi Press, 1993), 30; Michael Gold, *Change the World!* (New York: International Publishers, 1936), 29.

35. Ellison and Cannon, Raphael, and Thompson, "A Very Stern Discipline," *CRE,* 124.

36. "Editorial Statement," *Partisan Review* 4 (Dec. 1937): 3.

37. Harry Roskolenko, *When I Was Last on Cherry Street* (New York: Stein and Day, 1965), 164; Constance Ashton Meyers, "'We Were a Little Hipped on the Subject of Trotsky': Literary Trotskyists in the 1930s," *Cultural Politics: Radical Movements in Modern History,* ed. Jerold M. Starr (New York: Praeger, 1985), 153–154.

38. Ralph Ellison, "Jupiter Hammon," nd., New York Writers' Project: Harlem Section 1936–1941, Reel 3 "Miscegenation," SCRBC.

39. Ralph Ellison, "Woodson's *The Beginning of Miscegenation of the Whites and Blacks,*" 30 Sept. 1938, New York Writers' Project: Harlem Section 1936–1941, Reel 3 "Miscegenation," SCRBC.

40. Fabre, *Unfinished Quest,* 176.

41. Rena Fraden, *Blueprints for a Black Federal Theatre, 1935–1939* (New York: Cambridge University Press, 1994),116–117; Theodore Ward, Clipping File, SCRBC; Hatch-Billups Collection, Theodore Ward, interview by Camille Billops, 7 Apr. 1974, *The Book of Achievement: The World Over Featuring the Negro in Chicago: 1779–1929,* SCRBC.

42. Ellison, letter to Wright, 24 June 1946.

43. Ellison, letter to Wright, 11 May 1940.

44. Margaret Walker, *Richard Wright Daemonic Genius* (New York: Amistad, 1988), 120; Anna Grimshaw, "C. L. R. James: A Revolutionary Vision," *The C. L. R. James Reader* (Oxford, England: Blackwell, 1992), 8; Horace Cayton, *Long Old Road* (New York: Trident, 1965), 249.

45. C. L. R. James, "Stalin Ruins the Chinese Revolution," *The Future in the Present* (London: Allison and Busby, 1977), 52–53.

46. Martin Duberman, *Paul Robeson* (New York: Ballantine, 1989), 197. Duberman interviewed James in 1983.

47. Ellison, "World and the Jug," *SA,* 117; Ellison, letter to Wright, 11 May 1940.

48. André Malraux, *Man's Hope,* trans. Stuart Gilbert and Alistair McDonald (New York: Random House, 1938), 379, 391, 393, 397.

49. Ellison, untitled note, 3 Jan. 1939, New York Writers' Project: Harlem Section 1936–1941, Reel 2 "Economic History of the Negroes of New York," SCRBC.

50. William L. Patterson, *The Man Who Cried Genocide* (New York: International Publishers, 1971), 138–141.

51. Ralph Ellison, letter to Langston Hughes, 30 Jan. 1939, Box 54, Folder "Ellison, Ralph," LHP.

52. Mangione, *Dream,* 290, 309.

53. "Terrors of Nazis Related By Benes," *New York Times,* 3 June 1939, 4.

54. Walker, *Daemonic,* 128.

55. "Exiles' Woes Move Writers' Congress," *New York Times,* 5 June 1939, 20.

56. Babb, interview.

57. Ralph Ellison, "Slick Gonna Learn," *Direction* 2.5 (1939): 10–11, 14, 16.

58. Paul R. Gorman, *Left Intellectuals and Popular Culture in Twentieth Century America* (Chapel Hill: University of North Carolina Press, 1996), 111.

59. Fabre, *Unfinished Quest,* 200.

60. Mark Naison, *Communists in Harlem During the Depression* (New York: Grove Press, 1983), 136–137.

61. Ralph Ellison, "Judge Lynch in New York," *New Masses,* 15 Aug. 1939, 15.

62. Ralph Ellison, "Judge Lynch in New York," Literary and Scholarly Manuscripts Collection, SCRBC.

63. Ellison, "Judge Lynch," SCRBC.

64. Ellison, "Judge Lynch," *New Masses,* 16.

65. Ralph Ellison, *Slick,* Box 55 Folder "Original Typescripts I," REP.

66. Rampersad, *Life of Langston Hughes,* 374–375.

67. Angelo Herndon, "Negroes Have No Stake in This War, Wright Says," *Sunday Worker,* 11 Feb. 1940, 7.

68. Ralph Ellison, letter to Michel Fabre, 22 Jan. 1970; courtesy of Michel Fabre.

69. Miguel Unamuno, *The Tragic Sense of Life,* quoted in Victor Ouimette, *Reason Aflame: Unamuno and the Heroic Will* (New Haven: Yale University Press, 1974), 49.

70. Ellison, *Slick,* REP.

71. Walker, *Daemonic,* 127–146; Ralph Ellison and Michael S. Harper and Robert B. Stepto, "Study and Experience: An Interview with Ralph Ellison," *CRE,* 323.

72. Ellison and Hersey, "A Completion," *CRE,* 294; Ellison, letter to Wright, May 11, 1940; Ellison, interview for Constance Webb, 3 Feb. 1963; Ellison et al., "The Essential Ellison," *CRE,* 361–362; Constance Webb, *Richard Wright: A Biography* (New York: G.P. Putnam's Sons, 1968), 146–147. Webb's account of the break between Wright and Ellison over the issue of Ellison's fiction is greatly misleading. She takes an interview with Ellison in 1963 and proceeds to speciously offer her extrapolations as direct quotations. Her aim is to present a fawning and obsequious Ellison: "You are the master—I want to know if it's [his short story] any good." Her bias is evident, particularly because she treats this incident with Wright, which happened no earlier than 1939, on the same page as the men's introduction in 1937.

73. Ralph Ellison, "Ruling Class Southerner," *New Masses,* 5 Dec. 1939, 27.

74. Ralph Ellison, "Javanese Folklore," *New Masses,* 26 Dec. 1939, 26.

75. Mangione, *Dream,* 330.

76. Ann Banks, ed., *Harlem Document: Photographs 1932–1940* by Aaron Siskind (Providence, R.I.: Matrix, 1981), 7.

77. Ralph Ellison, "Folklore, Harlem Children's Rhymes," 15 Dec. 1939, and "Harlem Children's Rhymes," 31 Jan. 1940, WPA New York Folklore, Box A648, Folder "Ralph Ellison and Frank Byrd," Manuscript Division, Library of Congress.

78. Sidney Alexander, Ben Field, S. Funaroff, and Prudencia de Pereda, eds. *American Writing* (Prairie City, Ill.: James Decker Press, 1940).

79. Ralph Ellison, "Afternoon," *American Writing,* eds. Sidney Alexander et al. (Prairie City, Ill.: James Decker Press, 1948), 36–37.

80. Ralph Ellison, "The 'Good Life,'" *New Masses,* 20 Feb. 1940, 27.

81. Ralph Ellison, "TAC Negro Show," *New Masses,* 27 Feb. 1940, 30.

82. Ralph Ellison, "Hunters and Pioneers," *New Masses,* 19 Mar. 1940, 30.

83. William F. McDonald, *Federal Relief Administration and the Arts* (Columbus: Ohio State University Press, 1969), 688.

84. Fabre, *Unfinished Quest,* 178–180.

85. Ellison, letter to Wright, 14 Apr. 1940.

86. Benjamin Davis Jr., untitled, *Sunday Worker,* 14 Apr. 1940; Sec. 2:4, 6; reprinted in *Richard Wright: The Critical Reception,* 69, 74.

87. Abner Berry, interview, 15 Sept. 1977, Tape 1, Oral History of the American Left, New York University, Tamiment Library.

88. Karl Marx and Frederick Engels, *The Holy Family* (Moscow: Progress Publishers, 1975), 264.

89. Ellison, letter to Wright, 14 Apr. 1940.

90. Ellison, letter to Wright, 22 Apr. 1940.

91. Ellison, letter to Wright, 22 Apr. 1940.

92. "Art Knows No Boundaries," *New Masses,* 9 Jan. 1940, 10.

93. Ralph Ellison, "A Congress Jim Crow Didn't Attend," *New Masses,* 14 May 1940, 5.

94. Ellison, letter to Wright, 11 May 1940.

95. Ralph Ellison, letter to Michel Fabre, 3 Mar. 1982, courtesy of Michel Fabre.

96. Ellison, "A Congress."

97. Memorandum, *"This Is Not Our War,"* Box 32, Folder "National Negro Congress," REP.

98. Jessie Scott Campbell, letter to Langston Hughes, 11 Aug. 1943, Box 112, Folder "National Negro Congress," LHP.

99. Ralph Ellison, "The Birthmark," *New Masses,* 2 July 1940, 16.

100. Richard Wright, "Blueprint for Negro Writing," *New Challenge* 2 (1937): 53.

101. Ralph Ellison, "Stormy Weather," *New Masses,* 24 Sept. 1940, 20.

102. Ellison, letter to Wright, 11 May 1940.

103. Ellison, "Stormy Weather," 21.

104. Ellison, letter to Wright, 26 May 1940.

105. Ellison, interview for Constance Webb, 3 Feb. 1963.

106. Ralph Ellison, interview with Horace Cayton, 8 Sept. 1968, Horace Cayton Notes, Horace Cayton Papers, Southside Branch Library, Chicago, Ill.

Chapter 9. *New Negro at* Negro Quarterly: *1941–1942*

1. Quoted in Irving Howe and Lewis Coser, *The American Communist Party: A Critical History: 1919–1957* (Boston: Beacon Press, 1957), 416.

2. Ralph Ellison, letter to Richard Wright, 5 Aug. 1945, Richard Wright Papers, Box 97, Folder "Ellison, Ralph," RWP.

3. Ralph Ellison, interview for Constance Webb, 3 Feb. 1963, Richard Wright Papers, SCRBC.

4. Langston Hughes, letter to Franklin Folsom, 26 May 1941, Box 93, Folder "League of American Writers," LHP.

5. Franklin Folsom, letter to board members, 22 Sept. 1941, Box 87, Folder "League of American Writers," REP.

6. Henry Hart, *Official Program, League of American Writers Fourth American Writers Congress* (New York: New Union Press, 1941), 7.

7. Ellison, letter to Wright, 5 Aug. 1945.

8. Ralph Ellison, "Richard Wright and Recent Negro Fiction," *Direction* 4 (Summer 1941): 12, 13.

9. Wilson Record, *The Negro in the Communist Party* (1951: New York: Atheneum, 1971), 55–56.

10. See C. L. R. James, "The Revolutionary Answer to the Negro Problem," *The Future in the Present: Selected Writings* (London: Allison and Busby, 1977), 119–127.

11. Ralph Ellison, "Recent Negro Fiction," *New Masses,* 5 Aug. 1941, 24, 26.

12. Ralph Ellison, letter to Constance Webb, 7 July 1967, Richard Wright Papers, SCRBC; Constance Webb, *Richard Wright: A Biography* (New York: Putnam, 1967), n. 408.

13. Bill Chase, "All Ears," *Amsterdam-Star News,* 7 Feb. 1942, 8.

14. "Report of the Magazine and Clipper Committee," 30 May 1941, Box 87, Folder "League of American Writers," REP; Franklin Folsom, *Days of Anger, Days of Hope: A Memoir of the League of American Writers, 1937–1942* (Boulder, Colo.: University of Colorado Press, 1994), 201.

15. Ralph Ellison, untitled note [essay on Hemingway], nd. [ca. spring 1941], Box 100, Folder "Hemingway, Ernest unfinished essay on his themes," REP.

16. Ellison, letter to Wright, 3 Nov. 1941.

17. Angelo Herndon, letter to Ralph Ellison, 25 Nov. 1941, Box 60, Folder "Negro Quarterly," REP.

18. "Evenings with Negro Authors," circular, Box 94, Folder "Attaway, William and Ruth," RWP.

19. Ralph Ellison, "The Great Migration," *New Masses*, 2 Dec. 1941, 24.

20. Ellison, "Migration," *New Masses*, 2 Dec. 1941, 24.

21. Herbert Aptheker, personal interview, 11 June 1999.

22. Ralph Ellison and John Hersey, "A Completion of Personality: A Talk With Ralph Ellison," *CRE*, 296.

23. Ralph Ellison, "The World and the Jug," *SA*, 142; Michel Fabre, *The Unfinished Quest of Richard Wright*, trans. Isabel Barzun (New York: William Morrow, 1973), 236.

24. Fabre, *Unfinished*, 229.

25. P. E. Foxworth, Letters to director of Federal Bureau of Investigation, 9, 19, and 24, Nov. 1942, "Negro Quarterly," Federal Bureau of Investigation, File 100-HQ-115471.

26. Ralph Ellison, untitled note ["Let us consider the Harlem crime wave . . ."], np., Box 101, Folder "Let Us Consider the Harlem Crime Wave," REP.

27. Ralph Ellison, draft letter to Horace Cayton, nd. [ca. May 1942], Box 60, Folder "Negro Quarterly," REP.

28. Ralph Ellison, letter to Eugene Holmes, 2 May 1942, Box 60, Folder "Negro Quarterly," REP.

29. Ralph Ellison, letter to Kirker Quinn, 29 May 1942, Box 60, Folder "Negro Quarterly," REP.

30. Ralph Ellison, letter to John Barnes, 2 May 1942, Box 60, Folder "Negro Quarterly," REP.

31. "Guitar Ace Passes Away," *Amsterdam-Star News*, 7 Mar. 1942, 17.

32. "Woman Attempts Suicide in Teddy Wilson's Home," *Amsterdam-Star News*, 7 Mar. 1942, 1, 5.

33. Howe and Coser, *American Communist Party*, 316.

34. Louise Mally, letter to Ralph Ellison, 27 Jan. 1942, Box 87, Folder "League of American Writers," REP.

35. Nan Golden, letter to Ralph Ellison, 10 Mar. 1942, Box 87, Folder "League of American Writers," REP.

36. Ralph Ellison, letter to Julia Brice, 25 Aug. 1942, Box 60, Folder "Negro Quarterly," REP.

37. Ralph Ellison, letter to Langston Hughes, 12 Sept. 1942, Box 54, Folder "Ellison, Ralph," LHP.

38. Ralph Ellison, letter to Carson McCullers, nd. [ca. 1942], Box 60, Folder "Negro Quarterly," REP.

39. Ralph Ellison, letter to Stanley Edgar Hyman, 15 July 1942, Box 6, Folder "Ralph and Fanny Ellison," SHP.

40. Ralph Ellison, "Richard Wright and Recent Negro Fiction," *Direction* 4 (Summer 1941): 12.

41. Ellison, letter to Hyman, nd. [ca. Aug. 1942] ["I don't think you should underestimate . . ."].

42. Pearl Buck, "A Letter to Colored Americans," *Opportunity* 20 (Mar. 1942): 72.

43. Dashiell Hammett, letter to Ralph Ellison, nd. [ca. Mar. 1942], Box 60, Folder "Negro Quarterly," REP.

44. Abner Berry, " 'The Negro Quarterly' A Vigorous Journal," *Daily Worker,* 15 Sept. 1942, 7.

45. Ralph Ellison, "Transition," *Negro Quarterly* 1.1 (Spring 1942): 92.

46. Carl Lawrence, "Congress Casino Manager Victim of Thugs; Then Narrowly Misses Psychopathic Ward," *Amsterdam-Star News,* 4 Apr. 1942, 3.

47. J. Robert Smith, "Mental Patient Shot to Death," *Amsterdam-Star News,* 16 May 1942, 1.

48. Count Basie and Albert Murray, *Good Morning Blues: The Autobiography of Count Basie as told to Albert Murray* (New York: Da Capo, 1995), 249–250.

49. Ira Gilter, *Jazz Masters of the 40s* (New York: Da Capo, 1983), 11.

50. Ralph Ellison and Ron Welburn, "Ralph Ellison's Territorial Vantage," *CRE,* 313.

51. Ralph Ellison, "The Golden Age, Time Past," *SA,* 203.

52. Dizzy Gillespie with Al Fraser, *To Be, or Not To Bop: Memoirs, Dizzy Gillespie* (Garden City, N.Y.: Doubleday, 1979), 201.

53. "Program to Abolish Discrimination," *Negro Labor Victory Committee of Greater New York,* Box 60, Folder "Negro Quarterly," REP.

54. "Editorial Comment," *Negro Quarterly* 1.4 (Winter-Spring 1943): 298–299.

55. Robert O'Meally, personal interview, 31 Nov. 1995.

56. Ellison, untitled note ["Let us consider the Harlem crime wave . . ."], np.

57. Langston Hughes, letter to Ralph Ellison, 26 Oct. 1942, Box 60, Folder "Negro Quarterly," REP.

58. "Words Can Be Bullets," *New Masses,* 15 Dec. 1942, 2.

59. "Urban League Guild Sponsors Benefit Party," *Opportunity* 20 (Dec. 1942): 373.

Chapter 10. Labor of Love: 1943–1944

1. Add Bates, letter to Bill Campbell, 19 Feb. 1943, Box 60, Folder "Negro Quarterly," REP.

2. John Bunker, *Heroes in Dungarees: The Story of the American Merchant Marine in World War II* (Annapolis, Md.: Naval Institute Press, 1995), app. B 329–344.

3. Ralph Ellison, letter to Lloyd Mallan, 9 Feb. 1943, Box 60, Folder "Negro Quarterly," REP.

4. Richard Wright, *Black Boy* (New York: Harper, 1993), 43.

5. "Editorial Comment," *Negro Quarterly* 1.4 (Winter-Spring 1943): 301.

6. Marvel Cooke, "Herndon-Ellison Win Success as Negro Life Book Publishers," *Amsterdam-Star News,* 10 Apr. 1943, 24.

7. Unknown, letter to Ralph Ellison, 2 Apr. 1943, Box 60, Folder "Negro Quarterly," REP.

8. Louis Katz, letter to Ralph Ellison, 8 Apr. 1943, Box 60, Folder "Negro Quarterly," REP.

9. Ralph Ellison and John Hersey, "A Completion of Personality: A Talk With Ralph Ellison," *CRE,* 296.

10. "Editorial Aside," *Common Ground* 1.1 (Autumn 1940): 2.

11. Ralph Ellison, letter to Kenneth Burke, nd. [ca. 28 May 1943], ["Here are my very belated . . ."], KBP.

12. Ralph Ellison, untitled note ["My friendship with Stanley Hyman . . ."], Box 188, Folder "Biographies: Stanley Hyman," REP.

13. Ralph Ellison, "Eyewitness Story of Riot: False Rumors Spurred Mob," *New York Post* 2 Aug. 1943, 4.

14. John Henrik Clarke, personal interview, 8 Jan. 1997; Marvel Cooke, telephone interview, 26 Oct. 1996.

15. Ralph Ellison, interview with Dave Lacy, nd. 1992, Richard Wright film documentary, courtesy Avon Kirkland.

16. Ralph Ellison, "King of the Bingo Game," *Tomorrow* 4 (Nov. 1944): 29.

17. Ralph Ellison, "King of the Bingo Game" original manuscript, File "Ellison," James Weldon Johnson Papers, Beinecke Rare Book and Manuscript Library, Yale University.

18. Alexander Bloom, *Prodigal Sons: The New York Intellectuals and Their World* (New York: Oxford University Press, 1986), 135.

19. Saul Bellow, "Two Morning Monologues," *Partisan Review* 8.3 (May-June 1941): 234.

20. Kenneth Burke, letter to Malcolm Cowley, 16 Apr. 1945, *The Selected Correspondence of Kenneth Burke and Malcolm Cowley: 1915–1981,* ed. Paul Jay (New York: Viking, 1988), 266.

21. Ellison and Hersey, "A Completion," *CRE*, 295; Philip Rahv, "Disillusionment and Partial Answers," *Partisan Review* 15.5 (May 1948): 519–529; Alan Wald, *The New York Intellectuals: The Rise and Decline of the Anti-Stalinist Left from the 1930s to the 1980s* (Chapel Hill: University of North Carolina Press, 1987), 218–221.

22. "Editorial Comment," *Negro Quarterly* 1.4 (Winter-Spring 1943): 299.

23. Albert Murray, personal interview, 8 Jan. 1997.

24. Carl Lawrence, "Congress Casino Manager Victim of Thugs; Then Narrowly Misses Psychopathic Ward," *Amsterdam News,* 4 Apr. 1942, 3.

25. Ellison, untitled note ["My friendship with Stanley Hyman . . ."]; Edwin Seaver, introduction to *Cross Section* (New York: L.B. Fischer, 1944), viii.

26. "Notes on Contributors," *Cross Section,* 553, 554, 559.

27. Ralph Ellison, "Introduction to the Thirtieth Anniversary Edition of *Invisible Man*," *CERE,* 478.

28. Ralph Ellison, "In a Strange Country," *Tomorrow* 3 (July 1944): 42.

29. Henry Volkening, letter to Ralph Ellison, 19 May 1944, Box 53, Folder "*Invisible Man* Literary Agents," REP.

30. Fanny McConnell, letter to Langston Hughes, 4 Apr. 1938, Box 54, Folder "Ellison, Ralph," LHP; Jervis Anderson, "Going to the Territory," *New Yorker,* 22 Nov. 1976, 105.

31. Fanny McConnell, date book, nd. [ca. spring 1944], Box 74, Folder "Appointment Calendars 1944," REP.

32. Anderson, "Going to the Territory," 105.

33. Fanny McConnell, "A Broadway Taboo Is Lifted," *Opportunity* 22.4 (Fall 1944): 175.

34. Henry Volkening, letter to Ralph Ellison, 22 Aug. 1944, Box 53, Folder "*Invisible Man* Literary Agents," REP.

35. Ralph Ellison and Allen Geller, "An Interview with Ralph Ellison," *CRE,* 70.

36. Seaver, introduction to *Cross Section,* vii.

37. Richard Wright, letter to Ralph Ellison, nd. [ca. late Aug. 1944], Box 76, Folder "Richard Wright," REP.

38. Ralph Ellison, letter to Richard Wright, 5 Sept. 1944, Box 76, Folder "Richard Wright," REP; "This Agreement" (contract between Ralph Ellison and Reynal and Hitchcock), 28 Aug. 1944, Box 53, Folder "Literary Agents," REP.

39. Volkening, letter to Ellison, 27 Sept. 1944.

40. Ralph Ellison, letter to Richard Wright, 4 Sept. 1944.

41. Ralph Ellison and Steve Cannon, Lennox Raphael, and James Thompson, "A Very Stern Discipline," *CRE,* 127.

42. Ralph Ellison, "Black Yank in Britain," *Negro Digest* 2.11 (1944): 53–56.

43. Ralph Ellison, "New World A-Coming," *Tomorrow* 4 (Dec. 1944): 67.

44. Wright, letter to Ellison, nd. [ca. summer 1944], Box 97, Folder "Ellison, Ralph," RWP. ["This is in a hurry . . ."].

45. Ralph Ellison, "*An American Dilemma*: A Review," *SA,* 314, 317.

Chapter 11. *Portrait of the Artist as a Young Critic: 1945*

1. Richard Wright, diary entry, 7 Jan. 1945, Box 117, Folder 1860, RWP.

2. See Steve Chibnall, "Whistle and Zoot: the Changing Meaning of a Suit of Clothes," *History Workshop Journal* 20 (1985): 56–81; Stuart Cosgrove, "The Zoot-Suit and Style Warfare," *History Workshop Journal* 18 (1984): 77–91; and Eric Lott, "Double V, Double-Time: Bebop's Politics of Style," *Callaloo* 11.3 (1988): 597–605.

3. Dizzy Gillespie with Al Fraser, *To Be or Not to Bop: Memoirs, Dizzy Gillespie* (Garden City, N.Y.: Doubleday, 1979), 120.

4. Wright, diary, 22 Jan. 1945.

5. Wright, diary, 22 Jan. 1945.

6. Wright, diary, 23 Jan. 1945.

7. Ralph Ellison and Horace Cayton, interview notes, 8 Sept. 1968, Horace Cayton Papers, Southside Branch, Chicago Public Library; Ralph Ellison, interview for Constance Webb, 3 Feb. 1963, Richard Wright Papers, SCRBC.

8. Wright, diary, 28 Jan. 1945.

9. Wright, diary, 29 Jan. 1945.

10. Wright, diary, 2 Feb. 1945.

11. Ellison and Cayton, interview notes.

12. Chester Himes, *The Quality of Hurt* (New York: Paragon, 1990), 76.

13. Ralph Ellison, untitled notes [8 March 1945 Red Cross Menu], Box 52, Folder "Draft Notes 1942–1950," REP.

14. Ralph Ellison, letter to Richard Wright, 18 Aug. 1945, Box 97, Folder "Ellison, Ralph," RWP; Ellison, letter to Wright, 1 Feb. 1948.

15. Ellison and Cayton, interview notes; Julius Rosenwald Fund Grant Register, Julius Rosenwald Fund, Julius Rosenwald Fund Papers, Amistad Research Center, Tulane University.

16. Ralph Ellison, "Statement of Plan of Work," Julius Rosenwald Fund, courtesy of Michel Fabre.

17. R. L. Duffus, "Deep-South Memoir," *New York Times Book Review,* 4 Mar. 1945, 3, quoted in *Richard Wright: The Critical Reception,* ed. John N. Reilly (New York: Burt Franklin, 1978), 133; Lionel Trilling, "A Tragic Situation," *The Nation,* 7 April 1945, 391–392, quoted in *Richard Wright: The Critical Reception,* 151.

18. W. E. B. Du Bois, "Richard Wright Looks Back," *New York Herald Tribune Weekly Book Review,* 4 Mar. 1945, quoted in *Richard Wright: The Critical Reception,* 132–133.

19. Ralph Ellison, "Richard Wright's Blues," *SA,* 93, 92, 93.

20. Richard Wright, letter to Ralph Ellison, 25 July 1945, Box 27, Folder "Richard and Ellen Wright," REP.

21. Ellison, letter to Wright, 5 Aug. 1945.

22. Wright, letter to Ellison, 25 July 1945.

23. Ellison, "Richard Wright's Blues," *SA,* 78.

24. Ellison, letter to Wright, 5 Aug. 1945; Michel Fabre, "In Ralph Ellison's Own Precious Words," unpublished ms., courtesy Michel Fabre.

25. Ralph Ellison, letter to Kenneth Burke, 29 Nov. 1945, KBP.

26. Ellison, letter to Wright, 5 Aug. 1945.

27. Ellison, letter to Wright, 22 July 1945.

28. Ellison, letter to Wright, 5 Aug. 1945.

29. Ralph Ellison, letter to Stanley Edgar Hyman, 7 June 1945, Box 6, Folder "Ralph and Fanny Ellison," SHP.

30. James Joyce, *Ulysses* (1922; New York: Random House, 1934): 9, line 1.259–261.

31. Ralph Ellison, "Beating That Boy," *New Republic,* 22 Oct. 1945: 536.

32. Ellison, letter to Hyman, 16 Sept. 1945.

33. Ralph Ellison, letter to Sonia Grodka, 23 Oct. 1945, Box 59, Folder "Lectures," REP.

34. Marjorie Green, clip sheet, Associated Negro Press, Box 59, Folder "Lectures," REP; see also "Negro Writing Must Become Force for Transforming American Value" and "Negro Writer Speaks at Bennington," *Detroit Tribune,* Box 59, Folder "Lectures," REP.

35. Ralph Ellison, "American Negro Writing," Box 59, Folder "Lectures," REP.

36. Thomas Sancton, "Unfinished Business," *New Republic* 3 Dec. 1945: 770.

37. Ellison, letter to Hyman, 12 Dec. 1945.

Chapter 12. African American Thoreau: 1946

1. Ralph Ellison, letter to Kenneth Burke, 23 Nov. 1945, KBP.

2. Ralph Ellison, "The Booker T," *New Republic,* 18 Feb. 1946: 262.

3. Albert Maltz, "What Shall We Ask of Writers?" *New Masses,* 12 Feb. 1946, quoted in Irving Howe and Lewis Coser, *The American Communist Party: A Critical History (1919–1957)* (Boston: Beacon Hill, 1957), 316–317.

4. Ralph Ellison, letter to Richard Wright, 24 Aug. 1946, Box 97, Folder "Ellison, Ralph," RWP.

5. E. Franklin Frazier, letter to Ida Guggenheimer, 7 Dec. 1945, Ida Guggenheimer Papers, SCRBC.

6. Alfred Kazin, *New York Jew* (New York: Knopf, 1978), 41.

7. Dorothy Norman, "A World to Live In: Help for the Troubled in Harlem," *New York Post,* 18 Mar. 1946: 30.

8. Richard Wright, "Psychiatry Goes to Harlem," *Twice A Year* 14-15 (Fall-Winter) 1946–1947: 353.

9. Ralph Ellison, "Living with the Music," *SA,* 187–188, 193–196.

10. Ralph Ellison, "Introduction to the Thirtieth Anniversary Issue of *Invisible Man,*" *CERE,* 472–473.

11. Ralph Ellison, draft letter to Peggy Hitchcock, nd. [ca. 1945], Box 52, Folder "*Invisible Man* Draft's Notes," REP.

12. Fanny Ellison, letter to Langston Hughes, 28 May 1946, Box 54, Folder "Ellison, Ralph," LHP.

13. Ralph Ellison, letter to Stanley Edgar Hyman, 20 June 1946, Box 6, Folder "Ralph and Fanny Ellison," SHP.

14. Ralph Ellison, untitled note, Box 52, Folder 10 "*Invisible Man* Draft's Notes," REP.

15. "Harlem Pioneers with Mental Clinic," *Headlines and Pictures,* July 1946, np.

16. Frederic Wertham, "Pit Without Pendulum," *New Republic,* 8 Apr. 1946: 484.

17. Ralph Ellison, interview with Horace Cayton, 8 Sept. 1968, Horace Cayton Notes, Horace Cayton Papers, Southside Branch, Chicago Public Library.

18. Ellison, letter to Wright, 24 Aug. 1946.

19. Ralph Ellison, "Stepchild Fantasy," *Saturday Review,* 8 June 1946: 25–26.

20. Ellison, letter to Wright, 24 June 1946.

21. Ellison, letter to Wright, 24 Aug. 1946.

22. Ellison, untitled note ["One Saturday night . . ."], Box 52, Folder 9 "*Invisible Man* Draft's Notes," REP.

23. Ellison, "Stepchild Fantasy," 26.

24. Ellison, untitled note, Box 52, Folder 9 "*Invisible Man* Draft's Notes," REP.

25. Ellison, letter to Wright, 24 June 1946.

26. Horace Cayton, "Writing Schools: Mr. Cayton May Be Saying Reality Inhibits Only a Dark and Furtive Zone," *Pittsburgh Courier,* 15 June 1946: 7.

27. Ellison, untitled note [handwritten note on Fanny M. Buford stationery], Box 52, Folder 2 "*Invisible Man* Draft's Notes," REP.

28. Thomas Sancton, letter to Ralph Ellison, 3 June 1946, Box 52, Folder "Imprisoned in Words," REP.

29. Ellison, *Invisible Man* draft, 29 Mar. 1946, Box 49, Folder "Campus," REP.

30. Schedule "Conference of Psychologists and Writers," Box 76, Folder "Printed Material 1904, 1921–1955," REP.

31. Ralph Ellison, letter to Thomas Sancton, 16 June 1946, Box 52, Folder "Imprisoned in Words," REP.

32. Ralph Ellison, "Twentieth Century Fiction and the Black Mask of Humanity," *SA,* 35.

33. Sancton, letter to Ellison, 31 July 1946.

34. Chester Himes, *The Quality of Hurt: The Early Years* (New York: Paragon, 1990), 95.

35. Chester Himes, *The Lonely Crusade* (New York: Thunder's Mouth Press, 1990), 61.

36. Thomas Sancton, telegram to Ralph Ellison, 8 Nov. 1946, Box 52, Folder "Imprisoned in Words," REP.

37. Paul Kellog, letter to Ralph Ellison, 23 Dec. 1946, Box 52, Folder "Imprisoned in Words," REP.

38. Ralph Ellison, letter to Paul Kellog, 29 Dec. 1946, Box 52, Folder "Imprisoned in Words," REP.

39. Ralph Ellison, untitled notes ["I left the woods . . ."], Box 52, Folder 6 "*Invisible Man* Draft's Notes," REP. Same as Thoreau's conclusion to Walden (1858). Henry David Thoreau, *The Portable Thoreau,* ed. Carl Bode (New York: Viking, 1982), 562.

Chapter 13. Absurdly, an Invisible Man: 1947

1. Michel Fabre, *The Unfinished Quest of Richard Wright,* trans. Isabel Barzun (New York: William Morrow, 1973), 308.

2. Howard Fast, *Being Red* (Boston: Houghton Mifflin, 1990), 183.

3. Ralph Ellison, interview for Constance Webb, 3 Feb. 1963, Richard Wright Papers, SCRBC.

4. Malcolm Cowley, letter to Kenneth Burke, 9 Mar. 1944, *The Selected Correspondence of Kenneth Burke and Malcolm Cowley,* ed. Paul Jay (New York: Viking, 1988), 262.

5. Malcolm Cowley, "Prolegomena to Kenneth Burke," *The Flower and the Leaf* (New York: Viking, 1985), 210.

6. Ralph Ellison, letter to Kenneth Burke, 23 Nov. 1945, KBP.

7. Fanny Ellison, letter to Kenneth Burke, 5 June 1969, KBP; Ralph and Fanny Ellison, letter to Kenneth Burke, 23 Sept. 1946, KBP. In Fanny Ellison's 1969 letter she claims to have first visited Burke's home in 1947. In the 1946 letter, the couple thank Burke for "a day in the country."

8. Henry Volkening, letter to Ralph Ellison, 1 Feb. 1947, Box 53, Folder "*Invisible Man* Literary Agents," REP.

9. Richard J. Walton, *Henry Wallace, Harry Truman, and the Cold War* (New York: Viking, 1973), 142–143, 152.

10. Mary McCarthy, *The Oasis* (New York: Random House, 1949), 19–20.

11. Michael Shelden, *Friends of Promise: Cyril Connolly and the World of Horizon* (London: Hamish Hamilton, 1989), 7, 163.

12. Ralph Ellison, untitled note ["Secretary reveals contents . . ."], Box 52, Folder 6 "*Invisible Man* Draft's Notes," REP.

13. Ellison, untitled note ["Remember to draw Cleo's face . . ."], Box 52, Folder 6 "*Invisible Man* Draft's Notes," REP.

14. Ellison, untitled note ["Stanley Edgar Hyman . . ."], Box 52, Folder 5 "*Invisible Man* Draft's Notes," REP.

15. Ted Gioia, *The History of Jazz* (New York: Oxford University Press, 1997), 222–223.

16. Ellison, untitled note ["More notes . . ."], Box 53, Folder "Partial Draft Fragments," REP.

17. Volkening, letter to Ellison, 9 May 1947.

18. Fast, *Being Red,* 171–177.

19. Albert Erskine and Frank Taylor, letter to Richard Wright, 17 Apr. 1947, Box 105, Folder "Random House," RWP.

20. "Agreement Between Random House, Inc. and Ralph Ellison," 18 July 1947, Box 100, Folder "Random House Correspondence," REP.

21. Ralph Ellison, letter to Henry Volkening, 12 Oct. 1947, Box 53, Folder "Invisible Man Literary Agents," REP.

22. F. A. H., "Invisible Man," *Labor Great Books Program,* Box 53, Folder 2 "*Invisible Man* Reviews," REP.

23. Ellison, letter to Volkening, 1 Aug. 1947.

24. Ellison, letter to Burke, 25 Aug. 1947.

25. Ralph Ellison, letter to Stanley Edgar Hyman, 17 June 1947, Box 6, Folder "Ralph and Fanny Ellison," SHP.

26. Shirley Jackson, "Pillar of Salt," *The Lottery or the Adventures of James Harris* (Cambridge, Mass.: Robert Bentley, 1980), 252.

27. Ralph Ellison, letter to Langston Hughes, 25 Aug. 1947, Box 70, Folder "Ellison, Ralph," LHP.

28. Richard Wright, letter to Ralph Ellison, 4 Oct. 1946, Box 76, Folder "Richard and Ellen Wright," REP.

29. Norman D. Markowitz, *The Rise and Fall of the People's Century: Henry A. Wallace and American Liberalism* (New York: Free Press, 1973), 234.

30. Ellison, untitled note ["Your short piece in Horizon . . ."], Box 52, Folder 9 "*Invisible Man* Draft's Notes," REP.

31. Donat O'Donnell, "The Augustan Agony," *Irish Times,* 25 Oct. 1947: np.; Box 53, Folder 2 "*Invisible Man* Reviews," REP.

32. Saul Bellow, "Man Underground," *Commentary* 13 (June 1952): 608.

33. Quoted in Clive Fisher, *Cyril Connolly: A Nostalgic Life* (London: MacMillan, 1995), 273.

34. "Reflections," *Time,* 29 Nov. 1948: 30; "Land of the Middlebrow," *Time,* 20 Oct. 1947: 77–78.

35. Volkening, letter to Ellison, 6 Oct. 1947.

36. Fanny Ellison, letter to Frank Taylor, 16 Sept. 1947, Box 53, Folder "*Invisible Man* Literary Agents," REP.

37. Ellison, letter to Volkening, 12 Oct. 1947.

38. Volkening, letter to Ellison, 23 Oct. 1947.

39. Volkening, letter to Ellison, 23 Oct. 1947.

40. Ralph Ellison, "Battle Royal," *48: Magazine of the Year* 2 (Jan. 1948): 14–15, 20–21, 32.

41. Ernest Kaiser, telephone interview, 24 May 1999.

42. Wright, letter to Ellison, 3 Nov. 1947.

43. Ralph Ellison, letter to Charles Humboldt, 19 Dec. 1947, Charles Humboldt Papers, Series I, Box 2, Yale University Manuscripts and Archives.

Chapter 14. Progressive Isolation: 1948

1. Ralph Ellison and Steve Cannon, Ishmael Reed, and Quincy Troupe, "The Essential Ellison," *CRE,* 364.

2. Ralph Ellison, letter to Richard Wright, 1 Feb. 1948, Box 97, Folder "Ellison, Ralph," RWP.

3. Ralph Ellison, "Ralph Ellison Explains," *48: Magazine of the Year* 2 (May 1948): 145.

4. Ellison, letter to Wright, 1 Feb. 1948.

5. Ellison, letter to Wright, 5 Jan. 1948.

6. Ralph Ellison, untitled note ["Pictorial problem . . ."], Box 100, Folder "Harlem Is Nowhere," REP.

7. Ralph Ellison, "Harlem Is Nowhere," *SA,* 296.

8. Ellison, untitled note, Box 100, Folder "Harlem Is Nowhere," REP.

9. Ellison, "Harlem Is Nowhere," *SA,* 300.

10. Henry Volkening, letter to John H. Johnson, 5 Feb. 1948, Box 53, Folder "*Invisible Man* Literary Agents," REP.

11. Gordon Parks, telephone interview, 7 Mar. 2000.

12. Ralph Ellison, 1948 appointment calendar, Box 74, Folder "Appointment Calendars," REP.

13. Gordon Parks, *Voices in the Mirror* (New York: Anchor, 1990), 103–112.

14. Sanford Laskoff, *Max Lerner: Pilgrim in the Promised Land* (Chicago: University of Chicago Press, 1998), 144.

15. Jervis Anderson, *A. Philip Randolph: A Biographical Portrait* (1973; Berkeley: University of California Press, 1986), 276.

16. Richard Wright, letter to Ralph Ellison, 12 Jan. 1948, Box 27, Folder "Richard and Ellen Wright," REP.

17. Ellison, letter to Wright, 1 Feb. 1948.

18. Quoted in Fred Pfiel, "Policiers Noirs," *The Critical Response to Chester Himes,* ed. Charles Silet (Westport, Conn.: Greenwood, 1999), 38; Chester Himes, *The Quality of Hurt* (1972; New York: Paragon, 1990), 104.

19. Richard Wright, "Introduction to the French Edition," *Richard Wright: Books and Writers,* ed. Michel Fabre (Jackson: University of Mississippi Press, 1990), 209.

20. Ida Guggenheimer, letters to Richard Wright, 16 July 1945; 9 Aug. 1945; Box 98, Folder "Guggenheimer, Ida," RWP.

21. E. Franklin Frazier, letter to Ida Guggenheimer, 4 Jan. 1953, Ida Guggenheimer Papers, SCRBC.

22. Ellison, 1948 appointment calendar.

23. David Cesarani, *Homeless Mind* (New York: Free Press, 1998), 307; Ralph Ellison, letter to Richard Wright, nd. [ca. May 1948], Box 27, Folder "Richard and Ellen Wright," REP.

24. Jere Daniel, letter to Ralph Ellison, 19 Apr. 1948, Box 100, Folder "Harlem Is Nowhere," REP.

25. Ralph Ellison, "Introduction, Thirtieth Anniversary Edition," *CERE,* 471.

26. Ellison, letter to Wright, nd. [ca. summer 1948] ["Finally we met . . ."].

27. Ralph Ellison, letter to Stanley Edgar Hyman, 16 Aug. 1948, Box 6, Folder "Ralph and Fanny Ellison," SHP.

28. Richard Lauterbach, letter to Ralph Ellison, 17 May 1948, Box 100, Folder "Harlem Is Nowhere," REP.

29. "Next Month," *48: Magazine of the Year* 2 (June 1948): back cover.

30. Albert Murray, "Tuskegee and New York: 1950–1955," *TT,* 3.

31. Leslie Fiedler, "Come Back to the Raft Ag'in, Huck Honey," *Partisan Review* 15 (June 1948): 671, 664.

32. Ellison, letter to Hyman, 15 June 1948.

33. Ellison, untitled note ["At what point . . ."], Box 49, Folder "Emerson," REP.

34. Ellison, untitled note ["north . . ."], Box 49, Folder "Emerson," REP.

35. Ralph Ellison, letter to John Roche, 6 Nov. 1984, "'American Culture Is of a Whole': From the Letters of Ralph Ellison," *New Republic,* 1 Mar. 1999: 46.

36. Harvey Breit, "On the Nature of Modern Literary Criticism," *New York Times Book Review,* 11 July 1948: 6.

37. Ellison, letter to Hyman, 16 Aug. 1948.

38. Ralph Ellison, letter to Albert Murray, 2 June 1957, *TT,* 166.

39. Shirley Jackson, "The Lottery," *The Lottery, or The Adventures of James Harris* (New York: Farrar, Straus, Giroux, 1980), 301–302.

40. Aristotle, *Poetics,* trans. Ingram Bywater, *Introduction to Aristotle* 2nd rev. ed. (Chicago: University of Chicago Press, 1973), 680–C.7 l, 34–39.

41. Ralph Ellison, letter to Edward Weinfeld, 29 Sept. 1948, Box 100, Folder "Harlem Is Nowhere," REP.

Chapter 15. *Time Stands Still: 1949*

1. Ralph Ellison, letter to Stanley Edgar Hyman, 21 Feb. 1949, Box 6, Folder "Ralph and Fanny Ellison," SHP.

2. Chester Eisinger, *Fiction of the Forties* (Chicago: University of Chicago Press, 1963), 136.

3. William Barrett, "A Prize for Ezra Pound," *Partisan Review* 16 (Apr. 1949): 344–347; Samuel Sillen, "A Prize for Ezra Pound," *Masses and Mainstream* 2 (Apr. 1949): 3–6.

4. Allen Tate, "The Question of the Pound Award," *Partisan Review* 16 (May 1949): 520.

5. Ralph Ellison, letter to Albert Murray, 26 Feb. 1949, courtesy of Albert Murray.

6. Ellison, letter to Hyman, 21 Feb. 1949.

7. Irving Howe, "The Culture Conference," *Partisan Review* 16 (May 1949): 510.

8. Peter Manso, *Mailer: His Life and His Times* (New York: Penguin, 1985), 134–137.

9. Martin L. Duberman, *Paul Robeson* (New York: Ballantine Books, 1989), 342.

10. Anatole Broyard, *When Kafka Was the Rage* (New York: Vintage, 1997), 69–70.

11. Milton Klonsky, "Along the Midway of Mass Culture," *Partisan Review* 16 (April 1949): 362–363, 364.

12. James Baldwin, "Everybody's Protest Novel," *Notes of a Native Son* (Boston: Beacon, 1955), 22–23.

13. William Barrett, "The End of Modern Literature," *Partisan Review* 16 (Sept. 1949): 947.

14. Richard Wright, "The FB Eye Blues," *Richard Wright Reader,* eds. Ellen Wright and Michel Fabre (New York: Da Capo, 1997), 249.

15. Ralph Ellison, letter to Richard Wright, nd. [ca. October 1949] ["Your wire reached me"], Box 76, Folder "Richard Wright," REP.

16. Fanny Ellison, letter to Richard Wright, 7 Nov. 1949, Box 97, Folder "Ellison, Ralph," RWP.

17. Alexander Bloom, *Prodigal Sons* (New York: Oxford University Press, 1986), 188.

18. Lionel Trilling, *The Liberal Imagination* (New York: Scribner's, 1976), xv.

19. Doxey Wilkerson, "Negro Culture: Heritage and Weapon," *Masses and Mainstream* 2 (Aug. 1949): 22, 24, 21.

20. Ralph Ellison, "The Shadow and the Act," *SA,* 276, 280.

21. *Intruder in the Dust,* film directed by Clarence Brown, Metro-Goldwyn-Mayer, 1949.

22. Michael Denning, *The Cultural Front* (New York: Verso, 1996), 436–445.

23. Ellison, letter to Hyman, 27 Oct. 1949.

24. Ernest Kaiser, letter to author, May 1999.

25. Harold Cruse, *The Crisis of the Negro Intellectual* (1967; New York: Quill, 1984), 216.

26. Ellison, letter to Wright, nd. [ca. Sept. 1949] ["Finally we met . . ."].

Chapter 16. Cold War and Inauthentic Blacks: 1950

1. Ralph Ellison, letter to Richard Wright, 5 Aug. 1945, Box 97, Folder "Ellison, Ralph," RWP.

2. Ellison, letter to Wright, 21 Jan. 1953.

3. Langston Hughes, letter to Arna Bontemps, 9 July 1958, *Arna Bontemps—Langston Hughes, Letters 1925–1967,* ed. Charles Nichols (New York: Paragon House, 1980), 374.

4. Ralph Ellison, letter to Albert Murray, 24 Jan. 1950, *TT,* 7.

5. "Ralph Waldo Ellison," *Federal Bureau of Investigation,* FBI File.

6. Ralph Ellison, "Collaborator with His Own Enemy," *New York Times Book Review,* 19 Feb. 1950, sect 7: 4.

7. Ellison, letter to Murray, 16 Apr. 1950, *TT,* 12.

8. Ellison, letter to Murray, 24 Jan. 1950, *TT,* 8.

9. Herbert Ellison, personal interview, 18 May 1996.

10. Albert Murray, letter to Ralph Ellison, 27 Mar. 1950, *TT,* 11; Albert Murray, unpublished manuscript of literary correspondence with Ralph Ellison.

11. James Atlas, *Delmore Schwartz: The Life of an American Poet* (New York: Atlas, 1977), 296–297.

12. Ellison, letter to Murray, 16 Apr. 1950, *TT,* 13.

13. Ralph Ellison, *Invisible Man* original typescript, Box 147, Folder 6, REP.

14. Ralph Ellison, *Invisible Man* draft's episodes, Box 145, Folder "Leroy's Journal," REP, 492.

15. John P. Diggins, *The Proud Decades: America in War and Peace, 1941–1960* (New York: Norton, 1981), 89–92.

16. "Suggestions for RE from HF," Box 52, Folder *"Invisible Man* Draft's Notes 1942–1950," REP.

17. Norman Podhoretz, *Making It* (New York: Random House, 1967), 130.

18. Anatole Broyard, "The Inauthentic Negro," *Commentary* 10 (July 1950): 57, 63, 64.

19. Anatole Broyard, *Kafka Was the Rage* (New York: Vintage, 1997), 12; Ralph Ellison, letter to Stanley Edgar Hyman, 15 June 1948, SHP.

20. Diggins, *The Proud Decades,* 93.

21. Hughes, letter to Bontemps, 27 Dec. 1950, *Letters,* 277.

22. Ralph Ellison, interview, 30 Apr. 1983, quoted in Arnold Rampersad, *The Life of Langston Hughes,* vol. 2 (New York: Oxford University Press, 1988), 202.

Chapter 17. The Black Kafka and the Fight against Reality: 1951

1. Richard Gibson, "A No to Nothing," *Kenyon Review* 13 (Spring 1951): 254.

2. Ralph Ellison, letter to Albert Murray, 6 June 1951, *TT,* 20.

3. Ellison, letter to Murray, 6 June 1951, *TT,* 19.

4. Anatole Broyard, "Keep Cool, Man," *Commentary* 11 (April 1951): 361–362.

5. Langston Hughes, letter to Arna Bontemps, 1 May 1951, *Arna Bontemps—Langston Hughes, Letters 1925–1967,* ed. Charles Nichols (New York: Paragon House, 1980), 281.

6. Arna Bontemps, letter to Langston Hughes, 11 June 1951, *Letters,* 284.

7. Bontemps, letter to Hughes, 31 Dec. 1950, *Letters,* 278.

8. Joan Givner, *Katherine Anne Porter: A Life* (New York: Simon and Schuster, 1982), 311.

9. Ralph Ellison, *Invisible Man* Drafts, Box 143, Folder "Brotherhood," REP.

10. Ralph Ellison, *Invisible Man* original typescript, Box 147, Folder *"Invisible Man* Original Typescript," REP, np.

11. Ellison, *Invisible Man* original typescript.

12. Ellison, letter to Murray, 6 June 1951, *TT,* 21.

13. James Baldwin, "Many Thousands Gone," *Notes of a Native Son* (Boston: Beacon, 1955), 33, 42.

14. James Baldwin, introduction to *The Price of the Ticket* (New York: St. Martin's, 1985), xiii.

15. Baldwin, "Many Thousands," 42.

16. Baldwin, introduction, *Price*, xii–xiii.

17. Ralph Ellison, *Invisible Man* final typescript, Box 147, Folder "*Invisible Man* Final Typescript," REP, 610–611.

18. Albert Murray, letter to Ralph Ellison, 30 Dec. 1951, *TT*, 23.

Chapter 18. *The Briar Patch: 1952–1953*

1. Albert Erskine, letter to Ralph Ellison, 19 Mar. 1952, Box 154, Folder "Published Editions, Random House Correspondence," REP.

2. Fanny Ellison, letter to Langston Hughes, 2 Apr. 1952, Box 70, Folder "Ellison, Ralph and Fanny," LHP.

3. Ralph Ellison, letter to Albert Murray, 8 Jan. 1952, *TT*, 25.

4. Albert Murray, letter to Ralph Ellison, nd. [ca. Jan.-Feb. 1952] *TT*, 27.

5. Ellison, letter to Murray, 4 Feb. 1952, *TT*, 29.

6. Stephen Polcari, *Abstract Expressionism and the Modern Experience* (New York: Cambridge University Press, 1991), 33–34.

7. Jean Ennis, letter to Ralph Ellison, 25 June 1952, Box 154, Folder "Published Editions, Random House Correspondence," REP.

8. Delmore Schwartz, "Books," *Partisan Review* 19 (May-June 1952): 359.

9. William Barrett, "Black and Blue: A Negro Céline," *American Mercury* 74 (June 1952): 100, 104.

10. Saul Bellow, "Man Underground," *Commentary* 13 (June 1952): 608.

11. Irving Howe, "A Negro in America," *The Nation*, 6 May 1952: 454.

12. Ellison, letter to Murray, 4 Feb. 1952, *TT*, 29.

13. Saunders Redding, "Invisible Man," *Baltimore Afro-American*, 10 May 1952: 10.

14. Lloyd Brown, "The Deep Pit," *Masses and Mainstream* 5 (June 1952): 62.

15. John O. Killens, "Invisible Man," *Freedom* (June 1952): 7.

16. Abner Berry, "Ralph Ellison's Novel *Invisible Man* Shows Snobbery, Contempt for Negro People," *The Worker*, 1 June 1952: 7.

17. Irving Howe and Lewis Coser, *The American Communist Party: A Critical History* (Boston: Beacon Press, 1957), 296.

18. Ralph Ellison, letter to Richard Wright, 21 Jan. 1953, Box 97, Folder "Ellison, Ralph," RWP.

19. Chester Himes, *The Quality of Hurt* (1971; New York: Paragon, 1990), 136.

20. Ralph Ellison, interview with Horace Cayton, 8 Sept. 1968, Horace Cayton Papers, Horace Cayton Notes, Southside Branch, Chicago Public Library.

21. Ellison, letter to Wright, 21 Jan. 1953.

22. Chester Himes, *The End of a Primitive* (New York: Norton, 1997), 181, 189, 190, 191.

23. Arna Bontemps, letter to Langston Hughes, 8 Oct. 1953, *Arna Bontemps—Langston Hughes, Letters 1925–1967*, ed. Charles Nichols (New York: Paragon House, 1980), 315.

24. Royalty statement, Box 53, Folder "Random House Royalties," REP.

25. Bontemps, letter to Hughes, 2 May 1953, *Letters*, 307.

26. Langston Hughes, letter to Arna Bontemps, 22 Sept. 1953, *Letters*, 313.

27. Ralph Ellison, letter to Hugh McGovern, 27 Oct. 1952, Box 174, Folder "Interviews: The Denver Post 1952," REP.

28. Richard Wright, letter to Ralph Ellison, 21 Oct. 1952, Box 76, Folder "Richard Wright," REP.

29. Edmund Wilson, letter to Chauncey Hackett, 9 Dec. 1952, *Edmund Wilson, Letters on Literature and Politics: 1912–1972* (New York: Farrar, Straus and Giroux, 1977), 509.

30. Jeffrey Meyers, *Edmund Wilson: A Biography* (Boston: Houghton Mifflin, 1995): 337–338.

31. Ralph Ellison, letter to John H. Sengstacke, 15 Jan. 1953, Box 213, Folder "Award Citations," REP.

32. Dowdal Davis, letter to Ralph Ellison, 1 Apr. 1953, Box 214, Folder "Russwurm Award," REP.

33. Ellison, letter to Murray, 9 Apr. 1953, *TT*, 44–45.

34. "Book Medals Won by MacLeish, De Voto," *New York Times*, 28 Jan. 1953: 25.

35. Joseph Trimmer, preface to *The National Book Awards for Fiction* (Boston: G.K. Hall, 1978), vii–xxv.

36. Ralph Ellison, "Brave Words for a Startling Occasion," *SA*, 102, 104.

37. "Book Medals Won," *New York Times*, 25.

38. Ellison, letter to Wright, 21 Jan. 1953.

39. Murray, letter to Ellison, 20 Feb. 1953, *TT*, 39.

Index

Italicized page numbers refer to the illustrations.